Praise for *Eclipse: Building Commercial-Quality Plug-ins*

"I'm often asked, 'What are the best books about Eclipse?' Number one on my list, every time, is *Eclipse: Building Commercial-Quality Plug-ins*. I find it to be the clearest and most relevant book about Eclipse for the real-world software developer. Other Eclipse books focus on the internal Eclipse architecture or on repeating the Eclipse documentation, whereas this book is laser focused on the issues and concepts that matter when you're trying to build a product."

— *Bjorn Freeman-Benson*
Director, Open Source Process, Eclipse Foundation

"As the title suggests, this massive tome is intended as a guide to best practices for writing Eclipse plug-ins. I think in that respect it succeeds handily. Before you even think about distributing a plug-in you've written, read this book."

— *Ernest Friedman-Hill*
Sheriff, JavaRanch.com

"If you're looking for just one Eclipse plug-in development book that will be your guide, this is the one. While there are other books available on Eclipse, few dive as deep as *Eclipse: Building Commercial-Quality Plug-ins*."

— *Simon Archer*

"*Eclipse: Building Commercial-Quality Plug-ins* was an invaluable training aid for all of our team members. In fact, training our team without the use of this book as a base would have been virtually impossible. It is now required reading for all our developers and helped us deliver a brand-new, very complex product on time and on budget thanks to the great job this book does of explaining the process of building plug-ins for Eclipse."

— *Bruce Gruenbaum*

"This is easily one of the most useful books I own. If you are new to developing Eclipse plug-ins, it is a 'must-have' that will save you *lots* of time and effort. You will find lots of good advice in here, especially things that will help add a whole layer of professionalism and completeness to any plug-in. The book is very focused, well-structured, thorough, clearly written, and doesn't contain a single page of 'waffly page filler.' The diagrams explaining the relationships between the different components and manifest sections are excellent and aid in understanding how everything fits together. This book goes well beyond Actions, Views, and Editors, and I think everyone will benefit from the authors' experience. I certainly have."

— *Tony Saveski*

"The authors of this seminal book have decades of proven experience with the most productive and robust software engineering technologies ever developed. Their experiences have now been well applied to the use of Eclipse for more effective Java development. A must-have for any serious software engineering professional!"

— *Ed Klimas*

"Just wanted to also let you know this is an excellent book! Thanks for putting forth the effort to create a book that is easy to read *and* technical at the same time!"

— *Brooke Hedrick*

"The key to developing great plug-ins for Eclipse is understanding where and how to extend the IDE, and that's what this book gives you. It is a must for serious plug-in developers, especially those building commercial applications. I wouldn't be without it."

— *Brian Wilkerson*

Eclipse

Building Commercial-Quality Plug-ins
Second Edition

eclipse

SERIES EDITORS Erich Gamma ▪ Lee Nackman ▪ John Wiegand

Eclipse is a universal tool platform, an open extensible integrated development environment (IDE) for anything and nothing in particular. Eclipse represents one of the most exciting initiatives hatched from the world of application development in a long time, and it has the considerable support of the leading companies and organizations in the technology sector. Eclipse is gaining widespread acceptance in both the commercial and academic arenas.

The Eclipse Series from Addison-Wesley is the definitive series of books dedicated to the Eclipse platform. Books in the series promise to bring you the key technical information you need to analyze Eclipse, high-quality insight into this powerful technology, and the practical advice you need to build tools to support this evolutionary Open Source platform. Leading experts Erich Gamma, Lee Nackman, and John Wiegand are the series editors.

Titles in the Eclipse Series

Eclipse
Building Commercial-Quality Plug-ins
Second Edition

Eric Clayberg
Dan Rubel

♠Addison-Wesley

Upper Saddle River, NJ • Boston • Indianapolis • San Francisco
New York • Toronto • Montreal • London • Munich • Paris • Madrid
Capetown • Sydney • Tokyo • Singapore • Mexico City

Many of the designations used by manufacturers and sellers to distinguish their products are claimed as trademarks. Where those designations appear in this book, and the publisher was aware of a trademark claim, the designations have been printed with initial capital letters or in all capitals.

The authors and publisher have taken care in the preparation of this book, but make no expressed or implied warranty of any kind and assume no responsibility for errors or omissions. No liability is assumed for incidental or consequential damages in connection with or arising out of the use of the information or programs contained herein.

The publisher offers excellent discounts on this book when ordered in quantity for bulk purchases or special sales, which may include electronic versions and/or custom covers and content particular to your business, training goals, marketing focus, and branding interests. For more information, please contact:

U.S. Corporate and Government Sales
(800) 382-3419
corpsales@pearsontechgroup.com

For sales outside the United States please contact:

International Sales
international@pearsoned.com

Visit us on the Web: www.awprofessional.com

 This Book Is Safari Enabled

The Safari® Enabled icon on the cover of your favorite technology book means the book is available through Safari Bookshelf. When you buy this book, you get free access to the online edition for 45 days.

Safari Bookshelf is an electronic reference library that lets you easily search thousands of technical books, find code samples, download chapters, and access technical information whenever and wherever you need it.

To gain 45-day Safari Enabled access to this book:

* Go to http://www.awprofessional.com/safarienabled
* Complete the brief registration form
* Enter the coupon code CBIN-7SNH-GN25-UVHZ-SLX7

If you have difficulty registering on Safari Bookshelf or accessing the online edition, please e-mail customer-service@safaribooksonline.com.

Library of Congress Cataloging-in-Publication Data

Clayberg, Eric.
 Eclipse : building commercial-quality plug-ins / Eric Clayberg, Dan Rubel.-- 2nd ed.
  p. cm.
 Includes bibliographical references and index.
 ISBN 0-321-42672-X (pbk. : alk. paper)
 1. Computer software--Development. 2. Java (Computer program language) I. Rubel, Dan. II. Title.

 QA76.76.D47C574 2006
 005.1--dc22

                             2006004362

ISBN 0-321-42672-X

Text printed in the United States on recycled paper at Courier in Stoughton, Massachusetts.

First printing, March 2006

To our wives, Karen and Kathy,
and our children, Beth, Lauren, Lee, and David

Contents

Foreword

To the millions of developers, engineers, and users all over the world, Eclipse is an extensible platform for tool integration. To the hundreds of thousands of commercial customers using it to develop plug-ins or complete tool platforms, Eclipse represents a proven, reliable, scalable technology on which commercial products can be quickly designed, developed, and deployed.

To the thousands of students and researchers, Eclipse represents a stable platform for innovation, freedom, and experimentation. To all these individuals, groups, and organizations, Eclipse is a vendor-neutral platform to tool integration supported by a diverse Eclipse Ecosystem.

The Eclipse vendor-neutral platform is built on industry standards, which support a wide range of tools, platforms, and languages. The Eclipse Technology is royalty-free and has worldwide redistribution rights. The platform was designed from a clean slate to be extensible and to provide exemplarity tools. Eclipse development is based on rules of open source engagements. This includes open, transparent, merit-based, and collaborative development. All individuals can participate and contribute. All plans are developed in the public arena. This platform and the open source development process creates an environment for creativity, originality, and freedom. Eclipse is unparalleled in today's software-tool environment.

The software-tool industry is undergoing massive changes from the commoditization of the technology to the company consolidation. New technology efforts are being redesigned, while a common set of tooling infrastructure is adopted as an industry standard. Successful developers and development paradigms are being challenged to adopt new skills and new, more efficient methods. Old business models are being challenged with free software, and new business models are being developed.

The software-tool industry is deeply appreciative of Eric Clayberg and Dan Rubel for this authoritative book. This book provides the knowledge base so that developers, engineers, and users can learn and use the Eclipse Technology. This enables them to respond to these technology and industry change agents.

Eric and Dan leverage long careers of building software tooling. They each have extensive experience with using Smalltalk for seventeen years, Java for ten years, and Eclipse for six years. They have developed extensive vendor and customer relationships that enable them to experience firsthand the necessary elements for building successful software. They are able to combine this direct knowledge of the technology with the experiences of the users to create a book that provides an in-depth description of the process to build commercial-quality Eclipse extensions.

This book provides an introduction and overview to the new developer of the entire process of plug-in development, including all the best practices to achieve high-quality results. This is a reference book for experienced Eclipse developers. It discusses the APIs and demonstrates many samples and examples. Detailed tutorials are provided for both new and experienced developers. Eric and Dan leverage their broad knowledge of user interface (UI) development and present the Eclipse SWT UI. This establishes the building blocks for all Eclipse UI development. These authors articulate the development challenges of building tool software and establish proven in-depth solutions to the problems.

If you are a developer, engineer, or user wishing to build or use Eclipse, this book provides both a foundation and reference. It also provides the intellectual foundation to contribute to the open source Eclipse project and to develop commercial software.

—Skip McGaughey

Foreword

In the 1990s, when Java was in its infancy, learning the Java class libraries involved studying a handful of classes in four or five packages. The Java class libraries have grown in size and complexity, presenting a significant problem to developers wishing to learn Java today. Just like Java, the Eclipse platform has necessarily grown over the years, and therefore considerably more time and effort is required to learn Eclipse 3.1 than its predecessors. One of the principles of the Eclipse platform is that a plug-in should integrate seamlessly with the workbench and with other plug-ins. To achieve seamless integration, it is necessary for plug-in developers to understand the best practices, conventions, and strategies related to building software for Eclipse. *Eclipse: Building Commercial-Quality Plug-ins* covers everything you need to know to develop Eclipse plug-ins of which you will be proud.

Through the development of a **Favorites** plug-in, the Eclipse Standard Widget Toolkit (SWT) and JFace frameworks are thoroughly discussed, teaching you how to build professional-looking user interfaces such as views, editors, preferences pages, and dialogs. In addition to stock-in-trade subjects, such as user-interface design, lesser-understood Eclipse topics (for example, building features and product branding) are extensively covered, as well as the best discussion I have seen on using Ant to build a product from a single source that targets multiple versions of Eclipse.

Java developers new to Eclipse often have difficulty understanding the extension point mechanism and the critical link between a plug-in's declarative manifest and the Java code necessary to implement a plug-in's functional behavior. This book serves as a roadmap to using the Plug-in Development Environment (PDE) and the extension points defined by the Eclipse platform. It also provides the missing link that developers need to understand them aspects of a plug-in that should be described in the manifest, how to develop a plug-in using existing extension points, and how to contribute which other developers may further contribute.

When I first saw CodePro, I was both impressed with the productivity gains it brought to Eclipse and the extent to which its plug-ins integrated with the Eclipse platform. Having used CodePro for a while, it has become a part of my development toolkit that I cannot do without. By drawing on their extensive experience gained while developing CodePro, Eric and Dan have done an excellent job of capturing in this book those aspects of plug-in development necessary to create a high-quality and professional-looking Eclipse product.

—Simon Archer

Preface

When we were first exposed to Eclipse back in late 1999, we were struck by the magnitude of the problem IBM was trying to solve. IBM wanted to unify all its development environments on a single code base. At the time, the company was using a mix of technology composed of a hodgepodge of C/C++, Java, and Smalltalk.

Many of IBM's most important tools, including the award-winning Visual-Age for Java IDE, were actually written in Smalltalk—a wonderful language for building sophisticated tools, but one that was rapidly losing market share to languages like Java. While IBM had one of the world's largest collections of Smalltalk developers, there wasn't a great deal of industry support for it outside of IBM, and there were very few independent software vendors (ISVs) qualified to create Smalltalk-based add-ons.

Meanwhile, Java was winning the hearts and minds of developers worldwide with its promise of easy portability across a wide range of platforms, while providing the rich application programming interface (API) needed to build the latest generation of Web-based business applications. More important, Java was an object-oriented (OO) language, which meant that IBM could leverage the large body of highly skilled object-oriented developers it had built up over the years of creating Smalltalk-based tools. In fact, IBM took its premiere Object Technology International (OTI) group, which had been responsible for creating IBM's VisualAge Smalltalk and VisualAge Java environments (VisualAge Smalltalk was the first of the VisualAge brand family and VisualAge Java was built using it), and tasked the group with creating a highly extensible integrated development environment (IDE) construction set based in Java. Eclipse was the happy result.

OTI was able to apply its highly evolved OO skills to produce an IDE unmatched in power, flexibility, and extensibility. The group was able to replicate most of the features that had made Smalltalk-based IDEs so popular the decade before, while simultaneously pushing the state of the art in IDE development ahead by an order of magnitude.

The Java world had never seen anything as powerful or as compelling as Eclipse, and it now stands, with Microsoft's .NET, as one of the world's premier development environments. That alone makes Eclipse a perfect platform for developers wishing to get their tools out to as wide an audience as possible. The fact that Eclipse is completely free and open source is icing on the cake. An open, extensible IDE base that is available for free to anyone with a computer is a powerful motivator to the prospective tool developer.

It certainly was to us. At Instantiations and earlier at ObjectShare, we had spent the better part of a decade as entrepreneurs focused on building add-on tools for various IDEs. We had started with building add-ons for Digitalk's Smalltalk/V, migrated to developing tools for IBM's VisualAge Smalltalk, and eventually ended up creating tools for IBM's VisualAge Java (including our award-winning VA Assist product and our jFactor product, one of the world's first Java refactoring tools). Every one of these environments provided a means to extend the IDE, but they were generally not well-documented and certainly not standardized in any way. Small market shares (relative to tools such as VisualBasic) and an eclectic user base also afflicted these environments and, by extension, us.

As an Advanced IBM Business Partner, we were fortunate to have built a long and trusted relationship with the folks at IBM responsible for the creation of Eclipse. That relationship meant that we were in a unique position to be briefed on the technology and to start using it on a daily basis nearly a year and half before the rest of the world even heard about it. When IBM finally announced Eclipse to the world in mid-2001, our team at Instantiations had built some of the first demo applications IBM had to show. Later that year when IBM released its first Eclipse-based commercial tool, WebSphere Studio Application Developer v4.0 (v4.0 so that it synchronized with its then current VisualAge for Java v4.0), our CodePro product became the very first commercial add-on available for it (and for Eclipse in general) on the same day.

Currently, the CodePro product adds hundreds of enhancements to Eclipse and any Eclipse-based IDE. Developing CodePro over the last several years has provided us with an opportunity to learn the details of Eclipse development at a level matched by very few others (with the obvious exception of the IBM and OTI developers, who eat, sleep, and breathe this stuff on a daily basis). CodePro has also served as a testbed for many of the ideas and techniques presented in this book, providing us with a unique perspective from which to write.

Goals of the Book

This book provides an in-depth description of the process involved in building commercial-quality extensions for the Eclipse and the IBM Software Development Platform (SDP)—IBM's commercial version of Eclipse—development environments. To us, "commercial-quality" is synonymous with "commercial-grade" or "high-quality." Producing a *commercial-quality* plug-in means going above and beyond the minimal requirements needed to integrate with Eclipse. It means attending to all those details that contribute to the "fit and polish" of a commercial offering.

In the world of Eclipse plug-ins, very few people take the time to really go the extra mile, and most plug-ins fall into the open source, amateur category. For folks interested in producing high-quality plug-ins (which would certainly be the case for any software company wanting to develop Eclipse-based products), there are many details to consider. Our book is meant to encompass the entire process of plug-in development, including all the extra things that need to be done to achieve high-quality results. This book has several complementary goals:

- Provide a quick introduction to using Eclipse for new users
- Provide a reference for experienced Eclipse users wishing to expand their knowledge and improve the quality of their Eclipse-based products
- Provide a detailed tutorial on creating sophisticated Eclipse plug-ins suitable for new and experienced users

The first three chapters introduce the Eclipse development environment and outline the process of building a simple plug-in. The intention of these chapters is to help developers new to Eclipse quickly pull together a plug-in they can use to experiment with.

The first chapter, in particular, introduces the reader to the minimum set of Eclipse tools that he or she will need to build plug-ins. It is a fairly quick overview of the Eclipse IDE and relevant tools (one could write an entire book on that topic alone), and we would expect expert Eclipse users to skip that chapter entirely.

The second chapter introduces the example that we will use throughout most of the book and provides a very quick introduction to building a working plug-in from start to finish. The third chapter presents a high-level overview of the Eclipse architecture and the structure of plug-ins and extension points.

The fourth and fifth chapters cover the Standard Widget Toolkit (SWT) and JFace, which are the building blocks for all Eclipse user interfaces (UIs). These chapters can act as a stand-alone reference; they are intended to provide just enough detail to get you going. Both of these topics are rich enough to warrant entire books and several are currently available.

The subsequent chapters, comprising the bulk of this book, focus on describing each of the various aspects of plug-in development and providing the reader with in-depth knowledge of how to solve the various challenges involved. Each chapter focuses on a different aspect of the problem, and includes an overview, a detailed description, a discussion of challenges and solutions, diagrams, screenshots, cookbook-style code examples, relevant API listings, and a summary.

We have structured the book so that the most important material required for every plug-in project appears in the first half of it. Some of the packaging- and building-oriented material is placed at the end (for example, features and product builds). This organizational scheme left several topics that, while not critical to every plug-in, were important to the creation of commercial-quality plug-ins. These topics have been placed in the second half of the book in an order based on the importance of each and how it related to earlier material. Internationalization, for example, is one of those topics. It isn't critical, and it isn't even all that complicated when you get right down to it. It is, however, important to the book's premise, so we felt it was a topic we needed to include. Since we aren't assuming that the reader is an Eclipse expert (or even a plug-in developer), we have tried to take the reader through each of the important steps in as much detail as possible. While it is true that this is somewhat intro-ductory, it is also an area that most plug-in developers totally ignore and have little or no experience with.

Sometimes a developer needs a quick solution, while at other times that same developer needs to gain in-depth knowledge about a particular aspect of development. The intent is to provide several different ways for the reader to absorb and use the information so that both needs can be addressed. Relevant APIs are included in several of the chapters so that the book can be used as a stand-alone reference during development without requiring the reader to look up those APIs in the IDE. Most API descriptions are copied or para-phrased from the Eclipse platform Javadoc.

As the originators of Eclipse and a major consumer of Eclipse-based tech-nology, IBM is justifiably concerned that new plug-ins meet the same high-quality standards that IBM adheres to. To that end, IBM has established a rig-orous *Ready for Rational Software* (RFRS) certification program meant to ensure the availability of high-quality add-ons to Eclipse and the IBM Software Development Platform. RFRS certification should be one of the ultimate goals for anyone wishing to build and market Eclipse plug-ins. Every chapter covers any relevant RFRS certification criteria and strategies.

The examples provided as part of the chapters describe building various aspects of a concrete Eclipse plug-in that you will see evolve over the course of the book. When used as a reference rather than read cover-to-cover, you will typically start to look in one chapter for issues that are covered in another. To facilitate this type of searching, every chapter contains numerous forward and backward references to related material that appears in other chapters.

Intended Audience

The audience for this book includes Java tool developers wishing to build products that integrate with Eclipse and other Eclipse-based products, relatively advanced Eclipse users wishing to customize their environments, or anyone who is curious about what makes Eclipse tick. You do not need to be an expert Eclipse user to make use of this book because we introduce most of what you need to know to use Eclipse in Chapter 1, Using Eclipse Tools. While we don't assume any preexisting Eclipse knowledge, we do anticipate that the reader is a fairly seasoned developer with a good grasp of Java and at least a cursory knowledge of extensible markup language (XML).

Conventions Used in This Book

The following formatting conventions are used throughout the book.

Bold — the names of UI elements such as menus, buttons, field labels, tabs, and window titles

Italic — emphasize new terms and Web site addresses

`Courier` — code examples, references to class and method names, and filenames

`Courier Bold` — emphasize code fragments

"Quoted text" — quotation marks surrounding text indicates words to be entered by the user

What's New in the Second Edition

In this edition, we use the same **Favorites** view example as in the first edition, but have recreated the code from scratch to take advantage of pure Eclipse 3.1 and 3.2 APIs. All the screenshots are new and much of the text has been reworked. Some Eclipse concepts, such as actions, views, and editors are similar but with additional functionality and capabilities; other areas, such as the Eclipse plug-in infrastructure, have changed drastically due to the Eclipse shift toward an OSGi-based infrastructure. While all the chapters have been updated, the following is a sample of some of the sections that are new or have changed significantly in this second edition:

- Section 2.3, Reviewing the Generated Code, on page 71
- Section 2.4, Building a Product, on page 81
- Section 3.1, Structural Overview, on page 101
- Section 3.2, Plug-in Directory or JAR file, on page 104
- Section 3.3, Plug-in Manifest, on page 107
- Section 3.4, Plug-in Class, on page 114
- Section 3.5, Plug-in Model, on page 119
- Section 6.3, Object Actions, on page 224
- Section 6.6, Key Bindings, on page 251
- Section 7.3, View Actions, on page 283
- Section 7.4, Linking the View, on page 305
- Section 8.1, Editor Declaration, on page 326
- Section 8.5, Editor Actions, on page 354
- Section 9.4, Progress Monitor, on page 383
- Section 11.1, Dialogs, on page 405
- Section 11.2, Wizards, on page 430
- Section 12.3, Preference APIs, on page 467
- Section 13.3, Displaying Properties in the Properties View, on page 489
- Section 14.1, Builders, on page 499
- Section 15.5, Cheat Sheets, on page 563
- Section 16.2, Externalizing Plug-in Strings, on page 578
- Section 18.2, Branding, on page 631
- Section 18.3, Update Sites, on page 637
- Section 19.2, Building the Favorites Product, on page 671
- Section 20.2, Accessing Internal Code, on page 711
- Section 20.4, Opening a Browser or Creating an Email, on page 718
- Section 20.7, Label Decorators, on page 732

Acknowledgments

The authors would like to thank all those who have had a hand in putting this book together or who gave us their support and encouragement throughout the many months it took to create.

To our comrades at Instantiations, who gave us the time and encouragement to work on this book: Brent Caldwell, Doug Camp, Taylor Corey, Dianne Engles, Mark Johnson, Jeff Kraft, Brian MacDonald, Warren Martin, Nancy McClure, Carl McConnell, Steve Messick, Alexander Mitin, Tim O'Conner, Keerti Parthasarathy, Nate Putnam, Phil Quitslund, Mark Russell, Konstantin Scheglov, Chuck Shawan, Julie Taylor, Mike Taylor, Solveig Viste, Brian Wilkerson, and Jaime Wren.

To our agent, Laura Lewin, and the staff at Studio B, who encouraged us from day one and worked tirelessly on our behalf.

To our editors, Greg Doench and John Neidhart, our production editors, Elizabeth Ryan and Kathleen Caren, our copy editors, Marilyn Rash and Camie Goffi, our editorial assistant, Mary Kate Murray, our art director, Sandra Schroeder, our marketing manager, Beth Wickenhiser, and the staff at Pearson, for their encouragement and tremendous efforts in preparing this book for production.

To Simon Archer who contributed an unparalleled number of changes and suggestions to both editions of the book, and helped us improve them in almost every dimension.

To Linda Barney who helped us polish and edit the second edition.

To our technical reviewers who helped us enhance the book in many ways: Matt Lavin, Kevin Hammond, Mark Russell, Keerti Parthasarathy, Jaime Wren, Joe Bowbeer, Brian Wilkerson, Joe Winchester, David Whiteman, Boris Pruesmann, and Raphael Enns.

To the many readers of the first edition who contributed errata that have gone into this second edition: Bruce Gruenbaum, Tony Saveski, James Carroll, Tony Weddle, Karen Ploski, Brian Vosburgh, Peter Nye, Chris Lott, David Watkins, Simon Archer, Mike Wilkins, Brian Penn, Bernd Essann, Eric Hein, Dave Hewitson, Frank Parrott, William Beebe, Jim Norris, and Jim Wingard.

To the series editors, Erich Gamma, Lee Nackman, and John Weigand, for their thoughtful comments and for their ongoing efforts to make Eclipse the best development environment in the world.

We would also like to thank our wives, Karen and Kathy, for their endless patience, and our children, Beth, Lauren, Lee, and David, for their endless inspiration.

About the Authors

Eric Clayberg is Senior Vice President for Product Development for Instantiations, Inc. Eric is a seasoned software technologist, product developer, entrepreneur, and manager with more than seventeen years of commercial software development experience, including nine years of experience with Java and six years with Eclipse. He is the primary author and architect of more than a dozen commercial Java and Smalltalk add-on products, including the popular WindowBuilder Pro, CodePro, and the award-winning VA Assist product lines. He has a B.S. from MIT, an MBA from Harvard, and has cofounded two successful software companies— ObjectShare and Instantiations.

Dan Rubel is Chief Technology Officer for Instantiations, Inc. He is an entrepreneur and an expert in the design and application of OO technologies with more than seventeen years of commercial software development experience, including ten years of experience with Java and six years with Eclipse. He is the primary architect and product manager for several successful commercial products, including jFactor, jKit/GO, and jKit/Grid, and has played key design and leadership roles in other commercial products such as WindowBuilder Pro, VA Assist, and CodePro. He has a B.S. from Bucknell and is a cofounder of Instantiations.

Instantiations is an Advanced IBM Business Partner and developer of many commercial add-ons for Eclipse and IBM's VisualAge, WebSphere and Rational product lines. Instantiations is a member of the Eclipse Foundation and a contributor to the Eclipse open source effort with responsibility for the Eclipse Collaboration Tools project known as Koi and for the Eclipse Pollinate project (Beehive).

How to Contact Us

While we have made every effort to make sure that the material in this book is timely and accurate, Eclipse is a rapidly moving target and it is quite possible that you may encounter differences between what we present here and what you experience using Eclipse. The Eclipse UI has evolved considerably over the years, and the latest 3.1 and 3.2 releases are no exceptions. While we have targeted it at Eclipse 3.1 and 3.2 and used them for all of our examples, this book was completed before Eclipse 3.2 was finally locked down. That means that you may encounter various views, dialogs, and wizards that are subtly different from the screenshots herein.

- Questions about the book's technical content should be addressed to: *info@qualityeclipse.com*
- Sales questions should be addressed to Addison-Wesley at: *www.awprofessional.com/bookstoresales.asp*
- Source code for the projects presented can be found at: *www.qualityeclipse.com/projects*
- Errata can be found at: *www.qualityeclipse.com/errata*
- Tools used and described can be found at: *www.qualityeclipse.com/tools*

CHAPTER 1

Using Eclipse Tools

This chapter discusses using the Eclipse development environment to create Java applications and, more to the point, to create enhancements for Eclipse itself. We with an explanation of where to get Eclipse and how to set it up. This is followed by a quick introduction to the Eclipse user interface (UI) and how it can be customized. Next, this chapter introduces a number of important Eclipse tools and describes how they are used to create an initial Java project, navigate and search the environment, and create and edit Java code. Eclipse developers typically want to work as part of a team and share their code with other members of their team, so this chapter also includes the setup and use of the Concurrent Versions System (CVS), which ships as part of Eclipse. After creating an initial Java project and class, we follow up with details for executing, debugging, and testing the code that has been written.

1.1 Getting Started

Before using Eclipse, download it from the Web, install it, and set it up.

1.1.1 Getting Eclipse

The main Web site for Eclipse is *www.eclipse.org* (see Figure 1–1). On that page, you can see the latest Eclipse news and links to a variety of online resources, including articles, newsgroups, bug tracking (see Section 20.2.2, Bugzilla—Eclipse bug tracking system, on page 712), and mailing lists.

1

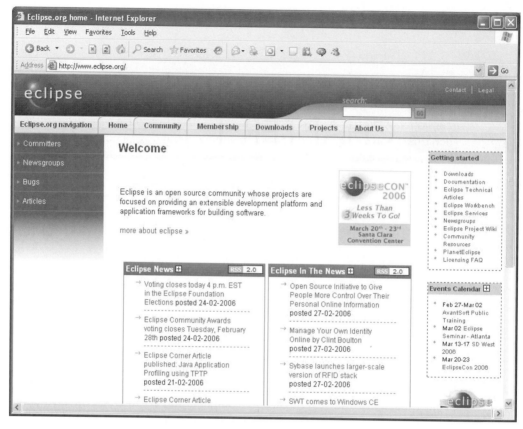

Figure 1–1   *Eclipse.org* home page.

The latest version of Eclipse can be downloaded from the main download page at *www.eclipse.org/downloads* (if this site is unavailable, a number of mirror sites around the world are available). Go ahead and download the latest release or stable build (also known as a *milestone*, as in Eclipse 3.2 M6). Typically, you should avoid *integration* or *nightly* builds unless you are involved in the development of Eclipse itself.

The download page for each release includes various notes concerning that release as well as links to every platform version. Eclipse supports a large number of platforms, including Windows, Linux, Solaris, HP, Mac OSX, and others. Choose the **Eclipse SDK** download link corresponding to your platform and save the Eclipse zip file to your computer's hard drive. This will generally be a very large file (>105 MB), so be patient unless you have sufficient bandwidth available to quickly download the file.

The download page includes a variety of other download links. You might also want to download the **Example plug-ins** file corresponding to your platform. Unless you have a specific need for one of the other downloads, you should ignore them for now.

> **Java Runtime Environment**   Eclipse is a Java program, but it does not include the Java Runtime Environment (JRE) necessary to make it run. Eclipse 3.1 and 3.2 can be used with any JRE newer than version 1.4, and most Java developers will already have a suitable JRE installed on their machines. If you don't have a JRE installed on your computer, you can download and install one from *java.sun.com*.

1.1.2   Installation

Once the Eclipse zip file has been successfully downloaded, unzip it to your hard drive. Eclipse does not modify the Windows registry, so it does not matter where it is installed. For the purposes of this book, assume that it has been installed into `C:\eclipse`. If you also downloaded any Eclipse examples, unzip them into the same location.

1.2   The Eclipse Workbench

To start Eclipse, double-click on the `eclipse.exe` file in the `C:\eclipse` directory. The first time Eclipse is launched, it displays a dialog in which you can select the location for your workspace directory (typically a directory underneath your user directory). To avoid seeing this dialog every time you start Eclipse, check the **Use this as the default and do not ask again** option.

> **Tip:** Creating a shortcut for launching Eclipse provides a way to specify an alternative workspace directory as well as increases the amount of memory allocated to the program. For example:
>
> ```
> C:\eclipse\eclipse.exe -data C:\MyWorkspace -vmargs -Xms128M -Xmx256M
> ```
>
> In this example, the workspace has been set to `C:\MyWorkspace`, the starting amount of memory to 128 MB, and the maximum amount of memory to 256 MB. Setting the workspace location is essential if you plan to migrate to newer versions of Eclipse in the future. A complete list of these and other command-line switches, such as `-vm` and `-showlocation`, can be found in the online help (see Chapter 15, Implementing Help) under **Workbench User Guide > Tasks > Running Eclipse**. For more on memory usage, see *www.qualityeclipse.com/doc/memory.html*.

In a few moments, the main Eclipse workbench window appears (see Figure 1–2). Normally, it consists of a main menu bar and toolbar as well as a number of tiled panes known as views and editors (these will be discussed in great detail in Chapters 7, Views, and 8, Editors). Initially, only a full-screen welcome page, known as the **Welcome** view, is visible and fills the entire workbench window.

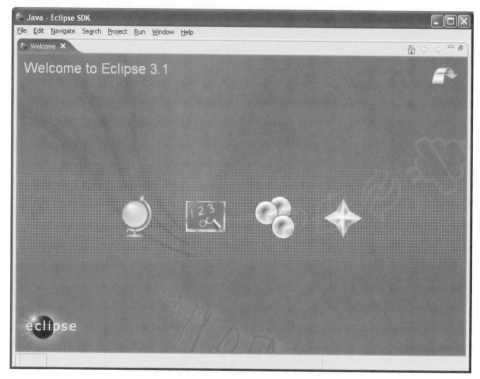

Figure 1–2   Eclipse workbench window.

The **Welcome** view opens automatically the first time that Eclipse is launched (it can be reopened at any time by using the **Help > Welcome** command). Take a moment to look it over as it provides links to other tools and resources to get you started with Eclipse such as an overview, tutorial, and a list of sample applications.

Closing the **Welcome** view (by clicking the "**X**" button on its title tab) will reveal several additional views (see Figure 1–3).

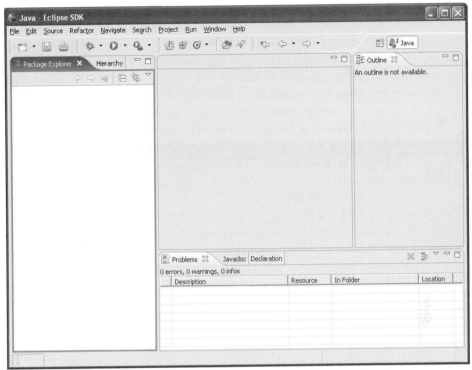

Figure 1–3   Workbench window with the Package Explorer view active.

1.2.1   *Perspectives, views, and editors*

Collectively, the combination of various views (e.g., **Package Explorer, Hierarchy, Outline, Problems, Javadoc,** and **Declaration**) and editors (used to work with various resources) visible within the Eclipse workbench are known as a *perspective*. A perspective can be thought of as one page within the Eclipse workbench. Multiple perspectives can be open at one time, and each has an icon (with or without a text description) visible in the perspective toolbar at the upper right corner of the workbench window. The perspective that is currently active has its name shown in the title bar of the window and its icon appears selected.

Views are typically used to navigate resources and modify properties of a resource. Any changes made within a view are saved immediately. By contrast, editors are used to view or modify a specific resource and follow the common open-save-close model.

Every perspective has its own set of views, but open editors are shared by all open perspectives. Only a single instance of any one view can be open in a given perspective, while any number of editors of the same type can be open at one time.

The currently active view or editor has its title bar highlighted. This is the view or editor that will be the recipient of any global actions such as cut, copy, or paste. All the other panes are inactive and their title bars appear grayed out. For instance, when you click on the **Package Explorer** view, its title bar becomes highlighted, indicating that it is active (see Figure 1–3), and the title bars of the other views turn gray, indicating that they are now inactive.

Views and editors can be resized by dragging the sizing border that appears on each side of the pane. Since Eclipse uses a tiled display for each of its panes, making one larger makes its neighbors smaller, and vice versa.

Panes can be moved around by dragging their individual title bars. If you drag a view onto another view, the two views will stack up with tabs indicating each of the views. Selecting a tab brings that view to the top of the stack. If a view is dropped into the sizing area between views, the view grabs a portion of the available area and inserts itself next to the view that previously occupied that space. The views that originally occupied that space shrink in size to accommodate the new view.

Right-clicking on a view's tab and selecting the **Fast View** command causes the view to dock to the *fast view* bar at the bottom edge of the window (you can drag the fast view bar to the left or right side of the window as well). Fast views remain docked to the fast view bar as icons until clicked on, at which point they expand to overlap most of the window area. Fast views are ideal for views that don't need to be seen all the time, but require a great deal of screen area when they are visible.

Right-clicking and selecting the **Detached** command causes the view to open into a separate, floating window that can be moved outside of the workbench area or that can float on top of the workbench area. Selecting the **Detached** command a second time will reattach the view into the workbench window.

Many different views are defined within Eclipse and only a few are visible when the workbench first opens. To add views to a perspective, select the **Window > Show View** command and choose the view you would like to see (or the **Other...** command to see a list of all views defined in the system).

Tip: Many third-party plug-ins are available, providing enhancements to the various Eclipse perspectives. For example, CodePro (see Appendix A, Eclipse Plug-ins and Resources) provides color-enhanced versions of the main Eclipse perspectives and views.

1.2.1.1   *Java perspectives*

At this point, we should quickly review the various perspectives you are most likely to use while developing plug-ins. The initial perspective shown in the workbench window is the **Java** perspective (see Figure 1–3).

Eclipse includes two perspectives for the development of Java code. Selecting the **Window > Open Perspective > Java** command opens the first, known as the **Java** perspective.

The primary view within the Java perspective is the **Package Explorer**. The **Package Explorer** shows the hierarchy of Java files and resources within the Java projects loaded into your workbench, providing a very Java-centric view of resources rather than a file-centric view.

For example, rather than showing Java packages as nested folders as in the **Navigator** view (see Section 1.2.1.2, Resource perspective, on page 9), the **Package Explorer** shows each package as a separate element in a flattened hierarchy. Any JAR file that is referenced within a project can also be browsed this way.

The second major Java perspective is the **Java Browsing** perspective. Selecting the **Window > Open Perspective > Java Browsing** command (see Figure 1–4) opens the **Java Browsing** perspective (see Figure 1–5).

Figure 1–4   Opening the Java Browsing perspective.

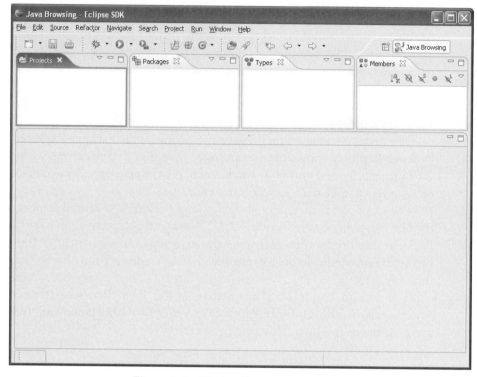

Figure 1–5 The Java Browsing perspective.

The **Java Browsing** perspective includes a series of linked views reminiscent of the browsers found in various Smalltalk integrated development environments (IDEs) or within IBM's VisualAge for Java IDE. The first view shows a list of loaded projects. Selecting a project shows its contained packages within the **Packages** view; selecting a package shows its types in the **Types** view; and selecting a type shows its members in the **Members** view. Selecting a method or field in the **Members** view will highlight that member in the corresponding editor.

> **Tip:** You can easily drag the individual views around to customize the layout to your taste. To get more vertical real estate associated with the editor area, consider stacking the four views vertically. Another common way to save some space in this perspective is to combine the **Projects** and **Packages** views into a single tabbed area, or drag the **Projects** view onto the fast view bar.

1.2.1.2   Resource perspective

While the **Java** perspectives provide tools for Java development, they are not ideal for reviewing all the resources in the workspace. The **Resource** perspective (see Figure 1-6) provides a hierarchical view of the files and folders within your system.

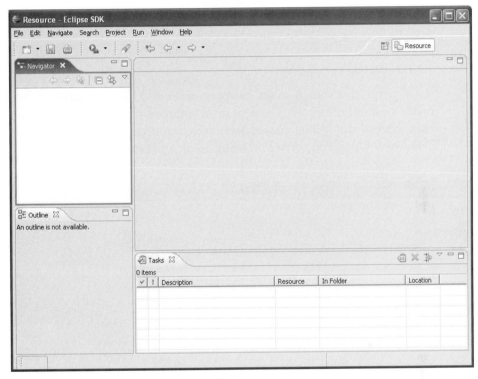

Figure 1–6   The Resource perspective.

The primary view within the **Resource** perspective is the **Navigator**, which presents a hierarchical view of the resources (projects, folders, and files) loaded in the workbench. The **Navigator** has its own toolbar and view menu (see Figure 1–7), which provide various viewing and filtering options. The view menu is accessed by clicking on the small down arrow on the right side of the view's toolbar.

Figure 1–7   The Navigator view.

1.2.1.3   Debug perspective

Each perspective shown so far has been optimized for the purpose of writing code or editing resources. The next most common type of perspective you will encounter is the **Debug** perspective, which you can access by selecting the **Window > Open Perspective > Debug** command (see Figure 1–8).

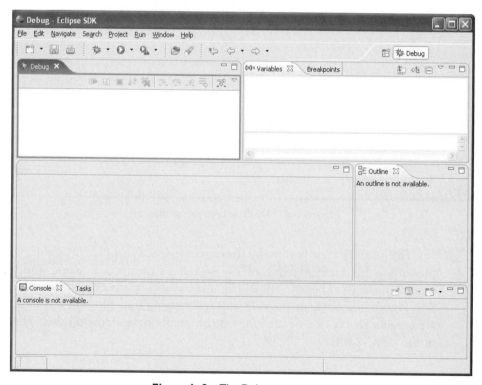

Figure 1–8   The Debug perspective.

As its name suggests, the **Debug** perspective is used to debug programs and easily find and correct runtime errors in Java code. You can step through individual statements within your code, set breakpoints, and inspect the values associated with individual variables. This is discusssed in more detail in Section 1.10.1, Setting breakpoints, on page 58.

1.2.2   Actions

In addition to the views and editors that make up the bulk of the display area, Eclipse includes a number of top-level and context menus and toolbar buttons that represent the various commands or actions available in the system.

1.2.2.1   Top-level menus

The basic Eclipse menu bar includes ten top-level menus: **File, Edit, Source, Refactor, Navigate, Search, Project, Run, Window,** and **Help** (see Figure 1–9). Additional menus may also be present depending on which add-on tools you have loaded or which perspectives and views you are using.

- The **File** menu provides actions to create new resources; save, close and print resources; refresh resources relative to their associated disk files; import and export resources; inspect the properties of resources; and exit the workbench.

- The **Edit** menu provides actions to work with the resources open in the editor area. It includes standard functions, such as cut, copy, and paste, as well as functions such as delete, select all, find, and replace.

- The **Source** menu provides commands to manipulate the current source such as adding and removing block comments, shifting left and right, formatting, organizing imports, and so on.

- The **Refactor** menu provides commands to refactor the selected Java elements. Sample refactorings include renaming fields and methods, moving elements, extracting methods and local variables, converting variables to fields, and so on.

Figure 1–9   The Java perspective menu bar and toolbar.

- The **Navigate** menu provides actions to traverse the resources loaded in the workbench. It provides commands that allow you to drill down into resources and then navigate within them much like you would with a Web browser.

- The **Search** menu provides access to workbench-wide search tools such as global file search, help search, Java search, and plug-in search. We will discuss searching in more detail later.

- The **Project** menu provides actions to manipulate the projects loaded in the workbench. You can open any closed project, close any open projects, and manually build either an individual project or all the projects in the workbench.

- The **Run** menu contains perspective-specific items for running or debugging your Java applications. It also includes an **External Tools** option that allows you to run any arbitrary external tool on the resources in your workbench.

- The **Window** menu includes items to open additional workbench windows, open different perspectives, and add any view to the current perspective. It also allows you to customize the current perspective and to access preferences for the entire workbench (more on this in Section 1.2.2.2).

- The **Help** menu provides access to various tips and tricks, software updates, information about the current workbench configuration, and general help on the entire environment.

1.2.2.2 Context menus

Right-clicking on any view or editor (except on the title bar) will reveal a context-sensitive popup menu. The contents of the menu depend not only on the view or editor that was clicked on, but also on the resources that were selected at the time. For example, Figure 1–10 shows three sample context menus.

The first sample is the context menu from the **Navigator** view when nothing is selected, the second example is the same context menu when a Java file is selected in the **Navigator** view, and the third shows the context menu that appears when a Java file is selected in the **Package Explorer** view. Note that some options, such as the **Refactor** submenu, only appear in certain views under the right circumstances.

Figure 1–10   Context menus.

1.2.2.3   Toolbars

Much like the context menus that appear when right-clicking in a view, the toolbar items that appear are context-sensitive depending on which perspective is in use and which editor has focus. Standard, common items appear first on the toolbar, with any editor-specific items at the end. When using the **Resource** perspective, the standard toolbar items visible by default include icons for creating new files, saving and printing resources, running external tools, accessing the search functions, and navigating recently accessed resources in browser style (see Figure 1–11).

Switching to the **Java** perspective (see Figure 1–9) causes several new icons to appear for running or debugging your Java applications and for creating new Java projects, packages, and files.

Figure 1–11   The Resource perspective menu bar and toolbar.

1.2.2.4 Customizing available actions

You do have some limited control over which items appear on the toolbar and on the main menu bar. Many commands are part of *command groups* known as *action sets* that can be selectively enabled and disabled using the **Customize Perspective** dialog. To customize the current perspective, select the **Window > Customize Perspective...** command, which opens the **Customize Perspective** dialog (see Figure 1–12). The toolbar and menu command groups are shown on the **Commands** page. Check the command groups you want to keep and uncheck all others. Use the **Shortcuts** page of the dialog to customize the entries on the **New, Open Perspective,** and **Show View** menus.

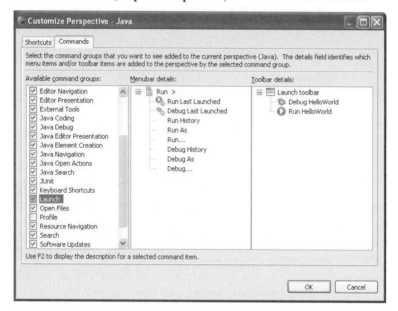

Figure 1–12   Customize Perspective dialog.

1.3   Setting Up Your Environment

The previous section briefly touched on customizing the current perspective, while this section goes into more detail on how to customize your Eclipse environment by changing various preferences. To customize Eclipse preferences, select the **Window > Preferences...** command, which opens the **Preferences** dialog (see Figure 1–13). Dozens of individual preference pages are grouped together in the hierarchy pane on the left side of the dialog. General workbench preferences are in the **General** group, while Java preferences are in the **Java** group. At the top of the dialog, a convenient filter field makes it easy to quickly find specific preference pages.

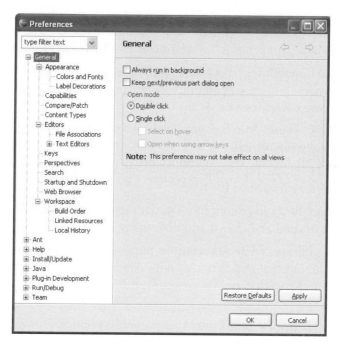

Figure 1–13   Preferences dialog.

Many hundreds of individual preferences can be accessed from the **Prefer-ences** dialog. Changing a value and clicking the **Apply** button locks in changes and allows you to continue setting other preferences. Clicking the **OK** button locks in changes and closes the dialog. The **Restore Defaults** button resets the preferences on the current page to the system's default values.

1.3.1   *Workbench preferences*

Most general Eclipse preferences can be found in the **General** category. Some highlights include:

- The **General** page determines whether opening a resource requires single- or double-clicking.

- The **Appearance** page determines whether view and editor tabs appear on the top or bottom.

- The **Appearance > Colors and Fonts** page provides options for customiz-ing colors and fonts for many different workspace elements such as stan-dard text font, dialog font, header font, error colors, and many others.

- The **Appearance > Label Decorations** page provides access to options that can enhance an item's icon and label. The **CVS** label decorator, for example, prepends a ">" character to all changed resources.

- The **Capabilities** page contains options for enabling and disabling various capabilities. Capabilities allow you to enable and disable various product features as a group.

- The **Compare/Patch** page allows you to control the behavior of the text comparison views.

- The **Content Types** page contains options for associating various content types with various file types.

- The **Editors** page contains a variety of options controlling how editors are opened and closed and how many can be open at one time.

- The **Editors > File Associations** page associates different editor types (both internal and external) with different file types. For example, if you wanted to associate Microsoft FrontPage with HTML files, you would do that here.

- The **Editors > Text Editors** page contains options controlling the appearance of editors such as the visibility of line numbers, current line highlighting, various item colors, and annotations.

- The **Keys** page provides options for customizing the key bindings for many commands in the system. It includes a predefined standard set of key bindings as well as a set of Emacs key bindings.

- The **Perspectives** page allows you to control which perspective is your default perspective and whether new perspectives are opened in the current window or in a new window.

- The **Search** page allows you to control the behavior of the **Search** view.

- The **Startup and Shutdown** page shows a list of any plug-ins requiring early activation. Most plug-ins are activated on first use, but some need to be activated on startup. This page provides the option of preventing those plug-ins from starting up early.

- The **Web Browser** page allows you to configure which Web browser is used when you open a Web page.

- The **Workspace** page contains various build and save options.

- The **Workspace > Build Order** page controls the order in which projects in your workspace are built.

- The **Workspace > Linked Resources** page allows you to define path variables used to provide relative references to linked resources.

- The **Workspace > Local History** page (see Figure 1–51) controls how many local changes are maintained. The default values are fairly small, so you should consider increasing them quite a bit. The more local history you keep, the more type and method versions you will be able to roll back to easily (see Section 1.7.4, Local history, on page 44 for tips on how to best use this feature).

1.3.2   Java preferences

Preferences specific to the Java development tools included in Eclipse can be found in the **Java** category of preferences. Some of the highlights include:

- The **Java** page provides options controlling the behavior of various Java views and editors.

- The **Appearance** page controls the appearance of Java elements in the various Java views.

- The **Build Path > Classpath Variables** page (see Figure 1–14) provides a place to define new classpath variables that can be added to a project's classpath.

- The **Code Style > Formatter** page (see Figure 1–39) controls the options the Eclipse Java code formatter uses to format Java code. It includes options for controlling brace position, new lines, line length, and white space usage.

- The **Code Style > Code Templates** page defines the naming conventions and default comments used in generated code for types, methods, fields, variables, and parameters.

- The **Compiler** page provides options for controlling the severity levels of various compilation and build path problems as well as various Java Development Kit (JDK) compliance options.

- The **Editor** page controls numerous options dealing with the appearance of elements within the Java editor (such as bracket matching, print margin, and current line highlighting), color highlighting of Java syntax (see Figure 1–38), the behavior and appearance of code assistance (see Figure 1–42), and problem annotations.

- The **Editor > Templates** page provides a place to define and edit various Javadoc and Java code templates (templates are common source code patterns that appear frequently in user-written code).

- The **Installed JREs** page provides options for specifying which JREs should be used with the workbench.

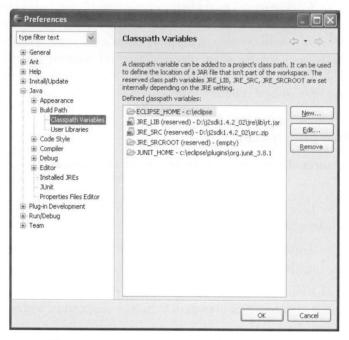

Figure 1–14   Classpath Variables preference page.

1.3.3 Importing and exporting preferences

Setting up multiple Eclipse workspaces or migrating from one Eclipse version to another can be inconvenient due to the difficulty of moving workspace preferences from one version to another. Likewise, configuring multiple users' workspaces with common settings, such as code formatting preferences and classpath variable settings, can also be very difficult.

The Eclipse **Export** and **Import** wizards include **Preferences** options that are intended to help solve this problem. Selecting **File > Export...** and then **Preferences** opens a wizard that prompts for the name of a preference export file (an .epf file) and records any non-default preference settings in it. Selecting **File > Import...** and then **Preferences** opens a wizard that is used to import a preference file. Options are provided to export your preferences at various levels of granularity. You can export all workspace preferences or specific ones.

This mechanism for exporting and importing preferences is less than ideal, however, because of problems handling various types of preferences such as classpath variables (which are exported using hard-coded paths rather than workspace-relative paths) and code templates (which are not exported at all).

1.4   Creating a Project

Earlier sections of this chapter introduced the Eclipse workbench and showed a number of ways to customize the environment. The next step is to actually use Eclipse to get some work done. This section takes you through the steps needed to create your first Eclipse project.

In the basic Eclipse environment, three different types of projects, simple, Java, and plug-in development, can be created.

1. **Simple** projects, as their name implies, are the simplest type of Eclipse project. They can contain any type of arbitrary resource, including text files, HTML files, and so on.

2. **Java** projects are used to hold the Java source code and resources needed to create a Java application. The next section describes the process of creating a Java project.

3. **Plug-in development** projects are used to create Eclipse plug-ins. This is the type of project that this book primarily concerns itself with, and Chapter 2, A Simple Plug-in Example, goes through a detailed example of how to create a plug-in project.

1.4.1   Using the new Java Project wizard

To create a new Java project, select the **File > New > Project...** command or click the 🔼 **New Java Project** toolbar button in the **Java** perspective to open the **New Project** wizard (see Figure 1–15). On the first page, select **Java Project** from the list and click the **Next** button. Under Eclipse 3.2, a filter field is available at the top of the wizard to make it easy to find specific project types.

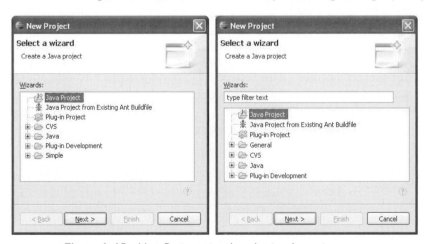

Figure 1–15   New Project wizard—selecting the project type.
The Eclipse 3.1 version is shown on the left and the Eclipse 3.2 version is
shown on the right. The Eclipse 3.2 version adds a filter field above the list of wizards.

On the second page of the wizard (see Figure 1–16), enter the name of the project (e.g., "First Project") and click the **Next** button. Note that this page also includes options for specifying the location of the project and its structure. By default, the project will be placed within the workspace directory and will use the project folder as the root for sources and class files.

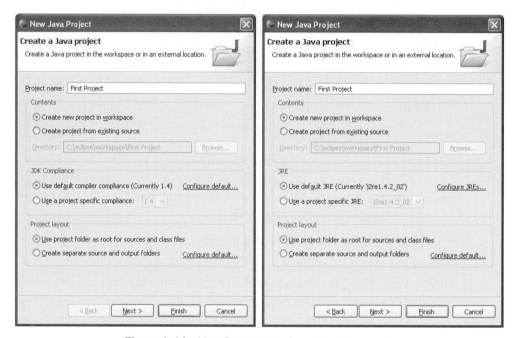

Figure 1–16   New Project wizard—naming the project.
The Eclipse 3.1 version is shown on the left and the Eclipse 3.2 version is shown on the right. Note the minor differences in terminology used in the center section of the pages.

The next page of the wizard (see Figure 1–17) contains build path settings for the Java project. The **Source** tab provides a place to add source folders, which act as roots for packages containing Java files. The **Projects** tab allows you to set up project dependencies by selecting other projects in the workbench on which this project depends.

> **Tip:** Traditionally, source files are placed in a separate source folder named **src** and the compiler output is in a **bin** directory. Placing these types of files in separate directories results in an easier build process. Use the **Java > Build Path** preference page to specify the default directory names used when creating new Java projects.

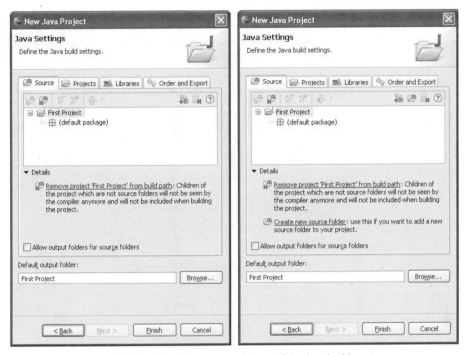

Figure 1–17 New Project wizard—specifying Java build settings.
The Eclipse 3.1 version is shown on the left and the Eclipse 3.2 version is shown on the right.
Note the addition of the **Create new source folder** option in the **Details**
section of the right page.

The **Libraries** tab is the place to add JAR files (either stored in the work-bench or out on the file system). The last tab, **Order and Export,** controls the order of build path elements and whether they are exported and visible to other projects that require this project.

The **Default output folder** field, at the bottom the page, is used to specify the default location where compilation output will be stored. When the **Finish** button is clicked, the new project is created and appears in the **Package Explorer** view or the **Navigator** view, depending on which perspective is active.

Differences between Eclipse 3.1 and 3.2 As you can see from the last three screenshots, there are a number of minor differences between Eclipse 3.1 and 3.2. For the most part, the differences won't impact your use of this book; however, differences will be highlighted whenever they are relevant or interesting.

1.4.2 .classpath and .project files

In addition to creating the project itself, two additional files are created—
.classpath and project. By default, both of those files as well as any other
files beginning with "." are hidden from view via a filter.

To show the files, select the **Filters...** command from the drop-down view
menu in the **Package Explorer** (see Figure 1–18), uncheck the **.* resources**
filter in the **Java Element Filters** dialog (see Figure 1–19) and click the **OK**
button.

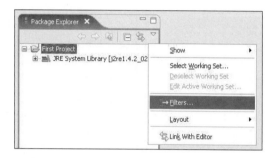

Figure 1–18   Filter menu.

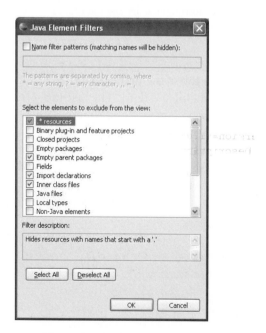

Figure 1–19   Filter dialog.

The `.classpath` file stores the *Java build path* for the project. It should look something like the following for the project you just created:

```
<?xml version="1.0" encoding="UTF-8"?>
<classpath>
    <classpathentry kind="src" path=""/>
    <classpathentry kind="con"
        path="org.eclipse.jdt.launching.JRE_CONTAINER"/>
    <classpathentry kind="output" path=""/>
</classpath>
```

Rather than editing the `.classpath` file directly, Eclipse provides a more user-friendly approach. Right-click on the project and select **Properties**. In the **Properties** dialog, selecting **Java Build Path** displays an interface similar to Figure 1–17 for editing the project's classpath.

> **Java Build Path** "Java classpath" is a generic term describing both the classpath used at compile-time and the classpath used at runtime. In Eclipse, the compile-time classpath is called the *Java build path*. When you are running or debugging Java application code, the runtime classpath is determined by the launch configuration (see Section 1.9.2, Launch configurations, on page 56). When you are developing Eclipse plug-ins, the runtime classpath is determined by the dependency declaration in the plug-in manifest (see Section 2.3.1, The Plug-in manifests, on page 71).

The `.project` file provides a complete description of the project suitable for recreating it in the workbench if it is exported and then imported. Your new project should look like the following:

```
<?xml version="1.0" encoding="UTF-8"?>
<projectDescription>
    <name>First Project</name>
    <comment></comment>
    <projects>
    </projects>
    <buildSpec>
        <buildCommand>
            <name>org.eclipse.jdt.core.javabuilder</name>
            <arguments></arguments>
        </buildCommand>
    </buildSpec>
    <natures>
        <nature>org.eclipse.jdt.core.javanature</nature>
    </natures>
</projectDescription>
```

The `nature` tag indicates what kind of project this is. The nature, `org.eclipse.jdt.core.javanature`, indicates that it is a Java project.

1.4.3 *Using the Java Package wizard*

To create a Java package, select **File > New > Package** or click the  **New Java Package** toolbar button to open the **New Java Package** wizard (see Figure 1-20). Enter the name of the package (e.g., "`com.qualityeclipse.sample`") and click the **Finish** button.

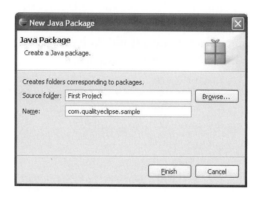

Figure 1–20   New Java Package wizard.

Note that the icon next to the new Java package name (see Figure 1–21) is hollow, indicating that it is empty. When one or more Java files are added to the package, the icon will appear in color.

Figure 1–21   New Java package in the Package Explorer.

1.4.4 *Using the Java Class wizard*

To create a Java class, select **File > New > Class** or click the  **New Java Class** toolbar button to open the **New Java Class** wizard, as shown in Figure 1-22. Enter the name of the class (e.g., "HelloWorld"), check the **public static**

void main(String[] args) checkbox, and click the **Finish** button. Note that the wizard presents numerous additional options for creating a new class, including its superclass, interfaces, and initial default methods.

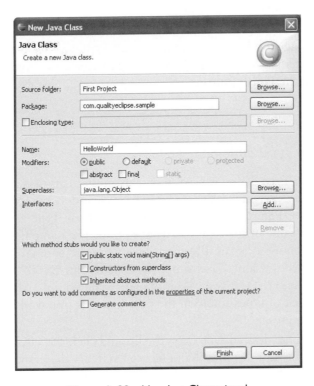

Figure 1–22 New Java Class wizard.

This process creates a new Java class (see Figure 1–23). The entry, **HelloWorld.java**, represents the file itself. Expanding that item reveals elements representing the class and its single "main" method. Note that the icon next to the package name is now in color, indicating that it is no longer empty.

Figure 1–23 New Java class in the Package Explorer.

1.5   Navigating

Eclipse includes a number of tools designed to make it easy to navigate the system and find information. This section discusses some of the tools accessible from the Eclipse **Navigate** menu.

> **Tip:** Many third-party plug-ins are available that provide various navigational enhancements for Eclipse (see Appendix A). For example, CodePro provides a **Java History** view that keeps track of any Java files you have accessed as well as a **Modified Type** view that track any types you have changed.

1.5.1   Open Type dialog

The **Open Type** dialog is used to quickly jump to any Java class in the system. Select the **Navigate > Open Type...** command (**Ctrl+Shift+T**) to open the dialog (see Figure 1–24) or click the 📂 **Open Type** toolbar button, then enter the name of the type you want to find. The name field allows wildcards and will show a list of all types that match the entered pattern. The dialog also provides CamelCase support, so entering "NPE" will find the class `NullPointerException`. If nothing is entered into the field, the dialog shows a list of types found in the past (the first time you access the dialog, it will be empty).

Select the desired type from the list and click the **OK** button to open that type in an editor. If more than one type matches the name, the package name qualifier will be displayed to the right of the type name.

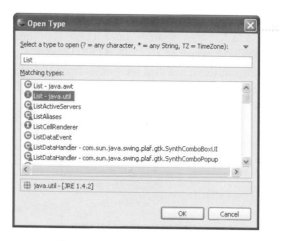

Figure 1–24   Open Type dialog.

1.5.2 Type Hierarchy view

The **Type Hierarchy** view shows the superclasses and subclasses of a given type (see Figure 1–25). The view also has options for showing just the supertype hierarchy (both superclasses and implemented interfaces) or subtype hierarchy (subclasses and interface implementers) of a type.

The **Type Hierarchy** view can be accessed in several different ways. The easiest way is to select the type name in an editor, then select the **Navigate > Open Type Hierarchy** command (or use the **F4** keyboard shortcut). Alternatively, select the **Navigate > Open Type in Hierarchy...** command (**Ctrl+Shift+H**) to open the **Open Type** dialog, as shown in Figure 1–24.

Figure 1–25   Type Hierarchy view.

1.5.3 Go to Line

To jump to a specific line of code within a file, use the **Navigate > Go to Line...** command (**Ctrl+L**). This opens a prompter for entering the desired line number (see Figure 1–26). Clicking the **OK** button jumps to that line in the editor.

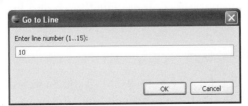

Figure 1–26   Line number prompter.

1.5.4 Outline view

The **Outline** view shows an outline of the structural elements of the selected editor. The contents vary depending on the type of editor in use. For example, when editing a Java class, the **Outline** view displays the classes, fields, and methods in the Java class being edited (see Figure 1–27).

The Java **Outline** view includes a number of options to control which elements are displayed within the outline. There are filters for hiding fields, static members, non-public members, and local types. In addition, there are options for sorting members (shown in definition order by default) and drilling down to the top-level type (normally, the outline starts at the file level).

Figure 1–27   Outline view.

1.6   Searching

In addition to the navigation tools available from the **Navigate** menu, Eclipse includes a number of powerful search tools accessible from the **Search** menu. The Eclipse **Search** dialog, accessible via the **Search > Search...** command (**Ctrl+H**) or the 🔍 **Search** toolbar button, acts as a portal to a number of different searching tools, including **File Search**, **Java Search**, and **Plug-in Search**. The two most important tools are **File Search** and **Java Search**.

1.6.1   File Search

The **File Search** tab (see Figure 1–28) of the **Search** dialog provides a way to find arbitrary files in the workbench by name or by the text they contain. To search for files containing a certain expression, enter that expression into the **Containing text** field. Various wildcards, such as "***** " to match any set of characters and "**?**" to match any single character, are supported. By default, the search is case-sensitive; to make it case-insensitive, uncheck the **Case sensitive** option. To perform complex text searches using regular expressions, turn on the **Regular expression** option.

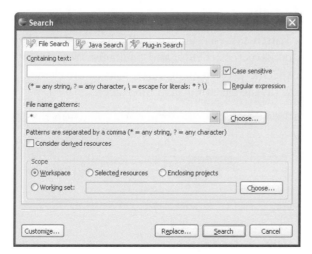

Figure 1–28 File Search tab.

To search for files by name, leave the **Containing text** field blank. To restrict a search to certain types of files or files containing a certain naming pattern, enter the file name expression into the **File name patterns** field.

The **Scope** fields provide another way to further restrict a search. The **Workspace** scope encompasses the entire workspace while the **Working set** scope limits a search to only those files contained in the selected working set. The **Selected resources** scope limits a search to only those files that have been selected in the active view (for example, the **Navigator** view or **Package Explorer** view), while the **Enclosing projects** scope limits a search to the projects containing the selected files.

For example, to search for all files containing the text "xml", enter that text into the **Containing text** field and leave the **File name patterns** field and **Scope** fields unchanged. When ready, click the **Search** button to find the matching files and display them in the **Search** view (see Figure 1–29). Clicking the **Replace** button rather than the **Search** button will perform the same search, but it will open up a **Replace** dialog where you can enter replacement text.

Figure 1–29 File search results.

Tip: If your goal is to search for various Java elements, such as types, methods, fields, and so on, the **Java Search** option is much more powerful than the **File Search** option.

1.6.2   Java Search

The **Java Search** tab (see Figure 1–30) locates Java elements such as types, methods, constructors, fields, and packages. You can use it to find declarations of a specific Java element, references to the element, or implementors of the element (in the case of a Java interface).

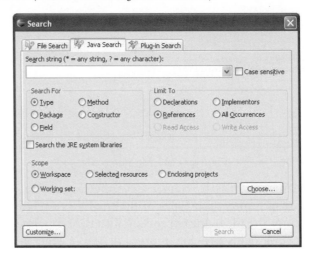

Figure 1–30   Java Search tab.

To search for elements with a specific name, enter the name in the **Search string** field (wildcards are supported). Depending on the kind of Java element you are interested in, select the **Type, Method, Package, Constructor,** or **Field** radio button. You can further limit search results to **Declarations, References, Implementors** (of Java interfaces), **All Occurrences, Read Access** (for fields), or **Write Access** (for fields).

As with the **File Search** tab, the **Scope** fields provide another way to restrict a search. The **Workspace** scope includes the entire workspace, the **Working set** scope limits the search to a specific working set, the **Selected resources** scope limits the search to the selected files in the active view, and the **Enclosing projects** scope limits the search to the projects containing the selected files.

> **Tip:** Consider building a reference project if you want to search the entire Eclipse plug-in source (see Section 20.1, Advanced Search—Reference Projects, on page 710).

For example, to search for all methods named "toLowerCase", enter that text into the **Search string** field, select the **Search For > Method** and **Limit To > Declarations** radio buttons, and leave the **Scope** fields unchanged. When ready, click the **Search** button to find the methods matching that name and to display them hierarchically in the **Search** view. Several options are available on the view toolbar for grouping the results by project, package, file, or class. Select the **Flat Layout** command from the view menu to see the results listed individually (see Figure 1–31).

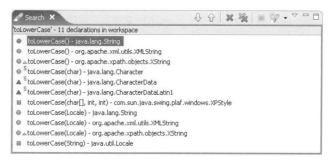

Figure 1–31   Java search results.

Double-clicking on any search result opens an editor on the file containing that result, highlights the search match in the text, and places a search marker in the left gutter area (also known as the marker bar, or left vertical ruler) of the editor (see Figure 1–32). Clicking the **Show Next Match** or **Show Previous Match** buttons (the up and down arrows) in the **Search** view selects the next or previous match (opening a new editor on a different file if necessary). You can also continue to search ("drill-down") using the context menus in the **Search** view.

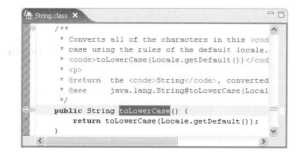

Figure 1–32   Editor showing search match and search marker.

1.6.3   Other Search menu options

The **Search** menu contains a number of dedicated, easy-to-use Java search commands that replicate the options found on the **Java Search** page of the **Search** dialog (see Figure 1–33).

Figure 1–33   Dedicated Java search commands.

Selecting a Java element either in a view or in a Java editor and then selecting the **Search > Declarations** command finds all elements with matching declarations in the workspace, the current project, the current type hierarchy, or
a specific working set. Likewise, selecting the **Search > References** command
finds all the places where the element is used. The **Search > Implementors,**
Search > Declarations, and **Search > Write Access** commands work similarly.
Note that the same commands are also available from the context menu in the
Java editor and the **Search** view.

1.6.4 Working sets

Working sets have been mentioned a number of times so far. They are used to
create a group of elements to act either as a filter in various views, such as
Navigator and **Package Explorer,** or as search scopes in the **Search** dialog or
any search menu. Working sets are extremely useful when you have a large
workspace containing many projects because they limit the scope of your code
and make many tasks easier.

To select a working set or to create a new one, choose **Scope > Working**
Set in the **Search** dialog, then click the **Choose** button. This opens the **Select**
Working Set dialog (see Figure 1–34). To use an existing working set, select it
from the list and click the **OK** button. To edit a working set, click the **Edit** button instead.

> **Tip:** Eclipse 3.2 adds the ability to select multiple working sets. This
> creates, in effect, a new *virtual* working set that merges the results
> from each of the selected sets. This makes it easier to create multiple,
> finer-grained working sets and then combine them in different
> combinations.

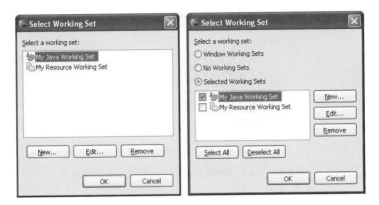

Figure 1–34   Select Working Set dialog.
The Eclipse 3.1 version is shown on the left, and the Eclipse 3.2 version is
shown on the right. Under Eclipse 3.2, multiple working sets can be selected.

Click the **New…** button to create a new working set. This opens the **New Working Set** dialog (see Figure 1–35). Four different types of working sets can be created: Resource, Java, Plug-ins, and Breakpoint working sets. Select the type of working set you want to create and click the **Next** button.

Figure 1–35   New Working Set dialog.

The next page of the **New Working Set** dialog facilitates defining new working sets (see Figure 1–36). Enter the desired name into the **Working set name** field and select the contents from the **Working set content** list. Clicking the **Finish** button closes the **New Working Set** dialog and adds the new working set to the **Select Working Set** dialog.

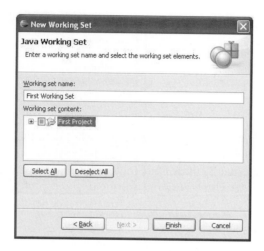

Figure 1–36   Define a New Working Set.

1.7   Writing Code

Now that your first Java project has created and you have explored different ways to navigate the system and find the items needed, it is time to start using Eclipse tools to write new code. Eclipse supports a number of different editor types, both internal and external, for editing types of resources. Double-clicking on a Java file, for example, opens the Java editor (see Figure 1-37).

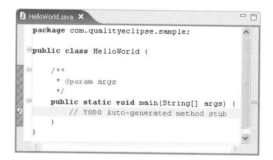

Figure 1–37   Java editor.

1.7.1   Java editor

The Java editor provides many features that focus on the job of editing Java code, including the following:

- Colored syntax highlighting (see Figure 1–37)
- User-defined code formatting
- Import organization and correction
- Context-sensitive code assistance
- "Quick fix" automatic problem correction

> **Tip:** Many former VisualAge for Java users loved the ability of that IDE to show only a single method at a time rather than the entire Java file. The Eclipse Java editor supports the same capability via the ▣ **Show Source of Selected Element Only** toolbar button. For it to work, you must give focus to an editor since the button is not enabled until you're actually editing some code. This is one of those options in Eclipse that should be a workspace preference rather than a toolbar button.

1.7.1.1 Colored syntax highlighting

The colored syntax highlighting feature controls how Java code will be depicted. Independent control over color and font style (plain or bold) is provided for multi- and single-line comments, keywords, strings, characters, task tags, and Javadoc elements via the **Java > Editor > Syntax Coloring** preference page (see Figure 1–38).

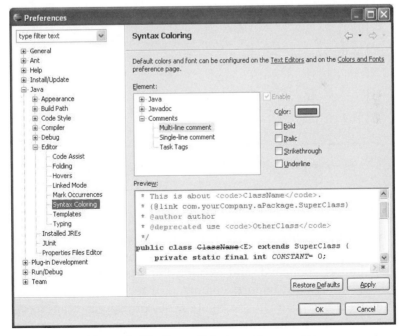

Figure 1–38 Syntax Coloring preference page.

1.7.1.2   User-defined code formatting

The code formatting feature controls how Java code will be formatted any time the **Source > Format** command is issued. A variety of options are provided for controlling brace position, new lines, line length, and white space usage through use of the **Java > Code Style > Formatter** preference page (see Figure 1–39).

> **Tip:** Alternate code formatters are available, including JIndent integration into Eclipse (*www.javadude.com/tools*).

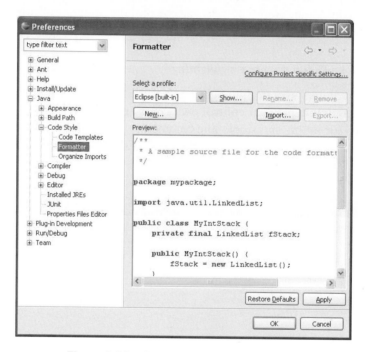

Figure 1–39   Code Formatter preference page.

1.7.1.3   Organizing Java import statements

The import organization feature provides an easy way to clean up the import statements within a Java file. New imports can be added using the **Source > Add Import** command, and existing imports can be cleaned up using the **Source > Organize Imports** command. The **Java > Code Style > Organize Imports** preference page (see Figure 1–40) provides a means to set the default order of import statements and the threshold above which wildcard imports will be used.

Tip: Set the threshold to 1 to cause packages to be imported with ".*"
immediately, or keep the default value at 99 to always import each type
individually depending on your coding style.

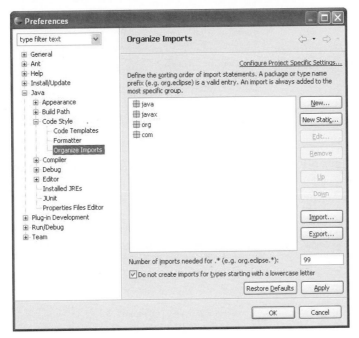

Figure 1–40   Organize Imports preference page.

1.7.1.4   Context-sensitive code assist

The context-sensitive code assist feature can help speed up the creation of Java
code quite dramatically. It can complete class names, method names, parameter names, and more. In Eclipse 3.2, CamelCase patterns, such as NPE, will
expand to full class names such as `NullPointerException`.

To use it, position the cursor at a location in your Java code needing a suggestion and select either the **Edit > Content Assist** command or hold the **Ctrl**
key down while pressing the **Space** key. This opens the popup code assist window (see Figure 1–41).

Tip: If the code assist window fails to open and the feature just beeps at you
instead, check your Java build path and then check your code because it
may have so many problems that the compiler cannot make sense of it.
Remember, the Java compiler is always working in the background!

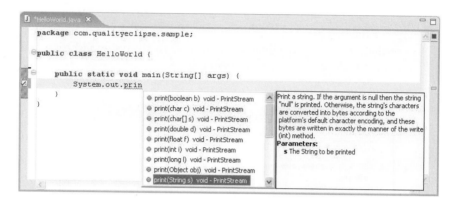

Figure 1–41   Code assistance in action.

The **Java > Editor > Code Assist** (**Content Assist** under Eclipse 3.2) preference page (see Figure 1–42) provides a number of options to control how the code assist feature acts when invoked.

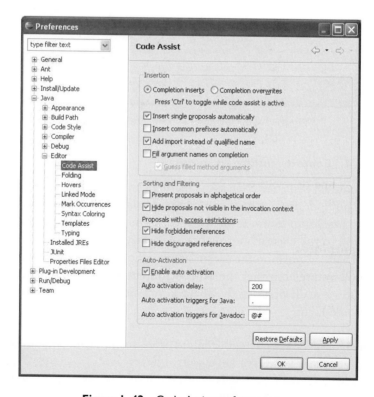

Figure 1–42   Code Assist preference page.

1.7.1.5 "Quick fix" automatic problem correction

The "quick fix" feature provides a way to easily fix common problems within the Java editor. Any time a problem is detected that can be fixed, a lightbulb icon is displayed in the marker bar (left vertical ruler) of the editor. Clicking on the icon opens a popup quick fix window (see Figure 1–43). Selecting the appropriate one from the list applies that fix to the Java source.

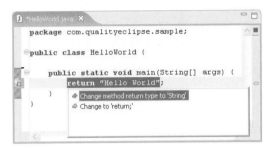

Figure 1–43 Quick fix in action.

Dozens of built-in quick fixes are available, including:

- Correcting missing or incorrect package declarations
- Removing unused and duplicate imports
- Changing the visibility of types, methods, and fields
- Renaming types, methods, and fields
- Removing unused private types, methods, and fields
- Creating new types, methods, and fields
- Fixing incorrect method arguments
- Adding or removing catch blocks
- Adding necessary cast operations

1.7.2 Templates

Templates are common source code patterns that appear frequently in user-written code. Eclipse has dozens of built-in templates and new ones are very easy to add.

To use a template, position the cursor at the desired position in your Java code, start to type the name of the template, and press **Ctrl+Space**. This opens the popup content assist window (see Figure 1–44). Note that some templates are parameterized with user-defined variables. Once a template has been expanded, use the **Tab** key to move between variables.

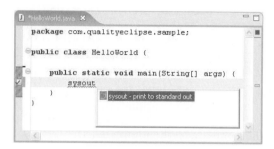

Figure 1–44   Template expansion in action.

As an example, open the `HelloWorld` class that was created in Section 1.4.4, Using the Java Class wizard, on page 24 then enter "sysout" and press **Ctrl+Space**. This expands the sysout template to `System.out.println();` with the cursor placed between the two parentheses. Type "Hello World" and press **Ctrl+S** to save your changes. This application will be run in Section 1.9, Running Applications, on page 54.

The **Java > Editor > Templates** preference page (see Figure 1–45) provides a place to add new templates and edit existing ones.

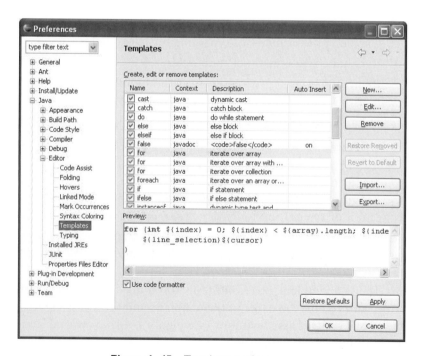

Figure 1–45   Templates preference page.

To add a new template, click the **New** button to open the **Edit Template** dialog (see Figure 1–46). Enter the name for the pattern in the **Name** field, its description in the **Description** field, and the code pattern itself in the **Pattern** field (note that code assist is not case-sensitive).

Eclipse supports two types of patterns, Java and Javadoc. Select the pattern type from the **Context** drop-down list. The **Insert Variable** button pops up a list of variables that can be inserted into the template. Click the **OK** button to add the template to the template list.

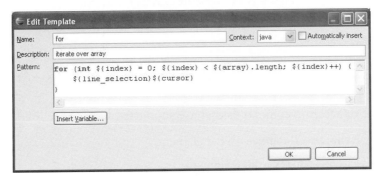

Figure 1–46   Edit Template dialog.

Tip: Some third-party plug-ins provide enhanced templates known as patterns (see Appendix A).

1.7.3 *Refactoring*

Refactoring is the process of changing a software system to improve its internal structure and reusability, without altering the external behavior of the program. It is a disciplined way of cleaning up code that minimizes the chances of introducing bugs. In essence, when developers refactor, they are improving the design of the code. Eclipse provides a very powerful and comprehensive collection of refactoring tools that make refactoring operations quick, easy, and reliable.

The Eclipse refactoring commands are available either from the Java editor's context menu or from the **Refactor** menu that is available from the main menu bar anytime a Java editor is open. The **Refactor** menu (see Figure 1–47) includes more than a dozen different refactoring commands that modify some aspect of a Java element and then update any references to it elsewhere in the workspace.

Figure 1–47   Refactor menu.

The refactoring commands that are supported include the following:

- **Rename**—Renames a Java element.

- **Move**—Moves a Java element.

- **Change Method Signature**—Changes method parameters (names, types, and order).

- **Convert Anonymous Class to Nested**—Converts an anonymous inner class to a named nested class.

- **Move Member Type to New File**—Converts a nested type into a top-level type.

- **Push Down**—Moves fields and methods from a class to one of its subclasses.

- **Pull Up**—Moves fields, methods, or member types from a class to one of its superclasses.

- **Extract Interface**—Creates a new interface from a collection of selected methods.

- **Generalize Type**—Generalizes the type of variable declarations, parameters, fields, and method return types.

- **Use Supertype Where Possible**—Replaces a type with one of its supertypes anywhere that transformation is possible.

- **Infer Generic Type Arguments**—Attempts to infer type parameters for all generic type references in a class, package, or project. This is especially useful when migrating from Java 1.4 code to Java 5.0 code.

- **Inline**—Inlines methods, constants, and local variables.

- **Extract Method**—Creates a new method based on the selected text in the current method and updates the current method to call the new method.

- **Extract Local Variable**—Creates a new local variable assigned to the selected expression and replaces the selection with a reference to the new variable.

- **Extract Constant**—Creates a static final field from the selected expression.

- **Introduce Parameter**—Replaces an expression with a parameter reference.

- **Introduce Factory**—Replaces a constructor invocation with a call to a new factory method.

- **Convert Local Variable to Field**—Converts a local variable into a field.

- **Encapsulate Field**—Replaces all direct references to a field with references to the field's getter and setter methods and creates those methods as necessary.

To use any refactoring command, select the Java element or expression that you would like to refactor and then select the refactoring command. Each refactoring dialog collects information appropriate to the task it needs to do. Once you have supplied that information (for example, the new method name as shown in Figure 1–48), click the **OK** button to complete the refactoring.

Figure 1–48   Rename Method dialog.

To preview the transformations that will be made by a refactoring method before they are committed, click the **Preview** button prior to clicking the **OK** button. The refactoring preview shows a hierarchy (a checkbox tree list) of the changes that will be made with text panes showing a before and after view of the affected code (see Figure 1-49). If you want to exclude a particular change from the refactoring operation, uncheck it in the tree list.

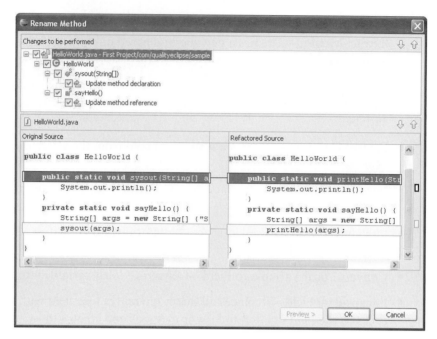

Figure 1–49   Rename Method preview.

> **Clean Up Wizard**   Eclipse 3.2 adds a **Clean Up** wizard that will fix multiple source problems (such as removing unused private fields and local variables) simultaneously. Access it using the **Source > Clean Up...** command.

1.7.4   Local history

Every time you make a change to a file and save it, a snapshot of that file at that moment in time is recorded to the Eclipse local history. This provides a way to revert back to an earlier version of a file or to compare the current version with an earlier version to see the changes that have been made. Every entry in the local history is identified by the date and time it was created.

Note that "local history" is really local to the machine; it is never stored in CVS or another source code repository. This means that the history is only available to you, not to other users. This might be a surprise to VisualAge for Java or ENVY users who expect "method editions" to be available in the repository.

> **External File Warning**   Local history is only saved for the files stored within your workspace. If you use Eclipse to edit external files, no local history is saved.

To compare the current state of a file with an earlier version, right-click on the file and select the **Compare With > Local History...** command from the context menu. This opens the **Compare with Local History** dialog (see Figure 1–50). Select any item in the history list to see a comparison relative to the current state of the file.

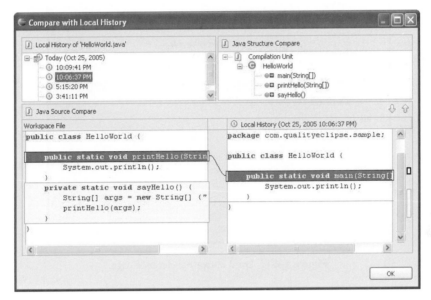

Figure 1–50   Compare with Local History dialog.

To replace the current version of a file with an earlier version, right-click on the file and select the **Replace With > Local History...** command from the context menu. This opens the **Replace from Local History** dialog, which is almost identical to the local history comparison dialog with the addition of **Replace** and **Cancel** buttons.

The **General > Workspace > Local History** preference page (see Figure 1-51) determines how much information is stored in local history. You can control how many days worth of changes are maintained, how many unique changes per file are maintained, and how large the entire local history is allowed to grow.

> **Tip:** Many former VisualAge for Java users loved the ability of that IDE to revert to any prior version of any method or class. The Eclipse local history feature provides a way to emulate that behavior on a local scale. There is no reason (other than disk space) to keep the Eclipse local history settings at the low values to which they default. Increasing the **Days to keep files** setting to 365, the **Entries per file** to 10,000, and the **Maximum file size (MB)** field to 100 will allow you to easily track an entire year of changes.

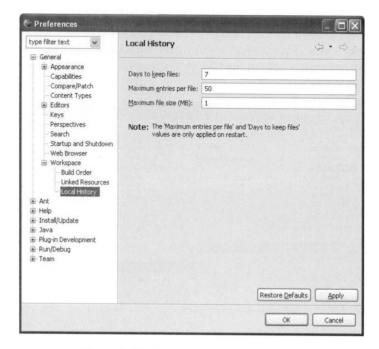

Figure 1–51   Local History preference page.

1.7.5   File extension associations

In addition to the built-in Java editor, Eclipse includes built-in editors for text files, plug-in development files (such as `plugin.xml`, `fragment.xml`, and `feature.xml`), and others.

You can change which editor is assigned to a specific file type using the **General > Editors > File Associations** preference page (see Figure 1–52). To change the editor, select the file type in the **File types** list, select the desired editor type in the **Associated editors** list, and click the **Default** button. If the desired editor type is not shown, use the **File types > Add** button to add it to the list.

To add an editor association for a file type not listed in the **File types** list, click the **File types > Add** button to reveal the **New File Type** dialog, as shown in Figure 1–53. For example, to add an editor for HTML files, enter "*.html" into the **File type** field and click the **OK** button.

Once the new file type has been added, an editor must be assigned to it. Click the **Associated editors > Add** button to open the **Editor Selection** dialog. By default, the various built-in editor types will be shown in the editor list.

Figure 1–52 File Associations preference page.

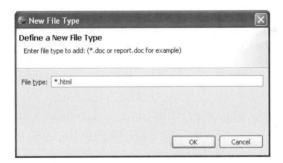

Figure 1–53 New File Type dialog.

To see a list of available external editors, select the **External Programs** radio button (see Figure 1–54). If you have an HTML editor (such as Microsoft FrontPage) installed in your system, select it from the list and click the **OK** button. That editor will be added to the **Associated editors** list and automatically made the default (assuming that no other default was in place).

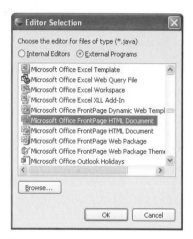

Figure 1–54   Editor Selection dialog.

> Tip: If you routinely edit XML files, the **XMLBuddy** plug-in, from
> *www.xmlbuddy.com*, is one of several XML editors integrated into
> Eclipse (see Appendix A). The XMLBuddy editor provides user-
> configurable syntax highlighting, Document Type Definition- (DTD-)
> driven code assist, XML validation, and many other features.

1.8   Team Development Using CVS

Typically, you will want to work as part of a team and share your code with
other team members. This section shows how to set up and use CVS, which
ships as part of Eclipse.

As team members work on different aspects of a project, changes are
made locally to their own workspaces. When they are ready to share changes
with other team members, they can commit them to the shared CVS repository. Likewise, when they want to get any changes made by other team members, they can update their workspaces with the contents of the repository. In
the event of conflicts (e.g., changes made to the same resource), Eclipse provides comparison and merge tools to resolve and integrate such changes.

CVS supports multiple streams of development known as *branches*. Each
branch represents an independent set of changes made to the same set of
resources. There may be multiple concurrent branches for various maintenance updates, bug fixes, experimental projects, and so on. The main branch,
known as the "HEAD," represents the primary flow of work within a project.

Just as the Eclipse local history feature records changes made to various resources over time, the CVS repository maintains a history of every committed change made to every resource over time. A resource may be compared with or replaced with any prior revision using tools similar to those used with the local history feature.

1.8.1   Getting started with CVS

To start using CVS with Eclipse, you will need to connect your Eclipse workspace to your CVS repository (see *www.cvshome.org* for information on setting up the repository). Start by opening either the **CVS Repository Exploring** perspective using the **Window > Open Perspective > Other...** command or the **CVS Repositories** view using the **Window > Show View > Other...** command. Next, right-click within the **CVS Repositories** view and select the **New > Repository Location...** command from the context menu (see Figure 1–55).

Figure 1–55   CVS Repositories view.

Within the **Add CVS Repository** dialog (see Figure 1–56), you need to specify the location of your repository and your login information. Enter the address of your CVS host into the **Host** field (e.g., "cvs.qualityeclipse.com") and the path of the repository relative to the host address into the **Repository path** field. Next, enter your user name and password into the **User** and **Password** fields, respectively, or leave them blank for anonymous access. If you need to use a different connect type than the default one, change that as well. When done, click the **Finish** button. Assuming that the CVS repository is found, it will show up in the **CVS Repositories** view.

> **Tip:** The **New Project** wizard also provides a convenient option for creating a new repository. Select **New > Project...** and then the **CVS > Checkout Projects from CVS** wizard. On the first page of that wizard, choose the **Create a new repository location** option and click **Next**. The second page of the wizard will look like the dialog shown in Figure 1-56.

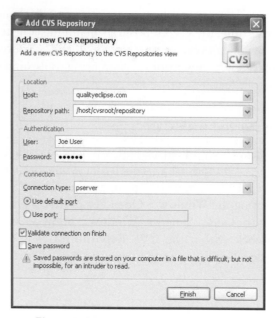

Figure 1–56   Add CVS Repository dialog.

1.8.2   Checking out a project from CVS

To check out a project from your CVS repository, expand the repository location and then the **HEAD** item until you see the project you want to load. Right-click on the project and select the **Check Out** command from the context menu (see Figure 1–57). This loads the project into your workspace.

Figure 1–57   Checking out a project.

To load the project into a specially configured project (e.g., a project outside your workspace), use the **Check Out As...** command instead.

> **Tip:** The **New Project** wizard also provides an option for checking out a project from an existing repository. Select **New > Project...** and then the **CVS > Checkout Projects from CVS** wizard. On the first page, choose the **Use existing repository location** option and the repository you wish to connect to and click **Next**. Selecting **Use an existing module** on the second page of the wizard will reveal a list of the projects in that repository. Select the desired projects and click the **Finish** button.

1.8.3 Synchronizing with the repository

Once changes have been made to the resources in the project, those changes should be committed back to the repository. Right-click on the resource (or the project containing the resource) and select the **Team > Synchronize with Repository** command (see Figure 1–58).

Figure 1–58   Team context menu.

After comparing the resources in the workspace to those in the repository, the **Synchronize** view opens (see Figure 1–59). The ▧ **Incoming Mode** icon causes the view to only show incoming changes, while the ▧ **Outgoing Mode** icon causes it to only show outgoing changes (the **Incoming/Outgoing Mode** is a third option).

Right-click on the outgoing changes and select the **Commit...** command to commit those changes to the repository. Right-click on any incoming changes and select the **Update** command to load the changes into your workspace.

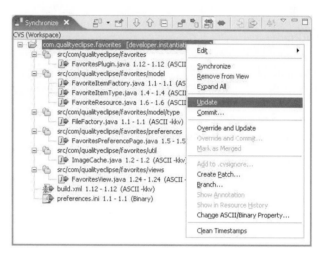

Figure 1–59   Synchronize view.

If any conflicts occur (e.g., changes made by you and by another developer), you will need to use the merge tools that are provided in the **Synchronize** view to resolve the conflicts and then commit the merged version to the repository.

1.8.4   Comparing and replacing resources

To compare the current state of a file with an earlier revision stored in the repository, right-click on the file and select the **Compare With > Revision...** command from the context menu. This opens the **Revision**s editor, which shows earlier revisions of the file made to the **HEAD** stream or any branch (see Figure 1–60). Select any item in the revision list to see a comparison relative to the current state of the file.

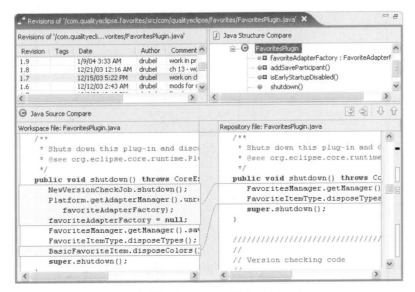

Figure 1–60   Compare with Revision editor.

A number of other resource comparison commands are also available. The **Compare With > Latest from Head** command compares the current state of the resource with the most recent version committed to a repository, and the **Compare With > Another Branch or Version...** command provides a way to compare a resource with a specific version or branch

To replace the current version of a file with an earlier revision, right-click on the file and select the **Replace With > Revision...** command from the context menu. This opens the same comparison editor as shown in Figure 1–60. Select any revision and right-click, then select the **Get Contents** command to load that version into the workspace.

1.8.5   CVS label decorators

To make it easier to see which resources are under repository control and which might have been changed but not committed, CVS provides a number of label decorations to augment the icons and labels of CVS-controlled resources. To turn on the CVS label decorators, use the **General > Appearance > Label Decorations** preference page (see Figure 1–61).

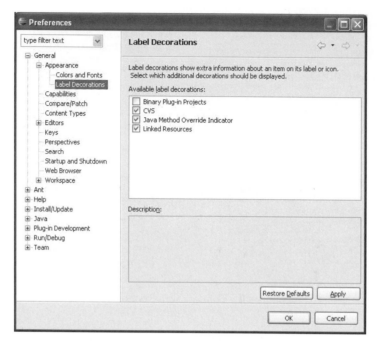

Figure 1-61   Label Decorations preference page.

The actual decorations added are controlled by the options on the **Team > CVS > Label Decorations** preference page. By default, outgoing changes are prefixed with ">".

> **Tip:** To make outgoing changes easier to see, CodePro includes a list colorization feature that changes the foreground or background color of any modified resource that is waiting to be committed to the repository. This and other third-party plug-ins are described in Appendix A.

1.9   Running Applications

Any Java application with a `main()` method, including the `.java` file created in Section 1.4.4, Using the Java Class wizard, on page 24 and enhanced in Section 1.7.2, Templates, on page 39, is marked with the runnable icon decoration (a small green triangle), indicating that it is runnable. This section shows the different ways to launch (run) a Java application.

1.9.1 Launching Java applications

The easiest way to run a Java application is to select the class and then select the **Run As > Java Application** command (**Ctrl+Shift+X, J**) from the **Run** menu or from the ● **Run** toolbar button (see Figure 1–62). This executes the main() method of the application and writes any output (in blue) and error text (in red) to the **Console** view (see Figure 1–63).

Figure 1–62   Run As > Java Application command.

Figure 1–63   Console view.

Once an application has been run, it can be run again by selecting it from the **Run > Run History** menu or from the ● **Run** toolbar button (see Figure 1–64). Clicking the ● **Run** toolbar button or pressing **Ctrl+F11** relaunches the last application you ran.

Figure 1–64   Run history.

1.9.2   Launch configurations

Whenever you run an application for the first time using the **Run As > Java Application** command, a *launch configuration* is created. A launch configuration records the information needed to launch a specific Java application. In addition to specifying the name of the Java class, the launch configuration can also specify program and virtual machine (VM) arguments, the JRE and classpath to use, and even the default perspectives to use when running or debugging the application.

A launch configuration can be edited using the launch configuration (**Run**) dialog accessible from the **Run > Run...** command (see Figure 1–65). The **Main** tab specifies the project and class to be run; the **Arguments** tab records the program parameters (as space-separated strings) and VM arguments; the **JRE** tab specifies the JRE to use (it defaults to the JRE specified in your **Java > Installed JREs** preferences); the **Classpath** tab is used to override or augment the default classpath used to find the class files needed to run the application; the **Source** tab specifies the location of the source files used to display the source of an application while debugging; the **Environment** tab is used to set environment variables; and the **Common** tab records information about where the launch configuration is stored and where standard input and output should be directed.

The **Eclipse Application** configuration is used specifically to test Eclipse plug-ins you are developing. It provides a mechanism for starting up another workbench with full control over which plug-ins are loaded, active, and debuggable. This is discussed in more detail in Chapter 2, A Simple Plug-in Example.

The **Java Applet** configuration type is very similar to the **Java Application** type, but it is specifically designed to be used with Java applets. In addition to the tabs available for Java applications, it adds a **Parameters** tab that specifies applet-specific information such as width, height, name, and applet parameters.

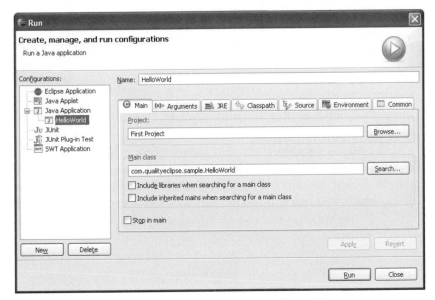

Figure 1–65   Launch configuration (Run) dialog.

The **JUnit** configuration is used to run JUnit test cases. *JUnit test cases* are a special type of Java application, so many of the configuration options are the same as for Java applications and applets. It adds a **Test** tab for specifying settings unique to the test case that will be executed. JUnit is discussed in more detail in Section 1.11, Introduction to Testing, on page 61.

The **JUnit Plug-in Test** configuration is used to run JUnit tests associated with an Eclipse plug-in. It is similar to the **Eclipse Application** configuration with the addition of the **Test** tab used by the JUnit configuration.

The **SWT Application** configuration is similar to the **Java Application** configuration and is designed to provide the appropriate runtime environment to launch an SWT application.

Tip: Eclipse supports hot code replacement during debug operations when using JDK 1.4 or above to run an application. If JDK 1.4 isn't your default JRE, you can specify it as the one to use when running or debugging an application by selecting it from the drop-down list on the **JRE** tab of the launch configurations dialog. If it isn't in the list, you can add it via the **New** button.

1.10   Introduction to Debugging

The previous section showed how to run a Java application using the options available under the **Run** menu. Any output or errors are written to the **Console** view. Placing `System.out.println()` statements at appropriate places in your code will give you limited debugging capabilities. Fortunately, Eclipse provides a much more effective debugging solution in the form of its integrated Java debugger.

The easiest way to debug a Java application is to select the class and then select the **Run > Debug As > Java Application** command (**Ctrl+Shift+D, J**) or the ⚙ **Debug** toolbar button. This opens the **Debug** perspective (see Figure 1–8), which you can use to step through individual statements within your code, set breakpoints, and inspect and change the values associated with individual variables. After you've run your application under the debugger the first time, you can use the **Run > Debug History** list to quickly run it again This list is also available from the **Debug** toolbar button's drop-down menu.

1.10.1   Setting breakpoints

To stop the debugger at a particular location in the code, set a breakpoint. At the location where you would like to set the breakpoint, right-click in the marker bar of the editor and select the **Toggle Breakpoint** command (see Figure 1–66). In addition to right-clicking, you can double-click the marker bar to the left of the line at which you want to place the breakpoint. A breakpoint marker appears next to the appropriate source code line.

Figure 1–66   Adding a breakpoint.

With one or more breakpoints set, the application runs until it encounters a breakpoint and then stops before executing the line with the breakpoint. The debugger shows which program threads are running and which ones have been suspended. It also shows the line of code at which execution has stopped and highlights that line of code in the editor (see Figure 1–67).

> **Tip:** If you are not hitting a breakpoint that you set, take a close look at how the breakpoint appears in the gutter. For an enabled breakpoint, you will see either a plain blue bullet or a blue bullet with a small checkmark. The checkmark icon appears only after launching the VM and the breakpoint exists in a loaded class.

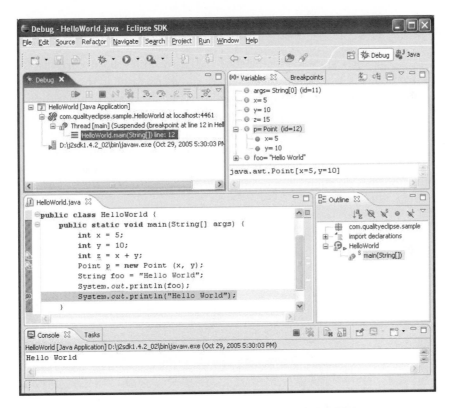

Figure 1–67 The debugger, stopping at a breakpoint.

> **Tip:** Check the **Remove terminated launches when a new launch is created** checkbox on the **Run/Debug > Launching** preference page to automatically clean up old launches.

1.10.2 Using the Debug view

After execution has stopped on a breakpoint, the **Debug** view presents various options for resuming execution, stepping through the program statement-by-statement, or terminating it altogether.

The ⏩ **Resume** button (also the **F8** key) in the **Debug** view resumes the execution of a program until it either ends on its own or encounters another breakpoint, while the ■ **Terminate** button stops execution of a program entirely.

The ⮑ **Step Into** button (also the **F3** key) executes the next expression in the highlighted statement, while the ⮑ **Step Over** button (also the **F6** key) steps over the highlighted statement and stops on the next statement.

1.10.3 Using the Variables view

The **Variables** view shows the state of the variables in the current stack frame (see Figure 1–68). Selecting a variable shows its value in the details pane at the bottom of the view. Primitive variable types show their values directly, while object types can be expanded to show their individual elements. You can change the value of a primitive in this view, but you can't change the value of object types unless you use the **Expressions** view (see Section 1.10.4, Using the Expressions view). Note that the variables listed in the **Variables** view change as you step through your program.

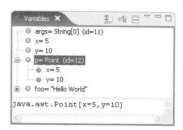

Figure 1–68   Variables view.

1.10.4 Using the Expressions view

The **Expressions** view (see Figure 1–69) provides a place to inspect values in the debugger and discover the results of various expressions entered into the editor, the detail pane of the **Variables** view, or the detail pane of the **Expressions** view.

To use the **Expressions** view, first select the expression to execute. This can be an existing expression or one that you enter. Next, select the **Watch, Display,** or **Inspect** command from the popup menu in the editor, the **Variables** view, or the **Expressions** view.

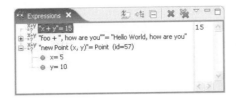

Figure 1–69 Expressions view.

If you select the **Display** command while an expression is selected in an editor, the results will be shown in the **Display** view. When an expression is selected in the **Variables** view or **Expressions** view, the results will be shown in the detail pane of that view.

If you select the **Inspect** command, a popup window containing the results of the expression appears. Pressing **Ctrl+Shift+I** will move the results to the **Expressions** view. As with the **Variables** view, primitive variable types show their values directly while object types can be expanded to show their individual elements.

1.11   Introduction to **Testing**

In addition to manually testing an application by running or debugging it, Eclipse supports the JUnit framework (see *www.junit.org*) for creating and running repeatable test cases.

1.11.1   *Creating test cases*

To create a test case, you first need to add the `junit.jar` file (from the `org.junit` plug-in) to your project as an external JAR using the Java **Build Path > Libraries** project property page.

Once this is done, select the class for which you want to create a test case, open the **New** wizard, and select the **Java > JUnit > JUnit Test Case** option. This invokes the **JUnit Test Case** wizard (see Figure 1–70), which creates a JUnit test case. If you forget to add the `junit.jar` to your project, the wizard will do this for you automatically.

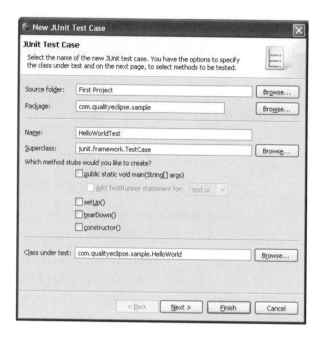

Figure 1–70   JUnit Test Case wizard.

By default, the name of the new test case is the name of the test class with the word "Test" added to the end. Optionally, you can have the wizard create `main()`, `setup()`, and `teardown()` methods as well as test methods for any public or protected method in the test class.

> Tip: CodePro includes a more advanced **Test Case** wizard that provides a number of enhancements over the Eclipse Test Case wizard, such as the ability to specify arbitrary test cases, generate better default code, and support the creation of test fixtures.

1.11.2   Running test cases

After a test case is created, select the test case class (or the project or package containing the test case) and then select the **Run > Run As > JUnit Test** command (**Alt+Shift+X, T**). This opens the **JUnit** view (see Figure 1–71), which shows the results of the test run. The **Failures** tab shows a list of the failures that were recorded in the test case, and the **Hierarchy** tab shows the entire test suite as a tree.

Figure 1–71 JUnit view.

If there are any test failures, correct the problem(s) and rerun the test by clicking on the ![] **Rerun Last Test** button in the **JUnit** view. Alternatively, rerun the last test by selecting it from the **Run** menu or toolbar button. If you need to customize the test configuration, select the **Run > Run...** command to open the launch configuration dialog (see Figure 1–65).

1.12 Summary

This chapter gave you a whirlwind tour of the major components of the Eclipse IDE that you will need to use to develop Eclipse plug-ins. At this point, you should be comfortable navigating the Eclipse UI and using the built-in Eclipse tools to create, edit, run, debug, and test your Java code.

The next chapter dives right in and gets our hands dirty creating the first Eclipse plug-in. Each succeeding chapter will introduce more and more layers of detail and slowly convert the plug-in from a simple example into a powerful tool that can be used on a daily basis while doing Eclipse development.

References

Eclipse-Overview.pdf (available from the *eclipse.org* Web site).

D'Anjou, Jim, Scott Fairbrother, Dan Kehn, John Kellerman, and Pat McCarthy, *The Java Developer's Guide to Eclipse, Second Edition*. Addison-Wesley, Boston, 2004.

Arthorne, John, and Chris Laffra, *Official Eclipse 3.0 FAQs*. Addison-Wesley, Boston, 2004.

Carlson, David, *Eclipse Distilled*. Addison-Wesley, Boston, 2005.

Eclipse Wiki (see *eclipsewiki.swiki.net*).

CVS (see *www.cvshome.org*).

Fowler, Martin, *Refactoring: Improving the Design of Existing Code*, Addison-Wesley, Boston, 1999 (*www.refactoring.com*).

Glezen, Paul, "Branching with Eclipse and CVS." IBM, July 3, 2003 (*www.eclipse.org/articles/Article-CVS-branching/eclipse_branch.html*).

JUnit (see *www.junit.org*).

CHAPTER 2

A Simple Plug-in Example

Before covering each area of commercial plug-in construction in-depth, it is useful to create a simple plug-in on which discussion and examples can be based. This chapter takes a step-by-step approach to creating a simple but fully operational plug-in that will be enhanced bit-by-bit during the course of this book. This process provides valuable firsthand experience using the Eclipse IDE and touches on every aspect of building and maintaining a commercial plug-in.

2.1 The Favorites Plug-in

The **Favorites** plug-in, which you'll build over the course of this book, displays a list of resources, lets you add and remove resources from the list, easily opens an editor on a selected resource, updates the list automatically as a result of events elsewhere in the system, and more. Subsequent chapters discuss aspects of commercial plug-in development in terms of enhancements to the **Favorites** plug-in.

This chapter starts the process by covering the creation of the **Favorites** plug-in in its simplest form using the following steps:

- Creating a plug-in project
- Reviewing the generated code
- Building a product
- Installing and running the product

2.2   Creating a Plug-in Project

The first step is to create a plug-in project using the Eclipse **New Project** wizard. In addition to creating a new project, this wizard has a number of different code generation options, such as views, editors, and actions, for creating sample plug-in code. To keep things simple and focus only on the essentials of plug-in creation, select the **Plug-in with a view** option, which is discussed in the next subsection.

2.2.1   New Plug-in Project wizard

From the **File** menu, select **New > Project** to launch the **New Project** wizard (see Figure 2–1). On this first page of the wizard, select **Plug-in Project** from the list and then click the **Next** button.

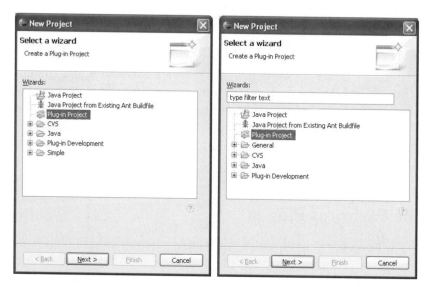

Figure 2–1   New Project wizard page 1—selecting a project type. The Eclipse 3.1 version is shown on the left, and the Eclipse 3.2 version is shown on the right.

On the next page of the wizard (see Figure 2–2), enter the name of the project; in this case, it's com.qualityeclipse.favorites, which is the same as the Favorites plug-in identifier. Chapter 3, Eclipse Infrastructure, discusses plug-in identifiers and other aspects of plug-in architecture in more detail. Fill in the other fields as shown and then click the **Next** button.

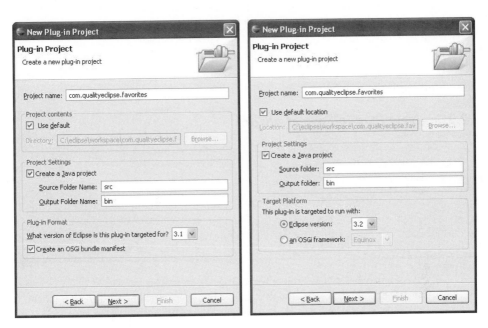

Figure 2–2   New Project wizard page 2—naming the project.
The Eclipse 3.1 version is shown on the left and the Eclipse 3.2 version is shown on the right. Note the minor differences in options available in the lower section of the page.

> **Tip:** A project can be named anything, but it is easier to name it the same as the plug-in identifier. By convention, this is the plug-in project-naming scheme that the Eclipse organization uses for most of its work. Because of this, the **New Project** wizard assumes that the project name and the plug-in identifier are the same.

2.2.2   *Define the plug-in*

Every plug-in has a META-INF/MANIFEST.MF file. In addition, it may contain a plugin.xml file and/or a Java class that represents the plug-in programmatically. The next wizard page displays options for generating both the plug-in manifest and plug-in Java class. Supply the **Plug-in ID**, **Plug-in Version**, **Plug-in Name** and more for the plug-in as shown in Figure 2–3 then click the **Next** button.

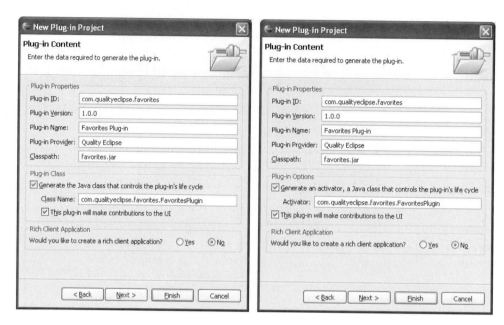

Figure 2–3   New Project wizard page 3—describing the plug-in.
The Eclipse 3.1 version is shown on the left, and the Eclipse 3.2 version is shown on the right.
Note the minor differences in terminology in the center section of the page.

Next, the **New Plug-in Project** wizard next displays the various plug-in pieces that can be automatically generated by the wizard (see Figure 2–4). There are many different options on this page for generating quite a bit of sample code. It is useful to try out each option and review the code that is generated; however for this example, select **Plug-in with a view** and then click the **Next** button.

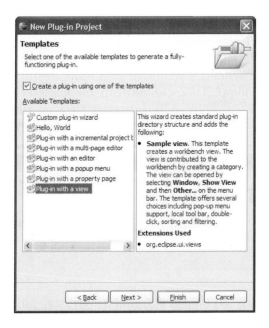

Figure 2–4   New Plug-in Project wizard page 4—selecting
a plug-in type.

2.2.3   Define the view

Selecting view code generation options is the next step in this process. Enter the values for this page (see Figure 2–5), uncheck the **Add the view to the resource perspective** checkbox to simplify the generated plug-in manifest file and click the **Next** button.

Finally, uncheck each of the code generation options on the last wizard page (see Figure 2–6). Each of these checkboxes represents code that could be generated as part of the **Favorites** view. These are covered in subsequent chapters. When you click the **Finish** button, the new plug-in project is created and the plug-in manifest editor is automatically opened (see Figure 2–9).

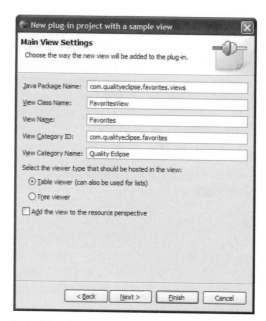

Figure 2–5   New Plug-in Project wizard page 5—defining the view.

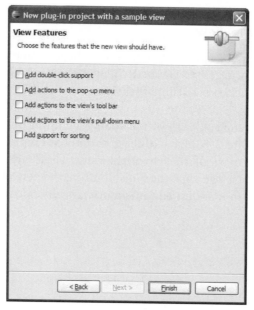

Figure 2–6   New Plug-in Project wizard page 6—code generation options for the view.

2.3   Reviewing the Generated Code

Reviewing the code generated by the **New Plug-in Project** wizard provides a brief look at the following major parts comprising the sample plug-in.

- The plug-in manifests
- The plug-in class
- The **Favorites** view

2.3.1   The Plug-in manifests

The plug-in manifest editor shows the contents of the two plug-in manifest files, `META-INF/MANIFEST.MF` and `plugin.xml`, which define how this plug-in relates to all the others in the system. This editor is automatically opened to its first page (see Figure 2–9) as a result of creating a new plug-in project. If the plug-in manifest editor is closed, double-clicking on either the `META-INF/MANIFEST.MF` or the `plugin.xml` file reopens the editor. The following is an overview of the manifest editor, while more detail on the plug-in manifest itself can be found in Chapter 3.

Although the editor is a convenient way to modify the plug-in's description, it's still useful to peek at the source behind the scenes to see how the editor's different parts relate to the underlying code. Click the **MANIFEST.MF** tab to display the source of the `META-INF/MANIFEST.MF` file that defines the runtime aspects of this plug-in (see Figure 2–7). The first two lines define it as an OSGi manifest file (see Section 3.3, Plug-in Manifest, on page 107). Subsequent lines specify plug-in name, version, identifier, classpath, and plug-ins on which this plug-in depends. All these aspects are editable using other pages in the plug-in manifest editor.

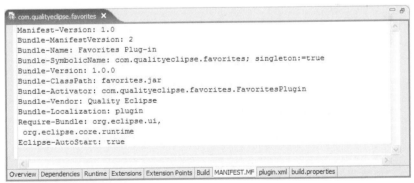

Figure 2–7   Plug-in manifest editor MANIFEST.MF page.

> **New in Eclipse 3.2**   The `Eclipse-AutoStart: true` directive in the `MANIFEST.MF` file has been replaced with `Eclipse-LazyStart: true`. Both directives have the same semantics; only the name has changed.

Clicking on the **plugin.xml** tab of the editor displays the `plugin.xml` file that defines the extension aspects of this plug-in (see Figure 2–8). The first line declares this to be an XML file, while subsequent lines specify plug-in extensions.

Figure 2–8   Plug-in manifest editor plugin.xml page.

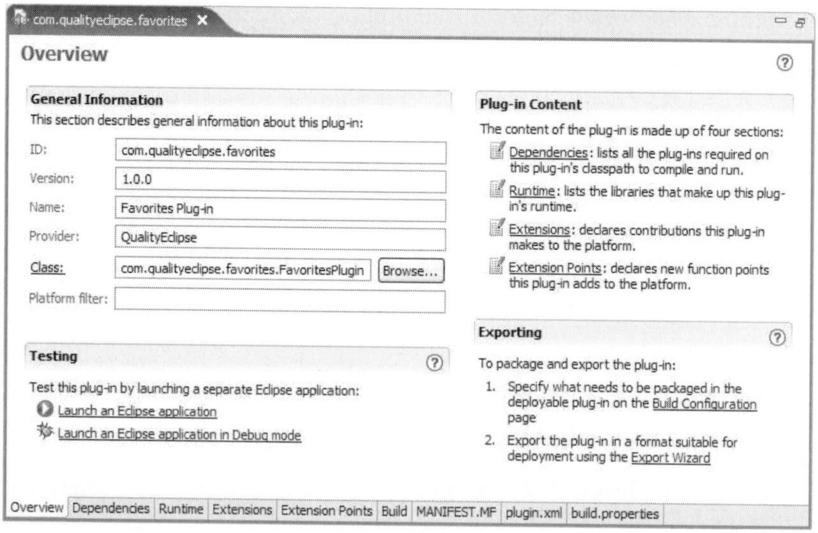

Figure 2–9   Plug-in manifest editor Overview page.

The **Overview** page of the manifest editor shows a summary of the plug-in manifest (see Figure 2–9). The section on this page describing general information, such as the plug-in identifier (ID), version, name, class, and provider, corresponds to the first chunk of source in the META-INF/MANIFEST.MF file:

```
Bundle-Name: Favorites Plug-in
Bundle-SymbolicName: com.qualityeclipse.favorites; singleton:=true
Bundle-Version: 1.0.0
Bundle-Activator: com.qualityeclipse.favorites.FavoritesPlugin
Bundle-Vendor: Quality Eclipse
```

You can edit the information on the **Overview** page or switch to the **MANIFEST.MF** page and edit the source directly.

> **Tip:** Making changes to any page other than the **plugin.xml** and **MANIFEST.MF** pages may cause the manifest editor to reformat the source. If you are particular about the formatting of either manifest file, then either use only the **plugin.xml** and **MANIFEST.MF** pages to perform editing or use another editor.
>
> *Caution:* The formatting rules of META-INF/MANIFEST.MF include some quite nonintuitive rules related to line length and line wrapping. Edit plugin.xml with care, and META-INF/MANIFEST.MF with caution!

The reliance of this plug-in on other plug-ins in the system appears on the **Dependencies** page of the plug-in manifest editor (see Figure 2–10).

Figure 2–10 Plug-in manifest editor Dependencies page.

This corresponds to the `Require-Bundle` chunk of source in the `META-INF/MANIFEST.MF` file:

```
Require-Bundle: org.eclipse.ui,
 org.eclipse.core.runtime
```

For the **Favorites** plug-in, this section indicates a dependency on the `org.eclipse.core.runtime` and `org.eclipse.ui` plug-ins. This dependency declaration differs from the **Favorites** project's Java build path (also known as the compile-time classpath) because the Java build path is a compile-time artifact, while the plug-in dependency declaration comes into play during plug-in execution. Because the project was created as a plug-in project and has the `org.eclipse.pde.PluginNature` nature (see Section 14.3, Natures, on page 525 for more on project natures), any changes to this dependency list will automatically be reflected in the Java build path, but not the reverse. If these two aspects of your plug-in get out of sync, then you can have a plug-in that compiles and builds but does not execute properly.

> **Tip:** Edit this dependency list rather than the Java build path so that the two are automatically always in sync.

Alternatively, the dependencies could have been expressed as **Imported Packages** on the **Dependencies** page of the manifest editor (see Figure 2–10 and the end of Section 3.3.3, Plug-in dependencies, on page 110). This would correspond to an `Import-Package` chunk of source in the `META-INF/ MANIFEST.MF` file looking something like this:

```
Import-Package: org.eclipse.ui.views,
 org.eclipse.core.runtime.model
```

The **Runtime** page of the manifest editor (see Figure 2–11) corresponds to the `Bundle-ClassPath` chunk of source in the `META-INF/MANIFEST.MF` file, which defines what libraries are delivered with the plug-in and used by the plug-in during execution, what package prefixes are used within each library (used to speed up plug-in loading time), and whether other plug-ins can reference the code in the library (see Section 20.2.5, Related plug-ins, on page 713 for more on package visibility). For the **Favorites** plug-in, all the code is contained in a single JAR file named `favorites.jar`, which contains classes that all use the "com.qualityeclipse.favorites" prefix:

```
Bundle-ClassPath: favorites.jar
```

The **Favorites** plug-in does not export any packages for other plug-ins to use or extend.

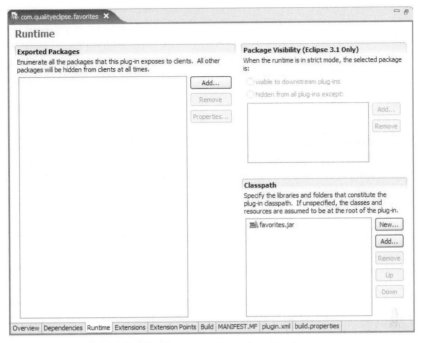

Figure 2–11 Plug-in manifest editor Runtime page.

The **Extensions** page (see Figure 2–12) displays how this plug-in augments the functionality already provided by other plug-ins in the system, and corresponds to the `<extension point="org.eclipse.ui.views">` chunk of XML in the `plugin.xml` file:

```
<extension
      point="org.eclipse.ui.views">
   <category
         name="Quality Eclipse"
         id="com.qualityeclipse.favorites">
   </category>
   <view
         name="Favorites"
         icon="icons/sample.gif"
         category="com.qualityeclipse.favorites"
         class="com.qualityeclipse.favorites.views.FavoritesView"
         id="com.qualityeclipse.favorites.views.FavoritesView">
   </view>
</extension>
```

The **Favorites** plug-in declares an extension to the `org.eclipse.ui` plug-in using the `org.eclipse.ui.views` extension point by providing an additional category of views named **Quality Eclipse** and a new view in that category named **Favorites**. Selecting an item in the tree on the left in the **Extensions** page causes the properties for that item to appear on the right. In this case, selecting **Favorites (view)** on the **Extensions** page displays the name, identifier, class, and more information about the **Favorites** view that is being declared. This corresponds to the XML attributes defined in the `<view>` chunk of XML shown previously.

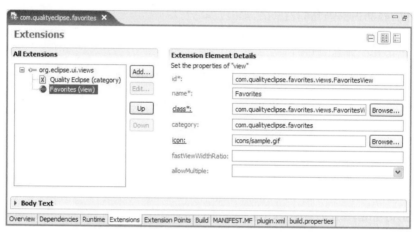

Figure 2–12   Plug-in manifest editor Extensions page.

Finally, the **Extension Points** page of the manifest editor (see Figure 2–13) facilitates the definition of new extension points so that other plug-ins can augment the functionality provided by this plug-in. At this time, the **Favorites** plug-in doesn't define any extension points and therefore cannot be augmented by other plug-ins (see Section 17.2, Defining an Extension Point, on page 597).

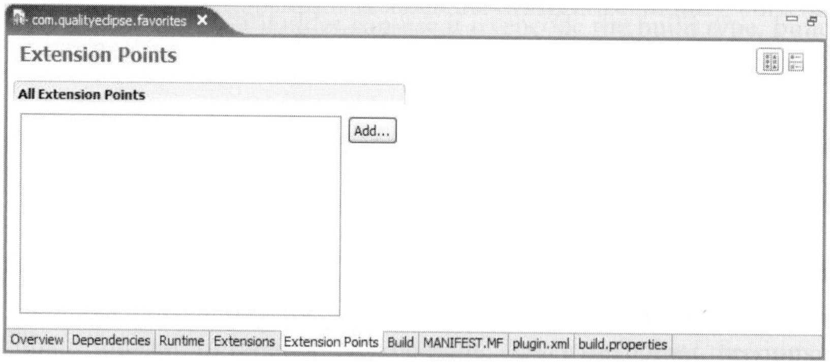

Figure 2–13   Plug-in manifest editor Extension Points page.

2.3.2   *The Plug-in class*

Every plug-in optionally can declare a class that represents the plug-in from a programmatic standpoint as displayed on the manifest editor's **Overview** page (see Figure 2–9). In the **Favorites** plug-in, this class is named com.quality-eclipse.favorites.FavoritesPlugin.

```
package com.qualityeclipse.favorites;

import org.eclipse.ui.plugin.*;
import org.eclipse.jface.resource.ImageDescriptor;
import org.osgi.framework.BundleContext;

/**
 * The main plugin class to be used in the desktop.
 */
public class FavoritesPlugin extends AbstractUIPlugin {

   // The shared instance.
   private static FavoritesPlugin plugin;

   /**
    * The constructor.
    */
   public FavoritesPlugin() {
      plugin = this;
   }

   /**
    * This method is called upon plug-in activation.
    */
   public void start(BundleContext context) throws Exception {
      super.start(context);
   }

   /**
    * This method is called when the plug-in is stopped.
    */
   public void stop(BundleContext context) throws Exception {
      super.stop(context);
      plugin = null;
   }

   /**
    * Returns the shared instance.
    */
   public static FavoritesPlugin getDefault() {
      return plugin;
   }
```

```
/**
 * Returns an image descriptor for the image file
 * at the given plug-in relative path.
 *
 * @param path
 *              the path
 * @return the image descriptor
 */
public static ImageDescriptor getImageDescriptor(String path) {
    return AbstractUIPlugin.imageDescriptorFromPlugin(
        "com.qualityeclipse.favorites", path);
}
}
```

When the plug-in is activated, the Eclipse system instantiates the plug-in class before loading any other classes in it. This single plug-in class instance is used by the Eclipse system throughout the life of the plug-in and no other instance is created.

Typically, plug-in classes declare a static field to reference this singleton so that it can be easily shared throughout the plug-in as needed. In this case, the **Favorites** plug-in defines a field named `plugin` that is assigned in the constructor and accessed using the `getDefault` method.

> **Tip:** The Eclipse system always instantiates exactly one instance of an active plug-in's `Plugin` class. You can add guard code to your `Plugin` class constructor to ensure that your own code does not create any new instances. For example:
>
> ```
> public FavoritesPlugin() {
>     if (plugin != null)
>         throw new IllegalStateException(
>             "Plug-in class already exists");
>     plugin = this;
> }
> ```

2.3.3   The Favorites view

In addition to the plug-in manifest and plug-in class, the **New Plug-in Project** wizard generated code for a simple view (in the following sample) called **Favorites**. At this point, the view creates and displays information from a sample model; in subsequent chapters, however, this view will be hooked up to a favorites model and will display information from the favorites items contained within that model.

```
package com.qualityeclipse.favorites.views;

import org.eclipse.swt.widgets.Composite;
import org.eclipse.ui.part.*;
import org.eclipse.jface.viewers.*;
import org.eclipse.swt.graphics.Image;
import org.eclipse.jface.action.*;
import org.eclipse.jface.dialogs.MessageDialog;
import org.eclipse.ui.*;
import org.eclipse.swt.widgets.Menu;
import org.eclipse.swt.SWT;

/**
 * This sample class demonstrates how to plug-in a new workbench
 * view. The view shows data obtained from the model. The sample
 * creates a dummy model on the fly, but a real implementation
 * would connect to the model available either in this or another
 * plug-in (e.g., the workspace). The view is connected to the
 * model using a content provider.
 * <p>
 * The view uses a label provider to define how model objects
 * should be presented in the view. Each view can present the
 * same model objects using different labels and icons, if
 * needed. Alternatively, a single label provider can be shared
 * between views in order to ensure that objects of the same type
 * are presented in the same way everywhere.
 * <p>
 */
public class FavoritesView extends ViewPart {
    private TableViewer viewer;

    /*
     * The content provider class is responsible for providing
     * objects to the view. It can wrap existing objects in
     * adapters or simply return objects as-is. These objects may
     * be sensitive to the current input of the view, or ignore it
     * and always show the same content (Task List, for
     * example).
     */

    class ViewContentProvider
        implements IStructuredContentProvider
    {
        public void inputChanged(
            Viewer v, Object oldInput, Object newInput) {
        }

        public void dispose() {
        }

        public Object[] getElements(Object parent) {
            return new String[] { "One", "Two", "Three" };
        }
    }
```

```java
/*
 * The label provider class is responsible for translating
 * objects into text and images that are displayed
 * in the various cells of the table.
 */
class ViewLabelProvider extends LabelProvider
   implements ITableLabelProvider
{
   public String getColumnText(Object obj, int index) {
      return getText(obj);
   }

   public Image getColumnImage(Object obj, int index) {
      return getImage(obj);
   }

   public Image getImage(Object obj) {
      return PlatformUI.getWorkbench().getSharedImages()
            .getImage(ISharedImages.IMG_OBJ_ELEMENT);
   }
}

/**
 * The constructor.
 */
public FavoritesView() {
}

/**
 * This is a callback that will allow us to create the viewer
 * and initialize it.
 */
public void createPartControl(Composite parent) {
   viewer = new TableViewer(
      parent, SWT.MULTI | SWT.H_SCROLL | SWT.V_SCROLL);
   viewer.setContentProvider(new ViewContentProvider());
   viewer.setLabelProvider(new ViewLabelProvider());
   viewer.setInput(getViewSite());
}

private void showMessage(String message) {
   MessageDialog.openInformation(
      viewer.getControl().getShell(), "Favorites", message);
}

/**
 * Passing the focus request to the viewer's control.
 */
public void setFocus() {
   viewer.getControl().setFocus();
}
}
```

2.4   Building a Product

Building a commercial product involves packaging up only those elements to be delivered in a form that the customer can install into his or her environment. You can build the product in several different ways, including manually or by using a Windows batch script, a UNIX shell script, or an Apache Ant script. You can deliver the end product as a single compressed file or as a stand-alone executable. For our purposes, the **Favorites** plug-in will be delivered with source code as a single compressed zip file.

2.4.1   Building manually

Building a product manually involves launching an Eclipse **Export** wizard, filling out a few fields, and clicking the **Finish** button. Select the **File > Export** command to launch the desired export wizard. On the first wizard page (see Figure 2–14), select **Deployable plug-ins and fragments** and then click the **Next** button.

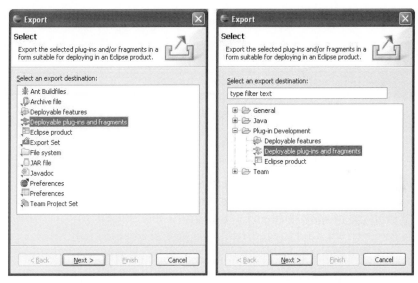

Figure 2–14   Export wizard page 1—choosing the type of export.
The Eclipse 3.1 version is shown on the left and the Eclipse 3.2 version is shown on the right. The Eclipse 3.2 version adds a filter field and categorized export types.

On the second page of the **Export** wizard (see Figure 2–15), select the plug-ins to be exported, enter the name of the zip file to contain the result, and select the options shown. In addition, specify that this export operation be saved as an Ant script in a file named `build-favorites.xml` in the `com.qualityeclipse.favorites` project, then click **Finish**.

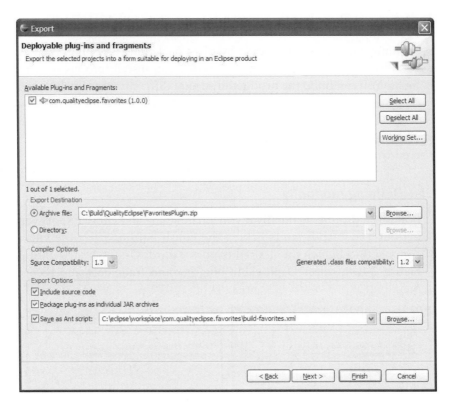

Figure 2–15   Export wizard page 2—specifying the zip file's contents.

The created zip file contains a single plug-in JAR file (a plug-in can be deployed as a single JAR file as of Eclipse 3.1):

```
plugins/com.qualityeclipse.favorites_1.0.0.jar
```

And that plug-in JAR file contains the plug-in and its source code as specified in the **Export** wizard:

```
favorites.jar
favoritessrc.zip
plugin.xml
icons/sample.gif
META-INF/MANIFEST.MF
```

Unfortunately, this process is manual, and therefore prone to errors. Manually building a product is fine once or twice, but what if a different person in the company needs to build the product? What happens as the product grows and encompasses more plug-ins? A commercial product needs a repeatable and reliable method for building it.

2.4.2   Building with Apache Ant

An Apache Ant script provides a reliable, flexible, and repeatable process for building a commercial plug-in project. There is a little more up-front work to set up an Ant script, but it is much less error-prone over time than building a product manually. For more information about Ant and constructing more complex build scripts, see Chapter 19.

Eclipse can generate simple Ant scripts. The prior section specified that the **Export** wizard generates an Ant script file named `build-favorites.xml` in the `com.qualityeclipse.favorites` project:

```
<?xml version="1.0" encoding="UTF-8"?>
<project default="plugin_export" name="build">
   <target name="plugin_export">
      <pde.exportPlugins
         destination="\Build\QualityEclipse"
         exportSource="true"
         exportType="zip"
         filename="FavoritesPlugin.zip"
         plugins="com.qualityeclipse.favorites"
         source="1.3"
         target="1.2"
         useJARFormat="true" />
   </target>
</project>
```

The preceding simple script works well from the Eclipse UI; however, unfortunately, the `pde.exportPlugins` and other `pde.export*` tasks are asynchronous and cannot be used in a headless environment (see Bugzilla entry 58413 at *bugs.eclipse.org/bugs/show_bug.cgi?id=58413*) making it difficult to build more than simple scripts.

If you want your build script to do more than just export plug-ins (see Section 3.2.1, Link files, on page 105), then you'll need a more complex Ant script similar to the following. For more on Ant and build scripts, see Chapter 19, Building a Product.

```xml
<?xml version="1.0" encoding="UTF-8"?>
<project default="plugin_export" name="build">
   <target name="plugin_export">

      <!-- Define build directories -->
      <property name="build.root"
         location="/Build/QualityEclipse" />
      <property name="build.temp"
         location="${build.root}/temp" />
      <property name="build.out"
         location="${build.root}/product" />

      <!-- Create build directories -->
      <delete dir="${build.temp}" />
      <mkdir dir="${build.temp}" />
      <mkdir dir="${build.out}" />

      <!-- Read the MANIFEST.MF -->
      <copy file="META-INF/MANIFEST.MF" todir="${build.temp}" />
      <replace file="${build.temp}/MANIFEST.MF">
         <replacefilter token=":=" value="=" />
         <replacefilter token=":" value="=" />
         <replacetoken>;</replacetoken>
         <replacevalue>
         </replacevalue>
      </replace>
      <property file="${build.temp}/MANIFEST.MF"/>

      <!-- Plugin locations -->
      <property name="plugin.dir" value=
         "com.qualityeclipse.favorites_${Bundle-Version}" />
      <property name="plugin.files" location=
         "${build.temp}/files/${plugin.dir}" />
      <property name="plugin.jar" location=
         "${build.temp}/jars/plugins/${plugin.dir}.jar" />
      <property name="product.zip" value=
         "${build.out}/Favorites_v${Bundle-Version}.zip" />

      <!-- Assemble the files -->
      <mkdir dir="${plugin.files}" />
      <jar destfile="${plugin.files}/favorites.jar">
         <fileset dir="bin" />
      </jar>
      <jar destfile="${plugin.files}/favoritessrc.zip">
         <fileset dir="src" />
      </jar>
      <copy todir="${plugin.files}">
         <fileset dir="." includes="META-INF/MANIFEST.MF" />
         <fileset dir="." includes="plugin.xml" />
         <fileset dir="." includes="icons/*.gif" />
      </copy>
```

```
        <!-- Assemble plug-in jar -->
        <mkdir dir="${build.temp}/jars/plugins" />
        <zip destfile="${plugin.jar}">
           <zipfileset dir="${plugin.files}">
              <include name="**/*.*" />
           </zipfileset>
        </zip>

        <!-- Assemble the product zip -->
        <zip destfile="${product.zip}">
           <fileset dir="${build.temp}/jars" />
        </zip>

   </target>
</project>
```

To execute this Ant script, right-click on the `build-favorites.xml` file and select **Run Ant...** (see Figure 2–16). When the Ant wizard appears, click on the **JRE** tab and select the **Run in the same JRE as the workspace** option (see Figure 2–17). Click the **Run** button to build the product.

Figure 2–16   The build.xml popup context menu.

> **Tip:** If your Ant script uses Eclipse-specific Ant tasks, such as `pde.exportPlugins`, then you must select the **Run in the same JRE as the workspace** option for your Ant script to execute properly.

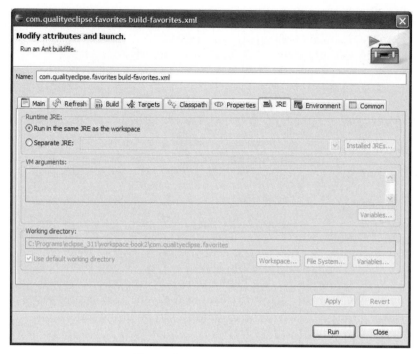

Figure 2–17   The Ant wizard.

2.5   Installing and Running the Product

To install the **Favorites** plug-in, do the following.

- Shut down Eclipse

- Unzip the `FavoritesPlugin.zip` file into your Eclipse directory
  (e.g., `C:/eclipse`)

- Verify that the favorites plug-in is in the `/plugins` directory
  (e.g., `C:/eclipse/plugins/com.qualityeclipse.`
  `favorites_1.0.0.jar`)

- Restart Eclipse

> **Tip:** Eclipse caches plug-in information in a configuration directory (see
> Section 3.4.5, Plug-in configuration files, on page 116). If you are
> installing a new version of your plug-in over an already installed one
> without incrementing the version number, then use the `-clean`
> command-line option when launching Eclipse so that it will rebuild its
> cached plug-in information.

After Eclipse has restarted, from the **Window** menu, select **Show View >
Other...** (see Figure 2–18) to open the **Show View** dialog (see Figure 2–19). In
the dialog, expand the **Quality Eclipse** category, select **Favorites,** and then
click the **OK** button. This causes the **Favorites** view to open (see Figure 2–20).

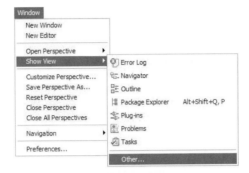

Figure 2–18   Show View > Other... from the Window menu.

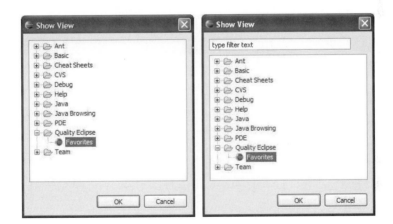

Figure 2–19   Show View dialog.
The Eclipse 3.1 version is shown on the left and the Eclipse 3.2 version is
shown on the right. The Eclipse 3.2 version adds a filter field.

Figure 2–20   The Favorites view in its initial
and simplest form.

2.6   Debugging the Product

Inevitably, during the course of producing a product, you'll need to debug a problem or you'll simply have to gain a better understanding of the code through a means more enlightening than just reviewing the source code. You can use the **Runtime Workbench** to determine exactly what happens during product execution so that you can solve problems.

2.6.1   Creating a configuration

The first step in this process is to create a configuration in which the product can be debugged. Start by selecting **Debug...** in the **Debug** toolbar menu (see Figure 2–21).

Figure 2–21   Debug menu.

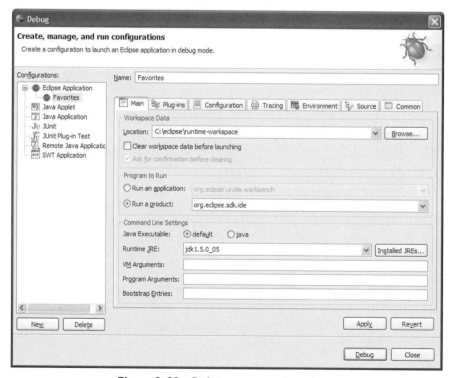

Figure 2–22   Defining a new configuration.

In the dialog that appears (see Figure 2–22), select **Eclipse Application** and then click the **New** button. Next, enter "Favorites" as the name of the configuration.

2.6.2   Selecting plug-ins and fragments

After the preceding, select the **Plug-ins** tab and the radio button labeled **Choose plug-ins and fragments to launch from the list** (see Figure 2–23). In the list of plug-ins, make sure that the **Favorites** plug-in is selected in the **Workspace Plug-ins** category but not in the **External Plug-ins** category.

> **Tip:** Plug-in projects specified in the configuration take precedence over plug-ins installed in Eclipse itself. If you have a plug-in project with the same identifier as a plug-in installed in Eclipse and want to use the installed plug-in in the **Runtime Workbench** rather than the plug-in project, uncheck the plug-in project in the **Workspace Plug-ins** category and check the installed plug-in in the **External Plug-ins** category.

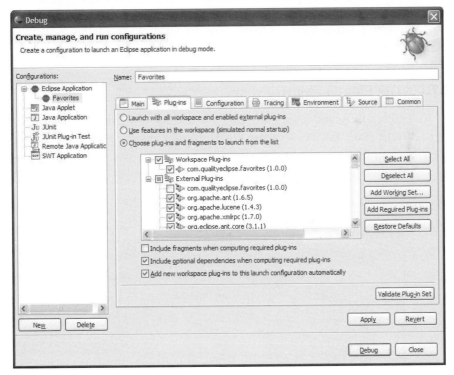

Figure 2–23   Selecting plug-ins in the configuration.

2.6.3   Launching the Runtime Workbench

Click the **Debug** button to launch the **Eclipse Application** in the **Runtime Workbench** to debug the product. Now that you've defined the configuration and used it once, it appears in the **Debug** toolbar menu (see Figure 2–21). Selecting it from that menu launches the **Runtime Workbench** without opening the **Configuration** wizard.

After clicking the **Debug** button in the **Configuration** wizard or selecting **Favorites** from the **Debug** toolbar menu, Eclipse opens a second workbench window (the **Runtime Workbench**, as opposed to the **Development Workbench**). This **Runtime Workbench** window executes the code in the projects contained in the **Development Workbench**. Making changes and setting breakpoints in the **Development Workbench** affects the execution of the **Runtime Workbench** (see Section 1.10, Introduction to Debugging, on page 58 for more about this).

2.7   PDE Views

The Plug-in Development Environment (PDE) provides several views for inspecting various aspects of plug-ins. To open the various PDE views, select **Window > Show View > Other...**; in the **Show View** dialog, expand both the **PDE** and **PDE Runtime** categories.

2.7.1   The Plug-in Registry view

The **Plug-in Registry** view displays a tree view of all plug-ins discovered in the current workspace (see Figure 2–24). Expanding the plug-in in the tree shows its components such as extension points, extensions, prerequisites, and run-time libraries. Selecting an element in the tree displays additional information about each element in the table to the right of the tree.

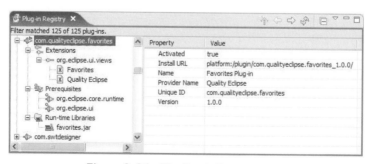

Figure 2–24   The Plug-in Registry view.

2.7.2 The Plug-ins view

The **Plug-ins** view shows a tree list of external plug-ins and plug-in projects in the current workspace and provides a quick way to review plug-ins that already exist (see Figure 2–25). In the tree, you can expand each external plug-in to browse the files located in the plug-in directory. Unfortunately, if that plug-in is contained in a JAR file rather than a directory (new in Eclipse 3.1), the files are not displayed in this view (see Bugzilla entry 89143 at *bugs.eclipse.org/bugs/show_bug.cgi?id=89143*). Double-clicking on a file element opens that file in an editor for viewing.

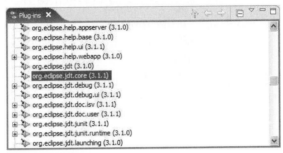

Figure 2–25   The Plug-ins view.

2.7.3 The Plug-in Dependencies view

The **Plug-in Dependencies** view shows a hierarchy of which plug-ins are dependent on which other plug-ins, which in turn are dependent on other plug-ins, and so on (see Figure 2–26). When the view opens, first right-click and select **Focus On...**, then select the `com.qualityeclipse.favorites` plug-in. Double-clicking on an element in the tree opens the plug-in manifest editor for the corresponding plug-in.

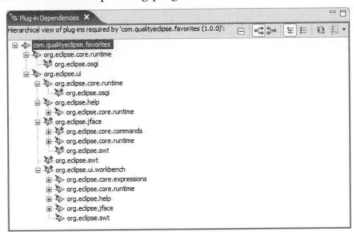

Figure 2–26   The Plug-in Dependencies view.

2.8   Writing Plug-in Tests

Eclipse is a continually moving target, and when building commercial plug-ins, tests are necessary to ensure that the product continues to function properly over multiple releases. If the goal was to develop and release a plug-in once, then manual testing would suffice; however, automated tests are better at preventing regressions from creeping into the product over time.

2.8.1   Test preparation

Before a test for the **Favorites** view can be created, you must modify the Favorites plug-in manifest so that the appropriate classes are visible to the test plug-in. Open the plug-in manifest editor by double-clicking on the `plugin.xml` file, then switch to the **Runtime** page (see Figure 2–11). In the **Exported Packages** section, click **Add...**, select the `com.qualityeclipse.favorites.views` package and save the changes by selecting **File > Save**.

Next, add the appropriate accessor so that the test can validate the view content. In the `FavoritesView` class, add the following method:

```
/**
 * For testing purposes only.
 * @return the table viewer in the Favorites view
 */
public TableViewer getFavoritesViewer() {
    return viewer;
}
```

> **Tip:** You can limit the visibility of your exported packages by specifying which plug-ins can access a package in the **Package Visibility** section of the **Runtime** page in the plug-in manifest editor (see Section 20.2.5, Related plug-ins, on page 713). Alternatively, you can place tests into a fragment so that no packages need to be exported (for more on fragments, see Section 16.3, Using Fragments, on page 587).

2.8.2   Creating a Plug-in test project

Use the same procedure as outlined in Section 2.2, Creating a Plug-in Project, on page 66, to create a new plug-in project with the following exceptions:

- Name the project **com.qualityeclipse.favorites.test**
- Put **favoritesTest.jar** on the classpath
- Change the plug-in class name to **com.qualityeclipse.favorites. test.FavoritesTestPlugin**
- Uncheck the **Create a plug-in using one of these templates** checkbox

After the project has been created, use the **Dependencies** page of the plug-in manifest editor (see Figure 2–10 on page 73) to add the following required plug-ins and then save the changes:

- **com.qualityeclipse.favorites**
- **org.junit**

2.8.3 Creating a Plug-in test

When a project has been created and the plug-in manifest modified, it's time to create a simple test for the **Favorites** plug-in (see the following code example). The goal of the test is to show the **Favorites** view, validate its content, and then hide the view.

```
package com.qualityeclipse.favorites.test;

import junit.framework.AssertionFailedError;
import junit.framework.TestCase;

import org.eclipse.core.runtime.Platform;
import org.eclipse.jface.viewers.ILabelProvider;
import org.eclipse.jface.viewers.IStructuredContentProvider;
import org.eclipse.jface.viewers.ITableLabelProvider;
import org.eclipse.jface.viewers.TableViewer;
import org.eclipse.swt.widgets.Display;
import org.eclipse.ui.PlatformUI;

import com.qualityeclipse.favorites.views.FavoritesView;

/**
 * The class <code>FavoritesViewTest</code> contains tests
 * for the class {@link
 *     com.qualityeclipse.favorites.views.FavoritesView}.
 *
 * @pattern JUnit Test Case
 * @generatedBy CodePro Studio
 */
public class FavoritesViewTest extends TestCase
{
    private static final String VIEW_ID =
        "com.qualityeclipse.favorites.views.FavoritesView";

    /**
     * The object that is being tested.
     *
     * @see com.qualityeclipse.favorites.views.FavoritesView
     */
    private FavoritesView testView;
```

```
/**
 * Construct new test instance.
 *
 * @param name the test name
 */
public FavoritesViewTest(String name) {
    super(name);
}


/**
 * Perform pre-test initialization.
 *
 * @throws Exception
 *
 * @see TestCase#setUp()
 */
protected void setUp() throws Exception {
    super.setUp();
    // Initialize the test fixture for each test
    // that is run.
    waitForJobs();
    testView = (FavoritesView)
        PlatformUI
            .getWorkbench()
            .getActiveWorkbenchWindow()
            .getActivePage()
            .showView(VIEW_ID);

    // Delay for 3 seconds so that
    // the Favorites view can be seen.
    waitForJobs();
    delay(3000);

    // Add additional setup code here.
}

/**
 * Perform post-test cleanup.
 *
 * @throws Exception
 *
 * @see TestCase#tearDown()
 */
protected void tearDown() throws Exception {
    super.tearDown();
    // Dispose of test fixture.
    waitForJobs();
    PlatformUI
        .getWorkbench()
        .getActiveWorkbenchWindow()
        .getActivePage()
        .hideView(testView);

    // Add additional teardown code here.
}
```

```
/**
 * Run the view test.
 */
public void testView() {
   TableViewer viewer = testView.getFavoritesViewer();
   Object[] expectedContent =
      new Object[] { "One", "Two", "Three" };
   Object[] expectedLabels =
      new String[] { "One", "Two", "Three" };

   // Assert valid content.
   IStructuredContentProvider contentProvider =
      (IStructuredContentProvider)
         viewer.getContentProvider();
   assertEquals(expectedContent,
      contentProvider.getElements(viewer.getInput()));

   // Assert valid labels.
   ITableLabelProvider labelProvider =
      (ITableLabelProvider) viewer.getLabelProvider();
   for (int i = 0; i < expectedLabels.length; i++)
      assertEquals(expectedLabels[i],
         labelProvider.getColumnText(expectedContent[i], 1));
}

/**
 * Process UI input but do not return for the
 * specified time interval.
 *
 * @param waitTimeMillis the number of milliseconds
 */
private void delay(long waitTimeMillis) {
   Display display = Display.getCurrent();

   // If this is the UI thread,
   // then process input.
   if (display != null) {
      long endTimeMillis =
         System.currentTimeMillis() + waitTimeMillis;
      while (System.currentTimeMillis() < endTimeMillis)
      {
         if (!display.readAndDispatch())
            display.sleep();
      }
      display.update();
   }
   // Otherwise, perform a simple sleep.
   else {
      try {
         Thread.sleep(waitTimeMillis);
      }
      catch (InterruptedException e) {
         // Ignored.
      }
   }
}
```

```java
/**
 * Wait until all background tasks are complete.
 */
public void waitForJobs() {
    while (Platform.getJobManager().currentJob() != null)
        delay(1000);
}


/**
 * Assert that the two arrays are equal.
 * Throw an AssertionException if they are not.
 *
 * @param expected first array
 * @param actual second array
 */
private void assertEquals(Object[] expected, Object[] actual) {
    if (expected == null) {
        if (actual == null)
            return;
        throw new AssertionFailedError(
            "expected is null, but actual is not");
    }
    else {
        if (actual == null)
            throw new AssertionFailedError(
                "actual is null, but expected is not");
    }

    assertEquals(
        "expected.length "
            + expected.length
            + ", but actual.length "
            + actual.length,
        expected.length,
        actual.length);

    for (int i = 0; i < actual.length; i++)
        assertEquals(
            "expected[" + i +
                "] is not equal to actual[" +
                i + "]",
            expected[i],
            actual[i]);
}
}
```

2.8.4   Running a Plug-in test

The next step after creating a test class is to configure and execute the test. Similar to creating a runtime configuration (see Section 2.6.1, Creating a configuration, on page 88), creating a test configuration involves right-clicking on the FavoritesViewTest in the **Package Explorer** and selecting the **Run As > JUnit Plug-in Test** command. This automatically builds a test configuration and executes the test. You should then see the Runtime Workbench appear, the **Favorites** view open, and the Runtime Workbench close. The **JUnit** view indicates that your test executed successfully and the **Favorites** view content has been validated (see Figure 2–27).

Figure 2–27   The JUnit view.

Right clicking on the FavoritesViewTest once again and selecting **Run As > Run...** opens the **Configuration** wizard (see Figure 2–28). Here you can specify whether a single test should be executed by itself or whether all tests in a project should be executed simultaneously.

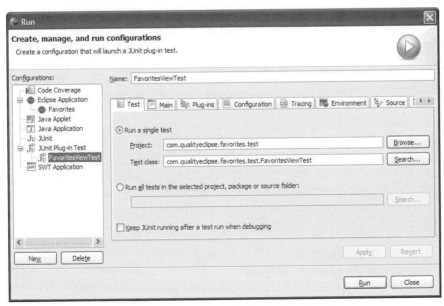

Figure 2–28   The test Configuration wizard.

2.8.5 *Uninstalling the Favorites plug-in*

Use the following steps to delete the **Favorites** plug-in from the **Development Workspace:**

1. Close the **Favorites** view.

2. Shut down Eclipse.

3. Delete the `com.quality.favorites_1.0.0.jar` file in the Eclipse plug-ins directory.

4. Restart Eclipse. If you get an error message (see Figure 2–29) when restarting, at least one of the **Favorites** views was not closed when Eclipse was shut down in Step 2.

5. Verify that the **Favorites** view is no longer available by opening the **Show View** dialog (see Figure 2–18) and verifying that the **Quality Eclipse** category is no longer present (see Figure 2–19).

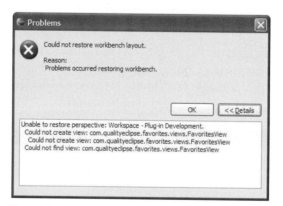

Figure 2–29   Problems dialog when restarting Eclipse.

2.9   **Summary**

This chapter covered the process of creating, running, debugging, inspecting, and testing a simple plug-in from start to finish. Subsequent chapters will cover every aspect of this process, plus more in much greater detail.

References

Chapter source (*www.qualityeclipse.com/projects/source-ch-02.zip*).

Gamma, Eric, and Kent Beck, *Contributing to Eclipse*. Addison-Wesley, Boston, 2003.

McAffer, Jeff, and Jean-Michel Lemieux, *Eclipse Rich Client Platform: Designing, Coding, and Packaging Java Applications*. Addison-Wesley, Boston, 2005.

CHAPTER 3

Eclipse Infrastructure

This chapter discusses the architecture behind the code generated in the previous chapter. Before diving deeper into every aspect of the program, it's time to step back and look at Eclipse as a whole.

The simple example plug-in that was started and described in Chapter 2—the **Favorites** plug-in—provides a concrete basis on which to discuss the Eclipse architecture.

3.1 Structural Overview

Eclipse isn't a single monolithic program, but rather a small kernel called a plug-in loader surrounded by hundreds (and potentially thousands) of plug-ins (see Figure 3–1) of which the **Favorites** example plug-in is one. Each plug-in may rely on services provided by another plug-in, and each may in turn provide services on which yet other plug-ins may rely.

This modular design lends itself to discrete chunks of functionality that can be more readily reused to build applications not envisioned by Eclipse's original developers.

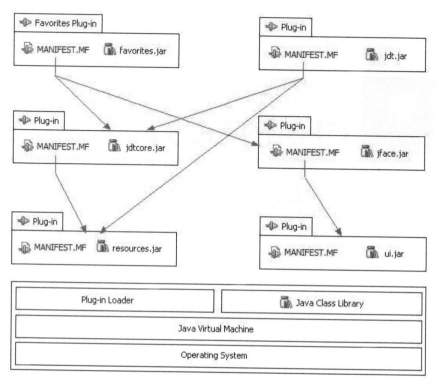

Figure 3–1   Eclipse plug-in structure.
An example of how plug-ins depend on one another.

3.1.1   *Plug-in structure*

The behavior of every plug-in is in code, yet the dependencies and services of a plug-in (see Section 2.3.1, The Plug-in manifests, on page 71) are declared in the MANIFEST.MF and plugin.xml files (see Figure 3–2). This structure facilitates lazy-loading of plug-in code on an as-needed basis, thus reducing both the startup time and the memory footprint of Eclipse.

On startup, the plug-in loader scans the MANIFEST.MF and plugin.xml files for each plug-in and then builds a structure containing this information. This structure takes up some memory, but it allows the loader to find a required plug-in much more quickly, and it takes up a lot less space than loading all the code from all the plug-ins all the time.

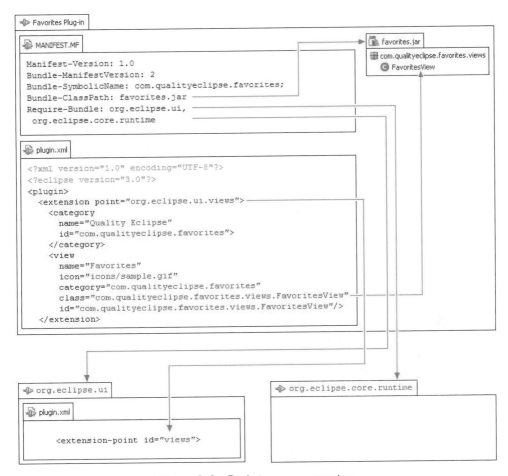

Figure 3–2   Declaring a new extension.
This is an example of how a new extension is declared in the plug-in manifest
with lines highlighting how the plug-in manifest references various plug-in artifacts.

Plug-ins Are Loaded But Not Unloaded   In Eclipse 3.1, plug-ins are loaded lazily during a session but not unloaded, causing the memory footprint to grow as the user requests more functionality. In future versions of Eclipse, this issue may be addressed by unloading plug-ins when they are no longer required (see *eclipse.org/equinox*; and for more specifics on deactivating plug-ins see *dev.eclipse.org/viewcvs/indextech.cgi/~checkout~/ equinoxhome/dynamicPlugins/deactivatingPlugins.html*).

3.1.2 Workspace

The Eclipse IDE displays and modifies files located in a ***workspace***. The work-space is a directory hierarchy containing both user files such as projects, source code, and so on, and plug-in state information such as preferences (see Section 3.4.4, Plug-in preferences, on page 116). The plug-in state informa-tion located in the workspace directory hierarchy is associated only with that workspace, yet the Eclipse IDE, its plug-ins, the plug-in static resources (see Section 3.4.3, Static plug-in resources, on page 115) and plug-in configuration files (see Section 3.4.5, Plug-in configuration files, on page 116) are shared by multiple workspaces.

3.2 Plug-in Directory or JAR file

The **Favorites** plug-in directory (or JAR file, see the first entry below) contains files similar to a typical plug-in, including `*.jar` files containing code, various images used by the plug-in, and the plug-in manifest.

> **favorites.jar**—A file containing the actual Java classes comprising the plug-in. Typically, the JAR file is named for the last segment in the plug-in's identifier, but it could have any name, as long as that name is declared in the `META-INF/MANIFEST.MF` file. In this case, since the **Favorites** plug-in identifier is `com.qualityeclipse.favorites`, the JAR file is named `favorites.jar`.

> **icons**—Image files are typically placed in an `icons` or `images` subdirec-tory and referenced in the `plugin.xml` and by the plug-in's various classes. Image files and other static resource files that are shipped as part of the plug-in can be accessed using methods in the plug-in class (see Section 3.4.3, Static plug-in resources, on page 115).

> **META-INF/MANIFEST.MF**—A file describing the runtime aspects of the plug-in such as identifier, version, and plug-in dependencies (see Sec-tion 2.3.1, The Plug-in manifests, on page 71 and see Section 3.3.2, Plug-in runtime, on page 110).

> **plugin.xml**—A file in XML format describing extensions and extension points (see Section 3.3.4, Extensions and extension points, on page 112).

The plug-in directory must have a specific name and be placed inside a specific directory so that Eclipse can find and load it. The directory name must be a concatenation of the plug-in identifier, an underscore, and the plug-in ver-sion in dot-separated form, as in:

```
com.qualityeclipse.favorites_1.0.0
```

The plug-in directory must be located in the `plugins` directory as a sibling to all the other Eclipse plug-ins, as is the case for the **Favorites** plug-in.

As of Eclipse 3.1, the plug-in can be delivered as a single JAR file containing the same files as a plug-in directory (see Section 2.4.1, Building manually, on page 81). If you wish to deliver the plug-in as a single JAR file rather than a directory of files, then it must be named in exactly the same way with a ".jar" suffix, as in

```
com.qualityeclipse.favorites_1.0.0.jar
```

Whenever we refer to a "plug-in directory," we are also referring to this alternate JAR file format.

3.2.1 Link files

Alternatively, plug-in directories comprising a product may be placed in a separate product-specific directory, and then a link file can be provided for Eclipse so that the program can find and load these plug-ins. Not only does this approach satisfy Ready for Rational Software (RFRS) requirements, but it also allows for multiple installations of Eclipse to be linked to the same set of plug-ins. You must make several modifications to the **Favorites** example so that it can use this alternate approach.

To begin, remove the existing **Favorites** plug-in in its current form from the **Development Workbench** using the steps outlined in Section 2.8.5, Uninstalling the Favorites plug-in, on page 98. Next, modify the Ant-based `build-favorites.xml` file so that the **Favorites** plug-in conforms to the new structure by inserting `QualityEclipse/Favorites/eclipse` in two places; then replace the following

```
<property name="plugin.jar" location=
    "${build.temp}/jars/plugins/${plugin.dir}.jar" />
```

with this (location must be on a single line)

```
<property name="plugin.jar" location=
    "${build.temp}/jars/QualityEclipse/Favorites/
        eclipse/plugins/${plugin.dir}.jar" />
```

Next, replace this:

```
<mkdir dir="${build.temp}/jars/plugins" />
```

with this (all on a single line):

```
<mkdir dir="${build.temp}/jars/QualityEclipse/Favorites/
    eclipse/plugins" />
```

When making these modifications, be sure that the location string is all on a single line; Ant does not handle paths that span multiple lines. When the modified `build-favorites.xml` is executed, the resulting zip file contains a new structure:

```
QualityEclipse/Favorites/eclipse/plugins/
    com.qualityeclipse.favorites_1.0.0.jar
```

The zip file can be unzipped to any location, but for this example, assume that the file is unzipped into the root directory of the C drive so that the plug-in directory is:

```
C:\QualityEclipse\Favorites\eclipse\plugins\
    com.qualityeclipse.favorites_1.0.0.jar
```

The locations for the Eclipse product directory and the Quality-Eclipse product directory are determined by the user and thus are not known at build time. Because of this, the link file that points to the Quality-Eclipse product directory must be manually created for now. Create the `links` subdirectory in the Eclipse product directory (e.g., `C:\eclipse\links`) and create a new file named `com.qualityeclipse.favorites.link` that contains this single line:

```
path=C:/QualityEclipse/Favorites
```

To do this in Windows, you can use Notepad to create and save the file as a `txt` file, which you can then rename appropriately. Note that the path in the `*.link` file must use forward slashes rather than backslashes. The new `*.link` file will be used by Eclipse once Eclipse has been restarted.

No Relative Paths in Link Files   Eclipse 3.1 does not allow link files to contain relative paths. This restriction may be changed in future versions (see *bugs.eclipse.org/bugs/show_bug.cgi?id=35037* for Bugzilla entry 35037).

3.2.2 *Hybrid approach*

Some products use a hybrid approach, delivering the product in multiple forms. When installing, the installer places product plug-ins directly in the Eclipse plug-ins directory, whereas when installing into Rational Application

Developer or any of the other Rational IDE family of products, the product plug-ins are placed in a separate product directory and a link file is created. In addition, these products are available in various zip file formats, each targeted at a specific type and version of an Eclipse or WebSphere product. This hybrid approach facilitates a simpler and smaller zip-based installation for Eclipse where Ready for Rational Software (RFRS) certification is not required, and a cleaner and easier installer-based installation for the Rational IDE family of products.

After you install the QualityEclipse product and create the link file as just described, the QualityEclipse product is ready for use. Verify that you have correctly installed the QualityEclipse product in its new location by restarting Eclipse and opening the **Favorites** view. After you have installed and verified the product, be sure to uninstall it by deleting the link file so that the JUnit tests described in Section 2.8, Writing Plug-in Tests, on page 92 will still run successfully.

3.3 Plug-in Manifest

As stated earlier, there are two files—MANIFEST.MF and plugin.xml—per plug-in defining various high-level aspects so that the plug-in does not have to load until you need its functionality. The format and content for these files can be found in the Eclipse help facility accessed by **Help > Help Contents**; look under **Platform Plug-in Developer Guide > Reference > Other Reference Information > OSGi Bundle Manifest** and **Plug-in Manifest**.

What is OSGi? Eclipse originally used a home-grown runtime model/mechanism that was designed and implemented specifically for Eclipse. This was good because it was highly optimized and tailored to Eclipse, but less than optimal because there are many complicated issues, and having a unique runtime mechanism prevented reusing the work done in other areas (e.g., OSGi, Avalon, JMX, etc.). As of Eclipse 3.0, a new runtime layer was introduced based upon technology from the OSGi Alliance (www.osgi.org) that has a strong specification, a good component model, supports dynamic behaviour, and is reasonably similar to the original Eclipse runtime. With each new release of Eclipse, the Eclipse runtime API and implementation (e.g. "plug-ins") continues to align itself more and more closely with the OSGi runtime model (e.g. "bundles").

3.3.1 Plug-in declaration

Within each bundle manifest, there are entries for name, identifier, version, plug-in class, and provider.

```
Bundle-Name: Favorites Plug-in
Bundle-SymbolicName: com.qualityeclipse.favorites; singleton:=true
Bundle-Version: 1.0.0
Bundle-Activator: com.qualityeclipse.favorites.FavoritesPlugin
Bundle-Vendor: Quality Eclipse
```

Strings in the plug-in manifest, such as the plug-in name, can be moved into a separate `plugin.properties` file. This process facilitates internationalization as discussed in Chapter 16, Internationalization.

3.3.1.1 Plug-in identifier

The plug-in identifier (`Bundle-SymbolicName`) is designed to uniquely identify the plug-in and is typically constructed using Java package naming conventions (e.g., `com.<companyName>.<productName>`, or in our case, `com.quality-eclipse.favorites`). If several plug-ins are all part of the same product, then each plug-in name can have four or even five parts to it as in `com.quality-eclipse.favorites.core` and `com.qualityeclipse.favorites.ui`.

3.3.1.2 Plug-in version

Every plug-in specifies its version (`Bundle-Version`) using three numbers separated by periods. The first number indicates the major version number, the second indicates the minor version number, and the third indicates the service level, as in `1.0.0`. You can specify an optional qualifier that can include alphanumeric characters as in `1.0.0.beta_1` or `1.0.0.2006-03-20` (no whitespace). Eclipse does not use or interpret this optional qualifier in any way, so the product builder can use it to encode the build type, build date, or other useful information.

> **Tip:** For an outline of the current use of version numbers and a proposed guideline for using plug-in version numbering to better indicate levels of compatibility, see *eclipse.org/equinox/documents/plugin-versioning.html.*

3.3.1.3 Plug-in name and provider

Both the name and the provider are human-readable text, so they can be anything and are not required to be unique. To see the names, versions, and providers of the currently installed plug-ins, select **Help > About Eclipse SDK** to open the **About** dialog (see Figure 3–3), and then click the **Plug-in Details** button to open the **Plug-ins** dialog (see Figure 3–4).

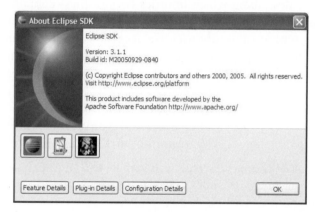

Figure 3–3   The About Eclipse SDK dialog, showing information about the Eclipse platform.

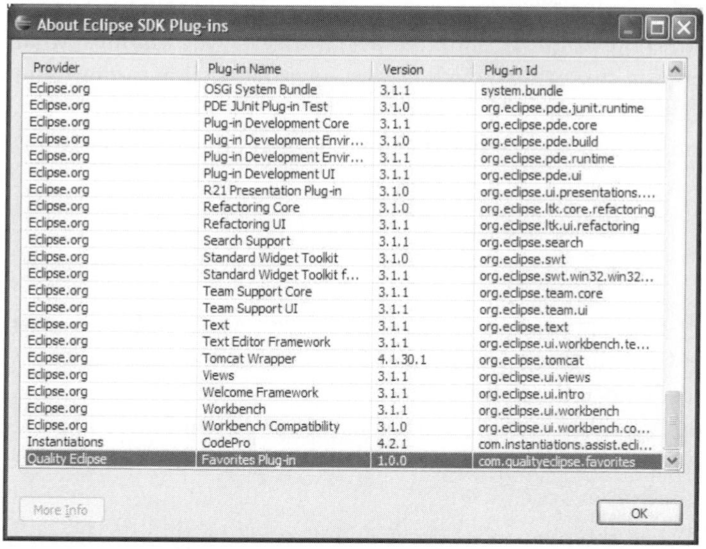

Figure 3–4   The About Eclipse SDK Plug-ins dialog, showing all the installed plug-ins with the Favorites plug-in highlighted at the bottom.

3.3.1.4   *Plug-in class declaration*

Optionally, every plug-in can specify a plug-in class (`Bundle-Activator`) as the **Favorites** plug-in does (see Section 3.4, Plug-in Class, on page 114).

3.3.2   *Plug-in runtime*

The `Bundle-ClassPath` declaration in the `MANIFEST.MF` file is a comma separated list describing which libraries (`*.jar` files) contain the plug-in code.
The `Export-Package` declaration is a comma-separated list indicating which
packages within those libraries are accessible to other plug-ins (see Section
20.2.4, How Eclipse is different, on page 713 and Section 20.2.5, Related
plug-ins, on page 713).

```
Bundle-ClassPath: favorites.jar
Export-Package: com.qualityeclipse.favorites.views
```

> **Tip:** When delivering your plug-in as a single JAR, the `Bundle-ClassPath`
> declaration should be empty so that Eclipse looks for classes in the plug-in
> JAR and not in a JAR inside your plug-in.

3.3.3   *Plug-in dependencies*

The plug-in loader instantiates a separate class loader for each loaded plug-in,
and uses the `Require-Bundle` declaration of the manifest to determine which
other plug-ins—thus which classes—will be visible to that plug-in during execution (see Section 20.9, Plug-in ClassLoaders, on page 742 for information
about loading classes not specified in the `Require-Bundle` declaration).

```
Require-Bundle: org.eclipse.ui,
 org.eclipse.core.runtime
```

If a plug-in has been successfully compiled and built but, during
execution, throws a `NoClassDefFoundError`, it may indicate that the plug-in
project's Java classpath is out of sync with the `Require-Bundle` declaration
in the `MANIFEST.MF` file. As discussed in Section 2.3.1, The Plug-in manifests,
on page 71, it is important to keep the classpath and the `Require-Bundle`
declaration in sync.

When the plug-in loader is about to load a plug-in, it scans the `Require-`
`Bundle` declaration of a dependent plug-in and locates all the required plug-
ins. If a required plug-in is not available, then the plug-in loader throws an
exception, generating an entry in the log file (see Section 3.6, Logging, on
page 122) and does not load the dependent plug-in. When a plug-in gathers
the list of plug-ins that extend an extension point it defines, it will not see any
disabled plug-ins. In this circumstance, no exception or log entry will be generated for the disabled plug-ins.

If a plug-in can successfully execute without a required plug-in, then that required plug-in can be marked as optional in the plug-in manifest. To do so, open the plug-in manifest editor and then switch to the **Dependencies** tab (see Figure 2–10 on page 73). Select the required plug-in, click the **Properties** button and then check the **Optional** checkbox in the Properties dialog (see Figure 3–5).

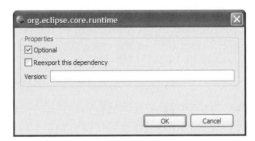

Figure 3–5 The required plug-in properties dialog.

Making this change in the plug-in manifest editor appends `;resolution:=optional` to the required plug-in in the `Require-Bundle` declaration so that it now looks something like this:

```
Require-Bundle: org.eclipse.ui,
 org.eclipse.core.runtime;resolution:=optional
```

If your plug-in requires not just any version of another plug-in, you can specify an exact version or a range of versions using the required plug-in properties dialog (see Figure 3–5). The following are some examples:

- **[3.0.0.test,3.0.0.test]**—requires a specific version
- **[3.0.0,3.0.1)**—requires version 3.0.0.x
- **[3.0.0,3.1.0)**—requires version 3.0.x
- **[3.0.0,3.2.0)**—requires version 3.0.x or 3.1.x
- **[3.0.0,4.0.0)**—requires version 3.x
- **3.0.0**—requires version 3.0.0 or greater

The general syntax for a range is

```
[ floor , ceiling )
```

where `floor` is the minimum version and `ceiling` is the maximum version. The first character can be `[` or `(` and the last character may be `]` or `)` where these characters indicate the following:

- [= floor is included in the range
- (= floor is **not** included in the range
-] = ceiling is included in the range
-) = ceiling is **not** included in the range

You can specify a floor or minimum version with no extra characters indicating that your plug-in needs any version greater than or equal to the specified version. Entering one of the preceding in the required plug-in properties dialog (see Figure 3–5) modifies the Require-Bundle declaration so that it now looks something like this:

```
Require-Bundle: org.eclipse.ui,
  org.eclipse.core.runtime;bundle-version="[3.0.0,3.1.0)"
```

Finally, check the **Reexport this dependency** checkbox (see Figure 3–5) to specify that the dependent plug-in classes are made visible (are (re)exported) to users of this plug-in. By default, dependent classes are not exported (i.e., they are not made visible).

Import-Package is similar to Require-Bundle except that Import-Package specifies names of packages that are required for execution rather than names of bundles. Using Import-Package can be thought of as specifying the service required whereas using Require-Bundle is like specifying the service provider. Import-Package makes it easier to swap out one bundle for another that provides the same service, but harder to know who is providing that service.

3.3.4   *Extensions and extension points*

A plug-in declares extension points so that other plug-ins can extend the functionality of the original plug-in in a controlled manner (see Section 17.1, The Extension Point Mechanism, on page 595). This mechanism provides a layer of separation so that the original plug-in does not need to know about the existence of the extending plug-ins at the time you build the original plug-in. Plug-ins declare extension points as part of their plug-in manifest, as in the views extension point declared in the org.eclipse.ui plug-in:

```
<extension-point
    id="views"
    name="%ExtPoint.views"
    schema="schema/views.exsd"/>
```

You can find documentation for this extension point in the Eclipse help (select **Help > Help Contents**, then in the **Help** dialog, select **Platform Plug-in Developer Guide > Reference > Extension Points Reference > Workbench > org.eclipse.ui.views**). It indicates that any plug-in using this extension point must provide the name of a class that implements the interface `org.eclipse.ui.IViewPart` (see Section 20.5, Types Specified in an Extension Point, on page 723).

Other plug-ins declare extensions to the original plug-in's functionality similar to the **Favorites** plug-in's view extensions. In this case, the **Favorites** plug-in declares a new category of views with the name **Quality Eclipse** and the class, `com.qualityeclipse.favorites.views.FavoritesView`, as a new type of view as follows:

```
<extension point="org.eclipse.ui.views">
   <category
        name="Quality Eclipse"
        id="com.qualityeclipse.favorites">
   </category>
   <view
        name="Favorites"
        icon="icons/sample.gif"
        category="com.qualityeclipse.favorites"
        class="com.qualityeclipse.favorites.views.FavoritesView"
        id="com.qualityeclipse.favorites.views.FavoritesView">
   </view>
</extension>
```

Each type of extension point may require different attributes to define the extension. Typically, ID attributes take a form similar to the plug-in identifier. The category ID provides a way for the **Favorites** view to uniquely identify the category that contains it. The `name` attribute of both the category and view is human-readable text, while the `icon` attribute specifies a relative path from the plug-in directory to the image file associated with the view.

This approach allows Eclipse to load information about the extensions declared in various plug-ins without loading the plug-ins themselves, thus reducing the amount of time and memory required for an operation. For example, selecting the **Windows > Show View > Other...** menu opens a dialog showing all the views provided by all the plug-ins known to Eclipse (see Section 2.5, Installing and Running the Product, on page 86). Because each type of view is declared in its plug-in's manifest, the Eclipse runtime can present a list of views to the user without actually loading each plug-in that contains the view.

3.4   Plug-in Class

By default, the plug-in class or `Bundle-Activator` provides methods for accessing static resources associated with the plug-in, and for accessing and initializing plug-in-specific preferences and other state information. A plug-in class is not required, but if specified in the plug-in manifest, the plug-in class is the first class notified after the plug-in loads and the last class notified when the plug-in is about to shut down (see Section 3.5.2, Plug-ins and Bundles, on page 120 and the source code listing in Section 2.3.2, The Plug-in class, on page 77).

> **Tip:** Historically, plug-ins have exposed their `Plugin` subclass as an entry point. To better control access to your plug-in's initialization, consider either a `Bundle-Activator` other than your `Plugin` subclass or moving public access methods to a new class and hiding your `Plugin` subclass.

3.4.1   Startup and shutdown

The plug-in loader notifies the plug-in class when the plug-in is loaded via the `start()` method and when the plug-in shuts down via the `stop()` method. These methods allow the plug-in to save and restore any state information between Eclipse sessions.

> **Be Careful When Overriding start() and stop()**   When overriding these methods, be careful; always call the superclass implementation, and only take the minimum action necessary so that you do not impact the speed or memory requirements during Eclipse startup or shutdown.

3.4.2   Early plug-in startup

Eclipse loads plug-ins lazily, so it may not call the `start()` method when it launches. Eclipse can provide resource change information indicating the changes that occurred while the plug-in was inactive (see Section 9.5, Delayed Changed Events, on page 387). If this is not enough and the plug-in *must* load

and start when Eclipse launches, the plug-in can use the
`org.eclipse.ui.startup` extension point by inserting the following into its
plug-in manifest:

```
<extension point="org.eclipse.ui.startup">
   <startup class="myPackage.myClass"/>
</extension>
```

Doing this requires that the `myPackage.myClass` class implement the
`org.eclipse.ui.IStartup` interface so that the workbench can call the
`earlyStartup()` method immediately after the UI completes its startup. For
more on early startup and the issues involved, see Section 20.10, Early Startup,
on page 747.

Like most plug-ins, the **Favorites** plug-in does not need to load and start
when Eclipse launches, so it does not use this extension point. If there is a need
for early startup, then place only what is necessary for it into a separate plug-
in and use the early startup extension point there so that the additional overhead of early startup has only a small impact on startup time and memory
footprint.

3.4.3 Static plug-in resources

Plug-ins can include images and other file-based resources that are installed
into the plug-in directory along with the plug-in manifest and library file.
These files are static in nature and shared between multiple workbench
incarnations. Declarations, such as actions, views, and editors, in the plug-in
manifest can reference resources such as icons stored in the plug-in installation
directory. Additionally, the plug-in class provides methods for locating and
loading these resources:

> `find (IPath path)`—Returns a uniform resource locator (URL) for the
> given path or null if the URL could not be computed or created.

> `openStream (IPath file)`—Returns an input stream for the specified
> file. The file path must be specified relative to the plug-in's installation
> location (the plug-in directory).

3.4.4 Plug-in preferences

Plug-in preferences and other workspace-specific state information are stored in the workspace metadata directory hierarchy. For example, if Eclipse is installed at `C:\eclipse` and the default workspace location is being used, then the **Favorites** preferences would be stored in:

```
C:/eclipse/workspace/.metadata/.plugins
        /com.qualityeclipse.favorites/pref_store.ini
```

The plug-in class provides methods for accessing plug-in preferences and other state-related files as follows:

`getPluginPreferences()`—Returns the preference store for this plug-in (see Section 12.3, Preference APIs, on page 467).

`getStateLocation()`—Returns the location in the local filesystem of the plug-in state area for this plug-in (see Section 7.5.2, Saving global view information, on page 311). If the plug-in state area did not exist prior to this call, it is created.

`savePluginPreferences()`—Saves the preference settings for this plug-in; it does nothing if the preference store does not need saving.

You can supply default preferences to a plug-in in several ways. In order to programmatically define default preference values, override the method `initializeDefaultPluginPreferences()`. Alternatively, you can specify default preferences in a `preferences.ini` file located in the plug-in directory (see Section 12.3.4, Specifying default values in a file, on page 472). Using this second approach also lets you easily internationalize the plug-in using a `preferences.properties` file (see Section 16.1, Externalizing the Plug-in Manifest, on page 576).

3.4.5 Plug-in configuration files

If you need to store plug-in information that needs to be shared among all workspaces associated with a particular Eclipse installation, then use the method `Platform.getConfigurationLocation()` and create a plug-in specific subdirectory. If Eclipse is installed in a read-only location, then `Platform.getConfigurationLocation()` will return `null`. You could add the following field and method to the `FavoritesPlugin` class to return a configuration directory for this plug-in. If Eclipse is installed in a read-only location, then this method would gracefully degrade by returning the workspace-specific state location rather than the configuration directory so that plug-in state information could still be stored and retrieved.

```
public static final String ID = "com.qualityeclipse.favorites";

public File getConfigDir() {
   Location location = Platform.getConfigurationLocation();
   if (location != null) {
      URL configURL = location.getURL();
      if (configURL != null
            && configURL.getProtocol().startsWith("file")) {
         return new File(configURL.getFile(), ID);
      }
   }
   // If the configuration directory is read-only,
   // then return an alternate location
   // rather than null or throwing an Exception.
   return getStateLocation().toFile();
}
```

Preferences can also be stored in the configuration directory by adding the following field and method to the `FavoritesPlugin` class.

> **Read-Only Installation**   Be warned that if Eclipse is installed in a read-only location, then this method will return `null`. In addition, neither the following code nor the Preferences object returned by the method below is thread safe.

```
private IEclipsePreferences configPrefs;

public Preferences getConfigPrefs() {
   if (configPrefs == null)
      configPrefs = new ConfigurationScope().getNode(ID);
   return configPrefs;
}
```

If you add the preceding method to your plug-in class, then you should also modify the `stop()` method to flush the configuration preferences to disk when Eclipse shuts down.

```
public void stop(BundleContext context) throws Exception {
   if (configPrefs != null) {
      configPrefs.flush();
      configPrefs = null;
   }
   plugin = null;
   super.stop(context);
}
```

When you launch a Runtime Workbench (see Section 2.6, Debugging the Product, on page 88), you can specify the configuration directory using the **Configration** page of the **Run** dialog (see Figure 3–6).

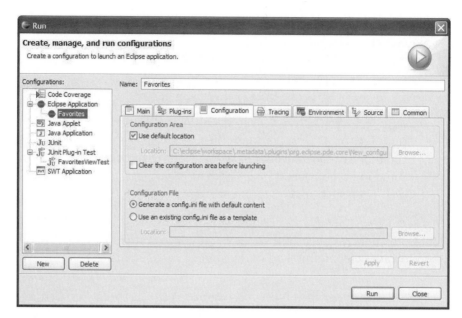

Figure 3–6   The Launch Configuration page for specifying the configuration directory.

3.4.6   *Plugin and AbstractUIPlugin*

All plug-in classes must implement the `BundleActivator` interface. Typically, UI-based plug-ins (plug-ins requiring the `org.eclipse.ui` plug-in) have a plug-in class that subclasses `AbstractUIPlugin`, while non-UI plug-ins subclass `Plugin`. Both classes provide basic plug-in services for the plug-in programmer, but there are important differences.

`AbstractUIPlugin` automatically saves plug-in preferences when the plug-in shuts down. When subclassing the `Plugin` class directly, modify the `stop()` method to always call `savePluginPreferences()` and `saveDialogSettings()` so that preferences will persist across sessions.

> **Older Preference Storage Methods**   `AbstractUIPlugin`
> provides alternate preferences storage methods and classes that you should not
> use. These methods, such as `getPreferenceStore()` and the associated
> `IPreferenceStore` interface, predate Eclipse 3.1 and the `Plugin` class
> preference methods, such as `getPluginPreferences()` and the associated
> class `Preferences`. They exist only for backward compatibility. These older
> preference storage methods do not provide any advantages when used in
> `AbstractUIPlugin`, so use the `Preferences` interface and associated
> methods unless the Eclipse API specifically requires the older interface (see
> Chapter 12, Preference Pages, for more on preferences).

Other methods provided by `AbstractUIPlugin` include:

`createImageRegistry()`—Returns a new image registry for this plug-in. You can use the registry to manage images that are used frequently by the plug-in. The default implementation of this method creates an empty registry. Subclasses can override this method if necessary.

`getDialogSettings()`—Returns the dialog settings for this UI plug-in (see Section 11.2.7, Dialog settings, on page 441). The dialog settings hold persistent state data for the various wizards and dialogs of this plug-in in the context of a workbench.

`getImageRegistry()`—Returns the image registry for this UI plug-in (see Section 4.4.3, Images, on page 181 and Section 7.7, Image Caching, on page 315).

`initializeImageRegistry(ImageRegistry reg)`—Initializes an image registry with images that are used frequently by the plug-in.

`loadDialogSettings()`—Loads the dialog settings for this plug-in by looking first for a `dialog_settings.xml` file in the plug-in's metadata directory, then for a file with the same name in the plug-in directory; failing both of these, it creates an empty settings object. This method can be overridden, although this is typically unnecessary.

3.5   Plug-in Model

When Eclipse first launches, it scans each of the plug-in directories and builds an internal model representing every plug-in it finds. This occurs by scanning each plug-in manifest without loading the plug-ins. The methods in the next two subsections are useful if you want to display information about plug-ins or perform operations based on specific plug-in characteristics without taking the time and memory usage hit associated with loading plug-ins.

3.5.1   Platform

The `org.eclipse.core.runtime.Platform` class provides information about the currently executing Eclipse environment. Using this class, you can obtain information about installed plug-ins (also known as Bundles), extensions, extension points, command line arguments, job manager (see Section 20.8, Background Tasks—Jobs API, on page 739), installation location, and more.

The following are some methods of note.

`asLocalURL(URL)`—Translates a plug-in-relative URL to a locally accessible URL.

`find(Bundle bundle, IPath path)`—Returns a URL to the resource in the specified bundle.

`getBundle(String)`—Returns the bundle with the specified unique identifier.

`getBundleGroupProviders()`—Returns an array of bundle providers that contain bundle groups that contain currently installed bundles.

`getExtensionRegistry()`—Returns extension and extension point information.

`getJobManager()`—Returns the platform job manager (see Section 20.8, Background Tasks—Jobs API, on page 739).

`getLog(Bundle)`—Returns the log for the specified bundle.

`getProduct()`—Returns the Eclipse product information.

`inDebugMode()`—Returns `true` if Eclipse is in debug mode, as it is when the user specifies the `-debug` command line argument.

`resolve(URL)`—Resolves a plug-in-relative URL to a URL native to the Java class library (e.g., file, http, etc.).

`run(ISafeRunnable)`—Runs the given runnable in a protected mode. Exceptions thrown in the runnable are logged and passed to the runnable's exception handler.

3.5.2 *Plug-ins and Bundles*

Information about the currently installed plug-ins, also known as Bundles, can be obtained using `Platform.getBundleGroupProviders()` or `Platform.getBundle(String)`. Accessing a plug-in class, also known as a bundle activator, requires the containing plug-in to be loaded whereas interacting with the `Bundle` interface does not carry such a penalty. If you already have a plug-in class, such as the **Favorites** plug-in, then you can obtain the `Bundle` interface for that plug-in by using something like this:

```
FavoritesPlugin.getDefault().getBundle()
```

After you obtain the `Bundle` object, several methods are of interest.

`getBundleId()`—Returns the bundle's unique identifier (a `long`), assigned by Eclipse when the bundle was installed.

`getEntry(String)`—Returns a URL for the specified `'/'`-separated bundle relative path name where `getEntry("/")` returns the bundle root. This provides access to resoures supplied with the plug-in that are typically read-only. Relative plug-in information should be written to the location provided by `Plugin.getStateLocation()`.

`getHeaders()`—Returns a dictionary of headers and values defined in the bundle's `MANIFEST.MF` file (see Section 3.3.1, Plug-in declaration, on page 108).

`getState()`—Returns the current state of a plug-in, such as `Bundle.UNINSTALLED`, `Bundle.INSTALLED`, `Bundle.RESOLVED`, `Bundle.STARTING`, `Bundle.STOPPING`, `Bundle.ACTIVE`.

`getSymbolicName()`—Returns the unique plug-in identifier (a `java.lang.String`), which is the same as the `Bundle-SymbolicName` declaration in the `MANIFEST.MF`.

The plug-in version number can be obtained using the `getHeaders()` method.

```
new PluginVersionIdentifier(
    bundle.getHeaders().get("Bundle-Version"))
```

3.5.3   *Plug-in extension registry*

You can access the plug-in extension registry using the `Plaform.getExtensionRegistry()` method. It contains plug-in descriptors, each representing a plug-in. The registry provides the following methods for extracting information about the various plug-ins without loading them (see Section 17.1, The Extension Point Mechanism, on page 595 for information on creating extension points).

`getConfigurationElementsFor(String extensionPointId)`—Returns all configuration elements from all extensions configured into the identified extension point.

`getExtensionPoint(String extensionPointId)`—Returns the extension point with the given extension point identifier in this plug-in registry.

Previously, extensions and extension-points did not change during execution, but that is slowly changing as the Eclipse plug-in model continues to align itself with OSGi. If you are interested in changes during execution, use `addRegistryChangeListener(IRegistryChangeListener)`.

> **Tip:** For more on the plug-in registry, activation, and lifecycle, check out the Equinox project at *www.eclipse.org/equinox*.

3.6   Logging

The RFRS requirements indicate that exceptions and other service-related information should be appended to a log file. To facilitate this, the plug-in class provides a method for accessing the plug-in logging mechanism via the `getLog()` method. For convenience, the `FavoritesLog` wraps the `ILog` interface returned by the `getLog()` method with several utility methods:

```
package com.qualityeclipse.favorites;

import org.eclipse.core.runtime.IStatus;
import org.eclipse.core.runtime.Status;

public class FavoritesLog {
```

The first group of methods that follow are for convenience, appending information, error messages, and exceptions to the log for the Favorites plug-in.

```
public static void logInfo(String message) {
    log(IStatus.INFO, IStatus.OK, message, null);
}

public static void logError(Throwable exception) {
    logError("Unexpected Exception", exception);
}

public static void logError(String message, Throwable exception) {
    log(IStatus.ERROR, IStatus.OK, message, exception);
}
```

Each of the preceding methods ultimately calls the following methods which create a status object (see Section 3.6.1, Status objects, on page 123) and then append that status object to the log.

```
public static void log(int severity, int code, String message,
      Throwable exception) {
   log(createStatus(severity, code, message, exception));
}

public static IStatus createStatus(int severity, int code,
      String message, Throwable exception) {
   return new Status(severity, FavoritesPlugin.ID, code,
         message, exception);
}

public static void log(IStatus status) {
   FavoritesPlugin.getDefault().getLog().log(status);
}
```

The `log()` and `createStatus()` methods take the following parameters.

`severity`—the severity; one of these:
   `IStatus.OK, IStatus.WARNING, IStatus.ERROR,`
   `IStatus.INFO, or IStatus.CANCEL`

`code`—the plug-in-specific status code or `IStatus.OK`

`message`—a human-readable message, localized to the current locale

`exception`—a low-level exception, or `null` if not applicable

3.6.1 Status objects

The `IStatus` type hierarchy in the `org.eclipse.core.runtime` package provides a mechanism for wrapping, forwarding, and logging the result of an operation, including an exception if there is one. A single error is represented using an instance of `Status` (see method `createStatus` in the previous source code), while a `MultiStatus` object that contains zero or more child status objects represents multiple errors.

When creating a framework plug-in that will be used by many other plug-ins, it is helpful to create status subtypes similar to `IResourceStatus` and `ResourceStatus`; however, for the **Favorites** plug-in, the existing status types that follow will do:

`IStatus`—A status object that represents the outcome of an operation. All `CoreExceptions` carry a status object to indicate what went wrong. Status objects are also returned by methods needing to provide details of failures (e.g., validation methods).

`IJavaModelStatus`—Represents the outcome of a Java model operation. Status objects are used inside `JavaModelException` objects to indicate what went wrong.

IResourceStatus—Represents a status related to resources in the
Resources plug-in and defines the relevant status code constants. Status
objects created by the **Resources** plug-in bear its unique identifier,
ResourcesPlugin.PI_RESOURCES, and one of these status codes.

MultiStatus—A concrete multistatus implementation, suitable either
for instantiating or subclassing.

OperationStatus—Describes the status of a request to execute, undo,
or redo an operation (see Section 6.6.2, Commands, on page 252).

Status—A concrete status implementation, suitable either for instantiating or subclassing.

TeamStatus—Returned from some Team operations or is the payload of
some exceptions of type TeamException.

3.6.2   *The Error Log view*

The PDE provides an **Error Log** view for inspecting the Eclipse log file. To
open the **Error Log** view, select **Window > Show View > Other...**, and in the
Show View dialog, expand the **PDE Runtime** category to find the **Error Log**
view (see Figure 3–7). Double-clicking on an entry opens a dialog showing
details for the error log entry. If Eclipse is installed in C:\Eclipse and the
default workspace location is being used, you can find the Eclipse log file at
C:\Eclipse\workspace\.metadata\.log.

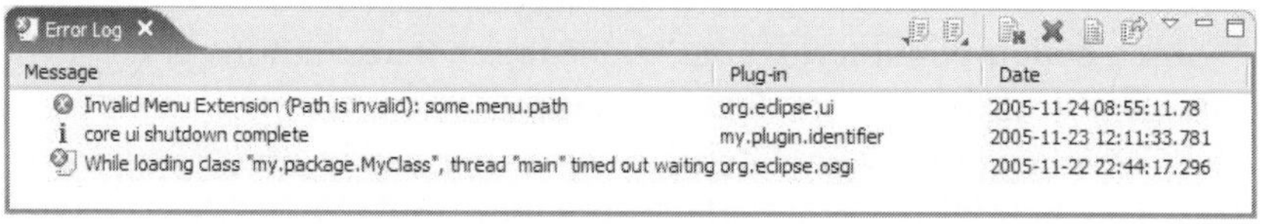

Message	Plug-in	Date
Invalid Menu Extension (Path is invalid): some.menu.path	org.eclipse.ui	2005-11-24 08:55:11.78
core ui shutdown complete	my.plugin.identifier	2005-11-23 12:11:33.781
While loading class "my.package.MyClass", thread "main" timed out waiting org.eclipse.osgi		2005-11-22 22:44:17.296

Figure 3–7   The Error Log view is provided by the Eclipse platform and displays
information and exceptions generated while Eclipse is running.

3.7   **Eclipse Plug-ins**

Commercial plug-ins are built on one or more base plug-ins that are shipped
as part of Eclipse. They are broken down into several groups, further separated into UI and Core, as follows. UI plug-ins contain aspects of a user interface or rely on other plug-ins that do, while you can use Core plug-ins in a
headless environment (an environment without a user interface).

Core—A general low-level group of non-UI plug-ins comprising basic services such as extension processing (see Chapter 9, Resource Change Tracking, on page 375), resource tracking (see Chapter 17, Creating New Extension Points, on page 595), and so on.

SWT—The Standard Widget Toolkit, a general library of UI widgets tightly integrated with the underlying operating system (OS), but with an OS-independent API (see Chapter 4, The Standard Widget Toolkit, on page 127).

JFace—A general library of additional UI functionality built on top of SWT (see Chapter 5, JFace Viewers, on page 185).

Workbench core—Plug-ins providing non-UI behavior specific to the Eclipse IDE itself, such as projects, project natures, and builders (see Chapter 14, Builders, Markers, and Natures, on page 497).

Workbench UI—Plug-ins providing UI behavior specific to the Eclipse IDE itself, such as editors, views, perspectives, actions, and preferences (see Chapters 6, 7, 8, 10, and 12).

Team—A group of plug-ins providing services for integrating different types of source code control management systems (e.g., CVS) into the Eclipse IDE.

Help—Plug-ins that provide documentation for the Eclipse IDE as part of the Eclipse IDE (see Chapter 15, Implementing Help, on page 539).

JDT core—Non-UI-based Java Development Tooling (JDT) plug-ins for the Eclipse IDE.

JDT UI—JDT UI plug-ins for the Eclipse IDE.

3.8 Summary

This chapter tried to give you a more in-depth understanding of Eclipse and its structure in relation to creating plug-ins. The next two chapters explore the user-interface elements that should be used to create your own plug-ins.

References

Chapter source (*www.qualityeclipse.com/projects/source-ch-03.zip*).

"Eclipse Platform Technical Overview," Object Technology International, Inc., February 2003, (*www.eclipse.org/whitepapers/eclipse-overview.pdf*).

Melhem, Wassim, et al., "PDE Does Plug-ins," IBM, September 8, 2003 (*www.eclipse.org/articles/Article-PDE-does-plugins/PDE-intro.html*).

Xenos, Stefan, "Inside the Workbench: A Guide to the Workbench Internals," IBM, October 20, 2005 (*www.eclipse.org/articles/Article-UI-Workbench/workbench.html*).

Bolour, Azad, "Notes on the Eclipse Plug-in Architecture," Bolour Computing, July 3, 2003 (*www.eclipse.org/articles/Article-Plug-in-architecture/plugin_architecture.html*).

Rufer, Russ, "Sample Code for Testing a Plug-in into Existence," Yahoo Groups Message 1571, Silicon Valley Patterns Group (*groups.yahoo.com/group/siliconvalleypatterns/message/1571*).

Gamma, Erich, Richard Helm, Ralph Johnson, and John Vlissides, *Design Patterns, Elements of Reusable Object-Oriented Software*. Addition-Wesley, Boston, 1995.

Buschmann, Frank, et al., *Pattern-Oriented Software Architecture*. John Wiley & Sons, Hoboken, NJ, 1996.

Estberg, Don, "How the Minimum Set of Platform Plug-ins Are Related," Eclipse Wiki (*eclipsewiki.editme.com/MinimumSetOfPlatformPlugins*).

Watson, Thomas, "Deprecation of Version-Match Attribute," equinox-dev email, April 30, 2004.

CHAPTER 4

The Standard Widget Toolkit

The **Standard Widget Toolkit** (SWT) is a thin layer on top of the platform's native controls. SWT provides the foundation for the entire Eclipse user interface (UI). This chapter begins with some history and philosophy of SWT, and then dives into using SWT to build applications. It covers most of the widgets commonly encountered and the layout managers used to arrange them within a window. The chapter concludes with a discussion of various resource management issues to be considered when using SWT.

4.1 SWT History and Goals

The roots of SWT go back more than a dozen years to work that Object Technology International, or OTI (then an independent pioneering OO software company and now a part of IBM), did when creating multiplatform, portable, native widget interfaces for Smalltalk (originally for OTI Smalltalk, which became IBM Smalltalk in 1993). IBM Smalltalk's Common Widget (CW) layer provided fast, native access to multiple platform widget sets while still providing a common API without suffering the "lowest common denominator" (LCD) problem typical of other portable graphical user interface (GUI) toolkits.

For many years, IBM had been using Smalltalk as its "secret weapon" when building development tools (even IBM's first Java IDE, VisualAge for Java, was written in Smalltalk); however, Smalltalk had deployment and configuration problems that ultimately doomed its long-term use at IBM.

Java's promise of universal portability and ubiquitous virtual machines (VMs) on every desktop was very appealing to the folks at IBM responsible for creating the next generation of development tools. In Java, OTI also saw another language to which it could apply its many talents.

Sun's initial attempt at providing a portable widget API, the Abstract Windowing Toolkit (AWT), suffered from both an overly complex interface to the native widgets and the LCD problem. It provided access to a minimal set of widgets, such as buttons, labels, and lists, common across most platforms but did not provide access to richer widgets such as tables, trees, and styled text. That, coupled with an anemic API, destined it to failure in the marketplace.

To solve the problems of AWT and to provide Java with a more powerful, extensible GUI library, Sun decided to abandon native widget interfaces and developed its own portable, emulated widget library officially known as the Java Foundation Classes (JFC)—more commonly known as Swing. Interestingly enough, this paralleled the developments in the Smalltalk world many years earlier when ParcPlace brought the world's first, truly portable, multiplatform GUI environment to market in a product called VisualWorks (many of the ex-ParcPlace engineers responsible for the portable, emulated GUI library in VisualWorks ended up working at Sun).

While Swing solved the LCD problem by providing a rich set of widgets, the emulation of the platform widgets left much to be desired. Swing applications ended up feeling like Swing applications, not the platform native applications they were meant to replace. Swing applications also suffered from performance problems not present in their native counterparts.

While AWT was able to run on the Java 2 Platform, Micro Edition (J2ME) devices, Swing could not because of the large runtime Java virtual machine (JVM) footprint and its reliance on fast native graphics to draw every emulated control. OTI was given the task within IBM of tooling for J2ME, and decided that AWT was not a good enough toolkit. It provided only a basic set of controls, and because its architecture necessitated using the JavaBeans component model, which allows null construction, it had a two-tiered object layer that used valuable JVM memory—something important to manage wisely on small devices.

Uncomfortable with the philosophy behind Swing and emulated widget libraries in general, and armed with extensive knowledge about how to correctly build native, portable, multiplatform widget libraries, OTI set out to correct the faults of both AWT and Swing and to produce the GUI library that AWT should have been. The result was the Standard Widget Toolkit. OTI used the same developers who created CW for Smalltalk to create SWT for Java.

SWT was designed to have as small a JVM footprint as possible. The CW had two layers, including an OS layer; however, for SWT, it was felt that a single layer was better, where each platform's implementation would be a set of completely optimized Java classes that went straight to native as soon as possible. The public API was the same, but it was not directed through an intermediate layer.

OTI used SWT to build VisualAge Micro Edition (VAME), their first IDE written in Java. When IBM decided to build a common tools platform (Eclipse) on which they could re-base their successful existing products, they initially built it using Swing. It was an early release of Swing in Java 1.2, and IBM was greatly disappointed with its performance and look-and-feel. There were memory leaks in Swing in addition to other defects, which led to its eventual abandonment.

One of the reasons SWT was chosen was because IBM's tooling effort was intended to compete head-to-head with Microsoft, and it was felt that SWT would give a rich enough UI experience. It was a huge risk at the time; SWT had not been ported to many platforms, and also by adopting SWT there was the potential that customers might say: "If Swing wasn't good enough for your toolkit, why should we use it?" Additionally, anyone writing plug-ins would have to use SWT instead of Swing—the fear was that there would be a natural antagonism toward learning this new application programming interface (API). There was also the possibility that SWT versus Swing would fragment the Java community. All these fears came true.

However, SWT has found a lot of favor with people who are now using it to program applications with the Eclipse Rich Client Platform (RCP) because they like its higher speed and platform integration. Arguably, Sun did take its eye off the ball with the 1.2 and 1.3 Swing releases. With JDK 1.4, Sun's Swing performance and its look-and-feel classes are much improved, so that developers who use it now have a greatly improved toolkit.

Without SWT threatening to become the new standard, it's difficult to know whether Sun would have done this work to try and catch up, so having the two toolkits is actually good for users of both. In the past, interoperability between the two toolkits was poor, although this has improved dramatically in Eclipse 3.0.

SWT is the foundation on which the entire Eclipse UI is based. It is fast, native, and multiplatform, but it does not suffer the LCD problem present in AWT or the look-and-feel problem present in Swing. SWT does this by taking a best-of-both-worlds approach: It uses native widgets whenever possible on a platform and supplements them with emulated widgets on platforms where they don't exist; a good example of this is the tree widget that exists in native form under Windows, but is emulated under Linux. The result is a rich, portable API for building GUI applications that adhere very closely the look-and-feel of each platform they support.

> **Note:** While providing a consistent, high-level, public API, under the covers SWT is very different from one platform to the next. SWT has a unique implementation for each platform and low-level SWT APIs map one to one with their platform counterparts. For a detailed discussion about how SWT interfaces to the native platform, see *www.eclipse.org/articles/Article-SWT-Design-1/SWT-Design-1.html*.

4.2   SWT Widgets

SWT provides a rich set of widgets that can be used to create either stand-alone Java applications or Eclipse plug-ins. Before going into detail about each of the widgets you are likely to use, it is instructive to explore a simple stand-alone SWT example.

4.2.1   Simple stand-alone example

Let's start by revisiting the simple Java project and `HelloWorld` application created in Chapter 1, Using Eclipse Tools.

4.2.1.1   Adding SWT to your project's classpath

Before you can start using SWT, the SWT libraries need to be added to your project's classpath. To add SWT support, do the following:

1. Download SWT for stand-alone applications. A standalone version of SWT is available on the same download page as the Eclipse SDK. Look for the section titled **SWT Binary and Source**. Do not extract the archive file, just save it to disk.

2. Select **File > Import...** to open the **Import** wizard.

3. Select **Existing Projects into Workspace** and click the **Next** button.

4. Choose **Select archive file** and use the **Browse...** button to locate the SWT stand-alone archive that you just downloaded.

5. Click the **Finish** button to finish importing the SWT project into your workspace.

6. Right-click on the project and select the **Properties** command to open the **Properties** dialog.

7. Select the **Java Build Path > Projects** tab and click the **Add** button.

8. Select the **org.eclipse.swt** project and click **OK** to finish adding the SWT libraries to your project's classpath (see Figure 4–1).

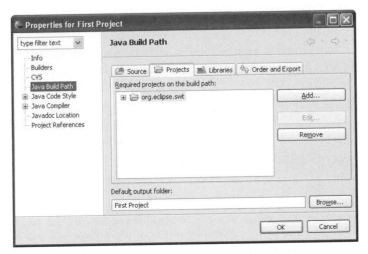

Figure 4–1 Java Build Path > Projects properties.

4.2.1.2 Standalone SWT code

Next, modify the `HelloWorld` class to convert it into a standalone SWT example. To do this, remove the contents of the `main()` method and replace it with the following:

```
1   public static void main(String[] args) {
2       Display display = new Display();
3       Shell shell = new Shell(display);
4       shell.setText("Hello World");
5       shell.setBounds(100, 100, 200, 50);
6       shell.setLayout(new FillLayout());
7       Label label = new Label(shell, SWT.CENTER);
8       label.setText("Hello World");
9       Color red = new Color(display, 255, 0, 0);
10      label.setForeground(red);
11      shell.open();
12      while (!shell.isDisposed()) {
13          if (!display.readAndDispatch()) display.sleep();
14      }
15      red.dispose();
16      display.dispose();
17  }
```

Note: After entering the new method text, select the **Source > Organize Imports** command (or press **Ctrl+Shift+O**) to add imports for all the referenced SWT classes.

The following examines each line in detail.

Line 2—Each SWT-based application has one `Display` instance that represents the link between the underlying platform and SWT. In addition to managing the SWT event loop, it also provides access to the platform resources SWT needs. It will be disposed in Line 16.

Line 3—Each window has a `Shell` representing the window frame with which the user interacts. It handles the familiar moving and sizing behavior common to all windows and acts as the parent for any widgets displayed within its bounds.

Line 4—The `setText()` method is used to set the title of the window frame.

Line 5—The `setBounds()` method is used to set the size and position of the window frame. In the example, the window frame will be 200 pixels wide, 50 pixels tall, and will be positioned 100x100 pixels from the top left corner of the screen.

Line 6—The `setLayout()` method sets the layout manager for the window frame. `FillLayout` is a simple layout that causes the single child widget to fill the entire bounds of its parent. SWT layout managers will be discussed in detail in Section 4.3, Layout Management, on page 170.

Line 7—This creates a simple label widget that has the shell as its parent and will display its text centered relative to itself.

Line 8—The `setText()` method is used to set the text of the label.

Line 9—This creates a `Color` instance with the color red. Note that you could use the red system color here as well:

```
Color red = display.getSystemColor(SWT.COLOR_RED);
```

Line 10—The `setForeground()` method sets the foreground color of the label.

Line 11—Up to this point, the window frame has not been visible. The `open()` method causes it to appear.

Line 12—The `while` loop continually checks whether the window frame has been closed.

Line 13—The `display` manages the event loop. The `readAndDispatch()` method reads events from the platform's event queue and dispatches them to the appropriate receiver. The method returns `true` as long as there is more work to be done and `false` when the event queue is empty (thus allowing the UI thread to sleep until there is more work to be done).

Lines 15 and 16—When the loop detects that the window has been disposed, it is necessary to dispose of the color, display, and any associated platform resources. Note that system colors should not be disposed.

4.2.1.3 Running the example

Normally, to launch a Java application, you would use the **Run As > Java Application** command. Doing so at this point will cause an "UnsatisfiedLink-Error" to be thrown, indicating that the SWT native library cannot be found. To avoid that problem, use the **Run As > SWT Application** command instead. This will create an SWT **launch configuration** (see Figure 4–2) that can be selected in the **Run** dialog.

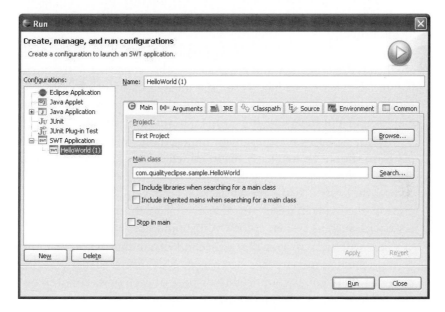

Figure 4–2   The Run dialog.

Click the dialog's **Run** button to launch the Java application (see Figure 4–3).

Figure 4–3   Running the standalone SWT application.

4.2.2 Widget lifecycle

One of SWT's goals is to be small and lean. To achieve this, a basic design decision was made that as much widget state as possible would be stored in the platform widget rather than in the SWT widget. This is in marked contrast to Swing, which maintains the entire widget state within the widget. By not duplicating the information maintained at the platform level, SWT widgets are very small with modest memory requirements.

One trade-off to this approach is that SWT widgets cannot properly exist by themselves. When an SWT widget is created, its underlying platform counterpart is immediately created. Almost all requests for widget state information go to the platform widget.

Most platforms require that widgets be created within the context of a specific parent, so SWT requires that a parent widget be supplied as one of its constructor arguments. Another requirement of many platforms is that certain *style* settings must be supplied at creation time (for example, buttons can be checkboxes, radio buttons, or simple buttons and text fields can be single- or multi-line).

Style bits are represented by `int` constants defined in the `SWT` class. Styles are then OR'ed together and passed as another constructor argument to create the initial style of a widget. Note that all styles are not supported on all platforms, so in many cases, the requested styles are treated as suggestions that may or may not have any effect on a particular platform.

Another platform requirement imposed on SWT is that resources for the platform should be explicitly disposed when they are no longer needed. This applies to the widgets themselves and any resources (e.g., graphics, fonts, and colors) they have used. The basic rule is: if you create a widget, you must destroy the widget using its `dispose()` method. If you use any system resources, such as system colors, you should not release them.

Fortunately, a widget that is a child of another widget is automatically destroyed when its parent is destroyed. This means that if you properly dispose of a shell, you do not need to dispose of each of its children because they will be disposed of automatically.

4.2.3   Widget events

An *event* is the mechanism that notifies an application when a user performs a mouse or keyboard action. The application can be notified about text entry, mouse clicks, mouse movements, focus changes, and so on. Events are handled by adding a listener to a widget. For example, a `SelectionListener` is used to inform the application that a `Button` has been pressed and released or that an item has been selected from a list box. As another example, all widgets support a `Dispose` event that is invoked just before a widget is destroyed.

For each type of event, SWT defines a listener interface (for example, `<EventName>Listener`); an event class; and, if necessary, an adapter class. Note that adapter classes are only provided in cases where the listener interface defines more than one method. Furthermore, for each widget that implements a specific event, there are corresponding `add<EventName>Listener` and `remove<EventName>Listener` methods.

Table 4–1 presents a list of the event types defined by SWT along with a description of when each event is generated and a list of the widgets that generate that event.

Table 4–1   Widget Events

Event Name	Generated When	Widgets
Arm	A menu item is armed (highlighted)	MenuItem
Control	A control is resized or moved	Control, TableColumn, Tracker
Dispose	A control is destroyed	Widget
Focus	A control gains or loses focus	Control
Help	The user requests help (e.g., by pressing the **F1** key)	Control, Menu, MenuItem
Key	A key is pressed or released	Control
Menu	A menu is hidden or shown	Menu
Modify	Text is modified	Combo, Text
Mouse	The mouse is pressed, released, or double-clicked	Control
MouseMove	The mouse moves over the control	Control
MouseTrack	The mouse enters, leaves, or hovers over the control	Control
Paint	A control needs to be repainted	Control
Selection	An item is selected in the control	Button, Combo, CoolItem, List, MenuItem, Sash, Scale, ScrollBar, Slider, StyledText, TabFolder, Table, TableColumn, TableTree, Text, ToolItem, Tree
Shell	The shell is minimized, maximized, activated, deactivated, or closed	Shell

continued

Table 4–1   Widget Events (continued)

Event Name	Generated When	Widgets
Traverse	The control is traversed (tabbed)	Control
Tree	A tree item is collapsed or expanded	Tree, TableTree
Verify	Text is about to be modified	Text, StyledText

Note: This table was adapted from the *Platform Plug-in Developer Guide for Eclipse.*

4.2.4   Abstract widget classes

All the UI objects in the system are derived from the abstract classes `Widget` and `Control` (see Figure 4–4). This section and the ones immediately following it discuss the major widget types and their major APIs. API descriptions are taken from the Eclipse platform Javadoc.

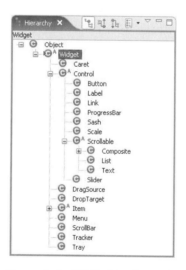

Figure 4–4   SWT widget hierarchy.

> **Note:** For every event, there is an `add<EventName>Listener` method and a corresponding `remove<EventName>Listener` method. Likewise, for every widget property, there is a `get<PropertyName>` and a `set<PropertyName>` method. In the interest of space, only the `add<EventName>Listener` and `set<PropertyName>` methods are listed. Each widget type has a constructor that requires the widget's parent as the first argument and the style (an int) as the second argument.

4.2.4.1 Widget

The `Widget` class is the abstract superclass of the following classes: `Caret`, `Control` (discussed below), `DragSource`, `DropTarget`, `Item`, `Menu` (discussed in Section 4.2.7), `ScrollBar`, and `Tracker`. Useful APIs include:

`addDisposeListener(DisposeListener)`—Adds the listener to the collection of listeners that will be notified when the widget is disposed.

`addListener(int, Listener)`—Adds the listener to the collection of listeners that will be notified when an event of the given type occurs.

`dispose()`—Disposes of the OS resources associated with the receiver and all its descendents.

`getData(String)`—Returns the application-defined property of the receiver with the specified name, or `null` if it has not been set.

`isDisposed()`—Returns `true` if the widget has been disposed and `false` otherwise.

`notifyListeners(int, Event)`—Notifies all the receiver's listeners for events of the given type that one such event has occurred by invoking the `handleEvent()` method.

`setData(String, Object)`—Sets the application-defined property of the receiver with the specified name to the given value.

`toString()`—Returns a string containing a concise, human-readable description of the widget.

4.2.4.2 Control

The `Control` class is the abstract superclass of all the dialog and window component classes such as `Button`, `Label`, `ProgressBar`, `Sash`, `Scrollable`, and `Slider` (each of these is described later in this chapter). Useful APIs include:

`addControlListener(ControlListener)`—Adds the listener to the collection of listeners that will be notified when the control is moved or resized by sending it one of the messages defined in the `ControlListener` interface.

`addFocusListener(FocusListener)`—Adds the listener to the collection of listeners that will be notified when the control gains or loses focus by sending it one of the messages defined in the `FocusListener` interface.

addHelpListener(HelpListener)—Adds the listener to the collection of listeners that will be notified when help events are generated for the control by sending it one of the messages defined in the HelpListener interface.

addKeyListener(KeyListener)—Adds the listener to the collection of listeners that will be notified when keys are pressed and released on the system keyboard by sending it one of the messages defined in the KeyListener interface.

addMouseListener(MouseListener)—Adds the listener to the collection of listeners that will be notified when mouse buttons are pressed and released by sending it one of the messages defined in the MouseListener interface.

addMouseMoveListener(MouseMoveListener)—Adds the listener to the collection of listeners that will be notified when the mouse moves by sending it one of the messages defined in the MouseMoveListener interface.

addMouseTrackListener(MouseTrackListener)—Adds the listener to the collection of listeners that will be notified when the mouse passes or hovers over controls by sending it one of the messages defined in the MouseTrackListener interface.

addPaintListener(PaintListener)—Adds the listener to the collection of listeners that will be notified when the receiver needs to be painted by sending it one of the messages defined in the PaintListener interface.

addTraverseListener(TraverseListener)—Adds the listener to the collection of listeners that will be notified when traversal events occur by sending it one of the messages defined in the TraverseListener interface.

getDisplay()—Returns the display on which the receiver was created.

getParent()—Returns the receiver's parent, which must be a Composite or null when the receiver is a shell that was created with null or a display for a parent.

getShell()—Returns the receiver's shell.

isDisposed()—Returns true if the widget has been disposed and false otherwise.

isEnabled()—Returns true if the receiver is enabled and all the receiver's ancestors are enabled and false otherwise.

`isVisible()`—Returns `true` if the receiver is visible and all the receiver's ancestors are visible and `false` otherwise.

`pack()`—Causes the receiver to be resized to its preferred size.

`redraw()`—Causes the entire bounds of the receiver to be marked as needing to be redrawn.

`setBackground(Color)`—Sets the receiver's background color to the color specified by the argument, or to the default system color for the control if the argument is `null`.

`setBounds(Rectangle)`—Sets the receiver's size and location to the rectangular area specified by the argument.

`setEnabled(boolean)`—Enables the receiver if the argument is `true` and disables it otherwise.

`boolean setFocus()`—Causes the receiver to have the keyboard focus such that all keyboard events will be delivered to it.

`setFont(Font)`—Sets the font that the receiver will use to paint textual information to the font specified by the argument, or to the default font for that kind of control if the argument is `null`.

`setForeground(Color)`—Sets the receiver's foreground color to the color specified by the argument, or to the default system color for the control if the argument is `null`.

`setLayoutData(Object)`—Sets the layout data associated with the receiver to the argument.

`setLocation(Point)`—Sets the receiver's location to the point specified by the argument that is relative to the receiver's parent (or its display if its parent is `null`).

`setRedraw(boolean)`—If the argument is `false`, causes subsequent drawing operations in the receiver to be ignored.

`setSize(Point)`—Sets the receiver's size to the point specified by the argument.

`setToolTipText(String)`—Sets the receiver's tool tip text to the argument, which may be `null`, indicating that no tool tip text should be shown.

`setVisible(boolean)`—Marks the receiver as visible if the argument is `true`, and marks it invisible otherwise.

`update()`—Forces all outstanding paint requests for the widget to be processed before this method returns.

4.2.4.3 Scrollable

The `Scrollable` class is the abstract superclass of all controls that can have scrollbars such as `Composite`, `List`, and `Text`. Useful APIs include:

> `getClientArea()`—Returns a rectangle describing the area of the receiver that is capable of displaying data (i.e., not covered by the "trimmings").

> `getHorizontalBar()`—Returns the receiver's horizontal scrollbar if it has one, and `null` if it does not.

> `getVerticalBar()`—Returns the receiver's vertical scrollbar if it has one, and `null` if it does not.

4.2.5 Top-level classes

As stated earlier, each SWT application needs a display and one or more shells (representing each window frame).

4.2.5.1 Display

The display represents the link between the underlying platform, the UI thread, and SWT. Although the `Display` constructors are public, under normal circumstances, you should not be constructing new instances (unless you are creating a standalone SWT application); instead, the following two static `Display` methods return an instance.

> `getCurrent()`—Returns the display associated with the currently running thread or `null` if the currently running thread is not a UI thread for any display.

> `getDefault()`—Returns the default display. This is the instance that was first created by the system.

Calls to SWT methods that create widgets or modify currently visible widgets must be made from the UI thread; otherwise, an `SWTException` is thrown indicating the call was made from a non-UI thread. A call to the previously listed `getCurrent()` method can be used to quickly determine whether or not the current thread is UI or non-UI. If the thread is non-UI, the following `Display` methods can be used to queue execution on the UI thread at the next available time.

> `asyncExec(Runnable)`—Causes the `run()` method of the runnable to be invoked by the UI thread at the next reasonable opportunity.

> `syncExec(Runnable)`—Causes the `run()` method of the runnable to be invoked by the UI thread at the next reasonable opportunity.

`timerExec(int, Runnable)`—Causes the `run()` method of the runnable to be invoked by the UI thread after the specified number of milliseconds have elapsed.

These methods, combined with the methods listed previously, can be used to update visible widgets when responding to resource change events (see the end of Section 9.2, Processing Change Events, on page 379), displaying error messages (see Section 20.4.3, OpenEmailAction, on page 720), or simply deferring execution until the widgets have been initialized (see Section 8.2.5, Label provider, on page 342).

In addition to managing the UI event loop, it also provides access to platform resources that SWT needs. Useful APIs include:

`addListener(int, Listener)`—Adds the listener to the collection of listeners that will be notified when an event of the given type occurs.

`beep()`—Causes the system hardware to emit a short sound (if it supports this capability).

`close()`—Requests that the connection between SWT and the underlying OS be closed.

`disposeExec(Runnable)`—Causes the `run()` method of the runnable to be invoked by the UI thread just before the display is disposed.

`findWidget(int)`—Given the OS handle for a widget, returns the instance of the `Widget` subclass, which represents it in the currently running application if such an instance exists, or `null` if no matching widget can be found.

`getActiveShell()`—Returns the currently active `Shell`, or `null` if no shell belonging to the currently running application is active.

`getBounds()`—Returns a rectangle describing the receiver's size and location.

`getClientArea()`—Returns a rectangle describing the area of the receiver that is capable of displaying data.

`getCursorControl()`—Returns the control that the onscreen pointer is currently over, or `null` if it is not currently over one of the controls built by the currently running application.

`getCursorLocation()`—Returns the location of the onscreen pointer relative to the top left corner of the screen.

`getData(String)`—Returns the application-defined property of the receiver with the specified name, or `null` if it has not been set.

getDoubleClickTime()—Returns the longest duration, in milliseconds, between two mouse button clicks that will be considered a double-click by the underlying OS.

getFocusControl()—Returns the control that currently has keyboard focus, or null if keyboard events are not currently going to any of the controls built by the currently running application.

getShells()—Returns an array containing all shells that have not been disposed and have the receiver as their display.

getSystemColor(int)—Returns the matching standard color for the given constant, which should be one of the color constants specified in the class SWT.

getSystemFont()—Returns a reasonable font for applications to use.

readAndDispatch()—Reads an event from the OS's event queue, dispatches it appropriately, and returns true if there is potentially more work to do, or false if the caller can sleep until another event is placed on the event queue.

setCursorLocation(Point)—Sets the location of the onscreen pointer relative to the top left corner of the screen.

setData(String, Object)—Sets the application-defined property of the receiver with the specified name to the given argument.

sleep()—Causes the UI thread to sleep (i.e., to be put in a state where it does not consume central processing unit [CPU] cycles) until an event is received or it is otherwise awakened.

update()—Forces all outstanding paint requests for the display to be processed before this method returns.

4.2.5.2   *Shell*

Every window has a shell representing the window frame with which the user interacts. The shell handles the familiar moving and sizing behavior common to all windows and acts as the parent for widgets displayed within its bounds (see Section 11.1.10, Opening a dialog—finding a parent shell, on page 428). Useful APIs include:

addShellListener(ShellListener)—Adds the listener to the collection of listeners that will be notified when operations are performed on the receiver by sending the listener one of the messages defined in the ShellListener interface.

close()—Requests that the window manager close the receiver in the same way it would be closed if the user clicked on the "close box" or performed some other platform-specific key or mouse combination that indicated the window should be removed.

dispose()—Disposes of the OS resources associated with the receiver and all its descendents.

getDisplay()—Returns the display on which the receiver was created.

getShell()—Returns the receiver's shell.

getShells()—Returns an array containing all shells that are descendents of the receiver.

isEnabled()—Returns true if the receiver is enabled and all the receiver's ancestors are enabled and false otherwise.

open()—Moves the receiver to the top of the drawing order for the display on which it was created (so that all other shells on that display, which are not the receiver's children, will be drawn behind it), marks it visible, sets focus to its default button (if it has one), and asks the window manager to make the shell active.

setActive()—Moves the receiver to the top of the drawing order for the display on which it was created (so that all other shells on that display, which are not the receiver's children, will be drawn behind it) and asks the window manager to make the shell active.

setEnabled(boolean enabled)—Enables the receiver if the argument is true and disables it otherwise.

setVisible(boolean visible)—Marks the receiver as visible if the argument is true and marks it invisible otherwise.

4.2.6   Useful widgets

Dozens of widgets are defined within the SWT class hierarchy. This section discusses the widgets most commonly used in plug-in development, such as labels, buttons, text fields, lists, tables, trees, containers, and tab folders. It also provides a list of useful APIs and creation styles for each widget.

4.2.6.1   Label

Labels are static controls that display either strings or images as their contents. They do not generate any special events and do not support any user interaction. Useful APIs include:

`setAlignment(int)`—Controls how text and images will be displayed in the receiver. Valid arguments include `SWT.LEFT`, `SWT.RIGHT`, and `SWT.CENTER`.

`setImage(Image)`—Sets the receiver's image to the argument, which may be `null`, indicating that no image should be displayed.

`setText(String)`—Sets the receiver's text.

Useful creation styles include:

`SWT.SHADOW_IN`—Creates an inset shadow around the widget.

`SWT.SHADOW_OUT`—Creates an outset shadow around the widget.

`SWT.SHADOW_NONE`—Creates a widget with no shadow.

`SWT.WRAP`—Causes the text of the widget to wrap onto multiple lines, if necessary.

`SWT.SEPARATOR`—Creates a single vertical or horizontal line.

`SWT.HORIZONTAL`—Creates a horizontal line.

`SWT.VERTICAL`—Creates a vertical line.

`SWT.LEFT`—Left-justifies the widget within its bounding box.

`SWT.RIGHT`—Right-justifies the widget within its bounding box.

`SWT.CENTER`—Centers the widget within its bounding box.

4.2.6.2   *Button*

Buttons provide a mechanism to initiate an action when clicked. They generate a `Selection` event when pressed and released. Buttons can display either strings or images as their contents. Depending on their style settings, buttons can represent a number of common UI element types such as pushbuttons, checkboxes, radio buttons, toggle buttons, and arrow buttons. Useful APIs include:

`addSelectionListener(SelectionListener)`—Adds the listener to the collection of listeners that will be notified when the control is selected by sending it one of the messages defined in the `SelectionListener` interface.

`getSelection()`—Returns `true` if the receiver is selected and `false` otherwise.

`setAlignment(int)`—Controls how text, images, and arrows will be displayed in the receiver.

setImage(Image)—Sets the receiver's image to the argument, which may be null, indicating that no image should be displayed.

setSelection(boolean)—Sets the selection state of the receiver if it is of type SWT.CHECK, SWT.RADIO, or SWT.TOGGLE.

setText(String)—Sets the receiver's text.

Useful creation styles include:

SWT.ARROW—Creates an arrow button widget.

SWT.CHECK—Creates a checkbox widget.

SWT.PUSH—Creates a pushbutton widget.

SWT.RADIO—Creates a radio button widget.

SWT.TOGGLE—Creates a toggle button widget.

SWT.UP—Creates an upward-pointing arrow button.

SWT.DOWN—Creates a downward-pointing arrow button.

SWT.LEFT—Creates a leftward-pointing arrow button or left-justifies the widget within its bounding box.

SWT.RIGHT—Creates a rightward-pointing arrow button or right-justifies the widget within its bounding box.

SWT.CENTER—Centers the widget within its bounding box.

The example code that follows (shown without a package statement) creates a window with a single pushbutton. Clicking on the pushbutton will change the text of the button (see Figure 4–5).

Figure 4–5   Button example.

```
import org.eclipse.swt.*;

import org.eclipse.swt.events.*;

import org.eclipse.swt.layout.*;

import org.eclipse.swt.widgets.*;


public class ButtonExample {
   public static void main(String[] args) {
      Display display = new Display();
      Shell shell = new Shell(display);
      shell.setText("Button Example");
      shell.setBounds(100, 100, 200, 100);
      shell.setLayout(new FillLayout());
      final Button button = new Button(shell, SWT.PUSH);
      button.setText("Click Me Now");
      button.addSelectionListener(new SelectionAdapter() {
         public void widgetSelected(SelectionEvent event) {
            button.setText("I Was Clicked");
         }
      });
      shell.open();
      while (!shell.isDisposed()) {
         if (!display.readAndDispatch()) display.sleep();
      }
      display.dispose();
   }
}
```

Relative to the first example in this chapter, the interesting lines in the preceding example are highlighted in bold. After the creation of the button, a selection listener is added in which a `SelectionAdapter` is created that overrides the `widgetSelected()` method.

4.2.6.3 Text

Text widgets provide text viewing and editing capabilities. If the user enters more text than can be accommodated within the widget, it will automatically scroll. Useful APIs include:

addModifyListener(ModifyListener)—Adds the listener to the collection of listeners that will be notified when the receiver's text is modified by sending it one of the messages defined in the `ModifyListener` interface.

addSelectionListener(SelectionListener)—Adds the listener to the collection of listeners that will be notified when the control is selected by sending it one of the messages defined in the `SelectionListener` interface.

`addVerifyListener(VerifyListener)`—Adds the listener to the collection of listeners that will be notified when the receiver's text is verified by sending it one of the messages defined in the `VerifyListener` interface.

`clearSelection()`—Clears the selection.

`copy()`—Copies the selected text.

`cut()`—Cuts the selected text.

`getSelectionText()`—Gets the selected text.

`getText()`—Gets the widget text.

`getText(int start, int end)`—Gets a range of text.

`insert(String)`—Inserts a string.

`paste()`—Pastes text from the clipboard.

`selectAll()`—Selects all the text in the receiver.

`setEchoChar(char echo)`—Sets the echo character.

`setEditable(boolean editable)`—Sets the editable state.

`setSelection(int start, int end)`—Sets the selection.

`setText(String)`—Sets the contents of the receiver to the given string.

`setTextLimit(int)`—Sets the maximum number of characters that the receiver is capable of holding to be the argument.

`setTopIndex(int)`—Sets the zero-relative index of the line that is currently at the top of the receiver.

Useful creation styles include:

`SWT.SINGLE`—Creates a single-line text widget.

`SWT.MULTI`—Creates a multi-line text widget.

`SWT.WRAP`—Causes widget's text to wrap onto multiple lines if necessary.

`SWT.READ_ONLY`—Creates a read-only text widget that cannot be edited.

`SWT.LEFT`—Creates a left-justified text widget.

`SWT.RIGHT`—Creates a right-justified text widget.

`SWT.CENTER`—Creates a center-justified text widget.

The example code that follows creates a window frame with a single-line text field, which only allows digits (0–9) to be entered (see Figure 4–6).

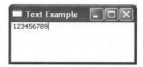

Figure 4–6   Text example.

```
import org.eclipse.swt.*;
import org.eclipse.swt.events.*;
import org.eclipse.swt.layout.*;
import org.eclipse.swt.widgets.*;

public class TextExample {
   public static void main(String[] args) {
      Display display = new Display();
      Shell shell = new Shell(display);
      shell.setText("Text Example");
      shell.setBounds(100, 100, 200, 100);
      shell.setLayout(new FillLayout());
      final Text text = new Text(shell, SWT.MULTI);
      text.addVerifyListener(new VerifyListener() {
         public void verifyText(VerifyEvent event) {
            event.doit = event.text.length() == 0
               || Character.isDigit(event.text.charAt(0));
         }
      });
      shell.open();
      while (!shell.isDisposed()) {
         if (!display.readAndDispatch()) display.sleep();
      }
      display.dispose();
   }
}
```

As in the previous example, interesting lines are highlighted in bold. After the creation of the text widget, a verify listener is added in which a `VerifyListener` is created that overrides the `verifyText()` method to verify that the character entered is a digit. Note: If the user deletes or backspaces over some text, the `event.text` will be empty.

4.2.6.4   List

List widgets present a list of items and allow the user to select one or more of them. Lists generate a `Selection` event when an item is selected. Useful APIs include:

> `add(String)`—Adds the argument to the end of the receiver's list.

> `addSelectionListener(SelectionListener)`—Adds the listener to the collection of listeners that will be notified when the receiver's selection changes by sending it one of the messages defined in the `SelectionListener` interface.

`deselect(int)`—Deselects the item at the given zero-relative index in the receiver.

`deselectAll()`—Deselects all selected items in the receiver.

`getItem(int)`—Returns the item at the given, zero-relative index in the receiver.

`getItemCount()`—Returns the number of items contained in the receiver.

`getItems()`—Returns an array of strings that are items in the receiver.

`getSelection()`—Returns an array of strings that are currently selected in the receiver.

`getSelectionCount()`—Returns the number of selected items contained in the receiver.

`getSelectionIndex()`—Returns the zero-relative index of the item that is currently selected in the receiver, or -1 if no item is selected.

`getSelectionIndices()`—Returns the zero-relative indices of the items that are currently selected in the receiver.

`indexOf(String)`—Gets the index of an item.

`remove(int)`—Removes the item from the receiver at the given zero-relative index.

`remove(String)`—Searches the receiver's list starting at the first item until an item is found that is equal to the argument and removes that item from the list.

`removeAll()`—Removes all the items from the receiver.

`select(int)`—Selects the item at the given zero-relative index in the receiver's list.

`selectAll()`—Selects all the items in the receiver.

`setItems(String[] items)`—Sets the receiver's items to be the given array of items.

`setSelection(int)`—Selects the item at the given zero-relative index in the receiver.

`setSelection(String[])`—Sets the receiver's selection to be the given array of items.

`setTopIndex(int)`—Sets the zero-relative index of the line that is currently at the top of the receiver.

Useful creation styles include:

SWT.SINGLE—Creates a single-selection list widget.

SWT.MULTI—Creates a multiple-selection list widget.

The following example creates a window frame with a single-selection list box. Clicking or double-clicking on an item will print the selection to the console (see Figure 4–7).

```java
import org.eclipse.swt.*;
import org.eclipse.swt.events.*;
import org.eclipse.swt.layout.*;
import org.eclipse.swt.widgets.*;

public class ListExample {
    public static void main(String[] args) {
        Display display = new Display();
        Shell shell = new Shell(display);
        shell.setText("List Example");
        shell.setBounds(100, 100, 200, 100);
        shell.setLayout(new FillLayout());
        final List list = new List(shell, SWT.SINGLE);
        list.setItems(new String[]
            {"First", "Second", "Third"});
        list.addSelectionListener(new SelectionAdapter() {
            public void widgetSelected(SelectionEvent event) {
                String[] selected = list.getSelection();
                if (selected.length > 0)
                    System.out.println(
                        "Selected: " + selected[0]);
            }
            public void widgetDefaultSelected(
                SelectionEvent event) {
                String[] selected = list.getSelection();
                if (selected.length > 0)
                    System.out.println(
                        "Default Selected: " + selected[0]);
            }
        });
        shell.open();
        while (!shell.isDisposed()) {
            if (!display.readAndDispatch()) display.sleep();
        }
        display.dispose();
    }
}
```

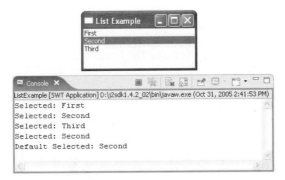

Figure 4–7 List example.

After the list widget is created, its contents are set using the `setItems()` method. Next, a selection listener is added in which a `SelectionAdapter` is created that overrides the `widgetSelected()` and `widgetDefaultSelected()` methods to print any items selected or double-clicked.

4.2.6.5 *Combo*

Similar to the list widget, the combo box widget allows the user to select a single item from a list of available items. Depending on how a combo is configured, it may also allow the user to enter a new value into the text field. The last selected or entered item is displayed in the text box. Useful APIs include:

`add(String)`—Adds the argument to the end of the receiver's list.

`addModifyListener(ModifyListener)`—Adds the listener to the collection of listeners that will be notified when the receiver's text is modified by sending it one of the messages defined in the `ModifyListener` interface.

`addSelectionListener(SelectionListener)`—Adds the listener to the collection of listeners that will be notified when the receiver's selection changes by sending it one of the messages defined in the `SelectionListener` interface.

`clearSelection()`—Sets the selection in the receiver's text field to an empty selection starting just before the first character.

`copy()`—Copies the selected text.

`cut()`—Cuts the selected text.

`deselect(int)`—Deselects the item at the given zero-relative index in the receiver's list.

`deselectAll()`—Deselects all selected items in the receiver's list.

getItem(int)—Returns the item at the given, zero-relative index in the receiver's list.

getItemCount()—Returns the number of items contained in the receiver's list.

getItems()—Returns an array of strings that are items in the receiver's list.

getSelectionIndex()—Returns the zero-relative index of the item that is currently selected in the receiver's list, or -1 if no item is selected.

getText()—Returns a string containing a copy of the contents of the receiver's text field.

indexOf(String)—Searches the receiver's list starting at the first item (index 0) until an item is found that is equal to the argument and returns the index of that item.

paste()—Pastes text from the clipboard.

remove(int)—Removes the item from the receiver's list at the given zero-relative index.

remove(String)—Searches the receiver's list starting at the first item until an item is found that is equal to the argument and removes that item from the list.

removeAll()—Removes all the items from the receiver's list.

select(int)—Selects the item at the given zero-relative index in the receiver's list.

setItems(String[] items)—Sets the receiver's list to be the given array of items.

setText(String)—Sets the contents of the receiver's text field to the given string.

setTextLimit(int)—Sets the maximum number of characters that the receiver's text field is capable of holding to be the argument.

Useful creation styles include:

SWT.DROP_DOWN—Creates a drop-down list widget. Editable drop-down list widgets are also known as combo boxes.

SWT.READ_ONLY—Creates a read-only drop-down list widget.

SWT.SIMPLE—Creates a combo widget in which the list is always present.

The following example creates a window frame with two combo widgets and a label widget. Selecting an item from the first or second combo box or entering a new value into the second combo box will change the label's contents to reflect the selection (see Figure 4–8).

Figure 4–8 Combo box example.

```
import org.eclipse.swt.*;
import org.eclipse.swt.events.*;
import org.eclipse.swt.layout.*;
import org.eclipse.swt.widgets.*;

public class ComboExample {
    public static void main(String[] args) {
        Display display = new Display();
        Shell shell = new Shell(display);
        shell.setText("Combo Example");
        shell.setBounds(100, 100, 200, 100);
        shell.setLayout(new FillLayout(SWT.VERTICAL));
        final Combo combo1 = new Combo(shell,SWT.READ_ONLY);
        final Combo combo2 = new Combo(shell,SWT.DROP_DOWN);
        final Label label = new Label(shell, SWT.CENTER);
        combo1.setItems(new String[]
           {"First", "Second", "Third"});
        combo1.setText("First");
        combo1.addSelectionListener(new SelectionAdapter() {
            public void widgetSelected(SelectionEvent event) {
                label.setText("Selected: " + combo1.getText());
            }
        });
        combo2.setItems(new String[]
           {"First", "Second", "Third"});
        combo2.setText("First");
        combo2.addModifyListener(new ModifyListener() {
            public void modifyText(ModifyEvent event) {
                label.setText("Entered: " + combo2.getText());
            }
        });
        shell.open();
        while (!shell.isDisposed()) {
            if (!display.readAndDispatch()) display.sleep();
        }
        display.dispose();
    }
}
```

After the creation of the combo widgets and the label widget, the contents of the combo widgets are set using the setItems() method and their initial selections (the contents of their text fields) with the setText() method. A selection listener is added to the first combo in which a `SelectionAdapter` is created that overrides the `widgetSelected()` method, and a modify listener is added to the second combo in which a `ModifyListener` is created that overrides the `modifyText()` method. Both methods update the contents of the label widget when their respective combo changes its selection.

4.2.6.6 *Table*

The table widget provides a vertical, multicolumn list of items showing a row of cells for each item in the list. The columns of the table are defined by one or more `TableColumn` instances, each of which defines its own heading, width, and alignment. Useful APIs include:

`addSelectionListener(SelectionListener)`—Adds the listener to the collection of listeners that will be notified when the receiver's selection changes by sending it one of the messages defined in the `SelectionListener` interface.

`deselect(int)`—Deselects the item at the given zero-relative index in the receiver.

`deselectAll()`—Deselects all selected items in the receiver.

`getColumn(int)`—Returns the column at the given, zero-relative index in the receiver.

`getColumns()`—Returns an array of `TableColumns` that are columns in the receiver.

`getItem(int)`—Returns the item at the given, zero-relative index in the receiver.

`getSelection()`—Returns an array of `TableItems` that are currently selected in the receiver.

`getSelectionCount()`—Returns the number of selected items contained in the receiver.

`getSelectionIndex()`—Returns the zero-relative index of the item that is currently selected in the receiver, or -1 if no item is selected.

`getSelectionIndices()`—Returns the zero-relative indices of the items that are currently selected in the receiver.

`indexOf(TableColumn)`—Searches the receiver's list starting at the first column (index 0) until a column is found that is equal to the argument and returns the index of that column.

`indexOf(TableItem)`—Searches the receiver's list starting at the first item (index 0) until an item is found that is equal to the argument and returns the index of that item.

`remove(int)`—Removes the item from the receiver at the given zero-relative index.

`removeAll()`—Removes all the items from the receiver.

`select(int)`—Selects the item at the given zero-relative index in the receiver.

`selectAll()`—Selects all the items in the receiver.

`setHeaderVisible(boolean)`—Marks the receiver's header as visible if the argument is `true`, and marks it invisible otherwise.

`setLinesVisible(boolean)`—Marks the receiver's lines as visible if the argument is `true`, and marks it invisible otherwise.

`setSelection(int)`—Selects the item at the given zero-relative index in the receiver.

`setSelection(TableItem[])`—Sets the receiver's selection to be the given array of items.

`setTopIndex(int)`—Sets the zero-relative index of the item that is currently at the top of the receiver.

Useful creation styles include:

`SWT.SINGLE`—Creates a single-selection table widget.

`SWT.MULTI`—Creates a multiple-selection table widget.

`SWT.CHECK`—Creates a checkbox table widget.

`SWT.FULL_SELECTION`—Creates a table widget with row selection (rather than cell selection).

Useful `TableColumn` APIs include:

`addControlListener(ControlListener)`—Adds the listener to the collection of listeners that will be notified when the control is moved or resized by sending it one of the messages defined in the `ControlListener` interface.

`addSelectionListener(SelectionListener)`—Adds the listener to the collection of listeners that will be notified when the control is selected by sending it one of the messages defined in the `Selection-Listener` interface.

`pack()`—Causes the receiver to be resized to its preferred size.

`setAlignment(int)`—Controls how text and images will be displayed in the receiver.

`setImage(Image)`—Sets the receiver's image to the argument, which may be `null`, indicating that no image should be displayed.

`setResizable(boolean)`—Sets the resizable attribute.

`setText(String)`—Sets the receiver's text.

`setWidth(int)`—Sets the width of the receiver.

Useful `TableItem` APIs include:

`getChecked()`—Returns `true` if the receiver is checked and `false` otherwise.

`getText(int)`—Returns the text stored at the given column index in the receiver, or empty string if the text has not been set.

`setBackground(Color)`—Sets the receiver's background color to the color specified by the argument, or to the default system color for the item if the argument is `null`.

`setChecked(boolean)`—Sets the checked state of the checkbox for this item.

`setForeground(Color)`—Sets the receiver's foreground color to the color specified by the argument, or to the default system color for the item if the argument is `null`.

`setGrayed(boolean)`—Sets the grayed state of the checkbox for this item.

`setImage(Image)`—Sets the receiver's image to the argument, which may be `null`, indicating that no image should be displayed.

`setImage(Image[])`—Sets the image for multiple columns in the table.

`setImage(int, Image)`—Sets the receiver's image at a column.

`setImageIndent(int)`—Sets the image indent.

`setText(int, String)`—Sets the receiver's text at a column.

`setText(String)`—Sets the receiver's text.

`setText(String[])`—Sets the text for multiple columns in the table.

The following example creates a two-column, two-item table. Clicking on an item causes the cell's contents to print to the console (see Figure 4–9).

```java
import org.eclipse.swt.*;
import org.eclipse.swt.events.*;
import org.eclipse.swt.layout.*;
import org.eclipse.swt.widgets.*;

public class TableExample {
    public static void main(String[] args) {
        Display display = new Display();
        Shell shell = new Shell(display);
        shell.setText("Table Example");
        shell.setBounds(100, 100, 200, 100);
        shell.setLayout(new FillLayout());
        final Table table = new Table(shell,
            SWT.SINGLE | SWT.BORDER | SWT.FULL_SELECTION);
        table.setHeaderVisible(true);
        table.setLinesVisible(true);
        TableColumn column1 =
            new TableColumn(table, SWT.NULL);
        column1.setText("Name");
        column1.pack();
        TableColumn column2 =
            new TableColumn(table, SWT.NULL);
        column2.setText("Age");
        column2.pack();
        TableItem item1 = new TableItem(table, SWT.NULL);
        item1.setText(new String[] {"Dan", "41"});
        TableItem item2 = new TableItem(table, SWT.NULL);
        item2.setText(new String[] {"Eric", "42"});
        table.addSelectionListener(new SelectionAdapter() {
            public void widgetSelected(SelectionEvent event) {
                TableItem[] selected = table.getSelection();
                if (selected.length > 0) {
                    System.out.println("Name: " +
                        selected[0].getText(0));
                    System.out.println("Age: " +
                        selected[0].getText(1));
                }
            }
        });
        shell.open();
        while (!shell.isDisposed()) {
            if (!display.readAndDispatch()) display.sleep();
        }
        display.dispose();
    }
}
```

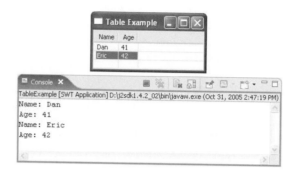

Figure 4–9   Table example.

The table widget is created with full selection behavior. Its headers are made visible with the `setHeaderVisble()` method and its lines are made visible with the `setLinesVisible()` method. Next, each column is created and its column header is set with the `setText()` method. The `pack()` method sets the size of each column to the maximum size of its contents. Each table row item is created next and cell contents are set with the `setText()` method (which expects an array of strings, one for each column). Finally, a selection listener is added to the table in which a `SelectionAdapter` is created that overrides the `widgetSelected()` method to print any items that are selected.

4.2.6.7 Tree

The tree widget is useful for displaying information in a hierarchical manner. A tree consists of a list of items composed of other items, which in turn can be composed of other items, and so on. A user navigates through a tree by expanding and collapsing items to view and hide their component items. Useful APIs include:

`addSelectionListener(SelectionListener)`—Adds the listener to the collection of listeners that will be notified when the receiver's selection changes by sending it one of the messages defined in the `SelectionListener` interface.

`addTreeListener(TreeListener)`—Adds the listener to the collection of listeners that will be notified when an item in the receiver is expanded or collapsed by sending it one of the messages defined in the `TreeListener` interface.

`deselectAll()`—Deselects all selected items in the receiver.

`getItemCount()`—Returns the number of items contained in the receiver that are direct item children of the receiver.

`getItems()`—Returns the items contained in the receiver that are direct item children of the receiver.

`getSelection()`—Returns an array of `TreeItems` that are currently selected in the receiver.

`getSelectionCount()`—Returns the number of selected items contained in the receiver.

`removeAll()`—Removes all the items from the receiver.

`selectAll()`—Selects all the items in the receiver.

`setSelection(TreeItem[])`—Sets the receiver's selection to be the given array of items.

`setTopItem(TreeItem)`—Sets the item that is currently at the top of the receiver.

Useful creation styles include:

`SWT.SINGLE`—Creates a single-selection tree widget.

`SWT.MULTI`—Creates a multiple-selection tree widget.

`SWT.CHECK`—Creates a checkbox tree widget.

Useful `TreeItem` APIs include:

`getChecked()`—Returns `true` if the receiver is checked and `false` otherwise.

`getExpanded()`—Returns `true` if the receiver is expanded and `false` otherwise.

`getItemCount()`—Returns the number of items contained in the receiver that are direct item children of the receiver.

`getItems()`—Returns an array of `TreeItems` that are the direct item children of the receiver.

`getParent()`—Returns the receiver's parent, which must be a `Tree`.

`getParentItem()`—Returns the receiver's parent item, which must be a `TreeItem` or `null` when the receiver is a root.

`setBackground(Color)`—Sets the receiver's background color to the color specified by the argument, or to the default system color for the item if the argument is `null`.

`setChecked(boolean)`—Sets the checked state of the receiver.

`setExpanded(boolean)`—Sets the expanded state of the receiver.

setForeground(Color)—Sets the receiver's foreground color to the color specified by the argument, or to the default system color for the item if the argument is null.

setGrayed(boolean grayed)—Sets the grayed state of the receiver.

setImage(Image)—Sets the receiver's image to the argument, which may be null, indicating that no image should be displayed.

setText(String)—Sets the receiver's text.

The following example creates a tree with three levels of items (see Figure 4–10). Clicking on an item causes its name to print to the console.

```java
import org.eclipse.swt.*;
import org.eclipse.swt.events.*;
import org.eclipse.swt.layout.*;
import org.eclipse.swt.widgets.*;

public class TreeExample {
    public static void main(String[] args) {
        Display display = new Display();
        Shell shell = new Shell(display);
        shell.setText("Tree Example");
        shell.setBounds(100, 100, 200, 200);
        shell.setLayout(new FillLayout());
        final Tree tree = new Tree(shell, SWT.SINGLE);
        for (int i = 1; i < 4; i++) {
            TreeItem grandParent = new TreeItem(tree, 0);
            grandParent.setText("Grand Parent - " + i);
            for (int j = 1; j < 4; j++) {
                TreeItem parent = new TreeItem(grandParent,0);
                parent.setText("Parent - " + j);
                for (int k = 1; k < 4; k++) {
                    TreeItem child = new TreeItem(parent, 0);
                    child.setText("Child - " + k);
                }
            }
        }
        tree.addSelectionListener(new SelectionAdapter() {
            public void widgetSelected(SelectionEvent event) {
                TreeItem[] selected = tree.getSelection();
                if (selected.length > 0) {
                    System.out.println("Selected: " +
                        selected[0].getText());
                }
            }
        });
        shell.open();
        while (!shell.isDisposed()) {
            if (!display.readAndDispatch()) display.sleep();
        }
        display.dispose();
    }
}
```

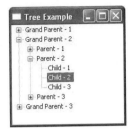

Figure 4–10   Tree example.

After the creation of the tree widget, new items are created and their labels are set with the `setText()` method. Many of the items have child items of their own. Finally, a selection listener is added in which a `SelectionAdapter` is created that overrides the `widgetSelected()` method to print a selected item.

4.2.6.8 Composite

The composite widget is used as a container for other widgets. The widget's children are widgets contained within the bounds of the composite and resize themselves relative to it. Useful APIs include:

`getChildren()`—Returns an array containing the receiver's children.

`layout()`—If the receiver has a layout, it asks the layout to set the size and location of the receiver's children.

`setLayout(Layout)`—Sets the layout that is associated with the receiver to be the argument, which may be `null`.

`setTabList(Control[])`—Sets the tabbing order for the specified controls to match the order in which they occur in the argument list.

Useful creation styles include:

`SWT.BORDER`—Creates a composite widget with a border.

`SWT.NO_RADIO_GROUP`—Prevents child radio button behavior.

`SWT.H_SCROLL`—Creates a composite widget with a horizontal scrollbar.

`SWT.V_SCROLL`—Creates a composite widget with a vertical scrollbar.

The following example expands on the earlier button example by inserting a composite widget between the shell and the button (see Figure 4–11).

```java
import org.eclipse.swt.*;
import org.eclipse.swt.events.*;
import org.eclipse.swt.widgets.*;

public class CompositeExample {
    public static void main(String[] args) {
        Display display = new Display();
        Shell shell = new Shell(display);
        shell.setText("Composite Example");
        shell.setBounds(100, 100, 200, 200);
        Composite composite = new Composite(
            shell,SWT.BORDER);
        composite.setBounds(25, 25, 150, 125);
        final Button button = new Button(composite,SWT.PUSH);
        button.setBounds(25, 25, 100, 75);
        button.setText("Click Me Now");
        button.addSelectionListener(new SelectionAdapter() {
            public void widgetSelected(SelectionEvent event) {
                button.setText("I Was Clicked");
            }
        });
        shell.open();
        while (!shell.isDisposed()) {
            if (!display.readAndDispatch()) display.sleep();
        }
        display.dispose();
    }
}
```

Figure 4–11   Composite example.

A composite widget is created as a child of the shell, and then the composite acts as the parent of the button widget. Note that the button is positioned relative to the composite, not the shell.

4.2.6.9   Group

Group widgets are a special type of composite widget that surround children with an etched border and an optional label. Each child widget is contained within the bounds of the group and resizes itself relative to it. Useful APIs include:

getChildren()—Returns an array containing the receiver's children.

layout()—If the receiver has a layout, it asks the layout to set the size and location of the receiver's children.

setLayout(Layout)—Sets the layout that is associated with the receiver to be the argument, which may be null.

setTabList(Control[])—Sets the tabbing order for the specified controls to match the order in which they occur in the argument list.

setText(String)—Sets the receiver's text, which is the string that will be displayed as the receiver's title, to the argument, which may not be null.

Useful creation styles include:

SWT.BORDER—Creates a composite widget with a border.

SWT.NO_RADIO_GROUP—Prevents child radio button behavior.

The example code that follows replaces the composite in the previous example with a group widget (see Figure 4–12).

Figure 4–12   Group example.

```
import org.eclipse.swt.*;
import org.eclipse.swt.events.*;
import org.eclipse.swt.widgets.*;

public class GroupExample {
    public static void main(String[] args) {
        Display display = new Display();
        Shell shell = new Shell(display);
        shell.setText("Group Example");
        shell.setBounds(100, 100, 200, 200);
        Group group = new Group(shell, SWT.NULL);
        group.setText("My Group");
        group.setBounds(25, 25, 150, 125);
        final Button button = new Button(group, SWT.PUSH);
        button.setBounds(25, 25, 100, 75);
        button.setText("Click Me Now");
        button.addSelectionListener(new SelectionAdapter() {
            public void widgetSelected(SelectionEvent event) {
                button.setText("I Was Clicked");
            }
        });
        shell.open();
        while (!shell.isDisposed()) {
            if (!display.readAndDispatch()) display.sleep();
        }
        display.dispose();
    }
}
```

A group widget is created as a child of the shell and acts as the parent of the button widget. In addition to the border, which is always present, the group widget also has a label.

4.2.6.10 Tab folder

The tab folder widget is used to organize information within a window frame into multiple pages that appear as a set of notebook tabs. Clicking on a tab brings that page to the front. Tabs can be labels with images and text. Useful APIs include:

addSelectionListener(SelectionListener)—Adds the listener to the collection of listeners that will be notified when the receiver's selection changes by sending it one of the messages defined in the SelectionListener interface.

TabItem getItem(int)—Returns the item at the given, zero-relative index in the receiver.

getItemCount()—Returns the number of items contained in the receiver.

`getItems()`—Returns an array of `TabItems` that are items in the receiver.

`getSelection()`—Returns an array of `TabItems` that are currently selected in the receiver.

`getSelectionIndex()`—Returns the zero-relative index of the item that is currently selected in the receiver, or -1 if no item is selected.

`indexOf(TabItem item)`—Searches the receiver's list starting at the first item (index 0) until an item is found that is equal to the argument, and returns the index of that item.

`setSelection(int)`—Selects the item at the given zero-relative index in the receiver.

Useful tab folder APIs include:

`getControl()`—Returns the control that is used to fill the client area of the tab folder when the user selects the tab item.

`setControl(Control control)`—Sets the control that is used to fill the client area of the tab folder when the user selects a tab item.

`setImage(Image)`—Sets the receiver's image to the argument, which may be `null`, indicating that no image should be displayed.

`setText(String)`—Sets the receiver's text.

`setToolTipText(String)`—Sets the receiver's tool tip text to the argument, which may be `null`, indicating that no tool tip text should be shown.

The example code that follows creates a tab folder with several tabs. Each tab contains a composite containing a single button (see Figure 4–13).

Figure 4–13   Tab folder example.

```
import org.eclipse.swt.*;
import org.eclipse.swt.events.*;
import org.eclipse.swt.layout.*;
import org.eclipse.swt.widgets.*;

public class TabFolderExample {
    public static void main(String[] args) {
        Display display = new Display();
        Shell shell = new Shell(display);
        shell.setText("TabFolder Example");
        shell.setBounds(100, 100, 175, 125);
        shell.setLayout(new FillLayout());
        final TabFolder tabFolder =
            new TabFolder(shell, SWT.BORDER);
        for (int i = 1; i < 4; i++) {
            TabItem tabItem =
                new TabItem(tabFolder, SWT.NULL);
            tabItem.setText("Tab " + i);
            Composite composite =
                new Composite(tabFolder, SWT.NULL);
            tabItem.setControl(composite);
            Button button = new Button(composite, SWT.PUSH);
            button.setBounds(25, 25, 100, 25);
            button.setText("Click Me Now");
            button.addSelectionListener(
                new SelectionAdapter(){
                public void widgetSelected(
                    SelectionEvent event) {
                    ((Button)event.widget)
                        .setText("I Was Clicked");
                }
            });
        }
        shell.open();
        while (!shell.isDisposed()) {
            if (!display.readAndDispatch()) display.sleep();
        }
        display.dispose();
    }
}
```

After the tab folder is created, several tab items are added. For each tab item, the setControl() method is used to fill its client area with a composite widget. A button widget is then added to each composite.

4.2.7 Menus

Menus provide an easy way for the user to trigger a variety of commands and actions. Top-level menus contain any number of menu item children. Useful menu APIs include the following:

addHelpListener(HelpListener)—Adds the listener to the collection
of listeners that will be notified when help events are generated for the
control by sending it one of the messages defined in the HelpListener
interface.

addMenuListener(MenuListener)—Adds the listener to the collection
of listeners that will be notified when menus are hidden or shown by
sending it one of the messages defined in the MenuListener interface.

getItem(int)—Returns the item at the given, zero-relative index in
the receiver.

getItemCount()—Returns the number of items contained in the
receiver.

getItems()—Returns an array of menu items that are the items in the
receiver.

getParentItem()—Returns the receiver's parent item, which must be a
menu item or null when the receiver is a root.

getParentMenu()—Returns the receiver's parent item, which must be a
menu or null when the receiver is a root.

indexOf(MenuItem item)—Searches the receiver's list starting at the
first item (index 0) until an item is found that is equal to the argument
and returns the index of that item.

setEnabled(boolean enabled)—Enables the receiver if the argument
is true and disables it otherwise.

setVisible(boolean visible)—Marks the receiver as visible if the
argument is true and marks it invisible otherwise.

Useful menu creation styles include:

SWT.BAR—Creates a menu bar.

SWT.DROP_DOWN—Creates a drop-down menu.

SWT.POP_UP—Creates a popup menu.

Useful menu item APIs include:

addArmListener(ArmListener)—Adds the listener to the collection of
listeners that will be notified when the Arm events are generated for the
control by sending it one of the messages defined in the ArmListener
interface.

`addHelpListener(HelpListener)`—Adds the listener to the collection of listeners that will be notified when the help events are generated for the control by sending it one of the messages defined in the `HelpListener` interface.

`addSelectionListener(SelectionListener)`—Adds the listener to the collection of listeners that will be notified when the control is selected by sending it one of the messages defined in the `SelectionListener` interface.

`getParent()`—Returns the receiver's parent, which must be a menu.

`getSelection()`—Returns `true` if the receiver is selected and `false` otherwise.

`isEnabled()`—Returns `true` if the receiver is enabled and all the receiver's ancestors are enabled and `false` otherwise.

`setAccelerator(int accelerator)`—Sets the widget accelerator.

`setEnabled(boolean enabled)`—Enables the receiver if the argument is `true` and disables it otherwise.

`setImage(Image)`—Sets the image the receiver will display to the argument.

`setMenu(Menu)`—Sets the receiver's pull-down menu to the argument.

`setSelection(boolean)`—Sets the selection state of the receiver.

`setText(String)`—Sets the receiver's text.

Useful menu item creation styles include:

`SWT.CHECK`—Creates a check menu that toggles on and off.

`SWT.CASCADE`—Creates a cascade menu with a submenu.

`SWT.PUSH`—Creates a standard menu item.

`SWT.RADIO`—Creates a radio button menu.

`SWT.SEPARATOR`—Creates a menu item separator.

The following example creates a menu bar with a single menu containing two menu items and a separator (see Figure 4–14).

Figure 4–14　Menu example.

```java
import org.eclipse.swt.*;
import org.eclipse.swt.events.*;
import org.eclipse.swt.widgets.*;

public class MenuExample {
    public static void main(String[] args) {
        Display display = new Display();
        final Shell shell = new Shell(display);
        shell.setText("Menu Example");
        shell.setBounds(100, 100, 200, 100);
        Menu bar = new Menu(shell, SWT.BAR);
        shell.setMenuBar(bar);
        MenuItem fileMenu = new MenuItem(bar, SWT.CASCADE);
        fileMenu.setText("&File");
        Menu subMenu = new Menu(shell, SWT.DROP_DOWN);
        fileMenu.setMenu(subMenu);
        MenuItem selectItem = new MenuItem(
            subMenu, SWT.NULL);
        selectItem.setText("&Select Me Now\tCtrl+S");
        selectItem.setAccelerator(SWT.CTRL + 'S');
        selectItem.addSelectionListener(
            new SelectionAdapter() {
            public void widgetSelected(SelectionEvent event) {
                System.out.println("I was selected!");
            }
        });
        MenuItem sep = new MenuItem(subMenu, SWT.SEPARATOR);
        MenuItem exitItem = new MenuItem(subMenu, SWT.NULL);
        exitItem.setText("&Exit");
        exitItem.addSelectionListener(new SelectionAdapter(){
            public void widgetSelected(SelectionEvent event) {
                shell.dispose();
            }
        });
        shell.open();
        while (!shell.isDisposed()) {
            if (!display.readAndDispatch()) display.sleep();
        }
        display.dispose();
    }
}
```

A menu widget is created as a child of the shell and set as the menu bar for the shell using the setMenuBar() method. Next, a cascade menu item is created as the parent for the **File** menu. A drop-down menu is then created as a child of the shell and associated with the **File** menu using the setMenu() method. Three menu items are then created as children of the drop-down menu (the second as a separator using the SWT.SEPARATOR creation style). The text of a menu item is set using the setText() method and the accelerator is set using the setAccelerator() method. To add behavior to the menu item, a selection listener is added in which a SelectionAdapter is created that overrides the widgetSelected() method.

4.3   Layout Management

In each of the examples presented in the previous section, the widget layouts are very simple. Widgets were either positioned relative to their parents using the setBounds() method (null layout) or they were designed to fill their parent entirely using a FillLayout. Eclipse provides several more powerful layout management algorithms that can be used to aesthetically place widgets under a variety of conditions.

Most layout managers in Eclipse trace their heritage to VisualAge for Smalltalk, and in particular, to the layout managers used to construct the wizards and dialogs in VisualAge for Java. As such, they were well thought out and thoroughly tested before ever being converted into Java as part of the Eclipse framework. Interestingly enough, the newest Eclipse layout manager, FormLayout, is based on the oldest and most powerful VisualAge for Smalltalk layout manager.

4.3.1   FillLayout

As you have seen, FillLayout provides an easy way for a widget (e.g., a list or a table) to completely fill its parent (see Figure 4–5 or 4–6 for an example). FillLayout does more than this, however, because it provides a way to lay out a group of widgets in single row or column such that each widget is the same size as all the other widgets in the group (see Figure 4–8 for an example).

The width and height of each widget matches the width and height of the widest and tallest widget in the group, and no options are provided to control the widget spacing, margins, or wrapping. FillLayout defines only this one significant attribute:

> type—Determines the orientation of the layout. Valid values are SWT.HORIZONTAL (the default) and SWT.VERTICAL.

FillLayout is ideal for creating a uniform row or column of widgets such as those found in a simple toolbar. The following example creates a row of buttons that are all the same size (see Figure 4–15).

Figure 4–15   FillLayout example.

```
import org.eclipse.swt.*;
import org.eclipse.swt.events.*;
import org.eclipse.swt.layout.*;
import org.eclipse.swt.widgets.*;

public class FillLayoutExample {
   public static void main(String[] args) {
      Button button;
      Display display = new Display();
      Shell shell = new Shell(display);
      shell.setText("FillLayout Example");
      shell.setBounds(100, 100, 400, 75);
      shell.setLayout(new FillLayout());
      for (int i = 1; i <= 8; i++) {
         button = new Button(shell, SWT.PUSH);
         button.setText("B" + i);
         button.addSelectionListener(
            new SelectionAdapter() {
            public void widgetSelected(
               SelectionEvent event) {
               System.out.println(
                  ((Button)event.widget).getText() +
                  " was clicked!");
            }
         });
      }
      shell.open();
      while (!shell.isDisposed()) {
         if (!display.readAndDispatch()) display.sleep();
      }
      display.dispose();
   }
}
```

By default, `FillLayout` is oriented horizontally. When buttons are added to the shell, they line up left to right with uniform widths and heights.

4.3.2 *RowLayout*

`RowLayout` is very similar to `FillLayout` in that it lays out widgets in columns or rows and has numerous additional options to control the layout. The spacing between widgets, as well as the margins between the widgets and the parent container, can be controlled. The widgets can be wrapped into multiple rows or columns or packed such that each widget will be the same size. `RowLayout` defines several significant attributes:

`justify`—Specifies whether the controls in a row should be fully justified, with any extra space placed between the controls.

`marginBottom`—Specifies the number of pixels of vertical margin that will be placed along the bottom edge of the layout. The default value is 3.

marginLeft—Specifies the number of pixels of horizontal margin that will be placed along the left edge of the layout. The default value is 3.

marginRight—Specifies the number of pixels of horizontal margin that will be placed along the right edge of the layout. The default value is 3.

marginTop—Specifies the number of pixels of vertical margin that will be placed along the top edge of the layout. The default value is 3.

pack—Specifies whether all controls in the layout take their preferred size. If pack is false, all controls will have the same size, which is the size required to accommodate the largest preferred height and width of all controls in the layout.

spacing—Specifies the number of pixels between the edge of one cell and the edge of its neighboring cell. The default value is 3.

type—Determines the orientation of the layout. Valid values are SWT.HORIZONTAL (the default) and SWT.VERTICAL.

wrap—Specifies whether a control will be wrapped to the next row if there is insufficient space on the current row.

The width and height of each widget in the layout can be controlled by using a RowData object, which can be assigned to widgets with the setLayoutData() method. RowData objects have two significant attributes:

width—Specifies the width of the cell in pixels.

height—Specifies the height of the cell in pixels.

The following example creates a row layout with 20 evenly spaced buttons inset from the edge of the window frame. Depending on the size and shape of the parent shell, the line of buttons wraps into one or more rows (see Figure 4–16).

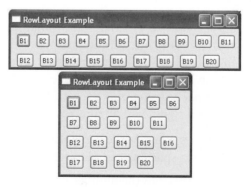

Figure 4–16   RowLayout example.

```java
import org.eclipse.swt.*;
import org.eclipse.swt.events.*;
import org.eclipse.swt.layout.*;
import org.eclipse.swt.widgets.*;

public class RowLayoutExample {
    public static void main(String[] args) {
        Button button;
        Display display = new Display();
        Shell shell = new Shell(display);
        shell.setText("RowLayout Example");
        shell.setBounds(100, 100, 400, 100);
        RowLayout layout = new RowLayout();
        layout.marginLeft = 10;
        layout.marginRight = 10;
        layout.marginTop = 10;
        layout.marginBottom = 10;
        layout.spacing = 10;
        shell.setLayout(layout);
        for (int i = 1; i <= 20; i++) {
            button = new Button(shell, SWT.PUSH);
            button.setText("B" + i);
            button.addSelectionListener(
                new SelectionAdapter() {
                public void widgetSelected(
                    SelectionEvent event) {
                    System.out.println(
                        ((Button)event.widget).getText() +
                        " was clicked!");
                }
            });
        }
        shell.open();
        while (!shell.isDisposed()) {
            if (!display.readAndDispatch()) display.sleep();
        }
        display.dispose();
    }
}
```

By default, `RowLayout` is oriented horizontally. The margin spacing between the buttons and the parent shell is set using the four margin attributes: `marginLeft`, `marginRight`, `marginTop`, and `marginBottom`. The spacing between widgets is set using the `spacing` attribute. After all the attributes have been set, the layout is assigned to the shell using the `setLayout()` method.

4.3.3 *GridLayout*

Most dialogs, wizards, and preference pages are laid out using `GridLayout`. It is both one of Eclipse's most frequently used layout classes and one of the most complicated. `GridLayout` arranges its children in a highly configurable grid of rows and columns, where many options are provided to control the sizing behavior of each child element.

`GridLayout` defines the following significant attributes.

`horizontalSpacing`—Specifies the number of pixels between the right edge of one cell and the left edge of its neighboring cell. The default value is `5`.

`makeColumnsEqualWidth`—Specifies whether all columns should be forced to the same width. The default is `false`.

`marginWidth`—Specifies the number of pixels used for the margin on the right and the left edge of the grid. The default value is `5`.

`marginHeight`—Specifies the number of pixels used for the margins on the top and bottom edge of the grid. The default value is `5`.

`numColumns`—Specifies the number of columns that should be used to make the grid. The default value is `1`.

`verticalSpacing`—Specifies the number of pixels between the bottom edge of one cell and the top edge of its neighboring cell. The default value is `5`.

The layout characteristics of each widget in the layout can be controlled by using a `GridData` object, which can be assigned to the widgets with the `setLayoutData()` method. `GridData` objects have the following significant attributes:

`grabExcessHorizontalSpace`—Specifies whether a cell should grow to consume extra horizontal space in the grid. After the cell sizes in the grid are calculated based on the widgets and their grid data, any extra space remaining in the composite will be allocated to those cells that grab excess space.

`grabExcessVerticalSpace`—Specifies whether a cell should grow to consume extra vertical space in the grid.

`heightHint`—Specifies a minimum height for the widget (and therefore for the row that contains it).

horizontalAlignment—Specifies the horizontal alignment of the widget within the cell. Valid values are SWT.BEGINNING, SWT.CENTER, SWT.END, and SWT.FILL. SWT.FILL means that the widget will be sized to consume the entire width of its grid cell.

horizontalIndent—Specifies the number of pixels between the widget and the left edge of its grid cell. The default value is 0.

horizontalSpan—Specifies the number of columns in the grid that the widget should span. By default, a widget consumes one cell in the grid. It can add additional cells horizontally by increasing this value. The default value is 1.

verticalAlignment—Specifies the vertical alignment of the widget within the cell. Valid values are SWT.BEGINNING, SWT.CENTER, SWT.END, and SWT.FILL. SWT.FILL means that the widget will be sized to consume the entire height of its grid cell.

verticalSpan—Specifies the number of rows in the grid the widget should span. By default, a widget takes up one cell in the grid. It can add additional cells vertically by increasing this value. The default value is 1.

widthHint—Specifies a minimum width for the widget (and therefore the column that contains it).

The example code that follows creates a two-column grid layout containing a two-column spanning label and two sets of labels and fields (see Figure 4–17).

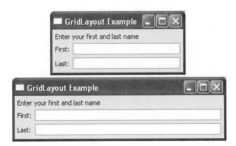

Figure 4–17   GridLayout example.

```
import org.eclipse.swt.*;
import org.eclipse.swt.layout.*;
import org.eclipse.swt.widgets.*;

public class GridLayoutExample {
   public static void main(String[] args) {
       Label label;
       Text text;
       GridData gridData;
       Display display = new Display();
       Shell shell = new Shell(display);
       shell.setText("GridLayout Example");
       shell.setBounds(100, 100, 200, 100);
       GridLayout layout = new GridLayout();
       layout.numColumns = 2;
       shell.setLayout(layout);

       label = new Label(shell, SWT.LEFT);
       label.setText("Enter your first and last name");
       gridData = new GridData();
       gridData.horizontalSpan = 2;
       label.setLayoutData(gridData);

       label = new Label(shell, SWT.LEFT);
       label.setText("First:");
       text = new Text(shell, SWT.SINGLE | SWT.BORDER);
       gridData = new GridData();
       gridData.horizontalAlignment = GridData.FILL;
       gridData.grabExcessHorizontalSpace = true;
       text.setLayoutData(gridData);

       label = new Label(shell, SWT.LEFT);
       label.setText("Last:");
       text = new Text(shell, SWT.SINGLE | SWT.BORDER);
       gridData = new GridData();
       gridData.horizontalAlignment = GridData.FILL;
       gridData.grabExcessHorizontalSpace = true;
       text.setLayoutData(gridData);

       shell.open();
       while (!shell.isDisposed()) {
          if (!display.readAndDispatch()) display.sleep();
       }
       display.dispose();
   }
}
```

The numColumn attribute specifies that the GridLayout should have two columns. The horizontalSpan attribute of the GridData object created for the first label specifies that it should span both columns. The GridData objects created have horizontalAlignment attributes that specify that each text field should fill the entire cell and `grabExcessHorizontalSpace` attributes that specify that each field should grab any horizontal space that is left over.

4.3.4 FormLayout

Nowhere does Eclipse show its VisualAge for Smalltalk roots more than in the `FormLayout` class that implements an attachment-based layout manager. `FormLayout` is the most powerful Eclipse layout manager and is a close replica of the layout management system first used in VisualAge for Smalltalk more than a decade earlier.

With attachment-based layout, you have independent control over the sizing behavior of each of the four sides of a widget. The top, bottom, left, and right sides can be independently attached to the sides of the parent container or the sides of any sibling widget within the same container using either fixed or relative offsets. This proves to be surprisingly powerful and can be used to emulate almost any of the other layout managers.

The `FormLayout` class is very simple and only specifies the margins of the container. The real power is in the `FormData` object, which holds up to four different `FormAttachment` objects (one for each side). `FormLayout` defines two significant attributes:

> `marginWidth`—Specifies the number of pixels of horizontal margin that will be placed along the left and right edges of the layout.
>
> `marginHeight`—Specifies the number of pixels of vertical margin that will be placed along the top and bottom edges of the layout.

`FormData` specifies several significant attributes:

> `top`—Specifies the attachment for the top side of the control.
>
> `bottom`—Specifies the attachment for the bottom side of the control.
>
> `left`—Specifies the attachment for the left side of the control.
>
> `right`—Specifies the attachment for the right side of the control.
>
> `width`—Specifies the preferred width in pixels of the control in the form.
>
> `height`—Specifies the preferred height in pixels of the control in the form.

FormAttachment specifies several significant attributes:

alignment—Specifies the alignment of the control side attached to a control. SWT.DEFAULT indicates that the widget should be attached to the adjacent side of the specified control. For top and bottom attachments, SWT.TOP, SWT.BOTTOM, and SWT.CENTER are used to indicate attachment of the specified side of the widget to the specified side of the control. For left and right attachments, SWT.LEFT, SWT.RIGHT, and SWT.CENTER are used to indicate attachment of the specified side of the widget to the specified side of the control. (For example, using SWT.TOP indicates that the top side of the attachment's widget should be attached to the top side of the specified control).

control—Specifies the target control to which the attachment's widget is attached.

denominator—Specifies the denominator of the "**a**" term in the equation $y = ax + b$, which defines the attachment.

numerator—Specifies the numerator of the "**a**" term in the equation $y = ax + b$, which defines the attachment.

offset—Specifies the offset in pixels of the control side from the attachment position; can be positive or negative. This is the "**b**" term in the equation $y = ax + b$, which defines the attachment.

The following example creates a simple form layout with two buttons in the lower right corner and a text field that fills the remaining space (see Figure 4–18 for a sketch of the window next to two examples of the running window at different sizes). The **Cancel** button is attached to the lower right corner while the **OK** button is attached to the bottom side of the window and to the left side of the **Cancel** button. The text field is attached to the top, left, and right sides of the window and to the top of the **Cancel** button.

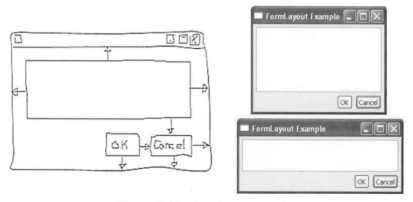

Figure 4–18   FormLayout example.

```
import org.eclipse.swt.*;
import org.eclipse.swt.layout.*;
import org.eclipse.swt.widgets.*;

public class FormLayoutExample {
    public static void main(String[] args) {
        FormData formData;
        Display display = new Display();
        final Shell shell = new Shell(display);
        shell.setText("FormLayout Example");
        shell.setBounds(100, 100, 220, 180);
        shell.setLayout(new FormLayout());

        Button cancelButton = new Button(shell, SWT.PUSH);
        cancelButton.setText("Cancel");
        formData = new FormData();
        formData.right = new FormAttachment(100,-5);
        formData.bottom = new FormAttachment(100,-5);
        cancelButton.setLayoutData(formData);

        Button okButton = new Button(shell, SWT.PUSH);
        okButton.setText("OK");
        formData = new FormData();
        formData.right = new FormAttachment(cancelButton,-5);
        formData.bottom = new FormAttachment(100,-5);
        okButton.setLayoutData(formData);

        Text text = new Text(shell, SWT.MULTI | SWT.BORDER);
        formData = new FormData();
        formData.top = new FormAttachment(0,5);
        formData.bottom = new FormAttachment(
            cancelButton,-5);
        formData.left = new FormAttachment(0,5);
        formData.right = new FormAttachment(100,-5);
        text.setLayoutData(formData);

        shell.open();
        while (!shell.isDisposed()) {
            if (!display.readAndDispatch()) display.sleep();
        }
        display.dispose();
    }
}
```

The FormData assigned to the **Cancel** button has a right and bottom attachment to the lower right corner of the shell. The first argument to each FormAttachment object is the percentage of the shell to attach initially (starting in the upper left corner with a 0% value). The value of 100 specifies the right and bottom sides, which are opposite the left and top sides.

The second argument represents the fixed offset from the attachment point (with positive values pointing right and down). The value of -5 indicates that the widget should be offset 5 pixels from the bottom and right sides.

Note that the left and top attachments are not specified. Leaving them blank will cause the widget to assume its preferred width and height.

The **OK** button is also attached to the bottom of the shell. Its right side is attached to the left side of the **Cancel** button rather than to the shell itself. This provides a way for the **OK** button to position itself relative to the preferred size of the **Cancel** button. This pattern can be particularly effective for internationalized applications where the text of the buttons (and thus their preferred sizes) is not known at design time.

Finally, the text field is attached with a fixed offset of 5 pixels from the left, right, and top sides of the shell. The bottom of the text field is attached with a 5-pixel offset to the top of the **Cancel** button.

4.4   Resource Management

Consistent with the design of the rest of SWT, colors, fonts, and images are also thin wrappers around their platform counterparts that must be explicitly destroyed when no longer needed.

The basic rule is: If you access a color, font, or image from somewhere else, you don't need to worry about it. On the other hand, if you create the resource, then you must destroy it when you are done with it. For any resources that you anticipate routinely accessing within your application, consider creating a resource manager to manage them and then destroy all the resources when your application exits.

4.4.1   Colors

Colors are created for a specific device (which can be `null`, representing the default device) and are described by three integer values representing each color component (red, green, and blue) in the range of 0 to 255 (e.g., `new Color(null, 255, 0, 0)` creates the color red). The foreground and background colors of widgets can be set using the `setForeground()` and `setBackground()` methods, respectively.

To use one of the colors predefined by the platform, such as window background color or button background color, you can use the `Display.getSystemColor(int)` method, which takes the identifier of the desired color as an argument. You don't need to dispose of any colors that you get this way.

4.4.2   Fonts

As with colors, fonts are also created for a specific device and are described by a font name (e.g., Arial, Times, etc.), a height in points, and a style (and combination of SWT.NORMAL, SWT.BOLD, or SWT.ITALIC). Fonts can be either created by specifying the name, height, and style directly or by referencing a FontData object that encodes those three values. For example, new Font(null, "Arial", 10, SWT.BOLD) creates a 10-point, bold Arial font. A widget's font can be set using the setFont() method.

4.4.3   Images

Images are frequently used in toolbars, buttons, labels, trees, and tables. Eclipse supports loading and saving images in a variety of common file formats such as GIF, JPEG, PNG, BMP (Windows bitmap), and ICO (Windows icon). Some formats, such as GIF, support transparency, which makes them ideal for use in toolbars and as item decorators in lists and tables.

Images are created for a specific device and are usually either loaded from a specific file or created from a device-independent ImageData object. For example, both of the following are equivalent:

```
Image img = new Image(null, "c:\\my_button.gif")
ImageData data = new ImageData("c:\\my_button.gif");
Image img = new Image(null, data);
```

On widgets that support images as part of their content, such as labels and buttons, use the setImage() method to set the widget's images. For information on image caching and ImageDescriptor, see Section 7.7, Image Caching, on page 315.

4.5   Summary

SWT is a well-designed native UI library for Java that is based on a long history of similar work done by IBM and OTI over the years. It is the native UI library of Eclipse itself and will be used extensively in any Eclipse plug-in that you create. SWT is also more than powerful enough to be used for creating standalone Java applications that don't require any of the other Eclipse frameworks.

SWT includes a rich collection of built-in widgets that are mapped to native-platform widgets whenever possible and are emulated when an appropriate widget is not present on a specific platform. SWT also includes a wide array of layout management classes ranging from the simple `FillLayout` to the more complex `GridLayout` and `FormLayout`. With these widgets and layout managers, you can create any user interface that you want to use for your plug-in.

References

Chapter source (*www.qualityeclipse.com/projects/source-ch-04-and-05.zip*).

Northover, Steve, and Mike Wilson, *SWT: The Standard Widget Toolkit*. Addison-Wesley, Boston, 2004.

Harris, Robert, and Rob Warner, *The Definitive Guide to SWT and JFACE*. Apress, Berkeley, CA, 2004.

Holder, Stephen, Stephen Holder, Stanford Ng, and Laurent Mihalkovic, *SWT/JFace in Action: GUI Design with Eclipse 3.0.*   Manning Publications, Greenwich, CT, 2004.

Cornu, Christophe, "A Small Cup of SWT," IBM OTI Labs, September 19, 2003 (*www.eclipse.org/articles/Article-small-cup-of-swt/pocket-PC.html*).

Winchester, Joe, "Taking a Look at SWT Images," IBM, September 10, 2003 (*www.eclipse.org/articles/Article-SWT-images/graphics-resources.html*).

Irvine, Veronika, "Drag and Drop—Adding Drag and Drop to an SWT Application," IBM, August 25, 2003 (*www.eclipse.org/articles/Article-SWT-DND/DND-in-SWT.html*).

Arthorne, John, "Drag and Drop in the Eclipse UI," IBM, August 25, 2003 (*www.eclipse.org/articles/Article-Workbench-DND/drag_drop.html*).

Bordeau, Eric, "Using Native Drag and Drop with GEF," IBM, August 25, 2003 (*www.eclipse.org/articles/Article-GEF-dnd/GEF-dnd.html)*.

Savarese, Daniel F., "Eclipse vs. Swing," JavaPro, December 2002 (*www.ftponline.com/javapro/2002_12/magazine/columns/proshop/default_pf.aspx*).

Majewski, Bo, "Using OpenGL with SWT," Cisco Systems, Inc., April 15, 2005 (*www.eclipse.org/articles/Article-SWT-OpenGL/opengl.html*).

Kues, Lynne, and Knut Radloff, "Getting Your Feet Wet with the SWT Styled-Text Widget," OTI, July 19, 2004 (*www.eclipse.org/articles/StyledText%201/article1.html*).

Kues, Lynne, and Knut Radloff, "Into the Deep End of the SWT StyledText Widget," OTI, September 18, 2002 (*www.eclipse.org/articles/Styled-Text%202/article2.html*).

Li, Chengdong, "A Basic Image Viewer," University of Kentucky, March 15, 2004 (*www.eclipse.org/articles/Article-Image-Viewer/Image_viewer.html*).

MacLeod, Caroly,n and Shantha Ramachandran, "Understanding Layouts in SWT," OTI, May 2, 2002 (*www.eclipse.org/articles/Understanding%20 Layouts/Understanding%20Layouts.htm*).

Northover, Steve, "SWT: The Standard Widget Toolkit—PART 1: Implementation Strategy for Java™ Natives," OTI, March 22, 2001 (*www.eclipse.org/ articles/Article-SWT-Design-1/SWT-Design-*1.html).

MacLeod, Carolyn, and Steve Northover, "SWT: The Standard Widget Toolkit—PART 2: Managing Operating System Resources," OTI, November 27, 2001 (*www.eclipse.org/articles/swt-design-2/swt-design-2.html*).

Moody, James, and Carolyn MacLeod, "SWT Color Model," OTI, April 24, 2001 (*www.eclipse.org/articles/Article-SWT-Color-Model/swt-color-model.htm*).

Irvine, Veronika, "ActiveX Support In SWT: How Do I Include an OLE Document or ActiveX Control in My Eclipse Plug-in?," OTI, March 22, 2001 (*www.eclipse.org/articles/Article-ActiveX%20Support%20in%20SWT/ ActiveX%20Support%20in%20SWT.html*).

CHAPTER 5

JFace Viewers

Although SWT provides a direct interface to the native platform widgets, it is limited to using simple data types—primarily strings, numbers, and images. This is fine for a large number of applications, but it represents a severe impedance mismatch when dealing with object-oriented (OO) data that needs to be presented in lists, tables, trees, and text widgets. This is where JFace viewers step in to provide OO wrappers around their associated SWT widgets.

5.1 List-Oriented Viewers

JFace list viewers, such as `ListViewer`, `TableViewer`, and `TreeViewer`, allow you to directly use your domain model objects (e.g., business objects such as Company, Person, Department, etc.) without needing to manually decompose them into their basic string, numerical, and image elements. The viewers do this by providing adapter interfaces for such things as retrieving an item's label (both image and text), for accessing an item's children (in the case of a tree), for selecting an item from a list, for sorting items in the list, for filtering items in the list, and for converting an arbitrary input into a list suitable for the underlying SWT widget (see Figure 5–1).

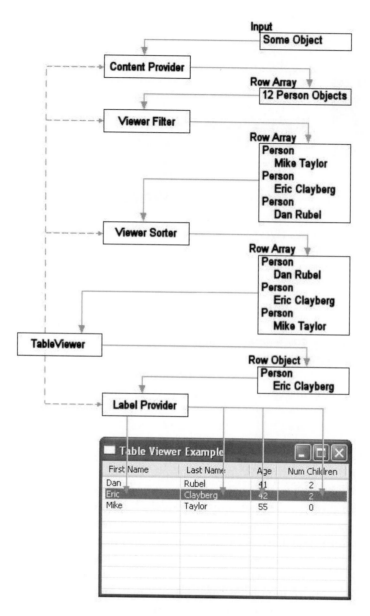

Figure 5–1   Relationship between viewers and adapters.

5.1.1   Label providers

A label provider is one of the most common adapter types used in list viewers. This provider is used to map a domain model object into one or more images and text strings displayable in the viewer's widget.

Figure 5–2   LabelProvider hierarchy.

   The two most common types of label providers are `ILabelProvider` (see Figure 5–2), used in lists and trees, and `ITableLabelProvider` (see Figure 5-3), used in tables. The former maps an item into a single image and text label while the latter maps an item into multiple images and text labels (one set for each column in the table). A label provider is associated with a viewer using the `setLabelProvider()` method.
   Useful APIs defined by `ILabelProvider` include:

   `getImage(Object)`—Returns the image for the label of the given element.

   `getText(Object)`—Returns the text for the label of the given element.

Useful APIs defined by `ITableLabelProvider` include:

   `getColumnImage(Object, int)`—Returns the label image for the given column of the given element.

   `getColumnText(Object, int)`—Returns the label text for the given column of the given element.

For an example of label providers, see Section 5.1.6, ListViewer class, on page 192.

Figure 5–3   TableLabelProvider hierarchy.

5.1.2   Content providers

A content provider is another common adapter type used in list viewers. This provider is used to map between a domain model object or a collection of domain model objects used as the input to the viewer and the internal list structure needed by the viewer itself.

The two most common types of content providers are IStructuredContentProvider, used in lists and tables, and ITreeContentProvider, used in trees (see Figure 5–4). The former maps a domain model input into an array while the latter adds support for retrieving an item's parent or children within a tree. A content provider is associated with a viewer using the setContentProvider() method. A domain model input is associated with a viewer using the setInput() method.

Figure 5–4   ContentProvider hierarchy.

Useful APIs defined by IStructuredContentProvider include:

getElements(Object)—Returns the elements to display in the viewer when its input is set to the given element.

inputChanged(Viewer, Object, Object)—Notifies this content provider that the given viewer's input has been switched to a different element.

Useful APIs added by ITreeContentProvider include:

Object[] getChildren(Object)—Returns the child elements of the given parent element. The difference between this method and the previously listed getElements(Object) method is that it is called to obtain the tree viewer's root elements, whereas getChildren(Object) is used to obtain the children of a given parent element in the tree (including a root).

getParent(Object)—Returns either the parent for the given element or null, indicating that the parent can't be computed.

hasChildren(Object)—Returns whether the given element has children.

For an example of content providers, see Section 5.1.6, ListViewer class, on page 192.

5.1.3 Viewer sorters

A viewer sorter (see Figure 5–5 for the `ViewerSorter` hierarchy) is used to sort the elements provided by the content provider (see Figure 5–1). If a viewer does not have a viewer sorter, the elements are shown in the order returned by the content provider. A viewer sorter is associated with a viewer using the `setSorter()` method.

Figure 5–5   ViewerSorter hierarchy.

The default sorting algorithm uses a two-step process. First, it groups elements into categories (ranked *0* through *n*); and second, it sorts each category based on the text labels returned by the label provider. By default, all items are in the same category, so all the items are sorted relative to their text labels. Your application can override the default categorization as well as the default comparison routine to use some criteria other than the item's text label.

Useful APIs defined by `ViewerSorter` include:

`category(Object)`—Returns the category of the given element.

`compare(Viewer, Object, Object)`—Returns a negative, zero, or positive number depending on whether the first element is less than, equal to, or greater than the second element.

`getCollator()`—Returns the collator used to sort strings.

`isSorterProperty(Object, String)`—Returns whether this viewer sorter would be affected by a change to the given property of the given element.

`sort(Viewer viewer, Object[])`—Sorts the given elements in place, modifying the given array.

For an example of viewer sorters, see Section 5.1.6, ListViewer class, on page 192.

5.1.4 Viewer filters

A viewer filter (see Figure 5–6 for the `ViewerFilter` hierarchy) is used to display a subset of the elements provided by the content provider (see Figure 5-1). If a view does not have a viewer filter, all the elements are displayed. A viewer filter is associated with a viewer using the `setFilter()` method.

Figure 5–6   ViewerFilter hierarchy.

Useful APIs defined by `ViewFilter` are listed next. Simple viewer filters need only to override the `select(Viewer, Object, Object)` method to determine whether an object should be visible in the viewer.

`filter(Viewer, Object, Object[])`—Filters the given elements for the given viewer. The default implementation of this method calls the following `select(Viewer, Object, Object)` method.

`isFilterProperty(Object, String)`—Returns whether this viewer filter would be affected by a change to the given property of the given element. The default implementation of this method returns `false`.

`select(Viewer, Object, Object)`—Returns whether the given element makes it through this filter.

5.1.5 StructuredViewer class

The `StructuredViewer` class is the abstract superclass of list viewers, table viewers, and tree viewers (see Figure 5–7).

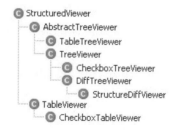

Figure 5–7   StructuredViewer hierarchy.

It defines a large number of useful APIs that are common to each class.

`addDoubleClickListener(IDoubleClickListener)`—Adds a listener for double-clicks in this viewer.

`addDragSupport(int, Transfer[], DragSourceListener)`—Adds support for dragging items out of this viewer via a user drag-and-drop operation.

`addDropSupport(int, Transfer[], DropTargetListener)`—Adds support for dropping items into this viewer via a user drag-and-drop operation.

`addFilter(ViewerFilter)`—Adds the given filter to this viewer and triggers refiltering and resorting of the elements.

`addHelpListener(HelpListener)`—Adds a listener for help requests in this viewer.

`addOpenListener(IOpenListener)`—Adds a listener for selection open in this viewer.

`addSelectionChangedListener(ISelectionChangedListener)`—Adds a listener for selection changes in this selection provider.

`addPostSelectionChangedListener(ISelectionChangedListener)`—Adds a listener for post-selection in this viewer.

`getSelection()`—The `StructuredViewer` implementation of this method returns the result as an `IStructuredSelection`.

`refresh()`—Refreshes this viewer completely with information freshly obtained from this viewer's model.

`refresh(boolean)`—Refreshes this viewer with information freshly obtained from this viewer's model.

`refresh(Object)`—Refreshes this viewer starting with the given element.

`refresh(Object, boolean)`—Refreshes this viewer starting with the given element.

`resetFilters()`—Discards this viewer's filters and triggers refiltering and resorting of the elements.

`setComparer(IElementComparer)`—Sets the comparator to use for comparing elements, or `null` to use the default `equals` and `hashCode` methods on the elements themselves.

`setContentProvider(IContentProvider)`—The implementation, `StructuredViewer`, of this method checks to ensure that the content provider is an `IStructuredContentProvider`.

`setData(String, Object)`—Sets the value of the property with the given name to the given value, or to `null` if the property is to be removed.

`setInput(Object)`—The `ContentViewer` implementation of this viewer method invokes `inputChanged` on the content provider and then the `inputChanged` hook method. The content provider's `getElements(Object)` method is called later with this input object as its argument to determine the root-level elements in the viewer.

`setSelection(ISelection, boolean)`—The `StructuredViewer` implementation of this method updates the current viewer selection based on the specified selection.

`setSorter(ViewerSorter)`—Sets this viewer's sorter and triggers refiltering and resorting of this viewer's element.

`setUseHashlookup(boolean)`—Configures whether this structured viewer uses an internal hash table to speed up the mapping between elements and SWT items.

`update(Object[], String[])`—Updates the given element's presentation when one or more of its properties changes.

`update(Object, String[])`—Updates the given element's presentation when one or more of its properties changes.

5.1.6 ListViewer class

The `ListViewer` class wraps the `List` widget and is used to view a collection of objects rather than a flat collection of strings. A list viewer needs to be configured with label and content providers. Useful APIs include:

`add(Object)`—Adds the given element to this list viewer.

`add(Object[])`—Adds the given elements to this list viewer.

`getControl()`—Returns the primary control associated with this viewer.

`getElementAt(int)`—Returns the element with the given index from this list viewer.

`getList()`—Returns this list viewer's list control.

`remove(Object)`—Removes the given element from this list viewer.

`remove(Object[])`—Removes the given elements from this list viewer.

`reveal(Object)`—Ensures that the given element is visible, scrolling the viewer if necessary.

`setLabelProvider(IBaseLabelProvider)`—The list viewer implementation of this `Viewer` framework method ensures that the given label provider is an instance of `ILabelProvider`.

The `Person` domain model class for the next few examples looks like the following.

```
public class Person {
    public String firstName = "John";
    public String lastName = "Doe";
    public int age = 37;
    public Person[] children = new Person[0];
    public Person parent = null;
```

```
public Person(String firstName, String lastName,
    int age) {
    this.firstName = firstName;
    this.lastName = lastName;
    this.age = age;
}
public Person(String firstName, String lastName,
    int age, Person[] children) {
    this(firstName, lastName, age);
    this.children = children;
    for (int i = 0; i < children.length; i++) {
        children[i].parent = this;
    }
}
public static Person[] example() {
    return new Person[] {
        new Person("Dan", "Rubel", 41, new Person[] {
            new Person("Beth", "Rubel", 11),
            new Person("David", "Rubel", 6)}),
        new Person("Eric", "Clayberg", 42, new Person[] {
            new Person("Lauren", "Clayberg", 9),
            new Person("Lee", "Clayberg", 7)}),
        new Person("Mike", "Taylor", 55)
    };
}
public String toString() {
    return firstName + " " + lastName;
}
}
```

The example code that follows creates a list viewer with a label provider, content provider, and viewer sorter (see Figure 5–8). Note: To run the JFace demos standalone, you need to add the following four entries to your **Java Build Path** (plug-in version numbers should match those used in your Eclipse installation).

```
ECLIPSE_HOME/plugins/org.eclipse.core.runtime_3.1.2.jar
ECLIPSE_HOME/plugins/org.eclipse.jface_3.1.1.jar
ECLIPSE_HOME/plugins/org.eclipse.jface.text_3.1.2.jar
ECLIPSE_HOME/plugins/org.eclipse.text_3.1.1.jar
```

Figure 5–8 ListViewer example.

```java
import org.eclipse.jface.viewers.*;
import org.eclipse.swt.*;
import org.eclipse.swt.layout.*;
import org.eclipse.swt.widgets.*;

public class ListViewerExample {
    public static void main(String[] args) {
        Display display = new Display();
        Shell shell = new Shell(display);
        shell.setText("List Viewer Example");
        shell.setBounds(100, 100, 200, 100);
        shell.setLayout(new FillLayout());
        final ListViewer listViewer =
            new ListViewer(shell, SWT.SINGLE);
        listViewer.setLabelProvider(
            new PersonListLabelProvider());
        listViewer.setContentProvider(
            new ArrayContentProvider());
        listViewer.setInput(Person.example());
        listViewer.setSorter(new ViewerSorter() {
            public int compare(
                Viewer viewer, Object p1, Object p2) {
                return ((Person) p1).lastName
                    .compareToIgnoreCase(((Person) p2).lastName);
            }
        });
        listViewer.addSelectionChangedListener(
            new ISelectionChangedListener() {
            public void selectionChanged(
                SelectionChangedEvent event) {
                IStructuredSelection selection =
                    (IStructuredSelection) event.getSelection();
                System.out.println("Selected: "
                    + selection.getFirstElement());
            }
        });
        listViewer.addDoubleClickListener(
            new IDoubleClickListener() {
            public void doubleClick(DoubleClickEvent event)
            {
                IStructuredSelection selection =
                    (IStructuredSelection) event.getSelection();
                System.out.println("Double Clicked: " +
                    selection.getFirstElement());
            }
        });
        shell.open();
        while (!shell.isDisposed()) {
            if (!display.readAndDispatch()) display.sleep();
        }
        display.dispose();
    }
}
```

After the list viewer has been created, the label provider is set by using the `setLabelProvider()` method and the content provider is set with the `setContentProvider()` method. `PersonListLabelProvider`, the label provider, returns a text label composed of the person's first and last names and does not return an icon. The class looks like this:

```
public class PersonListLabelProvider extends LabelProvider {
   public Image getImage(Object element) {
      return null;
   }
   public String getText(Object element) {
      Person person = (Person) element;
      return person.firstName + " " + person.lastName;
   }
}
```

For the content provider, use the built-in `ArrayContentProvider` class that maps an input collection to an array. The input object is set using the `setInput()` method. The viewer sorter defines a custom `compare()` method that sorts the elements based on a person's last name. Finally, a `selection-Changed` listener and a `doubleClick` listener are added that override the `selectionChanged()` method and the `doubleClick()` method, respectively.

5.1.7   *TableViewer class*

The `TableViewer` class wraps the `Table` widget. A table viewer provides an editable, vertical, multicolumn list of items, which shows a row of cells for each item in the list where each cell represents a different attribute of the item at that row. A table viewer needs to be configured with a label provider, a content provider, and a set of columns.

The `CheckboxTableViewer` enhances this further by adding support for graying out individual items and toggling on and off an associated checkbox with each item. Useful APIs include:

> `add(Object)`—Adds the given element to this table viewer. This method should be called (by the content provider) when a single element has been added to the model to cause the viewer to accurately reflect the model. This method only affects the viewer, not the model.

> `add(Object[])`—Adds the given elements to this table viewer. This method should be called (by the content provider) when elements have been added to the model to cause the viewer to accurately reflect the model. This method only affects the viewer, not the model.

`cancelEditing()`—Cancels a currently active cell editor.

`editElement(Object, int)`—Starts editing the given element.

`getElementAt(int)`—Returns the element with the given index from this table viewer.

`getTable()`—Returns this table viewer's table control.

`insert(Object, int)`—Inserts the given element into this table viewer at the given position.

`isCellEditorActive()`—Returns whether there is an active cell editor.

`remove(Object)`—Removes the given element from this table viewer. This method should be called (by the content provider) when a single element has been removed from the model to cause the viewer to accurately reflect the model. This method only affects the viewer, not the model.

`remove(Object[])`—Removes the given elements from this table viewer. This method should be called (by the content provider) when elements have been removed from the model in order to cause the viewer to accurately reflect the model. This method only affects the viewer, not the model.

`reveal(Object)`—Ensures that the given element is visible, scrolling the viewer if necessary.

`setCellEditors(CellEditor[])`—Sets the cell editors of this table viewer.

`setCellModifier(ICellModifier)`—Sets the cell modifier of this table viewer.

`setColumnProperties(String[])`—Sets the column properties of this table viewer.

`setLabelProvider(IBaseLabelProvider)`—The table viewer implementation of this `Viewer` framework method ensures that the given label provider is an instance of either `ITableLabelProvider` or `ILabelProvider`.

The `CheckboxTableViewer` adds the following useful APIs:

`addCheckStateListener(ICheckStateListener)`—Adds a listener for changes to the checked state of elements in this viewer.

`getChecked(Object)`—Returns the checked state of the given element.

`getCheckedElements()`—Returns a list of elements corresponding to checked table items in this viewer.

`getGrayed(Object)`—Returns the grayed state of the given element.

`getGrayedElements()`—Returns a list of elements corresponding to grayed nodes in this viewer.

`setAllChecked(boolean)`—Sets to the given value the checked state for all elements in this viewer.

`setAllGrayed(boolean)`—Sets to the given value the grayed state for all elements in this viewer.

`setChecked(Object, boolean)`—Sets the checked state for the given element in this viewer.

`setCheckedElements(Object[])`—Sets which nodes are checked in this viewer.

`setGrayed(Object, boolean)`—Sets the grayed state for the given element in this viewer.

`setGrayedElements(Object[])`—Sets which nodes are grayed in this viewer.

The example code that follows creates a table viewer with a label provider, content provider, and four columns (see Figure 5–9).

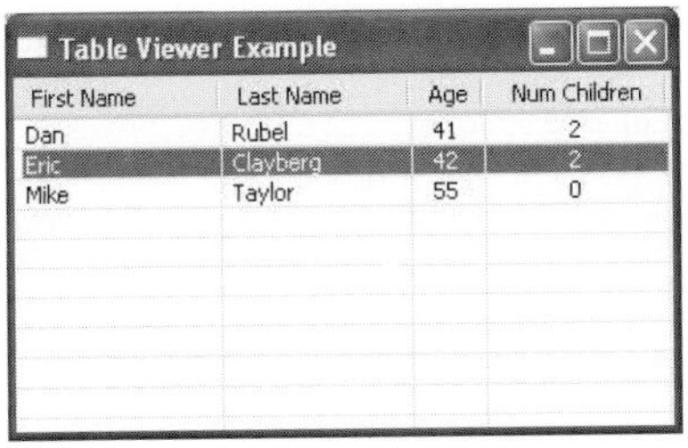

Figure 5–9   TableViewer example.

```
import org.eclipse.jface.viewers.*;
import org.eclipse.swt.*;
import org.eclipse.swt.layout.*;
import org.eclipse.swt.widgets.*;

public class TableViewerExample {
   public static void main(String[] args) {
      Display display = new Display();
      Shell shell = new Shell(display);
      shell.setText("Table Viewer Example");
      shell.setBounds(100, 100, 325, 200);
      shell.setLayout(new FillLayout());

      final TableViewer tableViewer = new TableViewer(
         shell, SWT.SINGLE | SWT.FULL_SELECTION);
      final Table table = tableViewer.getTable();
      table.setHeaderVisible(true);
      table.setLinesVisible(true);

      String[] columnNames = new String[] {
         "First Name", "Last Name", "Age", "Num Children"};
      int[] columnWidths = new int[] {
         100, 100, 35, 75};
      int[] columnAlignments = new int[] {
         SWT.LEFT, SWT.LEFT, SWT.CENTER, SWT.CENTER};
      for (int i = 0; i < columnNames.length; i++) {
         TableColumn tableColumn =
            new TableColumn(table, columnAlignments[i]);
         tableColumn.setText(columnNames[i]);
         tableColumn.setWidth(columnWidths[i]);
      }

      tableViewer.setLabelProvider(
         new PersonTableLabelProvider());
      tableViewer.setContentProvider(
         new ArrayContentProvider());
      tableViewer.setInput(Person.example());

      shell.open();
      while (!shell.isDisposed()) {
         if (!display.readAndDispatch()) display.sleep();
      }
      display.dispose();
   }
}
```

After creating the table viewer, the column headers and lines are made visible by calling the setHeaderVisible() and setLinesVisible() methods in the table viewer's underlying table. Four columns are then added to the table with different alignments. The header text and width of each column are set with the setText() and setWidth() methods (see Section 7.8, Auto-sizing Table Columns, on page 316).

The label provider is set using the setLabelProvider() method and the content provider is set with the setContentProvider() method. The label provider, PersonTableLabelProvider, returns a text label for each column in the table and does not return an icon. The class looks like this:

```
import org.eclipse.jface.viewers.*;
import org.eclipse.swt.graphics.*;

public class PersonTableLabelProvider
    extends LabelProvider
    implements ITableLabelProvider {
    public Image getColumnImage(
        Object element, int) {
      return null;
    }
    public String getColumnText(Object element, int index) {
        Person person = (Person) element;
        switch (index) {
          case 0 :
              return person.firstName;
          case 1 :
              return person.lastName;
          case 2 :
              return Integer.toString(person.age);
          case 3 :
              return Integer.toString(person.children.length);
          default :
              return "unknown " + index;
        }
    }
}
```

5.1.8   TreeViewer class

The TreeViewer class wraps the Tree widget. A tree viewer displays a hierarchical list of objects in a parent–child relationship. This viewer needs to be configured with label and content providers. The CheckboxTreeViewer enhances this further by adding support for graying out individual items and toggling on and off an associated checkbox with each item. Useful APIs include:

add(Object, Object)—Adds the given child element to this viewer as a child of the given parent element.

add(Object, Object[])—Adds the given child elements to this viewer as children of the given parent element.

addTreeListener(ITreeViewerListener)—Adds a listener for expanding and collapsing events in this viewer.

collapseAll()—Collapses all nodes of the viewer's tree, starting with the root.

`collapseToLevel(Object, int)`—Collapses the subtree rooted at the given element to the given level.

`expandAll()`—Expands all nodes of the viewer's tree, starting with the root.

`expandToLevel(int)`—Expands the root of the viewer's tree to the given level.

`expandToLevel(Object, int)`—Expands all ancestors of the given element so that the given element becomes visible in this viewer's tree control, and then expands the subtree rooted at the given element to the given level.

`getExpandedElements()`—Returns a list of elements corresponding to expanded nodes in this viewer's tree, including currently hidden ones that are marked as expanded but are under a collapsed ancestor.

`getExpandedState(Object)`—Returns whether the node corresponding to the given element is expanded or collapsed.

`Tree getTree()`—Returns this tree viewer's tree control.

`getVisibleExpandedElements()`—Gets the expanded elements that are visible to the user.

`isExpandable(Object)`—Returns whether the tree node representing the given element can be expanded.

`remove(Object)`—Removes the given element from the viewer.

`remove(Object[])`—Removes the given elements from this viewer.

`reveal(Object)`—Ensures that the given element is visible, scrolling the viewer if necessary.

`scrollDown(int, int)`—Scrolls the viewer's control down by one item from the given display-relative coordinates.

`scrollUp(int, int)`—Scrolls the viewer's control up by one item from the given display-relative coordinates.

`setAutoExpandLevel(int)`—Sets the auto-expand level.

`setContentProvider(IContentProvider)`—The implementation, `AbstractTreeViewer`, of this method checks to ensure that the content provider is an `ITreeContentProvider`.

`setExpandedElements(Object[])`—Sets which nodes are expanded in this viewer's tree.

`setExpandedState(Object, boolean)`—Sets whether the node corresponding to the given element is expanded or collapsed.

setLabelProvider(IBaseLabelProvider)—The tree viewer implementation of this Viewer framework method ensures that the given label provider is an instance of ILabelProvider.

CheckboxTreeViewer adds the following useful APIs:

addCheckStateListener(ICheckStateListener)—Adds a listener for changes to the checked state of elements in this viewer.

getChecked(Object)—Returns the checked state of the given element.

getCheckedElements()—Returns a list of checked elements in this viewer's tree, including currently hidden ones that are marked as checked but are under a collapsed ancestor.

getGrayed(Object)—Returns the grayed state of the given element.

getGrayedElements()—Returns a list of grayed elements in this viewer's tree, including currently hidden ones that are marked as grayed but are under a collapsed ancestor.

setChecked(Object, boolean)—Sets the checked state for the given element in this viewer.

setCheckedElements(Object[])—Sets which elements are checked in this viewer's tree.

setGrayChecked(Object, boolean)—Checks and grays the selection rather than calling both setGrayed and setChecked as an optimization.

setGrayed(Object, boolean)—Sets the grayed state for the given element in this viewer.

setGrayedElements(Object[])—Sets which elements are grayed in this viewer's tree.

setParentsGrayed(Object, boolean)—Sets the grayed state for the given element and its parents in this viewer.

setSubtreeChecked(Object, boolean)—Sets the checked state for the given element and its visible children in this viewer.

The following example creates a tree viewer with a label provider and content provider (see Figure 5–10).

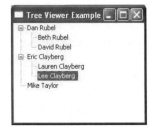

Figure 5–10   TreeViewer example.

```
import org.eclipse.jface.viewers.*;
import org.eclipse.swt.*;
import org.eclipse.swt.layout.*;
import org.eclipse.swt.widgets.*;

public class TreeViewerExample {
   public static void main(String[] args) {
      Display display = new Display();
      Shell shell = new Shell(display);
      shell.setText("Tree Viewer Example");
      shell.setBounds(100, 100, 200, 200);
      shell.setLayout(new FillLayout());

      final TreeViewer treeViewer =
         new TreeViewer(shell, SWT.SINGLE);
      treeViewer.setLabelProvider(
         new PersonListLabelProvider());
      treeViewer.setContentProvider(
         new PersonTreeContentProvider());
      treeViewer.setInput(Person.example());

      shell.open();
      while (!shell.isDisposed()) {
         if (!display.readAndDispatch()) display.sleep();
      }
      display.dispose();
   }
}
```

After creating the tree viewer, the label provider is set using the
setLabelProvider() method and the content provider with the
setContentProvider() method. The content provider, PersonTree-
ContentProvider, returns the parent and children of each item. The class
looks like this:

```
import org.eclipse.jface.viewers.*;

public class PersonTreeContentProvider
    extends ArrayContentProvider
    implements ITreeContentProvider {

    public Object[] getChildren(Object parentElement) {
        Person person = (Person) parentElement;
        return person.children;
    }

    public Object getParent(Object element) {
        Person person = (Person) element;
        return person.parent;
    }

    public boolean hasChildren(Object element) {
        Person person = (Person) element;
        return person.children.length > 0;
    }
}
```

5.2 Text Viewers

The `TextViewer` class wraps the `StyledText` widget (see Figure 5–11 for the `TextViewer` hierarchy). Individual runs of text may have different styles associated with them, including foreground color, background color, and bold. Text viewers provide a document model to the client and manage the conversion of the document to the styled text information used by the text widget.

Figure 5–11 TextViewer hierarchy.

Useful APIs include:

`addTextListener(ITextListener)`—Adds a text listener to this viewer.

`appendVerifyKeyListener(VerifyKeyListener)`—Appends a verify key listener to the viewer's list of verify key listeners.

`canDoOperation(int)`—Returns whether the operation specified by the given operation code can be performed.

changeTextPresentation(TextPresentation, boolean)—Applies the color information encoded in the given text presentation.

doOperation(int)—Performs the operation specified by the operation code on the target.

enableOperation(int, boolean)—Enables/disables the given text operation.

getSelectedRange()—Returns the range of the current selection in coordinates of this viewer's document.

getSelection()—Returns the current selection for this provider.

getTextWidget()—Returns the viewer's text widget.

isEditable()—Returns whether the shown text can be manipulated.

refresh()—Refreshes this viewer completely with information freshly obtained from the viewer's model.

setDocument(IDocument)—Sets the given document as the text viewer's model and updates the presentation accordingly.

setEditable(boolean)—Sets the editable mode.

setInput(Object)—Sets or clears the input for this viewer. The TextViewer implementation of this method calls setDocument(IDocument) with the input object if the input object is an instance of IDocument or with null if the input object is not.

setRedraw(boolean)—Enables/disables the redrawing of this text viewer.

setSelectedRange(int, int)—Sets the selection to the specified range.

setSelection(ISelection, boolean)—Sets a new selection for this viewer and optionally makes it visible.

setTextColor(Color)—Applies the given color to this viewer's selection.

setTextColor(Color, int, int, boolean)—Applies the given color to the specified section of this viewer.

setTextHover(ITextHover, String)—Sets this viewer's text hover for the given content type.

Figure 5–12   TextViewer example.

The following example creates a text viewer containing styled text (see Figure 5–12).

```
import org.eclipse.jface.text.*;
import org.eclipse.swt.*;
import org.eclipse.swt.custom.*;
import org.eclipse.swt.graphics.*;
import org.eclipse.swt.layout.*;
import org.eclipse.swt.widgets.*;

public class TextViewerExample {
    public static void main(String[] args) {
        Display display = new Display();
        Shell shell = new Shell(display);
        shell.setText("Text Viewer Example");
        shell.setBounds(100, 100, 225, 125);
        shell.setLayout(new FillLayout());

        final TextViewer textViewer =
            new TextViewer(shell, SWT.MULTI | SWT.V_SCROLL);

        String string = "This is plain text\n"
            + "This is bold text\n"
            + "This is red text";
        Document document = new Document(string);
        textViewer.setDocument(document);

        TextPresentation style = new TextPresentation();
        style.addStyleRange(
            new StyleRange(19, 17, null, null, SWT.BOLD));
        Color red = new Color(null, 255, 0, 0);
        style.addStyleRange(
            new StyleRange(37, 16, red, null));
        textViewer.changeTextPresentation(style, true);

        shell.open();
        while (!shell.isDisposed()) {
            if (!display.readAndDispatch()) display.sleep();
        }
        display.dispose();
    }
}
```

After creating the text viewer, a `Document` object is created that holds a string of text and is then assigned to the viewer. Next, a `TextPresentation` object is created to hold the style ranges. Two style ranges are added: one that sets a range of text to bold and a second that sets a range of text to the color red. The first argument to the `StyleRange` constructor is the index of the first character in the string to which the style should apply. The second argument is the number of characters that should be affected by the style. Finally, the style object is assigned to the viewer.

5.3 Summary

JFace viewers are used extensively in Eclipse plug-in development. List viewers provide OO wrappers around the basic Eclipse widgets, making it easier to directly deal with high-level domain objects rather than simple strings, numbers, and images. Likewise, text viewers make it easier to deal with text documents that require more complex text styling. Viewers are discussed in more detail in Chapter 7, Views.

References

Chapter source (*www.qualityeclipse.com/projects/source-ch-04-and-05.zip*).

Gauthier, Laurent, "Building and Delivering a Table Editor with SWT/JFace," Mirasol Op'nWorks, July 3, 2003 (*www.eclipse.org/articles/Article-Table-viewer/table_viewer.html*).

Grindstaff, Chris, "How to Use the JFace Tree Viewer," Applied Reasoning, May 5, 2002 (*www.eclipse.org/articles/treeviewer-cg/TreeViewerArticle.htm*).

CHAPTER 6

Actions

Actions, like everything else in Eclipse, are defined through various extension points so that new actions can be easily added at various points throughout the Eclipse framework. Actions appear in several different places throughout the Eclipse IDE, including the menu bar, toolbars, and context menus. Filters control when an action is visible and enabled for selection by a user.

This chapter covers all this with examples that show how to use actions and action sets in the example **Favorites** plug-in.

6.1 IAction versus IActionDelegate

An Eclipse *action* is composed of several parts, including the XML declaration of the action in the plug-in's manifest, the IAction object instantiated by the Eclipse UI to represent the action, and the IActionDelegate defined in the plug-in library containing the code to perform the action (see Figure 6–1).

This separation of the IAction object, defined and instantiated by the Eclipse user interface based on the plug-in's manifest and the IAction-Delegate defined in the plug-in's library, allows Eclipse to represent the action in a menu or toolbar without loading the plug-in that contains the operation until the user selects a specific menu item or clicks on the toolbar. Again, this approach represents one of the overarching themes of Eclipse: lazy plug-in initialization.

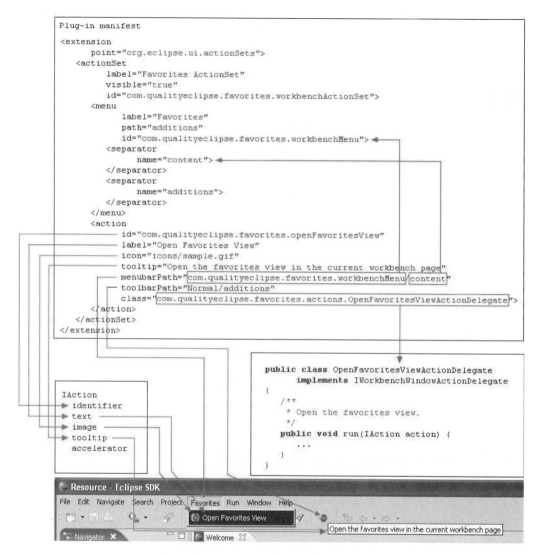

Figure 6–1 Action versus IActionDelegate.

There are several interesting subtypes of IActionDelegate.

IActionDelegate2—Provides lifecycle events to action delegates; if you are implementing IActionDelegate and need additional information, such as when to clean up before the action delegate is disposed, then implement IActionDelegate2 instead.

`IEditorActionDelegate`—Provides lifecycle events to action delegates associated with an editor (see Section 6.5.3, IEditorActionDelegate, on page 246).

`IObjectActionDelegate`—Provides lifecycle events to action delegates associated with a context menu (see Section 6.3.3, IObjectActionDelegate, on page 233).

`IViewActionDelegate`—Provides lifecycle events to action delegates associated with a view (see Section 6.4.3, IViewActionDelegate, on page 240).

`IWorkbenchWindowActionDelegate`—Provides lifecycle events to action delegates associated with the workbench window menu bar or toolbar.

6.2   Workbench Window Actions

Where and when an action appears is dependent on the extension point and filter used to define the action. This section discusses adding a new menu to the workbench menu bar and a new button to the workbench toolbar using the `org.eclipse.ui.actionSets` extension point (see Figure 6–1).

Both the menu item and toolbar button open the **Favorites** view when selected by a user. The user can already open the **Favorites** view (as outlined in Section 2.5, Installing and Running the Product, on page 86) but a top-level menu will really show off the new product by providing an easy way to find it.

> **Tip:** A top-level menu is a great way to show off a new product to a user, but be sure to read Section 6.2.9, Discussion, on page 222 concerning the pitfalls of this approach.

6.2.1   *Defining a workbench window menu*

To create a new menu to appear in the workbench menu bar, you have to create an **actionSet** extension in the **Favorites** plug-in manifest describing the new actions. That declaration must describe the location and content of the new menu and reference the action delegate class that performs the operation.

Open the **Favorites** plug-in manifest editor, select the **Extensions** tab, and click the **Add...** button (see Figure 6–2). You can also open the **New Extension** wizard by right-clicking to display the context menu, then select the **New > Extension...** command.

Figure 6–2   The Extensions page of the Manifest editor.

Select **org.eclipse.ui.actionSets** from the list of all available extension points (see Figure 6–3). If you can't locate **org.eclipse.ui.actionSets** in the list, then uncheck the **Show only extension points from the required plug-ins** checkbox. Click the **Finish** button to add this extension to the plug-in manifest.

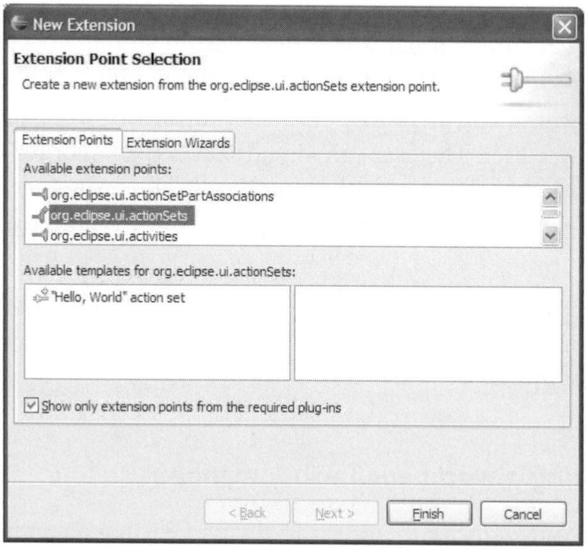

Figure 6–3   The New Extension wizard showing extension points.

Now, back in the **Extensions** page of the plug-in manifest editor, right-click on the **org.eclipse.ui.actionSets** extension and select **New > actionSet**. This immediately adds a new action set named **com.qualityeclipse.favorites.-actionSet1** in the plug-in manifest. Selecting this new action set displays the **properties on the right side of the editor.** Modify them as follows:

id—"com.qualityeclipse.favorites.workbenchActionSet"
The unique identifier used to reference the action set.

label—"Favorites ActionSet"
The text that appears in the **Customize Perspective** dialog.

visible—"true"
Determines whether the action set is initially visible. The user can show
or hide an action set by selecting **Window > Customize Perspective...,**
expanding the **Other** category in the **Customize Perspective** dialog, and
checking or unchecking the various action sets that are listed.

Next, add a menu that will appear in the workbench menu bar by right-
clicking on the action set you just added and selecting **New > menu**. Note that
the name of the new action set changes to **Favorites ActionSet** when the tree
selection changes. Select the new menu and set its attributes as follows (see
Figure 6–4):

id—"com.qualityeclipse.favorites.workbenchMenu"
The unique identifier used to reference this menu.

label—"Fa&vorites"
The name of the menu appearing in the workbench menu bar. The "&"
is for keyboard accessibility (see Section 6.6.5, Keyboard accessibility, on
page 255).

path—"additions"
The insertion point indicating where the menu will be positioned in the
menu bar (see Section 6.2.5, Insertion points, on page 215).

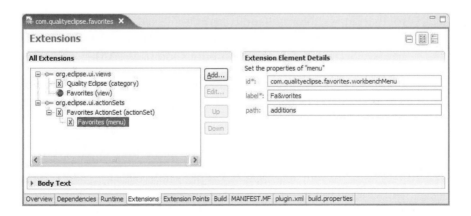

Figure 6–4   The Extensions page showing the Favorites menu's attributes.

6.2.2 Groups in a menu

Actions are added not to the menu itself, but to groups within the menu, so first some groups need to be defined. Right-click on the new **Favorites** menu and select **New > groupMarker**. Select the new *groupMarker* and change the **name** to "content" to uniquely identify that group within the **Favorites** menu. Add a second group to the **Favorites** menu; however, this time select **New > separator** and give it the name "additions".

A *separator* group has a horizontal line above the first menu item in the group, whereas a *groupMarker* does not have any line. The additions group is not used here, but it exists as a matter of course in case another plug-in wants to contribute actions to the plug-in's menu.

6.2.3 Defining a menu item and toolbar button

Finally, its time to define the action that appears in both the **Favorites** menu and the workbench toolbar. Right-click on the **Favorites ActionSet** and select **New > action**. Select this new action and enter the following values:

id—"com.qualityeclipse.favorites.openFavoritesView"
The unique identifier used to reference the action.

label—"Open Favo&rites View"
The text appearing in the **Favorites** menu. The "&" is for keyboard accessibility (see Section 6.6.5, Keyboard accessibility, on page 255).

menubarPath—"com.qualityeclipse.favorites.workbenchMenu/content"
The insertion point indicating where the action will appear in the menu (see Section 6.2.5, Insertion points, on page 215).

toolbarPath—"Normal/additions"
The insertion point indicating where the button will appear in the toolbar (see Section 6.2.5, Insertion points, on page 215).

tooltip—"Open the favorites view in the current workbench page"
The text that appears when the mouse hovers over the action's icon in the workbench toolbar.

Other attributes, which are discussed in subsequent sections, include the following:

allowLabelUpdate—Optional attribute indicating whether the retarget action allows the handler to override its label and tooltip. Only applies if the retarget attribute is `true`.

class—The `org.eclipse.ui.IWorkbenchWindowActionDelegate` delegate used to perform the operation is covered later (see Section 6.2.6, Creating an action delegate, on page 216). If the pulldown style is specified, then the class must implement the `org.eclipse.ui.IWorkbenchWindowPulldownDelegate` interface. The class is instantiated using its no argument constructor, but may be parameterized using the `IExecutableExtension` interface (see Section 20.5, Types Specified in an Extension Point, on page 723).

definitionId—The command identifier for the action, which allows a key sequence to be associated with it (see Section 6.6.4, Associating commands with actions, on page 255).

disabledIcon—The image displayed when the action is disabled. For more detail, see Section 6.2.4, Action images, on page 214.

enablesFor—An expression indicating when the action will be enabled (see Section 6.3.2, Action filtering and enablement, on page 227). If blank, then the action is always active unless overridden programmatically via the `IAction` interface.

helpContextId—The identifier for the help context associated with the action (covered in Chapter 15, Implementing Help).

hoverIcon—An image displayed when the cursor *hovers* over the action without being clicked. For more detail, see Section 6.2.4, Action images, on page 214.

icon—The associated image. For more detail, see Section 6.2.4, Action images, on page 214.

retarget—An optional attribute to retarget this action. When `true`, view and editor parts may supply a handler for this action using the standard mechanism for setting a global action handler (see Section 8.5.2.2, Top-level menu, on page 360) on their site using this action's identifier. If this attribute is `true`, the class attribute should not be supplied.

state—For an action with either the `radio` or `toggle` style, set the initial state to `true` or `false`.

style—An attribute defining the visual form of the action and having one of the following values:

push—A normal menu or toolbar item (the default style).

radio—A radio button-style menu or toolbar item where only one item at a time in a group of items all having the radio style can be active. See the **state** attribute.

toggle—A checked menu item or toggle tool item. See the **state** attribute.

pulldown—A submenu or drop-down toolbar menu. See the **class** attribute.

6.2.4   Action images

Next, associate an icon with the action that will appear in the workbench toolbar. Select the **Open Favorites View** action added in the previous section, then click the **Browse...** button that appears to the right of the **icon** field. In the resulting dialog, expand the tree and select the **sample.gif** item from the **icons** folder (see Figure 6–5). Click the **OK** button and **icons/sample.gif** will appear in the **icon** field.

The path appearing in the **icon** field and in the plugin.xml is relative to the plug-in's installation directory. Other image-related attributes include **hoverIcon** and **disabledIcon** for specifying the image that will be used when the mouse is hovered over the toolbar button and when the action is disabled, respectively.

Figure 6–5   The Resource Attribute Value dialog
for selecting an icon.

> **Creating Your Own Icons**   Several programs are available for creating and modifying images such as Jasc's Paint Shop Pro and Adobe's Photoshop Elements. Using one of these programs, you can create an icon from scratch or start with one of the many icons provided by Eclipse (for starters, see the \icons\full directories located within the plugins\org.eclipse.ui_3.1.2.jar or plugins\org.eclipse.jdt.ui_3.1.2.jar). Icons are typically *.gif files with a transparency color.

6.2.5 Insertion points

Because Eclipse is composed of multiple plug-ins—each one capable of contributing actions but not necessarily knowing about one another at build-time—the absolute position of an action or submenu within its parent is not known until runtime. Even during the course of execution, the position might change due to a sibling action being added or removed as the user changes a selection. For this reason, Eclipse uses *identifiers* to reference a menu, group, or action, and a path, known as an *insertion point*, for specifying where a menu or action will appear.

Every insertion point is composed of one or two identifiers separated by a forward slash, indicating the parent (a menu in this case) and group where the action will be located. For example, the **Open Favorites View** action's **menubar** attribute (see Section 6.2.3, Defining a menu item and toolbar button, on page 212 and Figure 6–1) is composed of two elements separated by a forward slash.

The first element, com.qualityeclipse.favorites. workbenchMenu, identifies the **Favorites** menu, while the second element, content, identifies the group within the **Favorites** menu. In some cases, such as when the parent is the workbench menu bar or a view's context menu, the parent is implied and thus only the group is specified in the insertion point.

Typically, plug-ins make allowances for other plug-ins to add new actions to their own menus by defining an empty group labeled "**additions**" in which the new actions will appear. The "**additions**" identifier is fairly standard throughout Eclipse, indicating where new actions or menus will appear, and is included in it as the IWorkbenchActionConstants.MB_ADDITIONS constant. For example, the **Favorites** menu specifies a **path** attribute (see Section 6.2.1, Defining a workbench window menu, on page 209) having the value "**additions**" that causes the **Favorites** menu to appear to the left of the

Window menu. Because the identifier for the **Window** menu is **window**, and if the **path** attribute of the **Favorites** menu is set to **"window/additions"**, then the **Favorites** menu will appear as a submenu in the **Window** menu itself rather than in the workbench menu bar.

Nested ActionSet Problem   Defining an action in an actionSet that contributes to a menu defined in a *different* actionSet can result in the following error in the Eclipse log file:

Invalid Menu Extension (Path is invalid): some.action.id

To work around this issue, define the menu in *both* actionSets. For more information, see Bugzilla entries #36389 and #105949.

The **toolbarPath** attribute is also an insertion point and has a structure identical to the **menubarPath** attribute, but indicates where the action will appear in the workbench toolbar rather than the menu bar. For example, the **toolbarPath** attribute of the **Open Favorites View** action (see Section 6.2.3, Defining a menu item and toolbar button, on page 212) is also composed of two elements separated by a forward slash: The first element, **Normal**, is the identifier of the workbench toolbar, while **additions**, the second element, is the group within that toolbar where the action will appear.

6.2.6   Creating an action delegate

The action is almost complete except for the action delegate, which contains the behavior associated with the action. The following are several ways that you can specify the action delegate associated with an action.

- Enter the fully qualified class name of action delegate in the **class** field.

- Click on the **class:** label that appears to the left of the **class** field to create a new action delegate class.

- Click on the **Browse...** button to the right of the **class** field to select an already existing action delegate.

Since you have not already created a class for the action, have Eclipse generate one that can be customized. Select the **Open Favorites View** action and click the **class:** label that appears to the left of the **class** field to open the **Java Attribute Editor** for the action's class (see Figure 6–6).

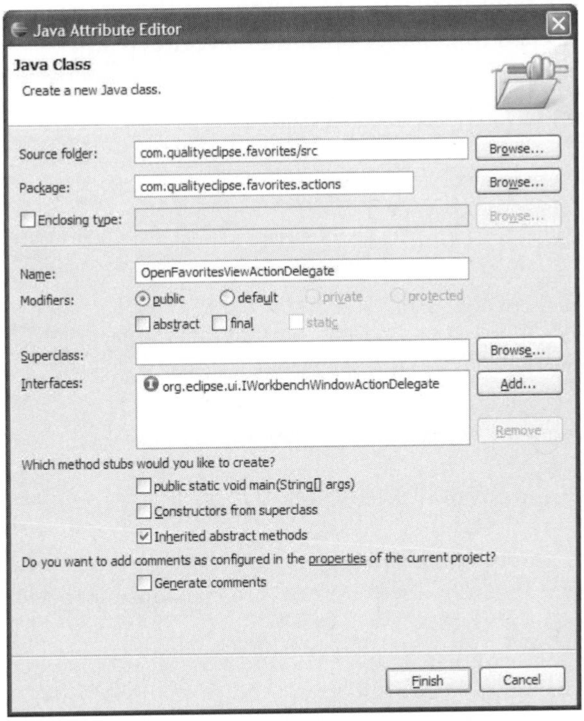

Figure 6-6   The Java Attribute Editor for an action's class.

Enter "com.qualityeclipse.favorites.actions" in the **Package** field and "OpenFavoritesViewActionDelegate" in the **Name** field. Click the **Finish** button to generate the new action delegate and open an editor on the new class.

After the class has been created and the editor opened, modify the class as follows so that the **Favorites** view will open when a user selects the action. Start by adding a new field and modifying the init() method to cache the window in which this action delegate is operating.

```
private IWorkbenchWindow window;

public void init(IWorkbenchWindow window) {
   this.window = window;
}
```

Next, add a constant to the FavoritesView class representing the unique identifier used to open the **Favorites** view.

```
public static final String ID =
   "com.qualityeclipse.favorites.views.FavoritesView";
```

Finally, modify the `run()` method of the `OpenFavoritesViewAction-Delegate` class to actually open the **Favorites View.**

```
public void run(IAction action) {

   // Get the active page.
   if (window == null)
      return;

   IWorkbenchPage page = window.getActivePage();
   if (page == null)
      return;

   // Open and activate the Favorites view.
   try {
      page.showView(FavoritesView.ID);
   }
   catch (PartInitException e) {
      FavoritesLog.logError("Failed to open the Favorites view", e);
   }
}
```

6.2.6.1   selectionChanged method

While the action declaration in the plug-in manifest provides the initial state of the action, the `selectionChanged()` method in the action delegate provides an opportunity to dynamically adjust the state, enablement, or even the text of the action using the `IAction` interface.

For example, the **enablesFor** attribute (see Section 6.3.2, Action filtering and enablement, on page 227) is used to specify the number of objects to select for an action to be enabled, but further refinement of this enablement can be provided by implementing the `selectionChanged()` method. This method can interrogate the current selection and call the `IAction.setEnabled()` method as necessary to update the action enablement.

In order for the action delegate's `selectionChanged()` method to be called, you need to call `getViewSite().setSelectionProvider(viewer)` in your view's `createPartControl()` method.

6.2.6.2   *run method*

The `run()` method is called when a user selects an action and expects an operation to be performed. Similar to the `selectionChanged()` method, the `IAction` interface can be used to change the state of an action dependent on the outcome of an operation.

> **Guard Code Needed**   Be aware that if the plug-in is not loaded and the user selects a menu option causing the plug-in to be loaded, the `selectionChanged()` method *may not be called* before the `run()` method, so the `run()` method still needs the appropriate guard code. In addition, the `run()` method executes in the main UI thread, so consider pushing long running operations into a background thread (see Section 20.8, Background Tasks—Jobs API, on page 739).

6.2.7   *Manually testing the new action*

Testing the modifications you have just made involves launching the **Runtime Workbench** as discussed in Chapter 2, A Simple Plug-in Example. If the **Favorites** menu does not appear in the **Runtime Workbench** menu bar or the **Favorites** icon cannot be found in the toolbar, try the following suggestions:

- Enable the action set by selecting **Window > Customize Perspective...** to open the **Customize Perspective** dialog. In the dialog, select the **Commands** tab, locate **Favorites ActionSet**, and make sure it is checked (see Figure 6–7).

- Reinitialize the perspective using **Window > Reset Perspective**.

- Close and reopen the perspective.

- If nothing else works, then try clearing the workspace data before launching the **Runtime Workbench**. To do this, select **Run...** in the launch menu, select the **Favorites** launch configuration, and check the **Clear workspace data before launching** checkbox. Click the **Run** button to launch the **Runtime Workbench**.

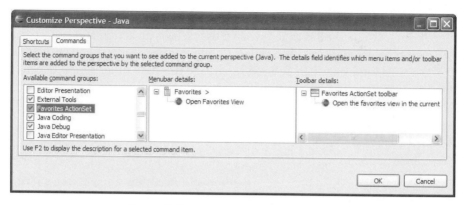

Figure 6–7   Customize Perspective dialog.

6.2.8   Adding a test for the new action

Before the work is complete, you need to devise a test for the new **Open Favorites View** action. You already have a FavoritesViewTest (see Section 2.8.3, Creating a Plug-in test, on page 93) from which to extract common test functionality.

Create a new superclass for all the tests called AbstractFavoritesTest, then pull up the delay(), assertEquals(), and waitForJobs() methods from the existing FavoritesViewTest. The VIEW_ID constant is the same as the FavoritesView.ID constant, so replace it with FavoritesView.ID. Next, create a new test subclassing AbstractFavoritesTest that exercises the new OpenFavoritesViewActionDelegate class.

```
package com.qualityeclipse.favorites.test;

import ...

public class OpenFavoritesViewTest extends AbstractFavoritesTest {
    public OpenFavoritesViewTest(String name) {
        super(name);
    }
}
```

Override the setUp() method to ensure that the system is in the appropriate state before the test executes.

```
protected void setUp() throws Exception {
    super.setUp();

    // Ensure that the view is not open.
    waitForJobs();
    IWorkbenchPage page = PlatformUI.getWorkbench()
        .getActiveWorkbenchWindow().getActivePage();
```

```
IViewPart view = page.findView(FavoritesView.ID);
if (view != null)
   page.hideView(view);

// Delay for 3 seconds so that
// the Favorites view can be seen.
waitForJobs();
delay(3000);
}
```

Finally, create the test method that exercises the `OpenFavoritesView-ActionDelegate` class.

```
public void testOpenFavoritesView() {

   // Execute the operation.
   (new Action("OpenFavoritesViewTest") {
      public void run() {
         IWorkbenchWindowActionDelegate delegate =
            new OpenFavoritesViewActionDelegate();
         delegate.init(PlatformUI.getWorkbench()
            .getActiveWorkbenchWindow());
         delegate.selectionChanged(this, StructuredSelection.EMPTY);
         delegate.run(this);
      }
   }).run();

   // Test that the operation completed successfully.
   waitForJobs();
   IWorkbenchPage page = PlatformUI.getWorkbench()
         .getActiveWorkbenchWindow().getActivePage();
   assertTrue(page.findView(FavoritesView.ID) != null);
}
```

After entering the preceding test, the following error will appear in the **Problems** view:

```
Access restriction: The type OpenFavoritesViewActionDelegate
is not accessible due to restriction on required project
com.qualityeclipse.favorites.
```

This indicates that the **com.qualityeclipse.favorites** plug-in does not provide access to the `OpenFavoritesViewActionDelegate` class to other plug-ins. To remedy this situation, open the plug-in manifest editor to the **Exported Packages** section (see Section 2.8.1, Test preparation, on page 92), click **Add...**, select the **com.qualityeclipse.favorites.actions** package, and save the changes.

Now everything is ready to execute the tests. Rather than launching each test individually, the FavoritesViewTest and OpenFavoritesViewTest can be combined into a single test suite named FavoritesTestSuite, which can be launched to execute both tests at once:

```
package com.qualityeclipse.favorites.test;

import ...

public class FavoritesTestSuite
{
   public static Test suite() {

      TestSuite suite =
         new TestSuite("Favorites test suite");

      suite.addTest(
         new TestSuite(FavoritesViewTest.class));

      suite.addTest(
         new TestSuite(OpenFavoritesViewTest.class));

      return suite;
   }
}
```

While individually launching tests is not a problem now with just two tests; in the future, as more tests are added for the **Favorites** plug-in, it can save time to have a single test suite. To launch the test suite, select **Run...** in the launch menu, select the FavoritesViewTest launch configuration that was created in Section 2.8.4, Running a Plug-in test, on page 97, and modify the target to be the new FavoritesTestSuite test suite.

6.2.9 *Discussion*

To define a top-level menu or not... that is the question. On the one hand, a top-level menu is a great way to promote a new product that has just been installed, providing a good way for a potential customer to become accustomed to new functionality. On the other hand, if every plug-in defined a top-level menu, then the menu bar would be cluttered and Eclipse would quickly become unusable. Additionally, the customer may become annoyed if he or she does not want to see the menu and continually has to use the multistep process outlined in Section 1.2.2.4, Customizing available actions, on page 14 to remove the menu. What to do?

Action sets are one answer to this question. They can be specified in the `plugin.xml` as visible everywhere in every perspective. Using the new `IActionSetDescriptor.setInitiallyVisible()` method, you can programmatically override the visibility specified in the `plugin.xml` so that the top-level menu no longer shows up in any newly opened perspectives. You can create a new action that removes your top-level menu from all current and future perspectives, by using `setInitiallyVisible()` in conjunction with `IWorkbenchPage.hideActionSet()`. Your product could contain a checkbox option in your Preference page (see Section 12.2, Preference Page APIs, on page 453) that uses this action to show or hide your top-level menu.

Note: We submitted a feature request and patch to Eclipse (see Bugzilla entry #39455 at *bugs.eclipse.org/bugs/show_bug.cgi?id=39455*) for the new `IActionSetDescriptor` API discussed here, and it was accepted and integrated into Eclipse 3.0 and 3.1. This is a good example of how users can contribute back to Eclipse (see Section 20.6.4, Submitting the change to Eclipse, on page 731), making it a better platform for everyone.

Another option is to tie your top-level menu or action set to a particular perspective (see Section 10.2.3, Adding action sets, on page 402). In this way, the menu and actions are only visible when that particular perspective is active. If one or more perspectives are particularly suited for the functionality added by your plug-in, then this may be your best approach.

What if an action is editor-related? Section 6.5.2, Defining an editor context action, on page 246 and Section 6.5.5, Defining an editor top-level action, on page 248 discuss adding menus and actions tied to a specific type of editor. With this approach, the top-level menu is only visible when an editor of that type is open.

The `org.eclipse.ui.actionSetPartAssociations` extension point provides yet another option, allowing an action set to be displayed whenever one or more specific types of views or editors are open, regardless of the perspective in which they are opened. This is an excellent way to ensure that specific actions appear in a wide range of perspectives without having to explicitly add the actions to those perspectives.

The remainder of this chapter focuses on providing actions in view-specific menus, or as operations directed at specific types of objects rather than top-level menus. In this way, the action will only be visible when it is needed and on the types of objects to which it applies. This approach avoids the top-level menu issue and prevents Eclipse from becoming cluttered. Various approaches for locally scoped actions are covered in subsequent sections.

6.3   Object Actions

Suppose you want to make it easy for the user to add files and folders to the
Favorites view. Object contributions are ideal for this because they appear in
context menus only when the selection in the current view or editor contains
an object compatible with that action (see Figure 6–8). In this manner, an
object contribution is available to the user when he or she needs the action,
yet not intrusive when the action does not apply.

6.3.1   *Defining an object-based action*

As in Section 6.2.1, Defining a workbench window menu, on page 209 and
subsequent sections, use the **Extensions** page of the plug-in manifest editor to
create the new object contribution. Click on the **Add** button to add an
org.eclipse.ui.popupMenus extension, then add an **objectContribution** with
the following attributes:

> **adaptable**—"true"
> Indicates that objects that adapt to IResource are acceptable targets
> (see Section 20.3, Adapters, on page 714).
>
> **id**—"com.qualityeclipse.favorites.popupMenu"
> The unique identifier for this contribution.
>
> **nameFilter**—Leave blank
> A wildcard filter specifying the names that are acceptable targets. For
> example, entering "*.java" would target only those files with names end-
> ing with .java. More on this in Section 6.3.2, Action filtering and
> enablement, on page 227.
>
> **objectClass**—"org.eclipse.core.resources.IResource"
> The type of object that is an acceptable target. Use the **Browse...** button
> at the right of the **objectClass** field to select the existing org.eclipse.
> core.resources.IResource class. If you want to create a new class,
> then click the **objectClass:** label to the left of the **objectClass** field.

Next, add an action to the new objectContribution with the following
attribute values, which are very similar to the action attributes covered in Section 6.2.3, Defining a menu item and toolbar button, on page 212.

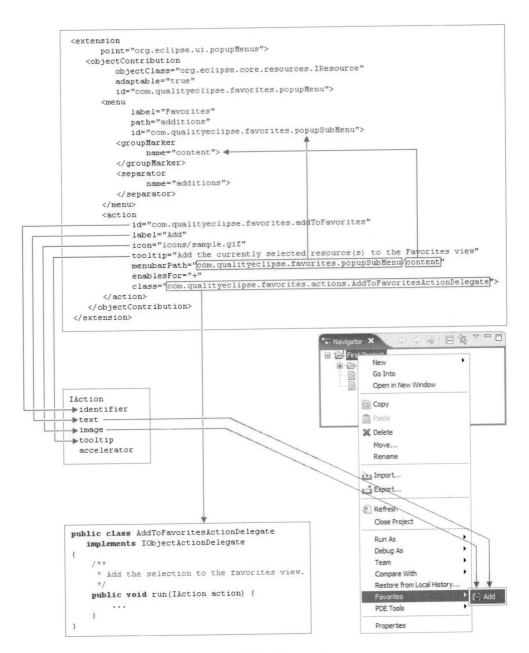

Figure 6–8   Object action.

class—"com.qualityeclipse.favorites.actions. AddToFavoritesAction-Delegate" The action delegate for the action that implements the `org.eclipse.ui.IObjectActionDelegate` interface (see Section 6.3.3, IObjectActionDelegate, on page 233). The class is instantiated using its no argument constructor, but can be parameterized using the `IExecutable-Extension` interface (see Section 20.5, Types Specified in an Extension Point, on page 723). The class can be specified in one of three different ways as in Section 6.2.6, Creating an action delegate, on page 216.

enablesFor—"+"
An expression indicating when the action will be enabled (see Section 6.3.2, Action filtering and enablement, on page 227).

id—"com.qualityeclipse.favorites.addToFavorites"
The unique identifier for the action.

label—"Add to Favorites"
The text that appears in the context menu for the action.

menubarPath—"additions"
The insertion point for the action (see Section 6.2.5, Insertion points, on page 215).

tooltip—"Add the selected resource(s) to the Favorites view"
The text that appears when the mouse hovers over the menu item in the context menu.

> **Multiple actions appear in reverse order:** Buried in the `org.eclipse.ui.popupMenu` extension point documentation is the following nugget of information: "If two or more actions are contributed to a menu by a single extension, the actions will appear in the reverse order of how they are listed in the `plugin.xml` file. This behavior is admittedly unintuitive. However, it was discovered after the Eclipse Platform API was frozen. Changing the behavior now would break every plug-in that relies on the existing behavior."

Other available action attributes not used in this example include:

helpContextId—The identifier for the help context associated with the action (see Chapter 15, Implementing Help).

icon—The associated image (see Section 6.2.4, Action images, on page 214).

overrideActionId—An optional attribute specifying the identifier for an action that the action overrides.

state—For an action with either the `radio` or `toggle` style, set the initial state to `true` or `false` (see Section 6.2.3, Defining a menu item and toolbar button, on page 212).

style—An attribute defining the visual form of the action. This is covered in Section 6.2.3, Defining a menu item and toolbar button, on page 212, with the exception that the `pulldown` style does not apply to object contributions.

6.3.2   *Action filtering and enablement*

In keeping with the lazy loading plug-in theme, Eclipse provides multiple declarative mechanisms for filtering actions based on the context, and enabling visible actions only when appropriate. Because they are declared in the plug-in manifest, these mechanisms have the advantage that they do not require the plug-in to be loaded for Eclipse to use them.

6.3.2.1   *Basic filtering and enablement*

In Section 6.3.1, Defining an object-based action, on page 224, the **nameFilter** and **objectClass** attributes are examples of filters, while the **enablesFor** attribute determines when an action will be enabled. When the context menu is activated, if a selection does not contain objects with names that match the wildcard **nameFilter** or are not of a type specified by the **objectClass** attribute, none of the actions defined in that object contribution will appear in the context menu. In addition, the **enablesFor** attribute uses the syntax in Table 6–1 to define exactly how many objects need to be selected for a particular action to be enabled:

Table 6–1   enabledFor attribute options

Syntax	Description
!	0 items selected.
?	0 or 1 items selected.
+	1 or more items selected.
multiple, 2+	2 or more items selected.
n	A precise number of items selected; for example, `enablesFor="4"` enables the action only when 4 are selected.
*	Any number of items selected.

The techniques listed in this table represent those most commonly used for limiting visibility and the enablement of actions; occasionally, a more refined approach is needed. The **visibility** and **filter** elements provide an additional means to limit an action's visibility, while the **selection** and **enablement** elements provide a more flexible way to specify when an action is enabled. Still further refinement of action enablement can be provided by using the `selectionChanged()` method in the action delegate, as discussed in Section 6.2.6, Creating an action delegate, on page 216.

6.3.2.2   *The visibility element*

The **visibility** element provides an alternate and more powerful way to specify when an object contribution's actions will be available to the user as compared with the object contribution's **nameFilter** and **objectClass**. For example, an alternate way to specify filtering for the object contribution just described would be:

```
<objectContribution ...>
   <visibility>
      <objectClass
         name="org.eclipse.core.resources.IResource"/>
   </visibility>
   ...the other stuff here...
</objectContribution>
```

If the action is to be visible only for resources that are not read-only, then the `visibility` object contribution might look like this:

```
<objectContribution ...>
   <visibility>
      <and>
         <objectClass
            name="org.eclipse.core.resources.IResource"/>
         <objectState name="readOnly" value="false"/>
      </and>
   </visibility>
   ... the other stuff here ...
</objectContribution>
```

As part of the `<visibility>` element declaration, you can use nested `<and>`, `<or>`, and `<not>` elements for logical expressions, plus the following Boolean expressions.

adapt—Adapts the selected object to the specified type then uses the new object in any child expressions. For example, if you wanted to adapt the selected object (see Section 20.3, Adapters, on page 714) to a resource and then test some resource object state, the expression would look like this:

```
<adapt type="org.eclipse.core.resources.IResource">
   <objectState name="readOnly" value="false"/>
</adapt>
```

The children of an **adapt** expression are combined using the **and** operator. The expression returns `EvaluationResult.NOT_LOADED` if either the adapter or the type referenced isn't loaded yet. It throws an `ExpressionException` during evaluation if the type name doesn't exist.

and—Evaluates `true` if all subelement expressions evaluate `true`.

instanceof—Compares the class of the selected object against a name. This is identical to the **objectClass** element, except that **instanceof** can be combined with other elements using the **and** and **or** elements.

not—Evaluates `true` if its subelement expressions evaluates `false`.

objectClass—Compares the class of the selected object against a name as shown above.

objectState—Compares the state of the selected object against a specified state similar to the **filter** element (see Section 6.3.2.3, The filter element, on page 230).

or—Evaluates `true` if one subelement expression evaluates `true`.

pluginState—Compares the plug-in state, indicating whether it is `installed` or `activated`. For example, an expression such as `<pluginState id="org.eclipse.pde" value="installed"/>` would cause an object contribution to be visible only if the `org.eclipse.pde` plug-in is installed, and an expression such as `<pluginState id="org.eclipse.pde" value="activated"/>` would cause an object contribution to be visible only if the `org.eclipse.pde` plug-in has been activated in some other manner.

systemProperty—Compares the system property. For example, if an object contribution should only be visible when the language is English, then the expression would be: `<systemProperty name="user.language" value="en"/>`

systemTest—Identical to the **systemProperty** element, except that **systemTest** can be combined with other elements using the **and** and **or** elements.

test—Evaluate the property state of the object. For example, if an object contribution should only be visible when a resource in a Java project is selected, then the expression would be:

```
<test
    property="org.eclipse.debug.ui.projectNature"
    value="org.eclipse.jdt.core.javanature"/>
```

The test expression returns `EvaluationResult.NOT_LOADED` if the property tester doing the actual testing isn't loaded yet. The set of testable properties can be extended using the `org.eclipse.core.expressions.propertyTesters` extension point. One example of this is the `org.eclipse.debug.internal.ui.ResourceExtender` class.

6.3.2.3   The filter element

The **filter** element is a simpler form of the **objectState** element discussed previously. For example, if the object contribution was to be available for any file that is not read-only, then the object contribution could be expressed like this:

```
<objectContribution ...>
    <filter name="readOnly" value="false"/>
    ... the other stuff here ...
</objectContribution>
```

As with the **objectState** element, the **filter** element uses the `IAction-Filter` interface to determine whether an object in the selection matches the criteria. Every selected object must either implement or adapt to the `IAction-Filter` interface (more on adapters in Chapter 20, Advanced Topics) and implement the appropriate behavior in the `testAttribute()` method to test the specified name/value pair against the state of the specified object. For resources, Eclipse provides the following built-in state comparisons as listed in the `org.eclipse.ui.IResourceActionFilter` class:

name—Comparison of the filename. "*" can be used at the start or end to represent "one or more characters."

extension—Comparison of the file extension.

path—Comparison against the file path. "*" can be used at the start or end to represent "one or more characters."

readOnly—Comparison of the read-only attribute of a file.

projectNature—Comparison of the project nature.

persistentProperty—Comparison of a persistent property on the selected resource. If the value is a simple string, then this tests for the existence of the property on the resource. If it has the format `propertyName=propertyValue`, this obtains the value of the property with the specified name and tests it for equality with the specified value.

projectPersistentProperty—Comparison of a persistent property on the selected resource's project with similar semantics to the `persistentProperty` listed above.

sessionProperty—Comparison of a session property on the selected resource with similar semantics to the `persistentProperty` just listed.

projectSessionProperty—Comparison of a session property on the selected resource's project with similar semantics to `persistentProperty`.

6.3.2.4   The selection element

The **selection** element is a technique for enabling an individual action based on its name and type, similar to the way that the **nameFilter** and **objectClass** attributes determine whether all actions in an object contribution are visible. For example, an alternate form for the object contribution using the **selection** element would be:

```
<objectContribution
      objectClass="java.lang.Object"
      id="com.qualityeclipse.favorites.popupMenu">
   <action
         label="Add to Favorites"
         tooltip="Add the selected resource(s) to the
               Favorites view"
         class="com.qualityeclipse.favorites.actions.
               AddToFavoritesActionDelegate"
         menubarPath="additions"
         enablesFor="+"
         id="com.qualityeclipse.favorites.addToFavorites">
   <selection
            class="org.eclipse.core.resources.IResource"
            name="*.java"/>
   </action>
</objectContribution>
```

With this declaration, the object contribution's actions would always be visible, but the **Add to Favorites** action would only be enabled if the selection contained only implementers of `IResource` that matched the name filter `*.java`.

6.3.2.5   The enablement element

The **enablement** element is a more powerful alternative to the **selection** element, supporting the same complex conditional logic expressions and comparisons as the **visibility** element (see Section 6.3.2.2, The visibility element, on page 228). For example, an alternate object contribution declaration to the one outlined in the previous section, but that produces the same behavior would be:

```
<objectContribution
      objectClass="java.lang.Object"
      id="com.qualityeclipse.favorites.popupMenu">
   <action
        label="Add to Favorites"
        tooltip="Add the selected resource(s)
               to the Favorites view"
        class="com.qualityeclipse.favorites.actions.
               AddToFavoritesActionDelegate"
        menubarPath="additions"
        enablesFor="+"
        id="com.qualityeclipse.favorites.addToFavorites">
      <enablement>
        <and>
           <objectClass
             name="org.eclipse.core.resources.IResource"/>
           <objectState name="name" value="*.java"/>
        </and>
      </enablement>
   </action>
</objectContribution>
```

6.3.2.6   *Content-sensitive object contributions*

There is a new mechanism for filtering actions based on resource content. This filtering is specified in the plug-in manifest (does not load your plug-in) and determines whether an action should be visible or enabled by inspecting a file's content. For example, the **Run Ant...** command is associated with resources named build.xml, but no others; what if your Ant script is located in a file called export.xml? This new mechanism can determine whether the **Run Ant...** command should be visible based on the first XML tag or DTD specified in the file. In this case, the org.eclipse.ant.core plug-in defines a new antBuildFile content type:

```
<extension point="org.eclipse.core.runtime.contentTypes">
   <content-type
      id="antBuildFile"
      name="%antBuildFileContentType.name"
      base-type="org.eclipse.core.runtime.xml"
      file-names="build.xml"
      file-extensions="macrodef,ent,xml"
      priority="normal">
      <describer
        class="org.eclipse.ant.internal.core.
           contentDescriber.AntBuildfileContentDescriber">
      </describer>
   </content-type>
</extension>
```

The preceding declaration associates the `antBuildFile` content type with the `AntBuildfileContentDescriber` class, which determines whether XML content is Ant content. The `antBuildFile` content type can then be used to specify action visibility and enablement, editor association, and more. For more about declaring and using your own content types, see the following:

- "Content Sensitive Object Contributions" at **eclipse.org > projects > The Eclipse Project > Platform > UI > Development Resources > Content Sensitive Object Contributions,** or browse *dev.eclipse.org/viewcvs/index. cgi/~checkout~/platform-ui-home/object-aware-contributions/ objCont.htm.*

- "Content types" in the Eclipse Help System at **Help > Help Contents > Platform Plug-in Developer Guide > Programmer's Guide > Runtime overview > Content types**

- "A central content type catalog for Eclipse" at *dev.eclipse.org/viewcvs/ index.cgi/platform-core-home/documents/content_types.html?rev=1.11*

- " Content types in Eclipse" at *eclipse.org/eclipse/platform-core/ planning/3.0/plan_content_types.html*

6.3.3 *IObjectActionDelegate*

Getting back to the **Favorites** plug-in, the next task is to create an action delegate that implements the `IObjectActionDelegate` interface, which performs the operation behind the new **Add to Favorites** menu item. Create a new `AddToFavoritesActionDelegate` class as described next. Since the **Favorites** view is not fully functional, the action displays a message rather than adding the selected items to the view (see Section 7.3.1, Model actions, on page 283 for more implementation details).

Start by selecting the action defined in Section 6.3.1, Defining an object-based action, on page 224 and then clicking on the **class:** label to the left of the class field. This opens the **Java Attribute Editor** dialog for creating a new Java class. Fill in the package and class name fields as necessary and be sure to add `IObjectActionDelegate` as the interface to implement, then click **Finish** to generate the new class.

Next, add a new field and modify the `setActivePart()` method to cache the view or editor in which the action appears:

```
private IWorkbenchPart targetPart;

public void setActivePart(IAction action, IWorkbenchPart part) {
   this.targetPart = part;
}
```

Finally, modify the `run()` method to open a message dialog indicating that this action was successfully executed. As mentioned before, this action delegate will be fleshed out in Section 7.3.1, Model actions, on page 283.

```
public void run(IAction action) {
   MessageDialog.openInformation(
        targetPart.getSite().getShell(),
        "Add to Favorites",
        "Triggered the " + getClass().getName() + " action");
}
```

6.3.4 *Creating an object-based submenu*

Menus can be contributed to a context menu in a manner similar to adding actions. If three or more similar actions are contributed, then think about placing those actions in a submenu rather than in the context menu itself. The **Favorites** plug-in only adds one action to the context menu, but let's place the action in a submenu rather than in the context menu itself.

To create the **Favorites** menu, right-click on the **com.qualityeclipse.-favorites.popupMenu** object contribution in the **Extensions** page of the plug-in manifest editor, and select **New > menu**. Enter the following values for this new menu:

> **id**—"com.qualityeclipse.favorites.popupSubMenu"
> The identifier for the submenu.
>
> **label**—"Favorites"
> The text appearing in the context menu as the name of the submenu.
>
> **path**—"additions"
> The insertion point that determines the location in the context menu where the submenu will appear (see Section 6.2.5, Insertion points, on page 215).

Next, add a **groupMarker** to the menu with the name "content" and a **separator** with the name "additions" (see Section 6.2.2, Groups in a menu, on page 212). Finally, modify the **Add to Favorites** action's attributes as follows so that the action will now be part of the new **Favorites** submenu:

> **label**—"Add"
> The text appearing in the submenu as the name of the action.
>
> **menubarPath**—"com.qualityeclipse.favorites.popupSubMenu/content"
> The insertion point that determines where the **Favorites** submenu action will appear (see Section 6.2.5, Insertion points, on page 215).

6.3.5   Manually testing the new action

When the **Favorites Runtime Workbench** configuration is launched (see Section 2.6, Debugging the Product, on page 88), any context menu activated on a workbench resource will contain the **Favorites** menu with the **Add** submenu item. Selecting this submenu item displays a message box notifying you that the action was indeed triggered correctly.

The **Favorites** action is only displayed when one or more objects are selected due to `enablesFor="+"` in the declaration shown in Section 6.3.2.5, The enablement element, on page 231. This means that when you test the **Favorites** menu, you must have at least one project created in your runtime workbench and select at least one resource in the **Navigator** view when you activate the context menu. If you right click without selecting anything, you will only see an abbreviated context menu that does not have the **Favorites** menu.

6.3.6   Adding a test for the new action

The last task is to create an automated test that triggers the action and validates the result. Because this operation displays a message rather than adding a resource to the **Favorites** view, the code that validates the results of this test will have to wait until the next chapter (see Section 7.6, Testing, on page 314), where the **Favorites** view will be more fully developed. For now, create the following new test case in the **Favorites** test project and then modify the **Favorites** test suite to include this new test (see Section 6.2.8, Adding a test for the new action, on page 220).

You can begin by creating a new `AddToFavoritesTest` class that extends `AbstractFavoritesTest` and adds it to the **Favorites** test suite.

```
package com.qualityeclipse.favorites.test;

import ...

public class AddToFavoritesTest extends AbstractFavoritesTest {

    public AddToFavoritesTest(String name) {
        super(name);
    }
```

Next add a field and override the `setUp()` method to create a temporary project called "TestProj" for the duration of this test. The `tearDown()` method deletes this temporary project when the test is complete.

To get these changes to properly compile, edit the **Favorites** test project's plug-in manifest and add the `org.eclipse.core.resources` plug-in to the **Required Plug-ins** list (see Figure 2–10 on page 73).

```
protected IProject project;

protected void setUp() throws Exception {
   super.setUp();
   IWorkspaceRoot root = ResourcesPlugin.getWorkspace().getRoot();
   project = root.getProject("TestProj");
   project.create(null);
   project.open(null);
}

protected void tearDown() throws Exception {
   super.tearDown();

   // Wait for a bit for the system to catch up
   // so that the delete operation does not collide
   // with any background tasks.
   delay(3000);
   waitForJobs();

   project.delete(true, true, null);
}
```

Finally, add the method that exercises the new menu item for adding objects to the **Favorites** view.

```
public void testAddToFavorites() throws CoreException {

   // Show the resource navigator and select the project.
   IViewPart navigator = PlatformUI.getWorkbench()
         .getActiveWorkbenchWindow().getActivePage().showView(
               "org.eclipse.ui.views.ResourceNavigator");
   StructuredSelection selection = new StructuredSelection(project);
   ((ISetSelectionTarget) navigator).selectReveal(selection);

   // Execute the action.
   final IObjectActionDelegate delegate
      = new AddToFavoritesActionDelegate();
   IAction action = new Action("Test Add to Favorites") {
      public void run() {
         delegate.run(this);
      }
   };
   delegate.setActivePart(action, navigator);
   delegate.selectionChanged(action, selection);
   action.run();

   // Add code here at a later time to verify that the
   // Add to Favorites action correctly added the
   // appropriate values to the Favorites view.
}
```

6.4   View Actions

There are several ways in which actions can be manifested as part of a view. For example, the **Members** view has toolbar buttons that appear in its title bar, a pull-down menu appearing at the right of the toolbar buttons, and a context menu containing yet more actions (see Figure 6–9). Actions are added to views using the extension point mechanism, similar to the discussions in the previous two sections. In addition, views can programmatically provide their own actions, bypassing the extension point mechanism (see Section 7.3, View Actions, on page 283).

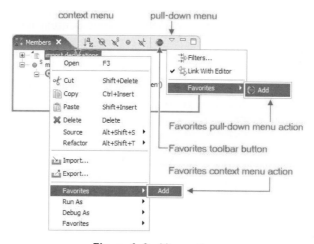

Figure 6–9   View actions.

6.4.1   *Defining a view context submenu*

Similar to an `objectContribution`, a `viewerContribution` is used to add a menu item to a context menu. Whereas an `objectContribution` causes a menu item to appear based on the selection in the viewer, a `viewer-Contribution` causes a menu item to appear based on the type of viewer. As with an `objectContribution`, the `viewerContribution` element can have a single `visibility` subelement that takes control when all its other subelements are visible to the user (see Section 6.3.2.2, The visibility element, on page 228).

The **Favorites** submenu shows up in several different types of views, but not in the **Members** view. It would probably be more appropriate to use the `objectContribution` approach discussed in Section 6.3, Object Actions, on page 224 to target objects contained in the **Members** view; however, use the `viewerContribution` instead as an example.

Start by right-clicking on the `popupMenu` extension that was added as part of Section 6.3.1, Defining an object-based action, on page 224 and select **New > viewerContribution**. Fill in the following attributes for the newly added `viewerContribution`.

id—"com.qualityeclipse.favorites.membersViewPopup"
The identifier for this view contribution.

targetID—"org.eclipse.jdt.ui.MembersView"
The identifier of the view's context menu to which the submenu will be added (see Section 20.6, Modifying Eclipse to Find Part Identifiers, on page 727).

Add the **Favorites** menu to the **Members** view context menu by right-clicking on the `viewerContribution` and selecting **New > menu**. Enter the following attributes for the new menu:

id—"com.qualityeclipse.favorites.membersViewPopupSubMenu"
The identifier for the **Favorites** menu in the **Members** view context menu.

label—"Favorites"
The text appearing in the **Members** view context menu as the name of the **Favorites** submenu.

path—"additions"
The insertion point that determines the location in the **Members** view context menu where the **Favorites** submenu will appear (see Section 6.2.5, Insertion points, on page 215).

Next, add a **groupMarker** to the menu with the name "content" and a **separator** with the name "additions" (see Section 6.2.2, Groups in a menu, on page 212).

6.4.2 *Defining a view context menu action*

Finally, add an action to the **Favorites** submenu by right-clicking on the `viewerContribution`, selecting **New > action**, and entering the following attributes for the new action:

class—"com.qualityeclipse.favorites.actions.
AddToFavoritesActionDelegate"
The fully qualified name of the class that implements the `org.eclipse.ui.IViewActionDelegate` interface and performs the action. In this case, the same action delegate used in the object contribution is used here as well, with a few modifications (see Section 6.4.3, IViewActionDelegate,

on page 240). The class is instantiated using its no argument constructor, but may be parameterized using the `IExecutableExtension` interface (see Section 20.5, Types Specified in an Extension Point, on page 723).

id—"com.qualityeclipse.favorites.addToFavoritesInMembersView"
The identifier for the action.

label—"Add"
The name of the action as it appears in the **Favorites** submenu.

menubarPath—"com.qualityeclipse.favorites.membersViewPopup SubMenu/content"
The insertion point that determines the location in the **Favorites** submenu where the action will appear (see Section 6.2.5, Insertion points, on page 215). If the action is to appear directly in the **Members** view context menu rather than in the **Favorites** submenu, use the value "additions" instead.

tooltip—"Add selected member's compilation unit to the Favorites view"
The text describing the action.

Other action attributes applicable but not used here include the following.

enablesFor—An expression indicating when the action will be enabled (see Section 6.3.2, Action filtering and enablement, on page 227).

helpContextId—The identifier for the help context associated with the action (see Chapter 15, Implementing Help).

icon—The associated image (see Section 6.2.4, Action images, on page 214).

overrideActionId—An optional attribute specifying the identifier for an action that the action overrides.

state—For an action with either the `radio` or `toggle` style, set the initial state to `true` or `false` (see Section 6.2.3, Defining a menu item and toolbar button, on page 212).

style—An attribute defining the visual form of the action. This is covered in Section 6.2.3, Defining a menu item and toolbar button, on page 212, with the exception that the `pulldown` style does not apply to object contributions.

You can also specify **selection** and **enablement** subelements to the action element similar to Section 6.3.2.4, The selection element, on page 231 and Section 6.3.2.5, The enablement element, on page 231.

6.4.3   *IViewActionDelegate*

The action delegate for a view contribution must implement the org.eclipse.
ui.IViewActionDelegate interface, so you need to modify the class AddTo-
FavoritesActionDelegate first introduced in Section 6.3.3, IObjectAction-
Delegate, on page 233. First, add the IViewActionDelegate interface to the
implements clause, and then add the following init() method to cache the target part. All other aspects of the action delegate stay the same.

```
public void init(IViewPart view) {
   this.targetPart = view;
}
```

6.4.4   *Defining a view toolbar action*

In addition to being in the **Favorites** submenu of the view context menu, the
action should appear as a toolbar button in the **Members** view (see Section
7.3.3, Toolbar buttons, on page 287, to programmatically add a toolbar button to a view). As in Section 6.2.1, Defining a workbench window menu, on
page 209, and subsequent sections, use the **Extensions** page of the plug-in
manifest editor to create the new view contribution. Click the **Add** button to
add an **org.eclipse.ui.viewActions** extension, then add a **viewContribution** to
that with the following attributes.

> **id**—"com.qualityeclipse.favorites.membersViewActions"
> The identifier for the view contribution.
>
> **targeted**—"org.eclipse.jdt.ui.MembersView"
> The identifier of the view to which the actions are added.

Next, add an action to the **Members** view toolbar by right-clicking on the
viewContribution, selecting **New > action**, and then entering the attributes
shown below for the new action. All the objectContribution action
attributes listed in Section 6.3.1, Defining an object-based action, on page 224
also apply to viewContribution actions.

> **class**—"com.qualityeclipse.favorites.actions.
> AddToFavoritesActionDelegate"
> The fully qualified name of the class that implements the org.eclipse.
> ui.IViewActionDelegate interface and performs the action. In this case,
> the same action delegate used in the object contribution is used here as
> well, with a few modifications (see Section 6.4.3, IViewActionDelegate, on
> page 240).
>
> **icon**—"icons/sample.gif"
> The icon displayed in the view's toolbar for the action.

id—"com.qualityeclipse.favorites.addToFavoritesInMembersView"
The identifier for the action.

toolbarPath—"additions"
The insertion point that determines the location in the **Members** view's toolbar where the action will appear (see Section 6.2.5, Insertion points, on page 215).

tooltip—"Add the selected items in the Members view to the Favorites view"
The text describing the action appearing in the hover help when the cursor is positioned over the toolbar button associated with the action.

6.4.5 *Defining a view pull-down submenu and action*

The same `viewContribution` extension described in the previous section is used to add a view pull-down submenu (see Section 7.3.2, Context menu, on page 283 to programmatically create a view pull-down menu). Typically, a view pull-down menu contains actions, such as sorting and filtering, specific to that view. To add the **Favorites** submenu and action to the **Members** view pull-down menu (not that it really needs to be there in addition to everywhere else its been added), right-click on the `viewContribution` extension, select **New > menu,** and then set the attributes of the newly created menu as follows:

id—"com.qualityeclipse.favorites.membersViewPulldownSubMenu"
The identifier for the **Favorites** menu in the **Members** view.

label—"Favorites"
The text appearing in the **Members** view pull-down menu as the name of the **Favorites** submenu.

path—"additions"
The insertion point, which determines the location in the **Members** view pull-down menu, where the **Favorites** submenu will appear (see Section 6.2.5, Insertion points, on page 215).

Next, add a **groupMarker** to the menu with the name "content" and a **separator** with the name "additions" (see Section 6.2.2, Groups in a menu, on page 212). Finally, the action defined in Section 6.4.4, Defining a view toolbar action, on page 240 can be modified to define a menu item in the menu just created as well as the toolbar button it already described by modifying some of its attributes.

label—"Add"
The name of the action appearing in the **Favorites** submenu.

menubarPath—"com.qualityeclipse.favorites.
membersViewPulldownSubMenu/content"
The insertion point, which determines the location in the **Favorites** submenu, where the action will appear (see Section 6.2.5, Insertion points,
on page 215). If the action was to appear directly in the **Members** view
pull-down menu rather than in the **Favorites** submenu, you would have
to use a value of "additions" instead.

6.4.6 Manually testing the new actions

When the modifications to the plug-in manifest and the action delegate are
complete, launching the **Runtime Workbench** and inspecting the **Members**
view will show the new **Favorites** submenu and the **Add to Favorites** toolbar
button.

6.4.7 Adding tests for the new actions

There is no need for any additional test cases other than the ones created in
Section 6.3.6, Adding a test for the new action, on page 235 because the same
action delegate is being reused. After the **Favorites** view is fleshed out as part
of Chapter 7, Views, more tests for new types of selections can be added.

6.4.8 View context menu identifiers

The context menu identifiers for some Eclipse views follow. For more information on how this list was generated, see Section 20.6, Modifying Eclipse to
Find Part Identifiers, on page 727.

Ant
```
id = org.eclipse.ant.ui.views.AntView
menuId = org.eclipse.ant.ui.views.AntView
```

Bookmarks
```
id = org.eclipse.ui.views.BookmarkView
menuId = org.eclipse.ui.views.BookmarkView
```

Breakpoints
```
id = org.eclipse.debug.ui.BreakpointView
menuId = org.eclipse.debug.ui.BreakpointView
```

Console
```
id = org.eclipse.ui.console.ConsoleView
menuId = org.eclipse.ui.console.ConsoleView
```

Debug
```
id = org.eclipse.debug.ui.DebugView
menuId = org.eclipse.debug.ui.DebugView
```

Display
```
id = org.eclipse.jdt.debug.ui.DisplayView
menuId = org.eclipse.jdt.debug.ui.DisplayView
```

Expressions
```
id = org.eclipse.debug.ui.ExpressionView
menuId = org.eclipse.debug.ui.VariableView.detail
menuId = org.eclipse.debug.ui.ExpressionView
```

Members
```
id = org.eclipse.jdt.ui.MembersView
menuId = org.eclipse.jdt.ui.MembersView
```

Memory
```
id = org.eclipse.debug.ui.MemoryView
menuId = org.eclipse.debug.ui.MemoryView.MemoryBlocksTreeViewPane
```

Navigator
```
id = org.eclipse.ui.views.ResourceNavigator
menuId = org.eclipse.ui.views.ResourceNavigator
```

Package Explorer
```
id = org.eclipse.jdt.ui.PackageExplorer
menuId = org.eclipse.jdt.ui.PackageExplorer
```

Packages
```
id = org.eclipse.jdt.ui.PackagesView
menuId = org.eclipse.jdt.ui.PackagesView
```

Problems
```
id = org.eclipse.ui.views.ProblemView
menuId = org.eclipse.ui.views.ProblemView
```

Projects
```
id = org.eclipse.jdt.ui.ProjectsView
menuId = org.eclipse.jdt.ui.ProjectsView
```

Registers
```
id = org.eclipse.debug.ui.RegisterView
menuId = org.eclipse.debug.ui.VariableView.detail
menuId = org.eclipse.debug.ui.RegisterView
```

Tasks
```
id = org.eclipse.ui.views.TaskList
menuId = org.eclipse.ui.views.TaskList
```

Threads and Monitors
```
id = org.eclipse.jdt.debug.ui.MonitorsView
menuId = org.eclipse.jdt.debug.ui.MonitorsView
```

Types
```
id = org.eclipse.jdt.ui.TypesView
menuId = org.eclipse.jdt.ui.TypesView
```

Variables
```
id = org.eclipse.debug.ui.VariableView
menuId = org.eclipse.debug.ui.VariableView.detail
menuId = org.eclipse.debug.ui.VariableView
```

6.5   Editor Actions

Actions can be added to editors in a way that is similar to how they are added to views. For example, the Java editor has a context menu, so naturally the **Favorites** action should show up there regardless of whether it's really needed (see Figure 6–10). In addition, editors can add actions to themselves bypassing the standard extension point mechanism. Some related sections include the following:

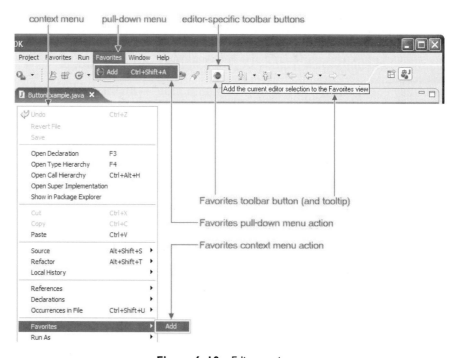

Figure 6–10   Editor actions.

- Section 8.5, Editor Actions, on page 354 for more on editor actions

- Section 14.2.4, Marker resolution—quick fix, on page 520 for an example of manipulating text in an editor

- Chapter 17, Creating New Extension Points, for more on extension points

6.5.1 Defining an editor context menu

To add the **Favorites** menu to the Java editor's context menu, revisit the **popupMenus** extension declared in Section 6.3.1, Defining an object-based action, on page 224, right-click, and then select **New > viewerContribution**. Enter the following attributes for the new viewer contribution. As with object contributions, the `visibility` subelement can be used to control when the menu and actions appear in the editor's context menu (see Section 6.3.2.2, The visibility element, on page 228).

> **id**—"com.qualityeclipse.favorites.compilationUnitEditorPopup"
> The identifier for the viewer contribution.

> **targetID**—"#CompilationUnitEditorContext"
> The identifier of the editor's context menu to which the actions will be added (see Section 20.6, Modifying Eclipse to Find Part Identifiers, on page 727).

Next, create the **Favorites** submenu in the editor's context menu by right-clicking on the new viewer contribution extension and selecting **New > menu**. Enter the following attributes for the new menu declaration.

> **id**—"com.qualityeclipse.favorites.compilationUnitEditorPopup SubMenu"
> The identifier for the **Favorites** menu in the editor's context menu.

> **label**—"Favorites"
> The text appearing in the editor's context menu as the name of the **Favorites** submenu.

> **path**—"additions"
> The insertion point that determines the location in the editor's context menu where the **Favorites** submenu will appear (see Section 6.2.5, Insertion points, on page 215).

Finally, add a **groupMarker** to the menu with the name "content" and a **separator** with the name "additions" (see Section 6.2.2, Groups in a menu, on page 212).

6.5.2 Defining an editor context action

Add the **Add to Favorites** action to the **Favorites** submenu by right-clicking on the viewer contribution defined in Section 6.5.1, Defining an editor context menu, on page 245 and selecting **New > action**. Enter the following action attributes.

> **class**—"com.qualityeclipse.favorites.actions.
> AddToFavoritesActionDelegate"
> The fully qualified name of the class that implements the `org.eclipse.`
> `ui.IEditorActionDelegate` interface and performs the action. The same action delegate used in the object contribution is used here as well, with a few modifications (see Section 6.3.3, IObjectActionDelegate, on page 233). The class is instantiated using its no argument constructor, but can be parameterized using the `IExecutableExtension` interface (see Section 20.5, Types Specified in an Extension Point, on page 723).

> **id**—"com.qualityeclipse.favorites.
> addToFavoritesInCompilationUnitEditor"
> The identifier for the action.

> **label**—"Add"
> The name of the action appearing in the **Favorites** submenu.

> **menubarPath**—"com.qualityeclipse.favorites.
> compilationUnitEditorPopupSubMenu/content"
> The insertion point that determines the location in the **Favorites** submenu where the action will appear (see Section 6.2.5, Insertion points, on page 215). To make the action appear directly in the editor's context menu rather than in the **Favorites** submenu, use a value of "additions" instead.

Other action attributes not listed here are the same as for the viewer contributions outlined in Section 6.4.2, Defining a view context menu action, on page 238.

6.5.3 IEditorActionDelegate

The action delegate for an editor contribution must implement the `org.eclipse.ui.IEditorActionDelegate` interface, so you must modify the `AddToFavoritesActionDelegate` class first introduced in Section 6.3.3, IObjectActionDelegate, on page 233.

First add the `IEditorActionDelegate` interface to the implements clause, and then add the following `setActiveEditor()` method to cache the target part. All other aspects of the action delegate can stay the same.

```
public void setActiveEditor(IAction action, IEditorPart editor) {
    this.targetPart = editor;
}
```

6.5.4   Defining an editor top-level menu

Using the `org.eclipse.ui.editorActions` extension point, you can define a workbench window menu and toolbar button that are only visible when an editor of a particular type is open. As discussed in Section 6.2.9, Discussion, on page 222, think twice before adding menus or toolbar buttons to the workbench window itself. The **Favorites** example doesn't really need this, but the following takes you through the process as a matter of course.

To start, click the **Add** button in the **Extensions** page of the plug-in manifest editor and add a new `org.eclipse.ui.editorActions` extension. Right-click on the new extension and select **New > editorContribution,** then enter the following `editorContribution` attributes.

id—"com.qualityeclipse.favorites.compilationUnitEditorActions"
The identifier for the editor contribution.

targetID—"org.eclipse.jdt.ui.CompilationUnitEditor"
The identifier of the type of editor that should be open for these menus and actions to be visible.

Add the **Favorites** menu by right-clicking on `editorContribution` and selecting **New > menu.** Enter the following attributes for the new menu.

id—"com.qualityeclipse.favorites.compilationUnitEditorPopup SubMenu"
The identifier for the **Favorites** menu.

label—"Favorites"
The text appearing in the workbench window menu bar as the name of the **Favorites** submenu.

path—"additions"
The insertion point that determines the location in the workbench window menu bar where the **Favorites** submenu will appear (see Section 6.2.5, Insertion points, on page 215).

Finally, add a **groupMarker** to the menu with the name "content" and a **separator** with the name "additions" (see Section 6.2.2, Groups in a menu, on page 212).

6.5.5 Defining an editor top-level action

Add an action to the **Favorites** menu by right-clicking on the editor-Contribution, selecting **New > action** and entering the following attributes shown for the new action. Similar to object contributions, the selection and enablement elements can be used to limit the visibility and enablement of the action (see Section 6.3.2.4, The selection element, on page 231 and Section 6.3.2.5, The enablement element, on page 231).

> **class**—"com.qualityeclipse.favorites.actions.
> AddToFavoritesActionDelegate"
> The fully qualified name of the class that implements the org.eclipse.
> ui.IEditorActionDelegate interface and performs the action. In this case, the action delegate used in the object contribution was modified in Section 6.5.3, IEditorActionDelegate, on page 246 and thus can be used here as well.
>
> **id**—"com.qualityeclipse.favorites.
> addToFavoritesInCompilationUnitEditor"
> The identifier for the action.
>
> **label**—"Add"
> The text appearing in the **Favorites** menu for the action.
>
> **menubarPath**—"com.qualityeclipse.favorites.
> compilationUnitEditorPopupSubMenu/content"
> The insertion point that indicates where the menu will be positioned in the menu bar (see Section 6.2.5, Insertion points, on page 215).

Other available action attributes that are not used in this example include the following:

> **definitionId**—The command identifier for the action, allowing a key sequence to be associated with the action. For more details, see Section 6.7, RFRS Considerations, on page 256.
>
> **enablesFor**—An expression indicating when the action will be enabled (see Section 6.3.2, Action filtering and enablement, on page 227). If blank, then the action is always active unless overridden programmatically by using the IAction interface.

helpContextId—The identifier for the help context associated with the action (see Section 15.3.1, Associating context IDs with items, on page 553).

hoverIcon—An image displayed when the mouse *hovers* over the action without being clicked (see Section 6.2.4, Action images, on page 214 for more detail).

icon—The associated image (see Section 6.2.4, Action images, on page 214 for more detail).

state—For an action with either the `radio` or `toggle` style, set the initial state to `true` or `false` (see Section 6.2.3, Defining a menu item and toolbar button, on page 212).

style—An attribute that defines the visual form of the action and that has one of the following values:

> `push`—A normal menu or toolbar item (the default style).
> `radio`—A radio button-style menu or toolbar item where only one item at a time in a group can be active (see the `state` attribute).
> `toggle`—A checked menu item or toggle tool item (see the `state` attribute).

toolbarPath—The insertion point that indicates where the button will appear in the toolbar (see Section 6.2.5, Insertion points, on page 215 for more detail).

tooltip—The text appearing when the mouse hovers over the action's icon in the workbench toolbar.

6.5.6   Defining an editor toolbar action

Similar to the way that workbench menu actions can be displayed as toolbar buttons, the editor action defined in Section 6.5.5, Defining an editor top-level action, on page 248 can be modified to show up in the workbench window toolbar by making the following modifications to its attributes:

`icon`—"icons/sample.gif"

`toolbarPath`—"Normal/additions"

`tooltip`—"Add the editor selection to the Favorites view"

6.5.7 *Adding tests for the new actions*

As stated in Section 6.4.7, Adding tests for the new actions, on page 242, tests will be added in Chapter 7, Views, for new types of selections to the same test case that was outlined in Section 6.3.6, Adding a test for the new action, on page 235.

6.5.8 *Editor context menu identifiers*

The following are the context menu identifiers for some Eclipse editors. For more information on how this list was generated, see Section 20.6, Modifying Eclipse to Find Part Identifiers, on page 727.

Ant Editor (`build.xml`)
```
id = org.eclipse.ant.ui.internal.editor.AntEditor
menuId = #TextEditorContext
menuId = #TextRulerContext
```

Class File Editor (`*.class`)
```
id = org.eclipse.jdt.ui.ClassFileEditor
menuId = #ClassFileEditorContext
menuId = #ClassFileRulerContext
```

Compilation Unit Editor (`*.java`)
```
id = org.eclipse.jdt.ui.CompilationUnitEditor
menuId = #CompilationUnitEditorContext
menuId = #CompilationUnitRulerContext
```

Default Text Editor
```
id = org.eclipse.ui.DefaultTextEditor
menuId = #TextEditorContext
menuId = #TextRulerContext
```

Snippet Editor (`*.jpage`)
```
id = org.eclipse.jdt.debug.ui.SnippetEditor
menuId = #JavaSnippetEditorContext
menuId = #JavaSnippetRulerContext
```

6.6 Key Bindings

Both workbench actions and editor actions can have accelerator keys associated with them (see Section 7.3.5, Keyboard actions, on page 288 for how to programmatically associate accelerator keys). Originally, the accelerator was specified as part of the action declaration, but that approach did not prevent multiple actions from declaring the same accelerator and did not allow the user to change key bindings. The new approach involves associating actions and key bindings with commands and grouping those commands into categories (see Figure 6–11). In addition, each command has a scope indicating when it will be available to the user, and it is part of a configuration so that the user can select between different configurations to get different key bindings (e.g., Emacs key bindings vs. Eclipse key bindings).

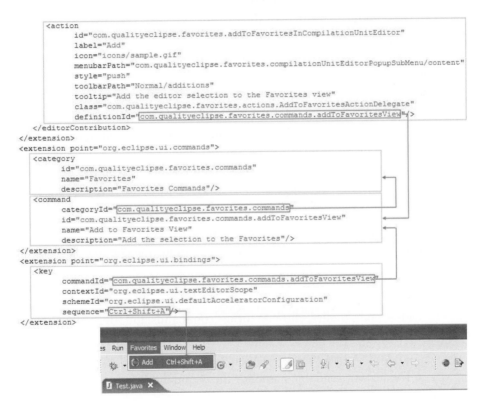

Figure 6–11   Key binding declaration.

6.6.1   Categories

Categories are used to group commands for presentation to the user. Categories appear in the **General > Keys** preference page as the first column in the table on the **View** tab and the **Command / Category** drop-down list on the **Modify** tab. To add a key binding for the **Add to Favorites** action, first you need to define a category. Create a new `org.eclipse.ui.commands` extension (see Section 6.2.1, Defining a workbench window menu, on page 209 for an example of how extensions are added), then right-click and select **New > category**. Enter the following attributes for the new category:

> **description**—"Favorites Commands"
> A description of the commands contained in the category.
>
> **id**—"com.qualityeclipse.favorites.commands"
> The unique identifier for the category.
>
> **name**—"Favorites"
> The text displayed to the user as the category name.

6.6.2   Commands

Commands are contained in categories and have key bindings associated with them. Actions then reference commands to associate key bindings. To add a command for the **Add to Favorites** action, right-click on the `org.eclipse.ui.commands` extension and select **New > command**. Enter the following attributes for the new command.

> **categoryId**—"com.qualityeclipse.favorites.commands"
> The identifier for the category that contains the command.
>
> **description**—"Add the selection to the Favorites"
> A description of the command.
>
> **id**—"com.qualityeclipse.favorites.commands.addToFavoritesView"
> The unique identifier for the command.
>
> **name**—"Add to Favorites View"
> The human-readable name for the command.

6.6.3   Key bindings

Commands do not reference key bindings; rather, key bindings are declared separately and reference commands. This allows for multiple key bindings to be associated with the same command. For example, the default accelerator for saving the contents of a file is **Ctrl+S**, but after switching to the Emacs configuration, the save accelerator becomes **Ctrl+X Ctrl+S**.

To add a key binding for the **Add to Favorites** action, create a new `org.eclipse.ui.bindings` extension (see Section 6.2.1, Defining a workbench window menu, on page 209 for an example of how extensions are added), then right-click and select **New > key**. Enter the following attributes for the new key binding. After completion, the **Favorites** key binding appears in the **Keys** preference page (see Figure 6–12).

> **commandId**—"com.qualityeclipse.favorites.commands.
> addToFavoritesView"
> The command triggered by the key binding.
>
> **contextId**—"org.eclipse.ui.textEditorScope"
> The context in which the key binding is available to the user. Some of the predefined scopes include:
>
> > `org.eclipse.ui.contexts.window`—the workbench window
> >
> > `org.eclipse.ui.textEditorScope`—text editors
> >
> > `org.eclipse.ui.contexts.dialog`—dialogs
> >
> > `org.eclipse.jdt.ui.javaEditorScope`—java editors
> >
> > `org.eclipse.debug.ui.debugging`—debugging views
> >
> > `org.eclipse.debug.ui.console`—console view

New contexts can be defined using the `org.eclipse.ui.contexts` extension point. If **contextId** is not specified, then it defaults to `org.eclipse.ui.contexts.window`.

> **schemeId**—"org.eclipse.ui.defaultAcceleratorConfiguration"
> The scheme containing the key binding. Typically, key bindings are added to the default Eclipse configuration, but alternate key bindings, such as "org.eclipse.ui. emacsAcceleratorConfiguration," can be added to other configurations. New schemes can be defined by declaring a new `scheme` element in the `org.eclipse.ui.bindings` extension.
>
> **sequence**—"Ctrl+Shift+A"
> The key sequence to assign to the command. Key sequences consist of one or more keystrokes, where a keystroke consists of a key on the keyboard, optionally pressed in combination with one or more of the following modifiers: Ctrl, Alt, Shift, Command, M1 (mapped to Ctrl or Command as appropriate on that platform), M2 (Shift) and M3 (Alt or Option as appropriate on that platform). Keystrokes are separated by spaces, and modifiers are separated by "+" characters. For example a key sequence of holding down the control key while pressing **X** followed

by holding down the control key while pressing **S** would be "**Ctrl+X Ctrl+S**". Special keys are represented by ARROW_DOWN, ARROW_LEFT, ARROW_RIGHT, ARROW_UP, BREAK, BS, CAPS_LOCK, CR, DEL, END, ESC, F1, F2, F3, F4, F5, F6, F7, F8, F9, F10, F11, F12, F13, F14, F15, FF, HOME, INSERT, LF, NUL, NUM_LOCK, NUMPAD_0, NUMPAD_1, NUMPAD_2, NUMPAD_3, NUMPAD_4, NUMPAD_5, NUMPAD_6, NUMPAD_7, NUMPAD_8, NUMPAD_9, NUMPAD_ADD, NUMPAD_DECIMAL, NUMPAD_DIVIDE, NUMPAD_ENTER, NUMPAD_EQUAL, NUMPAD_MULTIPLY, NUMPAD_SUBTRACT, PAGE_UP, PAGE_DOWN, PAUSE, PRINT_SCREEN, SCROLL_LOCK, SPACE, TAB, and VT. There are some alternative names for some common special keys. For example, both ESC and ESCAPE are the same, and CR, ENTER, and RETURN are all the same.

Other key binding attributes that are not used in the **Favorites** example include:

locale—An optional attribute indicating that the key binding is only defined for a specified locale. Locales are specified according to the format declared in `java.util.Locale`.

platform—An optional attribute indicating that the key binding is only defined for the specified platform. The possible values of the platform attribute are the set of the possible values returned by `org.eclipse.swt.SWT.getPlatform()`.

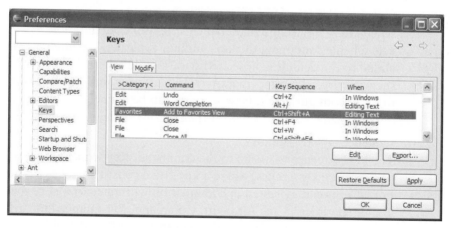

Figure 6–12 Keys preference page showing **Favorites** key binding.

6.6.4   Associating commands with actions

The final step in defining an accelerator for the **Favorites** example involves modifying the editor action defined in Section 6.5.5, Defining an editor top-level action, on page 248 to reference the new command created in Section 6.6.2, Commands, on page 252.

Select the editor action in the plug-in manifest and modify the **definitionId** attribute to have the value "com.qualityeclipse.favorites.commands.addToFavoritesView" so that the action now references the new command and associated key binding.

6.6.5   Keyboard accessibility

The keyboard can be used to select menu items in the workbench window. For example, if you press and release the **Alt** key and then press and release **F** (or press **Alt+F**), you will see the workbench window **File** menu drop down. If you look closely, you will see an underscore under at most one letter in each menu label and menu item label. When you are in this menu selection mode, pressing the letter with the underscore will activate that menu or menu command. Under some platforms, such as Windows XP, these underscores are not visible unless you activate menu selection mode.

In your plug-in manifest, you can specify which character in a menu's or menu item's label should have an underscore by preceding that character with the "&" character. For example, in the following declaration, the "&" before the letter "r" in the word "Favorites" causes that letter to have an underscore when you activate the menu selection mode (see Figure 6–13).

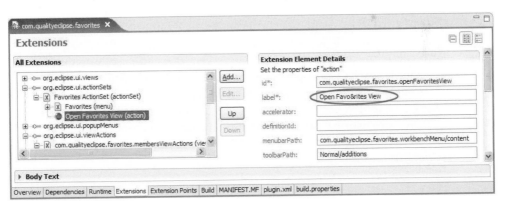

Figure 6–13   Plug-in manifest editor showing & for keyboard accessibility.

When viewing the XML for this same declaration, the & character appears as **&** because the & character has special meaning in XML.

```
<action
    class="com.qualityeclipse.....OpenFavoritesViewActionDelegate"
    icon="icons/sample.gif"
    id="com.qualityeclipse.favorites.openFavoritesView"
    label="Open Favo&amp;rites View"
    menubarPath="com.qualityeclipse.favorites.workbenchMenu/content"
    style="push"
    toolbarPath="Normal/additions"
    tooltip="Open the Favorites view in the current workbench page"/>
```

If you use this same approach with the **Favorites** menu declaration (see Section 6.2.1, Defining a workbench window menu, on page 209), you can use a sequence of keystrokes to open the **Favorites** view without touching the mouse.

- Press and release the **Alt** key to enter menu selection mode.
- Press and release "v" to get the **Favorites** menu to drop down.
- Press and release "r" to activate the **Open Favorites View** action.

  or

- Press **Alt+V** to get the **Favorites** menu to drop down.
- Press and release "r" to activate the **Open Favorites View** action.

> **Ready for Rational Software**   Starting with this chapter, we will list IBM's relevant RFRS certification requirements and briefly discuss what is required to pass each test. We will also endeavor to make sure that the ongoing **Favorites** example complies with any relevant requirements. The rule definitions themselves are quoted with permission from IBM's official *Ready for IBM Rational Software Integration Requirements* document. To obtain more information about the RFRS program, see Appendix B, Ready for Rational Software, or visit the IBM Web site at *www.developer.ibm.com/ isv/rational/ readyfor.html.*

6.7 RFRS Considerations

The "User Interface" section of the *RFRS Requirements* includes one best practice dealing with actions. It is derived from the Eclipse UI Guidelines.

6.7.1   Global action labels   (RFRS 5.3.5.1)

User Interface Guideline #3.3 is a **best practice** that states:

> *Adopt the labeling terminology of the workbench for **new, delete, add,** and **remove** actions. For consistency, any action that has a similar behavior to existing actions in the workbench should adopt the same terminology. When creating a resource, the term "**New**" should be used in an action or wizard. For instance, "**New File**", "**New Project**", and "**New Java Class**". The term "**Delete**" should be used when deleting an existing resource. When creating an object inside a resource (e.g., a tag in an XML file), the term "**Add**" should be used; the user is adding something to an existing resource. The term "**Remove**" should be used to remove an object from a resource.*

To pass this test, create a list of the actions defined by your application and demonstrate their use. Show that the terms **New, Delete, Add,** and **Remove** are used properly and consistently with the workbench. In the case of the examples presented earlier in this chapter, it is preferable to show the **Favorites** editor actions (see Figure 6–10) and describe their use to the reviewers.

6.8   Summary

An Eclipse user can trigger commands by using the workbench's pull-down menus or toolbar or by using the context menus defined for various views. Each of these is an example of an action. This chapter discussed how to create various actions and how to control their visibility and enablement state using filters.

References

Chapter source (*www.qualityeclipse.com/projects/source-ch-06.zip*).

Arsenault, Simon, "Contributing Actions to the Eclipse Workbench," 2003 (available on the *eclipse.org* Web site at *www.eclipse.org/articles*).

D'Anjou, Jim, Scott Fairbrother, Dan Kehn, John Kellerman, and Pat McCarthy, *The Java Developer's Guide to Eclipse, Second Edition.* Addison-Wesley, Boston, 2004.

CHAPTER 7

Views

Many plug-ins either add a new Eclipse view or enhance an existing one as a way to provide information to the user. This chapter covers creating a new view, modifying the view to respond to selections in the active editor or other views, and exporting the view's selection to the rest of Eclipse. In addition, it briefly touches on the differences between editors and views, and when one should be used instead of the other.

Views must implement the `org.eclipse.ui.IViewPart` interface. Typically, views are subclasses of `org.eclipse.ui.part.ViewPart` and thus indirectly subclasses of `org.eclipse.ui.part.WorkbenchPart`, inheriting much of the behavior needed to implement the `IViewPart` interface (see Figure 7–1).

Views are contained in a *view site* (an instance of the class, `org.eclipse.ui.IViewSite`), which in turn is contained in a *workbench page* (an instance of `org.eclipse.ui.IWorkbenchPage`). In the spirit of lazy initialization, the `IWorkbenchPage` instance holds on to instances of `org.eclipse.ui.IViewReference` rather than the view itself so that views can be enumerated and referenced without actually loading the plug-in that defines the view.

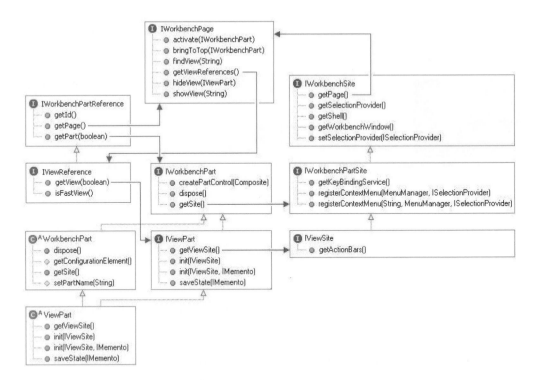

Figure 7–1   ViewPart classes.

Views share a common set of behaviors with editors via the superclass `org.eclipse.ui.part.WorkbenchPart` and the `org.eclipse.ui.IWorkbenchPart` interface but have some very important differences. Any action performed in a view should immediately affect the state of the workspace and the underlying resource(s), whereas editors follow the classic open-modify-save paradigm.

Editors appear in one area of Eclipse, while views are arranged around the outside of the editor area (see Section 1.2.1, Perspectives, views, and editors, on page 5). Editors are typically resource-based, while views may show information about one resource, multiple resources, or even something totally unrelated to resources at all.

Because there are potentially hundreds of views in the workbench, they are organized into categories. The **Show View** dialog presents a list of views organized by category (see Section 2.5, Installing and Running the Product, on page 86) so that a user can more easily find a desired view.

7.1 View Declaration

Three steps are involved in creating a new view:

- Define the view category in the plug-in manifest file.
- Define the view in the plug-in manifest file.
- Create the view part containing the code.

One way to do all this at once is to create the view when the plug-in itself is being created (see Section 2.2.3, Define the view, on page 69). If the plug-in already exists, then this becomes a three-step process.

7.1.1 Declaring a view category

First, to define a new view category, edit the plug-in manifest and navigate to the **Extensions** page. Click the **Add...** button to add the org.eclipse. ui.views extension if it is not already present (see Figure 7–2). Right-click the org.eclipse.ui.views extension and select **New > category** to add a new category if one does not exist already.

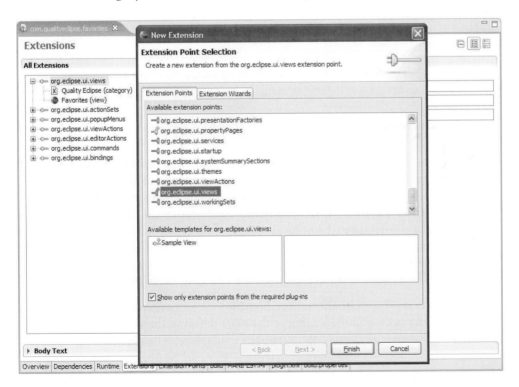

Figure 7–2 The New Extension wizard with the org.eclipse.ui.views extension point selected.

The properties for this category can be modified in the plug-in manifest editor (see Figure 7–3). For the category containing the **Favorites** view, the attributes would be as follows:

id—"com.qualityeclipse.favorites"
The unique identifier for the category.

name—"Quality Eclipse"
The human-readable name for the category that appears in the **Show View** dialog (see Figure 2–20 on page 87).

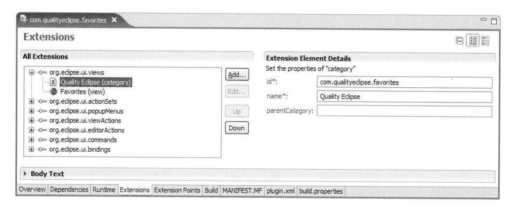

Figure 7–3   The Plug-in manifest editor showing the Quality Eclipse view category.

7.1.2   Declaring a view

When the view category has been defined, right-click again on the `org.eclipse.ui.views` extension in the **Extensions** page and select **New > view** to define a new view. Use the **Extension Element Details** section of the editor (see Figure 7–4) to modify the attributes of the view. For the **Favorites** view, the attributes would be as follows:

category—"com.qualityeclipse.favorites"
The unique identifier for the view category that contains this view.

class—"com.qualityeclipse.favorites.views.FavoritesView"
The fully qualified name of the class defining the view and implementing the `org.eclipse.ui.IViewPart` interface. The class is instantiated using its no argument constructor, but can be parameterized using the `IExecutableExtension` interface (see Section 20.5, Types Specified in an Extension Point, on page 723).

icon—"icons/sample.gif"
The image displayed in the upper left corner of the view and in the **Show View** dialog (see Figure 2–20 on page 87). Similar to an action image (see Section 6.2.4, Action images, on page 214), this path is relative to the plug-in's installation directory.

id—"com.qualityeclipse.favorites.views.FavoritesView"
The unique identifier for this view.

name—"Favorites"
The human-readable name for the view displayed in the view's title bar and the **Show View** dialog (see Figure 2–20 on page 87).

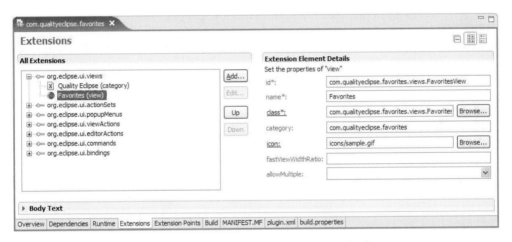

Figure 7–4   The Plug-in manifest editor view showing the Favorites view.

7.2   View Part

The code defining a view's behavior is found in a class implementing the `org.eclipse.ui.IViewPart` interface, typically by subclassing the `org.eclipse.ui.part.ViewPart` abstract class.

Section 2.3.3, The Favorites view, on page 78 reviewed the **Favorites** view in its simplest form.

7.2.1   View methods

IViewPart and its supertypes define the following methods.

`createPartControl(Composite)`—This method is *required* because it creates the controls comprising the view. Typically, this method simply calls more finely grained methods such as `createTable`, `createSort-Actions`, `createFilters`, and so on (see the next section).

dispose()—Cleans up any platform resources, such as images, clipboard, and so on, that were created by this class. This follows the *if you create it, you destroy it* theme that runs throughout Eclipse.

getAdapter(Class)—Returns the adapter associated with the specified interface so that the view can participate in various workbench actions. Adapters returned by views include IShowInSource, IShowInTarget, and IContributedContentsView, among others (see Section 20.3, Adapters, on page 714).

saveState(IMemento)—Saves the local state of this view, such as the current selection, current sorting, current filter, and so on (see Section 7.5.1, Saving local view information, on page 308).

setFocus()—This method is *required* because it sets focus to the appropriate control within the view (see the next section).

7.2.2 View controls

Views can contain any type and number of controls, but typically, a view such as the **Favorites** view contains a single table or tree control. The **Favorites** view could use the SWT table widget directly (org.eclipse.swt.widgets.Table —see Section 4.2.6.6, Table, on page 154); however, the higher-level JFace table viewer (org.eclipse.jface.viewers.TableViewer—see Section 5.1.7, Table Viewer class, on page 195) wraps the SWT table widget and is easier to use. It handles much of the underlying grunt work, allowing you to add, select, and remove model objects directly rather than dealing with the underlying instances of TableItem.

With this in mind, let's start by adding three new fields to the FavoritesView class:

```
private TableColumn typeColumn;
private TableColumn nameColumn;
private TableColumn locationColumn;
```

You should continue to enhance the createPartControl() method that was generated as part of building the **Favorites** plug-in (see Section 2.3.3, The Favorites view, on page 78) so that the table has three columns. The SWT.FULL_SELECTION style bit causes the entire row to be highlighted when the user makes a selection.

```
viewer = new TableViewer(parent,
   SWT.H_SCROLL | SWT.V_SCROLL | SWT.MULTI | SWT.FULL_SELECTION);
final Table table = viewer.getTable();

typeColumn = new TableColumn(table, SWT.LEFT);
typeColumn.setText("");
typeColumn.setWidth(18);

nameColumn = new TableColumn(table, SWT.LEFT);
nameColumn.setText("Name");
nameColumn.setWidth(200);

locationColumn = new TableColumn(table, SWT.LEFT);
locationColumn.setText("Location");
locationColumn.setWidth(450);

table.setHeaderVisible(true);
table.setLinesVisible(false);

viewer.setContentProvider(new ViewContentProvider());
viewer.setLabelProvider(new ViewLabelProvider());
viewer.setInput(getViewSite());
```

Later, when you want to get more involved, auto-size the columns in the table (see Section 7.8, Auto-sizing Table Columns, on page 316).

7.2.3 View model

A view can have its own internal model such as the **Favorites** view, it can use existing model objects such as an `IResource` and its subtypes, or it may not have a model at all. In this case, create:

- `IFavoriteItem`—An interface used to abstract the differences between different types of **Favorites** objects.

- `FavoritesManager`—Holds **Favorites** model objects.

- `FavoriteResource`—A class adapting a resource to the `IFavoriteItem` interface.

- `FavoriteJavaElement`—A class adapting a Java element to the `IFavoriteItem` interface.

The `IFavoriteItem` interface hides the differences between various types of **Favorites** objects. This enables the `FavoritesManager` and `Favorites-View` to deal with all **Favorites** items in a uniform manner. The naming convention followed, which is used in many places throughout Eclipse, is to prefix an interface with a capital "I" so that the interface name is `IFavoriteItem` rather than `FavoriteItem`, as one would expect (see Section 7.4.2, Adaptable objects, on page 306 for more on `IAdaptable`).

```
package com.qualityeclipse.favorites.model;

public interface IFavoriteItem
   extends IAdaptable
{
   String getName();
   void setName(String newName);
   String getLocation();
   boolean isFavoriteFor(Object obj);
   FavoriteItemType getType();
   String getInfo();

   static IFavoriteItem[] NONE = new IFavoriteItem[] {};
}
```

Later, **Favorites** items will be serialized so that they can be placed on the clipboard (see Section 7.3.7, Clipboard actions, on page 290) and saved to disk between Eclipse workbench sessions (see Section 7.5.2, Saving global view information, on page 311). To this end, the getInfo() method for each item must return enough state so that the item can be correctly reconstructed later.

The FavoriteItemType object returned by the getType() method is a type-safe enumeration that can be used for sorting and storing **Favorites** objects. It has a human-readable name associated with it for display purposes. Introducing the FavoriteItemType rather than a simple String or int allows the sort order to be separated from the human-readable name associated with a type of **Favorites** object.

```
package com.qualityeclipse.favorites.model;

import ...

public abstract class FavoriteItemType
   implements Comparable
{
   private static final ISharedImages PLATFORM_IMAGES =
      PlatformUI.getWorkbench().getSharedImages();
```

Next, you need to add a constructor plus some fields and accessors to the FavoriteItemType used by the **Favorites** view to sort and display **Favorites** items. Since the workbench already provides images for various types of resources, the FavoriteItemType object simply returns the appropriate shared image. To return custom images for other types of **Favorites** objects, you could cache those images during the life of the plug-in and dispose of them when the plug-in is shut down (see Section 7.7, Image Caching, on page 315).

```
private final String id;
private final String printName;
private final int ordinal;

private FavoriteItemType(String id, String name, int position) {
   this.id = id;
   this.ordinal = position;
   this.printName = name;
}

public String getId() {
   return id;
}

public String getName() {
   return printName;
}

public abstract Image getImage();
public abstract IFavoriteItem newFavorite(Object obj);
public abstract IFavoriteItem loadFavorite(String info);
```

The `FavoriteItemType` implements the `Comparable` interface, for sorting purposes, so must implement the `compareTo` method.

```
public int compareTo(Object arg) {
   return this.ordinal - ((FavoriteItemType) arg).ordinal;
}
```

Next, add public static fields for each of the known types of Favorites. For now, these instances are hard-coded; however, in the future, these instances will be defined by an extension point so that others can introduce new types of Favorites (see Section 17.3, Code Behind an Extension Point, on page 607). These new public static fields depend on the `org.eclipse.core.resources`, `org.eclipse.ui.ide`, and `org.eclipse.jdt.core` plug-ins, so use the **Dependencies** page of the plug-in manifest editor (see Figure 2–10 on page 73) to add these required plug-ins, and then save the changes.

```
public static final FavoriteItemType UNKNOWN
   = new FavoriteItemType("Unknown", "Unknown", 0)
{
   public Image getImage() {
      return null;
   }

   public IFavoriteItem newFavorite(Object obj) {
      return null;
   }
```

```
      public IFavoriteItem loadFavorite(String info) {
         return null;
      }
};

public static final FavoriteItemType WORKBENCH_FILE
      = new FavoriteItemType("WBFile", "Workbench File", 1)
{
   public Image getImage() {
      return PLATFORM_IMAGES
            .getImage(org.eclipse.ui.ISharedImages.IMG_OBJ_FILE);
   }

   public IFavoriteItem newFavorite(Object obj) {
      if (!(obj instanceof IFile))
         return null;
      return new FavoriteResource(this, (IFile) obj);
   }

   public IFavoriteItem loadFavorite(String info) {
      return FavoriteResource.loadFavorite(this, info);
   }
};

public static final FavoriteItemType WORKBENCH_FOLDER
      = new FavoriteItemType("WBFolder", "Workbench Folder", 2)
{
   public Image getImage() {
      return PLATFORM_IMAGES
            .getImage(org.eclipse.ui.ISharedImages.IMG_OBJ_FOLDER);
   }

   public IFavoriteItem newFavorite(Object obj) {
      if (!(obj instanceof IFolder))
         return null;
      return new FavoriteResource(this, (IFolder) obj);
   }

   public IFavoriteItem loadFavorite(String info) {
      return FavoriteResource.loadFavorite(this, info);
   }
};

... more of the same ...
```

Finally, create a static array containing all known types and a getTypes()
method that will return all known types.

```
private static final FavoriteItemType[] TYPES = {
   UNKNOWN, WORKBENCH_FILE, WORKBENCH_FOLDER, WORKBENCH_PROJECT,
   JAVA_PROJECT, JAVA_PACKAGE_ROOT, JAVA_PACKAGE,
   JAVA_CLASS_FILE, JAVA_COMP_UNIT, JAVA_INTERFACE, JAVA_CLASS};

public static FavoriteItemType[] getTypes() {
   return TYPES;
}
```

All **Favorites** views should show the same collection of **Favorites** objects, so the FavoritesManager is a singleton responsible for maintaining this global collection.

```
package com.qualityeclipse.favorites.model;

import ...

public class FavoritesManager {
   private static FavoritesManager manager;
   private Collection favorites;

   private FavoritesManager() {}

   public static FavoritesManager getManager() {
      if (manager == null)
         manager = new FavoritesManager();
      return manager;
   }

   public IFavoriteItem[] getFavorites() {
      if (favorites == null)
         loadFavorites();
      return (IFavoriteItem[]) favorites.toArray(
         new IFavoriteItem[favorites.size()]);
   }

   private void loadFavorites() {
      // temporary implementation
      // to prepopulate list with projects
      IProject[] projects = ResourcesPlugin.getWorkspace().getRoot()
            .getProjects();
      favorites = new HashSet(projects.length);
      for (int i = 0; i < projects.length; i++)
         favorites.add(new FavoriteResource(
               FavoriteItemType.WORKBENCH_PROJECT, projects[i]));
   }
```

The manager needs to look up existing **Favorites** objects and create new ones.

```
public IFavoriteItem newFavoriteFor(Object obj) {
   FavoriteItemType[] types = FavoriteItemType.getTypes();
   for (int i = 0; i < types.length; i++) {
      IFavoriteItem item = types[i].newFavorite(obj);
      if (item != null)
         return item;
   }
   return null;
}
```

```
public IFavoriteItem[] newFavoritesFor(Iterator iter) {
    if (iter == null)
        return IFavoriteItem.NONE;
    Collection items = new HashSet(20);
    while (iter.hasNext()) {
        IFavoriteItem item = newFavoriteFor((Object) iter.next());
        if (item != null)
            items.add(item);
    }
    return (IFavoriteItem[]) items.toArray(new IFavoriteItem[items
        .size()]);
}

public IFavoriteItem[] newFavoritesFor(Object[] objects) {
    if (objects == null)
        return IFavoriteItem.NONE;
    return newFavoritesFor(Arrays.asList(objects).iterator());
}

public IFavoriteItem existingFavoriteFor(Object obj) {
    if (obj == null)
        return null;
    Iterator iter = favorites.iterator();
    while (iter.hasNext()) {
        IFavoriteItem item = (IFavoriteItem) iter.next();
        if (item.isFavoriteFor(obj))
            return item;
    }
    return null;
}

public IFavoriteItem[] existingFavoritesFor(Iterator iter) {
    List result = new ArrayList(10);
    while (iter.hasNext()) {
        IFavoriteItem item = existingFavoriteFor(iter.next());

        if (item != null)
            result.add(item);
    }
    return (IFavoriteItem[]) result
        .toArray(new IFavoriteItem[result.size()]);
}

public void addFavorites(IFavoriteItem[] items) {
    if (favorites == null)
        loadFavorites();
    if (favorites.addAll(Arrays.asList(items)))
        fireFavoritesChanged(items, IFavoriteItem.NONE);
}

public void removeFavorites(IFavoriteItem[] items) {
    if (favorites == null)
        loadFavorites();
    if (favorites.removeAll(Arrays.asList(items)))
        fireFavoritesChanged(IFavoriteItem.NONE, items);
}
```

Since more than one view will be accessing the information, the manager must be able to notify registered listeners when the information changes. The FavoritesManager will only be accessed from the UI thread, so you do not need to worry about thread safety (see Section 4.2.5.1, Display, on page 140 for more about the UI thread).

```
private List listeners = new ArrayList();

public void addFavoritesManagerListener(
   FavoritesManagerListener listener
) {
   if (!listeners.contains(listener))
      listeners.add(listener);
}

public void removeFavoritesManagerListener(
   FavoritesManagerListener listener
) {
   listeners.remove(listener);
}

private void fireFavoritesChanged(
   IFavoriteItem[] itemsAdded, IFavoriteItem[] itemsRemoved
) {
   FavoritesManagerEvent event = new FavoritesManagerEvent(
      this, itemsAdded, itemsRemoved);
   for (Iterator iter = listeners.iterator(); iter.hasNext();)
      ((FavoritesManagerListener) iter.next())
            .favoritesChanged(event);
}
```

The FavoritesManager uses the FavoritesManagerListener and FavoritesManagerEvent classes to notify interested objects of changes.

```
package com.qualityeclipse.favorites.model;

public interface FavoritesManagerListener
{
   public void favoritesChanged(FavoritesManagerEvent event);
}

package com.qualityeclipse.favorites.model;

import java.util.EventObject;

public class FavoritesManagerEvent extends EventObject
{
   private static final long serialVersionUID = 3697053173951102953L;

   private final IFavoriteItem[] added;
   private final IFavoriteItem[] removed;
```

```
public FavoritesManagerEvent(
   FavoritesManager source,
   IFavoriteItem[] itemsAdded, IFavoriteItem[] itemsRemoved
) {
   super(source);
   added = itemsAdded;
   removed = itemsRemoved;
}

public IFavoriteItem[] getItemsAdded() {
   return added;
}

public IFavoriteItem[] getItemsRemoved() {
   return removed;
}
}
```

In the future, the FavoritesManager will be enhanced to allow the list to persist between Eclipse sessions (see Section 7.5.2, Saving global view information, on page 311), but for now, the list will be initialized with current workspace projects every time Eclipse starts. In addition, the current implementation will be extended in future chapters to include **Favorites** types added by other plug-ins (see Section 17.3, Code Behind an Extension Point, on page 607).

The FavoriteResource wraps an IResource object, adapting it to the IFavoriteItem interface.

```
package com.qualityeclipse.favorites.model;

import ...

public class FavoriteResource
   implements IFavoriteItem
{
   private FavoriteItemType type;
   private IResource resource;
   private String name;

   FavoriteResource(FavoriteItemType type, IResource resource) {
      this.type = type;
      this.resource = resource;
   }

   public static FavoriteResource loadFavorite(
      FavoriteItemType type, String info)
   {
      IResource res = ResourcesPlugin.getWorkspace().getRoot()
            .findMember(new Path(info));
      if (res == null)
         return null;
      return new FavoriteResource(type, res);
   }
```

```
public String getName() {
    if (name == null)
        name = resource.getName();
    return name;
}

public void setName(String newName) {
    name = newName;
}

public String getLocation() {
    IPath path = resource.getLocation().removeLastSegments(1);
    if (path.segmentCount() == 0)
        return "";
    return path.toString();
}

public boolean isFavoriteFor(Object obj) {
    return resource.equals(obj);
}

public FavoriteItemType getType() {
    return type;
}

public boolean equals(Object obj) {
    return this == obj || (
        (obj instanceof FavoriteResource)
        && resource.equals(((FavoriteResource) obj).resource));
}

public int hashCode() {
    return resource.hashCode();
}

public Object getAdapter(Class adapter) {
    if (adapter.isInstance(resource))
        return resource;
    return Platform.getAdapterManager().getAdapter(this, adapter);
}

public String getInfo() {
    return resource.getFullPath().toString();
}
}
```

Similar to the `FavoriteResource`, the `FavoriteJavaElement` adapts an `IJavaElement` object to the `IFavoriteItem` interface. Before creating this class, you'll need to add the `org.eclipse.jdt.ui` plug-in to the **Favorites** plug-in's manifest (see Figure 7–5).

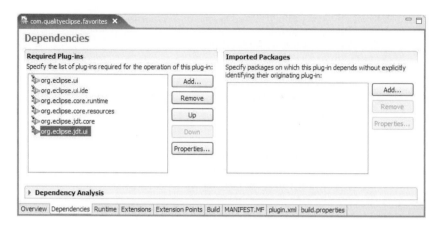

Figure 7–5   Plug-in manifest editor Dependencies page.

If the project is a plug-in project (see Section 2.2, Creating a Plug-in Project, on page 66), modifying the plug-in's manifest causes the project's Java build path to be automatically updated.

```
package com.qualityeclipse.favorites.model;

import ...

public class FavoriteJavaElement
   implements IFavoriteItem
{
   private FavoriteItemType type;
   private IJavaElement element;
   private String name;

   public FavoriteJavaElement(
      FavoriteItemType type, IJavaElement element
   ) {
      this.type = type;
      this.element = element;
   }

   public static FavoriteJavaElement loadFavorite(
      FavoriteItemType type, String info
   ) {
      IResource res = ResourcesPlugin.getWorkspace().getRoot()
            .findMember(new Path(info));
      if (res == null)
         return null;
      IJavaElement elem = JavaCore.create(res);
      if (elem == null)
         return null;
      return new FavoriteJavaElement(type, elem);
   }
```

```java
public String getName() {
    if (name == null)
        name = element.getElementName();
    return name;
}

public void setName(String newName) {
    name = newName;
}

public String getLocation() {
    try {
        IResource res = element.getUnderlyingResource();
        if (res != null) {
            IPath path = res.getLocation().removeLastSegments(1);
            if (path.segmentCount() == 0)
                return "";
            return path.toString();
        }
    }
    catch (JavaModelException e) {
        FavoritesLog.logError(e);
    }
    return "";
}

public boolean isFavoriteFor(Object obj) {
    return element.equals(obj);
}

public FavoriteItemType getType() {
    return type;
}

public boolean equals(Object obj) {
    return this == obj || (
        (obj instanceof FavoriteJavaElement)
        && element.equals(((FavoriteJavaElement) obj).element));
}

public int hashCode() {
    return element.hashCode();
}

public Object getAdapter(Class adapter) {
    if (adapter.isInstance(element))
        return element;
    IResource resource = element.getResource();
    if (adapter.isInstance(resource))
        return resource;
    return Platform.getAdapterManager().getAdapter(this, adapter);
}
```

```
    public String getInfo() {
        try {
            return element.getUnderlyingResource().getFullPath()
                    .toString();
        }
        catch (JavaModelException e) {
            FavoritesLog.logError(e);
            return null;
        }
    }
}
```

7.2.4 Content provider

When the model objects have been created, they need to be linked into the view. A content provider is responsible for extracting objects from an input object—in this case, the FavoritesManager—and handing them to the table viewer for displaying, one object in each row. Although the IStructured-ContentProvider does not specify this, the content provider has also been made responsible for updating the viewer when the content of Favorites-Manager changes.

After extracting the content provider that was automatically generated as part of the FavoritesView class (see Section 2.3.2, The Plug-in class, on page 77) and reworking it to use the newly created FavoritesManager, it looks something like the following code.

```
package com.qualityeclipse.favorites.views;

import ...

class FavoritesViewContentProvider
    implements IStructuredContentProvider, FavoritesManagerListener
{
    private TableViewer viewer;
    private FavoritesManager manager;

    public void inputChanged(
        Viewer viewer, Object oldInput, Object newInput
    ) {
        this.viewer = (TableViewer) viewer;
        if (manager != null)
            manager.removeFavoritesManagerListener(this);
        manager = (FavoritesManager) newInput;
        if (manager != null)
            manager.addFavoritesManagerListener(this);
    }

    public void dispose() {
    }
```

```
    public Object[] getElements(Object parent) {
        return manager.getFavorites();
    }

    public void favoritesChanged(FavoritesManagerEvent event) {
        viewer.getTable().setRedraw(false);
        try {
            viewer.remove(event.getItemsRemoved());
            viewer.add(event.getItemsAdded());
        }
        finally {
            viewer.getTable().setRedraw(true);
        }
    }
}
```

> **Tip:** The preceding method uses the `setRedraw` method to reduce the flicker when adding and removing multiple items from the viewer.

Extracting and modifying the content provider means that the calls to `setContentProvider` and `setInput` in the `createPartControl` method have changed as follows:

```
viewer.setContentProvider(new FavoritesViewContentProvider());
viewer.setInput(FavoritesManager.getManager());
```

7.2.5 *Label provider*

The label provider takes a table row object returned by the content provider and extracts the value to be displayed in a column. After refactoring the `FavoritesView.ViewLabelProvider` inner class (see Section 2.3.3, The Favorites view, on page 78) into a top-level class and reworking it to extract values from the newly created model object, it looks something like the following code.

```
package com.qualityeclipse.favorites.views;

import ...

class FavoritesViewLabelProvider extends LabelProvider
    implements ITableLabelProvider
{
    public String getColumnText(Object obj, int index) {
        switch (index) {
        case 0: // Type column
            return "";
```

```
        case 1: // Name column
            if (obj instanceof IFavoriteItem)
                return ((IFavoriteItem) obj).getName();
            if (obj != null)
                return obj.toString();
            return "";
        case 2: // Location column
            if (obj instanceof IFavoriteItem)
                return ((IFavoriteItem) obj).getLocation();
            return "";
        default:
            return "";
        }
    }

    public Image getColumnImage(Object obj, int index) {
        if ((index == 0) && (obj instanceof IFavoriteItem))
            return ((IFavoriteItem) obj).getType().getImage();
        return null;
    }
}
```

> **Tip:** If you are displaying workbench-related objects,
> `WorkbenchLabelProvider` and `WorkbenchPartLabelProvider`
> contain behavior for determining text and images for workbench resources
> implementing the `IWorkbenchAdapter` interface (see Section 20.3.4,
> IWorkbenchAdapter, on page 718). For lists and single-column trees and
> tables, implement `IViewerLabelProvider` to efficiently set text, image,
> font, and color by implementing a single `updateLabel()` method;
> otherwise, implement `IFontProvider` and `IColorProvider` to provide
> font and color information, respectively.

7.2.6 Viewer sorter

Although a content provider serves up row objects, it is the responsibility of
the `ViewerSorter` to sort the row objects before they are displayed. In the
Favorites view, there are currently three criteria by which items can be sorted
in either ascending or descending order:

- Name
- Type
- Location

The `FavoritesViewSorter` delegates sorting to three comparators, one
for each of the criteria just listed. In addition, the `FavoritesViewSorter` listens for mouse clicks in the column headers and resorts the table content
based on the column that was selected. Clicking on a column a second time
toggles the sort order.

```java
package com.qualityeclipse.favorites.views;
import ...

public class FavoritesViewSorter extends ViewerSorter
{
   // Simple data structure for grouping
   // sort information by column.
   private class SortInfo {
      int columnIndex;
      Comparator comparator;
      boolean descending;
   }

   private TableViewer viewer;
   private SortInfo[] infos;

   public FavoritesViewSorter(
      TableViewer viewer,
      TableColumn[] columns,
      Comparator[] comparators
   ) {
      this.viewer = viewer;
      infos = new SortInfo[columns.length];
      for (int i = 0; i < columns.length; i++) {
         infos[i] = new SortInfo();
         infos[i].columnIndex = i;
         infos[i].comparator = comparators[i];
         infos[i].descending = false;
         createSelectionListener(columns[i], infos[i]);
      }
   }

   public int compare(
      Viewer viewer, Object favorite1, Object favorite2
   ) {
      for (int i = 0; i < infos.length; i++) {
         int result = infos[i].comparator
            .compare(favorite1, favorite2);
         if (result != 0) {
            if (infos[i].descending)
               return -result;
            return result;
         }
      }
      return 0;
   }

   private void createSelectionListener(
      final TableColumn column, final SortInfo info
   ) {
      column.addSelectionListener(new SelectionAdapter() {
         public void widgetSelected(SelectionEvent e) {
            sortUsing(info);
         }
      });
   }
```

```
protected void sortUsing(SortInfo info) {
   if (info == infos[0])
      info.descending = !info.descending;
   else {
      for (int i = 0; i < infos.length; i++) {
         if (info == infos[i]) {
            System.arraycopy(infos, 0, infos, 1, i);
            infos[0] = info;
            info.descending = false;
            break;
         }
      }
   }
   viewer.refresh();
}
```

A new field in `FavoritesView` is introduced now to hold the sorter instance:

```
private FavoritesViewSorter sorter;
```

and the **Favorites** view `createPartControl(Composite)` method is modified to call the new method shown below. Later, the current sort order, as chosen by the user, must be preserved between Eclipse sessions (see Section 7.5.1, Saving local view information, on page 308).

```
private void createTableSorter() {
   Comparator nameComparator = new Comparator() {
      public int compare(Object o1, Object o2) {
         return ((IFavoriteItem) o1)
            .getName()
            .compareTo(
            ((IFavoriteItem) o2).getName());
      }
   };
   Comparator locationComparator = new Comparator() {
      public int compare(Object o1, Object o2) {
         return ((IFavoriteItem) o1)
            .getLocation()
            .compareTo(
            ((IFavoriteItem) o2).getLocation());
      }
   };
   Comparator typeComparator = new Comparator() {
      public int compare(Object o1, Object o2) {
         return ((IFavoriteItem) o1)
            .getType()
            .compareTo(
            ((IFavoriteItem) o2).getType());
      }
   };
```

```
    sorter = new FavoritesViewSorter(
       viewer,
       new TableColumn[] {
          nameColumn, locationColumn, typeColumn },
       new Comparator[] {
          nameComparator, locationComparator, typeComparator
       });
    viewer.setSorter(sorter);
}
```

7.2.7 Viewer filters

ViewerFilter subclasses determine which of the row objects returned by a content provider will be displayed and which will not. While there can be only one content provider, only one label provider, and only one sorter, there can be any number of filters associated with a viewer. When multiple filters are applied, only those items that satisfy all the applied filters will be displayed.

Similar to the sorting just discussed, the **Favorites** view can be filtered by:

- Name
- Type
- Location

Eclipse provides the org.eclipse.ui.internal.misc.StringMatcher type, which is ideal for wildcard filtering, but since the class is in an internal package, the first step is to copy the class into the com.qualityeclipse. favorites.util package. Although copying sounds horrid, there are already 10 copies of this particular class in various locations throughout Eclipse, all of them internal (see Section 20.2, Accessing Internal Code, on page 711 for more on internal packages and the issues that surround them).

After that is complete, the ViewerFilter class for filtering the **Favorites** view by name looks like this (see below). This viewer filter is hooked up to the **Favorites** view using an action delegate in Section 7.3.4, Pull-down menu, on page 287.

```
package com.qualityeclipse.favorites.views;

import ...

public class FavoritesViewNameFilter extends ViewerFilter
{
    private final StructuredViewer viewer;
    private String pattern = "";
    private StringMatcher matcher;
```

```
   public FavoritesViewNameFilter(StructuredViewer viewer) {
      this.viewer = viewer;
   }

   public String getPattern() {
      return pattern;
   }

   public void setPattern(String newPattern) {
      boolean filtering = matcher != null;
      if (newPattern != null && newPattern.trim().length() > 0) {
         pattern = newPattern;
         matcher = new StringMatcher(pattern, true, false);
         if (!filtering)
            viewer.addFilter(this);
         else
            viewer.refresh();
      }
      else {
         pattern = "";
         matcher = null;
         if (filtering)
            viewer.removeFilter(this);
      }
   }

   public boolean select(
      Viewer viewer,
      Object parentElement,
      Object element
   ) {
      return matcher.match(
         ((IFavoriteItem) element).getName());
   }
}
```

7.2.8 View selection

Now that the model objects and view controls are in place, other aspects of
the view, specifically actions, need a way to determine which **Favorites** items
are currently selected. Add the following method to the `FavoritesView` so
that actions can perform operations on the selected items.

```
public IFavoriteItem[] getSelectedFavorites() {
   IStructuredSelection selection =
      (IStructuredSelection) viewer.getSelection();
   IFavoriteItem[] items = new IFavoriteItem[selection.size()];
   Iterator iter = selection.iterator();
   int index = 0;
   while (iter.hasNext())
      items[index++] = (IFavoriteItem) iter.next();
   return items;
}
```

7.3   View Actions

A view action can appear as a menu item in a view's context menu, as a tool-bar button on the right side of a view's title bar, and as a menu item in a view's pull-down menu (see Figure 6–9 on page 237). This section covers adding an action to a view programmatically and registering that view so that others can contribute their own actions via the plug-in manifest, whereas Section 6.4, View Actions, on page 237 discussed adding an action using declarations in the plug-in manifest.

7.3.1   Model actions

Now that the model objects are in place, the AddToFavoritesAction-Delegate class introduced in Section 6.3.3, IObjectActionDelegate, on page 233, can be completed. With the modifications outlined below, the action delegate adds the selected items to the FavoritesManager, which then notifies the FavoritesViewContentProvider, which then refreshes the table to display the new information. In addition, the targetPart field is not being used any longer, so it and all references to it can be removed.

```
private ISelection selection;

public void selectionChanged(IAction action, ISelection selection) {
    this.selection = selection;
    action.setEnabled(!selection.isEmpty());
}

public void run(IAction action) {
    if (selection instanceof IStructuredSelection) {
        FavoritesManager mgr = FavoritesManager.getManager();
        Iterator iter = ((IStructuredSelection) selection).iterator();
        mgr.addFavorites(mgr.newFavoritesFor(iter));
    }
}
```

7.3.2   Context menu

Typically, views have context menus populated by actions targeted at the view or selected objects within it. There are several steps to create a view's context menu programmatically. If you want other plug-ins to contribute actions to your view's context menu via declarations in the plug-in manifest, then you must take several more steps to register your view (see Section 6.3, Object Actions, on page 224, Section 6.4.1, Defining a view context submenu, on page 237, and Section 6.4.2, Defining a view context menu action, on page 238 for information concerning how actions are contributed to a view's context menus via the plug-in manifest).

7.3.2.1 *Creating actions*

The first step is to create the actions that will appear in the context menu. For the **Favorites** view, an action that will remove the selected elements from the view is needed.

```
package com.qualityeclipse.favorites.actions;

import ...

public class RemoveFavoritesAction extends Action
{
    private FavoritesView view;

    public RemoveFavoritesAction(FavoritesView view, String text) {
        super(text);
        this.view = view;
    }

    public void run() {
        FavoritesManager.getManager().removeFavorites(
            view.getSelectedFavorites());
    }
}
```

In the `FavoritesView` class, create a new action field as follows:

```
private RemoveFavoritesAction removeAction;
```

and call the following new method from `createPartControl(Composite)` to initialize the field.

```
private void createActions() {
    IWorkbench workbench = PlatformUI.getWorkbench();
    ISharedImages platformImages = workbench.getSharedImages();
    removeAction = new RemoveFavoritesAction(this, "Remove");
    removeAction.setImageDescriptor(platformImages
        .getImageDescriptor(ISharedImages.IMG_TOOL_DELETE));
    removeAction.setDisabledImageDescriptor(platformImages
        .getImageDescriptor(ISharedImages.IMG_TOOL_DELETE_DISABLED));
    removeAction
        .setToolTipText("Remove the selected favorite items");
}
```

This same action is used later for keyboard-based actions (see Section 7.3.5, Keyboard actions, on page 288) and global actions (see Section 7.3.6, Global actions, on page 289).

7.3.2.2 Creating the context menu

The context menu must be created at the same time that the view is created, but because contributors add and remove menu items based on the current selection, its contents cannot be determined until just after the user clicks the right mouse button and just before the menu is displayed. To accomplish this, set the menu's RemoveAllWhenShown property to true so that the menu will be built from scratch every time, and add a menu listener to dynamically build the menu. In addition, the menu must be registered with the control so that it will be displayed and with the view site so that other plug-ins can contribute actions to it (see Section 6.3, Object Actions, on page 224). For the **Favorites** view, modify createPartControl() to call the following new createContextMenu() method.

```
private void createContextMenu() {
    MenuManager menuMgr = new MenuManager("#PopupMenu");
    menuMgr.setRemoveAllWhenShown(true);
    menuMgr.addMenuListener(new IMenuListener() {
        public void menuAboutToShow(IMenuManager m) {
            FavoritesView.this.fillContextMenu(m);
        }
    });
    Menu menu =
        menuMgr.createContextMenu(viewer.getControl());
    viewer.getControl().setMenu(menu);
    getSite().registerContextMenu(menuMgr, viewer);
}
```

7.3.2.3 Dynamically building the context menu

Every time the user clicks the right mouse button, the context menu's content must be rebuilt from scratch because contributors can add or remove actions based on the selected items. In addition, the context menu must contain a separator with the IWorkbenchActionConstants.MB_ADDITIONS constant, indicating where contributed actions can appear in the menu. The create ContextMenu() method (see Section 7.3.2.2, Creating the context menu, on page 285) calls the new fillContextMenu(IMenuManager) method shown here:

```
private void fillContextMenu(IMenuManager menuMgr) {
    boolean isEmpty = viewer.getSelection().isEmpty();
    removeAction.setEnabled(!isEmpty);
    menuMgr.add(removeAction);
    menuMgr.add(new Separator(
        IWorkbenchActionConstants.MB_ADDITIONS));
}
```

7.3.2.4   Selection provider

When object-based actions are defined (see Section 6.3, Object Actions, on page 224), they are targeted at the selected object rather than at the view. For object-based actions to appear in a view's context menu, the view must not only register the context menu (see Section 7.3.2.1, Creating actions, on page 284), but it must also publish its selection for any other registered listeners (see Section 7.4.1, Selection provider, on page 305). In addition, object-based actions are typically targeted at specific types of objects rather than all objects. This means that the selected object must implement the IAdaptable interface so that contributors can adapt the selected objects to any object they can interrogate and manipulate (see Section 7.4.2, Adaptable objects, on page 306).

7.3.2.5   Filtering unwanted actions

At this point, the **Favorites** view context menu appears as it should, but if your view publishes its selection as referenced in Section 7.3.2.4, on this page, and described in Section 7.4.1, Selection provider, on page 305, then the context menu will incorrectly contain the **Favorites** submenu with the **Add** menu item that was defined in Section 6.3.1, Defining an object-based action, on page 224. That **Favorites** submenu should appear everywhere else *except* in the **Favorites** view. To accomplish this, revisit the object contribution outlined in Section 6.3.1 and insert the following visibility element and change the adaptable attribute so that the object contribution looks like this:

```
<objectContribution
    objectClass="org.eclipse.core.resources.IResource"
    adaptable="false"
    id="com.qualityeclipse.favorites.popupMenu">
    ... etc ...
    <visibility>
      <not>
        <objectClass
          name="com.qualityeclipse.favorites.model.IFavoriteItem"/>
      </not>
    </visibility>
</objectContribution>
```

The modifications cause the **Favorites > Add** menu item to appear for resource selections but not for Java element selections. Duplicate the preceding objectContribution declaration, changing only the objectClass attribute as follows:

```
objectClass="org.eclipse.jdt.core.IJavaElement"
```

For more, see Section 6.3.2.2, The visibility element, on page 228.

7.3.3   Toolbar buttons

Next, programmatically add the remove action to the toolbar (see Section 6.4.4, Defining a view toolbar action, on page 240 for declaring a toolbar button using the plug-in manifest rather than programmatically). In addition, the state of this toolbar button needs to change based on the selection in the **Favorites** view. In the `FavoritesView` class, call the following new method from the `createPartControl(Composite)` method.

```
private void createToolbarButtons() {
   getViewSite().getActionBars().getToolBarManager()
      .add(removeAction);
   removeAction.setEnabled(false);
   viewer.addSelectionChangedListener(
      new ISelectionChangedListener() {
         public void selectionChanged(SelectionChangedEvent event) {
            removeAction.setEnabled(!event.getSelection().isEmpty());
         }
   });
}
```

7.3.4   Pull-down menu

This section will programmatically add an action to the **Favorites** view pull-down menu so that the name filter can be enabled and disabled (see Section 6.4.5, Defining a view pull-down submenu and action, on page 241 for defining a pull-down menu item in the plug-in manifest rather than programmatically). For now, the action will use a simple `InputDialog` to prompt for the name filter pattern, but this will be replaced with a specialized **Favorites** view filter dialog later in the book (see Section 11.1.2, Common SWT dialogs, on page 406).

```
package com.qualityeclipse.favorites.views;
import ...

public class FavoritesViewFilterAction extends Action {
   private final Shell shell;
   private final FavoritesViewNameFilter nameFilter;

   public FavoritesViewFilterAction(
      StructuredViewer viewer,
      String text
   ) {
      super(text);
      shell = viewer.getControl().getShell();
      nameFilter = new FavoritesViewNameFilter(viewer);
   }
```

```
public void run() {
   InputDialog dialog = new InputDialog(
      shell,
      "Favorites View Filter",
      "Enter a name filter pattern"
         + " (* = any string, ? = any character)"
         + System.getProperty("line.separator")
         + "or an empty string for no filtering:",
      nameFilter.getPattern(),
      null);
   if (dialog.open() == InputDialog.OK)
      nameFilter.setPattern(dialog.getValue().trim());
   }
}
```

The `createPartControl()` method is getting quite long and is in need of refactoring. After extracting the table columns as fields and extracting table creation and sorting into separate methods, the `createPartControl()` method is modified to call a new `createViewPulldownMenu()` method. This new method programmatically creates and initializes the **filter** field, and adds the new filter action to the **Favorites** view's pull-down menu (see Figure 7–6).

```
private FavoritesViewFilterAction filterAction;

private void createViewPulldownMenu() {
   IMenuManager menu =
      getViewSite().getActionBars().getMenuManager();
   filterAction =
      new FavoritesViewFilterAction(viewer, "Filter...");
   menu.add(filterAction);
}
```

Figure 7–6   Favorites view showing the view's pull-down menu.

7.3.5 Keyboard actions

Rather than using the mouse to activate the context menu and then selecting the **Remove** command to remove an item from the **Favorites** view (see Section 7.3.2, Context menu, on page 283), it would be quicker just to press the **Delete** key. This approach programmatically associates the **Delete** key with the `RemoveFavoritesAction` rather than defining the command via the

plug-in manifest as in Section 6.6, Key Bindings, on page 251. For this to
work, call the following `hookKeyboardActions()` method from the
`createPartControl()` method.

```
private void hookKeyboardActions() {
   viewer.getControl().addKeyListener(new KeyAdapter() {
      public void keyReleased(KeyEvent event) {
         handleKeyReleased(event);
      }
   });
}

protected void handleKeyReleased(KeyEvent event) {
   if (event.character == SWT.DEL && event.stateMask == 0) {
      removeAction.run();
   }
}
```

7.3.6   *Global actions*

Now that the `RemoveFavoritesAction` is available both in the context menu
(see Section 7.3.2.1, Creating actions, on page 284) and by pressing the **Delete**
key (see Section 7.3.5, Keyboard actions, on page 288), that same action
needs to be triggered when the user selects **Delete** from the **Edit** menu. The
interface `org.eclipse.ui.IWorkbenchActionConstants` defines a number
of constants, such as the following, for just this purpose.

- Undo
- Redo
- Cut
- Copy
- Paste
- Delete

Calling the following new method from the `createPartControl()` method
associates **Edit > Delete** with `RemoveFavoritesAction` when the **Favorites**
view is active.

```
private void hookGlobalActions() {
   getViewSite().getActionBars().setGlobalActionHandler(
      ActionFactory.DELETE.getId(), removeAction);
}
```

7.3.7 Clipboard actions

The three clipboard-related actions are cut, copy, and paste. For the **Favorites** view, you need to provide the ability to cut selected items out of the view, copy selected items, and paste new items into the view using three separate actions. To support these three actions, lazily create a clipboard object.

```
private Clipboard clipboard;

public Clipboard getClipboard() {
    if (clipboard == null)
        clipboard = new Clipboard(getSite().getShell().getDisplay());
    return clipboard;
}
```

In addition, the clipboard, if it is defined, must be cleaned up when the view is closed by extending the view's `dispose()` method.

```
public void dispose() {
    if (clipboard != null)
        clipboard.dispose();
    super.dispose();
}
```

7.3.7.1 Copy

The copy action translates selected **Favorites** items into various formats such as resources, and places that information into the clipboard. Transfer objects convert various formats, such as resources, into platform-specific byte streams and back so that information can be exchanged between different applications (see Section 7.3.8.3, Custom transfer types, on page 298 for more on transfer types). The following `CopyFavoritesAction` class will be added to handle copying items from the **Favorites** view.

```
package com.qualityeclipse.favorites.actions;

import ...

public class CopyFavoritesAction extends Action
{
    private FavoritesView view;

    public CopyFavoritesAction(FavoritesView view, String text) {
        super(text);
        this.view = view;
    }
```

```
public void run() {
   IFavoriteItem[] items = view.getSelectedFavorites();
   if (items.length == 0)
      return;
   try {
      view.getClipboard().setContents(
         new Object[] {
            asResources(items),
            asText(items), },
         new Transfer[] {
            ResourceTransfer.getInstance(),
            TextTransfer.getInstance(), });
   }
   catch (SWTError error) {
      // Copy to clipboard failed.
      // This happens when another application
      // is accessing the clipboard while we copy.
      // Ignore the error.
   }
}

public static IResource[] asResources(IFavoriteItem[] items) {
   List resources = new ArrayList();
   for (int i = 0; i < items.length; i++) {
      IResource res =
         (IResource) items[i].getAdapter(IResource.class);
      if (res != null)
         resources.add(res);
   }
   return (IResource[]) resources.toArray(
      new IResource[resources.size()]);
}

public static String asText(IFavoriteItem[] items) {
   StringBuffer buf = new StringBuffer();
   for (int i = 0; i < items.length; i++) {
      if (i > 0)
         buf.append(System.getProperty("line.separator"));
      buf.append(items[i].getName());
   }
   return buf.toString();
}
}
```

You need to create a field in `FavoritesView` to hold the copy action:

```
private CopyFavoritesAction copyAction;
```

then initialize that field in the `createActions()` method:

```
copyAction = new CopyFavoritesAction(this, "Copy");
copyAction.setImageDescriptor(platformImages
   .getImageDescriptor(ISharedImages.IMG_TOOL_COPY));
copyAction.setDisabledImageDescriptor(platformImages
   .getImageDescriptor(ISharedImages.IMG_TOOL_COPY_DISABLED));
copyAction.setToolTipText("Copy the selected favorite items");
```

and hook the action to the global copy (see Section 7.3.6, Global actions, on page 289) in the hookGlobalActions() method:

```
getViewSite().getActionBars().setGlobalActionHandler(
   ActionFactory.COPY.getId(), copyAction);
```

The copy action can also be added to the context menu by modifying the fillContextMenu() method (see Section 7.3.2.3, Dynamically building the context menu, on page 285) and to the view's toolbar (see Section 7.3.3, Toolbar buttons, on page 287).

7.3.7.2 Cut

The cut action is based on the copy and remove actions, first using the copy action to copy the selected **Favorites** items to the clipboard and then the remove action to remove the selected items from the **Favorites** view. It is initialized and used much like the copy operation described in the previous section.

```
package com.qualityeclipse.favorites.actions;

import ...

public class CutFavoritesAction extends Action
{
   private CopyFavoritesAction copyAction;
   private RemoveFavoritesAction removeAction;

   public CutFavoritesAction(
      CopyFavoritesAction copyAction,
      RemoveFavoritesAction removeAction,
      String text
   ) {
      super(text);
      this.copyAction = copyAction;
      this.removeAction = removeAction;
   }

   public void run() {
      copyAction.run();
      removeAction.run();
   }
}
```

7.3.7.3   Paste

The paste operation takes information that was previously added to the clipboard by another operation and adds it to the **Favorites** view. As with the copy operation (see Section 7.3.7.1, Copy, on page 290), transfer objects facilitate translation from platform-specific byte streams to objects, and the paste operation converts those objects into items that are added to the **Favorites** view. The initialization and use of the paste operation is much like the copy operation discussed in Section 7.3.7.1, Copy, on page 290.

```
package com.qualityeclipse.favorites.actions;
import ...

public class PasteFavoritesAction extends Action
{
   private FavoritesView view;

   public PasteFavoritesAction(FavoritesView view, String text) {
      super(text);
      this.view = view;
   }

   public void run() {
      if (pasteResources())
         return;
      if (pasteJavaElements())
         return;
      // Other transfer types here.
   }

   private boolean pasteResources() {
      ResourceTransfer transfer =
         ResourceTransfer.getInstance();
      IResource[] resources = (IResource[])
         view.getClipboard().getContents(transfer);
      if (resources == null || resources.length == 0)
         return false;
      FavoritesManager mgr = FavoritesManager.getManager();
      mgr.addFavorites(mgr.newFavoritesFor(resources));
      return true;
   }

   private boolean pasteJavaElements() {
      Transfer transfer =
         JavaUI.getJavaElementClipboardTransfer();
      IJavaElement[] elements = (IJavaElement[])
         view.getClipboard().getContents(transfer);
      if (elements == null || elements.length == 0)
         return false;
      FavoritesManager mgr = FavoritesManager.getManager();
      mgr.addFavorites(mgr.newFavoritesFor(elements));
      return true;
   }
}
```

7.3.8   Drag-and-drop support

The ability to add objects to the **Favorites** view from another view using the copy/paste actions is available, but it would be nice to allow objects to be dragged into and out of the **Favorites** view. To accomplish this, add *drag source* and *drop target* objects to the **Favorites** view by calling the following new method from the `createPartControl()` method. The `FavoritesDragSource` and `FavoritesDropTarget` types are defined in the next two sections.

```
private void hookDragAndDrop() {
   new FavoritesDragSource(this, viewer);
   new FavoritesDropTarget(this, viewer);
}
```

7.3.8.1   Dragging objects out of the Favorites view

The `FavoritesDragSource` type initializes the drag source operation and handles conversions of **Favorites** items into resource objects and text. This allows the user to drag and drop selected **Favorites** items elsewhere within Eclipse or into another drag-and-drop-enabled application such as Microsoft Word (see Figure 7–7).

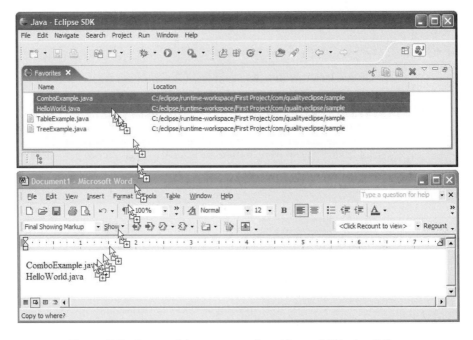

Figure 7–7   Drag-and-drop operationfrom Microsoft Word to Eclipse.

The constructor, called from the `hookDragAndDrop()` method (see Section 7.3.8, Drag-and-drop support, on page 294), initializes the drag source by:

- Creating a drag source—`new DragSource()`

- Specifying available operations—`DND.DROP_COPY`
  Multiple operations can be specified as in `DND.DROP_MOVE | DND.DROP_COPY` if items can be both moved and copied.

- Specifying available data types—Resources and text
  (For more, see Section 7.3.8.3, Custom transfer types, on page 298).

- Adding itself as a `DragSourceListener` to handle the data conversion from **Favorites** items to either resources or text.

When a user initiates a drag operation from the **Favorites** view, the `dragStart()` method is called to determine whether the drag operation can be performed. In this case, set the `event.doit` field to be `true` if there are **Favorites** items selected, otherwise set `event.doit` to `false` since the operation can only be performed when at least one **Favorites** item is selected. When the user drops the objects, the `dragSetData()` method is called to convert the selected items before the transfer occurs, and then the `dragFinish()` method is called after the transfer is complete.

```
package com.qualityeclipse.favorites.views;

import ...

public class FavoritesDragSource
   implements DragSourceListener
{
   private FavoritesView view;

   public FavoritesDragSource(
      FavoritesView view,
      TableViewer viewer
   ) {
      this.view = view;
      DragSource source =
         new DragSource(viewer.getControl(), DND.DROP_COPY);
      source.setTransfer(
         new Transfer[] {
            TextTransfer.getInstance(),
            ResourceTransfer.getInstance()});
      source.addDragListener(this);
   }

   public void dragStart(DragSourceEvent event) {
      event.doit = view.getSelectedFavorites().length > 0;
   }
```

```
public void dragSetData(DragSourceEvent event) {
    if (TextTransfer.getInstance()
        .isSupportedType(event.dataType)) {
        event.data =
            CopyFavoritesAction.asText(
                view.getSelectedFavorites());
    }
    else if (ResourceTransfer.getInstance()
        .isSupportedType(event.dataType)) {
        event.data =
            CopyFavoritesAction.asResources(
                view.getSelectedFavorites());
    }
}
public void dragFinished(DragSourceEvent event) {
    // If this was a MOVE operation,
    // then remove the items that were moved.
}
}
```

7.3.8.2 Dragging objects into the Favorites view

The FavoritesDropTarget type allows items to be added to the **Favorites** view by dragging them from another view. This allows the user to drag resources or Java elements from the **Resource Navigator** view or the **Java Package** view into the **Favorites** view.

The constructor, called from the hookDragAndDrop() method (see Section 7.3.8, Drag-and-drop support, on page 294), initializes the drop target by:

- Creating the drop target—new DropTarget()

- Specifying accepted operations—DND.DROP_MOVE | DND.DROP_COPY
  For convenience, specify that a move operation is allowed, but when the actual operation is performed, convert it to a copy operation.

- Specifying accepted data types—Resources and Java elements
  (For more, see Section 7.3.8.3, Custom transfer types, on page 298.)

- Adding itself as a DropTargetListener to handle data conversion from objects to **Favorites** items.

During the drag operation, there are several events that occur so that various drop targets can provide feedback to the user when the cursor enters, moves over, and exits a drag target. Since you need to add items to the **Favorites** view without removing them from their original location, and to make it convenient for the user so that he or she does not have to hold down the **Ctrl** key to perform the drag operation, implement the dragEnter() method to convert a move operation into a copy operation. The conversion

from a move operation to a copy operation is done in the `dragEnter()`
method in addition to the `drop()` method so that the user gets visual feedback
indicating that a copy will occur before the operation is performed.

When the user drops the objects on the **Favorites** view, the `drop()` method
is called to perform the operation. It converts the objects into **Favorites** items
and ensures that the operation is indeed a copy operation so that the objects
are not removed from their original locations.

```java
package com.qualityeclipse.favorites.views;
import ...
public class FavoritesDropTarget extends DropTargetAdapter
{
   public FavoritesDropTarget(
      FavoritesView view,
      TableViewer viewer) {
      DropTarget target =
         new DropTarget(
            viewer.getControl(),
            DND.DROP_MOVE | DND.DROP_COPY);
      target.setTransfer(
         new Transfer[] {
            ResourceTransfer.getInstance(),
            JavaUI.getJavaElementClipboardTransfer()});
      target.addDropListener(this);
   }

   public void dragEnter(DropTargetEvent event) {
      if (event.detail == DND.DROP_MOVE
         || event.detail == DND.DROP_DEFAULT) {
         if ((event.operations & DND.DROP_COPY) != 0)
            event.detail = DND.DROP_COPY;
         else
            event.detail = DND.DROP_NONE;
      }
   }

   public void drop(DropTargetEvent event) {
      FavoritesManager mgr = FavoritesManager.getManager();
      if (ResourceTransfer.getInstance()
         .isSupportedType(event.currentDataType)
         && (event.data instanceof IResource[])) {
         mgr.addFavorites(
            mgr.newFavoritesFor((IResource[]) event.data));
         event.detail = DND.DROP_COPY;
      } else if (JavaUI.getJavaElementClipboardTransfer()
         .isSupportedType(event.currentDataType)
         && (event.data instanceof IJavaElement[])) {
         mgr.addFavorites(
            mgr.newFavoritesFor((IJavaElement[]) event.data));
         event.detail = DND.DROP_COPY;
      } else
         event.detail = DND.DROP_NONE;
   }
}
```

7.3.8.3   *Custom transfer types*

Transfer objects convert various formats, such as resources, into platform-specific byte streams and back so that information can be exchanged between different applications. Eclipse provides several transfer types, including:

- ByteArrayTransfer
- EditorInputTransfer
- FileTransfer
- JavaElementTransfer
- MarkerTransfer
- PluginTransfer
- ResourceTransfer
- RTFTransfer
- TextTransfer

These transfer objects are useful for generic types of objects such as resources. If you are dragging objects specific to your application from one view to another, however, the transfered objects may not completely capture the information of the object being dragged. For example, if you were to drag a **Favorites** item from one **Favorites** view to another, and there was additional state information associated with the item, and a `ResourceTransfer` object was being used, then that additional state information would be lost.

Solving this problem requires building a custom transfer type such as the one that follows. A transfer type must be a subclass of the `org.eclipse.swt.dnd.Transfer` class, but subclassing `org.eclipse.swt.dnd.ByteArray-Transfer` is easier because of the additional behavior it provides. If a custom transfer type for **Favorites** items is built, then it would rely on functionality introduced in Section 7.5.2, Saving global view information, on page 311 and might be similar to the existing `ResourceTransfer` type.

```
package com.qualityeclipse.favorites.views;

import ...;

public class FavoritesTransfer extends ByteArrayTransfer
{
   private static final FavoritesTransfer INSTANCE =
      new FavoritesTransfer();

   public static FavoritesTransfer getInstance() {
      return INSTANCE;
   }
```

```
private FavoritesTransfer() {
    super();
}
```

Each `FavoritesTransfer` class must have a unique identifier to ensure that different Eclipse applications use `FavoritesTransfer` classes of different "types." The `getTypeIds()` and `getTypeNames()` methods return the platform-specfic IDs and names of the data types that can be converted using this transfer agent.

```
private static final String TYPE_NAME =
    "favorites-transfer-format:"
        + System.currentTimeMillis()
        + ":"
        + INSTANCE.hashCode();

private static final int TYPEID =
    registerType(TYPE_NAME);

protected int[] getTypeIds() {
    return new int[] { TYPEID };
}

protected String[] getTypeNames() {
    return new String[] { TYPE_NAME };
}
```

The `javaToNative()` method converts a Java representation of data to a platform-specific representation of the data, then returns that information by placing it in the `TransferData` argument.

```
protected void javaToNative(
    Object data,
    TransferData transferData) {

    if (!(data instanceof IFavoriteItem[])) return;
    IFavoriteItem[] items = (IFavoriteItem[]) data;

    /**
     * The serialization format is:
     *   (int) number of items
     * Then, the following for each item:
     *   (String) the type of item
     *   (String) the item-specific info glob
     */
    try {
        ByteArrayOutputStream out =
            new ByteArrayOutputStream();
```

```
            DataOutputStream dataOut =
                new DataOutputStream(out);
            dataOut.writeInt(items.length);
            for (int i = 0; i < items.length; i++) {
                IFavoriteItem item = items[i];
                dataOut.writeUTF(item.getType().getId());
                dataOut.writeUTF(item.getInfo());
            }
            dataOut.close();
            out.close();
            super.javaToNative(out.toByteArray(), transferData);
        }
        catch (IOException e) {
            // Send nothing if there were problems.
        }
    }
}
```

The `nativeToJava()` method converts a platform-specific representation of data to a Java representation.

```
protected Object nativeToJava(TransferData transferData) {
    /**
     * The serialization format is:
     *  (int) number of items
     * Then, the following for each item:
     *   (String) the type of item
     *   (String) the item-specific info glob
     */
    byte[] bytes =
        (byte[]) super.nativeToJava(transferData);
    if (bytes == null)
        return null;
    DataInputStream in =
        new DataInputStream(
            new ByteArrayInputStream(bytes));
    try {
        FavoritesManager mgr =
            FavoritesManager.getManager();
        int count = in.readInt();
        List items = new ArrayList(count);
        for (int i = 0; i < count; i++) {
            String typeId = in.readUTF();
            String info = in.readUTF();
            items.add(mgr.newFavoriteFor(typeId, info));
        }
        return (IFavoriteItem[]) items.toArray(
            new IFavoriteItem[items.size()]);
    }
    catch (IOException e) {
        return null;
    }
}
```

> **Tip:** In input/output (I/O) code like the preceding, consider using a `BufferedOutputStream` between the `ByteArrayOutputStream` and the `DataOutputStream`. While not always necessary, this can be a useful performance improvement.

7.3.9 Inline editing

Another feature you need to have is the ability to edit the name of the **Favorites** items directly in the **Favorites** view quickly and easily. It is arguable that it should trigger the rename action or refactoring so that the underlying resource or Java element will be renamed rather than just editing the name of the item itself, but things are kept simple for the purposes of demonstrating the inline editing function.

To perform inline editing of a **Favorites** item's name, a new action named `RenameFavoriteAction` is needed. When the user selects the **Rename** command in the context menu, a text field opens over the selected item's name in the **Favorites** view (see Figure 7–8). The user enters the new name into the text field and presses the **Return** key, which closes the editor and updates the item's name.

Figure 7–8 Favorites view showing the inline text field.

This new action is derived from `org.eclipse.ui.actions.Rename-ResourceAction` and uses two helper classes. The `TableEditor` is responsible for positioning and sizing the text field over the item being renamed. The `TextActionHandler` temporarily redirects all global editing commands like cut, copy, paste, clear, and select all to the text field rather than to the current Eclipse editor. This class has very little code specific to the **Favorites** view, and with a little refactoring, it could become a general-purpose inline edit action.

```
package com.qualityeclipse.favorites.actions;

import ...

public class RenameFavoriteAction extends Action
{
    private static final int COLUMN_TO_EDIT = 1;
```

```
private final FavoritesView view;
private final Table table;
private final TableEditor tableEditor;
private final TextActionHandler textActionHandler;
private Composite editorParent;
private Text editor;
private String originalText;

public RenameFavoriteAction(
   FavoritesView view,
   Table table,
   String text
) {
   super(text);
   this.view = view;
   this.table = table;
   tableEditor = new TableEditor(table);
   textActionHandler =
      new TextActionHandler(
         view.getViewSite().getActionBars());
}
```

When the action is executed, the run() method is called to create and show the cell editor.

```
public void run() {
   originalText = getTextToEdit();
   if (originalText == null)
      return;
   if (editor == null)
      createEditor();
   showEditor(originalText);
}

private void createEditor() {
   // Create the parent so that a simple border
   // can be painted around the text editor.
   editorParent = new Composite(table, SWT.NONE);
   TableItem[] tableItems = table.getSelection();
   tableEditor.horizontalAlignment = SWT.LEFT;
   tableEditor.grabHorizontal = true;
   tableEditor.setEditor(
      editorParent, tableItems[0], COLUMN_TO_EDIT);
   editorParent.setVisible(false);
   editorParent.addListener(SWT.Paint, new Listener() {
      public void handleEvent(Event e) {
         // Paint a simple border around the text editor.
         Point textSize = editor.getSize();
         Point parentSize = editorParent.getSize();
         int w = Math.min(
            textSize.x + 4, parentSize.x - 1);
         int h = parentSize.y - 1;
         e.gc.drawRectangle(0, 0, w, h);
      }
   });
```

```java
    // Create the editor itself.
    editor = new Text(editorParent, SWT.NONE);
    editorParent.setBackground(editor.getBackground());
    editor.addListener(SWT.Modify, new Listener() {
       public void handleEvent(Event e) {
          Point textSize =
             editor.computeSize(SWT.DEFAULT, SWT.DEFAULT);
          textSize.x += textSize.y;
          // Add extra space for new characters.
          Point parentSize = editorParent.getSize();
          int w = Math.min(textSize.x, parentSize.x - 4);
          int h = parentSize.y - 2;
          editor.setBounds(2, 1, w, h);
          editorParent.redraw();
       }
    });
    editor.addListener(SWT.Traverse, new Listener() {
       public void handleEvent(Event event) {
          //Workaround for Bug 20214 due to extra
          //traverse events.
          switch (event.detail) {
             case SWT.TRAVERSE_ESCAPE :
                //Do nothing in this case.
                disposeEditor();
                event.doit = true;
                event.detail = SWT.TRAVERSE_NONE;
                break;
             case SWT.TRAVERSE_RETURN :
                saveChangesAndDisposeEditor();
                event.doit = true;
                event.detail = SWT.TRAVERSE_NONE;
                break;
          }
       }
    });
    editor.addFocusListener(new FocusAdapter() {
       public void focusLost(FocusEvent fe) {
          saveChangesAndDisposeEditor();
       }
    });

    // Add a handler to redirect global cut, copy, etc.
    textActionHandler.addText(editor);
}

private void showEditor(String name) {
    editor.setText(name);
    editorParent.setVisible(true);
    Point textSize =
       editor.computeSize(SWT.DEFAULT, SWT.DEFAULT);
    textSize.x += textSize.y;
    // Add extra space for new characters.
    Point parentSize = editorParent.getSize();
    int w = Math.min(textSize.x, parentSize.x - 4);
    int h = parentSize.y - 2;
```

```
        editor.setBounds(2, 1, w, h);
        editorParent.redraw();
        editor.selectAll();
        editor.setFocus();
    }
```

After the user has finished editing the name, the cell editor event listeners call the `saveChangesAndDisposeEditor()` method to save the new name and dispose of the cell editor.

```
    protected void saveChangesAndDisposeEditor() {
        String newText = editor.getText();
        if (!originalText.equals(newText))
            saveChanges(newText);
        disposeEditor();
    }

    protected void disposeEditor() {
        textActionHandler.removeText(editor);
        if (editorParent != null) {
            editorParent.dispose();
            editorParent = null;
            editor = null;
            tableEditor.setEditor(null, null, COLUMN_TO_EDIT);
        }
    }

    protected String getTextToEdit() {
        String text = null;
        IFavoriteItem[] items = view.getSelectedFavorites();
        if (items.length == 1)
            text = items[0].getName();
        return text;
    }

    protected void saveChanges(String newText) {
        IFavoriteItem[] items = view.getSelectedFavorites();
        if (items.length == 1) {
            items[0].setName(newText);
            view.getFavoritesViewer().refresh(items[0]);
        }
    }
}
```

Next, add a new field, a new line in `createActions()` to initialize the field, and a new line to the `fillContextMenu()` method so that the new **Rename** item appears in the **Favorites** view's popup menu.

```
private RenameFavoriteAction renameAction;

renameAction = new RenameFavoriteAction(
    this, viewer.getTable(), "Rename");
menuMgr.add(renameAction);
```

One alternate approach is to hook this up so that the user can press **F2** to directly edit the item name, similar to the way that the **Delete** key was previously hooked to the delete action (see Section 7.3.5, Keyboard actions, on page 288). Another approach is to add a mouse listener so that **Alt+click** directly edits the item name by calling the following method from the createPartControl() method.

```
private void hookMouse() {
    viewer.getTable().addMouseListener(new MouseAdapter() {
        public void mouseUp(MouseEvent e) {
            if ((e.stateMask & SWT.ALT) != 0) {
                renameAction.run();
            }
        }
    });
}
```

7.4 Linking the View

In many situations, the current selection in the active view can affect the selection in other views, cause an editor to open, change the selected editor, or change the selection within an already open editor. For example, in the Java browsing perspective (see Section 1.2.1.1, Java perspectives, on page 7), changing the selection in the **Types** view changes the selection in both the **Projects** and the **Packages** views, changes the content displayed in the **Members** view, and changes the active editor. For a view to both publish its own selection and to consume the selection of the active part, it must be both a *selection provider* and a *selection listener*.

7.4.1 *Selection provider*

For a view to be a selection provider, it must register itself as a selection provider with the view site. In addition, each of the objects contained in the view should be adaptable (see the next section) so that other objects can adapt the selected objects into objects they can understand. In the **Favorites** view, register the view as a selection provider by adding the following to the createTableViewer() method:

```
getSite().setSelectionProvider(viewer);
```

7.4.2 Adaptable objects

The org.eclipse.core.runtime.IAdaptable interface allows an object to convert one type of object that it may not understand to another type of object that it can interrogate and manipulate (more on adapters in Section 20.3, Adapters, on page 714). For the **Favorites** view, this means that the IFavoritesItem interface must extend the IAdaptable interface, and the following two getAdapter() methods must be added to FavoriteResource and FavoriteJavaElement, respectively.

```
public Object getAdapter(Class adapter) {
   if (adapter.isInstance(resource))
      return resource;
   return Platform.getAdapterManager().getAdapter(this, adapter);
}

public Object getAdapter(Class adapter) {
   if (adapter.isInstance(element))
      return element;
   IResource resource = element.getResource();
   if (adapter.isInstance(resource))
      return resource;
   return Platform.getAdapterManager().getAdapter(this, adapter);
}
```

7.4.3 Selection listener

For a view to consume the selection of another part, it must add a selection listener to the page so that when the active part changes or the selection in the active part changes, it can react by altering its own selection appropriately. For the **Favorites** view, if the selection contains objects that can be adapted to the objects in the view, then the view should adjust its selection. To accomplish this, add a call at the end of the createPartControl() method to the following new hookPageSelection() method.

```
private ISelectionListener pageSelectionListener;

private void hookPageSelection() {
   pageSelectionListener = new ISelectionListener() {
      public void selectionChanged(
         IWorkbenchPart part,
         ISelection selection) {
            pageSelectionChanged(part, selection);
      }
   };
   getSite().getPage().addPostSelectionListener(
      pageSelectionListener);
}
```

```
protected void pageSelectionChanged(
    IWorkbenchPart part,
    ISelection selection
) {
    if (part == this)
        return;
    if (!(selection instanceof IStructuredSelection))
        return;
    IStructuredSelection sel = (IStructuredSelection) selection;
    IFavoriteItem[] items = FavoritesManager.getManager()
        .existingFavoritesFor(sel.iterator());
    if (items.length > 0)
        viewer.setSelection(new StructuredSelection(items), true);
}
```

Then add the following to the `dispose()` method to clean up when the **Favorites** view is closed.

```
if (pageSelectionListener != null)
    getSite().getPage().removePostSelectionListener(
        pageSelectionListener);
```

7.4.4   *Opening an editor*

When a user double-clicks on a file in the **Favorites** view, a file editor should open. To accomplish this, add a new method to the `MouseAdapter` in the `hookMouse` method of the `FavoritesView` class.

```
public void mouseDoubleClick(MouseEvent e) {
    OpenEditorActionDelegate.openEditor(
        getSite().getPage(), viewer.getSelection());
}
```

This method references a new static method in a new `OpenEditor-ActionDelegate` class. The new method examines the first element in the current selection, and if that element is an instance of `IFile`, opens an editor on that file.

```
public static void openEditor(
    IWorkbenchPage page, ISelection selection)
{
    // Get the first element.

    if (!(selection instanceof IStructuredSelection))
        return;
    Iterator iter = ((IStructuredSelection) selection).iterator();
    if (!iter.hasNext())
        return;
    Object elem = iter.next();
```

```
// Adapt the first element to a file.

if (!(elem instanceof IAdaptable))
    return;

IFile file = (IFile) ((IAdaptable) elem).getAdapter(IFile.class);
if (file == null)
    return;

// Open an editor on that file.

try {
    IDE.openEditor(page, file);
}
catch (PartInitException e) {
    FavoritesLog.logError(
        "Open editor failed: " + file.toString(), e);
}
}
}
```

7.5   Saving View State

Up to this point, the **Favorites** view contains only the current list of projects when the Eclipse session starts up. Items can be added to the **Favorites** view during the course of the session, but as soon as Eclipse is shut down, the changes are lost. In addition, the view's sort and filter information should be saved so that the view will be returned to the same state when the session is restarted. To accomplish all this, two different mechanisms are used.

7.5.1   Saving local view information

Eclipse provides a memento-based mechanism for saving view and editor state information. In this case, this mechanism is good for saving the sorting and filter state of a view because that information is specific to each individual view. It is not good for saving global information shared by multiple views, so that is tackled in the next section.

To save the sorting state, two methods should be added to the FavoritesViewSorter. The first method saves the current sort state as an instance of IMemento by converting the sort order and ascending/descending state into an XML-like structure. The second method takes a very guarded approach to reading and resetting the sort order and ascending/descending state from IMemento so that the sort state will be valid even if IMemento is not what was expected.

```
private static final String TAG_DESCENDING = "descending";
private static final String TAG_COLUMN_INDEX = "columnIndex";
private static final String TAG_TYPE = "SortInfo";
private static final String TAG_TRUE = "true";

public void saveState(IMemento memento) {
   for (int i = 0; i < infos.length; i++) {
      SortInfo info = infos[i];
      IMemento mem = memento.createChild(TAG_TYPE);
      mem.putInteger(TAG_COLUMN_INDEX, info.columnIndex);
      if (info.descending)
         mem.putString(TAG_DESCENDING, TAG_TRUE);
   }
}

public void init(IMemento memento) {
   List newInfos = new ArrayList(infos.length);
   IMemento[] mems = memento.getChildren(TAG_TYPE);
   for (int i = 0; i < mems.length; i++) {
      IMemento mem = mems[i];
      Integer value = mem.getInteger(TAG_COLUMN_INDEX);
      if (value == null)
         continue;
      int index = value.intValue();
      if (index < 0 || index >= infos.length)
         continue;
      SortInfo info = infos[index];
      if (newInfos.contains(info))
         continue;
      info.descending =
         TAG_TRUE.equals(mem.getString(TAG_DESCENDING));
      newInfos.add(info);
   }
   for (int i = 0; i < infos.length; i++)
      if (!newInfos.contains(infos[i]))
         newInfos.add(infos[i]);
   infos = (SortInfo[]) newInfos.toArray(
      new SortInfo[newInfos.size()]);
}
```

In addition to saving the sort state, the filter state needs to be saved. This is accomplished by adding the following two methods to the `Favorites-ViewFilterAction` type.

```
public void saveState(IMemento memento) {
   nameFilter.saveState(memento);
}

public void init(IMemento memento) {
   nameFilter.init(memento);
}
```

Then add two new methods to `FavoritesViewNameFilter`:

```
private static final String TAG_PATTERN = "pattern";
```

```
private static final String TAG_TYPE = "NameFilterInfo";

public void saveState(IMemento memento) {
   if (pattern.length() == 0)
      return;
   IMemento mem = memento.createChild(TAG_TYPE);
   mem.putString(TAG_PATTERN, pattern);
}

public void init(IMemento memento) {
   IMemento mem = memento.getChild(TAG_TYPE);
   if (mem == null)
      return;
   setPattern(mem.getString(TAG_PATTERN));
}
```

These new methods are hooked to the view by adding the following field and methods to the FavoritesView.

```
private IMemento memento;

public void saveState(IMemento memento) {
   super.saveState(memento);
   sorter.saveState(memento);
   filterAction.saveState(memento);
}

public void init(IViewSite site, IMemento memento)
   throws PartInitException
{
   super.init(site, memento);
   this.memento = memento;
}
```

The sorting and filter state cannot be restored immediately in the init() method shown above because the part control has not been created. Instead, the method caches IMemento for use later during the initialization process. You must then modify both the createTableSorter() method and the createViewPulldownMenu() method as shown next to restore the sorting and filter state before associating the sorter with the viewer and the filter action with the menu, respectively.

```
private void createTableSorter() {

   ... same code as in Section 7.2.6 on page 278 ...

   if (memento != null)
      sorter.init(memento);
   viewer.setSorter(sorter);
}
```

```
private void createViewPulldownMenu() {

    ... same code as in a Section 7.3.4 on page 287 ...

    if (memento != null)
        filterAction.init(memento);
    menu.add(filterAction);
}
```

Eclipse stores all memento-based view and editor state information in a single file:

```
<workspace>\.metadata\.plugins\org.eclipse.ui.workbench\workbench.xml
```

For example (reformatted so that it's easier to read):

```
<views>
  <view
    id="com.qualityeclipse.favorites.views.FavoritesView"
    partName="Favorites">
    <viewState>
      <SortInfo columnIndex="0" descending="true"/>
      <SortInfo columnIndex="1"/>
      <SortInfo columnIndex="2"/>
    </viewState>
  </view>
  <view id="org.eclipse.ui.views.TaskList" partName="Tasks">
    <viewState
      columnWidth0="19" columnWidth1="19" columnWidth2="288"
      columnWidth3="108" columnWidth4="216" columnWidth5="86"
      horizontalPosition="0" verticalPosition="0">
      <selection/>
    </viewState>
  </view>
  ...
</views>
```

7.5.2 Saving global view information

Now you need to save the state of the FavoritesManager, which is shared by all **Favorites** views. For this to occur, augment the FavoritesPlugin, the FavoritesManager, and each **Favorites** item with the ability to save their information so that they can be recreated later. In the FavoritesPlugin, augment the stop() method to call a new saveFavorites() method in the FavoritesManager.

```
FavoritesManager.getManager().saveFavorites();
```

The existing `loadFavorites()` method in the `FavoritesManager` must be revised as follows and new methods added so that the **Favorites** items will be lazily loaded when needed. Lazy initialization is the Eclipse theme, so the list will not be built until it is needed. In addition, a new `saveFavorites()` method must be added to store the **Favorites** items so that they can be restored when Eclipse is restarted.

```
private static final String TAG_FAVORITES = "Favorites";
private static final String TAG_FAVORITE = "Favorite";
private static final String TAG_TYPEID = "TypeId";
private static final String TAG_INFO = "Info";

private void loadFavorites() {
    favorites = new HashSet(20);
    FileReader reader = null;
    try {
        reader = new FileReader (getFavoritesFile());
        loadFavorites(XMLMemento.createReadRoot(reader));
    }
    catch (FileNotFoundException e) {
        // Ignored... no Favorites items exist yet.
    }
    catch (Exception e) {
        // Log the exception and move on.
        FavoritesLog.logError(e);
    }
    finally {
        try {
            if (reader != null) reader.close();
        } catch (IOException e) {
            FavoritesLog.logError(e);
        }
    }
}

private void loadFavorites(XMLMemento memento) {
    IMemento [] children = memento.getChildren(TAG_FAVORITE);
    for (int i = 0; i < children.length; i++) {
        IFavoriteItem item =
            newFavoriteFor(
                children[i].getString(TAG_TYPEID),
                children[i].getString(TAG_INFO));
        if (item != null)
            favorites.add(item);
    }
}

public IFavoriteItem newFavoriteFor(String typeId, String info) {
    FavoriteItemType[] types = FavoriteItemType.getTypes();
    for (int i = 0; i < types.length; i++)
        if (types[i].getId().equals(typeId))
            return types[i].loadFavorite(info);
    return null;
}
```

```
public void saveFavorites() {
    if (favorites == null)
        return;
    XMLMemento memento = XMLMemento.createWriteRoot(TAG_FAVORITES);
    saveFavorites(memento);
    FileWriter writer = null;
    try {
        writer = new FileWriter(getFavoritesFile());
        memento.save(writer);
    }
    catch (IOException e) {
        FavoritesLog.logError(e);
    }
    finally {
        try {
            if (writer != null)
                writer.close();
        }
        catch (IOException e) {
            FavoritesLog.logError(e);
        }
    }
}

private void saveFavorites(XMLMemento memento) {
    Iterator iter = favorites.iterator();
    while (iter.hasNext()) {
        IFavoriteItem item = (IFavoriteItem) iter.next();
        IMemento child = memento.createChild(TAG_FAVORITE);
        child.putString(TAG_TYPEID, item.getType().getId());
        child.putString(TAG_INFO, item.getInfo());
    }
}

private File getFavoritesFile() {
    return FavoritesPlugin
        .getDefault()
        .getStateLocation()
        .append("favorites.xml")
        .toFile();
}
```

The load and save methods interact with a file named favorites.xml,
which is located in the following workspace metadata subdirectory:
<workspace>\.metadata\.plugins\com.qualityeclipse.favorites.
The file content is in XML format and might look something like this:

```
<?xml version="1.0" encoding="UTF-8"?>
<Favorites>
    <Favorite
        Info="/First Project/com/qualityeclipse/sample
            /HelloWorld.java"
        TypeId="WBFile"/>
    <Favorite
        Info="/com.qualityeclipse.favorites/src"
        TypeId="WBFolder"/>
    ...
</Favorites>
```

> **Tip:** Eclipse can crash or lock up...not often, if ever, but it can. If it does, then the normal shutdown sequence is preempted and your plug-in will not get a chance to save its model state. To protect your data, you can register a save participant (ISaveParticipant) and store critical model states ("snapshots") at various times during the Eclipse session. The mechanism is the same as that used to receive resource change events when your plug-in is inactive (see Section 9.5, Delayed Changed Events, on page 387).

7.6 Testing

Now that the **Favorites** view has been modified, the JUnit tests for the **Favorites** view need to be updated to take the modifications into account. If the tests are run as they stand, you'll get the following failure.

```
testView(com.qualityeclipse.favorites.test.FavoritesViewTest)

junit.framework.AssertionFailedError: expected.length 3,
but actual.length 0 expected:<3> but was:<0>
  at junit.framework.Assert.fail(Assert.java:47)
  at junit.framework.Assert.failNotEquals(Assert.java:282)
  at junit.framework.Assert.assertEquals(Assert.java:64)
  at junit.framework.Assert.assertEquals(Assert.java:201)
  at com.qualityeclipse.favorites.test.FavoritesViewTest
        .assertEquals(FavoritesViewTest.java:125)
  at com.qualityeclipse.favorites.test.FavoritesViewTest
        .testView(FavoritesViewTest.java:93)
  at sun.reflect.NativeMethodAccessorImpl
        .invoke0(Native Method)
... etc ...
```

On closer inspection, this test is looking for the default viewer content (see Section 2.8.3, Creating a Plug-in test, on page 93). Since this default content has been removed in favor of real content (see Section 7.2.4, Content provider, on page 276), the test should be modified as follows:

```
public void testView() {
   TableViewer viewer = testView.getFavoritesViewer();

   Object[] expectedContent = new Object[] { };
   Object[] expectedLabels = new String[] { };

   ... code for the rest of the test ...
}
```

In a similar fashion, add code to the `AddToFavoritesTest` (see Section 6.3.6, Adding a test for the new action, on page 235) to assert the **Favorites** view content before and after the test. Since this type of assertion is duplicated in several places, it can be extracted into a new `assertFavorites-ViewContent` method and pushed up into the `AbstractFavoritesTest` class.

7.7   Image Caching

`Image` is a Java construct that wraps a native resource and thus must be properly managed. As with all other native wrappers in Eclipse, the rule is that if you create it, you must dispose of it to prevent memory leaks. `ImageDescriptor`, on the other hand, is a pure Java type that identifies a particular image without its associated native resource. It does not need to be managed and removed properly; rather, it will be automatically managed and disposed of by the Java garbage collector.

When a plug-in creates an instance of `Image`, it typically caches it in an object that maps the identifier for the image—typically an `ImageDescriptor`—to a particular image. Not only does the cache provide a way to remember which `Image` instances were created and thus need to be cleaned up, but it also keeps the same image from being loaded into memory more than once, preventing unnecessary usage of limited OS resources. Depending on where and when the image is used, the image cache may be disposed when the view closes, or it may be kept around for the life of the plug-in.

In the **Favorites** plug-in, if you need to load your own images (see Section 7.2.3, View model, on page 265), instantiate a class similar to the one below to cache loaded images. This class follows the Eclipse approach by lazily loading the images as they are requested rather than loading all images immediately when the plug-in starts or when the view is first opened. The plug-in's `stop()` method would be modified to call the `dispose()` method of this instance so that the images would be cleaned up when the plug-in is shut down.

```
package com.qualityeclipse.favorites.util;

import ...

public class ImageCache {
   private final Map imageMap = new HashMap();

   public Image getImage(ImageDescriptor imageDescriptor) {
      if (imageDescriptor == null)
         return null;
```

```
        Image image = (Image) imageMap.get(imageDescriptor);
        if (image == null) {
            image = imageDescriptor.createImage();
            imageMap.put(imageDescriptor, image);
        }
        return image;
    }

    public void dispose() {
        Iterator iter = imageMap.values().iterator();
        while (iter.hasNext())
            ((Image) iter.next()).dispose();
        imageMap.clear();
    }
}
```

Alternatively, you can use the class `org.eclipse.jface.resource.`
`ImageRegistry` or the `Plugin.getImageRegistry()` method.

> **Tip:** WindowBuilder Pro (see Appendix A, Eclipse Plug-ins and Resources)
> provides a `ResourceManager` that caches images, fonts, cursors, and so on.

7.8 Auto-sizing Table Columns

Another nice enhancement to the **Favorites** view is for the columns in the table
to be automatically resized to fit the current space. To do this, replace the table
layout by adding the following to `createTableViewer()` just under the
`table` variable assignment.

```
AutoResizeTableLayout layout = new AutoResizeTableLayout(table);
table.setLayout(layout);
```

Then create this class:

```
package com.qualityeclipse.favorites.util;

import ...

public class AutoResizeTableLayout extends TableLayout
    implements ControlListener {
    private final Table table;
    private List columns = new ArrayList();
    private boolean autosizing = false;

    public AutoResizeTableLayout(Table table) {
        this.table = table;
        table.addControlListener(this);
    }
```

```
public void addColumnData(ColumnLayoutData data) {
   columns.add(data);
   super.addColumnData(data);
}

public void controlMoved(ControlEvent e) {
}

public void controlResized(ControlEvent e) {
   if (autosizing)
      return;
   autosizing = true;
   try {
      autoSizeColumns();
   }
   finally {
      autosizing = false;
   }
}

private void autoSizeColumns() {
   int width = table.getClientArea().width;

   // XXX: Layout is being called with an invalid value
   // the first time it is being called on Linux.
   // This method resets the layout to null,
   // so we run it only when the value is OK.
   if (width <= 1)
      return;

   TableColumn[] tableColumns = table.getColumns();
   int size = Math.min(columns.size(), tableColumns.length);
   int[] widths = new int[size];
   int fixedWidth = 0;
   int numberOfWeightColumns = 0;
   int totalWeight = 0;

   // First calculate space occupied by fixed columns.
   for (int i = 0; i < size; i++) {
      ColumnLayoutData col =
         (ColumnLayoutData) columns.get(i);
      if (col instanceof ColumnPixelData) {
         int pixels = ((ColumnPixelData) col).width;
         widths[i] = pixels;
         fixedWidth += pixels;
      } else if (col instanceof ColumnWeightData) {
         ColumnWeightData cw = (ColumnWeightData) col;
         numberOfWeightColumns++;
         int weight = cw.weight;
         totalWeight += weight;
      } else {
         throw new IllegalStateException(
            "Unknown column layout data");
      }
   }
```

```
            // Do we have columns that have a weight?
            if (numberOfWeightColumns > 0) {
                // Now, distribute the rest
                // to the columns with weight.
                int rest = width - fixedWidth;
                int totalDistributed = 0;
                for (int i = 0; i < size; i++) {
                    ColumnLayoutData col =
                        (ColumnLayoutData) columns.get(i);
                    if (col instanceof ColumnWeightData) {
                        ColumnWeightData cw = (ColumnWeightData) col;
                        int weight = cw.weight;
                        int pixels =
                            totalWeight == 0
                                ? 0
                                : weight * rest / totalWeight;
                        if (pixels < cw.minimumWidth)
                            pixels = cw.minimumWidth;
                        totalDistributed += pixels;
                        widths[i] = pixels;
                    }
                }

                // Distribute any remaining pixels
                // to columns with weight.
                int diff = rest - totalDistributed;
                for (int i = 0; diff > 0; i++) {
                    if (i == size)
                        i = 0;
                    ColumnLayoutData col =
                        (ColumnLayoutData) columns.get(i);
                    if (col instanceof ColumnWeightData) {
                        ++widths[i];
                        --diff;
                    }
                }
            }

            for (int i = 0; i < size; i++) {
                if (tableColumns[i].getWidth() != widths[i])
                    tableColumns[i].setWidth(widths[i]);
            }
        }
    }
}
```

For each column, you will need to supply additional layout information. For example:

```
// fixed width column
layout.addColumnData(new ColumnPixelData(18));

// weighted column
layout.addColumnData(new ColumnWeightData(50));
```

The **Favorites** view can use the `AutoResizeTableLayout` class by modifying the code shown in Section 7.2.2, View controls, on page 264, after which the columns in the view will automatically be resized when the view is resized.

```
TableColumn typeColumn = new TableColumn(table, SWT.LEFT);
typeColumn.setText("");
//typeColumn.setWidth(18);
layout.addColumnData(new ColumnPixelData(18));


TableColumn nameColumn = new TableColumn(table, SWT.LEFT);
nameColumn.setText("Name");
//nameColumn.setWidth(200);
layout.addColumnData(new ColumnWeightData(200));


TableColumn locationColumn = new TableColumn(table, SWT.LEFT);
locationColumn.setText("Location");
//locationColumn.setWidth(450);
layout.addColumnData(new ColumnWeightData(200));
```

7.9   RFRS Considerations

The "User Interface" section of the *RFRS Requirements* includes seven items—five requirements and two best practices—dealing with views. All of them are derived from the Eclipse UI Guidelines.

7.9.1   *Views for navigation*   *(RFRS 3.5.15)*

User Interface Guideline #7.1 is a **requirement** that states:

> *Use a view to navigate a hierarchy of information, open an editor, or display the properties of an object.*

To pass this test, create a list of the views defined by your application and demonstrate how they are used to navigate information, open editors, or display the properties of some object. In the case of the examples presented earlier in this chapter, show the **Favorites** view (see Figure 10–4 on page 393) and describe its use to the reviewers. In particular, double-clicking on a file in the **Favorites** view will open the file in an editor.

7.9.2   Views save immediately   *(RFRS 3.5.16)*

User Interface Guideline #7.2 is a **requirement** that states:

> *Modifications made within a view must be saved immediately. For instance, if a file is modified in the **Navigator**, the changes must be committed to the workspace immediately. A change made in the **Outline** view must be committed to the edit model of the active editor immediately. For changes made in the **Properties** view, if the property is a property of an open edit model, it should be persisted to the edit model. If it is a property of a file, persist it to file. In the past, some views have tried to implement an editor-style lifecycle with a save action. This can cause confusion. The **File** menu within a workbench window contains a **Save** action, but it only applies to the active editor. It will not target the active view. This can lead to a situation where the **File > Save** action is in contradiction with the **Save** action within the view.*

For this test, show how changes made in your view are saved immediately. If your view updates an existing editor, make sure that the editor is immediately marked as dirty and shows the modification indicator (*). Further, show that the **Save** menu does not need to be invoked for the view to save its changes.

7.9.3   View initialization   *(RFRS 3.5.17)*

User Interface Guideline #7.8 is a **requirement** that states:

> *When a view first opens, derive the view input from the state of the perspective. The view may consult the perspective input or selection, or the state of another view. For instance, if the **Outline** view is opened, it will determine the active editor, query the editor for an outline model, and display the outline model.*

To pass this test, show that your view reflects the input state of the perspective (if appropriate). If your view is meant to show some attribute of the selected editor, make sure that when it is opened it displays the appropriate information. For the **Favorites** view, this requirement probably does not apply. The **Favorites** view could be extended to update its own selection to reflect the currently active editor.

7.9.4   View global actions   *(RFRS 3.5.18)*

User Interface Guideline #7.19 is a **requirement** that states:

> *If a view has support for **cut, copy, paste**, or any of the global actions, the same actions must be executable from the same actions in the window*

*menu and toolbar. The window menu contains a number of global actions, such as **cut**, **copy**, and **paste** in the **Edit** menu. These actions target the active part, as indicated by a shaded title area. If these actions are supported within a view, the view should hook these window actions so that selection in the window menu or toolbar produces the same result as selection of the same action in the view. The following are the supported global actions: **undo**, **redo**, **cut**, **copy**, **paste**, **print**, **delete**, **find**, **select all**, and **bookmark**.*

For this requirement, if your view implements any of the items on the global action list, show that those commands can also be invoked from the window menus and toolbars. For the **Favorites** view, show that the **Cut**, **Copy**, **Paste**, and **Delete** (**Remove**) commands can be invoked from the platform **Edit** menu.

7.9.5   Persist view state   *(RFRS 3.5.19)*

User Interface Guideline #7.20 is a **requirement** that states:

*Persist the state of each view between sessions. If a view is self-starting in the sense that its input is not derived from selection in other parts, the state of the view should be persisted between sessions. Within the workbench, the state of the **Navigator** view, including the input and expansion state, is saved between sessions.*

Show that your view persists its state between sessions. For the **Favorites** view, shut down and restart the workbench and show that the **Favorites** items appearing in the list are the same ones that were there when the workbench was shut down.

7.9.6   Register context menus   *(RFRS 5.3.5.8)*

User Interface Guideline #7.17 is a **best practice** that states:

Register all context menus in the view with the platform. In the platform, the menu and toolbar for a view are automatically extended by the platform. By contrast, the context menu extension is supported in collaboration between the view and the platform. To achieve this collaboration, a view must register each context menu it contains with the platform.

Show that the context menu of your view is extensible by the platform. If the platform defines commands that are appropriate for the objects contained in your view, those commands should appear in the view's context menu. For the **Favorites** view, show that common Eclipse commands such as "Replace

With" and "Compare With" appear when you right-click on a **Favorites** item (see Figure 7–9).

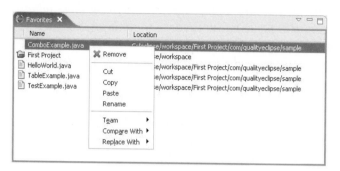

Figure 7–9   Favorites view showing platform contributions to the context menu.

7.9.7   Action filters for views   *(RFRS 5.3.5.9)*

User Interface Guideline #7.18 is a **best practice** that states:

> *Implement an action filter for each object type in the view. An action filter makes it easier for one plug-in to add an action to objects in a view defined by another plug-in. An action target is described using object type and attributes.*

As with the previous best practice, show that any commands contributed to your view's context menu are appropriate to the type of the selected object. Commands that don't apply should be filtered out. For the **Favorites** view, show that the platform commands contributed to the context menu are context-sensitive based on the type of object selected (see Figure 7–10).

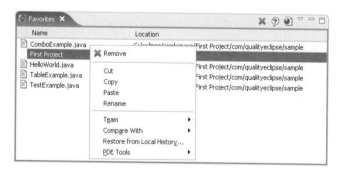

Figure 7–10   Favorites view showing that context menu items are filtered based on their type (projects show items other than files).

7.10   Summary

This chapter covered creating new views, modifying a view to respond to selections in the active editor or other views, and exporting a view's selection to the rest of Eclipse. The next chapter discusses editors, which are used to edit the state of individual resources.

References

Chapter source (*www.qualityeclipse.com/projects/source-ch-07.zip*).

D'Anjou, Jim, Scott Fairbrother, Dan Kehn, John Kellerman, and Pat McCarthy, *The Java Developer's Guide to Eclipse, Second Edition*. Addison-Wesley, Boston, 2004.

McAffer, Jeff, and Jean-Michel Lemieux, *Eclipse Rich Client Platform: Designing, Coding, and Packaging Java Applications*. Addison-Wesley, Boston, 2005.

Springgay, Dave, "Creating an Eclipse View," OTI, November 2, 2001 (*www.eclipse.org/articles/viewArticle/ViewArticle2.html*).

Liotta, Matt, "Extending Eclipse with Helpful Views," July 20, 2004 (*www.devx.com/opensource/Article/21562*).

CHAPTER 8

Editors

Editors are the primary mechanism for users to create and modify resources (e.g., files). Eclipse provides some basic editors such as text and Java source editors, along with some more complex multipage editors such as the plug-in manifest editor. Products that need to present their own editors can use the same extension points used by the built-in Eclipse editors. This chapter discusses creating a new **Properties** editor, hooking up actions to it, and linking the editor to the **Outline** view.

Editors must implement the `org.eclipse.ui.IEditorPart` interface. Typically, views are subclasses of `org.eclipse.ui.part.EditorPart` and thus indirectly subclasses of `org.eclipse.ui.part.WorkbenchPart`, inheriting much of the behavior needed to implement the `IEditorPart` interface (see Figure 8–1).

Editors are contained in an `org.eclipse.ui.IEditorSite`, which in turn is contained in an `org.eclipse.ui.IWorkbenchPage`. In the spirit of lazy initialization, `IWorkbenchPage` holds on to instances of `org.eclipse.ui.IEditorReference` rather than the editor itself so that editors can be enumerated and referenced without actually loading the plug-in defining the editor.

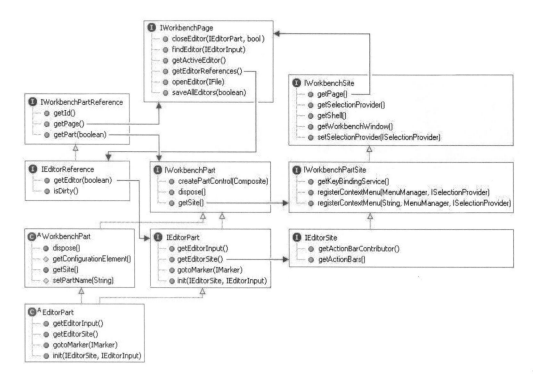

Figure 8–1   EditorPart classes.

Editors share a common set of behaviors with views via the `org.eclipse.ui.part.WorkbenchPart` superclass and `org.eclipse.ui.` `IWorkbenchPart` interface, but have some very important differences. Editors follow the classic open-modify-save paradigm, whereas any action performed in a view should immediately affect the state of the workspace and underlying resource(s).

Editors appear in one area of Eclipse, while views are arranged around the outside of the editor area. Editors are typically resource-based, while views can show information about one resource, multiple resources, or even something totally unrelated to resources such as available memory, network status, or builder errors.

8.1   Editor Declaration

There are two steps involved in creating a new editor:

- Define the editor in the plug-in manifest file (see Figure 8-2).
- Create the editor part containing the code.

One way to do all this at once is to create the editor when the plug-in is being created, similar to the way that views can be created (see Section 2.2.3, Define the view, on page 69). If the plug-in already exists, then this becomes a two-step process.

```xml
<extension point="org.eclipse.ui.editors">
   <editor
      id="com.qualityeclipse.favorites.editors.PropertiesEditor"
      extensions="properties"
      name="Properties Editor"
      icon="icons/sample.gif"
      contributorClass=
         "com.qualityeclipse.favorites.editors.PropertiesEditorContributor"
      class="com.qualityeclipse.favorites.editors.PropertiesEditor"/>
</extension>
```

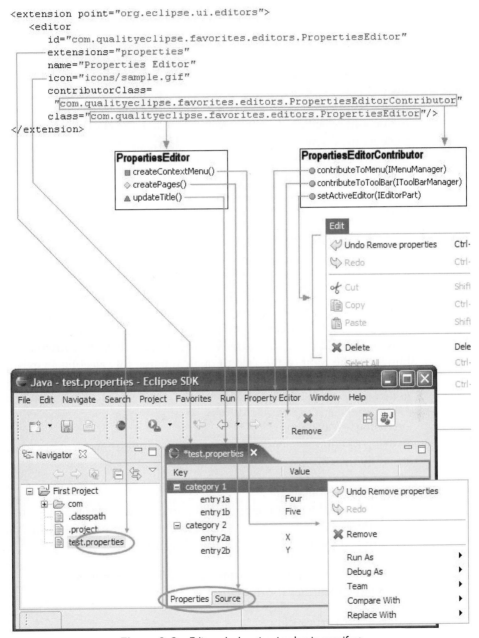

Figure 8–2 Editor declaration in plug-in manifest.

The first step in creating an editor is to define the editor in the plug-in manifest (see Figure 8–2). On the **Extensions** page of the plug-in manifest editor, click the **Add...** button in the upper right corner, select **org.eclipse.ui. editors**, and finally click **Finish**. Next, right-click on **org.eclipse.ui.editors** and select **New > editor** to add an editor extension. Select the new editor extension to display the properties on the right and then enter the following values.

class—"com.qualityeclipse.favorites.editors.PropertiesEditor"
The fully qualified name of the class defining the editor and implementing `org.eclipse.ui.IEditorPart` (see Section 8.2, Editor Part, on page 330). Click the **Browse...** button to the right of the field to open a dialog and select an existing editor part. Click the **class** label on the left to generate a new one. The attribute's class, command, and launcher are mutually exclusive. The class is instantiated using its no argument constructor, but can be parameterized using the `IExecutableExtension` interface (see Section 20.5, Types Specified in an Extension Point, on page 723).

contributorClass—"com.qualityeclipse.favorites.editors. PropertiesEditorContributor"
The fully qualified name of a class that implements `org.eclipse.ui. IEditorActionBarContributor` and adds new actions to the workbench menu and toolbar, reflecting the features of the editor type (see Section 8.5.2, Editor contributor, on page 357). This attribute should only be defined if the class attribute is defined. Click the **Browse...** button to the right of the field to open a dialog for selecting an existing editor contributor. Click the **contributorClass** on the left to generate a new one.

extensions—"properties"
A string of comma-separated file extensions indicating file types understood by the editor.

icon—"icons/sample.gif"
The image displayed at the upper left corner of the editor. Similar to action images (see Section 6.2.4, Action images, on page 214), this path is relative to the plug-in's installation directory.

id—"com.qualityeclipse.favorites.editors.PropertiesEditor"
The unique identifier for this editor.

name—"Properties Editor"
The human-readable name for the editor.

Other attributes that are not used in this example include:

command—A command to run to launch an external editor. The executable command must be located on the system path or in the plug-in's directory. The attribute's class, command, and launcher are mutually exclusive.

default—"true" or "false" (blank = `false`)
If `true`, this editor will be used as the default editor for the type. This is only relevant in the case where more than one editor is registered for the same type. If an editor is not the default for the type, it can still be launched using the **Open with...** submenu for the selected resource.

filenames—A string containing comma-separated filenames indicating filenames understood by the editor. For instance, an editor that understands plug-in and fragment manifest files can register `plugin.xml`, `fragment.xml`.

launcher—The name of a class that implements `org.eclipse.ui.IEditorLauncher` and opens an external editor. The attribute's class, command, and launcher are mutually exclusive.

matchingStrategy—the name of a class that implements `org.eclipse.ui.IEditorMatchingStrategy`. This attribute should only be defined if the class attribute is defined and allows the editor extension to provide its own algorithm for matching the input of one of its editors to a given editor input. This is used to find a matching editor during `openEditor()` and `findEditor()`.

In addition, the **editor** element can have one or more **contentTypeBinding** subelements, each specifying a **contentTypeId**. The **contentTypeId** references an `org.eclipse.core.runtime.contentTypes` extension and indicates that the editor can contain that type of content. The **contentTypes** extension can more accurately define whether a file should be associated with a partiular editor than by file extension alone.

After filtering files by name and extension, the content type uses a *describer*—an instance of `IContentDescriber` or `ITextContentDescriber`—to scan the content of a file before determining whether a file contains a particular type of content. Eclipse provides several built-in describers including the following:

`BinarySignatureDescriber`—A content describer for binary formats that present some simple signature at a known, fixed offset. There are three parameters: "signature," "offset," and "required"—the first one being mandatory.

signature—a sequence of hex codes, one for each byte. For example, "CA FE BA BE" would be a signature for Java class files.

offset—an integer indicating the offset where the signature's first byte is to be found.

required—a boolean (default is `true`) indicating whether the absence of a signature should deem the contents validity status as `IContent-Describer.INVALID` or `IContentDescriber.INDETERMINATE`.

`XMLRootElementContentDescriber`—A content describer for detecting the name of the top-level element or the DTD system identifier in an XML file. Two parameters are supported: "dtd" and "element."

8.2   Editor Part

The code defining the editor's behavior is found in a class implementing the `org.eclipse.ui.IEditorPart` interface, typically by subclassing either the `org.eclipse.ui.part.EditorPart` abstract class or `org.eclipse.ui.part.MultiPageEditorPart`. The **Properties** editor subclasses `MultiPage-EditorPart` and provides two pages for the user to edit its content.

8.2.1   Editor methods

Here are the `EditorPart` methods.

`createPartControl(Composite)`—Creates the controls comprising the editor. Typically, this method simply calls more finely grained methods such as `createTree`, `createTextEditor`, and so on.

`dispose()`—This method is automatically called when the editor is closed and marks the end of the editor's lifecycle. It cleans up any platform resources, such as images, clipboard, and so on, which were created by this class. This follows the *if you create it, you destroy it* theme that runs throughout Eclipse.

`doSave(IProgressMonitor)`—Saves the contents of this editor. If the save is successful, the part should fire a property changed event (`PROP_DIRTY` property), reflecting the new dirty state. If the save is canceled via user action, or for any other reason, the part should invoke `setCanceled` on the `IProgressMonitor` to inform the caller (see Section 9.4, Progress Monitor, on page 383).

`doSaveAs()`—This method is *optional*. It opens a **Save As** dialog and saves the content of the editor to a new location. If the save is successful, the part should fire a property changed event (`PROP_DIRTY` property), reflecting the new dirty state.

`gotoMarker(IMarker)`—Sets the cursor and selection state for this editor as specified by the given marker.

`init(IEditorSite, IEditorInput)`—Initializes this editor with the given editor site and input. This method is automatically called shortly after editor construction; it marks the start of the editor's lifecycle.

`isDirty()`—Returns whether the contents of this editor have changed since the last save operation.

`isSaveAsAllowed()`—Returns whether the "Save As" operation is supported by this part.

`setFocus()`—Asks this part to take focus within the workbench. Typically, this method simply calls `setFocus()` on one of its child controls.

`MultiPageEditorPart` provides the following additional methods:

`addPage(Control)`—Creates and adds a new page containing the given control to this multipage editor. The control may be `null`, allowing it to be created and set later using `setControl`.

`addPage(IEditorPart, IEditorInput)`—Creates and adds a new page containing the given editor to this multipage editor. This also hooks a property change listener onto the nested editor.

`createPages()`—Creates the pages of this multipage editor. Typically, this method simply calls more finely grained methods such as `ceatePropertiesPage`, `createSourcePage`, and so on.

`getContainer()`—Returns the composite control containing this multipage editor's pages. This should be used as the parent when creating controls for individual pages. That is, when calling `addPage(Control)`, the passed control should be a child of this container.

`setPageImage(int, Image)`—Sets the image for the page with the given index.

`setPageText(int, String)`—Sets the text label for the page with the given index.

8.2.2   *Editor controls*

The new `PropertiesEditor` is a multipage editor containing **Properties** and **Source** pages. The **Properties** page contains a tree displaying the property key/value pairs, while the **Source** page displays the text as it appears in the file itself. These pages showcase building an editor out of individual controls (**Properties** page) and nesting one type of editor inside another (**Source** page).

Start by creating a new subclass of `MultiPageEditorPart`. The new `PropertiesEditor` class contains an `init()` method ensuring that the appropriate type of content is being edited.

```
package com.qualityeclipse.favorites.editors;

import ...
import com.qualityeclipse.favorites.FavoritesLog;

public class PropertiesEditor extends MultiPageEditorPart
{
   public void init(IEditorSite site, IEditorInput input)
     throws PartInitException
   {
      if (!(input instanceof IFileEditorInput))
         throw new PartInitException(
            "Invalid Input: Must be IFileEditorInput");
      super.init(site, input);
   }
```

Next, add two fields plus methods to create the **Source** and **Properties** pages.

```
private TreeViewer treeViewer;
private TextEditor textEditor;

protected void createPages() {
   createPropertiesPage();
   createSourcePage();
   updateTitle();
}

void createPropertiesPage() {
   treeViewer = new TreeViewer(
      getContainer(), SWT.MULTI | SWT.FULL_SELECTION);
   int index = addPage(treeViewer.getControl());
   setPageText(index, "Properties");
}

void createSourcePage() {
   try {
      textEditor = new TextEditor();
      int index = addPage(textEditor, getEditorInput());
      setPageText(index, "Source");
   }
   catch (PartInitException e) {
      FavoritesLog.logError("Error creating nested text editor", e);
   }
}

void updateTitle() {
   IEditorInput input = getEditorInput();
   setPartName(input.getName());
   setTitleToolTip(input.getToolTipText());
}
```

When the focus shifts to the editor, the setFocus() method is called; it must then redirect focus to the appropriate editor based on which page is currently selected.

```
public void setFocus() {
    switch (getActivePage()) {
        case 0:
            treeViewer.getTree().setFocus();
            break;
        case 1:
            textEditor.setFocus();
            break;
    }
}
```

When the user directly or indirectly requests that a marker be revealed, ensure that the **Source** page is active then redirect the request to the text editor. You could do something different when the **Properties** page is active, but that would require additional editor model infrastructure.

```
public void gotoMarker(IMarker marker) {
    setActivePage(1);
    ((IGotoMarker) textEditor.getAdapter(IGotoMarker.class))
        .gotoMarker(marker);
}
```

Three methods are involved in saving editor content. If the isSaveAsAllowed() method returns false, then the doSaveAs() method is never called.

```
public boolean isSaveAsAllowed() {
    return true;
}

public void doSave(IProgressMonitor monitor) {
    textEditor.doSave(monitor);
}

public void doSaveAs() {
    textEditor.doSaveAs();
    setInput(textEditor.getEditorInput());
    updateTitle();
}
```

This code defines a very simple editor. When the editor is opened, the first page is an empty tree (the content will be added in the next section), while the second page is an embedded text editor (see Figure 8–3). The editor handles all the normal text editing operations on the second page thanks to the embedded text editor, but the first page needs work.

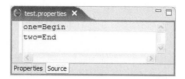

Figure 8–3   The Properties editor's Source page.

First, you need to add columns to the tree by adding two new fields plus additional functionality to the createPropertiesPage() method. Later, if you want the display to look more polished, auto-size the columns in the tree similar to the way the **Favorites** view is auto-sized. (see Section 7.8, Auto-sizing Table Columns, on page 316).

```
private TreeColumn keyColumn;
private TreeColumn valueColumn;

void createPropertiesPage() {
   treeViewer = new TreeViewer(
      getContainer(), SWT.MULTI | SWT.FULL_SELECTION);

   Tree tree = treeViewer.getTree();
   tree.setHeaderVisible(true);

   keyColumn = new TreeColumn(tree, SWT.NONE);
   keyColumn.setText("Key");
   keyColumn.setWidth(150);

   valueColumn = new TreeColumn(tree, SWT.NONE);
   valueColumn.setText("Value");
   valueColumn.setWidth(150);

   int index = addPage(tree);
   setPageText(index, "Properties");
}
```

When run, the **Properties** editor now displays two empty columns on the **Properties** page (see Figure 8–4).

Figure 8–4   Properties editor's Properties page.

8.2.3   *Editor model*

The next step is to hook up the tree so that content in the text editor appears in the tree. To accomplish this, you need to build a model capable of parsing the text editor's content, and then attach that model, along with a label provider, to the tree. Of course, there is lots of room for improvement in this model, such as splitting out the parsing, refactoring code into a separate class, and enhancing the parser to handle multiline values; however, it will do for the purposes of this demonstration.

Start this process by introducing a new PropertyElement superclass for all property model objects.

```
package com.qualityeclipse.favorites.editors;

public abstract class PropertyElement
{
    public static final PropertyElement[] NO_CHILDREN = {};
    private PropertyElement parent;

    public PropertyElement(PropertyElement parent) {
        this.parent = parent;
    }

    public PropertyElement getParent() {
        return parent;
    }

    public abstract PropertyElement[] getChildren();

    public abstract void removeFromParent();
}
```

A PropertyEntry object represents a key/value pair in the property file. Note that the next three classes are all interdependent and should be added to your project at the same time.

```
package com.qualityeclipse.favorites.editors;

public class PropertyEntry extends PropertyElement
{
    String key;
    String value;

    public PropertyEntry(
        PropertyCategory parent, String key, String value
    ) {
        super(parent);
        this.key = key;
        this.value = value;
    }
```

```java
    public String getKey() {
       return key;
    }

    public String getValue() {
       return value;
    }

    public PropertyElement[] getChildren() {
       return NO_CHILDREN;
    }

    public void setKey(String text) {
       if (key.equals(text))
          return;
       key = text;
       ((PropertyCategory) getParent()).keyChanged(this);
    }

    public void setValue(String text) {
       if (value.equals(text))
          return;
       value = text;
       ((PropertyCategory) getParent()).valueChanged(this);
    }

    public void removeFromParent() {
       ((PropertyCategory) getParent()).removeEntry(this);
    }
}
```

A `PropertyCategory` represents a group of related property entries with a comment preceding the group indicating the name. The category can extract its name and entries from a reader object.

```java
package com.qualityeclipse.favorites.editors;
import ...

public class PropertyCategory extends PropertyElement
{
   private String name;
   private List entries;

   public PropertyCategory(
      PropertyFile parent, LineNumberReader reader
   ) throws IOException {
      super(parent);

      // Determine the category name from comments.
      while (true) {
         reader.mark(1);
         int ch = reader.read();
         if (ch == -1)
            break;
```

```
            reader.reset();
            if (ch != '#')
               break;
            String line = reader.readLine();
            if (name == null) {
               line = line.replace('#', ' ').trim();
               if (line.length() > 0)
                  name = line;
            }
         }
         if (name == null)
            name = "";

         // Determine the properties in this category.
         entries = new ArrayList();
         while (true) {
            reader.mark(1);
            int ch = reader.read();
            if (ch == -1)
               break;
            reader.reset();
            if (ch == '#')
               break;
            String line = reader.readLine();
            int index = line.indexOf('=');
            if (index != -1) {
               String key = line.substring(0, index).trim();
               String value = line.substring(index + 1).trim();
               entries.add(new PropertyEntry(this, key, value));
            }
         }
      }

      public String getName() {
         return name;
      }

      public Collection getEntries() {
         return entries;
      }

      public PropertyElement[] getChildren() {
         return (PropertyElement[]) entries.toArray(
            new PropertyElement[entries.size()]);
      }

      public void setName(String text) {
         if (name.equals(text))
            return;
         name = text;
         ((PropertyFile) getParent()).nameChanged(this);
      }
```

```
   public void addEntry(PropertyEntry entry) {
      if (!entries.contains(entry)) {
         entries.add(entry);
         ((PropertyFile) getParent()).entryAdded(
            this, entry);
      }
   }

   public void removeEntry(PropertyEntry entry) {
      if (entries.remove(entry))
         ((PropertyFile) getParent()).entryRemoved(
            this, entry);
   }

   public void removeFromParent() {
      ((PropertyFile) getParent()).removeCategory(this);
   }

   public void keyChanged(PropertyEntry entry) {
      ((PropertyFile) getParent()).keyChanged(this, entry);
   }

   public void valueChanged(PropertyEntry entry) {
      ((PropertyFile) getParent()).valueChanged(this, entry);
   }
}
```

The `PropertyFile` object ties it all together.

```
package com.qualityeclipse.favorites.editors;

import ...

import com.qualityeclipse.favorites.FavoritesLog;

public class PropertyFile extends PropertyElement
{
   private PropertyCategory unnamedCategory;
   private List categories;
   private List listeners = new ArrayList();

   public PropertyFile(String content) {
      super(null);
      categories = new ArrayList();

      LineNumberReader reader =
         new LineNumberReader(new StringReader(content));
      try {
         unnamedCategory = new PropertyCategory(this, reader);
         while (true) {
            reader.mark(1);
            int ch = reader.read();
            if (ch == -1)
               break;
```

```java
            reader.reset();
            categories.add(
               new PropertyCategory(this, reader));
         }
      }
      catch (IOException e) {
         FavoritesLog.logError(e);
      }
   }

   public PropertyElement[] getChildren() {
      List children = new ArrayList();
      children.addAll(unnamedCategory.getEntries());
      children.addAll(categories);
      return (PropertyElement[]) children.toArray(
         new PropertyElement[children.size()]);
   }

   public void addCategory(PropertyCategory category) {
      if (!categories.contains(category)) {
         categories.add(category);
         categoryAdded(category);
      }
   }

   public void removeCategory(PropertyCategory category) {
      if (categories.remove(category))
         categoryRemoved(category);
   }

   public void removeFromParent() {
      // Nothing to do.
   }

   void addPropertyFileListener(
     PropertyFileListener listener) {
      if (!listeners.contains(listener))
         listeners.add(listener);
   }

   void removePropertyFileListener(
      PropertyFileListener listener) {
      listeners.remove(listener);
   }

   void keyChanged(PropertyCategory category,PropertyEntry entry) {
      Iterator iter = listeners.iterator();
      while (iter.hasNext())
         ((PropertyFileListener) iter.next())
            .keyChanged(category, entry);
   }
```

```
void valueChanged(PropertyCategory category, PropertyEntry entry)
{
   Iterator iter = listeners.iterator();
   while (iter.hasNext())
      ((PropertyFileListener) iter.next())
         .valueChanged(category, entry);
}

void nameChanged(PropertyCategory category) {
   Iterator iter = listeners.iterator();
   while (iter.hasNext())
      ((PropertyFileListener) iter.next())
         .nameChanged(category);
}

void entryAdded(PropertyCategory category, PropertyEntry entry) {
   Iterator iter = listeners.iterator();
   while (iter.hasNext())
      ((PropertyFileListener) iter.next())
         .entryAdded(category, entry);
}

void entryRemoved(PropertyCategory category, PropertyEntry entry)
{
   Iterator iter = listeners.iterator();
   while (iter.hasNext())
      ((PropertyFileListener) iter.next())
         .entryRemoved(category, entry);
}

void categoryAdded(PropertyCategory category) {
   Iterator iter = listeners.iterator();
   while (iter.hasNext())
      ((PropertyFileListener) iter.next())
         .categoryAdded(category);
}

void categoryRemoved(PropertyCategory category) {
   Iterator iter = listeners.iterator();
   while (iter.hasNext())
      ((PropertyFileListener) iter.next())
         .categoryRemoved(category);
}
}
```

The PropertyFileListener interface is used by the ProperyFile to notify registered listeners, such as PropertiesEditor, that changes have occurred in the model.

```
package com.qualityeclipse.favorites.editors;

public interface PropertyFileListener
{
   void keyChanged(
      PropertyCategory category,
      PropertyEntry entry);

   void valueChanged(
      PropertyCategory category,
      PropertyEntry entry);

   void nameChanged(
      PropertyCategory category);

   void entryAdded(
      PropertyCategory category,
      PropertyEntry entry);

   void entryRemoved(
      PropertyCategory category,
      PropertyEntry entry);

   void categoryAdded(
      PropertyCategory category);

   void categoryRemoved(
      PropertyCategory category);
}
```

8.2.4   *Content provider*

All these model objects are useless unless they can be properly displayed in the tree. To accomplish this, you need to create a content provider and label provider. The content provider provides the rows appearing in the tree along with parent/child relationships, but not the actual cell content.

```
package com.qualityeclipse.favorites.editors;

import ...

public class PropertiesEditorContentProvider
   implements ITreeContentProvider
{
   public void inputChanged(
      Viewer viewer, Object oldInput, Object newInput
   ) { }

   public Object[] getElements(Object element) {
      return getChildren(element);
   }
```

```
public Object[] getChildren(Object element) {
   if (element instanceof PropertyElement)
      return ((PropertyElement) element).getChildren();
   return null;
}

public Object getParent(Object element) {
   if (element instanceof PropertyElement)
      return ((PropertyElement) element).getParent();
   return null;
}

public boolean hasChildren(Object element) {
   if (element instanceof PropertyElement)
      return ((PropertyElement) element).getChildren().length > 0;
   return false;
}

public void dispose() {
}
}
```

8.2.5 Label provider

The label provider converts the row element object as returned by the content provider into images and text that can be displayed in the table cells.

```
package com.qualityeclipse.favorites.editors;

import ...

public class PropertiesEditorLabelProvider extends LabelProvider
   implements ITableLabelProvider
{
   public Image getColumnImage(Object element, int columnIndex) {
      return null;
   }

   public String getColumnText(Object element, int columnIndex) {
      if (element instanceof PropertyCategory) {
         PropertyCategory category =
            (PropertyCategory) element;
         switch (columnIndex) {
            case 0 :
               return category.getName();
            case 1 :
               return "";
         }
      }
```

```
            if (element instanceof PropertyEntry) {
               PropertyEntry entry = (PropertyEntry) element;
               switch (columnIndex) {
                  case 0 :
                     return entry.getKey();
                  case 1 :
                     return entry.getValue();
               }
            }

            if (element == null)
               return "<null>";
            return element.toString();
         }
      }
```

Finally, you need to add a new initTreeContent() method, called from the createPages() method, to associate the new content and label providers with the tree. This method is followed by another new method to synchronize the text editor's content with the tree's content. The call to asyncExec() ensures that the updateTreeFromTextEditor method is executed in the UI thread (see Section 4.2.5.1, Display, on page 140 for more on the UI thread). The updateTreeFromTextEditor() method indirectly references code in the org.eclipse.jface.text plug-in, so it must be added to the **Favorites** plug-in's manifest (see Figure 2–10 on page 73).

```
private PropertiesEditorContentProvider treeContentProvider;

void initTreeContent() {
   treeContentProvider = new PropertiesEditorContentProvider();
   treeViewer.setContentProvider(treeContentProvider);
   treeViewer.setLabelProvider(new PropertiesEditorLabelProvider());

   // Reset the input from the text editor's content
   // after the editor initialization has completed.
   treeViewer.setInput(new PropertyFile(""));
   treeViewer.getTree().getDisplay().asyncExec(new Runnable() {
      public void run() {
         updateTreeFromTextEditor();
      }
   });
   treeViewer.setAutoExpandLevel(TreeViewer.ALL_LEVELS);
}

void updateTreeFromTextEditor() {
   PropertyFile propertyFile = new PropertyFile(
      textEditor
         .getDocumentProvider()
         .getDocument(textEditor.getEditorInput())
         .get());
   treeViewer.setInput(propertyFile);
}
```

When all this has been accomplished, the **Properties** editor's **Properties** page will have some content (see Figure 8–5).

Figure 8–5   Properties editor with new content.

8.3   Editing

When the **Properties** page displays the content in a tree, it is important to edit the content without having to switch to the **Source** page (see Section 14.2.4, Marker resolution—quick fix, on page 520 for an example of manipulating the content in an existing text editor).

8.3.1   Cell editors

Cell editors use identifiers rather than a column index to identify what aspect of a particular object is being edited. Before creating the cell editors, first create some constants used as identifiers.

```
public static final String VALUE_COLUMN_ID = "Value";
public static final String KEY_COLUMN_ID = "Key";
```

Then, assign property identifiers to each column by adding a new `initTreeEditors()` method, which is called from `createPages()`.

```
treeViewer.setColumnProperties(
   new String[] { KEY_COLUMN_ID, VALUE_COLUMN_ID });
```

Cell editors are created by adding code to the `initTreeEditors()` method:

```
final TextCellEditor keyEditor =
   new TextCellEditor(treeViewer.getTree());
final TextCellEditor valueEditor =
   new TextCellEditor(treeViewer.getTree());
treeViewer.setCellEditors(
   new CellEditor[] { keyEditor, valueEditor });
```

8.3.2 *Cell modifiers*

Cell editors know nothing about the model being edited, which is where cell
modifiers come in. Cell modifiers adapt the underlying model to an interface
understood by cell editors so that the cell editors can present the correct value
to the user and update the model with new values when a user has made modifications. Add this new code to the `initTreeEditors()` method:

```
treeViewer.setCellModifier(
   new PropertiesEditorCellModifier(this, treeViewer));
```

Then, create a new class to handle this editor/model interaction.

```
package com.qualityeclipse.favorites.editors;

import ...

public class PropertiesEditorCellModifier
   implements ICellModifier
{
   private PropertiesEditor editor;

   public PropertiesEditorCellModifier(
      PropertiesEditor editor,
      TreeViewer viewer
   ) {
      this.editor = editor;
   }

   public boolean canModify(Object element, String property) {
      if (property == PropertiesEditor.KEY_COLUMN_ID) {
         if (element instanceof PropertyCategory)
            return true;
         if (element instanceof PropertyEntry)
            return true;
      }
      if (property == PropertiesEditor.VALUE_COLUMN_ID){
         if (element instanceof PropertyEntry)
            return true;
      }
      return false;
   }

   public Object getValue(Object element, String property) {
      if (property == PropertiesEditor.KEY_COLUMN_ID) {
         if (element instanceof PropertyCategory)
            return ((PropertyCategory) element).getName();
         if (element instanceof PropertyEntry)
            return ((PropertyEntry) element).getKey();
      }
```

```
        if (property == PropertiesEditor.VALUE_COLUMN_ID){
            if (element instanceof PropertyEntry)
                return ((PropertyEntry) element).getValue();
        }
        return null;
    }

    public void modify(Object item, String property, Object value) {
        // Null indicates that the validator rejected the value.
        if (value == null)
            return;

        Object element = item;
        if (element instanceof TreeItem)
            element = ((TreeItem) element).getData();

        String text = ((String) value).trim();
        if (property == PropertiesEditor.KEY_COLUMN_ID) {
            if (element instanceof PropertyCategory)
                ((PropertyCategory) element).setName(text);
            if (element instanceof PropertyEntry)
                ((PropertyEntry) element).setKey(text);
        }
        if (property == PropertiesEditor.VALUE_COLUMN_ID){
            if (element instanceof PropertyEntry)
                ((PropertyEntry) element).setValue(text);
        }
    }
}
```

The `modify(Object, String, Object)` method changes the editor model (see Figure 8-6), which then calls a new `treeModified()` method in the `PropertiesEditor` class to notify any interested members that the editor's content has been modified. This happens via a new `PropertyFileListener` listener created in the next section.

```
public void treeModified() {
    if (!isDirty())
        firePropertyChange(IEditorPart.PROP_DIRTY);
}
```

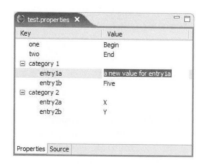

Figure 8–6   Properties editor with modified cell value.

8.3.3 Change listeners

When a user edits a value, the model generates a change event to notify registered listeners. The next step is to hook up a change listener in the PropertiesEditor class so that you can be notified of events and update the tree appropriately. First, add a new PropertyFileListener.

```
private final PropertyFileListener propertyFileListener =
   new PropertyFileListener()
{
   public void keyChanged(
      PropertyCategory category, PropertyEntry entry
   ) {
      treeViewer.update(entry, new String[] { KEY_COLUMN_ID });
      treeModified();
   }

   public void valueChanged(
      PropertyCategory category, PropertyEntry entry
   ) {
      treeViewer.update(entry, new String[] { VALUE_COLUMN_ID });
      treeModified();
   }

   public void nameChanged(PropertyCategory category) {
      treeViewer.update(category, new String[] { KEY_COLUMN_ID });
      treeModified();
   }

   public void entryAdded(
      PropertyCategory category, PropertyEntry entry
   ) {
      treeViewer.refresh();
      treeModified();
   }

   public void entryRemoved(
      PropertyCategory category, PropertyEntry entry
   ) {
      treeViewer.refresh();
      treeModified();
   }

   public void categoryAdded(PropertyCategory category) {
      treeViewer.refresh();
      treeModified();
   }

   public void categoryRemoved(PropertyCategory category) {
      treeViewer.refresh();
      treeModified();
   }
};
```

Next, modify the `updateTreeFromTextEditor()` method, as folows so that the listener is removed from the old editor model before it is discarded and added to the new editor model.

```
void updateTreeFromTextEditor() {
    PropertyFile propertyFile = (PropertyFile) treeViewer.getInput();
    propertyFile.removePropertyFileListener(propertyFileListener);
    propertyFile = new PropertyFile(
        textEditor
            .getDocumentProvider()
            .getDocument(textEditor.getEditorInput())
            .get());
    treeViewer.setInput(propertyFile);
    propertyFile.addPropertyFileListener(propertyFileListener);
}
```

8.3.4 Cell validators

Cell editors have validators to prevent invalid input from reaching model objects. Whenever a user modifies a cell editor's content, the `isValid(Object)` method returns an error message if the object represents an invalid value, or `null` if the value is valid. Assign each cell editor a validator in the `initTreeEditors()` method as follows:

```
keyEditor.setValidator(new ICellEditorValidator() {
    public String isValid(Object value) {
        if (((String) value).trim().length() == 0)
            return "Key must not be empty string";
        return null;
    }
});
valueEditor.setValidator(new ICellEditorValidator() {
    public String isValid(Object value) {
        return null;
    }
});
```

Whenever a user enters an invalid value, you have to decide how the user will be notified that the value is invalid. In this case, add an `ICellEditor-Listener` in the `initTreeEditors()` method so that the error message will appear in the window's status line (see Figure 8–7). For a more prominent error message, the editor's header area could be redesigned to allow an error image and message to be displayed just above the tree rather than in the workbench's status line.

```
keyEditor.addListener(new ICellEditorListener() {
    public void applyEditorValue() {
        setErrorMessage(null);
    }
```

```
public void cancelEditor() {
    setErrorMessage(null);
}
public void editorValueChanged(
    boolean oldValidState,
    boolean newValidState
) {
    setErrorMessage(keyEditor.getErrorMessage());
}
void setErrorMessage(String errorMessage) {
    getEditorSite().getActionBars().getStatusLineManager()
        .setErrorMessage(errorMessage);
}
});
```

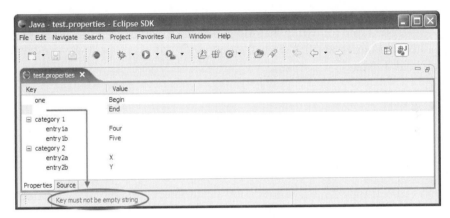

Figure 8–7   Error message in status line indicating invalid input.

8.3.5   *Editing versus selecting*

Before editing is added in the tree, a user could easily select one or more rows, but now the cell editor is always open. One possible solution is to only open the editor when the **Alt** key is held down, but select one or more rows when it is not. To accomplish this, some additional `PropertiesEditor` code needs to be added to capture the state of the **Alt** key by adding a listener in the `init-TreeEditors()` method. This same approach could be used to capture the state of any modifier key.

```
private boolean isAltPressed;

private void initTreeEditors() {
    ... existing code here ...
    treeViewer.getTree().addKeyListener(new KeyListener() {
        public void keyPressed(KeyEvent e) {
            if (e.keyCode == SWT.ALT)
                isAltPressed = true;
        }
```

```
        public void keyReleased(KeyEvent e) {
            if (e.keyCode == SWT.ALT)
                isAltPressed = false;
        }
    });
}

public boolean shouldEdit() {
    if (!isAltPressed)
        return false;
    // Must reset this value here because if an editor
    // is opened, we don't get the Alt key up event.
    isAltPressed = false;
    return true;
}
```

Next, the following method in `PropertiesEditorCell-Modifier` needs to be modifed so that the cell editor will only be opened when the **Alt** key is held down.

```
public boolean canModify(Object element,String property) {
    if (property == PropertiesEditor.KEY_COLUMN_ID) {
        if (element instanceof PropertyCategory)
            return editor.shouldEdit();
        if (element instanceof PropertyEntry)
            return editor.shouldEdit();
    }
    if (property == PropertiesEditor.VALUE_COLUMN_ID){
        if (element instanceof PropertyEntry)
            return editor.shouldEdit();
    }
    return false;
}
```

8.4 Editor Lifecycle

Typical editors go through an open-modify-save-close lifecycle. When the editor is opened, the `init(IEditorSite, IEditorInput)` method is called to set the editor's initial content. When the user modifies the editor's content, the editor must notify others that its content is now "dirty" by using the `firePropertyChange(int)` method. When a user saves the editor's content, the `firePropertyChange(int)` method must be used again to notify registered listeners that the editor's content is no longer dirty. Eclipse automatically registers listeners to perform various tasks based on the value returned by the `isDirty()` method, such as updating the editor's title, adding or removing an asterisk preceding the title, and enabling the **Save** menu. Finally, when the editor is closed, the editor's content is saved if the `isDirty()` method returns true.

8.4.1 Dirty editors

You need to ensure that the editor knows whether its content has been modified by the user since the last save operation. To do this, introduce this new field to track whether the current page has been modified relative to the other pages:

```
private boolean isPageModified;
```

Whenever the current page's content has been modified, you need to set the new isPageModified field. Whenever the tree is modified, the cell modifier calls the treeModified() method (see Section 8.3.2, Cell modifiers, on page 345), where the new isPageModified field can be set.

```
public void treeModified() {
    boolean wasDirty = isDirty();
    isPageModified = true;
    if (!wasDirty)
        firePropertyChange(IEditorPart.PROP_DIRTY);
}
```

Whenever the text editor is modified, the MultiPageEditorPart's addPage() method uses the handlePropertyChange(int) method (see the createSourcePage() method in Section 8.2.2, Editor controls, on page 331) to notify others when the editor's content has changed. You can override this method to set the isPageModified field as appropriate:

```
protected void handlePropertyChange (int propertyId) {
    if (propertyId == IEditorPart.PROP_DIRTY)
        isPageModified = isDirty();
    super.handlePropertyChange(propertyId);
}
```

Finally, you need to let other registered listeners know when the editor's content is dirty. The MultiPageEditorPart's isDirty() method appropriately returns true for the nested text editor on the **Source** page, but knows nothing about modifications to the tree. Overriding this method to add this knowledge causes the **Save** menu item to be enabled and the editor's title to be updated at the appropriate time.

```
public boolean isDirty() {
    return isPageModified || super.isDirty();
}
```

8.4.2 Switching pages

When switching between the **Properties** and **Source** pages, any edits made in the **Properties** page must automatically carry over to the **Source** page, and vice versa. To accomplish this, override the pageChange(int) method to update the page content as follows:

```
protected void pageChange(int newPageIndex) {
   switch (newPageIndex) {
      case 0 :
         if (isDirty())
            updateTreeFromTextEditor();
         break;
      case 1 :
         if (isPageModified)
            updateTextEditorFromTree();
         break;
   }
   isPageModified = false;
   super.pageChange(newPageIndex);
}
```

The updateTreeFromTextEditor() method has already been defined (see Section 8.2.3, Editor model, on page 335), but the updateTextEditorFromTree() method has not, so add it now.

```
void updateTextEditorFromTree() {
   textEditor
      .getDocumentProvider()
      .getDocument(textEditor.getEditorInput())
      .set(((PropertyFile) treeViewer.getInput()).asText());
}
```

The updateTextEditorFromTree() method calls a new asText() method in the PropertyFile. The new asText() method reverses the parsing process in the PropertyFile's constructor (see Section 8.2.3, Editor model, on page 335) by reassembling the model into a textual representation.

```
public String asText() {
   StringWriter stringWriter = new StringWriter(2000);
   PrintWriter writer = new PrintWriter(stringWriter);
   unnamedCategory.appendText(writer);
   Iterator iter = categories.iterator();
   while (iter.hasNext()) {
      writer.println();
      ((PropertyCategory) iter.next()).appendText(writer);
   }
   return stringWriter.toString();
}
```

The asText() method calls a new appendText(PrintWriter) method in PropertyCategory:

```
public void appendText(PrintWriter writer) {
   if (name.length() > 0) {
      writer.print("# ");
      writer.println(name);
   }
   Iterator iter = entries.iterator();
   while (iter.hasNext())
      ((PropertyEntry) iter.next()).appendText(writer);
}
```

which then calls a new appendText(PrintWriter) method in Property-Entry:

```
public void appendText(PrintWriter writer) {
   writer.print(key);
   writer.print(" = ");
   writer.println(value);
}
```

8.4.3 Saving content

Because the current implementation uses the nested text editor to save content into the file being edited, changes on the **Properties** page will not be noticed unless the user switches to the **Source** page. The following methods must be modified to update the nested text editor before saving. Since save operations are typically long-running operations, the progress monitor is used to communicate progress to the user (see Section 9.4, Progress Monitor, on page 383).

```
public void doSave(IProgressMonitor monitor) {
   if (getActivePage() == 0 && isPageModified)
      updateTextEditorFromTree();
   isPageModified = false;
   textEditor.doSave(monitor);
}

public void doSaveAs() {
   if (getActivePage() == 0 && isPageModified)
      updateTextEditorFromTree();
   isPageModified = false;
   textEditor.doSaveAs();
   setInput(textEditor.getEditorInput());
   updateTitle();
}
```

8.5   Editor Actions

Editor actions can appear as menu items in the editor's context menu, as toolbar buttons in the workbench's toolbar, and as menu items in the workbench's menu (see Figure 6–10 on page 244). This section covers adding actions to an editor programmatically, whereas Section 6.5, Editor Actions, on page 244 discussed adding actions by using declarations in the plug-in manifest (see Section 14.2.4, Marker resolution—quick fix, on page 520 for an example of manipulating the content in an existing text editor).

8.5.1   Context menu

Typically, editors have context menus populated by actions targeted at the editor or at selected objects within the editor. There are several steps to creating an editor's context menu and several more steps to register the editor so that others can contribute actions (see Section 6.3, Object Actions, on page 224, Section 6.5.1, Defining an editor context menu, on page 245, and Section 6.5.2, Defining an editor context action, on page 246 for information concerning how actions are contributed to an editor's context menus via the plug-in manifest).

8.5.1.1   Creating actions

The first step is to create the menu item actions that will appear in the context menu. The **Properties** editor needs an action that will remove the selected tree elements from the editor. In addition, this action adds a selection listener to facilitate keeping its enablement state in sync with the current tree selection.

```
package com.qualityeclipse.favorites.editors;

import ...

public class RemovePropertiesAction extends Action
{
   private final PropertiesEditor editor;
   private final TreeViewer viewer;

   private ISelectionChangedListener listener =
      new ISelectionChangedListener() {
      public void selectionChanged(SelectionChangedEvent e) {
         setEnabled(!e.getSelection().isEmpty());
      }
   };
```

```
public RemovePropertiesAction(
   PropertiesEditor editor,
   TreeViewer viewer,
   String text,
   ImageDescriptor imageDescriptor
) {
   super(text, imageDescriptor);
   this.editor = editor;
   this.viewer = viewer;
   setEnabled(false);
   viewer.addSelectionChangedListener(listener);
}

public void run() {
   ISelection sel = viewer.getSelection();
   Tree tree = viewer.getTree();
   tree.setRedraw(false);
   try {
      Iterator iter = ((IStructuredSelection) sel).iterator();
      while (iter.hasNext())
         ((PropertyElement) ((Object) iter.next()))
            .removeFromParent();
   }
   finally {
      tree.setRedraw(true);
   }
}
}
```

Tip: As shown in the preceding code, use the tree's `setRedraw(boolean)` method to reduce flashing when making more than one modification to a control or its model.

In `PropertiesEditor`, create a new field to hold the action and then call the following new method from `createPages()` method to initialize the field.

```
private RemovePropertiesAction removeAction;

private void createActions() {
   ImageDescriptor removeImage = PlatformUI.getWorkbench()
      .getSharedImages().getImageDescriptor(
         ISharedImages.IMG_TOOL_DELETE);
   removeAction =
      new RemovePropertiesAction(
         this, treeViewer, "Remove", removeImage);
}
```

This same action is used later for keyboard-based actions (see Section 8.5.2.4, Keyboard actions, on page 361) and global actions (see Section 8.5.2.1, Global actions, on page 358).

8.5.1.2   Creating the context menu

The context menu must be created at the same time as the editor. However, because contributors can add and remove menu items based on the selection, its contents cannot be determined until just after the user clicks the right mouse button and just before the menu is displayed. To accomplish this, set the menu's RemoveAllWhenShown property to true so that the menu will be built from scratch every time, and add a menu listener to dynamically build the menu. In addition, the menu must be registered with the control so that it will be displayed, and with the editor site so that other plug-ins can contribute actions to it (see Section 6.4, View Actions, on page 237).

For the **Properties** editor, modify createPages() to call this new createContextMenu() method:

```
private void createContextMenu() {
   MenuManager menuMgr = new MenuManager("#PopupMenu");
   menuMgr.setRemoveAllWhenShown(true);
   menuMgr.addMenuListener(new IMenuListener() {
      public void menuAboutToShow(IMenuManager m) {
         PropertiesEditor.this.fillContextMenu(m);
      }
   });
   Tree tree = treeViewer.getTree();
   Menu menu = menuMgr.createContextMenu(tree);
   tree.setMenu(menu);
   getSite().registerContextMenu(menuMgr,treeViewer);
}
```

8.5.1.3   Dynamically building the context menu

Every time a user clicks the right mouse button, the context menu's content must be rebuilt from scratch because contributors can add actions based on the editor's selection. In addition, the context menu must contain a separator with the IWorkbenchActionConstants.MB_ADDITIONS constant, indicating where those contributed actions will appear in the context menu. The createContextMenu() method (see the previous section) calls this new fillContextMenu(IMenuManager) method:

```
private void fillContextMenu(IMenuManager menuMgr) {
   boolean isEmpty = treeViewer.getSelection().isEmpty();
   removeAction.setEnabled(!isEmpty);
   menuMgr.add(removeAction);
   menuMgr.add(
      new Separator(IWorkbenchActionConstants.MB_ADDITIONS));
}
```

When this functionality is in place, the context menu, containing the **Remove** menu item plus items contributed by others, will appear (see Figure 8–8).

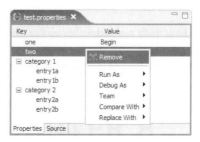

Figure 8–8   The Properties editor's context menu.

8.5.2   *Editor contributor*

An instance of `org.eclipse.ui.IEditorActionBarContributor` manages the installation and removal of global menus, menu items, and toolbar buttons for one or more editors. The manifest specifies which contributor, typically a subclass of `org.eclipse.ui.part.EditorActionBarContributor` or `org.eclipse.ui.part.MultiPageEditorActionBarContributor`, is associated with which editor type (see Section 8.1, Editor Declaration, on page 326). The platform then sends the following events to the contributor, indicating when an editor has become active or inactive, so that the contributor can install or remove menus and buttons as appropriate.

> `dispose()`—This method is automatically called when the contributor is no longer needed. It cleans up any platform resources, such as images, clipboard, and so on, which were created by this class. This follows the *if you create it, you destroy it* theme that runs throughout Eclipse.

> `init(IActionBars, IWorkbenchPage)`—This method is called when the contributor is first created.

> `setActiveEditor(IEditorPart)`—This method is called when an associated editor becomes active or inactive. The contributor should insert and remove menus and toolbar buttons as appropriate.

The `EditorActionBarContributor` class implements the `IEditorActionBarContributor` interface, caches the action bar and workbench page, and provides two new accessor methods.

> `getActionBars()`—Returns the contributor's action bars provided to the contributor when it was initialized.

> `getPage()`—Returns the contributor's workbench page provided to the contributor when it was initialized.

The `MultiPageEditorActionBarContributor` class extends `Editor-ActionBarContributor`, providing a new method to override instead of the `setActiveEditor(IEditorPart)` method.

> `setActivePage(IEditorPart)`—Sets the active page of the multipage editor to the given editor. If there is no active page, or if the active page does not have a corresponding editor, the argument is `null`.

8.5.2.1 *Global actions*

By borrowing from `org.eclipse.ui.editors.text.TextEditorAction-Contributor` and `org.eclipse.ui.texteditor.BasicTextEditor-ActionContributor`, you will create your own contributor for the **Properties** editor. This contributor hooks up global actions (e.g., **cut, copy, paste**, etc. in the **Edit** menu) appropriate not only to the active editor but also to the active page within the editor.

```
package com.qualityeclipse.favorites.editors;

import ...

public class PropertiesEditorContributor
   extends EditorActionBarContributor
{
   private static final String[] WORKBENCH_ACTION_IDS = {
      ActionFactory.DELETE.getId(),
      ActionFactory.UNDO.getId(),
      ActionFactory.REDO.getId(),
      ActionFactory.CUT.getId(),
      ActionFactory.COPY.getId(),
      ActionFactory.PASTE.getId(),
      ActionFactory.SELECT_ALL.getId(),
      ActionFactory.FIND.getId(),
      IDEActionFactory.BOOKMARK.getId(),
   };
   private static final String[] TEXTEDITOR_ACTION_IDS = {
      ActionFactory.DELETE.getId(),
      ActionFactory.UNDO.getId(),
      ActionFactory.REDO.getId(),
      ActionFactory.CUT.getId(),
      ActionFactory.COPY.getId(),
      ActionFactory.PASTE.getId(),
      ActionFactory.SELECT_ALL.getId(),
      ActionFactory.FIND.getId(),
      IDEActionFactory.BOOKMARK.getId(),
   };

   public void setActiveEditor(IEditorPart part) {
      PropertiesEditor editor = (PropertiesEditor) part;
      setActivePage(editor, editor.getActivePage());
   }
```

```
public void setActivePage(
   PropertiesEditor editor,
   int pageIndex
) {
   IActionBars actionBars = getActionBars();
   if (actionBars != null) {
      switch (pageIndex) {
         case 0 :
            hookGlobalTreeActions(editor, actionBars);
            break;
         case 1 :
            hookGlobalTextActions(editor, actionBars);
            break;
      }
      actionBars.updateActionBars();
   }
}

private void hookGlobalTreeActions(
   PropertiesEditor editor,
   IActionBars actionBars
) {
   for (int i = 0; i < WORKBENCH_ACTION_IDS.length; i++)
      actionBars.setGlobalActionHandler(
         WORKBENCH_ACTION_IDS[i],
         editor.getTreeAction(WORKBENCH_ACTION_IDS[i]));
}

private void hookGlobalTextActions(
   PropertiesEditor editor,
   IActionBars actionBars
) {
   ITextEditor textEditor = editor.getSourceEditor();
   for (int i = 0; i < WORKBENCH_ACTION_IDS.length; i++)
      actionBars.setGlobalActionHandler(
         WORKBENCH_ACTION_IDS[i],
         textEditor.getAction(TEXTEDITOR_ACTION_IDS[i]));
}
}
```

Now modify the **Properties** editor to add accessor methods for the contributor.

```
public ITextEditor getSourceEditor() {
   return textEditor;
}

public IAction getTreeAction(String workbenchActionId) {
   if (ActionFactory.DELETE.getId().equals(workbenchActionId))
      return removeAction;
   return null;
}
```

Append the following lines to the `pageChange()` method to notify the contributor when the page has changed so that the contributor can update the menu items and toolbar buttons appropriately.

```
IEditorActionBarContributor contributor =
    getEditorSite().getActionBarContributor();
if (contributor instanceof PropertiesEditorContributor)
    ((PropertiesEditorContributor) contributor)
        .setActivePage(this, newPageIndex);
```

8.5.2.2 Top-level menu

Next, add the **remove** action to a top-level menu for the purpose of showing how it is accomplished. In this case, instead of referencing the action directly as done with the context menu (see Section 8.5.1, Context menu, on page 354), you will use an instance of `org.eclipse.ui.actions.RetargetAction`, or more specifically, `org.eclipse.ui.actions.LabelRetargetAction`, which references the **remove** action indirectly via its identifier. You'll be using the `ActionFactory.DELETE.getId()` identifier, but could use any identifier so long as `setGlobalActionHandler(String, IAction)` is used to associate the identifier with the action. To accomplish all this, add the following to the `PropertiesEditorContributor`.

```
private LabelRetargetAction retargetRemoveAction =
    new LabelRetargetAction(ActionFactory.DELETE.getId(), "Remove");

public void init(IActionBars bars, IWorkbenchPage page) {  ·
    super.init(bars, page);
    page.addPartListener(retargetRemoveAction);
}

public void contributeToMenu(IMenuManager menuManager) {
    IMenuManager menu = new MenuManager("Property Editor");
    menuManager.prependToGroup(
        IWorkbenchActionConstants.MB_ADDITIONS,
        menu);
    menu.add(retargetRemoveAction);
}

public void dispose() {
    getPage().removePartListener(retargetRemoveAction);
    super.dispose();
}
```

Once in place, this code causes a new top-level menu to appear in the workbench's menu bar (see Figure 8–9).

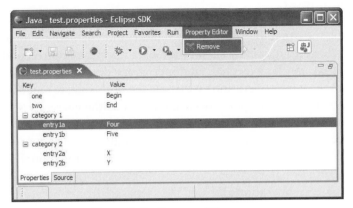

Figure 8–9   Property Editor menu.

8.5.2.3   Toolbar buttons

You can use the same retargeted action (see previous section) to add a button to the workbench's toolbar by including the following code in `Properties-EditorContributor`.

```
public void contributeToToolBar(IToolBarManager manager) {
   manager.add(new Separator());
   manager.add(retargetRemoveAction);
}
```

8.5.2.4   Keyboard actions

By using the **remove** action again (see Section 8.5.1.1, Creating actions, on page 354), you can hook in the **Delete** key by modifying the `initTreeEditors()` method introduced earlier (see Section 8.3.5, Editing versus selecting, on page 349) so that when a user presses it, the selected property key/value pairs in the tree will be removed.

```
private void initTreeEditors() {
   ... existing code ...
   treeViewer.getTree().addKeyListener(new KeyListener() {
      public void keyPressed(KeyEvent e) {
         if (e.keyCode == SWT.ALT)
            isAltPressed = true;
         if (e.character == SWT.DEL)
            removeAction.run();
      }
      public void keyReleased(KeyEvent e) {
         if (e.keyCode == SWT.ALT)
            isAltPressed = false;
      }
   });
}
```

8.5.3　Undo/Redo

Adding the capability for a user to undo and redo actions involves separating user edits into actions visible in the user interface and the underlying operations that can be executed, undone, and redone. Typically each action will instantiate a new operation every time the user triggers that action. The action gathers the current application state, such as the currently selected elements, and the operation caches that state so that it can be executed, undone and redone independent of the original action. An instance of IOperationHistory manages the operations in the global undo/redo stack (see Figure 8–10). Each operation uses one or more associated undo/redo contexts to keep operations for one part separate from operations for another.

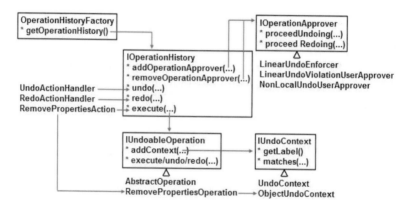

Figure 8–10　The Eclipse undo/redo infrastructure

In this case, you need to split the RemovePropertiesAction (see Section 8.5.1.1, Creating actions, on page 354), moving some functionality into a new RemovePropertiesOperation class. The AbstractOperation superclass implements much of the required IUndoableOperation interface.

```
public class RemovePropertiesOperation extends AbstractOperation
{
   private final TreeViewer viewer;
   private final PropertyElement[] elements;

   public RemovePropertiesOperation(
      TreeViewer viewer, PropertyElement[] elements
   ) {
      super(getLabelFor(elements));
      this.viewer = viewer;
      this.elements = elements;
   }
```

The constructor calls the `getLabelFor()` method to generate a human-readable label for the operation based on the currently selected elements. This label appears wherever the undo/redo actions appears such as on the **Edit** menu.

```
private static String getLabelFor(PropertyElement[] elements) {
   if (elements.length == 1) {
      PropertyElement first = elements[0];
      if (first instanceof PropertyEntry) {
         PropertyEntry propEntry = (PropertyEntry) first;
         return "Remove property " + propEntry.getKey();
      }
      if (first instanceof PropertyCategory) {
         PropertyCategory propCat = (PropertyCategory) first;
         return "Remove category " + propCat.getName();
      }
   }
   return "Remove properties";
}
```

The `execute()` method prompts the user to confirm the operation and removes the specified properties. If the `info` argument is not `null`, then it can be queried for a UI context in which to prompt the user for information during execution. If the monitor argument is not `null`, then it can be used to provide progress feedback to the user during execution. This method is only called the first time the operation is executed.

```
public IStatus execute(IProgressMonitor monitor, IAdaptable info)
   throws ExecutionException
{
   // If a UI context has been provided,
   // then prompt the user to confirm the operation.

   if (info != null) {
      Shell shell = (Shell) info.getAdapter(Shell.class);
      if (shell != null) {
         if (!MessageDialog.openQuestion(
            shell,
            "Remove properties",
           "Do you want to remove the currently selected properties?"
         ))
            return Status.CANCEL_STATUS;
      }
   }

   // Perform the operation.

   return redo(monitor, info);
}
```

The execute() method calls the redo() method to perform the actual property removal. This method records information about the elements being removed in two additional fields so that this operation can be undone. The arguments passed to the redo() method are identical to those supplied to the execute() method described before.

```java
private PropertyElement[] parents;
private int[] indexes;

public IStatus redo(IProgressMonitor monitor, IAdaptable info)
    throws ExecutionException
{
    // Perform the operation, providing feedback to the user
    // through the progress monitor if one is provided.

    parents = new PropertyElement[elements.length];
    indexes = new int[elements.length];

    if (monitor != null)
        monitor.beginTask("Remove properties", elements.length);

    Tree tree = viewer.getTree();
    tree.setRedraw(false);
    try {
        for (int i = elements.length; --i >= 0;) {
            parents[i] = elements[i].getParent();
            PropertyElement[] children = parents[i].getChildren();
            for (int index = 0; index < children.length; index++) {
                if (children[index] == elements[i]) {
                    indexes[i] = index;
                    break;
                }
            }
            elements[i].removeFromParent();

            if (monitor != null)
                monitor.worked(1);
        }
    }
    finally {
        tree.setRedraw(true);
    }

    if (monitor != null)
        monitor.done();

    return Status.OK_STATUS;
}
```

The undo() method reverses the current operation by reinserting the removed elements into the model.

```
public IStatus undo(IProgressMonitor monitor, IAdaptable info)
   throws ExecutionException
{
   Tree tree = viewer.getTree();
   tree.setRedraw(false);
   try {
      for (int i = 0; i < elements.length; i++) {
         if (parents[i] instanceof PropertyCategory)
            ((PropertyCategory) parents[i]).addEntry(indexes[i],
                  (PropertyEntry) elements[i]);
         else
            ((PropertyFile) parents[i]).addCategory(indexes[i],
                  (PropertyCategory) elements[i]);
      }
   }
   finally {
      tree.setRedraw(true);
   }
   return Status.OK_STATUS;
}
```

The preceding undo() method inserts elements back into the model at exactly the same position from where they were removed. This necessitates some refactoring of the PropertyCategory addEntry() method (see Section 8.2.3, Editor model, on page 335 for more on the editor model).

```
public void addEntry(PropertyEntry entry) {
   addEntry(entries.size(), entry);
}

public void addEntry(int index, PropertyEntry entry) {
   if (!entries.contains(entry)) {
      entries.add(index, entry);
      ((PropertyFile) getParent()).entryAdded(
         this, entry);
   }
}
```

Here is a similar refactoring of the PropertyFile addCategory() method.

```
public void addCategory(PropertyCategory category) {
   addCategory(categories.size(), category);
}

public void addCategory(int index, PropertyCategory category) {
   if (!categories.contains(category)) {
      categories.add(index, category);
      categoryAdded(category);
   }
}
```

Rather than removing the selected properties, the RemoveProperties-Action must now build an array of properties to be removed and then pass that to a new instance of RemovePropertiesOperation. The operation is passed to the editor's undo/redo manager for execution along with a UI context for prompting the user and a progress monitor for user feedback. If there is an exception during execution, you could use a ExceptionsDetailsDialog (see Section 11.1.9, Details dialog, on page 420) rather than the following MessageDialog.

```
public void run() {

   // Build an array of properties to be removed.
   IStructuredSelection sel =
      (IStructuredSelection) viewer.getSelection();
   Iterator iter = sel.iterator();
   int size = sel.size();
   PropertyElement[] elements = new PropertyElement[size];
   for (int i = 0; i < size; i++)
      elements[i] = (PropertyElement) ((Object) iter.next());

   // Build the operation to be performed.
   RemovePropertiesOperation op =
      new RemovePropertiesOperation(viewer, elements);
   op.addContext(editor.getUndoContext());

   // The progress monitor so the operation can inform the user.
   IProgressMonitor monitor = editor.getEditorSite().getActionBars()
         .getStatusLineManager().getProgressMonitor();

   // An adapter for providing UI context to the operation.
   IAdaptable info = new IAdaptable() {
      public Object getAdapter(Class adapter) {
         if (Shell.class.equals(adapter))
            return editor.getSite().getShell();
         return null;
      }
   };

   // Execute the operation.
   try {
      editor.getOperationHistory().execute(op, monitor, info);
   }
   catch (ExecutionException e) {
      MessageDialog.openError(
         editor.getSite().getShell(),
         "Remove Properties Error",
         "Exception while removing properties: " + e.getMessage());
   }
}
```

The preceding `run()` method calls some new methods in `PropertiesEditor`.

```
public IOperationHistory getOperationHistory() {

    // The workbench provides its own undo/redo manager
    //return PlatformUI.getWorkbench()
    //    .getOperationSupport().getOperationHistory();

    // which, in this case, is the same as the default undo manager
    return OperationHistoryFactory.getOperationHistory();
}

public IUndoContext getUndoContext() {

    // For workbench-wide operations, we should return
    //return PlatformUI.getWorkbench()
    //    .getOperationSupport().getUndoContext();

    // but our operations are all local, so return our own content
    return undoContext;
}
```

This `undoContext` must be initialized along with undo and redo actions in the `createActions()` method (see Section 8.5.1.1, Creating actions, on page 354 for the original `createActions()` method).

```
private UndoActionHandler undoAction;
private RedoActionHandler redoAction;
private IUndoContext undoContext;

private void createActions() {
    undoContext = new ObjectUndoContext(this);
    undoAction = new UndoActionHandler(getSite(), undoContext);
    redoAction = new RedoActionHandler(getSite(), undoContext);
    ... existing code ...
}
```

These new undo and redo actions should appear in the context menu, so modify the `fillContextMenu()` method.

```
private void fillContextMenu(IMenuManager menuMgr) {
    menuMgr.add(undoAction);
    menuMgr.add(redoAction);
    menuMgr.add(new Separator());
    ... existing code ...
}
```

Then, modify the `getTreeAction()` method to return the new undo and redo actions so that they will be hooked to the global undo and redo actions that appear in the **Edit** menu.

```
public IAction getTreeAction(String workbenchActionId) {
   if (ActionFactory.UNDO.getId().equals(workbenchActionId))
      return undoAction;
   if (ActionFactory.REDO.getId().equals(workbenchActionId))
      return redoAction;
   if (ActionFactory.DELETE.getId().equals(workbenchActionId))
      return removeAction;
   return null;
}
```

Finally, the undo/redo stack for the **Source** page is separate from the undo/redo stack for the **Properties** page, so add the following line to the pageChange() method to clear the undo/redo stack when the page changes.

```
getOperationHistory().dispose(undoContext, true, true, false);
```

A better solution similar to what has already been discussed, but not implemented here, would be to merge the two undo/redo stacks into a single unified undo/redo stack shared between both the **Properties** and **Source** pages.

If operations share a common undo context but also have some contexts that are not shared, then there exists the possibility that operations from one context will be undone in a linear fashion; however, some operations from another context may be skipped. To allieviate this problem, you can register an instance of IOperationApprover to ensure that an operation will not be undone without all prior operations being undone first.

This interface also provides a way to confirm undo and redo operations that affect contexts outside the active editor and not immediately apparent to the user. The Eclipse platform contains the following subclasses of IOperationApprover useful when managing undo/redo operations with overlapping contexts.

LinearUndoEnforcer—An operation approver that enforces a strict linear undo. It does not allow the undo or redo of any operation that is not the latest available operation in all of its undo contexts.

LinearUndoViolationUserApprover—An operation approver that prompts the user to see whether linear undo violations are permitted. A linear undo violation is detected when an operation being undone or redone shares an undo context with another operation appearing more recently in the history.

NonLocalUndoUserApprover—An operation approver that prompts the user to see whether a nonlocal undo should proceed inside an editor. A non-local undo is detected when an operation being undone or redone affects elements other than those described by the editor itself.

The Eclipse SDK contains a basic undo/redo example as part of the `eclipse-examples-3.1.2-win32.zip` download. It provides additional undo/redo code not covered here such as an `UndoHistoryView` and an implementation of `IOperationApprover` for approving the undo or redo of a particular operation within an operation history.

8.5.4   Clipboard actions

Clipboard-based actions for an editor are identical to their respective view-based operations (see Section 7.3.7, Clipboard actions, on page 290).

8.6   Linking the Editor

The selection in the active editor can be linked to the views that surround it in a technique similar to linking view selections (see Section 7.4, Linking the View, on page 305). In addition, the editor can provide content for the **Outline** view by implementing the `getAdapter(Class)` method something like this (see Section 7.4.2, Adaptable objects, on page 306 for more about adapters):

```
private PropertiesOutlinePage outlinePage;

public Object getAdapter(Class adapter) {
   if (adapter.equals(IContentOutlinePage.class)) {
      if (outlinePage == null)
         outlinePage = new PropertiesOutlinePage();
      return outlinePage;
   }
   return super.getAdapter(adapter);
}
```

The `PropertiesOutlinePage` class implements `IContentOutlinePage`, typically by extending `ContentOutlinePage` and implementing a handful of methods. These methods are similar to the methods discussed earlier in this chapter and in the previous chapter; thus, they are not covered in detail here.

8.7   RFRS Considerations

The "User Interface" section of the *RFRS Requirements* includes eleven items—five requirements and six best practices—dealing with editors. All of them are derived from the Eclipse UI Guidelines.

8.7.1   Using an editor to edit or browse   (RFRS 3.5.9)

User Interface Guideline #6.1 is a **requirement** that states:

> *Use an editor to edit or browse a file, document, or other input object. This requirement tests that editors are used to edit files (or similar inputs) and views are used to aid navigation (e.g., Navigator) or handle simple modification tasks (e.g., Properties view). Editors must open on double- or single-click (depending on the workbench's single-click behavior preference) from the resource. While views may open simultaneously with the editor, it is improper to open only a view when the input follows an open-save-close lifecycle. Views must not retarget editor actions, contribute to the common toolbar, or otherwise substitute for proper editor behavior and appearance.*

For this test, demonstrate the editors provided by your plug-in. Show the file, document, or other input type that they are used to edit or browse. Based on the examples presented in this chapter, show how the **Property File** editor is used to edit property files.

8.7.2   Editor lifecycle   (RFRS 3.5.10)

User Interface Guideline #6.2 is a **requirement** that states:

> *Modifications made in an editor must follow an open-save-close lifecycle model. When an editor first opens, the editor's contents should be unmodified (clean). If the contents are modified, the editor should communicate this change to the platform. In response, an asterisk should appear in the editor's tab. The modifications should be buffered within the edit model until such time as the user explicitly saves them. At that point, the modifications should be committed to the model storage.*

To pass this test, open your editor on a file and show that the editor is initially unmodified. Then make a change using the editor and show that an asterisk appears in the editor's tab. Finally, save the editor and show that the changes have been committed to the file and that the editor has gone back to its unmodified state. See Section 8.4, Editor Lifecycle, on page 350 for more information about editor lifecycles.

8.7.3   Accessing global actions   *(RFRS 3.5.11)*

User Interface Guideline #6.9 is a **requirement** that states:

> *If an editor has support for **cut, copy, paste**, or any of the global actions, the same actions must be executable from the same actions in the window menu and toolbar. The window menu contains a number of global actions, such as **cut, copy**, and **paste** in the **Edit** menu. These actions target the active part, as indicated by a shaded title area. If these actions are supported within an editor, the editor should hook into these window actions so that selection in the window menu or toolbar produces the same result as selection of the same action in the editor. The editor should not ignore these actions and contribute duplicate actions to the window menu or toolbar. The following are the supported global actions:*
>
> > *a. Undo*
> > *b. Redo*
> > *c. Cut*
> > *d. Copy*
> > *e. Paste*
> > *f. Print*
> > *g. Delete*
> > *h. Find*
> > *i. Select all*
> > *j. Bookmark*

Show that your editor supports any relevant global actions such as **cut, copy**, and **paste**. Trigger those actions from within your editor and then show that they may also be triggered from the workbench's menu bar with the same effect. For the **Properties** editor, you would show that global actions, such as **delete**, can be accessed within both the **Properties** and **Source** pages of the editor. See Section 8.5.2.1, Global actions, on page 358 for more about hooking up global actions.

8.7.4   Closing when the object is deleted   *(RFRS 3.5.12)*

User Interface Guideline #6.16 is a **requirement** that states:

> *If the input to an editor is deleted and the editor contains no changes, the editor should be closed. When a resource is deleted from one of the navigators (e.g., Navigator view, J2EE view, Data view, or DBA Explorer view in SDP), the handling of any editor that is currently open on that*

resource depends on whether the editor has any unsaved changes. If the editor does not contain any changes since the resource was last saved then the editor should be immediately closed.

Show that your editor is closed automatically any time an input object to your editor (e.g., a specific resource) is deleted. For the **Properties** editor, you would create a new properties file, open it with the **Properties** editor, and then delete the file in the **Navigator** view. If you implement your editor using the editor framework described in this chapter, the framework should automatically enforce this guideline.

8.7.5 *Synchronize external changes*   *(RFRS 3.5.14)*

User Interface Guideline #6.30 is a **requirement** that states:

> *If modifications to a resource are made outside the workbench, users should be prompted to either override the changes made outside the workbench or back out of the Save operation when the save action is invoked in the editor.*

Open your editor on a file and make a change. Next, modify the file outside Eclipse. Finally, switch back to Eclipse and attempt to save the file. Show that you are prompted to override the external changes or to cancel the save operation. If you implement your editor using the editor framework described in this chapter, the framework should automatically enforce this guideline.

8.7.6 *Registering editor menus*   *(RFRS 5.3.5.2)*

User Interface Guideline #6.14 is a **best practice** that states:

> *Register with the platform all context menus in the editor. In the platform, the menu and toolbar for an editor are automatically extended by the platform. By contrast, context menu extension is supported in collaboration between the editor and the platform. To achieve this collaboration, an editor must register each context menu it contains with the platform.*

To pass this test, show that your editor's context menus have been registered with the platform. If they are properly registered, you should see the system contributing appropriate context menu items. See Section 8.5.1, Context menu, on page 354 for more about context menus.

8.7.7 Editor action filters   (RFRS 5.3.5.3)

User Interface Guideline #6.15 is a **best practice** that states:

> *Implement an action filter for each object type in the editor. An action fil-*
> *ter makes it easier for one plug-in to add an action to objects in an editor*
> *defined by another plug-in.*

For this test, show that menu action filtering is in effect for the objects edited by your editor. See Section 6.3.2, Action filtering and enablement, on page 227 for more about using action filters and Section 8.5.1.2, Creating the context menu, on page 356 for more about building context menus that can be extended by other plug-ins.

8.7.8 Unsaved editor modifications   (RFRS 5.3.5.4)

User Interface Guideline #6.17 is a **best practice** that states:

> *If the input to an editor is deleted and the editor contains changes, the edi-*
> *tor should give the user a chance to save the changes to another location,*
> *and then close.*

Start by opening your editor on a file and then making a change. Next, select the file in the **Navigator** view and delete it. Show that a warning message is displayed, informing the user that the editor contains unsaved changes. To pass the best practice component of this guideline, the user should be given the option to save the file to another location. If you implement your editor using the editor framework described in this chapter, the framework should automatically enforce this guideline.

8.7.9 Prefix dirty resources   (RFRS 5.3.5.5)

User Interface Guideline #6.18 is a **best practice** that states:

> *If a resource is dirty, prefix the resource name presented in the editor tab*
> *with an asterisk.*

This is essentially a subset of Guideline #14. Edit a file with your editor and show that the filename is prefixed with an asterisk. If you implement your editor using the editor framework described in this chapter, the framework should automatically enforce this guideline.

8.7.10   Editor outline view   (RFRS 5.3.5.6)

User Interface Guideline #6.20 is a **best practice** that states:

> *If the data within an editor is too extensive to see on a single screen, and will yield a structured outline, the editor should provide an outline model to the* **Outline** *view. In Eclipse, there is a special relationship between each editor and the* **Outline** *view. When an editor is opened, the* **Outline** *view will connect to the editor and ask it for an outline model. If the editor answers with an outline model, that model will be displayed in the* **Out-line** *view whenever the editor is active. The outline is used to navigate through the edit data, or interact with the edit data at a higher level of abstraction.*

For this test, open your editor and show that it updates the contents of the **Outline** view and allows the data's structure to be navigated. If a different instance of your editor is selected, show that the **Outline** view's contents change appropriately. See Section 8.4, Editor Lifecycle, on page 350 for information about linking an editor to the **Outline** view.

8.7.11   Synchronize with outline view   (RFRS 5.3.5.7)

User Interface Guideline #6.21 is a **best practice** that states:

> *Notification about location between an editor and the* **Outline** *view should be two-way. Context menus should be available in the* **Outline** *view as appropriate.*

Select an item in the **Outline** view and show that it selects the corresponding item in the editor. Next, select an item in the editor and show that it selects the corresponding item in the **Outline** view.

8.8   Summary

This chapter went into detail about how to create new editors for editing and browsing resources in the workbench. It showed how to set up a multipage editor, handle the editor lifecycle, and create various editor actions.

References

Chapter source (*www.qualityeclipse.com/projects/source-ch-08.zip*).

Deva, Prashant, "Folding in Eclipse Text Editors," March 11, 2005 (*www.eclipse.org/articles/Article-Folding-in-Eclipse-Text-Editors/folding.html*).

Ho, Elwin, "Creating a Text-Based Editor for Eclipse," HP, June 2003 (*devresource.hp.com/drc/technical_white_papers/eclipeditor/index.jsp*).

CHAPTER 9

Resource Change Tracking

The Eclipse system generates resource change events indicating, for example, the files and folders that have been added, modified, and removed during the course of an operation. Interested objects can subscribe to these events and take whatever action is necessary to keep themselves synchronized with Eclipse.

To demonstrate resource change tracking, the **Favorites** view will be modified (see Chapter 7, Views) so that whenever a resource is deleted, you can remove the corresponding element from the **Favorites** view.

9.1   IResourceChangeListener

Eclipse uses the interface `org.eclipse.core.resources.IResource-ChangeListener` to notify registered listeners when a resource has changed. The `FavoritesManager` (see Section 7.2.3, View model, on page 265) needs to keep its list of **Favorites** items synchronized with Eclipse. This is done by implementing the `org.eclipse.core.resources.IResourceChange-Listener` interface and registering for resource change events.

In addition, the `FavoritesPlugin stop()` method must be modified to call the new `FavoritesManager shutdown()` method so that the manager is no longer notified of resource changes once the plug-in has been shut down. Now, whenever a resource change occurs, Eclipse will call the `resourceChanged()` method.

```
public class FavoritesManager
   implements IResourceChangeListener
{
   private FavoritesManager() {
      ResourcesPlugin.getWorkspace().addResourceChangeListener (
         this, IResourceChangeEvent.POST_CHANGE);
   }

   public static void shutdown() {
      if (manager != null) {
         ResourcesPlugin.getWorkspace()
            .removeResourceChangeListener(manager);
         manager.saveFavorites();
         manager = null;
      }
   }

   public void resourceChanged(IResourceChangeEvent e) {
      // Process events here.
   }
   ... existing code from Section 7.2.3, View model, on page 265 ...
}
```

9.1.1 IResourceChangeEvent

FavoritesManager is only interested in changes that have already occurred and therefore uses the IResourceChangeEvent.POST_CHANGE constant when subscribing to change events. Several IResourceChangeEvent constants that can be used in combination to specify when an interested object should be notified of resource changes are provided by Eclipse. Below is the list of valid constants as they appear in the IResourceChangeEvent Javadoc.

PRE_BUILD—Before-the-fact report of builder activity (see Section 14.1, Builders, on page 499).

PRE_CLOSE—Before-the-fact report of the impending closure of a single project as returned by getResource().

PRE_DELETE—Before-the-fact report of the impending deletion of a single project as returned by getResource().

POST_BUILD—After-the-fact report of builder activity (see Section 14.1, Builders, on page 499).

POST_CHANGE—After-the-fact report of creations, deletions, and modifications to one or more resources expressed as a hierarchical resource delta as returned by getDelta().

The IResourceChangeEvent interface also defines several methods that can be used to query its state.

findMarkerDeltas(String, boolean)—Returns all marker deltas of the specified type that are associated with resource deltas for this event. Pass true as the second parameter if you want to include subtypes of the specified type.

getBuildKind()—Returns the kind of build that caused the event.

getDelta()—Returns a resource delta, rooted at the workspace, describing the set of changes that happened to resources in the workspace.

getResource()—Returns the resource in question.

getSource()—Returns an object identifying the source of this event.

getType()—Returns the type of event being reported.

9.1.2   IResourceDelta

Each individual change is encoded as an instance of a resource delta that is represented by the IResourceDelta interface. Eclipse provides several different constants that can be used in combination to identify the resource deltas handled by the system. Below is the list of valid constants as they appear in the IResourceDelta Javadoc.

ADDDED—Delta kind constant indicating that the resource has been added to its parent.

ADDED_PHANTOM—Delta kind constant indicating that a phantom resource has been added at the location of the delta node.

ALL_WITH_PHANTOMS—The bit mask that describes all possible delta kinds, including those involving phantoms.

CHANGED—Delta kind constant indicating that the resource has been changed.

CONTENT—Change constant indicating that the content of the resource has changed.

DESCRIPTION—Change constant indicating that a project's description has changed.

ENCODING—Change constant indicating that the encoding of the resource has changed.

MARKERS—Change constant indicating that the resource's markers have changed.

MOVED_FROM—Change constant indicating that the resource was moved from another location.

MOVED_TO—Change constant indicating that the resource was moved to another location.

NO_CHANGE—Delta kind constant indicating that the resource has not been changed in any way.

OPEN—Change constant indicating that the resource was opened or closed.

REMOVED—Delta kind constant indicating that the resource has been removed from its parent.

REMOVED_PHANTOM—Delta kind constant indicating that a phantom resource has been removed from the location of the delta node.

REPLACED—Change constant indicating that the resource has been replaced by another at the same location (i.e., the resource has been deleted and then added).

SYNC—Change constant indicating that the resource's sync status has changed.

TYPE—Change constant indicating that the type of the resource has changed.

The IResourceDelta class also defines numerous useful APIs as follows:

accept(IResourceDeltaVisitor)—Visits resource deltas that are ADDED, CHANGED, or REMOVED. If the visitor returns true, the resource delta's children are also visited.

accept(IResourceDeltaVisitor, boolean)—Same as above but optionally includes phantom resources.

accept(IResourceDeltaVisitor, int)—Same as above but optionally includes phantom resources and/or team private members.

findMember(IPath)—Finds and returns the descendent delta identified by the given path in this delta, or null if no such descendent exists.

getAffectedChildren()—Returns resource deltas for all children of this resource that were ADDED, CHANGED, or REMOVED.

getAffectedChildren(int)—Returns resource deltas for all children of this resource whose kind is included in the given mask.

getFlags()—Returns flags that describe in more detail how a resource has been affected.

getFullPath()—Returns the full, absolute path of this resource delta.

getKind()—Returns the kind of this resource delta.

getMarkerDeltas()—Returns the changes to markers on the corresponding resource.

getMovedFromPath()—Returns the full path (in the "before" state) from which this resource (in the "after" state) was moved.

getMovedToPath()—Returns the full path (in the "after" state) to which this resource (in the "before" state) was moved.

getProjectRelativePath()—Returns the project-relative path of this resource delta.

getResource()—Returns a handle for the affected resource.

9.2   Processing Change Events

The POST_CHANGE resource change event is expressed not as a single change, but as a hierarchy describing one or more changes that have occurred. Events are batched in this manner for efficiency; reporting each change as it occurs to every interested object would dramatically slow down the system and reduce responsiveness to the user. To see this hierarchy of changes, add the following code to the FavoritesManager.

```
public void resourceChanged(IResourceChangeEvent e) {
   System.out.println(
      "FavoritesManager - resource change event");
   try {
      event.getDelta().accept(new IResourceDeltaVisitor() {
         public boolean visit(IResourceDelta delta)
            throws CoreException
         {
            StringBuffer buf = new StringBuffer(80);
            switch (delta.getKind()) {
               case IResourceDelta.ADDED:
                  buf.append("ADDED");
                  break;
               case IResourceDelta.REMOVED:
                  buf.append("REMOVED");
                  break;
               case IResourceDelta.CHANGED:
                  buf.append("CHANGED");
                  break;
               default:
                  buf.append("[");
                  buf.append(delta.getKind());
                  buf.append("]");
                  break;
            }
            buf.append(" ");
            buf.append(delta.getResource());
            System.out.println(buf);
            return true;
         }
      });
   }
   catch (CoreException ex) {
      FavoritesLog.logError(ex);
   }
}
```

The preceding code will generate a textual representation of the hierarchical structure describing the resource changes in the system. To see this code in action, launch the **Runtime Workbench** (see Section 2.6, Debugging the Product, on page 88) and open the **Favorites** view. In the **Runtime Workbench**, create a simple project and then add folders and files as shown here (see Figure 9–1).

Figure 9–1   Navigator view.

During the creation process, you will see output generated to the **Console** view describing the resource change events that were sent by Eclipse. The FavoritesManager is specifically interested in the deletion of resources, and when you delete these two files, you'll see the following in the **Console** view:

```
FavoritesManager - resource change event
CHANGED R/
CHANGED P/Test
CHANGED F/Test/folder1
CHANGED F/Test/folder1/folder2
REMOVED L/Test/folder1/folder2/file1.txt
REMOVED L/Test/folder1/folder2/file2.txt
```

The next step is to modify the FavoritesManager methods to do something with this information. The modifications will enable the Favorites-Manager to remove **Favorites** items that reference resources that have been removed from the system.

```
public void resourceChanged(IResourceChangeEvent e) {
   Collection itemsToRemove = new HashSet();
   try {
      event.getDelta().accept(new IResourceDeltaVisitor() {
         public boolean visit(IResourceDelta delta)
            throws CoreException
         {
            if (delta.getKind() == IResourceDelta.REMOVED) {
               IFavoriteItem item =
                  existingFavoriteFor(delta.getResource());
               if (item != null)
                  itemsToRemove.add(item);
            }
            return true;
         }
      });
   }
```

```
        catch (CoreException ex) {
            FavoritesLog.logError(ex);
        }
        if (itemsToRemove.size() > 0)
            removeFavorites(
                (IFavoriteItem[]) itemsToRemove.toArray(
                    new IFavoriteItem[itemsToRemove.size()])));
    }
```

When the preceding code is in place, launch the **Runtime Workbench** to test this modification by creating a file in a project, adding that file as a **Favorites** item to the **Favorites** view, and then deleting the file from the project. The file is removed, but the **Favorites** item is not removed as it should be. Looking in the .log file (see Section 3.6.2, The Error Log view, on page 124) reveals the following exception:

```
org.eclipse.swt.SWTException: Invalid thread access
```

This indicates that an SWT component, such as the table in the **Favorites** view, is being accessed from a thread other than the UI thread (see Section 4.2.5.1, Display, on page 140 for more about Display.getDefault() and the UI thread). To alleviate this problem, modify the FavoritesView-ContentProvider favoritesChanged() method as shown below to ensure that the viewer is accessed on the UI thread.

```
public void favoritesChanged(final FavoritesManagerEvent event) {
    // If this is the UI thread, then make the change.
    if (Display.getCurrent() != null) {
        updateViewer(event);
        return;
    }

    // otherwise, redirect to execute on the UI thread.
    Display.getDefault().asyncExec(new Runnable() {
        public void run() {
            updateViewer(event);
        }
    });
}

private void updateViewer(final FavoritesManagerEvent event) {
    // Use the setRedraw method to reduce flicker
    // when adding or removing multiple items in a table.
    viewer.getTable().setRedraw(false);
    try {
        viewer.remove(event.getItemsRemoved());
        viewer.add(event.getItemsAdded());
    } finally {
        viewer.getTable().setRedraw(true);
    }
}
```

9.3 Batching Change Events

Anytime a UI plug-in modifies resources, it should wrap the resource modification code by subclassing org.eclipse.ui.actions.WorkspaceModify-Operation. The primary consequence of using this operation is that events that typically occur as a result of workspace changes (e.g., the firing of resource deltas, performance of autobuilds, etc.) are deferred until the outermost operation has successfully completed. In the **Favorites** view, if you want to implement a delete operation that removed the resources themselves rather than just the **Favorites** items that referenced the resources, then it might be implemented as shown below.

The run() method, inherited from WorkspaceModifyOperation and called by an Action or IActionDelegate, first calls the execute() method and then fires a single change event containing all the resources changed by the execute() method.

```
package com.qualityeclipse.favorites.actions;

import ...

public class DeleteResourcesOperation
   extends WorkspaceModifyOperation
{
   private final IResource[] resources;

   public DeleteResourcesOperation(IResource[] resources) {
      this.resources = resources;
   }

   protected void execute(IProgressMonitor monitor)
      throws
         CoreException,
         InvocationTargetException,
         InterruptedException
   {
      monitor.beginTask("Deleting resources...", resources.length);
      for (int i = 0; i < resources.length; i++) {
         if (monitor.isCanceled())
            break;
         resources[i].delete(
            true, new SubProgressMonitor(monitor, 1));
      }
      monitor.done();
   }
}
```

If you are modifying resources in a headless Eclipse environment or in a plug-in that does not rely on any UI plug-ins, the WorkspaceModify-Operation class is not accessible. In this case, use the IWorkspace.run() method to batch change events.

```
protected void execute(IProgressMonitor monitor)
    throws CoreException
{
    ResourcesPlugin.getWorkspace().run(new IWorkspaceRunnable() {
        public void run(IProgressMonitor monitor) throws CoreException
        {
            monitor.beginTask(
                "Deleting resources...", resources.length);
            for (int i = 0; i < resources.length; i++) {
                resources[i].delete(
                    true, new SubProgressMonitor(monitor, 1));
            }
            monitor.done();
        }
    }, monitor);
}
```

9.4   Progress Monitor

For long-running operations, the progress monitor indicates what the operation is doing and an estimate of how much more there is left to be done. In the preceding code, a progress monitor was used to communicate with the user, indicating that resources were being deleted and how many resources needed to be deleted before the operation completed (see methods in previous sections and the redo() method in Section 8.5.3, Undo/Redo, on page 362).

In addition, since DeleteResourcesOperation interacts with the user interface, isCanceled() is called periodically to see if the user has canceled the operation. There is nothing more frustrating than looking at a long running operation with a cancel button only to find out that the cancel button has no effect.

9.4.1   IProgressMonitor

The org.eclipse.core.runtime.IProgressMonitor interface provides methods for indicating when an operation has started, how much has been done, and when it is complete.

beginTask(String, int)—Called once by the operation to indicate that the operation has started and approximately how much work must be done before it is complete. This method must be called exactly once per instance of a progress monitor.

done()—Called by the operation to indicate that it is complete.

isCanceled()—The operation should periodically poll this method to see whether the user has requested that the operation be canceled.

setCanceled(boolean)—This method is typically called by UI code setting the canceled state to true when the user clicks on the **Cancel** button during an operation.

setTaskName(String)—Sets the task name displayed to the user. Usually, there is no need to call this method because the task name is set by beginTask(String, int).

worked(int)—Called by the operation to indicate that the specified number of units of work has been completed.

The IProgressMonitorWithBlocking interface extends IProgress-Monitor for monitors that want to support feedback when an activity is blocked due to concurrent activity in another thread. If a running operation ever calls the setBlocked method listed below, it must eventually call clearBlocked before the operation completes.

clearBlocked()—Called by an operation to indicate that the operation is no longer blocked.

setBlocked(IStatus)—Called by an operation to indicate that this operation is blocked by some background activity.

9.4.2 Classes for displaying progress

Eclipse provides several classes that either implement the IProgressMonitor interface or provide a progress monitor via the IRunnableWithProgress interface. These classes are used under different circumstances to notify the user of the progress of long-running operations.

SubProgressMonitor—A progress monitor passed by a parent operation to a suboperation so that the suboperation can notify the user of progress as a portion of the parent operation (see Section 9.3, Batching Change Events, on page 382).

NullProgressMonitor—A progress monitor that supports cancellation but does not provide any user feedback. Suitable for subclassing.

ProgressMonitorWrapper—A progress monitor that wrappers another progress monitor and forwards IProgressMonitor and IProgress-MonitorWithBlocking methods to the wrapped progress monitor. Suitable for subclassing.

WorkspaceModifyOperation—An operation that batches resource change events and provides a progress monitor as part of its execution (see Section 9.3, Batching Change Events, on page 382).

ProgressMonitorPart—An SWT composite consisting of a label displaying the task and subtask name, and a progress indicator to show progress.

`ProgressMonitorDialog`—Opens a dialog that displays progress to the user and provides a progress monitor used by the operation to relate that information.

`TimeTriggeredProgressMonitorDialog`—Waits for a specified amount of time during operation execution *then* opens a dialog that displays progress to the user and provides a progress monitor used by the operation to relate that information. If the operation completes *before* the specified amount of time, then no dialog is opened. This is an internal workbench class but listed here because the concept and its functionality is interesting. For more, see Section 9.4.4, IProgressService, on page 386 and Bugzilla entry 123797 at *bugs.eclipse.org/bugs/show_bug.cgi?id=123797*.

`WizardDialog`—When opened, optionally provides progress information as part of the wizard. The wizard implements the `IRunnableContext`, and thus the operation can call `run(boolean, boolean, IRunnable-WithProgress)` and display progress in the wizard via the provided progress monitor (see Section 11.2.3, IWizardContainer, on page 434 and Section 11.2.6, Wizard example, on page 439).

9.4.3 Workbench window status bar

The workbench window provides a progress display area along the bottom edge of the window. Use the `IWorkbenchWindow.run()` method to execute the operation and the progress monitor passed to `IRunnableWithProgress` will be the progress monitor in the status bar. For example, the following snippet from an action delegate (see Section 6.2.6, Creating an action delegate, on page 216 for more on creating action delegates) shows simulated progress in the status bar:

```
private IWorkbenchWindow window;
public void init(IWorkbenchWindow window) {
   this.window = window;
}
public void run(IAction action) {
   try {
      window.run(true, true, new IRunnableWithProgress() {
         public void run(IProgressMonitor monitor)
            throws InvocationTargetException, InterruptedException {
            monitor.beginTask("simulate status bar progress:", 20);
            for (int i = 20; i > 0; --i) {
               monitor.subTask("seconds left = " + i);
               Thread.sleep(1000);
               monitor.worked(1);
            }
            monitor.done();
         }
      });
   }
}
```

```
      catch (InvocationTargetException e) {
        FavoritesLog.logError(e);
      }
      catch (InterruptedException e) {
        // User canceled the operation... just ignore.
      }
  }
```

If you have a view or editor, you can obtain the containing IWorkbench-Window via IWorkbenchPart, which both IViewPart and IEditorPart extend.

```
IWorkbenchWindow window
    = viewOrEditor.getWorkbenchSite().getWorkbenchWindow();
```

You can also obtain the progress monitor in the status bar directly via the IStatusLineManager interface.

```
viewPart.getViewSite().getActionBars()
    .getStatusLineManager().getProgressMonitor()
```

or:

```
editorPart.getEditorSite().getActionBars()
    .getStatusLineManager().getProgressMonitor()
```

9.4.4 IProgressService

Yet another mechanism for displaying progress in the workbench is using the IProgressService interface. While the run() method in IWorkbench-Window displays progress in the status bar, the IProgressService interface displays progress using a subclass of ProgressMonitorDialog named TimeTriggeredProgressMonitorDialog. Although you could use a ProgressMonitorDialog, IProgressService only opens a progress dialog if the operation takes longer to execute than a specified amount of time (currently 800 milliseconds).

```
window.getWorkbench().getProgressService().run(true, true,
    new IRunnableWithProgress() {
      public void run(IProgressMonitor monitor)
         throws InvocationTargetException, InterruptedException
      {
         monitor.beginTask("Simulated long running task #1", 60);
         for (int i = 60; i > 0; --i) {
           monitor.subTask("seconds left = " + i);
           if (monitor.isCanceled()) break;
           Thread.sleep(1000);
           monitor.worked(1);
         }
         monitor.done();
      }
    });
```

Typically, jobs are executed in the background (see Section 20.8, Background Tasks—Jobs API, on page 739), but the `IProgressService` provides the `showInDialog()` method for executing them in the foreground.

9.5   Delayed Changed Events

Eclipse uses lazy initialization—only load a plug-in when it is needed. Lazy initialization presents a problem for plug-ins that need to track changes. How does a plug-in track changes when it is not loaded?

Eclipse solves this problem by queuing change events for a plug-in that is not loaded. When the plug-in is loaded, it receives a single resource change event containing the union of the changes that have occurred during the time it was not active. To receive this event, your plug-in must register to be a save participant when it is started up, as follows.

```
public static void addSaveParticipant() {
    ISaveParticipant saveParticipant = new ISaveParticipant(){
        public void saving(ISaveContext context)
            throws CoreException
        {
            // Save any model state here.
            context.needDelta();
        }
        public void doneSaving(ISaveContext context) {}
        public void prepareToSave(ISaveContext context)
            throws CoreException {}
        public void rollback(ISaveContext context) {}
    };

    ISavedState savedState;
    try {
        savedState = ResourcesPlugin
            .getWorkspace()
            .addSaveParticipant   (
                FavoritesPlugin.getDefault(),
                saveParticipant);
    }
    catch (CoreException e) {
        FavoritesLog.logError(e);
        // Recover if necessary.
        return;
    }

    if (savedState != null)
        savedState.processResourceChangeEvents(
            FavoritesManager.getManager());
}
```

Tip: Even though Eclipse is based on lazy plug-in initialization, it does provide a mechanism for plug-ins to start when the workbench itself starts. To activate at startup, the plug-in must extend the `org.eclipse.ui.startup` extension point and implement the `org.eclipse.ui.IStartup` interface. Once the plug-in is started, the workbench will call the plug-in's `earlyStartup()` method (see Section 3.4.2, Early plug-in startup, on page 114). A workbench preference option gives the user the ability to prevent a plug-in from starting early, so make sure that if your plug-in takes advantage of this extension point, it degrades gracefully in the event that it is not started early.

9.6 Summary

This chapter demonstrated how to process resource change events propagated by the system. Anytime a resource is added, modified, or removed, a corresponding change event is generated. Responding to these events provides a way for your plug-in to stay synchronized with the Eclipse environment.

References

Chapter source (*www.qualityeclipse.com/projects/source-ch-09.zip*).

Arthorne, John, "How You've Changed! Responding to Resource Changes in the Eclipse Workspace," OTI, November 23, 2004 (*www.eclipse.org/articles/Article-Resource-deltas/resource-deltas.html*).

CHAPTER 10

Perspectives

Perspectives are a way to group Eclipse views and actions for a particular task such as coding or debugging. Larger Eclipse enhancements that involve multiple plug-ins may provide their own perspectives. Smaller Eclipse enhancements that involve only one or two plug-ins and provide only one or two new Eclipse views typically enhance existing perspectives rather than provide entirely new perspectives.

This chapter will further extend the **Favorites** example by creating a new perspective for hosting the **Favorites** view and show how to add the **Favorites** view to existing perspectives.

10.1 Creating a Perspective

To create a new perspective, extend the `org.eclipse.ui.perspectives` extension point and then define the layout of the perspective by creating a perspective factory class implementing the `IPerspectiveFactory` interface (see Figure 10–1).

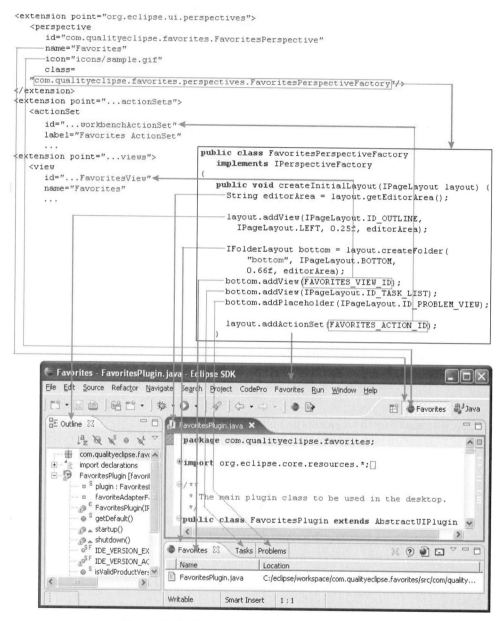

Figure 10–1   Perspective declaration and behavior.

10.1.1   Perspective extension point

Start by opening the **Favorites** plug-in manifest editor, selecting the **Extensions** tab, and clicking the **Add** button. When the **New Extension** wizard opens, select **org.eclipse.ui.perspectives** from the list of all available extension points (see Figure 10–2). Click the **Finish** button to add this extension to the plug-in manifest.

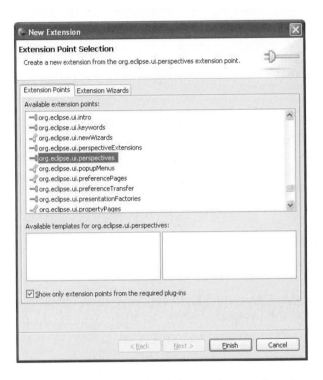

Figure 10–2   The New Extension wizard showing the org.eclipse.ui.perspectives extension point selected.

Now, back in the **Extensions** page of the plug-in manifest editor, right-click on the `org.eclipse.ui.perspectives` extension and select **New > perspective**. This immediately adds a perspective named `com.quality-eclipse.favorites.perspective1` in the plug-in manifest. Clicking on this new perspective displays its properties on the right side of the editor (see Figure 10–3). Modify them as follows:

id—"com.qualityeclipse.favorites.FavoritesPerspective"
The unique identifier used to reference the perspective.

name—"Favorites"
The text label associated with the perspective.

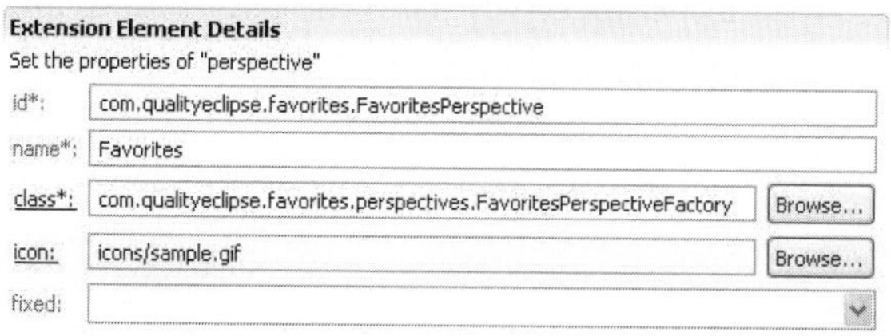

Figure 10–3   The extension element details for the Favorites perspective.

class—"com.qualityeclipse.favorites.perspectives.FavoritesPerspective-Factory"
The class describing the layout of the perspective. The class is instantiated using its no argument constructor, but can be parameterized using the IExecutableExtension interface (see Section 20.5, Types Specified in an Extension Point, on page 723).

icon—"icons/sample.gif"
The icon associated with the perspective.

If you switch to the **plugin.xml** page of the plug-in manifest editor, you will see the following new section of XML defining the new perspective:

```
<extension point="org.eclipse.ui.perspectives">
   <perspective
      class="com.qualityeclipse.favorites.perspectives.
             FavoritesPerspectiveFactory"
      icon="icons/sample.gif"
      id="com.qualityeclipse.favorites.FavoritesPerspective"/>
      name="Favorites"
</extension>
```

10.1.2   Perspective factories

When specifying the name of a perspective factory class, clicking on the **Browse...** button next to the **class** field will open a class selection editor, in which an existing class can be selected. Clicking on the **class:** label to the right of the **class** field will open a **Java Attribute Editor** dialog in which a new class (conforming to the IPerspectiveFactory interface) can be created (see Figure 10–4).

Figure 10–4 The Java Class Selection wizard.

The `IPerspectiveFactory` interface defines a single method, `createInitialLayout()`, which specifies the initial page layout and visible action sets for the perspective. The factory is only used to define the initial layout of the perspective and is then discarded. By default, the layout area contains space for the editors, but no views. The factory can add additional views, which are placed relative to the editor area or to another view.

Open the newly created `FavoritesPerspectiveFactory` class and modify it as follows so that the **Favorites** view will appear below the editor area and the standard **Outline** view will be shown to its left.

```
package com.qualityeclipse.favorites.perspectives;

import org.eclipse.ui.*;

public class FavoritesPerspectiveFactory
    implements IPerspectiveFactory
{
    private static final String FAVORITES_VIEW_ID =
        "com.qualityeclipse.favorites.views.FavoritesView";
```

```
private static final String FAVORITES_ACTION_ID =
    "com.qualityeclipse.favorites.workbenchActionSet";

public void createInitialLayout(IPageLayout layout) {
    // Get the editor area.
    String editorArea = layout.getEditorArea();

    // Put the Outline view on the left.
    layout.addView(
        IPageLayout.ID_OUTLINE,
        IPageLayout.LEFT,
        0.25f,
        editorArea);

    // Put the Favorites view on the bottom with
    // the Tasks view.
    IFolderLayout bottom =
        layout.createFolder(
            "bottom",
            IPageLayout.BOTTOM,
            0.66f,
            editorArea);
    bottom.addView(FAVORITES_VIEW_ID);
    bottom.addView(IPageLayout.ID_TASK_LIST);
    bottom.addPlaceholder(IPageLayout.ID_PROBLEM_VIEW);

    // Add the Favorites action set.
    layout.addActionSet(FAVORITES_ACTION_ID);
  }
}
```

Within the `createInitialLayout()` method, the `addView()` method is used to add the standard **Outline** view to the left of the editor area such that it takes up 25 percent of the horizontal area within the window. Using the `createFolder()` method, a folder layout is created to occupy the bottom third of the layout below the editor area. The **Favorites** view and standard **Tasks** view are added to the folder layout so that each will appear stacked with a tab inside the folder.

Next, a placeholder for the standard **Problems** view is added to the folder. If a user opened the **Problems** view, it would open in the location specified by the placeholder. Finally, the **Favorites** action set is made visible by default within the perspective.

When opened, the new **Favorites** perspective will look something like what's shown Figure 10–5.

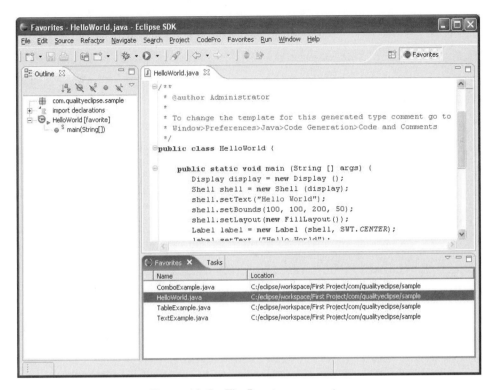

Figure 10–5   The Favorites perspective.

10.1.3   IPageLayout

As seen in the previous section, the IPageLayout interface defines the proto-col necessary to support just about any possible perspective layout. It defines many useful APIs, including the following:

addActionSet(String)—Adds an action set with the given ID to the page layout.

addFastView(String)—Adds the view with the given ID to the page layout as a fast view.

addFastView(String, float)—Adds the view with the given ID to the page layout as a fast view with the given width ratio.

addNewWizardShortcut(String)—Adds a creation wizard to the **File New** menu.

addPerspectiveShortcut(String)—Adds a perspective shortcut to the **Perspective** menu.

`addPlaceholder(String, int, float, String)`—Adds a placeholder for a view with the given ID to the page layout.

`addShowInPart(String)`—Adds an item to the **Show In** prompter.

`addShowViewShortcut(String)`—Adds a view to the **Show View** menu.

`addStandaloneView(String, boolean, int, float, String)`—Adds a stand-alone view with the given ID to this page layout. A stand-alone view cannot be docked together with other views.

`addView(String, int, float, String)`—Adds a view with the given ID to the page layout.

`createFolder(String, int, float, String)`—Creates and adds a folder with the given ID to the page layout.

`createPlaceholderFolder(String, int, float, String)`—Creates and adds a placeholder for a new folder with the given ID to the page layout.

`getEditorArea()`—Returns the special ID for the editor area in the page layout.

`getViewLayout(String)`—Returns the layout for the view or placeholder with the given compound ID in this page layout.

`setEditorAreaVisible(boolean)`—Shows or hides the editor area for the page layout.

`setFixed(boolean)`—Sets whether this layout is fixed. In a fixed layout, layout parts cannot be moved or zoomed, and the initial set of views cannot be closed.

10.2 Enhancing an Existing Perspective

In addition to creating a new perspective, you can also extend an existing perspective by adding new views, placeholders, shortcuts, and action sets. To illustrate this, you can add several extensions to the standard **Resource** perspective.

To extend an existing perspective, open the **Favorites** plug-in manifest editor, select the **Extensions** tab, and click the **Add** button to open the **New Extension** wizard. Select the `org.eclipse.ui.perspectiveExtensions` extension point from the list of available extension points (see Figure 10–6).

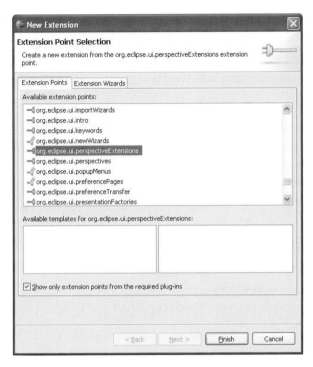

Figure 10–6   The New Extension wizard showing the org.eclipse.ui.perspectiveExtensions
extension point selected.

On the **Extensions** page of the plug-in manifest editor, right-click on the
`org.eclipse.ui.perspectiveExtensions` extension and select **New >
perspectiveExtension**. This immediately adds a perspective extension named
`com.qualityeclipse.favorites.perspectiveExtension1` to the plug-in
manifest. Click on this new perspective extension to display its properties and
change the **targetID** field to "`org.eclipse.ui.resourcePerspective`" (see
Figure 10–7). This will change the name of the perspective extension as seen
on the **Extensions** page.

Figure 10–7   The extension element details showing the
perspective extension's attributes.

When the perspective extension has been created, a number of different
extension types can be added, including views, placeholders, action sets, as
well as shortcuts for views, perspectives, and the new wizards.

10.2.1 Adding views and placeholders

A view can be either directly added to an existing perspective or a placeholder can be added so that when the user opens the view it appears in the correct place. As an example, add the **Favorites** view to the standard **Resource** perspective.

On the **Extensions** page, click on the newly created **org.eclipse.ui.resource-Perspective** extension and select **New > view**. This immediately adds a perspective view extension named com.quality-eclipse.favorites.view1 to the plug-in manifest. Clicking on this new extension shows its properties, which should be modified as follows (see Figure 10–8).

id—"com.qualityeclipse.favorites.views.FavoritesView"
The unique identifier of the **Favorites** view.

relationship—"stack"
This specifies how the view should be oriented relative to the target view.

relative—"org.eclipse.ui.views.TaskList"
The view relative to which the added view should be oriented.

visible—"true"
The view should be initially visible.

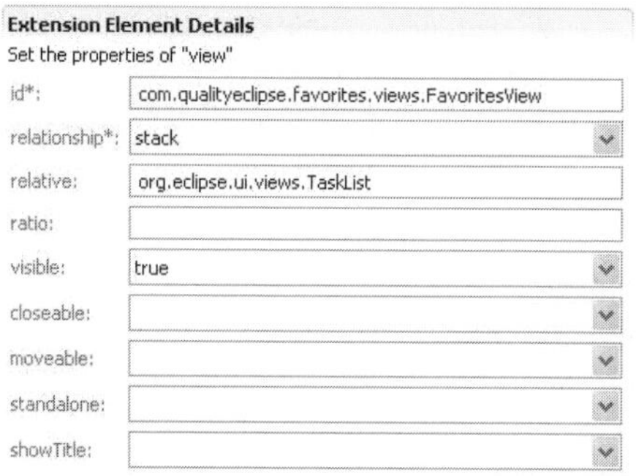

Figure 10–8   The extension element details showing the perspective
view extension's attributes.

The name of the perspective view extension as seen on the **Extensions** page will change to reflect the id entered.

In addition to being stacked in a folder relative to another view, the added view could be placed at the left, right, above, or below the view specified in the **relative** field, or added as a fast view in the left toolbar. If the new view is added at the left, right, above, or below, the **ratio** of space that the new view takes from the old view can also be specified.

If the **visible** field is specified as `true`, the new view will open when the perspective is opened. If it is set to `false`, the view will not open automatically. Rather, a placeholder will be established that defines the initial location of the view, if it is ever opened by a user.

Switching to the **plugin.xml** page of the plug-in manifest editor, you will see the following new section of XML defining the new perspective extension.

```
<extension point="org.eclipse.ui.perspectiveExtensions">
   <perspectiveExtension
      targetID="org.eclipse.ui.resourcePerspective">
      <view
         id="com.qualityeclipse.favorites.views.FavoritesView">
         relationship="stack"
         relative="org.eclipse.ui.views.TaskList"
         visible="true"
      </view>
   </perspectiveExtension>
</extension>
```

When the **Resource** perspective is opened, the **Favorites** view will appear stacked relative to the **Tasks** view (see Figure 10–9).

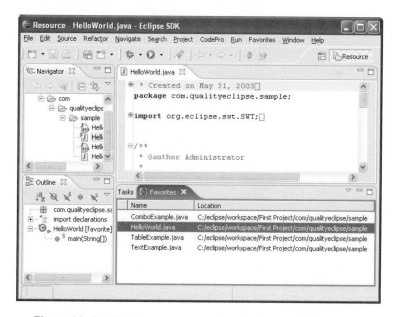

Figure 10–9   The Resource perspective showing the Favorites view.

10.2.2   Adding shortcuts

Shortcuts for quickly accessing related views, perspectives, and new wizards can also be added to a perspective. As an example, add shortcuts for accessing the **Favorites** view and perspective to the **Resources** perspective.

Start by adding a view shortcut for accessing the **Favorites** view from the **Resource** perspective. On the **Extensions** page, right-click on the `org.eclipse.ui.resourcePerspective` extension and select **New > view-Shortcut**. This adds a view shortcut extension named `com.quality-eclipse.favorites.viewShortcut1` to the plug-in manifest. Click on it to show its properties and then change the **id** field to "`com.quality-eclipse.favorites.views.FavoritesView`" (see Figure 10–10). This will change the name of the view shortcut extension as seen on the **Extensions** page.

Extension Element Details
Set the properties of "viewShortcut"
id*: com.qualityeclipse.favorites.views.FavoritesView

Figure 10–10   The extension element details showing the view
shortcut extension's attributes.

When the **Resource** perspective is opened, this will add a shortcut to the **Favorites** view on the **Window > Show View** menu (see Figure 10–11).

Figure 10–11   The Show View menu showing the Favorites shortcut.

Next, add a perspective shortcut for accessing the **Favorites** perspective from the **Resource** perspective. On the **Extensions** page, right-click on the `org.eclipse.ui.resourcePerspective` extension and select **New > perspectiveShortcut**. This adds a perspective shortcut extension named

com.qualityeclipse.favorites.perspectiveShortcut1 to the plug-in
manifest. Click on it to show its properties and then change the **id** field to
"com.qualityeclipse.favorites.FavoritesPerspective" (see Figure
10–12). This will change the name of the perspective shortcut extension as
seen on the **Extensions** page.

Figure 10–12   The extension element details showing the perspective
shortcut extension's attributes.

When the **Resource** perspective is opened, this will add a shortcut to the
Favorites view on the **Window > Open Perspective** menu (see Figure 10–13).

Figure 10–13   The Open Perspective menu showing the Favorites shortcut.

If you switch to the plug-in manifest editor's **plugin.xml** page, you will see this
added section of XML defining the new view and perspective shortcuts:

```
<extension point="org.eclipse.ui.perspectiveExtensions">
   <perspectiveExtension
      targetID="org.eclipse.ui.resourcePerspective">
      ...
      <viewShortcut
         id="com.qualityeclipse.favorites.views.FavoritesView"/>
      <perspectiveShortcut
         id="com.qualityeclipse.favorites.FavoritesPerspective"/>
   </perspectiveExtension>
</extension>
```

10.2.3   Adding action sets

Groups of commands (menu items and toolbar buttons) defined in action sets can also be added to a perspective (see Chapter 6, Actions, for more about adding actions). As an example, add the **Favorites** action set to the **Resources** perspective.

On the **Extensions** page, right-click on the `org.eclipse.ui.resource-Perspective` extension and select **New > actionSet**. This adds an action set extension, `com.qualityeclipse.favorites.actionSet1`, to the plug-in manifest.

Click on this action set to reveal its properties and change the **id** field to "`com.qualityeclipse.favorites.workbenchActionSet`" (see Figure 10–14). This will change the action set extension's name as seen on the **Extensions** page.

Figure 10–14   The extension element details showing the action set extension's attributes.

If you switch to the **plugin.xml** page of the plug-in manifest editor, you will see the following added section of XML defining the new action set extension.

```
<extension point="org.eclipse.ui.perspectiveExtensions">
   <perspectiveExtension
      targetID="org.eclipse.ui.resourcePerspective">
      ...
      <actionSet
         id="com.qualityeclipse.favorites.workbenchActionSet"/>
   </perspectiveExtension>
</extension>
```

With the above enhancements in place, the new perspective and perspective extensions will now be visible on the **Extensions** page (see Figure 10–15).

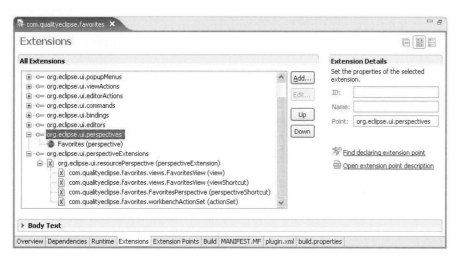

Figure 10–15   The Extensions page showing the new perspective and perspective extensions.

10.3 RFRS Considerations

The "User Interface" section of the *RFRS Requirements* includes three best practices dealing with perspectives. All of them are derived from the Eclipse UI Guidelines.

10.3.1   *Create for long-lived tasks*   *(RFRS 5.3.5.10)*

User Interface Guideline #8.1 is a **best practice** that states:

> *Create a new perspective type for long-lived tasks that involve the perfor-*
> *mance of smaller, non-modal tasks. A new perspective type should be cre-*
> *ated when there is a group of related tasks that would benefit from a*
> *predefined configuration of actions and views, and these tasks are long-*
> *lived. A task-oriented approach is imperative*

To pass this test, create a list of the perspectives defined by your application and demonstrate their use. For every perspective, describe the views, shortcuts, new wizard items, and action sets that are included. In the case of the examples presented earlier in this chapter, show the **Favorites** perspective (see Figure 10–5) and describe its use to the reviewers.

10.3.2   Extend existing perspectives   (RFRS 5.3.5.11)

User Interface Guideline #8.2 is a **best practice** that states:

> To expose a single view or two views, extend an existing perspective type.
> If a plug-in contributes a small number of views, and these augment an
> existing task, it is better to add those views to an existing perspective. For
> instance, if you create a view that augments the task of Java code creation,
> don't create a new perspective. Instead, add it to the existing Java perspec-
> tive. This strategy provides better integration with the existing platform.

For this test, simply create a list of any views that your application adds
to other existing perspectives. In the case of the earlier examples, show the
Favorites view added to the **Resource** perspective (see Figure 10–9).

10.3.3   Add actions to window menu   (RFRS 5.3.5.15)

User Interface Guideline #8.6 is a **best practice** that states:

> Populate the window menu bar with actions and action sets that are
> appropriate to the task orientation of the perspective, and any larger
> workflow.

For this test, provide a list of any action sets that have been added to any
perspectives. For the **Favorites** view, list things such as the **Favorites** action set
that was added to the **Resource** perspective in Section 10.2.3, Adding action
sets, on page 402.

10.4   Summary

Perspectives provide a way to group views and actions together to support a
specific task. This chapter described how to create a new perspective, to define
its default layout, and to add various extensions to it.

References

Chapter source (*www.qualityeclipse.com/projects/source-ch-10.zip*).

Springgay, Dave, "Using Perspectives in the Eclipse UI," OTI, August 27,
2001 (*www.eclipse.org/articles/using-perspectives/PerspectiveArticle.html*).

Lorimer, R. J., "Eclipse: Create Your Own Perspective," April 8, 2005
(*www.javalobby.org/java/forums/t18187.html*).

CHAPTER 11

Dialogs and Wizards

Good UI guidelines suggest that developers construct modeless Eclipse editors
and views, but there are times when a modal dialog or wizard is appropriate.
This chapter lays out Eclipse's dialog and wizard framework, discusses when
a dialog or wizard should be used instead of a view or editor, provides various
examples, and discusses Eclipse's various built-in dialog classes.

11.1 Dialogs

Whenever information is requested from or presented to the user in a modeless fashion, it allows the user to freely interact with all the resources in the
workbench. Windows, pages, editors, and views are all examples of modeless
UI constructs that do not restrict the order in which the user interacts with
them. Dialogs are typically modal, restricting the user to either entering the
information requested or canceling the operation. The only time a modal UI
construct should be used is when programming restrictions require a gathering or dissemination of information before any other processing can continue
and, even then, for as short a time as possible.

   In one case, the program could present two different versions of a file
using a dialog. Unfortunately, this approach prevents the user from switching
back and forth between the comparison and some other UI construct such as
another editor or view. A better approach would be to present that same information in a comparison editor.

   Creating a new project represents a different situation. In that case, the
operation must gather all the necessary information sequentially before the

operation can be performed. The user has requested the operation and typically does not need to interact with another aspect of the program until all the information is gathered and the operation is complete. In this case, a dialog or wizard is warranted.

11.1.1 SWT dialogs versus JFace dialogs

There are two distinct dialog hierarchies in Eclipse that should not be confused. SWT dialogs (`org.eclipse.swt.Dialog`) are Java representations of built-in platform dialogs such as a file dialog or font dialog; as such, they are not portable or extendable. JFace dialogs (`org.eclipse.jface.dialogs.Dialog`) are platform-independent dialogs on which wizards are built. SWT dialogs are only briefly discussed, while JFace dialogs are covered in detail.

11.1.2 Common SWT dialogs

Eclipse includes several SWT dialog classes that provide platform-independent interfaces to underlying platform-specific dialogs:

`ColorDialog`—Prompts the user to select a color from a predefined set of available colors.

`DirectoryDialog`—Prompts the user to navigate the filesystem and select a directory. Valid styles include `SWT.OPEN` for selecting an existing directory and `SWT.SAVE` for specifying a new directory.

`FileDialog`—Prompts the user to navigate the filesystem and select or enter a filename. Valid styles include `SWT.OPEN` for selecting an existing file and `SWT.SAVE` for specifying a new file.

`FontDialog`—Prompts the user to select a font from all available fonts.

`MessageBox`—Displays a message to the user. Valid icon styles are shown in Table 11–1.

Valid button styles include:

```
SWT.OK
SWT.OK | SWT.CANCEL
SWT.YES | SWT.NO
SWT.YES | SWT.NO | SWT.CANCEL
SWT.RETRY | SWT.CANCEL
SWT.ABORT | SWT.RETRY | SWT.IGNORE
```

`PrintDialog`—Prompts the user to select a printer and various print-related parameters prior to starting a print job.

Table 11–1 Icon Styles

Constant	Icon
SWT.ICON_ERROR	
SWT.ICON_INFORMATION	
SWT.ICON_QUESTION	
SWT.ICON_WARNING	
SWT.ICON_WORKING	

With any of these SWT dialogs, one of the following modal styles can be specified:

`SWT.MODELESS`—Modeless dialog behavior.

`SWT.PRIMARY_MODAL`—Modal behavior with respect to the parent shell.

`SWT.APPLICATION_MODAL`—Modal behavior with respect to the application.

`SWT.SYSTEM_MODAL`—Modal behavior with respect to the entire system.

11.1.3 *Common JFace dialogs*

There are many JFace dialogs that can be either instantiated directly or reused via subclassing.

Abstract dialogs

`AbstractElementListSelectionDialog`—An abstract dialog to select elements from a list of elements.

`IconAndMessageDialog`—The abstract superclass of dialogs that have an icon and a message as the first two widgets.

`SelectionDialog`—An abstract dialog for displaying and returning a selection.

`SelectionStatusDialog`—An abstract base class for dialogs with a status bar and **OK/Cancel** buttons. The status message must be passed over as a `StatusInfo` object and can be an error, warning, or okay. The **OK** button is enabled or disabled depending on the status.

`StatusDialog`—An abstract base class for dialogs with a status bar and **OK/Cancel** buttons.

`TitleAreaDialog`—An abstract dialog having a title area for displaying a title and an image as well as a common area for displaying a description, a message, or an error message.

File dialogs

`SaveAsDialog`—A standard "Save As" dialog that solicits a path from the user. The `getResult()` method returns the path. Note that the folder at the specified path might not exist and might need to be created.

Information dialogs

`ErrorDialog`—A dialog to display one or more errors to the user, as contained in an `IStatus` object. If an error contains additional detailed information, then a **Details** button is automatically supplied, which shows or hides an error details viewer when pressed by the user (see Section 11.1.9, Details dialog, on page 420 for a similar dialog that meet RFRS criteria).

`MessageDialog`—A dialog for showing messages to the user.

`MessageDialogWithToggle`—A `MessageDialog` that also allows the user to adjust a toggle setting. If a preference store is provided and the user selects the toggle, then the user's answer (yes/ok or no) will persist in the store (see Section 12.3.2, Accessing preferences, on page 469). If no store is provided, then this information can be queried after the dialog closes.

Resource dialogs

`ContainerSelectionDialog`—A standard selection dialog that solicits a container resource from the user. The `getResult()` method returns the selected container resource.

`NewFolderDialog`—A dialog used to create a new folder. Optionally, the folder can be linked to a filesystem folder.

`ProjectLocationMoveDialog`—A dialog used to select the location of a project for moving.

`ProjectLocationSelectionDialog`—A dialog used to select the name and location of a project for copying.

ResourceListSelectionDialog—Shows a list of resources to the user with a text entry field for a string pattern used to filter the list of resources.

ResourceSelectionDialog—A standard resource selection dialog that solicits a list of resources from the user. The getResult() method returns the selected resources.

TypeFilteringDialog—A selection dialog that allows the user to select a file editor.

Selection dialogs

CheckedTreeSelectionDialog—A dialog to select elements out of a tree structure.

ContainerCheckedTreeViewer—An enhanced CheckedTree-SelectionDialog dialog with special checked/gray state on the container (non-leaf) nodes.

ElementListSelectionDialog—A dialog to select elements out of a list of elements.

ElementTreeSelectionDialog—A dialog to select elements out of a tree structure.

ListDialog—A dialog that prompts for one element from a list of elements. Uses IStructuredContentProvider to provide the elements and ILabelProvider to provide their labels.

ListSelectionDialog—A standard dialog that solicits a list of selections from the user. This class is configured with an arbitrary data model represented by content and label provider objects. The getResult() method returns the selected elements.

TwoPaneElementSelector—A list selection dialog with two panes. Duplicated entries will be folded together and are displayed in the lower pane (qualifier).

Miscellaneous dialogs

InputDialog—A simple input dialog for soliciting an input string from the user.

MarkerResolutionSelectionDialog—A dialog to allow the user to select from a list of marker resolutions.

ProgressMonitorDialog—A modal dialog that displays progress during a long-running operation (see Section 9.4, Progress Monitor, on page 383).

`TaskPropertiesDialog`—Shows the properties of a new or existing task, or a problem.

`WizardDialog`—A dialog displaying a wizard and implementing the `IWizardContainer` interface (see Section 11.2.3, IWizardContainer, on page 434).

11.1.4   Creating a JFace dialog

The default implementation of the `Dialog` class creates a dialog containing a content area for dialog-specific controls and a button bar below containing **OK** and **Cancel** buttons (see Figure 11–1).

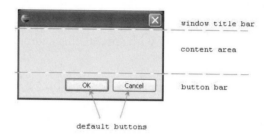

Figure 11–1   Default dialog structure.

Typically, new dialogs are created by subclassing `org.eclipse.jface.` `dialogs.Dialog` and overriding a handful of methods to customize the dialog for a particular purpose.

`buttonPressed(int)`—Called when a button created by the `createButton` method is clicked by the user. The default implementation calls `okPressed()` if the **OK** button is pressed and `cancelPressed()` if the **Cancel** button is pressed.

`cancelPressed()`—Called when the user presses the **Cancel** button. The default implementation sets the return code to `Window.CANCEL` and closes the dialog.

`close()`—Closes the dialog, disposes of its shell, and removes the dialog from its window manager (if it has one).

`createButton(Composite, int, String, boolean)`—Creates and returns a new button in the button bar with the given identifier and label. This method is typically called from the `createButtonsForButtonBar` method.

`createButtonBar(Composite)`—Lays out a button bar and calls the `createButtonsForButtonBar` method to populate it. Subclasses can override `createButtonBar` or `createButtonsForButtonBar` as necessary.

`createButtonsForButtonBar(Composite)`—Creates buttons in the button bar. The default implementation creates **OK** and **Cancel** buttons in the lower right corner. Subclasses can override this method to replace the default buttons, or extend this method to augment them using the `createButton` method.

`createContents(Composite)`—Creates and returns this dialog's contents. The default implementation calls `createDialogArea` and `createButtonBar` to create the dialog area and button bar, respectively. Subclasses should override these methods rather than `createContents`.

`createDialogArea(Composite)`—Creates and returns the content area for the dialog above the button bar. Subclasses typically call the superclass method and then add controls to the returned composite.

`okPressed()`—Called when the user presses the **OK** button. The default implementation sets the return code to `Window.OK` and closes the dialog.

`open()`—Opens this dialog, creating it first if it has not yet been created. This method waits until the user closes the dialog, and then returns the dialog's return code. A dialog's return codes are dialog-specific, although two standard return codes are predefined: `Window.OK` and `Window.CANCEL`.

`setShellStyle(int)`—Sets the shell style bits for creating the dialog. This method has no effect after the shell is created. Valid style bits include:

```
SWT.MODELESS
SWT.PRIMARY_MODAL
SWT.APPLICATION_MODAL
SWT.SYSTEM_MODAL
SWT.SHELL_TRIM
SWT.DIALOG_TRIM
SWT.BORDER
SWT.CLOSE
SWT.MAX
SWT.MIN
SWT.RESIZE
SWT.TITLE
```

setReturnCode(int)—Sets the dialog's return code that is returned by the open() method.

Dialog also provides some related utility methods:

applyDialogFont(Control)—Applies the dialog font to the specified control and recursively to all child controls that currently have the default font.

getImage(String)—Returns the standard dialog image with the given key (one of the Dialog.DLG_IMG_* constants). These images are managed by the dialog framework and must not be disposed by another party.

shortenText(String, Control)—Shortens the specified text so that its width in pixels does not exceed the width of the given control, by inserting an ellipsis ("...") as necessary.

11.1.5 Dialog units

If you are positioning controls in the dialog area based on absolute positioning (null layout) rather than using a layout manager, such as GridLayout or FormLayout, then problems may arise when a different font is used. If the dialog is sized for a font with one pixel size and the user has his or her system set for a font in a different pixel size, then the controls will be either too big or too small for the font used. To alleviate this problem, you should position and size the controls based on the font's average character size or based on *dialog units* (see Figure 11–2).

Figure 11–2 Dialog units superimposed over the letter "T."

Dialog units are based on the current font and are independent of the display device; thus, they can be used to position controls within a dialog, independent of the font being used. They are defined as one-quarter of the average width of a character and one-eighth of the average height of a character.

```
dialog unit X = average character width / 4
dialog unit Y = average character height / 8
```

Therefore, use the following to convert from dialog units to pixels.

```
pixelX = (dialog unit X * average character width) / 4
pixelY = (dialog unit Y * average character height) / 8
```

The Eclipse dialog framework provides several convenient methods for converting dialog units or character sizes into pixel sizes.

`convertHeightInCharsToPixels(int)`—Returns the number of pixels corresponding to the height of the given number of characters.

`convertHorizontalDLUsToPixels(int)`—Returns the number of pixels corresponding to the given number of horizontal dialog units.

`convertVerticalDLUsToPixels(int)`—Returns the number of pixels corresponding to the given number of vertical dialog units.

`convertWidthInCharsToPixels(int)`—Returns the number of pixels corresponding to the width of the given number of characters.

11.1.6 Initial dialog location and size

The default behavior for dialogs as implemented by the dialog framework is to initially position a dialog on top of its parent window specified in the dialog's constructor. To provide a different initial location or size for a dialog, you would override the following methods as necessary.

`getInitialLocation(Point)`—Returns the initial location to use for the dialog. The default implementation centers the dialog horizontally (half the difference to the left and half to the right) and vertically (one-third above and two-thirds below) relative to the parent shell or display bounds if there is no parent shell. The parameter is the initial size of the dialog, as returned by `getInitialSize()` method.

`getInitialSize()`—Returns the initial size to use for the dialog. The default implementation returns the preferred size of the dialog based on the dialog's layout and controls using the `computeSize` method.

11.1.7   Resizable dialogs

By default, subclasses of `Dialog` are not resizable, but there are examples of resizable dialogs within the Eclipse framework such as:

`org.eclipse.jdt.internal.ui.compare.ResizableDialog.`

Unfortunately, this dialog is within an internal package, thus, should not be reused outside of its defining plug-in (see Section 20.2, Accessing Internal Code, on page 711). The first step to making your wizard resizable is to include the `SWT.RESIZE` and `SWT.MAX` styles when the dialog is created to allow the user to resize the dialog and display the maximize window button, as follows:

```
public ResizableDialog(Shell parentShell) {
    super(parentShell);
}

public ResizableDialog(IShellProvider parentShell) {
    super(parentShell);
    setShellStyle(getShellStyle() | SWT.RESIZE | SWT.MAX);
}
```

Next, to preserve the size and location of the dialog across invocations, subclasses of this new class must supply a location in which to store values. For more about `IDialogSettings` see Section 11.2.7, Dialog settings, on page 441.

```
protected abstract IDialogSettings getDialogSettings();
```

Methods for loading the bounds from the dialog settings and saving the bounds into the dialog settings are neeed, as follows:

```
private static final String TAG_X = "x";
private static final String TAG_Y = "y";
private static final String TAG_WIDTH = "width";
private static final String TAG_HEIGHT = "height";

private Rectangle loadBounds() {
    IDialogSettings settings = getDialogSettings();
    try {
        return new Rectangle(
            settings.getInt(TAG_X),
            settings.getInt(TAG_Y),
            settings.getInt(TAG_WIDTH),
            settings.getInt(TAG_HEIGHT));
    }
    catch (NumberFormatException e) {
        return null;
    }
}
```

```
private void saveBounds(Rectangle bounds) {
   IDialogSettings settings = getDialogSettings();
   settings.put(TAG_X, bounds.x);
   settings.put(TAG_Y, bounds.y);
   settings.put(TAG_WIDTH, bounds.width);
   settings.put(TAG_HEIGHT, bounds.height);
}
```

You need to override the getInitialLocation() and getInitial-
Size() methods so that, when the dialog is first opened, its prior location and
size are restored.

```
protected Rectangle cachedBounds;

protected Point getInitialSize() {

   // Track the current dialog bounds.
   getShell().addControlListener(new ControlListener() {
      public void controlMoved(ControlEvent arg0) {
         cachedBounds = getShell().getBounds();
      }
      public void controlResized(ControlEvent arg0) {
         cachedBounds = getShell().getBounds();
      }
   });

   // Answer the size from the previous incarnation.
   Rectangle b1 = getShell().getDisplay().getBounds();
   Rectangle b2 = loadBounds();
   if (b2 != null)
      return new Point(
         b1.width < b2.width ? b1.width : b2.width,
         b1.height < b1.height ? b2.height : b2.height);

   return super.getInitialSize();
}

protected Point getInitialLocation(Point initialSize) {

   // Answer the location from the previous incarnation.
   Rectangle displayBounds =
      getShell().getDisplay().getBounds();
   Rectangle bounds = loadBounds();
   if (bounds != null) {
      int x = bounds.x;
      int y = bounds.y;
      int maxX = displayBounds.x + displayBounds.width
         - initialSize.x;
      int maxY = displayBounds.y + displayBounds.height
         - initialSize.y;
      if (x > maxX)
         x = maxX;
      if (y > maxY)
         y = maxY;
```

```
          if (x < displayBounds.x)
             x = displayBounds.x;
          if (y < displayBounds.y)
             y = displayBounds.y;
          return new Point(x, y);
      }
      return super.getInitialLocation(initialSize);
}
```

Finally, override the `close` method to save the dialog bounds for future incarnations:

```
public boolean close() {
    boolean closed = super.close();
    if (closed && cachedBounds != null)
       saveBounds(cachedBounds);
    return closed;
}
```

11.1.8 Favorites view filter dialog

As an example, create a specialized filter dialog for the **Favorites** view that presents the user the option of filtering content based on name, type, or location (see Section 7.2.7, Viewer filters, on page 281 and Section 7.3.4, Pull-down menu, on page 287). The dialog restricts itself to presenting and gathering information from the user and providing accessor methods for the filter action. Start by creating a new `FavoritesFilterDialog` class:

```
package com.qualityeclipse.favorites.dialogs;

import ...

public class FavoritesFilterDialog extends Dialog
{
   private String namePattern;
   private String locationPattern;
   private Collection selectedTypes;

   public FavoritesFilterDialog(
      Shell parentShell,
      String namePattern,
      String locationPattern,
      FavoriteItemType[] selectedTypes
   ) {
      super(parentShell);
      this.namePattern = namePattern;
      this.locationPattern = locationPattern;
      this.selectedTypes = new HashSet();
      for (int i = 0; i < selectedTypes.length; i++)
         this.selectedTypes.add(selectedTypes[i]);
   }
```

Next, override the `createDialogArea()` method to create the various fields that appear in the upper area of dialog.

```
private Text namePatternField;
private Text locationPatternField;

protected Control createDialogArea(Composite parent) {
    Composite container = (Composite) super.createDialogArea(parent);
    final GridLayout gridLayout = new GridLayout();
    gridLayout.numColumns = 2;
    container.setLayout(gridLayout);

    final Label filterLabel = new Label(container, SWT.NONE);
    filterLabel.setLayoutData(new GridData(GridData.BEGINNING,
        GridData.CENTER, false, false, 2, 1));
    filterLabel.setText("Enter a filter (* = any number of "
        + "characters, ? = any single character)"
        + "\nor an empty string for no filtering:");

    final Label nameLabel = new Label(container, SWT.NONE);
    nameLabel.setLayoutData(new GridData(GridData.END,
        GridData.CENTER, false, false));
    nameLabel.setText("Name:");

    namePatternField = new Text(container, SWT.BORDER);
    namePatternField.setLayoutData(new GridData(GridData.FILL,
        GridData.CENTER, true, false));

    final Label locationLabel = new Label(container, SWT.NONE);
    final GridData gridData = new GridData(GridData.END,
        GridData.CENTER, false, false);
    gridData.horizontalIndent = 20;
    locationLabel.setLayoutData(gridData);
    locationLabel.setText("Location:");

    locationPatternField = new Text(container, SWT.BORDER);
    locationPatternField.setLayoutData(new GridData(GridData.FILL,
        GridData.CENTER, true, false));

    final Label typesLabel = new Label(container, SWT.NONE);
    typesLabel.setLayoutData(new GridData(GridData.BEGINNING,
        GridData.CENTER, false, false, 2, 1));
    typesLabel.setText("Select the types of favorites to be shown:");

    final Composite typeCheckboxComposite = new Composite(container,
        SWT.NONE);
    final GridData gridData_1 = new GridData(GridData.FILL,
        GridData.FILL, false, false, 2, 1);
    gridData_1.horizontalIndent = 20;
    typeCheckboxComposite.setLayoutData(gridData_1);
    final GridLayout typeCheckboxLayout = new GridLayout();
    typeCheckboxLayout.numColumns = 2;
    typeCheckboxComposite.setLayout(typeCheckboxLayout);

    return container;
}
```

Next create a new `createTypeCheckboxes()` method, called at the end of the `createDialogArea()` method, to create one checkbox for each type.

```
private Map typeFields;

protected Control createDialogArea(Composite parent) {
    ... existing code ...
    createTypeCheckboxes(typeCheckboxComposite);
    return container;
}

private void createTypeCheckboxes(Composite parent) {
    typeFields = new HashMap();
    FavoriteItemType[] allTypes = FavoriteItemType.getTypes();
    for (int i = 0; i < allTypes.length; i++) {
        final FavoriteItemType eachType = allTypes[i];
        if (eachType == FavoriteItemType.UNKNOWN)
            continue;
        final Button button = new Button(parent, SWT.CHECK);
        button.setText(eachType.getName());
        typeFields.put(eachType, button);
        button.addSelectionListener(new SelectionAdapter() {
            public void widgetSelected(SelectionEvent e) {
                if (button.getSelection())
                    selectedTypes.add(eachType);
                else
                    selectedTypes.remove(eachType);
            }
        });
    }
}
```

Add the `initContent()` method that is called at the end of the `createDialogArea()` method to initialize the various fields in the dialog:

```
protected Control createDialogArea(Composite parent) {
    ... existing code ...
    createTypeCheckboxes(typeCheckboxComposite);
    initContent();
    return container;
}

private void initContent() {
    namePatternField.setText(namePattern != null ? namePattern : "");
    namePatternField.addModifyListener(new ModifyListener() {
        public void modifyText(ModifyEvent e) {
            namePattern = namePatternField.getText();
        }
    });

    locationPatternField
            .setText(locationPattern != null ? locationPattern : "");
```

```
        locationPatternField.addModifyListener(new ModifyListener() {
            public void modifyText(ModifyEvent e) {
                locationPattern = locationPatternField.getText();
            }
        });

        FavoriteItemType[] allTypes = FavoriteItemType.getTypes();
        for (int i = 0; i < allTypes.length; i++) {
            FavoriteItemType eachType = allTypes[i];
            if (eachType == FavoriteItemType.UNKNOWN)
                continue;
            Button button = (Button) typeFields.get(eachType);
            button.setSelection(selectedTypes.contains(eachType));
        }
    }
}
```

Override the `configureShell()` method to set the dialog title:

```
protected void configureShell(Shell newShell) {
    super.configureShell(newShell);
    newShell.setText("Favorites View Filter Options");
}
```

Finally, add accessor methods for clients to extract the settings specified by the user when the dialog was opened:

```
public String getNamePattern() {
    return namePattern;
}

public String getLocationPattern() {
    return locationPattern;
}

public FavoriteItemType[] getSelectedTypes() {
    return (FavoriteItemType[]) selectedTypes
        .toArray(new FavoriteItemType[selectedTypes.size()]);
}
```

The filter action (see `FavoritesViewFilterAction` in Section 7.3.4, Pull-down menu, on page 287) must be modified to fill the dialog with the current filter settings, open the dialog, and process the specified filter settings if the user closes the dialog using the **OK** button. If the dialog is closed using the **Cancel** button or any other way besides the **OK** button, the changes are discarded as per standard dialog operation guidelines. The type and location view filters referenced in the following code are left as an exercise for the reader.

```
public void run() {
    FavoritesFilterDialog dialog =
        new FavoritesFilterDialog(
            shell,
            nameFilter.getPattern(),
            typeFilter.getTypes(),
            locationFilter.getPattern());
    if (dialog.open() != InputDialog.OK)
        return;
    nameFilter.setPattern(dialog.getNamePattern());
    locationFilter.setPattern(dialog.getLocationPattern());
    typeFilter.setPattern(dialog.getSelectedTypes());
}
```

Getting the preceding `run()` method to compile involves adding a new `FavoritesViewLocationFilter` and `FavoritesViewTypeFilter` similar to the existing `FavoritesViewNameFilter`. When these changes are complete, the filter dialog presents the filter settings to the user when the **Filter...** menu item is selected (see Figure 11–3).

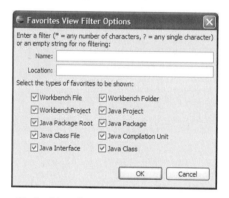

Figure 11–3 New Favorites View Filter Options dialog.

11.1.9   Details dialog

One of the RFRS criteria includes identifying the plug-in and plug-in creator when reporting problems to the user. In other words, whenever the application needs to report an error message or exception to the user, the plug-in's unique identifier, version, and creator must be visible in the dialog. The `org.eclipse.jface.dialogs.ErrorDialog` can display exception information in a details section that is shown or hidden using a **Details** button, but it does not display the necessary product information as required by RFRS standards. To satisfy this requirement, `ExceptionDetailsDialog` was created (see Figure 11–4).

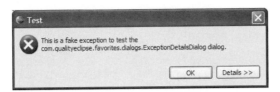

Figure 11–4 Details dialog with details hidden.

When the **Details** button is pressed, the dialog resizes itself to show additional information (see Figure 11–5).

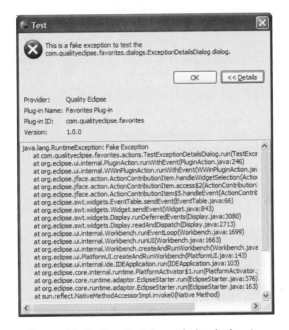

Figure 11–5 Details dialog with details showing.

The `ExceptionDetailsDialog` class implements this expanding details behavior.

```
package com.qualityeclipse.favorites.dialogs;
import ...
public class ExceptionDetailsDialog extends AbstractDetailsDialog {
   private final Object details;
   private final Plugin plugin;

   public ExceptionDetailsDialog(Shell parentShell, String title,
         Image image, String message, Object details, Plugin plugin)
   {
      this(new SameShellProvider(parentShell), title, image, message,
            details, plugin);
   }
```

```
public ExceptionDetailsDialog(IShellProvider parentShell,
    String title, Image image, String message, Object details,
    Plugin plugin)
{
    super(parentShell, getTitle(title, details), getImage(image,
        details), getMessage(message, details));

    this.details = details;
    this.plugin = plugin;
}
```

There are several utility methods that build content based on information provided in constructor arguments. The getTitle() method returns the title based on the provided title and details object.

```
public static String getTitle(String title, Object details) {
    if (title != null)
        return title;
    if (details instanceof Throwable) {
        Throwable e = (Throwable) details;
        while (e instanceof InvocationTargetException)
            e = ((InvocationTargetException) e).getTargetException();
        String name = e.getClass().getName();
        return name.substring(name.lastIndexOf('.') + 1);
    }
    return "Exception";
}
```

The getImage() method returns the image based on the provided image and details object.

```
public static Image getImage(Image image, Object details) {
    if (image != null)
        return image;
    Display display = Display.getCurrent();
    if (details instanceof IStatus) {
        switch (((IStatus) details).getSeverity()) {
            case IStatus.ERROR :
                return display.getSystemImage(SWT.ICON_ERROR);
            case IStatus.WARNING :
                return display.getSystemImage(SWT.ICON_WARNING);
            case IStatus.INFO :
                return display.getSystemImage(SWT.ICON_INFORMATION);
            case IStatus.OK :
                return null;
        }
    }
    return display.getSystemImage(SWT.ICON_ERROR);
}
```

The getMessage() method and helper methods build up a message based on the message and details objects provided.

```
public static String getMessage(String message, Object details) {
   if (details instanceof Throwable) {
      Throwable e = (Throwable) details;
      while (e instanceof InvocationTargetException)
         e = ((InvocationTargetException) e).getTargetException();
      if (message == null)
         return e.toString();
      return MessageFormat.format(
         message, new Object[] { e.toString() });
   }
   if (details instanceof IStatus) {
      String statusMessage = ((IStatus) details).getMessage();
      if (message == null)
         return statusMessage;
      return MessageFormat.format(
         message, new Object[] { statusMessage });
   }
   if (message != null)
      return message;
   return "An Exception occurred.";
}

public static void appendException(PrintWriter writer, Throwable ex)
{
   if (ex instanceof CoreException) {
      appendStatus(writer, ((CoreException) ex).getStatus(), 0);
      writer.println();
   }
   appendStackTrace(writer, ex);
   if (ex instanceof InvocationTargetException)
      appendException(writer, ((InvocationTargetException) ex)
            .getTargetException());
}

public static void appendStatus(
   PrintWriter writer, IStatus status, int nesting
) {
   for (int i = 0; i < nesting; i++)
      writer.print("  ");
   writer.println(status.getMessage());
   IStatus[] children = status.getChildren();
   for (int i = 0; i < children.length; i++)
      appendStatus(writer, children[i], nesting + 1);
}

public static void appendStackTrace(
   PrintWriter writer, Throwable ex
) {
   ex.printStackTrace(writer);
}
```

When the **Details** button is clicked, the superclass determines whether the details area needs to be shown or hidden and, as necessary, calls the `createDetailsArea()` method to create the content for the details area.

```java
protected Control createDetailsArea(Composite parent) {

    // Create the details area.
    Composite panel = new Composite(parent, SWT.NONE);
    panel.setLayoutData(new GridData(GridData.FILL_BOTH));
    GridLayout layout = new GridLayout();
    layout.marginHeight = 0;
    layout.marginWidth = 0;
    panel.setLayout(layout);

    // Create the details content.
    createProductInfoArea(panel);
    createDetailsViewer(panel);

    return panel;
}

protected Composite createProductInfoArea(Composite parent) {

    // If no plugin specified, then nothing to display here.
    if (plugin == null)
        return null;

    Composite composite = new Composite(parent, SWT.NULL);
    composite.setLayoutData(new GridData());
    GridLayout layout = new GridLayout();
    layout.numColumns = 2;
    layout.marginWidth = convertHorizontalDLUsToPixels(
        IDialogConstants.HORIZONTAL_MARGIN);
    composite.setLayout(layout);

    Dictionary bundleHeaders = plugin.getBundle().getHeaders();
    String pluginId = plugin.getBundle().getSymbolicName();
    String pluginVendor =
        (String) bundleHeaders.get("Bundle-Vendor");
    String pluginName = (String) bundleHeaders.get("Bundle-Name");
    String pluginVersion =
        (String) bundleHeaders.get("Bundle-Version");

    new Label(composite, SWT.NONE).setText("Provider:");
    new Label(composite, SWT.NONE).setText(pluginVendor);
    new Label(composite, SWT.NONE).setText("Plug-in Name:");
    new Label(composite, SWT.NONE).setText(pluginName);
    new Label(composite, SWT.NONE).setText("Plug-in ID:");
    new Label(composite, SWT.NONE).setText(pluginId);
    new Label(composite, SWT.NONE).setText("Version:");
    new Label(composite, SWT.NONE).setText(pluginVersion);

    return composite;
}
```

```
protected Control createDetailsViewer(Composite parent) {
   if (details == null)
      return null;

   Text text = new Text(parent, SWT.MULTI | SWT.READ_ONLY
         | SWT.BORDER | SWT.H_SCROLL | SWT.V_SCROLL);
   text.setLayoutData(new GridData(GridData.FILL_BOTH));

   // Create the content.
   StringWriter writer = new StringWriter(1000);
   if (details instanceof Throwable)
      appendException(new PrintWriter(writer), (Throwable) details);
   else if (details instanceof IStatus)
      appendStatus(new PrintWriter(writer), (IStatus) details, 0);
   text.setText(writer.toString());

   return text;
}
```

The `ExceptionDetailsDialog` class is built on top of the more generic
`AbstractDetailsDialog` class. This abstract dialog has a details section that
can be shown or hidden by the user but subclasses are responsible for providing the content of the details section.

```
package com.qualityeclipse.favorites.dialogs;

import ...

public abstract class AbstractDetailsDialog extends Dialog
{
   private final String title;
   private final String message;
   private final Image image;

   public AbstractDetailsDialog(Shell parentShell, String title,
         Image image, String message)
   {
      this(new SameShellProvider(parentShell),title,image,message);
   }

   public AbstractDetailsDialog(IShellProvider parentShell,
         String title, Image image, String message)
   {
      super(parentShell);

      this.title = title;
      this.image = image;
      this.message = message;

      setShellStyle(SWT.DIALOG_TRIM | SWT.RESIZE
            | SWT.APPLICATION_MODAL);
   }
```

The `configureShell()` method is responsible for setting the title:

```
protected void configureShell(Shell shell) {
   super.configureShell(shell);
   if (title != null)
      shell.setText(title);
}
```

The `createDialogArea()` method creates and returns the contents of the upper part of this dialog (above the button bar). This includes an image, if specified, and a message.

```
protected Control createDialogArea(Composite parent) {
   Composite composite = (Composite) super.createDialogArea(parent);
   composite.setLayoutData(new GridData(GridData.FILL_HORIZONTAL));

   if (image != null) {
      ((GridLayout) composite.getLayout()).numColumns = 2;
      Label label = new Label(composite, 0);
      image.setBackground(label.getBackground());
      label.setImage(image);
      label.setLayoutData(new GridData(
            GridData.HORIZONTAL_ALIGN_CENTER
               | GridData.VERTICAL_ALIGN_BEGINNING));
   }

   Label label = new Label(composite, SWT.WRAP);
   if (message != null)
      label.setText(message);
   GridData data = new GridData(GridData.FILL_HORIZONTAL
         | GridData.VERTICAL_ALIGN_CENTER);
   data.widthHint = convertHorizontalDLUsToPixels(
      IDialogConstants.MINIMUM_MESSAGE_AREA_WIDTH);
   label.setLayoutData(data);
   label.setFont(parent.getFont());

   return composite;
}
```

Override the `createButtonsForButtonBar()` method to create **OK** and **Details** buttons.

```
private Button detailsButton;

protected void createButtonsForButtonBar(Composite parent) {
   createButton(parent, IDialogConstants.OK_ID,
         IDialogConstants.OK_LABEL, false);
   detailsButton = createButton(parent, IDialogConstants.DETAILS_ID,
         IDialogConstants.SHOW_DETAILS_LABEL, false);
}
```

The `buttonPressed()` method is called when either the **OK** or **Details** buttons is pressed. Override this method to alternately show or hide the details area if the **Details** button is pressed.

```
private Control detailsArea;
private Point cachedWindowSize;

protected void buttonPressed(int id) {
   if (id == IDialogConstants.DETAILS_ID)
      toggleDetailsArea();
   else
      super.buttonPressed(id);
}

protected void toggleDetailsArea() {
   Point oldWindowSize = getShell().getSize();
   Point newWindowSize = cachedWindowSize;
   cachedWindowSize = oldWindowSize;

   // Show the details area.
   if (detailsArea == null) {
      detailsArea = createDetailsArea((Composite) getContents());
      detailsButton.setText(IDialogConstants.HIDE_DETAILS_LABEL);
   }

   // Hide the details area.
   else {
      detailsArea.dispose();
      detailsArea = null;
      detailsButton.setText(IDialogConstants.SHOW_DETAILS_LABEL);
   }

   /*
    * Must be sure to call
    *    getContents().computeSize(SWT.DEFAULT, SWT.DEFAULT)
    * before calling
    *    getShell().setSize(newWindowSize)
    * since controls have been added or removed.
    */

   // Compute the new window size.
   Point oldSize = getContents().getSize();
   Point newSize = getContents().computeSize(
      SWT.DEFAULT, SWT.DEFAULT);
   if (newWindowSize == null)
      newWindowSize = new Point(oldWindowSize.x, oldWindowSize.y
         + (newSize.y - oldSize.y));
```

```
    // Crop new window size to screen.
    Point windowLoc = getShell().getLocation();
    Rectangle screenArea =
       getContents().getDisplay().getClientArea();
    if (newWindowSize.y > screenArea.height
          - (windowLoc.y - screenArea.y))
       newWindowSize.y = screenArea.height
             - (windowLoc.y - screenArea.y);

    getShell().setSize(newWindowSize);
    ((Composite) getContents()).layout();
}
```

Finally, subclasses must implement `createDetailsArea()` to provide content for the area of the dialog made visible when the **Details** button is clicked.

```
protected abstract Control createDetailsArea(Composite parent);
```

11.1.10 Opening a dialog—finding a parent shell

When constructing a new dialog, you need to know either the parent shell or an object that can provide a parent shell (an object that has a `getShell()` method or implements the `IShellProvider` interface). You can specify `null` for the parent shell, but this will prevent proper association of the dialog with its parent; if the dialog is modal as many dialogs are, then specifying the correct parent shell or shell provider will prevent the user from being able to activate the parent window before closing the dialog. So the question becomes: How do you obtain the parent shell?

IWorkbenchWindowActionDelegate (see example code in Section 6.2.6, Creating an action delegate, on page 216)—If you have an action delegate, then Eclipse provides the workbench window from which a shell can be obtained. Immediately after the action delegate is instantiated, Eclipse calls the `init()` method with the workbench window as the argument. Cache this window and pass the window's shell as an argument when constructing your dialog:

```
private IWorkbenchWindow window;

public void init(IWorkbenchWindow window) {
   this.window = window;
}
```

```
public void run(IAction action) {
    Shell parentShell = window.getShell();
    MyDialog dialog = new MyDialog(parentShell, ...);
    ... etc ...
}
```

IObjectActionDelegate (see Section 6.3.3, IObjectActionDelegate, on page 233)—If you have an action in a context menu, Eclipse provides the target part from which a shell provider can be obtained. Before the run() method is called, Eclipse calls setActivePart() with the target part. Cache this part and pass the site containing the part as an argument when constructing your dialog.

```
private IWorkbenchPart targetPart;

public void setActivePart(IAction action, IWorkbenchPart targetPart)
{
    this.targetPart = targetPart;
}

public void run(IAction action) {
    IWorkbenchPartSite site = targetPart.getSite();
    MyDialog dialog = new MyDialog(site, ...);
    ... etc ...
}
```

IViewPart or IEditorPart (see Section 7.2, View Part, on page 263 or Section 8.2, Editor Part, on page 330)—If you have a view or editor, then, similar to the preceding code, you can obtain a shell provider:

```
IShellProvider shellProvider = viewOrEditor.getSite();
```

PlatformUI—The platform UI provides the workbench window from which a shell can be obtained.

```
Shell parentShell =
    PlatformUI.getWorkbench().getActiveWorkbenchWindow().getShell();
```

Display (see Section 4.2.5.1, Display, on page 140)—If all else fails, you can obtain the shell of the active window from Display.

```
Shell parentShell = Display.getDefault().getActiveShell();
```

11.2   Wizards

org.eclipse.jface.wizard.WizardDialog is a specialized subclass of
Dialog (see Figure 11–6) that is used when a modal operation requires a
particular sequence for its information collection or when a single screen has
too many fields. Wizards have a title area along the top; a content area in
the middle showing the wizard pages; a progress bar as needed; and **Help,
Next, Back, Finish,** and **Cancel** buttons (or some subset) along the bottom (see
Figure 11–7). The title area contains the wizard's title, description, an optional
image, and an error, warning, or informational message as required.

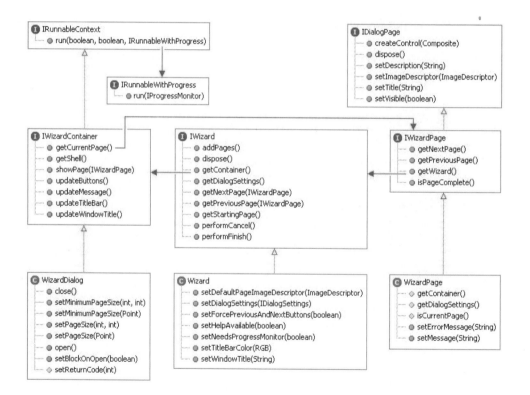

Figure 11–6   Wizard class hierarchy.

Figure 11–7   Default wizard dialog structure.

11.2.1   IWizard

Rather than subclass WizardDialog, you should subclass org.eclipse.
jface.wizard.Wizard, which implements the org.eclipse.jface.
wizard.IWizard interface for use with WizardDialog. The WizardDialog
uses the IWizard interface to obtain the pages to be displayed and to notify
the wizard of user interaction. The concrete wizard class provides much of the
IWizard behavior, allowing you to focus on a subset of the IWizard interface.
The wizard's task is to create and initialize the pages it contains, handle any
special customized flow and information between pages, and execute the
operation when the **Finish** button is pressed.

addPages()—Subclasses should override this method to add the appropriate pages by calling addPage().

canFinish()—Returns whether this wizard could be finished without
further user interaction. Typically, this is used by the wizard container to
enable or disable the **Finish** button.

createPageControls(Composite)—Creates this wizard's controls in
the given parent control.

dispose()—Cleans up any native resources, such as images, clipboard,
and so on, that were created by this class. This follows the *if you create
it, you destroy it* theme that runs throughout Eclipse.

getContainer()—Returns the wizard container in which this wizard is
being displayed.

getDefaultPageImage()—Returns the default page image for this wizard.

getDialogSettings()—Returns the dialog settings for this wizard page.

getNextPage(IWizardPage)—Returns the wizard page to be shown after the specified wizard page, or null if none. The default implementation shows pages in the order in which they were added to the wizard, so subclasses need only to override this method to implement a custom page flow.

getPreviousPage(IWizardPage)—Returns the wizard page to be shown before the specified wizard page, or null if none. The default implementation shows pages in the order in which they were added to the wizard, so subclasses need only to override this method to implement a custom page flow.

getStartingPage()—Answers the first page to be displayed in the wizard. The default implementation answers the first wizard page added to the wizard, so subclasses need only to override this method if the starting page is not the first page added.

performCancel()—Called by the wizard container if the wizard is canceled. Subclasses need only to override this method to provide any custom cancel processing. Return true if the wizard container can be closed, or false if it should remain open.

performFinish()—Called by the wizard container when the **Finish** button is pressed. Subclasses should override this method to perform the wizard operation and return true to indicate that the wizard container should be closed, or false if it should remain open.

setDefaultPageImageDescriptor(ImageDescriptor)—Sets the image displayed in the wizard's title area if the current wizard page does not specify an image.

setHelpAvailable(boolean)—Sets whether help is available and whether the **Help** button is visible.

setNeedsProgressMonitor(boolean)—Sets whether this wizard needs a progress monitor. If true, then space is reserved below the page area and above the buttons for a progress bar and progress message to be displayed (see Section 9.4, Progress Monitor, on page 383).

setTitleBarColor(RGB)—Sets the color of the title area.

setWindowTitle(String)—Sets the window title.

11.2.2   IWizardPage

Wizards use the `org.eclipse.jface.wizard.IWizardPage` interface to communicate with the pages they contain. Typically, you will subclass the `org.eclipse.jface.wizard.WizardPage` class, accessing and overriding the following methods, rather than implementing the `IWizardPage` interface. The wizard page's task is to present a page of information to the user, validate any information entered by the user on that page, and provide accessors for the wizard to gather the information entered.

`createControl(Composite)`—Creates the controls comprising this wizard page.

`dispose()`—Cleans up any native resources, such as images, clipboard, and so on, that were created by this class. This follows the *if you create it, you destroy it* theme that runs throughout Eclipse.

`getContainer()`—Returns the wizard container for this wizard page.

`getDialogSettings()`—Returns the dialog settings for this wizard page.

`getWizard()`—Returns the wizard that hosts this wizard page.

`setDescription(String)`—Sets the descriptive text appearing in the wizard's title area.

`setErrorMessage(String)`—Sets or clears the error message for this page.

`setImageDescriptor(ImageDescriptor)`—Sets the image that appears in the wizard's title area.

`setMessage(String)`—Sets or clears the message for this page.

`setPageComplete(boolean)`—Sets whether this page is complete. This forms the basis for determining whether the **Next** and **Finish** buttons are enabled.

`setTitle(String)`—Sets the title that appears in the title area of the wizard, not the title on the shell.

`setVisible(boolean)`—Sets the visibility of this dialog page. Subclasses can extend this method (being sure to call the superclass method) to detect when a page becomes the active page.

One approach for validating information entered by a user on a wizard page is for each field to have a listener that calls an `updatePageComplete()` method in the wizard page (snipped from Section 11.2.8, Page content based on selection, on page 441).

```
sourceFileField = new Text(container, SWT.BORDER);
sourceFileField.addModifyListener(new ModifyListener()  {
   public void modifyText(ModifyEvent e) {
      updatePageComplete();
   }
});
```

This `updatePageComplete()` method would be responsible for checking the content in each field, displaying an error message as appropriate, and calling the `setPageComplete()` method (see Section 11.2.8, Page content based on selection, on page 441 for an example). The `pageComplete` attribute is used by the wizard container to determine whether the **Next** and **Finish** buttons should be enabled.

> **New in Eclipse 3.2**   The `org.eclipse.jface.fieldassist` package adds images, hover text, content proposals, and auto type-ahead to fields in forms, dialogs, and wizards. This functionality can help a user understand and enter information into a form-based user interface.

11.2.3 IWizardContainer

The wizard uses the `org.eclipse.jface.wizard.IWizardContainer` interface to communicate with the context in which it is being displayed.

`getCurrentPage()`—Returns the current page being displayed.

`getShell()`—Returns the shell for this wizard container.

`run(boolean, boolean, IRunnableWithProgress)`—Runs the given runnable in the context of the wizard dialog. The first argument "fork" indicates whether the runnable should be executed in a separate thread. The second argument "cancelable" indicates whether the user should be allowed to cancel the operation while it is in progress (see Section 4.2.5.1, Display, on page 140 for more on the UI thread).

`showPage(IWizardPage)`—Shows the specified wizard page. This should not be used for normal next/back page flow, but exists for custom page flow such as double-clicking in a list.

`updateButtons()`—Adjusts the enable state of the **Back, Next,** and **Finish** buttons to reflect the state of the active page in this container.

`updateMessage()`—Updates the message shown in the message line to reflect the state of the currently active page in this container.

`updateTitleBar()`—Updates the title bar (title, description, and image) to reflect the state of the active page in this container.

`updateWindowTitle()`—Updates the window title to reflect the state of the wizard.

In addition to `IWizardContainer`, `WizardDialog` implements both `IWizardContainer2` and `IPageChangeProvider`. In your wizard, you can obtain the container using `getContainer()` and then test to see whether it implements either of these interfaces to access additional functionality.

`addPageChangedListener(IPageChangedListener)`—Adds a listener for page changes in this page change provider.

`getSelectedPage()`—Returns the currently selected page in the dialog.

`removePageChangedListener(IPageChangedListener)`—Removes the given page change listener from this page change provider.

`updateSize()`—Updates the window size to reflect the state of the current wizard.

11.2.4   Nested wizards

One wizard can contain one or more nested wizards such as the **Import** and **Export** wizards. The `org.eclipse.jface.wizard.WizardSelectionPage` class provides behavior for managing one or more nested wizards. When a nested wizard can be determined, a `WizardSelectionPage` subclass calls the `setSelectedNode()` method. When a user clicks the **Next** button, the `WizardSelectionPage` class uses that information via the `org.eclipse.jface.wizard.IWizardNode` interface to create and manage the nested wizard.

11.2.5   Launching a wizard

You can hook a wizard into the Eclipse framework using one of the predefined wizard extension points, or you can manually launch a wizard as a result of a user action.

11.2.5.1   Wizard extension points

If you want Eclipse to automatically provide an action delegate and display your wizard in a predefined location, you can extend one of the following wizard extension points.

`org.eclipse.ui.exportWizards`—Adds a nested wizard in the **Export** wizard, which is displayed by selecting the **File > Export...** command. Wizard classes associated with this extension point must implement the `org.eclipse.ui.IExportWizard` interface.

org.eclipse.ui.importWizards—Adds a nested wizard in the **Import** wizard, which is displayed by selecting **File > Import...**. Wizard classes associated with this extension point must implement the org.eclipse. ui.IImportWizard interface.

org.eclipse.ui.newWizards—Adds a nested wizard in the **New** wizard, which is displayed by selecting **File > New > Other...**. Wizard classes associated with this extension point must implement the org.eclipse. ui.INewWizard interface.

These three extension points share several common attributes:

class—The wizard class to be launched by the parent wizard. This wizard must implement the appropriate interface for the extension point as outlined earlier. The class is instantiated using its no argument constructor, but can be parameterized using the IExecutableExtension interface (see Section 20.5, Types Specified in an Extension Point, on page 723).

icon—The icon associated with this wizard, similar to action images (see Section 6.2.4, Action images, on page 214).

id—The unique identifier for the wizard.

name—The human-readable name for the wizard.

You can specify a filter for both org.eclipse.ui.exportWizards and org.eclipse.ui.importWizards extension points using the selection subelement. By using a filter, your export or import wizard only appears when the appropriately named or typed element is selected.

The org.eclipse.ui.newWizards extension point requires an additional category attribute to identify how wizards are to be hierarchically organized. This category is declared using the same extension point with the following attributes:

id—The unique identifier for the category.

name—The human-readable name for the category.

parentCategory—The unique identifier for the category in which the category will appear, if there is one.

The org.eclipse.ui.newWizards extension point also allows you to specify a primaryWizard. A primary wizard is emphasized in the new wizard dialog and exists so that product managers can emphasize a set of wizards for their products. This element is not intended to be used by plug-in developers.

If a wizard declared using one of the aforementioned extension points implements the IExecutableExtension interface, then Eclipse will communicate additional initialization information encoded in the declaration to the wizard using that interface (see Section 20.5, Types Specified in an Extension Point, on page 723).

You can use the plug-in manifest editor to quickly create a wizard class with stub methods that is hooked into one of the wizard extension points. In the plug-in manifest editor, navigate to the **Extensions** page and click the **Add...** button to add, for example, an org.eclipse.ui.newWizards extension (see Section 6.2.1, Defining a workbench window menu, on page 209 for an example of adding extensions). Then, right-click on the org.eclipse.ui.newWizards extension in the plug-in manifest editor and select **New > wizard**. Select the wizard extension that was added to edit its properties (see Figure 11–8).

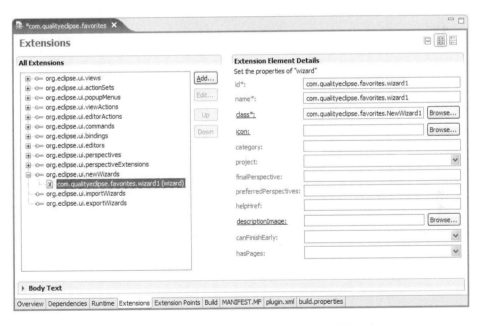

Figure 11–8   The extension element details showing newWizard extension.

Clicking on the **class:** label to the right of the **class** field will open a **Java Attribute Editor** dialog in which a new class can be created (see Figure 11–9).

Figure 11–9   Java Attribute Editor dialog showing class creation.

Completing the required fields generates a new Java class and hooks that class into the plug-in manifest. The folowing are the generated plug-in manifest entry and stub Java wizard class.

```
<extension point="org.eclipse.ui.newWizards">
   <wizard
      name="com.qualityeclipse.favorites.wizard1"
      class="com.qualityeclipse.favorites.NewWizard1"
      id="com.qualityeclipse.favorites.wizard1">
   </wizard>
</extension>

package com.qualityeclipse.favorites;
import ...

public class NewWizard1 extends Wizard
   implements INewWizard
{
   public void init(
      IWorkbench workbench, IStructuredSelection selection
   ) {
      // Initialization code here.
   }
```

```
public boolean performFinish() {
    // Perform operation here.
    return false;
}
}
```

11.2.5.2 Manually launching a wizard

Alternatively, you can launch a wizard from an action delegate. In this case, implement an `IObjectActionDelegate` (see Section 6.3.3, IObjectAction-Delegate, on page 233) with a `run()` method that launches the **Extract Strings** wizard (see next section).

```
public void setActivePart(IAction action, IWorkbenchPart targetPart)
{
    this.targetPart = targetPart;
}

public void selectionChanged(IAction action, ISelection selection) {
    this.selection =
        selection instanceof IStructuredSelection
            ? (IStructuredSelection) selection
            : null;
}

public void run(IAction action) {
    IWorkbenchPartSite site = targetPart.getSite();
    IWorkbenchWindow window = site.getWorkbenchWindow();
    ExtractStringsWizard wizard = new ExtractStringsWizard();
    wizard.init(window.getWorkbench(), selection);
    WizardDialog dialog = new WizardDialog(window.getShell(), wizard);
    dialog.open();
}
```

11.2.6 Wizard example

For the example, you will create a two-page wizard for extracting strings from a `plugin.xml` file and placing those strings into a separate `plugin.properties` file as specified by the RFRS requirements. The wizard is responsible for instantiating the two pages, facilitating communication from the first page to the second, and gathering information from the two pages and performing the operation when the user presses the **Finish** button. The operation is performed in a separate thread so that the user can cancel the operation (see Section 9.4, Progress Monitor, on page 383 and Section 4.2.5.1, Display, on page 140 for more about the UI thread).

In the following code example, the `init()` method is called directly by the action delegate, while the `addPages()` method is called indirectly by the dialog framework when the wizard dialog is created and opened. This approach parallels the INewWizard interface so that this wizard can easily implement that interface and thus be launched by **File > New > Other....**

```
package com.qualityeclipse.favorites.wizards;
import ...
public class ExtractStringsWizard extends Wizard
      implements INewWizard
{
   private IStructuredSelection initialSelection;
   private SelectFilesWizardPage selectFilesPage;
   private SelectStringsWizardPage selectStringsPage;

   public void init(
      IWorkbench workbench, IStructuredSelection selection
   ) {
      initialSelection = selection;
   }
   public void addPages() {
      setWindowTitle("Extract");
      selectFilesPage = new SelectFilesWizardPage();
      addPage(selectFilesPage);
      selectStringsPage = new SelectStringsWizardPage();
      addPage(selectStringsPage);
      selectFilesPage.init(initialSelection);
   }
```

When the user has finished entering information and clicks the **Finish** button, the performFinish() method is called to perform the operation. In this example, the finish method uses functionality provided by the wizard container to perform the operation on a separate thread so that the UI stays responsive during the operation and so that the user can cancel the operation.

```
public boolean performFinish() {
   try {
      getContainer().run(true, true, new IRunnableWithProgress() {
         public void run(IProgressMonitor monitor)
            throws InvocationTargetException, InterruptedException
         {
            performOperation(monitor);
         }
      });
   }
   catch (InvocationTargetException e) {
      FavoritesLog.logError(e);
      return false;
   }
   catch (InterruptedException e) {
      // User canceled, so stop but don't close wizard.
      return false;
   }
   return true;
}
```

```
private void performOperation(IProgressMonitor monitor) {
   ExtractedString[] extracted = selectStringsPage.getSelection();
   // Perform the operation here.
}
```

11.2.7 Dialog settings

Dialog settings can be used to store current values for a wizard or dialog to use the next time the wizard or dialog is opened. In this case, instantiate and cache the dialog settings object in the wizard's constructor for use by the various wizard pages. The getSection() call is used to isolate settings for this wizard from settings for other wizards. Each page can then use the various IDialogSetting get() and put() methods to load and save values across sessions.

```
public ExtractStringsWizard() {
   IDialogSettings favoritesSettings =
      FavoritesPlugin.getDefault().getDialogSettings();
   IDialogSettings wizardSettings =
      favoritesSettings.getSection("ExtractStringsWizard");
   if (wizardSettings == null)
      wizardSettings =
         favoritesSettings.addNewSection("ExtractStringsWizard");
   setDialogSettings(favoritesSettings);
}
```

11.2.8 Page content based on selection

The first page of the **Extract Strings** wizard displays **Source File** and **Destination File** text fields, each with a **Browse...** button to the right (see Figure 11–10). The createControl() method creates and aligns each of the wizard page controls.

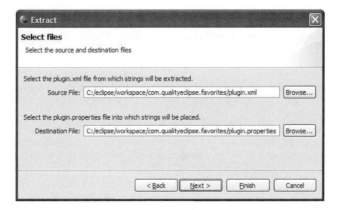

Figure 11–10   The Extract Strings wizard.

```java
package com.qualityeclipse.favorites.wizards;

import ...

public class SelectFilesWizardPage extends WizardPage
{
   private Text sourceFileField;
   private Text destinationFileField;
   private IPath initialSourcePath;

   public SelectFilesWizardPage() {
      super("selectFiles");
      setTitle("Select files");
      setDescription(
         "Select the source and destination files");
   }

   public void createControl(Composite parent) {
      Composite container = new Composite(parent, SWT.NULL);
      final GridLayout gridLayout = new GridLayout();
      gridLayout.numColumns = 3;
      container.setLayout(gridLayout);
      setControl(container);

      final Label label = new Label(container, SWT.NONE);
      final GridData gridData = new GridData();
      gridData.horizontalSpan = 3;
      label.setLayoutData(gridData);
      label.setText(
         "Select the plugin.xml file " +
         "from which strings will be extracted.");

      final Label label_1 = new Label(container, SWT.NONE);
      final GridData gridData_1 =
         new GridData(GridData.HORIZONTAL_ALIGN_END);
      label_1.setLayoutData(gridData_1);
      label_1.setText("Source File:");

      sourceFileField = new Text(container, SWT.BORDER);
      sourceFileField.addModifyListener(new ModifyListener() {
         public void modifyText(ModifyEvent e) {
            updatePageComplete();
         }
      });
      sourceFileField.setLayoutData(
         new GridData(GridData.FILL_HORIZONTAL));

      final Button button = new Button(container, SWT.NONE);
      button.addSelectionListener(new SelectionAdapter() {
         public void widgetSelected(SelectionEvent e) {
            browseForSourceFile();
         }
      });
      button.setText("Browse...");
```

```
    final Label label_2 = new Label(container, SWT.NONE);
    final GridData gridData_2 = new GridData();
    gridData_2.horizontalSpan = 3;
    label_2.setLayoutData(gridData_2);

    final Label label_3 = new Label(container, SWT.NONE);
    final GridData gridData_3 = new GridData();
    gridData_3.horizontalSpan = 3;
    label_3.setLayoutData(gridData_3);
    label_3.setText(
        "Select the plugin.properties file " +
        "into which strings will be placed.");

    final Label label_4 = new Label(container, SWT.NONE);
    final GridData gridData_4 = new GridData();
    gridData_4.horizontalIndent = 20;
    label_4.setLayoutData(gridData_4);
    label_4.setText("Destination File:");

    destinationFileField =
        new Text(container, SWT.BORDER);
    destinationFileField.addModifyListener(
        new ModifyListener() {
            public void modifyText(ModifyEvent e) {
                updatePageComplete();
            }
        });
    destinationFileField.setLayoutData(
        new GridData(GridData.HORIZONTAL_ALIGN_FILL));

    final Button button_1 =
        new Button(container, SWT.NONE);
    button_1
        .addSelectionListener(new SelectionAdapter() {
        public void widgetSelected(SelectionEvent e) {
            browseForDestinationFile();
        }
    });
    button_1.setText("Browse...");

    initContents();
    }
}
```

As always, the goal is to save time for the user. If the user has already selected something in the workbench, you want to populate the wizard page based on that information. For this wizard page, the init() method analyzes the current selection and caches the result, while the initContents() method initializes the field content based on that cached result.

```
public void init(ISelection selection) {
   if (!(selection instanceof IStructuredSelection))
      return;
   // Find the first plugin.xml file.
   Iterator iter = ((IStructuredSelection) selection).iterator();
   while (iter.hasNext()) {
      Object item = (Object) iter.next();
      if (item instanceof IJavaElement) {
         IJavaElement javaElem = (IJavaElement) item;
         try {
            item = javaElem.getUnderlyingResource();
         }
         catch (JavaModelException e) {
            // Log and report the exception.
            e.printStackTrace();
            continue;
         }
      }
      if (item instanceof IFile) {
         IFile file = (IFile) item;
         if (file.getName().equals("plugin.xml")) {
            initialSourcePath = file.getLocation();
            break;
         }
         item = file.getProject();
      }
      if (item instanceof IProject) {
         IFile file = ((IProject) item).getFile("plugin.xml");
         if (file.exists()) {
            initialSourcePath = file.getLocation();
            break;
         }
      }
   }
}

private void initContents() {
   if (initialSourcePath == null)
      return;
   IPath rootLoc = ResourcesPlugin.getWorkspace()
      .getRoot().getLocation();
   IPath path = initialSourcePath;
   if (rootLoc.isPrefixOf(path))
      path = path
         .setDevice(null)
         .removeFirstSegments(rootLoc.segmentCount());
   sourceFileField.setText(path.toString());
   destinationFileField.setText(
      path
         .removeLastSegments(1)
         .append("plugin.properties")
         .toString());
   updatePageComplete();
   setMessage(null);
   setErrorMessage(null);
}
```

Wizards provide a message area just below the title in which feedback can be provided. Generally, this area is used to indicate to the user that additional information needs to be entered before proceeding to the next wizard page or performing the operation. In this case, the updatePageComplete() method is called once after initial contents are determined and again by various text field listeners anytime the content changes. This method then inspects the current text field contents, displays an error or warning message, and enables or disables the **Next** and **Finish** buttons as appropriate.

```
private void updatePageComplete() {
    setPageComplete(false);

    IPath sourceLoc = getSourceLocation();
    if (sourceLoc == null || !sourceLoc.toFile().exists()) {
        setMessage(null);
        setErrorMessage("Please select an existing plugin.xml file");
        return;
    }

    IPath destinationLoc = getDestinationLocation();
    if (destinationLoc == null) {
        setMessage(null);
        setErrorMessage(
            "Please specify a plugin.properties file"
                + " to contain the extracted strings");
        return;
    }
    setPageComplete(true);

    IPath sourceDirPath = sourceLoc.removeLastSegments(1);
    IPath destinationDirPath = destinationLoc.removeLastSegments(1);
    if (!sourceDirPath.equals(destinationDirPath)) {
        setErrorMessage(null);
        setMessage(
            "The plugin.properties file is typically"
                + " located in the same directory"
                + " as the plugin.xml file",
            WARNING);
        return;
    }

    if (!destinationLoc.lastSegment().equals("plugin.properties")) {
        setErrorMessage(null);
        setMessage(
            "The destination file is typically"
                + " named plugin.properties",
            WARNING);
        return;
    }

    setMessage(null);
    setErrorMessage(null);
}
```

When the user clicks the **Browse** button, the selection listener calls the browseForSourceFile() method to prompt the user for a source file. You also need a similar method called browseForDestinationFile() to be called when the other **Browse** button is clicked, plus accessors for source and destination locations.

```
protected void browseForSourceFile() {
    IPath path = browse(getSourceLocation(), false);
    if (path == null)
        return;
    IPath rootLoc = ResourcesPlugin.getWorkspace()
        .getRoot().getLocation();
    if (rootLoc.isPrefixOf(path))
        path = path
            .setDevice(null)
            .removeFirstSegments(rootLoc.segmentCount());
    sourceFileField.setText(path.toString());
}


private IPath browse(IPath path, boolean mustExist) {
    FileDialog dialog = new FileDialog(getShell(),
            mustExist ? SWT.OPEN : SWT.SAVE);
    if (path != null) {
        if (path.segmentCount() > 1)
            dialog.setFilterPath(path.removeLastSegments(1)
                .toOSString());
        if (path.segmentCount() > 0)
            dialog.setFileName(path.lastSegment());
    }
    String result = dialog.open();
    if (result == null)
        return null;
    return new Path(result);
}


public IPath getSourceLocation() {
    String text = sourceFileField.getText().trim();
    if (text.length() == 0)
        return null;
    IPath path = new Path(text);
    if (!path.isAbsolute())
        path = ResourcesPlugin.getWorkspace().getRoot().getLocation()
            .append(path);
    return path;
}
```

11.2.9 Page content based on previous page

The second page of the wizard contains a checkbox list of key/value pairs that can be extracted from the source file (see Figure 11–11).

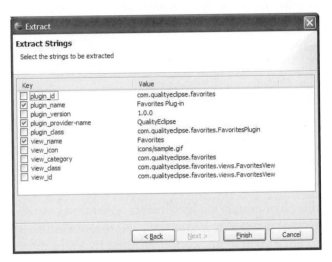

Figure 11–11 Second page of the Extract Strings wizard.

```
package com.qualityeclipse.favorites.wizards;
import ...

public class SelectStringsWizardPage extends WizardPage
{
    private CheckboxTableViewer checkboxTableViewer;
    private IPath sourceLocation;
    private ExtractedStringsModel stringModel;

    public SelectStringsWizardPage() {
        super("selectStrings");
        setTitle("Extract Strings");
        setDescription("Select the strings to be extracted");
    }

    public void createControl(Composite parent) {
        Composite container = new Composite(parent, SWT.NULL);
        container.setLayout(new FormLayout());
        setControl(container);

        checkboxTableViewer =
            CheckboxTableViewer.newCheckList(container, SWT.BORDER);
        checkboxTableViewer.setContentProvider(
            new ExtractedStringsContentProvider());
        checkboxTableViewer.setLabelProvider(
            new ExtractedStringsLabelProvider());
```

```
      final Table table = checkboxTableViewer.getTable();
      final FormData formData = new FormData();
      formData.bottom = new FormAttachment(100, 0);
      formData.right = new FormAttachment(100, 0);
      formData.top = new FormAttachment(0, 0);
      formData.left = new FormAttachment(0, 0);
      table.setLayoutData(formData);
      table.setHeaderVisible(true);

      final TableColumn tableColumn =
          new TableColumn(table, SWT.NONE);
      tableColumn.setWidth(200);
      tableColumn.setText("Key");

      final TableColumn tableColumn_1 =
          new TableColumn(table, SWT.NONE);
      tableColumn_1.setWidth(250);
      tableColumn_1.setText("Value");
   }
```

Rather than initializing its contents when first created, this page updates its contents whenever it becomes visible by overriding the setVisible() method. You also need an accessor method to return the selected strings.

```
public void setVisible(boolean visible) {
   if (visible) {
      IPath location =
         ((ExtractStringsWizard) getWizard()).getSourceLocation();
      if (!location.equals(sourceLocation)) {
         sourceLocation = location;
         stringModel = new ExtractedStringsModel(sourceLocation);
         checkboxTableViewer.setInput(stringModel);
      }
   }
   super.setVisible(visible);
}

public ExtractedString[] getSelection() {
   Object[] checked = checkboxTableViewer.getCheckedElements();
   int count = checked.length;
   ExtractedString[] extracted = new ExtractedString[count];
   System.arraycopy(checked, 0, extracted, 0, count);
   return extracted;
}
```

There are also two model classes, ExtractedString and Extracted-StringsModel, and two viewer helper classes, ExtractedStringsContent-Provider and ExtractedStringsLabelProvider, similar to classes already covered earlier in the book. This classes can be found as part of the example code that is downloadable from the QualityEclipse Web site (*www.quality-eclipse.com*). For more on these types of classes, see the following:

- Section 7.2.3, View model, on page 265
- Section 7.2.4, Content provider, on page 276
- Section 7.2.5, Label provider, on page 277

11.3 RFRS Considerations

The "User Interface" section of the *RFRS Requirements* includes five items—four requirements and one best practice—dealing with wizards. Most of them are derived from the Eclipse UI Guidelines.

11.3.1 *Wizard look and feel*   *(RFRS 3.5.2)*

User Interface Guideline #5.2 is a **requirement** that states:

> *Each wizard must contain a header with a banner graphic and a text area for user feedback. It must also contain* **Back**, **Next**, **Finish**, *and* **Cancel** *buttons in the footer. A one-page wizard does not need to have the* **Back** *and* **Next** *buttons.*

Show that your wizards conform to the standard wizard look and feel. Make sure that they contain the proper buttons in the correct order as well as an appropriate banner graphic.

11.3.2 *Open new file in editor*   *(RFRS 3.5.6)*

User Interface Guideline #5.9 is a **requirement** that states:

> *If a new file is created, open the file in an editor. If a group of files is created, open the most important, or central file, in an editor.*

If your wizard creates a file, show that it automatically opens in an editor when the wizard is finished. For the **Extract Strings** wizard, you would show that the `plugin.properties` file is opened after the wizard creates it.

11.3.3 *New project switches perspective*   *(RFRS 3.5.7)*

User Interface Guideline #5.10 is a **requirement** that states:

> *If a new project is created, change the active perspective to suit the project type.*

If your plug-in provides a new project wizard and an associated perspective, show that the system automatically switches to your perspective when your wizard is used to create a new project.

11.3.4 Show new object   (RFRS 3.5.8)

User Interface Guideline #5.11 is a **requirement** that states:

> *If a single new object is created, select and reveal the new object in the appropriate view. In cases where the creation of a resource results in the creation of project or folder resources, the wizard should propose reasonable default locations.*

If your wizard creates a file, show that it is automatically selected in the appropriate view. For the **Extract Strings** wizard, you would show that the `plugin.properties` file is selected in the **Navigator** view after the wizard creates it.

11.3.5 One-page wizard buttons   (RFRS 5.3.5.13)

Best practice #1 states:

> *A one-page wizard must contain the **Finish** and **Cancel** buttons, and should also contain grayed-out **Back** and **Next** buttons.*

If your plug-in contains any one-page wizards, show that it contains the appropriate buttons in the correct state.

11.4 Summary

This chapter introduced a number of the common SWT and JFace dialog classes that you will encounter when developing Eclipse plug-ins. When a built-in dialog or wizard isn't available that meets your needs, you can create your own using the techniques described in this chapter.

References

Chapter source (*www.qualityeclipse.com/projects/source-ch-11.zip*).

Klinger, Doina, "Creating JFace Wizards," IBM UK, December 16, 2002 (*www.eclipse.org/articles/Article-JFace%20Wizards/wizardArticle.html*).

Fatima, Azra, "Wizards in Eclipse: An Introduction to Working with Platform and Custom Wizards," HP, August 2003 (*devresource.hp.com/drc/technical_articles/wizards/index.jsp*).

CHAPTER 12

Preference Pages

Most Eclipse plug-ins provide user-configurable preferences for controlling how they will execute and display information. The *preference framework* provides a mechanism for displaying these options to the user and saving the values across multiple Eclipse sessions. This chapter discusses how to create an Eclipse preference page and the techniques for recording and restoring a plug-in's preferences.

12.1   Creating a Preference Page

You need to contribute a preference page that will allow users to select the columns that will be visible to the **Favorites** product. To accomplish this, create an `org.eclipse.ui.preferencePages` extension in the plug-in manifest. Fortunately, Eclipse provides a wizard for creating preference pages.

Open the **Favorites** `plugin.xml` file and switch to the **Extensions** page. Click the **Add...** button to open the **New Extension** wizard, select `org.eclipse.ui.preferencePages` from the extension point list and **Preference Page** in the template list, and then click **Next** (see Figure 12–1). On the following page, modify the **Page Class Name** and **Page Name** to "Favorites-PreferencePage" and "Favorites," respectively (see Figure 12–2) and click **Finish**.

Click on the new **Favorites (page)** extension under the `org.eclipse.ui.preferencePages` extension on the **Extensions** page to reveal its properties. In the extension element details area, you'll see the following attributes as described in the Eclipse online help. Change the `id` attribute to "com.qualityeclipse.favorites.prefs.view".

Figure 12–1   New Extension wizard.

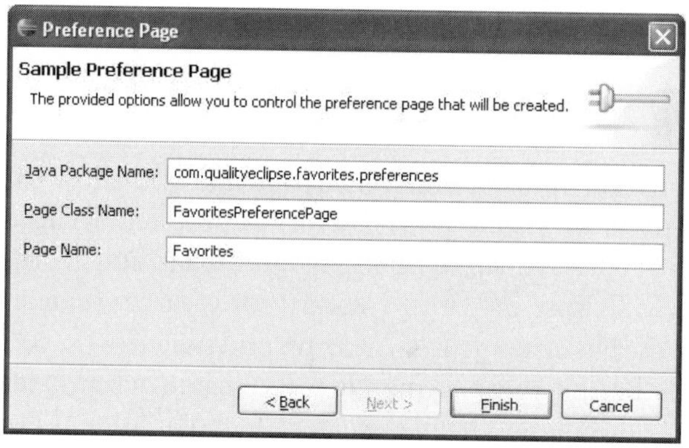

Figure 12–2   Sample Preference Page wizard.

id—A unique name that will be used to identify this page.

name—A human-readable name that appears in the preference page hierarchy on the left side of the workbench **Preferences** dialog.

class —The fully qualified name of the class that implements the `org.eclipse.ui.IWorkbenchPreferencePage` interface. The class is instantiated using its no argument constructor, but can be parameterized using the `IExecutableExtension` interface (see Section 20.5, Types Specified in an Extension Point, on page 723).

category —The **Preferences** dialog box provides for a hierarchical grouping of the pages. For this reason, a page can optionally specify a `category` attribute. This attribute represents a path composed of parent page IDs separated by "/". If this attribute is omitted or if any of the parent nodes in the path cannot be found, the page will be added at the root level (see Section 12.2.6, Nested preference pages, on page 464).

If you launch the **Runtime Workbench**, open the workbench **Preferences** dialog, and select **Favorites**, you'll see the sample **Favorites** preference page created by the **New Extension** wizard (see Figure 12–3).

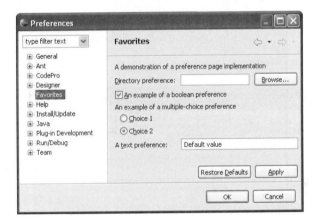

Figure 12–3   Sample Favorites preference page.

12.2   Preference Page APIs

Before modifing the preference page to suit our purposes, examine what was generated by the wizard (see Figure 12–4). The plug-in manifest contains the name, identifier, and fully qualified name of the class defining the page's content and behavior, as listed in the previous section. Preference pages must implement the `org.eclipse.ui.IWorkbenchPreferencePage` interface, and the abstract classes, `org.eclipse.jface.preference.PreferenceP-age` and `org.eclipse.jface.preference.FieldEditorPreferencePage`, provide much of the infrastructure for that purpose.

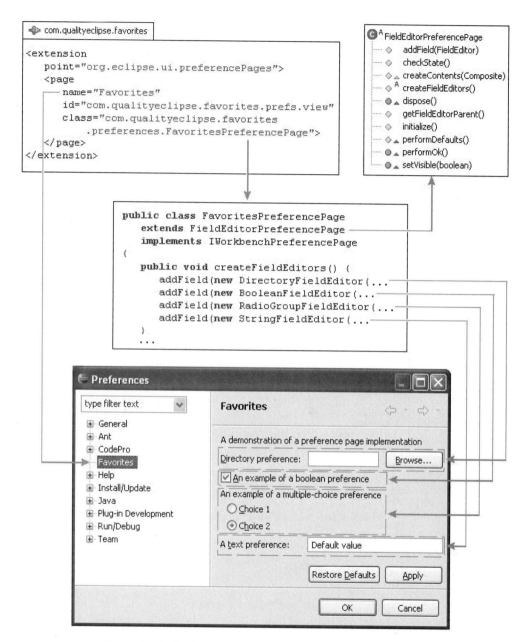

Figure 12–4 Preference page declaration, classes, and presentation.

In addition to the `FavoritesPreferencePage` class, the wizard also created two additional classes, `PreferenceConstants` and `Preference-Initializer`, which will be dicussed later in this chapter.

12.2.1 FieldEditorPreferencePage

The preference page extends `FieldEditorPreferencePage`, which, along with the various editor classes in the `org.eclipse.jface.preference.*` package, provide a quick and easy way to present and capture simple preferences. Subclasses of `FieldEditorPreferencePage` need only to implement the `createFieldEditors()` and `init()` methods to display a simple preference page; however, the following are several other methods of which you need to be aware for more involved preference pages.

`addField(FieldEditor)`—Called from the `createFieldEditors()` method to add a field to the page.

`checkState()`—Called by `FieldEditorPreferencePage` to validate the page content. The `FieldEditorPreferencePage` implementation of this method asks each field to validate its content and calls `setValid()` with the result. Override this method to perform additional page validation.

`createContents(Composite)`—Creates the composite in which field editors appear. Typically, subclasses override the `createFieldEditors()` method instead.

`createFieldEditors()`—Creates the field editors that appear in the preference page. Subclasses should call `getFieldEditorParent()` and `addField()` once for each field created. The parent returned by `getFieldEditorParent()` should not be used for more than one editor as the parent may change for each field editor depending on the layout style of the page.

`dispose()`—Cleans up any native resources allocated by this page. Typically, there is no need to override this method because the `FieldEditorPreferencePage` implementation of `dispose()` handles cleanup for all fields.

`getFieldEditorParent()`—Returns the parent to be used when creating a field editor. The parent returned should not be used for more than one editor as the parent may change for each field editor depending on the page's layout style.

`initialize()`—Called by `createContents()` after the fields have been created to initialize the field contents. Typically, there is no need to override this method because `FieldEditorPreferencePage` asks each field to initialize itself.

`isValid()`—Returns whether the contents of this preference page are currently valid.

`performDefaults()`—Loads all fields with their default values. Typically, there is no need to override this method because `FieldEditor-PreferencePage` asks each field to reset its content to its default value.

`performOk()`—Saves the field editor values in the preferences store. Typically, there is no need to override this method because `Field-EditorPreferencePage` asks each field to save its contents.

`setValid(boolean)`—Sets whether the contents of this preference page are currently valid.

`setVisible(boolean)`—Called to show or hide the page. Subclasses may extend this method.

12.2.2   Field editors

A field editor is designed to load, display, edit, and save a particular preference setting. The `org.eclipse.jface.preference` package provides many different field editors, some of which have already been discussed. Some editors contain a single control, while others contain several. Every editor has `Field-Editor` as its common superclass, providing `FieldEditorPreferencePage` with a common way to access editors. Table 12–1 displays a list of the field editors in the `org.eclipse.jface.preference` package, plus others available as public APIs elsewhere throughout Eclipse.

Table 12–1   PreferencePage Field Editors

Field Editor	Description
`BooleanFieldEditor` 	A checkbox representation of a Boolean.
`ColorFieldEditor` 	A label and button where the button displays the color preference and opens a color chooser when clicked.
`DirectoryFieldEditor` 	A label, text field, and button for choosing a directory. The button opens a directory chooser when clicked.

Table 12–1   PreferencePage Field Editors (continued)

`FileFieldEditor` File: [_____] [Browse...]	A label, text field, and button for selecting a file preference. The button opens a file chooser when clicked. The editor can optionally enforce an absolute file path and filter against specific file extensions.
`FontFieldEditor` Font: GillSans-regular-12 [Change...]	A label, font name, and button for selecting a font. The button opens a font chooser when clicked.
`IntegerFieldEditor` Integer [0_____]	A label and text field for selecting an integer. This editor can optionally enforce a value within a range.
`PathEditor` Path: D:\eclipse3.1 D:\eclipse3.0.2 D:\eclipse2.1.3 [New...] [Remove] [Up] [Down]	A label, list, and group of buttons for selecting zero or more paths. The **New...** button opens a directory chooser, while the other buttons manipulate paths already in the list.
`RadioGroupFieldEditor` Radio Group ⦿ Choice 1 ◯ Choice 2	A label and series of radio buttons for selecting one of several properties. Optionally, the radio buttons can be grouped and displayed in multiple columns.
`ScaleFieldEditor` Scale: [—slider—]	A label and slider for selecting a range of integer values.
`StringFieldEditor` String: [_____]	A label and text field for entering a string value.

Field editors are designed around the concept of *create them and forget them*. In other words, you create a field editor with all that it needs to know about the preferences it is to represent, and then the field editor, in combination with the `FieldEditorPreferencePage`, handles the rest.

Field editors excel at presenting and manipulating simple types of preferences such as strings, integers, colors, and so on. If your preferences lend themselves to simple values such as these, then field editors will save you the hassle of writing code to load, display, validate, and store these simple preferences. If the data you wish to present is more structured and complex, then you may need to build your preference page without field editors, subclassing `PreferencePage` rather than `FieldEditorPreferencePage`. If you need to interact with a field editor directly or to create a new type of field editor, here are some of the field editor methods you might need to know:

`adjustForNumColumns(int)`—Adjusts the horizontal span of the field editor's basic controls.

`dispose()`—Cleans up any native resources allocated by this editor.

`doFillIntoGrid(Composite, int)`—Creates the controls comprising the editor.

`doLoad()`—Initializes the editor content with the current value from the preferences store.

`doLoadDefault()`—Initializes the editor content with the default value.

`doStore()`—Saves the current editor value into the preferences store.

`fireStateChanged(String, boolean, boolean)`—Informs the field editor's listener, if it has one, about a change to Boolean-valued properties. Does nothing if the old and new values are the same.

`fireValueChanged(String, Object, Object)`—Informs the field editor's listener, if it has one, about a change to a property.

`getLabelControl()`—Returns the label that is part of the editor or `null` if none.

`getLabelControl(Composite)`—Returns the label that is part of the editor. Creates the label if label text has been specified either in the constructor or the `setLabelText()` method.

`getLabelText()`—Returns the label text specified either in the constructor or the `setLabelText()` method.

`getNumberOfControls()`—Returns the number of controls comprising the editor. This value is passed to the `doFillIntoGrid(Composite, int)` method.

`getPreferenceName()`—Returns the name/key of the preference displayed by the editor.

`getPreferenceStore()`—Returns the preferences store containing the preference being edited.

`isValid()`—Returns whether the editor's contents are valid. Subclasses should override this method along with the `presentsDefaultValue()` method.

`load()`—Loads the current value from the preferences store into the editor. Subclasses should override the `doLoad()` method rather than this method.

`loadDefault()`—Loads the default value into the editor. Subclasses should override the `doLoadDefault()` method rather than this method.

`presentsDefaultValue()`—Returns whether the editor is currently displaying the default value.

`refreshValidState()`—Determines whether the editor's content is valid. Subclasses should override this method to perform the validation and the `isValid()` method to return the state.

`setFocus()`—Sets focus to the editor. Subclasses may override this method to set focus to a particular control within the editor.

`setLabelText(String)`—Sets the text to appear in the label associated with the editor.

`setPreferenceName(String)`—Sets the name of the preference being displayed by the editor.

`setPreferenceStore(IPreferenceStore)`—Sets the preferences store in which the editor's value is saved.

`setPresentsDefaultValue(boolean)`—Sets whether the editor is displaying the default value.

`setPropertyChangeListener(IPropertyChangeListener)`—Sets the property change listener that should be notified via the `fireState-Changed()` or `fireValueChanged()` methods when the editor's content has changed.

showErrorMessage(String)—Convenient method for displaying an error message at the top of the preference page.

showMessage(String)—Convenient method for displaying a message at the top of the preference page.

store()—Saves the editor's current value into the preferences store. Subclasses should override doStore() rather than this method.

12.2.3   *PreferencePage*

FieldEditorPreferencePage assumes that all the preferences on the page are field editors and handles most of the work involved in loading, validating, and saving field editor content. For more complex preference pages, you can use PreferencePage, which is the superclass of FieldEditor-PreferencePage, instead. The downside is that you must do more of the work yourself.

createContents(Composite)—Creates the controls for the preference page.

doGetPreferenceStore()—Answers a page-specific preferences store or null to use the container's preferences store. Subclasses may override this method as necessary.

getPreferenceStore()—Answers the preferences store for this preference page.

isValid()—Returns whether the contents of the preference page are currently valid.

performDefaults()—Loads all fields with their default values.

performOk()—Saves all field values in the preferences store.

setErrorMessage(String)—Used to display an error message at the top of the preference page when a field's value is invalid.

setMessage(String, int)—Used to display a message at the top of the preference page.

setValid(boolean)—Sets whether the contents of the preference page are currently valid.

If you use PreferencePage, you can still use the various types of field editors, but you must do more of the work—loading, validating, and saving values—yourself. The extra work involves adding some method calls when the field editors are constructed; for example:

```
protected Control createContents(Composite parent) {
   ...
   editor = new BooleanFieldEditor(
      "boolean", "Boolean", parent);
   editor.setPreferencePage(this);
   editor.setPreferenceStore(getPreferenceStore());
   editor.load();
   ...
}
```

and when the user resets the values to their defaults:

```
protected void performDefaults() {
   editor.loadDefault();
   ...
   super.performDefaults();
}
```

and when the user decides to save the current preference value:

```
public boolean performOk() {
   ...
   editor.store();
   return true;
}
```

and to perform any additional validation other than what is enforced by the field.

12.2.4   Favorites preference page

For the **Favorites** view, you need one Boolean preference for every column, indicating whether that column is to be visible in the **Favorites** view. First, modify the generated PreferenceConstants class to define preference constants that can be shared by various classes in the **Favorites** product.

```
public class PreferenceConstants
{
   public static final String
      FAVORITES_VIEW_NAME_COLUMN_VISIBLE =
         "favorites.view.name.column.visible";
   public static final String
      FAVORITES_VIEW_LOCATION_COLUMN_VISIBLE =
         "favorites.view.location.column.visible";
}
```

The FavoritesPreferencePage is then modified to display these two preferences using Boolean preference field editors.

```java
public class FavoritesPreferencePage
   extends FieldEditorPreferencePage
   implements IWorkbenchPreferencePage
{
   private BooleanFieldEditor namePrefEditor;
   private BooleanFieldEditor locationPrefEditor;

   public FavoritesPreferencePage() {
      super(GRID);
      setPreferenceStore(
         FavoritesPlugin.getDefault().getPreferenceStore());
      setDescription("Favorites view column visibility:");
   }

   public void init(IWorkbench workbench) {
   }

   public void createFieldEditors() {
      namePrefEditor = new BooleanFieldEditor(
         PreferenceConstants.FAVORITES_VIEW_NAME_COLUMN_VISIBLE,
         "Show name column", getFieldEditorParent());
      addField(namePrefEditor);
      locationPrefEditor = new BooleanFieldEditor(
         PreferenceConstants.FAVORITES_VIEW_LOCATION_COLUMN_VISIBLE,
         "Show location column", getFieldEditorParent());
      addField(locationPrefEditor);
   }
}
```

Now, when the **Favorites** preference page is displayed, it shows the two-column visibility preferences (see Figure 12–5).

Figure 12–5   Favorites preference page with column visibility.

12.2.5   *Validation*

The preference page looks good (see Figure 12–5), but there are two problems. First, the visibility for the name and location columns should default to `true`; that problem is addressed in Section 12.3.3, Specifying default values programmatically, on page 471 and Section 12.3.4, Specifying default values in a file, on page 472. Second, at least one column should be visible at all times. Field editors enforce local validation of their own contents based on the type of editor and the parameters specified during creation. If you want validation between various editors, then you must enforce it yourself in the `PreferencePage` class by overriding the `FieldEditorPreferencePage` `checkState()` method.

```
protected void checkState() {
   super.checkState();
   if (!isValid())
      return;
   if (!namePrefEditor.getBooleanValue()
      && !locationPrefEditor.getBooleanValue()) {
      setErrorMessage("Must have at least one column visible");
      setValid(false);
   }
   else {
      setErrorMessage(null);
      setValid(true);
   }
}
```

The `FieldEditorPropertyPage` listens for `FieldEditor.IS_VALID` property change events and then calls `checkState()` and `setValid()` as necessary. The Boolean field editors are never in an invalid state and thus do not issue `FieldEditor.IS_VALID` property change events, only `FieldEditor.VALUE` property change events. You must override the `FieldEditorPreferencePage` `propertyChange()` method to call the `checkState()` method when the `FieldEditor.VALUE` property change event is received.

```
public void propertyChange(PropertyChangeEvent event) {
   super.propertyChange(event);
   if (event.getProperty().equals(FieldEditor.VALUE)) {
      if (event.getSource() == namePrefEditor
         || event.getSource() == locationPrefEditor)
         checkState();
   }
}
```

Now, when both preferences are unchecked, an error message is displayed across the top of the preference page and the **Apply** and **OK** buttons are disabled (see Figure 12–6).

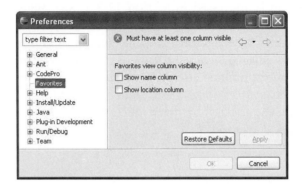

Figure 12–6   Favorites preference page with error message.

12.2.6   *Nested preference pages*

Nested preference pages provide a mechanism for hierarchically organizing related preference pages when a single page is not enough. Typically, the parent page contains root-level preferences or even just information, while the child preference pages focus on specific aspects.

To create a nested preference page in the **Favorites** product (see Figure 12–7), add a new declaration in the plug-in manifest where the `category` attribute specifies the parent preference page (see the `category` attribute in Section 12.1, Creating a Preference Page, on page 451). If Eclipse cannot find a parent page with the specified identifier, the preference page appears at the root level.

```
<page
   name="Nested Prefs"
   category="com.qualityeclipse.favorites.prefs.view"
   class="com.qualityeclipse.favorites
      .preferences.NestedPreferencePage"
   id="com.qualityeclipse.favorites.prefs.nested"/>
```

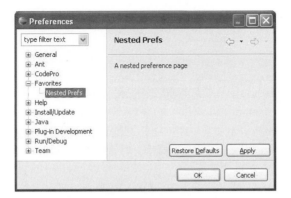

Figure 12–7   Nested preference pages.

Preference pages can be nested any number of levels deep by specifying the identifier for the parent preference page, prefixed by the identifier for the grandparent preference page, prefixed by the identifier for the great-grandparent preference page, and so on, each separated by the '/' character. For instance, to add a **Favorites** preference page nested two levels deep, the declaration might look like this:

```
<page
    name="Nested Prefs 2"
    category="com.qualityeclipse.favorites.prefs.view
        /com.qualityeclipse.favorites.prefs.nested"
    class="com.qualityeclipse.favorites
        .preferences.NestedPreferencePage2"
    id="com.qualityeclipse.favorites.prefs.nested2"/>
```

Tip: The root preference page can contain basic information about the product, while the child preference pages contain the actual preferences. For example, the root preference page in Figure 12–8 contains information about the product, including version and build date, where the product is installed, information about the company producing the product, and buttons for generating email.

Figure 12–8   Root-level preference page.

12.2.7 Tabbed preference pages

Tabbed preference pages are another approach for organizing more preferences than will fit on a page (see Figure 12–9). In this case, tabs across the top of the preference page (see Section 4.2.6.10, Tab folder, on page 164) provide separation between groups of related preferences. The advantage is that tabbed preference pages are located on a single page, and thus one page can handle any interrelated field validation.

The disadvantage is that the FieldEditorPreferencePage cannot be used for this purpose, so you must do more of the work yourself, basing your preference page on the PreferencePage class instead (see Section 12.2.3, PreferencePage, on page 460). Of course, both nested pages and tabbed pages can be used in the same product as needed.

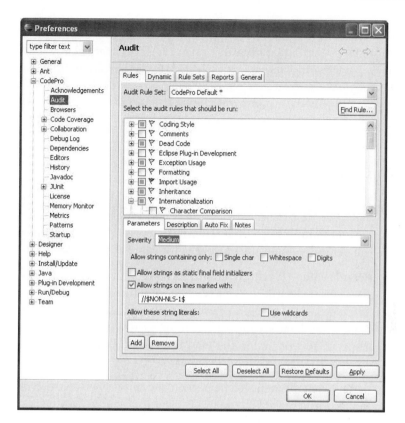

Figure 12–9 Tabbed preference page.

12.3 Preference APIs

The Preference API included in Eclipse provides simple string-based key/value pair storage in a flat structure. The plug-in infrastructure provides every plug-in with its own preference storage file named pref_store.ini, located in the workspace metadata area. For example, if you use the **Favorites** preference page created in the previous sections to change column visibility, then examining the pref_store.ini file in <workspace>\.metadata\.plugins\com.qualityeclipse.favorites directory reveals:

```
#Mon Mar 20 12:00:00 EST 2006
favorites.view.name.column.visible=true
favorites.view.location.column.visible=true
```

> **Tip:** If you have highly structured preference data that does not lend itself to simple, independent key/value pairs, then you might consider storing those preference elements in an XML-formatted preference file that is located in the plug-in's metadata area, similar to the way that the `FavoritesManager` stores its information (see Section 7.5.2, Saving global view information, on page 311).

12.3.1　Default preferences

Every preference has the following three values associated with it:

current value—Each preference has a current value, which is the same as the default value if the current value has not been specified.

default value—Each preference has a default value, which is the same as the default-default value if the default value has not been specified. The default value can be programmatically specified (see Section 12.3.3, Specifying default values programmatically, on page 471) or specified in a special file located in the plug-in's installation directory (see Section 12.3.4, Specifying default values in a file, on page 472).

default-default value—The default-default value is hard-coded into the Eclipse preference system and is used if no current value and no default value is specified for the preference in question.

The default-default values hard-coded into the Eclipse system depend on the API being used to access the preference. In Table 12–2, the default-default value on the right is returned by a method with the return type shown on the left if no current value and no default value have been specified for a preference.

Table 12–2　Default Preference Values

Preference Method Return Type	Default-Default Value
Boolean	false
double	0.0
float	0.0f
int	0
long	0L
String	" "

The contents of the preference file represent only those preferences whose values are *different* from the preference's default value. If the preference's current value is the same as the preference's default value, then that value is *not* written into the preference file.

12.3.2 Accessing preferences

There are two APIs for accessing preferences in Eclipse:

- `org.eclipse.core.runtime.Preferences`
- `org.eclipse.jface.preference.IPreferenceStore`

As covered in Section 3.4.6, Plugin and AbstractUIPlugin, on page 118 there is no advantage to using the older `IPreferenceStore` interface, so you need to concentrate on the newer `Preferences` interface and related API.

The preferences for a particular plug-in can be accessed using the `getPluginPreferences()` method in the plug-in class itself. The `Preferences` object returned by that method has many convenient methods for accessing the underlying string-based preference values in a variety of formats, including Boolean, int, long, and so on.

`getBoolean(String)`—Returns the preference value as a `Boolean`. A value other than `true` is interpreted as `false`.

`getDefaultBoolean(String)`—Returns the default preference value as a `Boolean`. A value other than `true` is interpreted as `false`.

`getDefaultDouble(String)`—Returns the default preference value as a `double`. A value that does not represent a double is interpreted as `0.0`.

`getDefaultFloat(String)`—Returns the default preference value as a `float`. A value that does not represent a float is interpreted as `0.0f`.

`getDefaultInt(String)`—Returns the default preference value as an `int`. A value that does not represent an int is interpreted as `0`.

`getDefaultLong(String)`—Returns the default preference value as a `long`. A value that does not represent a long is interpreted as `0L`.

`getDefaultString(String)`—Returns the default preference value as a string.

`getDouble(String)`—Returns the preference value as a `double`. A value that does not represent a double is interpreted as `0.0`.

getFloat(String)—Returns the preference value as a float. A value that does not represent a float is interpreted as 0.0f.

getInt(String)—Returns the preference value as an int. A value that does not represent an int is interpreted as 0.

getLong(String)—Returns the preference value as a long. A value that does not represent a long is interpreted as 0L.

getString(String)—Returns the preference value as a string.

isDefault(String)—Returns true if the current value of the specified preference is the same as its default value.

setDefault(String, boolean)—Sets the default value of the specified preference to a Boolean.

setDefault(String, double)—Sets the default value of the specified preference to a double.

setDefault(String, float)—Sets the default value of the specified preference to a float.

setDefault(String, int)—Sets the default value of the specified preference to an int.

setDefault(String, String)—Sets the default value of the specified preference to a string.

setDefault(String, long)—Sets the default value of the specified preference to a long.

setToDefault(String)—Sets the current value of the specified preference to its default value.

setValue(String, boolean)—Sets the value of the specified preference to a Boolean.

setValue(String, double)—Sets the value of the specified preference to a double.

setValue(String, float)—Sets the value of the specified preference to a float.

setValue(String, int)—Sets the value of the specified preference to an int.

setValue(String, String)—Sets the value of the specified preference to a string.

setValue(String, long)—Sets the value of the specified preference to a long.

In addition, there are various methods for loading, saving, and checking the state of a preference object.

`contains(String)`—Returns whether the given preference has a value that is not the default value or a default value that is not the default-default value.

`defaultPropertyNames()`—Returns a list containing the names of all preferences that have default values other than their default-default value.

`load(InputStream)`—Loads the non-default-valued preferences for the preference object from the specified `InputStream` using `java.util. Properties.load()`. Default preference values are not affected.

`needsSaving()`—Returns whether at least one preference value has changed since the last time preferences were saved (see `store()`).

`propertyNames()`—Returns a list containing the names of all preferences that have current values other than their default value.

`store(OutputStream, String)`—Saves the non-default-valued preferences to the specified `OutputStream` using `Properties.store()`, and resets the `dirty` flag so that `needsSaving()` will return `false` until a preference value is modified.

> **Note:** As covered in Section 3.4.6, Plugin and AbstractUIPlugin, on page 118, if your plug-in class is a subclass of `org.eclipse.core.runtime.Plugin` rather than `org.eclipse.ui.plugin.AbstractUIPlugin`, you must modify the `stop()` method to always call the `savePluginPreferences()` method so that preferences will persist across sessions.

12.3.3 Specifying default values programmatically

Default values can be specified programmatically using the `Preferences` API when a plug-in is first started. Extend the `initializeDefault-Preferences()` method of your plug-in's preference initializer class and call the various `setDefault*` methods. For the **Favorites** product, modify the `PreferenceInitializer` class created earlier in the chapter and implement the `initializeDefaultPreferences()` method to set the default value for the name column visibility preference. Now, when the **Favorites** preference page is displayed for the first time, the **Show name column** preference will already be checked.

```
public class PreferenceInitializer
   extends AbstractPreferenceInitializer {
   public void initializeDefaultPreferences() {
      IPreferenceStore store = FavoritesPlugin.getDefault()
        .getPreferenceStore();
      store.setDefault(
        PreferenceConstants.FAVORITES_VIEW_NAME_COLUMN_VISIBLE,true);
   }
}
```

The `PreferenceInitializer` class is referenced in the `plugin.xml` file by the `org.eclipse.core.runtime.preferences` extension point. This extension point was automatically extended by the **Preference Page** template used earlier.

```
<extension point="org.eclipse.core.runtime.preferences">
   <initializer class="com.qualityeclipse.favorites.
                        preferences.PreferenceInitializer"/>
</extension>
```

Now that you have programmatically specified `true` as the default value for the name column visibility preference, the only time it will appear in the `pref_store.ini` file is when the preference is *not* `true`.

12.3.4   *Specifying default values in a file*

Default preferences can also be specified in a special `preferences.ini` file located in the plug-in's installation directory. This file has an identical format to the `pref_store.ini` file (see Section 12.3, Preference APIs, on page 467) and can be installed when the plug-in is installed. The advantage to placing default values in a file is that it extracts them from the code, making them more easily changeable without modifying code. The disadvantage is that default values specified in this way cannot be dynamically adjusted as they can if they are specified programmatically; however, typically, a default preference specification does not need that type of flexibility. For the **Favorites** product, you will add a new `preferences.ini` file in the project root containing a single line specifying a default value for the location column visibility:

```
favorites.view.location.column.visible=true
```

> **Tip:** You can use the **General > Editors > File Associations** page in the workbench **Preferences** dialog (see Section 1.3.1, Workbench preferences, on page 15) to associate the internal text editor with any `*.ini` file so that double-clicking on the `preferences.ini` file will open a text editor on the file within Eclipse.

To complete the process, the build script must be modified to include this new `preferences.ini` file as part of the product (see Chapter 19, Building a Product, for more on building the product). Now that you have specified `true` as the default value for the location column visibility preference, the only time it will appear in the `pref_store.ini` file is when the preference is *not* `true`.

12.3.5   Hooking up the Favorites view

Now that the **Favorites** preference page is in place, you can hook up these preferences to the **Favorites** view. First, extract the initial column widths into constants using **Extract Constant** refactoring:

```
private static final int NAME_COLUMN_INITIAL_WIDTH = 200;
private static final int LOCATION_COLUMN_INITIAL_WIDTH = 450;
```

Next, you will create a new `updateColumnWidths()` method that is called from the `createPartControl(Composite)` method right after the table has been created.

```
private void updateColumnWidths() {
    Preferences prefs = FavoritesPlugin
        .getDefault().getPluginPreferences();

    boolean showNameColumn = prefs.getBoolean(
        PreferenceConstants.FAVORITES_VIEW_NAME_COLUMN_VISIBLE);
    nameColumn.setWidth(
        showNameColumn
            ? NAME_COLUMN_INITIAL_WIDTH
            : 0);

    boolean showLocationColumn = prefs.getBoolean(
        PreferenceConstants.FAVORITES_VIEW_LOCATION_COLUMN_VISIBLE);
    locationColumn.setWidth(
        showLocationColumn
            ? LOCATION_COLUMN_INITIAL_WIDTH
            : 0);
}
```

When these two changes are in place, the **Favorites** view will show the name and location columns as specified in the **Favorites** preference page.

12.3.6   Listening for preference changes

When the **Favorites** view is first opened, the columns conform to the settings specified on the **Favorites** preference page, but what if the preferences are changed while the **Favorites** view is already open? For the **Favorites** view to stay synchronized with the preferences specified on the **Favorites** preference page, you need to add listeners to the object containing the preferences. Back in the `FavoritesView`, you can add a new `propertyChangeListener` field that listens for property change events and calls `updateColumnWidths()` as appropriate.

```
private final IPropertyChangeListener propertyChangeListener
   = new IPropertyChangeListener() {
   public void propertyChange(PropertyChangeEvent event) {
      if (event.getProperty().equals(
            FAVORITES_VIEW_NAME_COLUMN_VISIBLE_PREF)
       || event.getProperty().equals(
            FAVORITES_VIEW_LOCATION_COLUMN_VISIBLE_PREF))
         updateColumnWidths();
   }
};
```

This new `propertyChangeListener` must be added as a listener when the view is created at the end of the `createPartControl()` method.

```
FavoritesPlugin
   .getDefault()
   .getPluginPreferences()
   .addPropertyChangeListener(propertyChangeListener);
```

The listener must be removed in the `dispose()` method when the view is closed.

```
FavoritesPlugin
   .getDefault()
   .getPluginPreferences()
   .removePropertyChangeListener(propertyChangeListener);
```

12.4   RFRS Considerations

The "User Interface" section of the *RFRS Requirements* includes a single requirement dealing with preferences. It is derived from the Eclipse UI Guidelines.

12.4.1   Preferences dialog use   **(RFRS 3.5.25)**

User Interface Guideline #15.1 is a **requirement** that states:

> *Global options will be exposed within the **Preferences** dialog. A new preference page must be created when you need to expose global options to the user. For instance, the global preferences for Java compilation are exposed as a group of preference pages in the **Preferences** dialog. If these preferences are changed, they affect the entire Java plug-in.*

To pass this test, show a sample of your product's preference pages and demonstrate that the preference settings control global options in it. Change a preference and then shut down and restart Eclipse to show that the preference's value properly persists. For the **Favorites** preferences, you would show that the column visibility options globally affect the columns shown in all **Favorites** views open in any perspective.

12.5   Summary

Almost any significant plug-in will contain global options controlling its execution and interaction with the user. This chapter explored the Eclipse preference page API and discussed the choices open to the developer for creating both simple and complex preference pages. It also demonstrated how to persist preference settings across workspace sessions.

References

Chapter source (*www.qualityeclipse.com/projects/source-ch-12.zip*).

Creasey, Tod, "Preferences in the Eclipse Workbench UI," August 15, 2002 (*www.eclipse.org/articles/Article-Preferences/preferences.htm*).

Cooper, Ryan, "Simplifying Preference Pages with Field Editors,"August 21, 2002 (*www.eclipse.org/articles/Article-Field-Editors/field_editors.html*).

CHAPTER 13

Properties

Whereas preferences apply to plug-ins or chunks of functionality, properties apply to resources or other objects that appear in the Eclipse environment. One typical way to access an object's properties is to select the **Properties** command from its context menu, opening the **Properties** dialog. Another way is to open the **Properties** view, which displays properties for the object that has been selected.

This chapter covers the creation of a property on a particular object and the display of that property in both the object's **Properties** dialog and the **Properties** view.

13.1 Creating Properties

You want to add properties for color and comments to the **Favorites** product. The Color property will determine the color used to display an item in the **Favorites** view, while the comment property will be displayed as an item's hover help.

Since properties are associated with objects, you must decide which type of object will contain properties. The Color property will be added to **Favorites** items; when an item is removed from the **Favorites** view, the Color property will be discarded. Conversely, you want the comment property to be associated with the resource behind the **Favorites** items so that when the resource is removed and then added to the **Favorites** view, the comment property will be preserved.

13.1.1   FavoriteItem properties

A property can be associated with an object in many different ways, but typically, a property value is accessed through *get* and *set* methods on the object itself. For **Favorites** items, accessor methods need to be added to the IFavoriteItem interface for the new Color property:

```
Color getColor();
void setColor(Color color);
```

Because this property is to be implemented identically across all **Favorites** items, you will place this behavior into a new abstract superclass called BasicFavoriteItem, which all your other item types will extend.

```
package com.qualityeclipse.favorites.model;

import ...

public class BasicFavoriteItem
{
    private Color color;

    public Color getColor() {
        if (color == null)
            return getDefaultColor();
        return color;
    }

    public void setColor(Color color) {
        this.color = color;
    }

    public static Color getDefaultColor() {
        if (defaultColor == null)
            defaultColor = getColor(new RGB(0, 0, 0));
        return defaultColor;
    }

    public static void setDefaultColor(Color color) {
        defaultColor = color;
    }
}
```

There are two types of properties: persistent and session. Persistent properties are preserved across multiple workbench sessions, while session property values are discarded when Eclipse exits. To persist the `Color` property across multiple sessions, you would need to modify the loading and saving methods outlined in Section 7.5.2, Saving global view information, on page 311. This is left as an exercise for the reader, and for now, the `Color` property will not be preserved across sessions.

A `Color` object has an underlying OS resource and must be managed properly. Add the `BasicFavoriteItem` utility methods to cache, reuse, and dispose of colors:

```
private static final Map colorCache = new HashMap();
private static Color defaultColor;

public static Color getColor(RGB rgb) {
    Color color = (Color) colorCache.get(rgb);
    if (color == null) {
        Display display = Display.getCurrent();
        color = new Color(display, rgb);
        colorCache.put(rgb, color);
    }
    return color;
}

public static void disposeColors() {
    Iterator iter = colorCache.values().iterator();
    while (iter.hasNext())
        ((Color) iter.next()).dispose();
    colorCache.clear();
}
```

When the **Favorites** plug-in shuts down, you must clean up any `Color` objects that you have been managing. Add the following line to the `FavoritesPlugin.stop()` method:

```
BasicFavoriteItem.disposeColors();
```

13.1.2   *Resource properties*

Eclipse has a generic mechanism for associating properties with resources that you can use to store resource comments. Methods in `IResource` provide both session properties, which are discarded when Eclipse exits, and persistent properties, which are preserved across multiple workspace sessions. Both types of properties can be used to determine whether an action should be visible (see Section 6.3.2.3, The filter element, on page 230).

`getPersistentProperty(QualifiedName)`—Returns the value of the persistent property of the resource identified by the given key, or `null` if this resource has no such property. These properties are preserved across different sessions.

`getSessionProperty(QualifiedName)`—Returns the value of the session property of the resource identified by the given key, or `null` if this resource has no such property. These properties are discarded when Eclipse exits.

`setPersistentProperty(QualifiedName, String)`—Sets the value of the persistent property of the resource identified by the given key. If the supplied value is `null`, the persistent property is removed from the resource. These properties are preserved across different sessions.

`setSessionProperty(QualifiedName, Object)`—Sets the value of the session property of the resource identified by the given key. If the supplied value is `null`, the session property is removed from the resource.

The `QualifiedName` argument in these methods is the key used to store and retrieve a property value. By convention, a key is composed of the plug-in identifier and a string identifying a property within the plug-in. For the **Favorites** product, define a constant key for the `comment` property in the `BasicFavoriteItem` class:

```
public static final QualifiedName COMMENT_PROPKEY =
   new QualifiedName(FavoritesPlugin.ID, "comment");
```

As discussed earlier, there are two types of properties: persistent and session. Persistent properties are preserved across multiple workbench sessions, while session property values are discarded when Eclipse exits. You want the `comment` property to persist across multiple workbench sessions, so use the `getPersistentProperty()` and `setPersistentProperty()` methods like this:

```
String comment =
   resource.getPersistentProperty(
      BasicFavoriteItem.COMMENT_PROPKEY);
```

```
resource.setPersistentProperty(
   BasicFavoriteItem.COMMENT_PROPKEY,
   comment);
```

If a resource object does not have a **Favorites** comment associated with it, then you want to display a default comment. Add `BasicFavoriteItem` utility methods to access the default comment.

```
public static final String COMMENT_PREFKEY = "defaultComment";

public static String getDefaultComment() {
   return FavoritesPlugin.getDefault().getPluginPreferences()
      .getString(COMMENT_PREFKEY);
}

public static void setDefaultComment(String comment) {
   FavoritesPlugin.getDefault().getPluginPreferences()
      .setValue(COMMENT_PREFKEY, comment);
}
```

13.2   Displaying Properties in the Properties Dialog

Now that you have defined the properties, you want to display and edit those properties in a **Properties** dialog. First, add a page to the existing resource **Properties** dialog to display and edit the `comment` property. Second, open a **Properties** dialog on **Favorites** items selected in the **Favorites** view to display and edit both the `Color` and `comment` properties.

13.2.1   Declaring a Property page

To create a new **Property** page appearing in a resource's **Properties** dialog, you need to declare the page in the **Favorites** plug-in manifest. The declaration references the new `FavoriteResourcePropertyPage` class, which handles creation and user interaction in the new page (see Figure 13–1).

To create the **Property** page declaration in the plug-in manifest, edit the **Favorites** `plugin.xml`, switch to the **Extensions** page, and click **Add....** In the **New Extensions** dialog, select `org.eclipse.ui.propertyPages` and click **Finish.**

```
<extension point="org.eclipse.ui.propertyPages">
   <page
      objectClass="org.eclipse.core.resources.IResource"
      adaptable="false"
      name="Favorite Properties"
      icon="icons/sample.gif"
      id="com.qualityeclipse.favorites.resourcePropertyPage"
      class="com.qualityeclipse.favorites.properties
            .FavoriteResourcePropertyPage"/>
</extension>
```

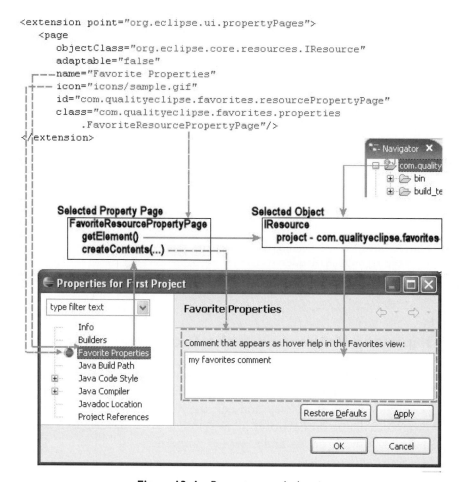

Figure 13–1   Property page declaration.

In the **Extensions** page of the plug-in manifest editor, right-click on
`org.eclipse.ui.propertyPages` and select **New > page.** Click on the new
`com.qualityeclipse.favorites.page1` page declaration to edit its properties, and enter the following attributes.

> **id**—"com.qualityeclipse.favorites.resourcePropertyPage"
> A unique name used to identify the **Property** page.
>
> **name**—"Favorite Properties"
> A human-readable name for the **Property** page.

objectClass—"org.eclipse.core.resources.IResource"
A fully qualified name of the class for which the page is registered. You want the **Favorites** properties to appear for all resources.

class—"com.qualityeclipse.favorites.properties.
FavoriteResourcePropertyPage"
A fully qualified name of the class that implements `org.eclipse.ui.
IWorkbenchPropertyPage`. Click on the **class** button at the left of the class attribute value to automatically generate the `FavoriteResource-
PropertyPage` class.

icon—"icons/sample.gif"
A relative path to an icon displayed in the UI along with the name attribute. Use the **Browse...** button at the right of the icon attribute value to select the `sample.gif` file in the **Favorites** project.

nameFilter—Leave blank
An optional attribute that allows conditional registration on a wildcard match applied to the target object name. You don't want to use a filter for the **Favorites** properties, but if you wanted to limit it to only Java source files, enter "`*.java`".

adaptable—"false"
A flag that indicates whether types that adapt to `IResource` should use the **Property** page. This flag is used if **objectClass** adapts to `IResource`. The default value is `false`.

category—Leave blank
A path indicating the location of the page in the properties tree. The path can be either a parent node ID or a sequence of IDs separated by "/", representing the full path from the root node.

If you set the **adaptable** attribute to `true`, then the selected object is adapted to an `IResource` using the `IAdaptable` interface. The advantage of this is that one **Property** page declaration would cause the **Favorites Property** page to appear for any object that adapted to a resource such as `IJavaElement`; you would not need to add a separate **Property** page declaration for `IJavaElement` or `IFavoriteItem`. The downside is that the framework automatically adapts the selected object from its original type to a resource object before the page gets the selection.

Because `IFavoriteItem` is itself adaptable to `IResource`, the `getEle-
ment()` method would return a resource rather than the currently selected instance of `IFavoriteItem`, preventing the **Property** page from accessing

information specific to the selected IFavoriteItem. To work around this problem, you have to set the **adaptable** attribute to false and create two additional **Property** page declarations.

Add a new **Property** page declaration containing the same information as the original except for the objectClass attribute.

objectClass = "org.eclipse.jdt.core.IJavaElement"

Add another **Property** page declaration containing the same information as the previous declarations except for the following attributes. The FavoriteItemPropertyPage is a refinement of the FavoriteResource-PropertyPage page containing an additional property field.

class = "com.qualityeclipse.favorites.properties .FavoriteItemPropertyPage"

objectClass = "com.qualityeclipse.favorites.model.IFavoriteItem"

> **Tip:** Most **Property** pages do not have an associated icon. If you associate an icon with your **Property** page, then the list of **Property** pages looks funny with all the blank space in front of all the other **Property** page names. To illustrate this point, an icon is associated with the Favorites **Property** page (shown in Figure 13–2), but we recommend that you do not do this.

One way to narrow down the resources to which the **Property** page applies is to add the nameFilter attribute as just described. Another way is to add a filter subelement by right-clicking on the **Favorites Property** page declaration in the **Extensions** page of the plug-in manifest editor and selecting **New > filter.** The filter subelement specifies an attribute name and value.

name—The name of an object attribute.

value—The value of an object attribute. In combination with the **name** attribute, the name/value pair is used to define the target object for a **Property** page.

The selected object for which properties are being displayed must have the specified value for that attribute before the **Property** page is displayed. For example, to display a **Property** page for read-only files, you would specify a filter subelement with name="readOnly" and value="true". To use the filter subelement, the selected object must implement the org.eclipse.ui. IActionFilter interface. Eclipse workbench resource types, such as IFile and IFolder, currently implement this interface.

13.2.2   *Creating a resource Property page*

When the **Property** page declaration is complete, you need to fill in the
FavoriteResourcePropertyPage class stub generated by the Java attribute
editor, starting with some fields and the createContents() method. Since
FavoriteResourcePropertyPage extends PropertyPage and inherits
behavior from the **Preference** page framework (see Section 12.2.3, Preference-
Page, on page 460), the createContents() method is called to create and
initialize the page controls (see Figure 13–2).

```
private Text textField;

protected Control createContents(Composite parent) {
   Composite panel = new Composite(parent, SWT.NONE);
   GridLayout layout = new GridLayout();
   layout.marginHeight = 0;
   layout.marginWidth = 0;
   panel.setLayout(layout);

   Label label = new Label(panel, SWT.NONE);
   label.setLayoutData(new GridData());
   label.setText(
      "Comment that appears as hover help in the Favorites view:");

   textField = new Text(panel, SWT.BORDER | SWT.MULTI | SWT.WRAP);
   textField.setLayoutData(new GridData(GridData.FILL_BOTH));
   textField.setText(getCommentPropertyValue());

   return panel;
}
```

The PropertyPage class contains a getElement() accessor method for
retrieving the object whose properties are being edited. Create accessor methods for getting and setting the comment associated with the current element:

```
protected String getCommentPropertyValue() {
   IResource resource =
      (IResource) getElement().getAdapter(IResource.class);
   try {
      String value =
         resource.getPersistentProperty(
            BasicFavoriteItem.COMMENT_PROPKEY);
      if (value == null)
         return BasicFavoriteItem.getDefaultComment();
      return value;
   }
   catch (CoreException e) {
      FavoritesLog.logError(e);
      return e.getMessage();
   }
}
```

```
protected void setCommentPropertyValue(String comment) {
   IResource resource =
      (IResource) getElement().getAdapter(IResource.class);
   String value = comment;
   if (value.equals(BasicFavoriteItem.getDefaultComment()))
      value = null;
   try {
      resource.setPersistentProperty(
         BasicFavoriteItem.COMMENT_PROPKEY,
         value);
   }
   catch (CoreException e) {
      FavoritesLog.logError(e);
   }
}
```

Because FavoriteResourcePropertyPage extends PropertyPage and inherits behavior from the **Preference** page framework (see Section 12.2.3, PreferencePage, on page 460), the performOk() method is called when the **OK** button is clicked, giving the **Property** page an opportunity to save its values.

```
public boolean performOk() {
   setCommentPropertyValue(textField.getText());
   return super.performOk();
}
```

When all this is in place, opening the **Properties** dialog for the **Favorites** project displays the **Favorites Property** page (see Figure 13–2).

Figure 13–2   Favorites resource Property page for Favorites project.

13.2.3 Creating a Favorites item resource page

Having successfully added a **Property** page to the resource **Properties** dialog, now you want to display a similar **Property** page with an additional field for instances of `IFavoriteItem`. Whereas the resource **Property** page described in the previous section only displayed a `comment` property, this new `FavoriteItemPropertyPage` will extend `FavoriteResourceProperty-Page` to add a field for displaying the `Color` property. Begin by creating the new class and adding the `createContents()` method.

```
private ColorSelector colorSelector;

protected Control createContents(Composite parent) {
   Composite panel = new Composite(parent, SWT.NONE);
   GridLayout layout = new GridLayout();
   layout.numColumns = 2;
   layout.marginHeight = 0;
   layout.marginWidth = 0;
   panel.setLayout(layout);

   Label label = new Label(panel, SWT.NONE);
   label.setLayoutData(new GridData());
   label.setText("Color of item in Favorites View:");

   colorSelector = new ColorSelector(panel);
   colorSelector.setColorValue(getColorPropertyValue());
   colorSelector.getButton().setLayoutData(
      new GridData(100, SWT.DEFAULT));

   Composite subpanel = (Composite) super.createContents(panel);
   GridData gridData = new GridData(GridData.FILL_BOTH);
   gridData.horizontalSpan = 2;
   subpanel.setLayoutData(gridData);

   return panel;
}
```

Create accessor methods for getting and setting the color of the selected **Favorites** item.

```
protected RGB getColorPropertyValue() {
   IFavoriteItem item = (IFavoriteItem) getElement();
   Color color = item.getColor();
   return color.getRGB();
}

protected void setColorPropertyValue(RGB rgb) {
   IFavoriteItem item = (IFavoriteItem) getElement();
   Color color = BasicFavoriteItem.getColor(rgb);
   if (color.equals(BasicFavoriteItem.getDefaultColor()))
      color = null;
   item.setColor(color);
}
```

Create a `performOk()` method to store the color value back into the selected **Favorites** item:

```
public boolean performOk() {
   setColorPropertyValue(colorSelector.getColorValue());
   return super.performOk();
}
```

13.2.4   Opening the Properties dialog

You have created a new, refined `FavoriteItemPropertyPage` for displaying **Favorites** item properties, but that page will only appear in a **Properties** dialog opened on an instance of `IFavoriteItem`. To open the **Properties** dialog on an instance of `IFavoriteItem`, you need to add a **Properties** command to the end of the **Favorites** view context menu.

Eclipse already provides an action for opening the **Properties** dialog, so add the following lines to the end of the `FavoritesView.fillContext-Menu()` method.

```
menuMgr.add(new Separator());
menuMgr.add(new PropertyDialogAction(getSite(), viewer));
```

Now, selecting **Properties** in the **Favorites** view context menu displays the **Properties** dialog for the selected **Favorites** item (see Figure 13–3).

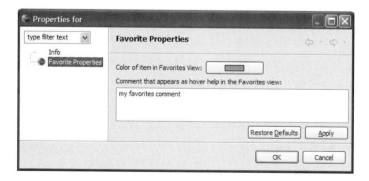

Figure 13–3   Favorites item Property page for Favorites project.

13.3   Displaying Properties in the Properties View

Another place that properties can be displayed and edited is in the **Properties** view. The **Properties** view examines the workbench selection to determine whether the selected objects support the org.eclipse.ui.views. properties.IPropertySource interface. An object can support the IPropertySource interface by either directly implementing IProperty-Source or by implementing the getAdapter() method to return an object that implements the IPropertySource interface (see Figure 13–4).

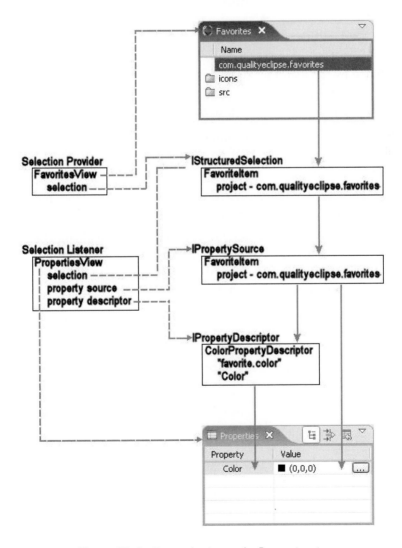

Figure 13–4   From selection to the Properties view.

13.3.1 Properties view API

The IPropertySource interface provides a descriptor for each property to be displayed in the **Properties** view, as well as methods for getting and setting property values. The id argument in the methods that follow is the identifier associated with the descriptor for that property.

getPropertyDescriptors()—Returns an array of descriptors, one for each property to be displayed in the **Properties** view.

getPropertyValue(Object)—Returns the value of the property that has the specified identifier.

isPropertySet(Object)—Returns true if the property specified by the identifier has a value different than its default value.

resetPropertyValue(Object)—Sets the value of the property specified by the identifier to its default value.

setPropertyValue(Object, Object)—Sets the value of the property specified by the identifier to the specified value.

Optionally, objects can implement the IPropertySource2 interface to allow an easier indication of properties that have a default value and can be reset.

isPropertyResettable(Object)—Returns whether the value of the property with the specified id can be reset to a default value.

isPropertySet(Object)—Very similar to the identical method in IPropertySource except, if an object implements IPropertySource2, then this method should return true rather than false if the referenced property does not have a meaningful default value.

Property descriptors—objects that implement the IPropertyDescriptor interface—contain a property identifier and create a property editor as necessary for the **Properties** view. Eclipse provides some implementations of the IPropertyDescriptor interface (see Figure 13–5).

Figure 13–5   IPropertyDescriptor hierarchy.

Instances of `PropertyDescriptor` are constructed with a property identifier and a display name for the property. If an object has many properties, then it's useful to group similar properties visually by calling `setCategory()` on each descriptor in the group.

Other useful methods include:

`setAlwaysIncompatible(boolean)`—Sets a flag indicating whether the property descriptor is to be considered always incompatible with any other property descriptor. Setting this flag prevents a property from displaying during multiple selections.

`setCategory(String)`—Sets the name of the category to which the property belongs. Properties belonging to the same category are grouped together visually. This localized string is shown to the user. If the category is not set on any of the descriptors, the property will appear at the top level in the **Properties** view without being grouped. If the category is set on at least one descriptor, then any descriptors with an unset category will appear in a miscellaneous category.

`setDescription(String)`—Sets a brief description of the property. This localized string is shown to the user when the property is selected.

`setFilterFlags(String[])`—Sets a list of filter types to which the property belongs. The user is able to toggle the filters to show/hide properties belonging to a filter type. Currently, the only valid value for these flags is `IPropertySheetEntry.FILTER_ID_EXPERT`.

`setHelpContextIds(Object)`—Sets the help context ID for the property. Even though the method name is plural, only a string can be specified, indicating the singular associated help context (see Section 15.3.1, Associating context IDs with items, on page 553).

`setLabelProvider(ILabelProvider)`—Sets the label provider for the property. The label provider is used to obtain the text (and possible image) for displaying the value of this property.

`setValidator(ICellEditorValidator)`—Sets the input validator for the cell editor for this property descriptor.

13.3.2 Favorite properties in the Properties view

For the **Favorites** product, you want to display the `Color` property and a `Hash Code` property. Using `setAlwaysIncompatible(true)`, you specify that the `Hash Code` property should appear in the **Properties** view only when the **Show Advanced Properties** option is turned on. The **Favorites** view is already a workbench selection provider (see Section 7.4.1, Selection provider, on page 305), so the **Properties** view is already examining the selected **Favorites** items. All that's left is for `BasicFavoriteItem` to implement the `IProperty-Source2` interface.

```
private static final String COLOR_ID = "favorite.color";
private static final ColorPropertyDescriptor
COLOR_PROPERTY_DESCRIPTOR =
   new ColorPropertyDescriptor(COLOR_ID, "Color");

private static final String HASH_ID = "favorite.hash";
private static final TextPropertyDescriptor HASH_PROPERTY_DESCRIPTOR
  = new TextPropertyDescriptor(HASH_ID, "Hash Code");
static {
   HASH_PROPERTY_DESCRIPTOR.setCategory("Other");
   HASH_PROPERTY_DESCRIPTOR.setFilterFlags(
      new String[] {IPropertySheetEntry.FILTER_ID_EXPERT });
   HASH_PROPERTY_DESCRIPTOR.setAlwaysIncompatible(true);
}

private static final IPropertyDescriptor[] DESCRIPTORS =
   { COLOR_PROPERTY_DESCRIPTOR, HASH_PROPERTY_DESCRIPTOR };

public Object getEditableValue() {
   return this;
}

public IPropertyDescriptor[] getPropertyDescriptors() {
   return DESCRIPTORS;
}

public Object getPropertyValue(Object id) {
   if (COLOR_ID.equals(id))
      return getColor().getRGB();
   if (HASH_ID.equals(id))
      return new Integer(hashCode());
   return null;
}

public boolean isPropertyResettable(Object id) {
   if (COLOR_ID.equals(id))
      return true;
   return false;
}
```

```
public boolean isPropertySet(Object id) {
   if (COLOR_ID.equals(id))
      return getColor() != getDefaultColor();
   if (HASH_ID.equals(id)) {
      // Return true for indicating that hash
      // does not have a meaningful default value.
      return true;
   }
   return false;
}

public void resetPropertyValue(Object id) {
   if (COLOR_ID.equals(id))
      setColor(null);
}

public void setPropertyValue(Object id, Object value) {
   if (COLOR_ID.equals(id))
      setColor(getColor((RGB) value));
}
```

Now, when an item is selected in the **Favorites** view, the **Properties** view displays the Color property for that item. When the **Show Advanced Properties** option is turned on, the Hash Code property appears (see Figure 13–6).

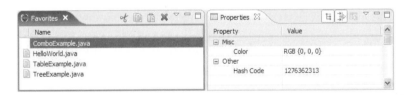

Figure 13–6   Properties view showing expert properties.

13.4   Property Pages Reused as Preference Pages

Since PropertyPage inherits from PreferencePage, with a little work you can reuse a **Property** page as a **Preference** page. In this case, you want to reuse the FavoriteItemPropertyPage as a **Preference** page for specifying the Color and comment properties' default values. To accomplish this, create a new FavoriteDefaultsPreferencePage as a subclass of FavoriteItem-PropertyPage, which implements org.eclipse.ui.IWorkbench-PreferencePage and overrides the property accessor methods.

```
package com.qualityeclipse.favorites.properties;

import ...

public class FavoriteDefaultsPreferencePage
   extends FavoriteItemPropertyPage
   implements IWorkbenchPreferencePage
{
   public void init(IWorkbench workbench) {
   }

   protected RGB getColorPropertyValue() {
      return BasicFavoriteItem.getDefaultColor().getRGB();
   }

   protected void setColorPropertyValue(RGB rgb) {
      BasicFavoriteItem.setDefaultColor(
         BasicFavoriteItem.getColor(rgb));
   }

   protected String getCommentPropertyValue() {
      return BasicFavoriteItem.getDefaultComment();
   }

   protected void setCommentPropertyValue(String comment) {
      BasicFavoriteItem.setDefaultComment(comment);
   }
}
```

Then, create a new **Preference** page declaration in the **Favorites** plug-in manifest (see Section 12.1, Creating a Preference Page, on page 451) with the following attributes:

category = "com.qualityeclipse.favorites.prefs.view"

class = "com.qualityeclipse.favorites.properties
     .FavoriteDefaultsPreferencePage"

id = "com.qualityeclipse.favorites.prefs.defaults"

name = "Defaults"

When complete, the **Defaults** preference page appears in the workbench **Preferences** dialog as a child of the **Favorites** preference page (see Figure 13–7).

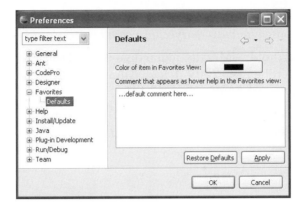

Figure 13–7 Favorite Defaults preference page.

13.5 RFRS Considerations

The "User Interface" section of the *RFRS Requirements* includes one require-ment dealing with properties. It is derived from the Eclipse UI Guidelines.

13.5.1 *Properties views for quick access*   *(RFRS 3.5.21)*

User Interface Guideline #10.1 is a requirement that states:

*Use the **Properties** view to edit the properties of an object when quick access is important, and you will switch quickly from object to object.*

To pass this test, show which objects in your plug-in have properties that are editable using the **Properties** view. For the **Favorites** view, you would show that each **Favorites** item shows its color and hash code within the **Properties** view (see Figure 13–6).

13.6 Summary

Many plug-ins will need to create and manage their own plug-in-specific resources. While preferences are global settings applicable to entire plug-ins and chunks of functionality, properties are local settings applicable to a single resource. This chapter explored the Eclipse property API and discussed the various choices open to the developer for accessing properties using the **Prop-erties** view or the **Properties** dialog. It also demonstrated how to persist prop-erties across workspace sessions.

References

Chapter source (*www.qualityeclipse.com/projects/source-ch-13.zip*).

Daum, Berthold, "Mutatis mutandis—Using Preference Pages as Property Pages," October 24, 2003 (*www.eclipse.org/articles/Article-Mutatis-mutandis/overlay-pages.html*).

Johan, Dicky, "Take Control of Your Properties," May 20, 2003 (*www.eclipse.org/articles/Article-Properties-View/properties-view.html*).

CHAPTER 14

Builders, Markers, and Natures

Incremental project builders, also knows as *builders*, automatically execute whenever a resource in an associated project changes. For example, when a Java source file is created or revised, Eclipse's incremental Java compiler annotates the source file and generates a class file. Because Java class files can be entirely regenerated by the compiler from the Java source files, they are known as *derived resources*.

Markers are used to annotate locations within a resource. For example, the Eclipse Java compiler annotates source files by adding markers to indicate compilation errors, deprecated member usage, bookmarks, and so on. These markers show up along the left margin, which is sometimes referred to as the *gutter*, when editing a Java file, and in the **Problems** view or **Tasks** view as appropriate.

Project *natures* are used to associate projects and builders (see Figure 14–1). The Java nature of a project makes it a Java project and associates the Eclipse incremental Java compiler.

The goal of this chapter is to discuss builders, markers, and natures in the context of a new `plugin.properties` file auditor in the **Favorites** product. The properties auditor is implemented as a builder and cross-references property keys in the `plugin.xml` with entries in the `plugin.properties` file. Markers are used to report problems that the auditor finds; keys in the `plugin.xml` that are not declared in the `plugin.properties` file are marked as missing, while keys in the `plugin.properties` file that are not referenced in the `plugin.xml` file are marked as unused. A new project nature is created to associate the auditor with a project.

```
<extension point="org.eclipse.core.resources.natures"
    id="propertiesAuditor"
    name="Favorites Properties Auditor">
    <builder id="com ... propertiesFileAuditor"/>
    <requires-nature id="org.eclipse.jdt.core.javanature"/>
    <requires-nature id="org.eclipse.pde.PluginNature"/>
    <one-of-nature id="pluginAuditors"/>
    <runtime>
        <run class="com ... PropertiesAuditorNature"/>
    </runtime>
</extension>
                    <extension point="org.eclipse.core.resources.builders"
                        id="propertiesFileAuditor">
                        <builder hasNature="true">
                            <run class="com ... PropertiesFileAuditor"/>
                        </builder>
                    </extension>
```

```
public class PropertiesAuditorNature
    implements IProjectNature
{
    public void configure() throws CoreException {
        PropertiesFileAuditor.addBuilderToProject(project);
        new Job("Properties File Audit") {
            protected IStatus run(IProgressMonitor monitor) {
                try {
                    project.build(
                        PropertiesFileAuditor.FULL_BUILD,
                        PropertiesFileAuditor.BUILDER_ID,
                        null, monitor);
                }
                catch (CoreEx
                    FavoritesL        public class PropertiesFileAuditor
                }                     extends IncrementalProjectBuilder
                return Status     {
            }                         protected IProject[] build(
        }.schedule();                     int kind,
    }                                     Map args,
                                          IProgressMonitor monitor)
    public void deconfigur             throws CoreException
        removeBuilderFromPr        {
        deleteAuditMarkers(            if (shouldAudit(kind)) {
    }                                     ResourcesPlugin.getWorkspace().run(
}                                             new IWorkspaceRunnable() {
                                                  public void run(IProgressMonitor monitor)
                                                      throws CoreException
                                                  {
                                                      auditPluginManifest(monitor);
                                                  }
                                              }, monitor);
                                          }
                                          return null;
                                      }
                                  }
```

Figure 14–1   Builders and natures.

14.1 Builders

A builder is scoped to a project. When one or more resources in a project change, the builders associated with the project are notified. If these changes have been batched (see Section 9.3, Batching Change Events, on page 382), the builder receives a single notification containing a list of all the changed resources rather than individual notifications for each changed resource.

> **Tip:** If you want a global builder not associated with any specific project, hook into the early startup extension point (see Section 3.4.2, Early plug-in startup, on page 114) and add a workspace resource change listener (see Section 9.1, IResourceChangeListener, on page 375). The downside of this approach is that the builder will consume memory and execution cycles regardless of whether it is really needed.

Builders process the list of changes and update their *build state* by regenerating the necessary derived resources (see Section 14.1.3, Derived resources, on page 509), annotating source resources, and so on. Builders are notified when a resource changes, such as when a user saves a modified Java source file, and thus are executed quite frequently. Because of this, a builder must execute incrementally, meaning that it must rebuild only those derived resources that have changed.

If the Eclipse Java compiler rebuilt all the Java source files in the project every time a single Java source file was saved, it would bring Eclipse to its knees.

14.1.1 Declaring a builder

The first step in creating the `plugin.properties` auditor involves adding a builder declaration to the **Favorites** plug-in manifest. Open the plug-in manifest editor on the **Favorites** `plugin.xml` file, switch to the **Extensions** page, and add an `org.eclipse.core.resources.builders` extension (see Figure 14–2).

Figure 14–2   The New Extension wizard showing the org.eclipse.core.resources.builders
extension point selected.

Click on the `org.eclipse.core.resources.builders` extension to
edit its properties, and set the `id` attribute for the extension (see Figure 14–3).

id—"propertiesFileAuditor"
The last segment of the builder's unique identifier. If the declaration
appears in the `com.qualityeclipse.favorites` plug-in, then the
builder's fully qualified identifier is `com.qualityeclipse.favorites.`
`propertiesFileAuditor`.

Figure 14–3   The plug-in manifest editor showing the builder's extension.

Right-click on the extension and select **New > builder** in the context menu. The builder element has these two attributes (see Figure 14–4).

hasNature—"true"
A Boolean indicating whether the builder is owned by a project nature. If `true` and no corresponding nature is found, this builder will not run, but will remain in the project's build spec. If the attribute is not specified, it is assumed to be `false`.

isConfiguarble—Leave blank
A Boolean indicating whether the builder allows customization of which build triggers it will respond to. If `true`, clients will be able to use the API `ICommand.setBuilding` to specify whether this builder should be run for a particular build trigger. If the attribute is not specified, it is assumed to be `false`.

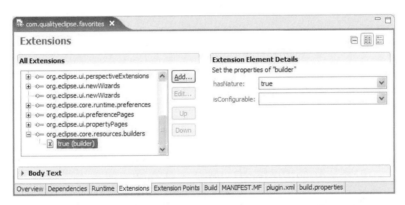

Figure 14–4 The plug-in manifest editor showing the builder's attributes.

Right-click on the builder element and select **New > run** in the context menu to associate a Java class with the builder. The Java class will provide behavior for the builder. The `run` element has only one attribute (see Figure 14–5), `class`, specifying the Java class to be executed.

Click the **class:** label to the right of the **class** field and use the **Java Attribute Editor** to create a new class in the **Favorites** project with the specified package and class name.

class—"com.qualityeclipse.favorites.builder.PropertiesFileAuditor"
The fully qualified name of a subclass of `org.eclipse.core.resources.IncrementalProjectBuilder`. The class is instantiated using its no argument constructor but can be parameterized using the `IExecutableExtension` interface (see Section 20.5.1, Parameterized types, on page 724).

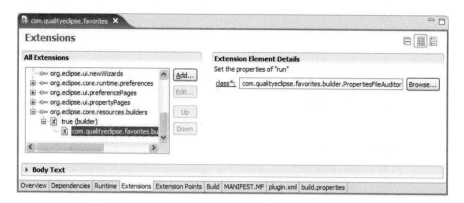

Figure 14–5   The plug-in manifest editor showing the run attributes.

The complete declaration in the **Favorites** plug-in manifest should look like this:

```
<extension
   id="propertiesFileAuditor"
   point="org.eclipse.core.resources.builders">
   <builder hasNature="true">
      <run class=
      "com.qualityeclipse.favorites.builder.PropertiesFileAuditor"/>
   </builder>
</extension>
```

14.1.2   IncrementalProjectBuilder

The class specified in the declaration of the previous section must be a subclass of `IncrementalProjectBuilder`, and at the very least, should implement the `build()` and `clean()` methods. The `build()` method is called by Eclipse when the builder should either incrementally or fully build related files and markers. This method has several arguments providing build information and a mechanism for displaying progress to the user.

kind—The kind of build being requested. Valid values include: `FULL_BUILD`, `INCREMENTAL_BUILD`, and `AUTO_BUILD`.

args—A map of builder-specific arguments keyed by argument name (key type: `String`, value type: `String`) or `null`, indicating an empty map.

monitor—A progress monitor, or `null` if progress reporting and cancellation are not desired.

The `kind` argument can have one of the following several values.

FULL_BUILD—The builder should rebuild all derived resources and perform its work as if it has not been executed before.

CLEAN_BUILD—The builder should delete all derived resources and markers before performing a full build (see the discussion of the clean() method that follows).

INCREMENTAL_BUILD—The builder should only rebuild those derived resources that need to be updated and only perform the work that is necessary based on its prior build state.

AUTO_BUILD—Same as INCREMENTAL_BUILD, except that the build was an automatically triggered incremental build (auto-building ON).

Calling IWorkspace.build() or IProject.build() whenever the build kind is CLEAN_BUILD triggers the clean() method prior to calling the build() method with the build kind equal to FULL_BUILD. The clean() method should discard any additional state that has been computed as a result of previous builds including all derived resources and all markers of type IMarker.PROBLEM. The platform will take care of discarding the builder's last built state (no need to call forgetLastBuiltState()). The following are several interesting methods in IncrementalProjectBuilder.

build(int, Map, IProgressMonitor)—Overridden by subclasses to perform the build operation. See the description earlier in this section and the implementation example later in this section.

clean(IProgressMonitor)—Similar to build(), except all derived resources, generated markers, and previous state should be discarded before building.

forgetLastBuiltState()—Requests that this builder forget any state it may be caching regarding previously built states. This may need to be called by a subclass if the build process is interrupted or canceled (see checkCancel() method later in this section).

getCommand()—Returns the build command associated with this builder which may contain project-specific configuration information (see Section 14.1.4, Associating a builder with a project, on page 509).

getDelta(IProject)—Returns the resource delta recording the changes in the given project since the last time the builder was run, or null if no such delta is available. See Section 9.2, Processing Change Events, on page 379 for details on processing resource change events and the shouldAudit() method later on in this section.

getProject()—Returns the project with which this builder is associated.

isInterrupted()—Returns whether an interrupt request has been made for this build. Background auto-build is interrupted when another thread tries to modify the workspace concurrently with the build thread. See shouldAudit() method later on in this section.

setInitializationData(IConfigurationElement, String, Object)—Called immediately after the builder is instantiated with configuration information specified in the builder's declaration (see Section 20.5.1, Parameterized types, on page 724).

After declaring the builder in the previous section, you must implement PropertiesFileAuditor, a subclass of org.eclipse.core.resources. IncrementalProjectBuilder, to perform the operation. When the build() method is called, the PropertiesFileAuditor builder delegates to shouldAudit() to see whether an audit should be performed and, if necessary, to auditPluginManifest() to perform the audit.

```
package com.qualityeclipse.favorites.builder;

import ...

public class PropertiesFileAuditor
    extends IncrementalProjectBuilder
{
    protected IProject[] build(
        int kind,
        Map args,
        IProgressMonitor monitor
    ) throws CoreException
    {
        if (shouldAudit(kind)) {
            auditPluginManifest(monitor);
        }

        return null;
    }

    ... other methods discussed later inserted here ...
}
```

The shouldAudit() method checks for FULL_BUILD, or if the plugin.xml or plugin.properties files of a project have changed (see Section 9.2, Processing Change Events, on page 379). If a builder has never been invoked before, then getDelta() returns null.

```
private boolean shouldAudit(int kind) {
    if (kind == FULL_BUILD)
        return true;
    IResourceDelta delta = getDelta(getProject());
    if (delta == null)
        return false;
    IResourceDelta[] children = delta.getAffectedChildren();
    for (int i = 0; i < children.length; i++) {
        IResourceDelta child = children[i];
        String fileName = child.getProjectRelativePath().lastSegment();
        if (fileName.equals("plugin.xml")
            || fileName.equals("plugin.properties"))
            return true;
    }
    return false;
}
```

If the `shouldAudit()` method determines that the manifest and properties files should be audited, then the `auditPluginManifest()` method is called to scan the `plugin.xml` and `plugin.properties` files and correlate the key/value pairs; any keys appearing in `plugin.xml` should have a corresponding key/value pair in `plugin.properties`. Before each lengthy operation, check to see whether the build has been interrupted or canceled. After each lengthy operation, you report progress to the user (see Section 9.4, Progress Monitor, on page 383); while this is not strictly necessary, it is certainly polite. If you do prematurely exit your build process, you may need to call `forgetLastBuildState()` before exiting so that a full rebuild will be performed the next time.

```
public static final int MISSING_KEY_VIOLATION = 1;
public static final int UNUSED_KEY_VIOLATION = 2;

private void auditPluginManifest(IProgressMonitor monitor) {
    monitor.beginTask("Audit plugin manifest", 4);
    IProject proj = getProject();

    if (checkCancel(monitor)) {
        return;
    }
    Map pluginKeys = scanPlugin(getProject().getFile("plugin.xml"));
    monitor.worked(1);

    if (checkCancel(monitor)) {
        return;
    }
    Map propertyKeys = scanProperties(
        getProject().getFile("plugin.properties"));
    monitor.worked(1);
```

```
   if (checkCancel(monitor)) {
      return;
   }

   Iterator iter = pluginKeys.entrySet().iterator();
   while (iter.hasNext()) {
      Map.Entry entry = (Map.Entry) iter.next();
      if (!propertyKeys.containsKey(entry.getKey()))
         reportProblem(
            "Missing property key",
            ((Location) entry.getValue()),
            MISSING_KEY_VIOLATION,
            true);
   }
   monitor.worked(1);

   if (checkCancel(monitor)) {
      return;
   }

   iter = propertyKeys.entrySet().iterator();
   while (iter.hasNext()) {
      Map.Entry entry = (Map.Entry) iter.next();
      if (!pluginKeys.containsKey(entry.getKey()))
         reportProblem(
            "Unused property key",
            ((Location) entry.getValue()),
            UNUSED_KEY_VIOLATION,
            false);
   }
   monitor.done();
}

private boolean checkCancel(IProgressMonitor monitor) {
   if (monitor.isCanceled()) {
      // Discard build state if necessary.
      throw new OperationCanceledException();
   }

   if (isInterrupted()) {
      // Discard build state if necessary.
      return true;
   }
   return false;
}
```

The auditPluginManifest() method delegates scanning the
plugin.xml and plugin.properties to two separate scan methods.

```
private Map scanPlugin(IFile file) {
    Map keys = new HashMap();
    String content = readFile(file);
    int start = 0;
    while (true) {
        start = content.indexOf("\"%", start);
        if (start < 0)
            break;
        int end = content.indexOf('"', start + 2);
        if (end < 0)
            break;
        Location loc = new Location();
        loc.file = file;
        loc.key = content.substring(start + 2, end);
        loc.charStart = start + 1;
        loc.charEnd = end;
        keys.put(loc.key, loc);
        start = end + 1;
    }
    return keys;
}

private Map scanProperties(IFile file) {
    Map keys = new HashMap();
    String content = readFile(file);
    int end = 0;
    while (true) {
        end = content.indexOf('=', end);
        if (end < 0)
            break;
        int start = end - 1;
        while (start >= 0) {
            char ch = content.charAt(start);
            if (ch == '\r' || ch == '\n')
                break;
            start--;
        }
        start++;
        String found = content.substring(start, end).trim();
        if (found.length() == 0
                || found.charAt(0) == '#'
                || found.indexOf('=') != -1)
            continue;
        Location loc = new Location();
        loc.file = file;
        loc.key = found;
        loc.charStart = start;
        loc.charEnd = end;
        keys.put(loc.key, loc);
        end++;
    }
    return keys;
}
```

The following two scan methods read the file content into memory using the `readFile()` method.

```
private String readFile(IFile file) {
    if (!file.exists())
        return "";
    InputStream stream = null;
    try {
        stream = file.getContents();
        Reader reader =
            new BufferedReader(
                new InputStreamReader(stream));
        StringBuffer result = new StringBuffer(2048);
        char[] buf = new char[2048];
        while (true) {
            int count = reader.read(buf);
            if (count < 0)
                break;
            result.append(buf, 0, count);
        }
        return result.toString();
    }
    catch (Exception e) {
        FavoritesLog.logError(e);
        return "";
    }
    finally {
        try {
            if (stream != null)
                stream.close();
        }
        catch (IOException e) {
            FavoritesLog.logError(e);
            return "";
        }
    }
}
```

The `reportProblem()` method appends a message to standard output. In subsequent sections, this method will be enhanced to generate markers instead (see Section 14.2.2, Creating and deleting markers, on page 515).

```
private void reportProblem(
    String msg, Location loc, int violation, boolean isError
) {
    System.out.println(
        (isError ? "ERROR: " : "WARNING: ")
            + msg + " \""
            + loc.key + "\" in "
            + loc.file.getFullPath());
}
```

The `Location` inner class is defined as an internal data holder with no associated behavior.

```
private class Location
{
   IFile file;
   String key;
   int charStart;
   int charEnd;
}
```

When hooked up to a project (see Section 14.1.4, Associating a builder with a project, on page 509 and Section 14.3.7, Associating a nature with a project, on page 532), the builder will append problems similar to the following to standard output.

```
ERROR: Missing property key "favorites.category.name"
   in /Test/plugin.xml
ERROR: Missing property key "favorites.view.name"
   in /Test/plugin.xml
WARNING: Unused property key "two"
   in /Test/plugin.properties
WARNING: Unused property key "three"
   in /Test/plugin.properties
```

14.1.3 Derived resources

Derived resources are ones that can be fully regenerated by a builder. Java class files are derived resources because the Java compiler can fully regenerate them from the associated Java source file. When a builder creates a derived resource, it should mark that file as derived using the `IResource.setDerived()` method. A team provider can then assume that the file does not need to be under version control by default.

> `setDerived(boolean)`—Sets whether this resource subtree is marked as derived. This operation does not result in a resource change event and does not trigger auto-builds.

14.1.4 Associating a builder with a project

Using a nature to associate a builder with a project is the preferred approach (see Section 14.3, Natures, on page 525), but you can associate builders with projects without using a nature. You could create an action in a workbench window (see Section 6.2.6, Creating an action delegate, on page 216) that calls the following `addBuilderToProject()` method to associate your auditor with the currently selected projects. Alternatively, you could, on startup, cycle through all the projects in the workbench and call the following `addBuilderToProject()` method. If you do not use a project nature, then be sure to set the `hasNature` attribute to `false` (see Figure 14–4 on page 501).

There are no advantages or disadvantages to associating a builder with a
project using an action delegate as opposed to using a project nature, but in
this case, you will create a project nature to make the association (see Section
14.3, Natures, on page 525). Place the following in the favorites
PropertiesFileAuditor class.

```
public static final String BUILDER_ID =
   FavoritesPlugin.ID + ".propertiesFileAuditor";

public static void addBuilderToProject(IProject project) {

   // Cannot modify closed projects.
   if (!project.isOpen())
      return;

   // Get the description.
   IProjectDescription description;
   try {
      description = project.getDescription();
   }
   catch (CoreException e) {
      FavoritesLog.logError(e);
      return;
   }

   // Look for builder already associated.
   ICommand[] cmds = description.getBuildSpec();
   for (int j = 0; j < cmds.length; j++)
      if (cmds[j].getBuilderName().equals(BUILDER_ID))
         return;

   // Associate builder with project.
   ICommand newCmd = description.newCommand();
   newCmd.setBuilderName(BUILDER_ID);
   List newCmds = new ArrayList();
   newCmds.addAll(Arrays.asList(cmds));
   newCmds.add(newCmd);
   description.setBuildSpec(
      (ICommand[]) newCmds.toArray(
         new ICommand[newCmds.size()]));
   try {
      project.setDescription(description, null);
   }
   catch (CoreException e) {
      FavoritesLog.logError(e);
   }
}
```

Every workbench project contains a .project file (see Section 1.4.2,
.classpath and .project files, on page 22) that contains build commands. Executing this method causes the following to appear in the buildSpec section
of the project's .project file.

```
<buildCommand>
   <name>
      com.qualityeclipse.favorites.propertiesFileAuditor
   </name>
   <arguments>
</arguments>
</buildCommand>
```

In addition to the `addBuilderToProject()` method, you would need a corresponding `removeBuilderFromProject()` method:

```java
public static void removeBuilderFromProject(IProject project) {

   // Cannot modify closed projects.
   if (!project.isOpen())
      return;

   // Get the description.
   IProjectDescription description;
   try {
      description = project.getDescription();
   }
   catch (CoreException e) {
      FavoritesLog.logError(e);
      return;
   }

   // Look for builder.
   int index = -1;
   ICommand[] cmds = description.getBuildSpec();
   for (int j = 0; j < cmds.length; j++) {
      if (cmds[j].getBuilderName().equals(BUILDER_ID)) {
         index = j;
         break;
      }
   }
   if (index == -1)
      return;

   // Remove builder from project.
   List newCmds = new ArrayList();
   newCmds.addAll(Arrays.asList(cmds));
   newCmds.remove(index);
   description.setBuildSpec(
      (ICommand[]) newCmds.toArray(
         new ICommand[newCmds.size()]));
   try {
      project.setDescription(description, null);
   }
   catch (CoreException e) {
      FavoritesLog.logError(e);
   }
}
```

14.1.5 Invoking builders

Normally, the build process for a project is triggered either by the user selecting a build action or by the workbench during an auto-build in response to a resource change. If need be, you can trigger the build process programmatically using one of the following methods:

IProject

> `build(int, IProgressMonitor)`—Runs the build processing on the project, causing *all* associated builders to be run. The first argument indicates the kind of build, `FULL_BUILD`, `INCREMENTAL_BUILD` or `CLEAN_BUILD` (see Section 14.1.2, IncrementalProjectBuilder, on page 502).

> `build(int, String, Map, IProgressMonitor)`—Triggers a single builder to be run on the project. The first argument indicates the kind of build, `FULL_BUILD`, `INCREMENTAL_BUILD` or `CLEAN_BUILD` (see Section 14.1.2, IncrementalProjectBuilder, on page 502), while the second specifies which builder is to be run.

IWorkspace

> `build(int, IProgressMonitor)`—Runs the build processing on all open projects in the workspace. The first argument indicates the kind of build, `FULL_BUILD`, `INCREMENTAL_BUILD` or `CLEAN_BUILD` (see Section 14.1.2, IncrementalProjectBuilder, on page 502).

14.2 Markers

Markers are used to annotate specific locations within a resource. For example, the Eclipse Java compiler not only produces class files from source files, but it also annotates the source files by adding markers to indicate compilation errors, deprecated code usage, and so on. Markers do not modify the resources they annotate, but instead are stored in the workspace metadata area. Markers are automatically updated by editors so that when a user edits a file, they are repositioned or deleted appropriately. Rather than sending messages to the **console**, you want the `PropertiesFileAuditor` to create a marker indicating where a problem exists (see Figure 14–6).

Figure 14–6 Marker declaration and data structures.

14.2.1 Marker types

Markers are grouped by marker type. Every marker type has an identifier and zero or more supermarker types but no behavior. New marker types are declared in terms of existing ones. Marker types added by the org.eclipse. core.resources plug-in appear as constants in IMarker and include:

org.eclipse.core.resources.bookmark—IMarker.BOOKMARK— The super type of marker that appears in the **Bookmarks** view.

`org.eclipse.core.resources.marker`—`IMarker.MARKER`—The root supertype of all markers.

`org.eclipse.core.resources.problemmarker`—`IMarker.PROBLEM` —The supertype of marker that appears in the **Problems** view.

`org.eclipse.core.resources.taskmarker`—`IMarker.TASK`—The supertype of marker that appears in the **Tasks** view.

`org.eclipse.core.resources.textmarker`—`IMarker.TEXT`—The supertype of all text-based markers.

For the purposes here, you want to introduce a new marker type for the plug-in manifest audit results. Switch to the **Extensions** page of the plug-in manifest editor and click the **Add...** button to add an `org.eclipse.core.resources.markers` extension. Select the newly added extension in the tree on the left and specify "auditmarker" as the ID and "Properties Auditor Marker" as the name in the fields on the right (see Figure 14–7).

You want your markers to appear in the **Problems** view, so specify `org.eclipse.core.resources.problemmarker` as a supertype by right-clicking on the markers' extension and selecting **New > super.** Click on the new `super` element and enter "org.eclipse.core.resources.problemmarker" for the type attribute. The markers relate to a range of sources in the plug-in manifest or plug-in properties files, so specify `org.eclipse.core.resources.textmarker` as well using the same procedure.

You want your markers to persist across multiple sessions, so right-click on the `markers` declaration and select **New > persistent.** Click on the new `persistent` element and enter "true" for the value attribute.

You inherit several marker attributes from the marker super types specified earlier, but want to associate two new attributes with the audit marker. Right-click on the `markers` declaration and select **New > attribute.** Click on the new `attribute` element and enter "key" for the value attribute. Repeat this process to specify the "violation" attribute.

Once complete, the new marker type declaration looks like this:

```
<extension
    id="auditmarker"
    point="org.eclipse.core.resources.markers"
    name="Properties Auditor Marker">
    <super type="org.eclipse.core.resources.problemmarker"/>
    <super type="org.eclipse.core.resources.textmarker"/>
    <attribute name="key"/>
    <attribute name="violation"/>
    <persistent value="true"/>
</extension>
```

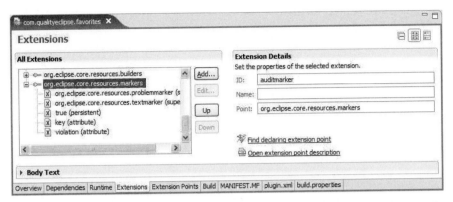

Figure 14–7 The New Extension wizard showing the markers extension point selected.

The aforementioned declaration specifies the marker's local identifier; the full identifier is the plug-in identifier plus the local identifier that is added as a constant in `PropertiesFileAuditor`.

```
private static final String MARKER_ID =
    FavoritesPlugin.ID + ".auditmarker";
```

14.2.2 *Creating and deleting markers*

You want to create one marker for each problem that is found, but first you must remove any old markers. To accomplish this, add the following lines in the `auditPluginManifest()` method:

```
private void auditPluginManifest(IProgressMonitor monitor) {
    monitor.beginTask("Audit plugin manifest", 4);

    if (!deleteAuditMarkers(getProject())) {
        return;
    }

    if (checkCancel(monitor)) {
        return;
    }

    ... etc ...
}
```

which calls the following new method to delete all existing markers in the specified project.

```
public static boolean deleteAuditMarkers(IProject project) {
   try {
      project.deleteMarkers(
         MARKER_ID, false, IResource.DEPTH_INFINITE);
      return true;
   }
   catch (CoreException e) {
      FavoritesLog.logError(e);
      return false;
   }
}
```

Next, add two constants and rework the `reportProblem()` method (see Section 14.1.2, IncrementalProjectBuilder, on page 502) to create a marker and set marker attributes (see the next section) to indicate problems. The revised method not only creates a marker but sets various marker attributes, which are discussed in the next section.

```
public static final String KEY = "key";
public static final String VIOLATION = "violation";

private void reportProblem(
   String msg, Location loc, int violation, boolean isError)
{
   try {
      IMarker marker = loc.file.createMarker(MARKER_ID);
      marker.setAttribute(IMarker.MESSAGE, msg + ": " + loc.key);
      marker.setAttribute(IMarker.CHAR_START, loc.charStart);
      marker.setAttribute(IMarker.CHAR_END, loc.charEnd);
      marker.setAttribute(
         IMarker.SEVERITY,
         isError
            ? IMarker.SEVERITY_ERROR
            : IMarker.SEVERITY_WARNING);
      marker.setAttribute(KEY, loc.key);
      marker.setAttribute(VIOLATION, violation);
   }
   catch (CoreException e) {
      FavoritesLog.logError(e);
      return;
   }
}
```

Finally, creating and setting attributes, and deleting markers generates resource change events. For efficiency, modify the `build()` method to wrap the call to `auditPluginManifest()` in a `IWorkspaceRunnable` so that events will be batched and sent when the operation has completed (see Section 9.3, Batching Change Events, on page 382):

```
protected IProject[] build(
   int kind,
   Map args,
   IProgressMonitor monitor
) throws CoreException
{
   if (shouldAudit(kind)) {
      ResourcesPlugin.getWorkspace().run(
         new IWorkspaceRunnable() {
            public void run(IProgressMonitor monitor)
               throws CoreException
            {
               auditPluginManifest(monitor);
            }
         },
         monitor
      );
   }
   return null;
}
```

When this is in place, the problems reported by the PropertiesFile-
Auditor appear in the **Problems** view rather than the **Console** view (see Figure
14–8). In addition, the markers appear as small warning and error icons along
the left side of the plugin.xml and plugin.properties editors.

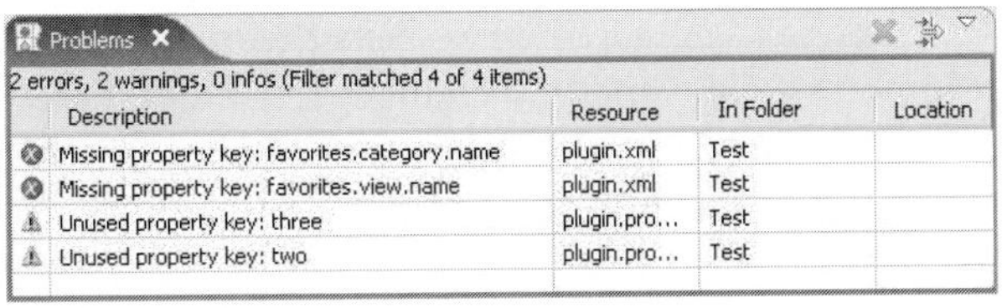

Figure 14–8   Problems view containing problems found by the auditor.

14.2.3   Marker attributes

Marker attributes take the form of key/value pairs, where the key is a string
and the value can be a string, an integer, or a Boolean. IMarker methods for
accessing attributes include:

getAttribute(String)—Returns the attribute with the given name.
The result is an instance of a string, an integer, or a Boolean.
Returns null if the attribute is undefined.

getAttribute(String, boolean)—Returns the Boolean-valued
attribute with the given name. Returns the given default value if the
attribute is undefined, the marker does not exist, or it is not a Boolean
value.

getAttribute(String, int)—Returns the integer-valued attribute with the given name. Returns the given default value if the attribute is undefined, the marker does not exist, or it is not an integer value.

getAttribute(String, String)—Returns the string-valued attribute with the given name. Returns the given default value if the attribute is undefined, the marker does not exist, or it is not a string value.

getAttributes()—Returns a map of the attributes for the marker. The map has String keys and values that are string, integer, Boolean, or null. If the marker has no attributes, then null is returned.

getAttributes(String[])—Returns the attributes with the given names. The result is an array whose elements correspond to the elements of the given attribute name array. Each element is a string, integer, Boolean, or null.

setAttribute(String, boolean)—Sets the Boolean-valued attribute with the given name. This method changes resources; these changes will be reported in a subsequent resource change event, including an indication that this marker has been modified.

setAttribute(String, int)—Sets the integer-valued attribute with the given name. This method changes resources; these changes will be reported in a subsequent resource change event, including an indication that this marker has been modified.

setAttribute(String, Object)—Sets the attribute with the given name. The value must be a string, integer, Boolean, or null. If the value is null, the attribute is considered to be undefined. This method changes resources; these changes will be reported in a subsequent resource change event, including an indication that this marker has been modified.

setAttributes(String[], Object[])—Sets the given attribute key/value pairs on this marker. The values must be string, integer, Boolean, or null. If a value is null, the new value of the attribute is considered to be undefined. This method changes resources; these changes will be reported in a subsequent resource change event, including an indication that this marker has been modified.

`setAttributes(Map)`—Sets the attributes for this marker to be the ones contained in the given map. The values must be instances of a `string`, `integer`, or `Boolean`. Attributes previously set on the marker but not included in the given map are considered to be removals. Passing a `null` parameter is equivalent to removing all marker attributes. This method changes resources; these changes will be reported in a subsequent resource change event, including an indication that this marker has been modified.

Marker attributes are declared in the plug-in manifest for documentation purposes, but are not used during compilation or execution. For example, in the marker type declaration, two new attributes were declared for the marker type named `key` and `violation`. Alternatively, they could be documented using XML `<!-- -->` comments, but we recommend using the `attribute` declaration below because future versions of Eclipse might use them.

```
<extension
    id="auditmarker"
    point="org.eclipse.core.resources.markers"
    name="Properties Auditor Marker">
    <super type="org.eclipse.core.resources.problemmarker"/>
    <super type="org.eclipse.core.resources.textmarker"/>
    <attribute name="key"/>
    <attribute name="violation"/>
    <persistent value="true"/>
</extension>
```

The `org.eclipse.core.resources` plug-in introduces several attributes used commonly throughout Eclipse. The following attribute keys are defined in `IMarker`.

CHAR_END—Character end marker attribute. An integer value indicating where a text marker ends. This attribute is zero-relative to the file and exclusive.

CHAR_START—Character start marker attribute. An integer value indicating where a text marker starts. This attribute is zero-relative to the file and inclusive.

DONE—Done marker attribute. A Boolean value indicating whether a marker (e.g., a task) is considered done.

LINE_NUMBER—Line number marker attribute. An integer value indicating the line number for a text marker. This attribute is 1-relative.

LOCATION—Location marker attribute. The location is a human-readable (localized) string that can be used to distinguish between markers on a resource. As such, it should be concise and aimed at users. The content and form of this attribute is not specified or interpreted by the platform.

MESSAGE—Message marker attribute. A localized string describing the nature of the marker (e.g., a name for a bookmark or task). The content and form of this attribute is not specified or interpreted by the platform.

PRIORITY—Priority marker attribute. A number from the set of constants defined in IMarker: PRIORITY_HIGH, PRIORITY_LOW, and PRIORITY_NORMAL.

SEVERITY—Severity marker attribute. A number from the set of constants defined in IMarker: SEVERITY_ERROR, SEVERITY_WARNING, and SEVERITY_INFO.

TRANSIENT—Transient marker attribute. A Boolean value indicating whether the marker (e. g., a task) is considered transient even if its type is declared as persistent.

USER_EDITABLE—User-editable marker attribute. A Boolean value indicating whether a user should be able to manually change the marker (e.g., a task). The default is true.

In the revised reportProblem() method (see Section 14.2.2, Creating and deleting markers, on page 515), several marker attributes were set that are later interpreted by Eclipse. The **Problems** view uses the IMarker. MESSAGE and IMarker.LOCATION attributes to populate the **Description** and **Location** columns. Editors use the IMarker.CHAR_START and IMarker. CHAR_END attributes to determine what range of text should be highlighted.

14.2.4 Marker resolution—quick fix

Now that you can generate markers, the user can quickly jump to the location of a problem by double-clicking on the corresponding entry in the **Problems** view, but no help with fixing the problem is provided. Using marker resolution, you can provide an automated mechanism for fixing the problems that your builder identifies.

Create a new org.eclipse.ui.ide.markerResolution extension (see Figure 14–9), add a markerResolutionGenerator nested element (see Figure 14–10), and specify the marker type as "com.qualityeclipse. favorites.auditmarker."

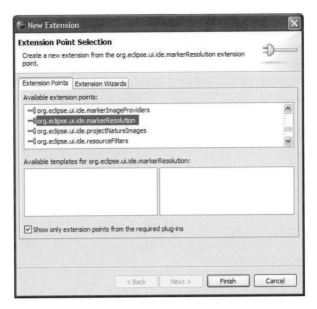

Figure 14–9   The New Extension wizard showing the org.eclipse.ui.ide.markerResolution
extension point selected.

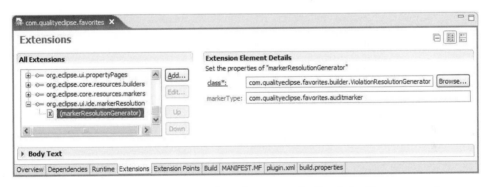

Figure 14–10   The Plug-in manifest editor showing markerResolutionGenerator attributes.

Use the **Java Attribute Editor** to generate a marker resolution class named
`ViolationResolutionGenerator` in the package `com.qualityeclipse.`
`favorites.builder`. When complete, the declaration should look something
like this:

```
<extension point="org.eclipse.ui.ide.markerResolution">
   <markerResolutionGenerator
      markerType="com.qualityeclipse.favorites.auditmarker"
      class="com.qualityeclipse.favorites.builder
         .ViolationResolutionGenerator">
   </markerResolutionGenerator>
</extension>
```

The `ViolationResolutionGenerator` class provides possible resolution for the user for any `com.qualityeclipse.favorites.auditmarker` marker by using the `org.eclipse.ui.IMarkerResolutionGenerator2` interface (the `IMarkerResolutionGenerator2` interface was introduced in Eclipse 3.0, providing additional functionality and replacing the now deprecated `IMarker-ResolutionGenerator`).

```java
package com.qualityeclipse.favorites.builder;

import ...

public class ViolationResolutionGenerator
    implements IMarkerResolutionGenerator2
{
    public boolean hasResolutions(IMarker marker) {
        switch (getViolation(marker)) {
            case PropertiesFileAuditor.MISSING_KEY_VIOLATION :
                return true;
            case PropertiesFileAuditor.UNUSED_KEY_VIOLATION :
                return true;
            default :
                return false;
        }
    }

    public IMarkerResolution[] getResolutions(IMarker marker){
        List resolutions = new ArrayList();
        switch (getViolation(marker)) {
            case PropertiesFileAuditor.MISSING_KEY_VIOLATION :
                resolutions.add(
                    new CreatePropertyKeyResolution());
                break;
            case PropertiesFileAuditor.UNUSED_KEY_VIOLATION :
                resolutions.add(
                    new DeletePropertyKeyResolution());
                resolutions.add(
                    new CommentPropertyKeyResolution());
                break;
            default :
                break;
        }

        return (IMarkerResolution[]) resolutions.toArray(
            new IMarkerResolution[resolutions.size()]);
    }

    private int getViolation(IMarker marker) {
        return marker.getAttribute(PropertiesFileAuditor.VIOLATION, 0);
    }
}
```

The ViolationResolutionGenerator class returns one or more instances of org.eclipse.ui.IMarkerResolution2 (similar to IMarker-ResolutionGenerator2, IMarkerResolution2 was introduced in Eclipse 3.0, replacing the now deprecated IMarkerResolution), indicating the possible resolutions for a violation. For example, an instance of Create-PropertyKeyResolution is returned for missing property key violations:

```
package com.qualityeclipse.favorites.builder;

import ...

public class CreatePropertyKeyResolution
   implements IMarkerResolution2
{
   public String getDescription() {
      return "Append a new property key/value pair"
         + " to the plugin.properties file";
   }

   public Image getImage() {
      return null;
   }

   public String getLabel() {
      return "Create a new property key";
   }
}
```

If the user selects this resolution, the run() method is executed, opening or activating the properties editor and appending a new property key/value pair.

```
public void run(IMarker marker) {

   // Get the corresponding plugin.properties.
   IFile file = marker.getResource().getParent().getFile(
      new Path("plugin.properties"));
   if (!file.exists()) {
      ByteArrayInputStream stream =
         new ByteArrayInputStream(new byte[] {});
      try {
         file.create(stream, false, null);
      }
      catch (CoreException e) {
         FavoritesLog.logError(e);
         return;
      }
   }
```

```
// Open or activate the editor.
IWorkbenchPage page = PlatformUI.getWorkbench()
      .getActiveWorkbenchWindow().getActivePage();

IEditorPart part;
try {
   part = IDE.openEditor(page, file, true);
}
catch (PartInitException e) {
   FavoritesLog.logError(e);
   return;
}

// Get the editor's document.
if (!(part instanceof ITextEditor)) {
   return;
}

ITextEditor editor = (ITextEditor) part;
IDocument doc = editor.getDocumentProvider()
   .getDocument(new FileEditorInput(file));

// Determine the text to be added.
String key;
try {
   key = (String) marker.getAttribute(PropertiesFileAuditor.KEY);
}
catch (CoreException e) {
   FavoritesLog.logError(e);
   return;
}

String text = key + "=Value for " + key;

// If necessary, add a newline.
int index = doc.getLength();
if (index > 0) {
   char ch;
   try {
      ch = doc.getChar(index - 1);
   }
   catch (BadLocationException e) {
      FavoritesLog.logError(e);
      return;
   }

   if (ch != '\r' || ch != '\n') {
      text = System.getProperty("line.separator") + text;
   }
}
```

```
    // Append the new text.
    try {
        doc.replace(index, 0, text);
    }
    catch (BadLocationException e) {
        FavoritesLog.logError(e);
        return;
    }

    // Select the value so the user can type.
    index += text.indexOf('=') + 1;
    editor.selectAndReveal(index, doc.getLength() - index);
}
```

14.2.5   Finding markers

You can query a resource for all its markers or all its markers of a given type.
If the resource is a container, such as folder, project, or the workspace root,
you can request all markers for that container's children as well. The depth
can be zero (just that container), one (the container and its direct children), or
infinite (the resource and all direct and indirect children). For example, to
retrieve all markers associated with a folder and its children to an infinite
depth, you might use an expression like this:

```
IMarker[] markers;
try {
    markers = myFolder.findMarkers(
        IMarker.PROBLEM, true, IResource.DEPTH_INFINITE);
}
catch (CoreException e) {
    // Log the exception and bail out.
}
```

14.3   Natures

A nature is used to associate a project with functionality such as a builder, a
tool, or a process. A nature can also be used to determine whether an action
should be visible (see Section 6.3.2.3, The filter element, on page 230).
Whereas a marker has only limited functionality but can be applied to any
resource, a nature is designed to contain additional functionality but can only
be applied to projects. A marker applies only to a resource in a single workspace, while a nature is part of a project and thus is shared by multiple developers.

The Java nature is what makes a project a Java project, distinguishing it from all other types of projects. When a nature, such as the Java nature, is added to a project, the project's .project file (see Section 1.4.2, .classpath and .project files, on page 22) is modified to include the nature's identifier (see Section 14.1.4, Associating a builder with a project, on page 509) and the nature has the opportunity to configure the project.

For example, the Java nature configures a project by adding the Java compiler as a build command. A nature also causes a project to be treated differently by the workbench; for instance, only projects that possess the Java nature are displayed by the **Package Explorer** view. When a nature is removed, it has the opportunity to deconfigure or remove aspects of itself from the project. The following are several natures defined within Eclipse that provide various types of behavior.

org.eclipse.jdt.core.javanature—Associates the Eclipse incremental Java compiler with a project and causes the project to appear in Java-related views such as the **Package Explorer** view.

org.eclipse.pde.PluginNature—Associates the plug-in manifest and extension point schema builders with a project, validating the content of the plugin.xml file and updating the project's Java build path based on its plug-in dependency declaration (see Section 2.3.1, The Plug-in manifests, on page 71).

org.eclipse.pde.FeatureNature—Associates the feature builder with a project, validating the content of the feature.xml file (see Section 18.1.2, Feature manifest files, on page 623).

org.eclipse.pde.UpdateSiteNature—Associates the site builder with a project, validating the content of the site.xml file (see Section 18.3.2, The site.xml file, on page 639).

14.3.1 Declaring a nature

For the **Favorites** product, you want a new propertiesAuditor nature to associate the property file audit builder with a project. Begin by creating a new org.eclipse.core.resources.natures extension in the **Favorites** plug-in manifest. Switch to the **Extensions** page, click the **Add...** button, select org.eclipse.core.resources.natures, and then click **Finish** (see Figure 14–11).

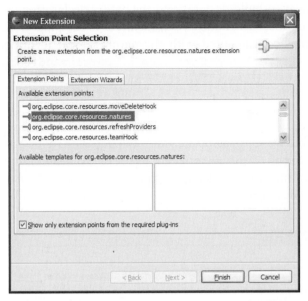

Figure 14–11   The New Extension wizard showing the natures extension point selected.

Click on the new extension to edit the properties, change the `id` to "propertiesAuditor", and change the `name` to "Favorites Properties Auditor" (see Figure 14–12). The nature declaration should look like this:

```
<extension
   id="propertiesAuditor"
   name="Favorites Properties Auditor"
   point="org.eclipse.core.resources.natures">
</extension>
```

Figure 14–12   The extension details showing the nature's attributes.

Similar to build declarations, the nature declaration contains the nature's local identifier. The nature's full identifier is the plug-in identifier containing the nature concatenated with the nature's local identifier, or in this case, com.qualityeclipse.favorites.propertiesAuditor.

14.3.2 Associating builders and natures

Now you want to associate your builder with your nature. Click on the org.eclipse.core.resources.natures extension point and select **New > builder**. Enter the builder id, which in this case is "com.qualityeclipse. favorites.propertiesFileAuditor" (see Figure 14–13).

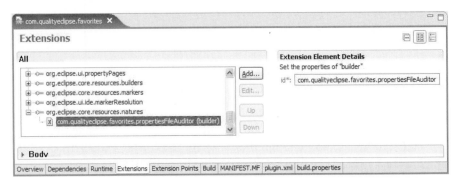

Figure 14–13   The extension element details showing the builder's attributes.

In addition, return to the builder declaration (see Section 14.1.1, Declaring a builder, on page 499) and modify the hasNature attribute to be "true." After this has been accomplished, the nature declaration should look like this:

```
<extension
    id="propertiesAuditor"
    name="Favorites Properties Auditor"
    point="org.eclipse.core.resources.natures">
    <builder id="com.qualityeclipse.favorites
            .propertiesFileAuditor"/>
</extension>
```

These changes ensure that the builder will be omitted from a project's build process if the nature is not associated with the project. If you want your builder to work regardless of whether your nature is present, then omit this from your nature's declaration.

14.3.3 IProjectNature

Natures can have behavior to configure and deconfigure a project. Similar to the Java nature, you want the nature to add your builder to the project's build spec. Right-click on the `org.eclipse.core.resources.natures` extension point and select **New > runtime**, then right-click on the (runtime) nested element and select **New > run**. In the plug-in manifest editor, click on the "class" label at the left of the **class** field, then use the **Java Attribute Editor** to generate a new class named `PropertiesAuditorNature` in the `com.quality-eclipse.favorites.builder` package. When this is complete, the nature declaration should look like this:

```
<extension
   id="propertiesAuditor"
   name="Favorites Properties Auditor"
   point="org.eclipse.core.resources.natures">
   <builder id="com.qualityeclipse.favorites
      .propertiesFileAuditor"/>
   <runtime>
      <run class="com.qualityeclipse.favorites.builder
         .PropertiesAuditorNature"/>
   </runtime>
</extension>
```

The class specified in the nature declaration must implement the `org.eclipse.core.resources.IProjectNature` interface. When the nature is added to a project, this class is instantiated and the `setProject()` method is called, followed by the `configure()` method; the `deconfigure()` method is called when the nature is removed from a project.

Similar to the Java nature, you want the nature to add your builder to the project's build spec via the `addBuilderToProject()` method (see Section 14.1.4, Associating a builder with a project, on page 509) and trigger a build in the background (see Section 20.8, Background Tasks—Jobs API, on page 739) when the project is configured. When the nature is removed from the project, the build spec is modified and all audit markers are removed.

```
package com.qualityeclipse.favorites.builder;

import ...

public class PropertiesAuditorNature implements IProjectNature
{
   private IProject project;

   public IProject getProject() {
      return project;
   }
```

```
public void setProject(IProject project) {
   this.project = project;
}

public void configure() throws CoreException {
   PropertiesFileAuditor.addBuilderToProject(project);
   new Job("Properties File Audit") {
      protected IStatus run(IProgressMonitor monitor) {
         try {
            project.build(
               PropertiesFileAuditor.FULL_BUILD,
               PropertiesFileAuditor.BUILDER_ID,
               null,
               monitor);
         }
         catch (CoreException e) {
            FavoritesLog.logError(e);
         }
         return Status.OK_STATUS;
      }
   }.schedule();
}

public void deconfigure() throws CoreException {
   PropertiesFileAuditor.removeBuilderFromProject(project);
   PropertiesFileAuditor.deleteAuditMarkers(project);
}
}
```

14.3.4 Required natures

A dependency of one nature on another nature can be expressed in the nature's declaration (see Section 14.3.1, Declaring a nature, on page 526). When the required nature is not present or not enabled, Eclipse disables the nature having the requirement. For example, the propertiesAuditor nature depends on the Java nature and PDE nature. If you were to express this in your nature's declaration, it would look like this:

```
<extension
   id="propertiesAuditor"
   name="Favorites Properties Auditor"
   point="org.eclipse.core.resources.natures">
   <builder id="com.qualityeclipse.favorites
      .propertiesFileAuditor">
   </builder>
   <runtime>
      <run class="com.qualityeclipse.favorites.builder
         .PropertiesAuditorNature"/>
   </runtime>
   <requires-nature id="org.eclipse.jdt.core.javanature"/>
   <requires-nature id="org.eclipse.pde.PluginNature"/>
</extension>
```

14.3.5 Conflicting natures

The conflict of one nature with one or more other natures can also be expressed in the nature's declaration. In your nature's declaration, add a one-of-nature nested element specifying the name of a set of natures. If any other nature specifies the same string in a one-of-nature nested element and is added to the same project as your nature, then Eclipse will disable both natures.

```
<extension
   id="propertiesAuditor"
   name="Favorites Properties Auditor"
   point="org.eclipse.core.resources.natures">
   <builder id="com.qualityeclipse.favorites
      .propertiesFileAuditor">
   </builder>
   <runtime>
      <run class="com.qualityeclipse.favorites.builder
         .PropertiesAuditorNature"/>
   </runtime>
   <requires-nature id="org.eclipse.jdt.core.javanature"/>
   <requires-nature id="org.eclipse.pde.PluginNature"/>
   <one-of-nature id="pluginAuditors">
</extension>
```

14.3.6 Nature image

A project nature can have an image associated with it using the `org.eclipse.ui.ide.projectNatureImages` extension point. The specified image is displayed over the top right corner of the standard project image. For example, the `org.eclipse.jdt.ui` plug-in associates an image of a "J" with the Java nature so that the icon for all Java projects has a small blue "J" at the top right corner.

```
<extension point="org.eclipse.ui.ide.projectNatureImages">
   <image
      icon="icons/full/ovr16/java_ovr.gif"
      natureId="org.eclipse.jdt.core.javanature"
      id="org.eclipse.ui.javaProjectNatureImage"/>
</extension>
```

The nature here does not define the type of project so much as associate the properties audit tool with the project, so it is not appropriate to supply a project nature image.

14.3.7 Associating a nature with a project

Similar to associating a builder with a project (see Section 14.1.4, Associating a builder with a project, on page 509), you can associate a nature with a project by modifying the project's description. To demonstrate this, build an action delegate that toggles the propertiesAuditor nature for a project. First, create an action declaration to add a new command in the top-level **Favorites** menu (see Section 6.2.1, Defining a workbench window menu, on page 209).

```
<extension point="org.eclipse.ui.actionSets">
   <actionSet
      label="Favorites ActionSet"
      visible="true"
      id="com.qualityeclipse.favorites.workbenchActionSet">
      ...
      <action
         label="Add/Remove propertiesAuditor project nature"
         class="com.qualityeclipse.favorites.actions
            .ToggleProjectNatureActionDelegate"
         menubarPath="com.qualityeclipse.favorites
            .workbenchMenu/content"
         id="com.qualityeclipse.favorites.toggleProjectNature"\>
   </actionSet>
</extension>
```

Next, create an action delegate (see Section 6.2.6, Creating an action delegate, on page 216) that checks the natures associated with every selected project and adds the propertiesAuditor nature to each one that does not have that nature associated with it and removes that nature from all other selected projects. Typically, a nature is added to or removed from a project as part of a larger process such as creating a Java project, but this action delegate suffices to show the mechanics of how it is accomplished.

```
package com.qualityeclipse.favorites.actions;

import ...

public class ToggleProjectNatureActionDelegate
   extends ActionDelegate
   implements IWorkbenchWindowActionDelegate
{
   private static final String NATURE_ID =
      FavoritesPlugin.ID + ".propertiesAuditor";

   private final Set projects = new HashSet();

   public void init(IWorkbenchWindow window) {
      // Ignored.
   }
}
```

When the selection changes, the `selectionChanged()` method caches the currently selected projects and updates the action enablement and checked state based on that seletion.

```
public void selectionChanged(IAction action, ISelection selection) {
    updateSelectedProjects(selection);
    if (projects.size() > 0) {
        action.setEnabled(true);
        boolean checked;

        try {
            checked = project.isOpen()
                && project.hasNature(NATURE_ID);
        }
        catch (CoreException e) {
            checked = false;
            FavoritesLog.logError(e);
        }

        action.setEnabled(true);
        action.setChecked(checked);
    }
    else {
        action.setEnabled(false);
        action.setChecked(false);
    }
}

private void updateSelectedProjects(ISelection selection) {
    projects.clear();
    if (!(selection instanceof IStructuredSelection))
        return;
    for (
        Iterator iter = ((IStructuredSelection) selection).iterator();
        iter.hasNext();
    ) {
        Object elem = iter.next();
        if (!(elem instanceof IResource)) {
            if (!(elem instanceof IAdaptable))
                continue;
            elem = ((IAdaptable) elem).getAdapter(IResource.class);
            if (!(elem instanceof IResource))
                continue;
        }
        if (!(elem instanceof IProject)) {
            elem = ((IResource) elem).getProject();
            if (!(elem instanceof IProject))
                continue;
        }

        projects.add(elem);
    }
}
```

When the action delegate is selected, it adds the nature to or removes the nature from the selected projects so that the project's plug-in properties are audited.

```java
public void run(IAction action) {
    for (Iterator iter = projects.iterator(); iter.hasNext();) {
        final IProject project = (IProject) iter.next();

        // Cannot modify closed projects.
        if (!project.isOpen()) {
            continue;
        }

        // Get the description.
        IProjectDescription description;
        try {
            description = project.getDescription();
        }
        catch (CoreException e) {
            FavoritesLog.logError(e);
            continue;
        }

        // Toggle the nature.
        List newIds = new ArrayList();
        newIds.addAll(Arrays.asList(description.getNatureIds()));

        int index = newIds.indexOf(NATURE_ID);
        if (index == -1) {
            newIds.add(NATURE_ID);
        } else {
            newIds.remove(index);
        }

        description.setNatureIds(
            (String[]) newIds.toArray(new String[newIds.size()]));

        // Save the description.
        try {
            project.setDescription(description, null);
        }
        catch (CoreException e) {
            FavoritesLog.logError(e);
        }
    }
}
```

14.4 RFRS Considerations

The "Build" section of the *RFRS Requirements* includes six items—three requirements and three best practices—dealing with builders.

14.4.1 *Use builders to convert resources* (RFRS 3.8.1)

Requirement #1 states:

> *Any extension that converts resources from one format into another where the resources are synchronized, such as compilers, must use the build APIs and* `org.eclipse.core.resources.builders` *extension point.*

To pass this requirement, start by showing your builder in action. Describe how it is invoked and what resources it transforms. Turn off the **Build automatically** preference on the **General > Workspace** preference page and show that your builder does not run. Invoke the **Project > Rebuild Project** command to show that your builder correctly processes any accumulated changes.

14.4.2 *Do not replace existing builders* (RFRS 3.8.3)

Requirement #2 states:

> *Extensions cannot replace the builders associated with project natures provided by the workbench, or by other vendors.*

Start by configuring a project to use your builder. Open the project's `.project` file to show that your builder has been added and that none of the existing builders, such as `org.eclipse.jdt.core.javabuilder`, have been removed.

14.4.3 *Do not misuse the term "build"* (RFRS 5.3.8.1)

Best Practice #3 states:

> *The term "build" should not be overloaded to have a meaning other than build processing triggered using the Eclipse build APIs. That is, do not use the term "build" in your product implementation or documentation to describe a process that is not implemented as a builder in the workbench.*

Show any places in your product documentation where the term "build" is used and confirm that any such uses are related to your plug-in's builders.

14.4.4　Mark created resources as "derived"　　　　(RFRS 5.3.8.2)

Best Practice #4 states:

> Resources created by builders should be identified as derived when they are not source (as in .java), or some other type of artifact that can be or will be modified by the user, or are required for deployment to a runtime platform.

For this test, demonstrate that any resources created by your builder are marked as derived. In the case of a .class file created by the Java compiler, you would open the **Properties** dialog and show that the **Derived** option has been checked (see Figure 14–14).

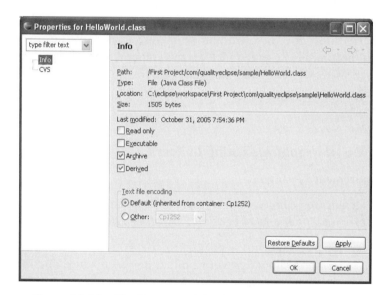

Figure 14–14　　The Properties dialog for the HelloWorld.class file.

14.4.5　Respond to clean-build requests　　　　　(RFRS 5.3.8.3)

Best Practice #5 states:

> Builders should respond to CLEAN_BUILD requests. A CLEAN_BUILD request asks the builder to forget any additional build state it has maintained privately using an overridden version of the clean() method. A user-invoked clean request is followed by a FULL_BUILD request.

For this test, check that the outputs of the builder in question exist and note their timestamp using the **Properties** view. Invoke a CLEAN_BUILD request (**Projects > Clean…**). Verify that the outputs of the builder being tested have been recreated (check timestamps) and that the builder ran to completion without errors (check the error log).

14.4.6   Use IResourceProxy when possible   *(RFRS 5.3.8.4)*

Best Practice #6 states:

> *Builders often need to process all the resources in a project when an* IncrementalProjectBuilder.FULL_BUILD *has been requested. There is an improved technique available starting with Eclipse 2.1. An* IResourceProxyVisitor *should be used in place of an* IResource-Visitor. *The proxy visitor provides access to lightweight* IResourceProxy *objects. These can return a real* IResource *object when required, but when not required, they result in improved overall builder performance for full builds.*

To pass this test, you should avoid using IResourceVisitor objects and use IResourceProxyVistor objects instead. Search your plug-in source code for references to IResourceVisitor and explain why IResourceProxy-Visitor could not be used instead.

14.4.7   Builders must be added by natures   *(RFRS 5.3.8.5)*

Best Practice #7 states:

> *A builder must be added to a project by a nature. The nature implementation, as identified in the* org.eclipse.core.resources.natures *extension, will add any builders required as part of the* configure() *method.*

For this test, show your nature definition in the plugin.xml file. Create a project with your nature and demonstrate that the builder is automatically configured. Add your nature to an existing project's .project file and show that your builder is invoked as soon as the file is saved.

14.5   Summary

This chapter went into detail about how to create builders, markers, and natures. Builders execute in response to resource changes within a project. Builders can create new, derived resources or tag existing resources with markers. Markers are used to tag locations within a resource, while natures are used to tag entire projects and configure any associated builders.

References

Chapter source (*www.qualityeclipse.com/projects/source-ch-14.zip*).

Arthorne, John, "Project Builders and Natures," IBM OTI Labs, 2003 (*www.eclipse.org/articles/Article-Builders/builders.html*).

Glozic, Dejan and Jeff McAffer, "Mark My Words: Using Markers to Tell Users about Problems and Tasks," IBM OTI Labs, 2001 (*www.eclipse.org/articles/Article-Mark%20My%20Words/Mark%20My%20Words.html*).

CHAPTER 15

Implementing Help

No matter how wonderful and easy-to-use your plug-in might be, eventually, users will have questions about how some feature works or they might want further detail on some operation or setting. Fortunately, Eclipse provides a comprehensive framework for including online help within applications.

This chapter begins with an overview of how to access the Eclipse help system and then follows up with a discussion of how to implement help for your application. After that, there is a discussion about how to add context-sensitive (F1) help and then an illustration of how to programmatically access the help system. It finishes up with a discussion of how to guide the user through a series of tasks using a cheat sheet.

15.1 Using Help

Users can access your full product documentation by using the **Help > Help Contents** menu (see Figure 15–1), which opens the Eclipse **Help** window (see Figure 15–2). The **Help** window is separate from the Eclipse workbench window, which makes it easy to switch back and forth between the two.

In early versions of Eclipse, the **Help** window was originally implemented as its own perspective. This made it difficult to access the help system while working with various workbench facilities (especially modal dialogs or wizards).

Figure 15–1   The Eclipse Help menu.

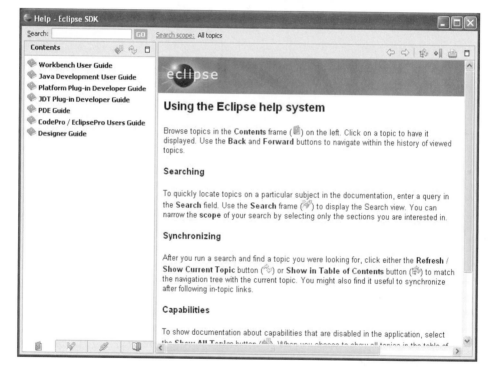

Figure 15–2   The Eclipse Help window.

The **Help** window has several major components. At the upper left is a
Search field. Entering a search term and clicking the **Go** button will cause the
help system to search all the help topics in the system. Putting quotes around
the search term causes an *exact match* search rather than the default *stemmed
search*. A *stemmed search* uses word roots and will yield more hits than an
exact match search, but it is not as helpful when searching for an exact word
or phrase.

At the right of the **Search** field is a link that is used to set the search scope. Clicking on the **Search scope** link will open the **Select Search Scope** dialog (see Figure 15–3).

Figure 15–3   The Select Search Scope dialog.

Within this dialog, you can choose to search all available topics or select a set of topics defined as a working set. Clicking the **New...** button in the dialog will allow you to create a new working set composed of top-level help topics (see Figure 15–4). Click the **OK** button in both dialogs to return to the **Help** window.

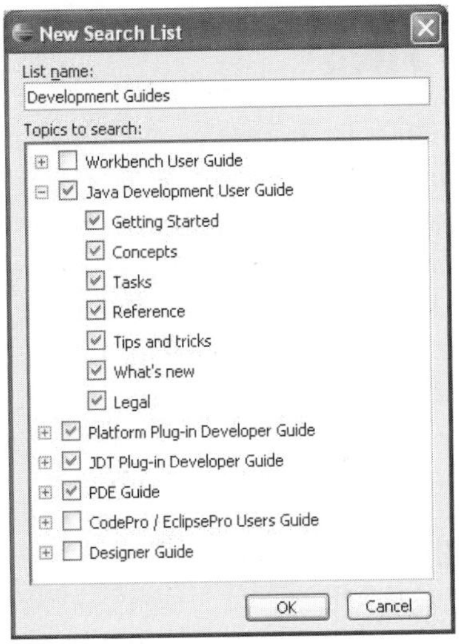

Figure 15–4   The New Search List dialog.

Below the search fields is a list of top-level help books available in the system. Here you will find built-in help books such as the Eclipse *Workbench User Guide* and *Platform Plug-in Developer Guide*, as well as books contributed by other plug-ins. Each book can be expanded to show its individual help topics. Selecting a help topic will display that help page in the content area to the right of the topic list (see Figure 15–5).

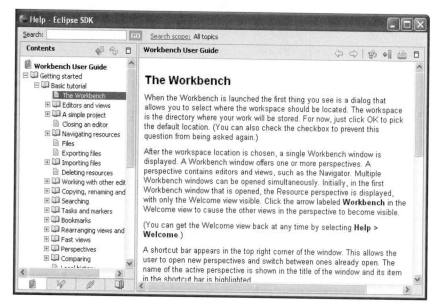

Figure 15–5   The Help window showing a selected help topic.

15.2   Implementing Help

Eclipse provides the infrastructure necessary to plug your own help documentation into the environment. Eclipse doesn't care how the help files are created and will happily uses content created in HTML or PDF format (you can even create dynamic, "active," help using XHTML if you want to). Your help can either be integrated into main plug-in or it can be placed into its own standalone plug-in (this is the common practice in the base Eclipse plug-ins).

After you have created your help content, assuming simple Hypertext Markup Language (HTML) files for the moment, integrating them into Eclipse involves four simple steps:

1. Create a new plug-in project to contain your help plug-in.
2. Set up your help file directory structure within the project.
3. Update the table of contents (toc) files to reference your help files.
4. Update the plug-in manifest to reference the toc files.

15.2.1   Creating a new help project

Because of the power of the Eclipse project creation wizards, most of the files needed to set up your help project can be generated automatically. You will begin by using the **New Project** wizard to create a new **Plug-in Project** (see Figure 15–6). There are quite a few steps involved in creating a project, but they are worth the time given how much of the project structure will be created automatically.

Figure 15–6   The New Project wizard.

On the first page of the **New Plug-in Project** wizard (see Figure 15–7), enter "com.qualityeclipse.favorites.help" as the project name. Leave the **Use default** checkbox checked so that the project is created within the default workspace. Finally, uncheck the **Create a Java project** option since you don't want any Java files to be created.

On the second page of the wizard (see Figure 15–8), leave the plug-in ID as "com.qualityeclipse.favorites.help", and change the name to "Favorites Help." Since you disabled the Java project option and don't plan to execute any Java code, there is no need for a plug-in startup class.

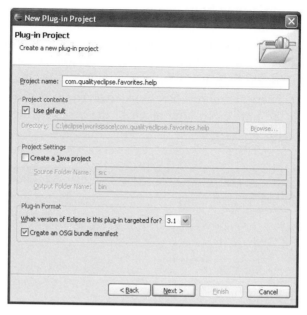

Figure 15–7   The New Plug-in Project wizard.

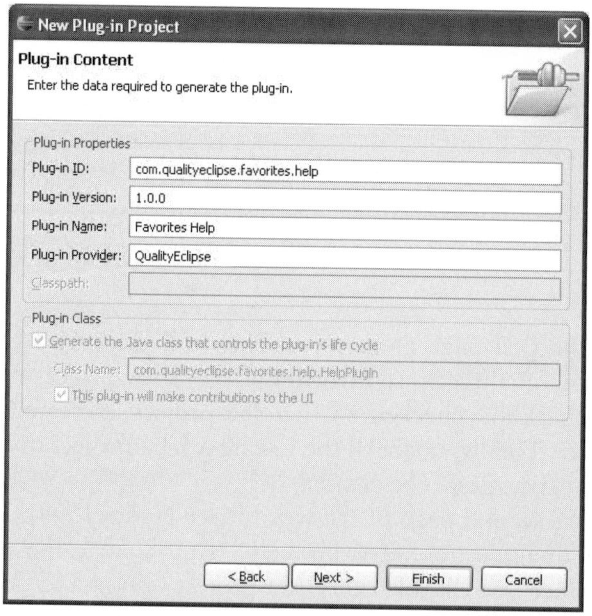

Figure 15–8   The Plug-in Content page.

Click the **Finish** button to create the project. The initial project configuration will contain a number of files including the initial project manifest file, MANIFEST.MF, which is automatically opened in the manifest file editor (see Figure 15–9). If you switch to the **MANIFEST.MF** page of the editor, you should see the following content:

```
Manifest-Version: 1.0
Bundle-ManifestVersion: 2
Bundle-Name: Favorites Help
Bundle-SymbolicName: com.qualityeclipse.favorites.help
Bundle-Version: 1.0.0
Bundle-Vendor: QualityEclipse
Bundle-Localization: plugin
```

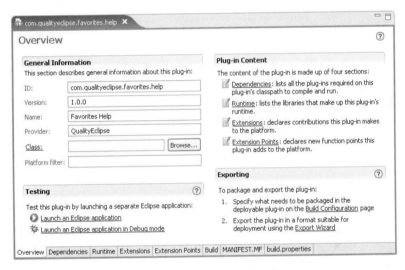

Figure 15–9   The Plug-in manifest file Overview page.

At this point, you have an empty project without any help content. Switch to the **Extensions** page of the manifest editor and click the **Add...** button to open the **New Extension** wizard. Switch to the **Extensions Wizards** tab and select **Help Content** in the right-hand list (see Figure 15–10).

On the next page of the wizard (see Figure 15–11), set the **Label for table of contents** field to "Favorites Guide". This is the name of the book that will show up as a top-level item in the **Help** window's contents pane. Next, select the **Primary** option. This will create a primary toc file. Primary toc files represent the top-level items in the **Help** window. Any number of toc files can exist in the project, but they will all be subordinate to one or more primary toc files.

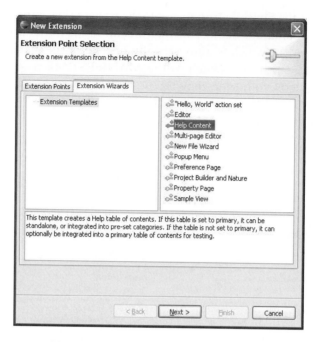

Figure 15–10   The Extension Wizard page.

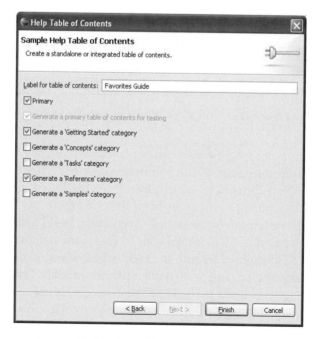

Figure 15–11   The Help Table of Contents page.

Finally, you are given the choice of creating one or more of several predefined secondary toc files covering major topic areas within the help documentation. Creating secondary toc files is optional. All your help files may be easily referenced from your main toc file. Partitioning help using multiple secondary toc files provides more granularity and makes it easier for several people to update different parts of the documentation without colliding. Here, select the options for creating **Getting Started** and **Reference** categories to illustrate how the various files are structured. Click **Finish** to complete the process and generate all the files.

15.2.2   Plug-in manifest files

Given the options selected earlier, a variety of files will be created (see Figure 15–12), including several dummy HTML files and the following XML files: `plugin.xml`, `toc.xml`, `tocgettingstarted.xml`, and `tocreference.xml`.

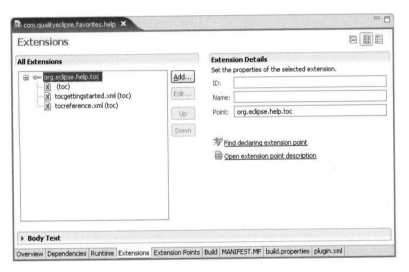

Figure 15–12   The Extensions page of the manifest editor.

If you switch to the **plugin.xml** page of the editor, you should see the following content.

```
<?xml version="1.0" encoding="UTF-8"?>
<?eclipse version="3.0"?>
<plugin>
   <extension
        point="org.eclipse.help.toc">
      <toc
           file="toc.xml"
           primary="true"/>
      <toc file="tocgettingstarted.xml"/>
      <toc file="tocreference.xml"/>
   </extension>
</plugin>
```

The most important thing here is the extension of the **org.eclipse.help.toc** extension point. This extension point is used to specify the primary and secondary toc files. The `file` attribute is used to specify the names of the toc files that will be used, while the `primary` attribute indicates whether an individual toc file should appear as a top-level book in the help topics list in the **Help** window. Any toc files without the `primary` attribute set to `true` will not show up unless they are linked to from one or more of the primary toc files.

The **org.eclipse.help.toc** extension point also defines an additional, rarely used `extradir` attribute that specifies the name of a directory that contains additional documentation files. Unless they are referenced by a specific topic element in one of the toc files, these files won't be accessible via the topics list, but they will be indexed and accessible via the help search facility.

15.2.3   *Table of contents (toc) files*

Next, let's take a look at a couple of the generated toc files. The `toc.xml` file represents the primary help topic entry for the plug-in and looks like this:

```
<?xml version="1.0" encoding="UTF-8"?>
<?NLS TYPE="org.eclipse.help.toc"?>

<toc label="Favorites Guide" topic="html/toc.html">
   <topic label="Getting Started">
      <anchor id="gettingstarted"/>
   </topic>
   <topic label="Reference">
      <anchor id="reference"/>
   </topic>
</toc>
```

Within the toc file, the `label` attributes specify the text that is displayed in the topic list, while the `topic` attribute specifies a link to a single documentation page that should be displayed when that topic is selected.

The structure of this toc file illustrates how the help topic tree can be built out of multiple, nested toc files. Eclipse supports two different approaches to building the help topic tree: top-down nesting and bottom-up composition. The aforementioned toc file illustrates the latter. In bottom-up composition, the toc file will define various *anchor points* to which other toc files can contribute additional topics.

Here, two subtopics have been defined for the documentation—"Getting Started" and "Reference"—each of which defines an anchor point (essentially an empty container for other toc files to fill). Note that each of these subtopics could have also defined its own hard-coded documentation links (you will see an example of this in the next toc file you examine).

Next, examine one of the two remaining toc files (both follow the same pattern, so you only need to look at one of them). The `tocgettingstarted.xml` file looks like this:

```xml
<?xml version="1.0" encoding="UTF-8"?>
<?NLS TYPE="org.eclipse.help.toc"?>

<toc label="Getting Started" link_to="toc.xml#gettingstarted">
    <topic label="Main Topic"
       href="html/gettingstarted/maintopic.html">
        <topic label="Sub Topic"
            href="html/gettingstarted/subtopic.html" />
    </topic>
    <topic label="Main Topic 2">
        <topic label="Sub Topic 2"
            href="html/gettingstarted/subtopic2.html" />
    </topic>
</toc>
```

This toc file provides topic links to the actual HTML files representing the plug-in's documentation using the `href` attributes (you will replace the default boilerplate generated by the wizard with links to the documentation files later). The most interesting aspect of this toc file is the use of the `link_to` attribute to link this file to the `gettingstarted` anchor in the main toc file.

> **Tip:** Note that your plug-in help pages are not limited to only linking in to your own anchor points. The core Eclipse documentation provides numerous anchor points to which you can attach help files. If your plug-in augments one of the basic Eclipse functions, linking your help pages to the appropriate section of the Eclipse docs is a nice touch.

Both of the toc files just reviewed provide an example of bottom-up composition with the secondary toc files linking to the primary toc file while the primary toc file has no knowledge of the secondary toc files. This approach closely mirrors the extension point concept used within Eclipse. The opposite approach of top-down nesting switches this around such that the main toc file will directly link to the secondary toc files.

Converting these two toc files to use the top-down approach is simple. First, replace the anchor attributes in the primary toc file with link attributes pointing to the secondary toc files. The toc.xml file will now look like this:

```
<?xml version="1.0" encoding="UTF-8"?>
<?NLS TYPE="org.eclipse.help.toc"?>

<toc label="Favorites Guide" topic="html/toc.html">
   <topic label="Getting Started">
      <link toc="tocgettingstarted.xml"/>
   </topic>
   <topic label="Reference">
      <link toc="tocreference.xml"/>
   </topic>
</toc>
```

Next, you can remove the link_to attribute from the secondary toc files as it is no longer needed.

> Tip: The top-down approach provides better control over the visibility of which files are included in the help documentation and does not provide any opportunities for other entities to augment the help provided by the plug-in. Conversely, the bottom-up approach provides a great deal of flexibility in structuring the help documentation and organically growing it over time with additional contributions both from within and outside the plug-in.

Internationalization   If your application needs to support multiple languages, your toc files and documentation files may be translated into multiple languages and placed into specially named subdirectories of your plug-in's root directory (for more information, see Chapter 16, Internationalization).

The translated files should be placed into the nl/<language> or nl/<language>/<country> directory, where <language> and <country> represent the two-letter codes used to signify the target language and country. For example, Brazilian translations would be placed into the nl/pt/br directory, while standard Portuguese translations would be placed into the nl/pt directory.

The help system will first look in the nl/<language>/<country> directory. If nothing is found there, the nl/<language> will be used instead. If no translation for the target language is found, it will default to using the files found in the root of the plug-in directory.

15.2.4   *Creating HTML content*

In addition to the XML files, the wizard creates several dummy HTML files.

```
html/
    gettingstarted/
        maintopic.html
        subtopic.html
        subtopic2.html
    reference/
        maintopic.html
        subtopic.html
        subtopic2.html
    toc.html
```

Assume that you create your own documentation files for the **Favorites** view with the following structure:

```
html/
    gettingstarted/
        installation.html
        favorites_view.html
        adding_favorites.html
        removing_favorites.html
    reference/
        view.html
        actions.html
        preferences.html
    toc.html
```

The, you would need to update the two secondary toc files. For example, the `tocgettingstarted.xml` file, would end up looking like this:

```
<?xml version="1.0" encoding="UTF-8"?>
<?NLS TYPE="org.eclipse.help.toc"?>

<toc label="Getting Started">
  <topic label="Installation"
    href="html/gettingstarted/installation.html"/>
  <topic label="Favorites View"
    href="html/gettingstarted/favorites_view.html">
    <topic label="Adding Favorites"
      href="html/gettingstarted/adding_favorites.html" />
    <topic label="Removing Favorites"
      href="html/gettingstarted/removing_favorites.html" />
  </topic>
</toc>
```

> **Tip:** If your application needs more than a handful of help files, you might consider placing all of them into a single ZIP file. If you package your help files into a file called `doc.zip` (preserving the same directory structure), Eclipse will be able to find them. Eclipse will look for help files in the `doc.zip` file before looking for them in the plug-in directory.

With these changes, the help plug-in is functionally complete! Launching Eclipse with this new help plug-in in place will add the **Favorites Guide** to the list of books in the **Help** window (see Figure 15–13).

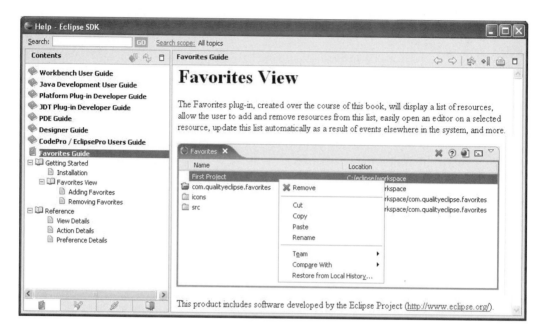

Figure 15–13   The Help window showing the *Favorites Guide*.

Dynamic Help Content in Eclipse 3.2   The Eclipse 3.2 help system supports dynamic help composition using XHTML. Help pages can use Eclipse-specific markup to provide filtering based on os/ws/arch values, enabled capabilities, existence of plug-ins, etc. Content may also be reused in multiple documents by using a new `<include>` tag. These features allow the help content to adapt to the context at the time of viewing. For more information on using XHTML in Eclipse, see: *www.eclipse.org/eclipse/platform-ua/proposals/xhtml/HelpDynamicContent.html.*

15.3   Context-Sensitive Help (F1)

Eclipse provides support for context-sensitive help for widgets, windows, actions, and menus using the **F1** key. This help can appear either in a floating "infopop" window or within the dynamic **Help** view depending on the user's **Help** preferences. The context-sensitive help that appears can contain a small amount of help for the selected item as well as links to more detailed documentation. For example, opening the Eclipse **Hierarchy** view and pressing **F1** will show context-sensitive help (see Figure 15–14) containing links relevant to the **Hierarchy** view as well as to views in general.

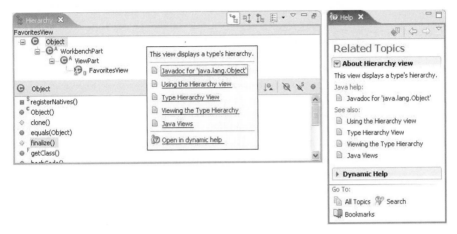

Figure 15–14   The Hierarchy view showing its associated context-sensitive help in an infopop window on the left and the dynamic Help view on the right.

To add context-sensitive help to an item, you need to associate a context ID with the item, provide a short description of the item, and create a list of links relevant to the item.

15.3.1   *Associating context IDs with items*

Whenever a user opens the **Favorites** view and presses **F1**, it would be best to have the context-sensitive help appear. First, you need to associate a context ID with the view using the `setHelp()` method from `org.eclipse.ui.help.` `IWorkbenchHelpSystem`.

The context ID is a string with the form `<plug-in-id>.<local-context-id>`, where `<plug-in-id>` is the unique plug-in identifier for the plug-in defining the workbench view or editor and `<local-context-id>` is an identifier unique within that plug-in identifying the context. The `<local-context-id>` can be composed of any alphanumeric characters and an underscore ("_"), but must not contain any whitespace or periods ("."). In this case, the `<plug-in-id>` is "com.qualityeclipse.favorites" and you have chosen a `<local-context-id>` of "favorites_view" for your **Favorites** view, so the context ID is "com.qualityeclipse.favorites.favorites_view".

Since the **Favorites** view consists of a single table widget, you will associate the help context ID with the table widget itself. Begin by creating a `setHelpContextIDs()` method in the `FavoritesView` class that looks like the following:

```
// FavoritesView.java
private void setHelpContextIDs() {
   IWorkbenchHelpSystem helpSystem =
      getSite().getWorkbenchWindow().getWorkbench().getHelpSystem();

   helpSystem.setHelp(
      viewer.getControl(),
      "com.qualityeclipse.favorites.favorites_view");
}
```

The, you can call this method from the existing `createPartControl()` method in the `FavoritesView` class.

Help contexts are inherited by child controls. In this case, a help context was assigned to the **Favorites** viewer control, which has no children. If you were to assign a help context to a composite, then its children will inherit the same help context unless you specifically override it by calling `setHelp()` on a child control.

The **Favorites** view also defines several different actions with which you would like to associate help context IDs. Do this by enhancing the `setHelpContextIDs()` method as follows:

```
private void setHelpContextIDs() {
   IWorkbenchHelpSystem helpSystem =
      getSite().getWorkbenchWindow().getWorkbench().getHelpSystem();

   // Assign a context ID to the view.
   helpSystem.setHelp(
      viewer.getControl(),
      "com.qualityeclipse.favorites.favorites_view");

   // Assign context IDs to the actions.
   helpSystem.setHelp(copyAction,
      "com.qualityeclipse.favorites.copyAction");
   helpSystem.setHelp(cutAction,
      "com.qualityeclipse.favorites.cutAction");
   helpSystem.setHelp(pasteAction,
      "com.qualityeclipse.favorites.pasteAction");
   helpSystem.setHelp(removeAction,
      "com.qualityeclipse.favorites.removeAction");
   helpSystem.setHelp(renameAction,
      "com.qualityeclipse.favorites.renameAction");
}
```

Help context IDs can also be assigned to actions defined within the plug-in manifest file by defining a `helpContextId` attribute. For example, you can enhance the definition of the "Open Favorites View" action like this:

```
<action
    class="com.qualityeclipse.favorites.actions.
            OpenFavoritesViewActionDelegate"
    icon="icons/sample.gif"
    id="com.qualityeclipse.favorites.openFavoritesView"
    label="Open Favorites View"
    menubarPath="com.qualityeclipse.favorites.workbenchMenu/content"
    style="push"
    toolbarPath="Normal/additions"
    tooltip="Open the favorites view in the current workbench page"
    helpContextId="favorites_view"/>
```

Note that if local context identifiers are used in the plug-in manifest, then the unique identifier for the declaring plug-in is prepended to make the full context identifier.

15.3.2   IWorkbenchHelpSystem API

The `IWorkbenchHelpSystem` interface defines a number of useful APIs for assigning help context IDs and programmatically displaying help, such as:

`displayContext(IContext context, int x, int y)`—Displays context-sensitive help for the given context.

`displayDynamicHelp()`—Displays the dynamic entire help for the current UI context.

`displayHelp()`—Displays the entire help bookshelf.

`displayHelp(IContext context)`—Displays context-sensitive help for the given context.

`displayHelp(String contextId)`—Calls the help support system to display the given help context ID.

`displayHelpResource(String href)`—Displays the help content for the help resource with the given uniform resource locator (URL).

`displaySearch()`—Displays the help search system.

`hasHelpUI()`—Returns whether there is a UI help system installed.

`isContextHelpDisplayed()`—Returns whether the context-sensitive help window is currently being displayed.

`search(String expression)`—Starts the search using the help search system.

`setHelp(Control control, String contextId)`—Sets the given help context ID on the given control.

`setHelp(IAction action, String contextId)`—Sets the given help context ID on the given action.

`setHelp(MenuItem item, String contextId)`—Sets the given help context ID on the given menu item.

`setHelp(Menu menu, String contextId)`—Sets the given help context ID on the given menu.

15.3.3   Creating context-sensitive help content

When context IDs have been assigned to views, you need to create the content for each help item, which consists of a description and a set of links. This content is described in one or more context manifest files in XML format. For the items assigned context IDs in the previous section, the `contexts.xml` file might look like this:

```
<contexts>
   <context
      id="favorites_view">
      <description>This is the Favorites view.</description>
      <topic href="html/gettingstarted/favorites_view.html"
         label="Using the Favorites View"/>
      <topic href="html/gettingstarted/installation.html"
         label="Installing the Favorites View"/>
      <topic href="html/reference/preferences.html"
         label="Favorites View Preferences"/>
   </context>
   <context id="copyAction">
      <description>
         This command copies a Favorites item from the view.
      </description>
      <topic href="html/gettingstarted/actions.html"
         label="Favorites View Actions"/>
   </context>
   <context id="cutAction">
      <description>
         This command cuts a Favorites item from the view.
      </description>
      <topic href="html/gettingstarted/actions.html"
         label="Favorites View Actions"/>
   </context>
   <context id="pasteAction">
      <description>
         This command pastes a Favorites item to the view.
      </description>
      <topic href="html/gettingstarted/actions.html"
         label="Favorites View Actions"/>
   </context>
```

```
<context id="removeAction">
   <description>
      This command removes a Favorites item.
   </description>
   <topic href="html/gettingstarted/actions.html"
      label="Favorites View Actions"/>
</context>
<context id="renameAction">
   <description>
      This command renames a Favorites item.
   </description>
   <topic href="html/gettingstarted/actions.html"
      label="Favorites View Actions"/>
</context>
</contexts>
```

Within the `contexts.xml` file, each context ID is described by its own *context element*. Each context element has a *description element* and zero or more *topic elements* that link to the actual documentation. Each topic element has an `href` attribute providing the link and a `label` attribute describing the text of the link, as it will appear in the context-sensitive help.

15.3.4   Context extension point

Now that context IDs have been associated with the view and actions and the context for each help item has been defined, you need to update your `plugin.xml` file to point to the `contexts.xml` file and associate it with the main plug-in. The built-in Eclipse wizards make this easy.

Start by opening the `plugin.xml` file in the help project and switching to the **Extensions** page (see Figure 15–15). Next, click the **Add...** button.

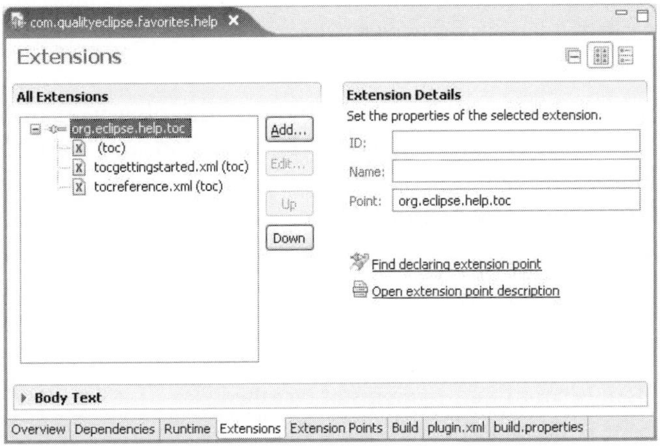

Figure 15–15   The Favorites Help manifest file showing the Extensions page.

When the **New Extension** wizard opens, select `org.eclipse.help.`
`contexts` from the list of all available extension points (see Figure 15–16). If
you don't see `org.eclipse.help.contexts` in the list, uncheck the **Show
only extension points from the required plug-ins** checkbox. Click the **Finish**
button to add this extension to the plug-in manifest.

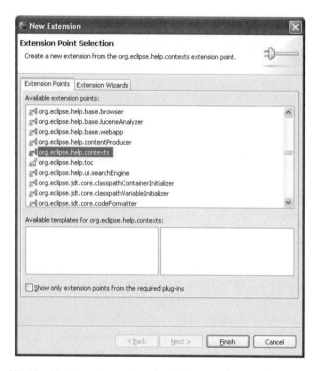

Figure 15–16   The New Extension wizard showing the org.eclipse.help.contexts
extension point selected.

Now, back in the **Extensions** page of the plug-in manifest editor, right-
click on the **org.eclipse.help.contexts** extension and select **New > contexts**.
This immediately adds a context item to the plug-in manifest. Clicking on this
new context item reveals the properties so that they can be modified as follows
(see Figure 15–17):

file—"contexts.xml"
The name of the context's XML file.

plugin—"com.qualityeclipse.favorites"
The text label associated with the perspective.

Extension Element Details
Set the properties of "contexts"

file*: contexts.xml   Browse...

plugin: com.qualityeclipse.favorites

Figure 15–17   The extension element details showing Favorites
context file attributes.

If you switch to the **plugin.xml** page of the plug-in manifest editor, you
will see the following new section of XML defining the new context file:

```
<extension
   point="org.eclipse.help.contexts">
   <contexts
      file="contexts.xml"
      plugin="com.qualityeclipse.favorites">
   </contexts>
</extension>
```

The plugin attribute is important for associating this context file with the
com.qualityeclipse.favorites plug-in. If that is not specified, the context file is associated with the local plug-in in which it is defined.

Note that multiple context files from different plug-ins can be associated
with the context ID. This allows one plug-in to extend the context help provided by another.

Now that you have completed the definition of the context-sensitive help,
you can test it by opening the **Favorites** view and pressing **F1**. The help content
for the "favorites_view" context ID should appear in the **Help** view (see Figure 15–18) or the floating infopop window.

Figure 15–18   The Help view showing context-sensitive
help for the Favorites view.

15.3.5   Marker help

The `org.eclipse.ui.ide.markerHelp` extension point allows plug-ins to associate a help context ID with a particular marker type. Chapter 14, Builders, Markers, and Natures, had one marker type representing two different violations, so you needed to further qualify the help declaration, creating one declaration for each type of violation. The expression `<attribute name="violation" value="1"/>` indicates that the help context should only be applied to markers having a `violation` attribute with a value of '1'.

```
<extension point="org.eclipse.ui.ide.markerHelp">
   <markerHelp
      markerType="com.qualityeclipse.favorites.auditmarker"
      helpContextId="com.qualityeclipse.favorites
         .violationHelp1">
      <attribute name="violation" value="1"/>
   </markerHelp>
   <markerHelp
      markerType="com.qualityeclipse.favorites.auditmarker"
      helpContextId="com.qualityeclipse.favorites
         .violationHelp2">
      <attribute name="violation" value="2"/>
   </markerHelp>
</extension>
```

The help content for the violation markers is defined as part of the `contexts.xml` file (see Section 15.3.3, Creating context-sensitive help content, on page 556).

15.4   Accessing Help Programmatically

So far, you have seen how to integrate help into the Eclipse **Help** window and access it using standard Eclipse mechanisms such as the **Help > Help Contents** menu and the **F1** key. There may be times when you want to provide help in ways other than the standard mechanisms.

As seen earlier, the `IWorkbenchHelpSystem` interface defines a large number of useful APIs. This section concentrates on a couple of the `display` methods.

To programmatically open the **Help** window, call the `displayHelp()` method without an argument. To programmatically open context-sensitive help for a specific context ID, call the `displayHelp()` method with the context ID string as the single argument. For example, to open the context-sensitive help associated with the **Favorites** view, use the following code.

```
PlatformUI.getWorkbench().getHelpSystem().displayHelp(
    "com.qualityeclipse.favorites.favorites_view");
```

15.4.1 Opening a specific help page

The most interesting API, however, is the `displayHelpReource()` method, which takes a single string argument representing the path to the help page to be displayed. For example, to open the main help page for the **Favorites** plug-in, use the following code:

```
PlatformUI.getWorkbench().getHelpSystem().displayHelpResource(
    "/com.qualityeclipse.favorites.help/html/toc.html");
```

The path argument is composed of the ID of the plug-in containing the help file and the path to the resource relative to the plug-in root directory. Based on this last example, you can easily add a custom help button to the toolbar of the **Favorites** view (see Figure 15–19) by creating the following method in the `FavoritesView` class and calling it from the `createPartControl()` method.

```
private void addHelpButtonToToolBar() {
    final IWorkbenchHelpSystem helpSystem =
        getSite().getWorkbenchWindow().getWorkbench().getHelpSystem();
    Action helpAction = new Action() {
        public void run() {
            helpSystem.displayHelpResource(
                "/com.qualityeclipse.favorites.help" +
                "/html/toc.html");
        }
    };
    helpAction.setToolTipText("Open the Favorites view help");
    helpAction.setImageDescriptor(
        ImageDescriptor.createFromFile(
            FavoritesView.class, "help.gif"));
    getViewSite()
        .getActionBars()
        .getToolBarManager()
        .add(helpAction);
}
```

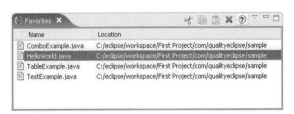

Figure 15–19 The Favorites view with the new help button showing.

15.4.2 Opening a Web page

In addition to opening a specific help page in the Eclipse **Help** window, you might want to open a Web browser on a specific Web page. Eclipse includes a class, `org.eclipse.swt.program.Program`, which is used to launch external programs, including the system Web browser. In particular, you are interested in the `launch()` method, which takes a string encoding the path to the program to be launched or the URL of the Web page to be accessed.

You can now add a button to the **Favorites** view's toolbar (see Figure 15-20) that will open a specific Web page (use the Web page for this book as an example). Do this by adding the following method to the `FavoritesView` class and calling it from the `createPartControl()` method.

```
private void addWebButtonToToolBar() {
   Action webAction = new Action() {
      public void run() {
         Program.launch("http://www.qualityeclipse.com");
      }
   };

   webAction.setToolTipText("Open a web page");
   webAction.setImageDescriptor(
      ImageDescriptor.createFromFile(
         FavoritesView.class, "web.gif"));

   getViewSite()
      .getActionBars()
      .getToolBarManager()
      .add(webAction);
}
```

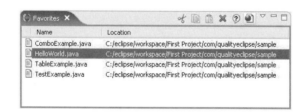

Figure 15–20   The Favorites view with the new Web button showing

This technique works very well for Windows but will not work on other platforms such as Linux. For an alternative approach that will work on any platform, see Section 20.4, Opening a Browser or Creating an Email, on page 718.

> **Tip:** You can use this technique to generate an email message from your application back to your sales or support group. For example, executing the following:
>
> ```
> Program.launch(
>     "mailto:info@qualityeclipse.com" +
>     "?Subject=Information Request")
> ```
>
> will generate an email message with the subject `Information Request`. Embedding a "`?Body=`" tag gives you the ability to pre-populate the body of the message with information such as the user's Eclipse configuration.

15.5   Cheat Sheets

In addition to the static help provided through the Eclipse Help system and the context-sensitive help provided through the dynamic **Help** view and infopop windows, Eclipse includes *cheat sheets* that are designed to walk you through a series of steps to complete a task and automatically launch any required tools.

15.5.1   Using a cheat sheet

Users can access your product's cheat sheets via the **Help > Cheat Sheets...** menu (see Figure 15–21).

Figure 15–21   The Eclipse Cheat Sheets
menu item.

This will open the Eclipse **Cheat Sheet Selection** dialog (see Figure 15–22). Available cheat sheets are grouped by category. Double-click on a cheat sheet or select one and click the **OK** button.

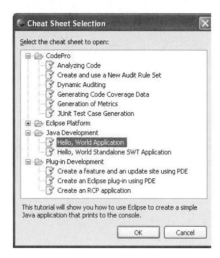

Figure 15–22   The Cheat Sheet selection dialog.

The selected cheat sheet will open as a view (see Figure 15–23). Only one cheat sheet can be active at one time, so any currently open cheat sheet will be closed first. Every cheat sheet starts with an introduction followed by a set of steps. After reading the introduction, you can begin working with the cheat sheet by clicking on the **Click to Begin** button. This will expand and highlight the next step. Use the **Click to Perform** button to execute the task associated with that step. Once completed, the next task in the sequence will be highlighted. If a step is optional, you may also skip it with the **Click to Skip** button. After the last step in the cheat sheet is completed, it will automatically restart.

Figure 15–23   An example cheat sheet.

15.5.2   Creating a simple cheat sheet

Creating a cheat sheet requires several steps. Start by opening the `plugin.xml` file in the help project and switching to the **Extensions** page. Next, click the **Add...** button. When the **New Extension** wizard opens, uncheck the **Show only extension points from the required plug-ins** checkbox and select `org.eclipse.ui.cheatsheets.cheatSheetContent` from the list of all available extension points (see Figure 15–24). Click the **Finish** button to add this extension to the plug-in manifest. Answer **Yes** when asked whether to add a dependency on the `org.eclipse.ui.cheatsheets` plug-in.

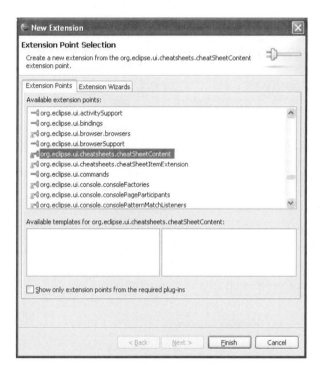

Figure 15–24   The New Extension wizard showing the org.eclipse.ui.cheatsheets.cheatSheetContent extension point selected.

Every cheat sheet must exist in a category, so create one before creating the cheat sheet itself. In the **Extensions** page of the plug-in manifest editor, right-click on the **org.eclipse.ui.cheatsheets.cheatSheetContent** extension and select **New > category**. This adds a category to the manifest. Clicking on this new category item reveals the properties so that they can be modified as follows (see Figure 15–25).

id—"com.qualityeclipse.favorites.cheatSheets"
The `id` of the cheat sheet category.

name—"Favorites"
The name of the cheat sheet category.

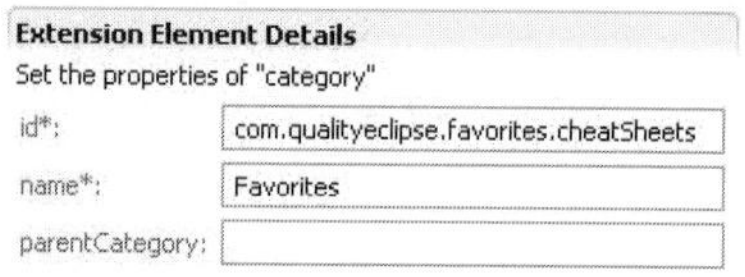

Figure 15–25　The Extension Element Details showing Favorites category attributes.

After creating the category, you can create the cheat sheet itself. Right-click on the **org.eclipse.ui.cheatsheets.cheatSheetContent** extension and select **New > cheatsheet** to add it to the manifest. Clicking on this new cheat sheet item reveals the properties so that they can be modified as follows (see Figure 15–26).

id—"com.qualityeclipse.favorites.cheatsheet"
The `id` of the cheat sheet.

name—"Adding a favorite to the Favorites view"
The name of the cheat sheet.

category—"com.qualityeclipse.favorites.cheatSheets"
The category in which to place the cheat sheet.

contentFile—"cheatsheets/FavoritesCheatSheet.xml"
The path of the cheat sheet content file.

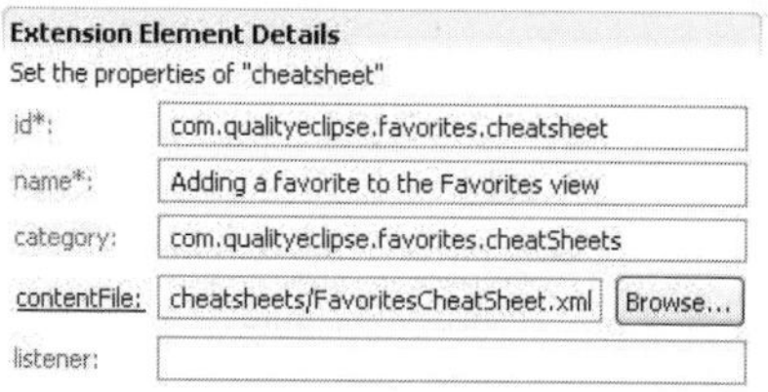

Figure 15–26　The Extension Element Details showing Favorites cheat sheet attributes.

If you switch to the **plugin.xml** page of the plug-in manifest editor, you will see the following new section of XML defining the new cheat sheet and category:

```
<extension
   point="org.eclipse.ui.cheatsheets.cheatSheetContent">
   <category
      id="com.qualityeclipse.favorites.cheatSheets"
      name="Favorites"/>
   <cheatsheet
      category="com.qualityeclipse.favorites.cheatSheets"
      contentFile="cheatsheets/FavoritesCheatSheet.xml"
      id="com.qualityeclipse.favorites.cheatsheet"
      name="Adding a favorite to the Favorites view"/>
</extension>
```

After creating the cheat sheet, you should add a brief description that will be displayed in the **Cheat Sheet Selection** dialog. Add the following to the <cheatsheet> section of the above XML.

```
<description>
   This cheat sheet will show you how to add
   an item to the Favorites view.
</description>
```

The final step is to create the cheat sheet content file. Use the **File > New > File** command and enter "cheatsheets/FavoritesCheatSheet.xml" to create a blank content file. At a minimum, cheat sheets must have an introduction and at least one cheat sheet item, so enter the following into the Favorites-CheatSheet.xml file.

```
<?xml version="1.0" encoding="UTF-8"?>
<cheatsheet title="Adding a favorite to the Favorites view">
   <intro>
      <description>
         This cheat sheet will show you how to add an item
         to the Favorites view.
      </description>
   </intro>
   <item title="Select a file">
      <description>
         Select the file that should be a favorite.
      </description>
   </item>
</cheatsheet>
```

Now that you have completed the definition of the cheat sheet, test it by lauching the Runtime Workbench, opening the **Cheat Sheet Selection** dialog (see Figure 15–27), selecting the **Favorites > Adding a favorite to the Favorites view** item, and then clicking **OK**.

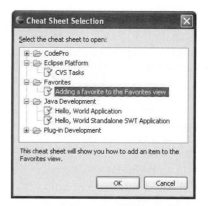

Figure 15–27   The Cheat Sheet Selection dialog showing
the Favorites cheat sheet.

The new Favorites cheat sheet will appear in a new view with its introduction initially expanded (see Figure 15–28).

Figure 15–28   The Favorites Cheat Sheet.

15.5.3   Adding cheat sheet actions

At this point, the cheat sheet is completely static without any interactive elements. Cheat sheets can have active content defined by Eclipse actions. Once the user has selected a file during the first step in the cheat sheet, it would be nice to add a second step that would add that file to the **Favorites** view.

The main plug-in already has an AddToFavoritesActionDelegate class defined (see Section 6.3.3, IObjectActionDelegate, on page 233), which you can use to derive an AddToFavoritesAction class that looks like this:

```
package com.qualityeclipse.favorites.actions;

import ...

public class AddToFavoritesAction extends Action {

   public void run() {
      ISelection selection = PlatformUI
         .getWorkbench()
         .getActiveWorkbenchWindow()
         .getActivePage()
         .getSelection(JavaUI.ID_PACKAGES);

      if (selection instanceof IStructuredSelection) {
         FavoritesManager mgr = FavoritesManager.getManager();
         Iterator iter =
            ((IStructuredSelection) selection).iterator();
         mgr.addFavorites(mgr.newFavoritesFor(iter));
      }
   }
}
```

Note that the above `AddToFavoritesAction` class is rather simple in that it assumes a selection in the **Java Packages** view. It could be improved by allowing a selection in any view but will suffice for the purposes here.

Next, you need to add a new item to the cheat sheet definition, so add the following into the `FavoritesCheatSheet.xml` file.

```
<?xml version="1.0" encoding="UTF-8"?>
<cheatsheet title="Adding a favorite to the Favorites view">
   ...
   <item
      href="/com.qualityeclipse.favorites.help
            /html/gettingstarted/adding_favorites.html"
      title="Select the Favorites > Add command">
      <action
         pluginId="com.qualityeclipse.favorites"
         class="com.qualityeclipse.favorites.actions.
               AddToFavoritesAction"/>
      <description>
         Select the Favorites > Add command.
      </description>
   </item>
   ...
</cheatsheet>
```

The `href` tag is optional and used to link a help page with the cheat sheet task. The link needs to be fully qualified with the name of the plug-in containing the help page, followed by the plug-in relative path to the help page. Even if the help page is in the same plug-in as the cheat sheet, the link must be fully qualified.

The `action` element describes what action will be invoked by the cheat sheet task. The `pluginId` attribute contains the ID of the plug-in containing the action class (the main plug-in in this case). The `class` attribute specifies the fully qualified name of the action class. Any simple action that implements `IAction` can be used here. For more complex actions that require additional parameters or state information from the cheat sheet itself, you can subclass the `org.eclipse.ui.cheatsheets.ICheatSheetAction` class instead.

Now that you have added a second step to the cheat sheet, you can test it as done earlier. After completing the first step of selecting a file, the second step will appear (see Figure 15–29). Use the **Click to Perform** ▷ button to execute the task and add the selected file to the **Favorites** view. Clicking on the **Open Related Help** ⑦ button will open the help page associated with adding an item to the **Favorites** view.

Figure 15–29   The Favorites Cheat Sheet
showing the second task.

15.6   RFRS Considerations

The "Help" section of the *RFRS Requirements* includes nine items—one requirement and eight best practices—dealing with help.

15.6.1   *Provide help through help system*   (RFRS 3.7.2)

Requirement #1 states:

> *Help for the Extension's Eclipse user interface should be provided through the Eclipse help system integrated to it. This includes the interface (menu items, toolbar entries, etc.) used to launch externally integrated*

vendor tools. Help for portions of your tool that are not tightly integrated to Eclipse may be provided through any existing help system it may use.

To pass this requirement, open the plug-in manifest for your help plug-in and point out the use of the `org.eclipse.help.toc` extension point. For the **Favorites** view, point to the following lines from the `plugin.xml` file.

```
<extension point="org.eclipse.help.toc">
   <toc file="toc.xml" primary="true"/>
   <toc file="tocgettingstarted.xml"/>
   <toc file="tocreference.xml"/>
</extension>
```

Next, open up the Eclipse **Help** window and show that your plug-in's help book appears in the main topic list. For the **Favorites** view, you would show that *Favorites Guide* appears in the list (see Figure 15–13 on page 552).

If your plug-in includes online help that is not provided through the Eclipse help system, show it here.

15.6.2 *Provide all help via the help system* (RFRS 5.3.7.1)

Best Practice #2 states:

Provide all help for your plug-in through the Eclipse help system integrated to the Eclipse UI.

As with *Requirement #1*, open the plug-in manifest for your help plug-in and point out the use of the `org.eclipse.help.toc` extension point. Open the Eclipse **Help** window and show that your help book is available. This best practice is actually a refinement of *Requirement #1*, where the only difference is that, to pass this test, your plug-in should provide all its online help through the Eclipse help system.

15.6.3 *Context help activated using F1* (RFRS 5.3.7.2)

Best Practice #3 states:

Context help, if available, should be activated through F1. For products that are tightly integrated, this requires that help be associated with one or more of the SWT or JFace widgets used to construct the user interface.

To pass this test, provide scenarios where pressing **F1** will show context-sensitive infopops for your plug-in. For the **Favorites** view, you would show the infopop associated with that view (see Figure 15–18 on page 559).

15.6.4   Implement active help   *(RFRS 5.3.7.3)*

Best Practice #4 states:

> *Implement active helps for topics that are best illustrated by using work-bench actions. For example, consider a topic called "Importing external plug-ins." Instead of telling the user to go to the workbench and select* **File > Import,** *and then select* **External Plug-ins and Fragments** *and click* **Next,** *the topic could simply say "Click here to open the Import External Fragments wizard." The link would call a class you have defined, which in turn would open the wizard on that page.*

Passing this test is much more difficult as it requires implementing one or more active help elements. Show how your active help elements call back into your plug-in to launch various wizards or other commands. For more information on creating active help, see the "Active Help" topic in the *Platform Plug-in Developer Guide* included in the online Eclipse documentation.

15.6.5   Use of stand-alone help   *(RFRS 5.3.7.4)*

Best Practice #5 states:

> *If help is not tightly integrated to the Eclipse UI, then use stand-alone help or a Web server-based information center.*

This test is basically the reverse of *Best Practice #2,* so only one or the other can be passed (good thing they are not both listed as requirements). For this test, demonstrate any non-workbench-based help provided with your application. For the **Favorites** view, the Web page access button added earlier might qualify.

15.6.6   Use of additional documentation   *(RFRS 5.3.7.5)*

Best Practice #6 states:

> *If additional documentation is provided (beyond readme files), it should be included in one of the plug-in directories used to implement the product or provide integrated help. This might be in a* \doc *subdirectory or a plug-in directory with a name such as* co.tool.doc.

> *Last-minute additions to the documentation or other product guidance that did not make it into the integrated documentation should be included in a readme file in the plug-in directory.*

To pass this test, show any additional documentation provided with your plug-in such as readme files or evaluation guides.

15.6.7 Provide an overview of tasks flow   *(RFRS 5.3.5.34)*

Best Practice #7 states:

> *Give an overview of the tasks' flow. One or two sentences describing what is "produced/generated/created" when the user completes all the steps in the cheat sheet; in addition to this, information about sample scenarios or code can be added here. Break the information into separate paragraphs.*

To pass this test, access one of the cheat sheets defined for your plug-in and show that it includes an introductory paragraph providing an overview of the tasks' flow.

15.6.8 Illustrate only one task   *(RFRS 5.3.5.35)*

Best Practice #8 states:

> *Each step in a cheat sheet must only illustrate one task and involve using only one tool (wizard, dialog or editor etc.).*
>
> *a. If a task using more than one tool, you should implement one step per tool.*
>
> *b. If the step requires user to perform the action without launching any tool, it is a manual step. Item description must instruct the user to press the appropriate button after the task has been completed.*

To pass this test, access one of the cheat sheets defined for your plug-in and show that each step illustrates only one task and involves only one tool.

15.6.9 Provide help link with each step   *(RFRS 5.3.5.36)*

Best Practice #9 states:

> *Each step must have a help link with information specific to the task described in the step. The help link shows additional information to help user understand the task, complete that step, or get more advanced options relating to the task. More help links can be placed in the launched page.*

To pass this test, access one of the cheat sheets defined for your plug-in and show that it includes a help link with information specific to each step.

15.7 Summary

After introducing the Eclipse help system, this chapter illustrated how to create and integrate your own online help. It showed how to make your help available from within the Eclipse **Help** window as well as by using the context-sensitive **F1** key. The chapter also illustrated how to guide your user through complex tasks using cheat sheets.

References

Chapter source (*www.qualityeclipse.com/projects/source-ch-15.zip*).

Adams, Greg, and Dorian Birsan, "Help Part 1, Contributing a Little Help," August 9, 2002 (*www.eclipse.org/articles/Article-Online%20Help%20for%202_0/help1.htm*)

Ford, Neal, "Centralizing Help in Eclipse," ThoughtWorks, June 21, 2005 (*www-128.ibm.com/developerworks/opensource/library/os-eclipsehelp*)

Zink, Lori, "Understanding Eclipse Online Help," HP, February 2005 (*devresource.hp.com/drc/resources/eclipsedoc/index.jsp*)

"*Dynamic Content in Eclipse Help System Pages*," Eclipse.org, December 2005 (*www.eclipse.org/eclipse/platform-ua/proposals/xhtml/HelpDynamicContent.html*)

Eclipse Help: **Platform Plug-in Developer Guide > Programmer's Guide > Plugging in help**

CHAPTER 16

Internationalization

If a plug-in developer's audience is to be wider than a single country, such as the United States, then internationalization becomes an important aspect of development. Both Eclipse and the underlying Java runtime environments provide APIs for separating language and UI-related issues from the code. This chapter covers the techniques involved and provides examples of internationalizing the example plug-in.

Every application—and an Eclipse plug-in is no exception—includes dozens of human-readable strings that present themselves to the user in windows, dialogs, and menus. Isolating those strings so that they can be localized (translated) for different countries and languages is the most important step in internationalizing your plug-in.

The strings that present themselves to the user of a plug-in come from different types of files. The plug-in manifest file contains the names for views and perspectives and labels for menus and actions. The plug-in's `about.ini` file (discussed in more detail in Chapter 18, Features, Branding, and Updates) contains the text shown in the Eclipse **About** dialog.

Other strings visible in the plug-in's interface, such as widget labels and error message text, come from the Java classes implementing the plug-in. Different techniques and tools exist for externalizing the strings found in these various files.

16.1   Externalizing the Plug-in Manifest

The plug-in manifest file contains a variety of strings for identifying elements of the plug-in. Some strings, such as plug-in identifiers and the unique IDs associated with extensions, do not need to be translated as they are never shown to the user. In fact, translating identifiers and unique IDs will likely break your plug-in. Other strings, such as the names of views and the labels of actions, need to be translated as they are seen by the user.

Externalizing the human-readable strings from the plug-in manifest file is straightforward. The file `plugin.properties` (a standard Java resource bundle file which you will create) contains the extracted strings. As an example, start with the following fragment from the **Favorites** plug-in manifest.

```
<plugin
   ...
   <extension point="org.eclipse.ui.views">
      <category
            name="Quality Eclipse"
            id="com.qualityeclipse.favorites">
      </category>
      <view
            name="Favorites"
            icon="icons/sample.gif"
            category="com.qualityeclipse.favorites"
            class="com.qualityeclipse.favorites.
                  views.FavoritesView"
            id="com.qualityeclipse.favorites.
                  views.FavoritesView">
      </view>
   </extension>
   ...
</plugin>
```

The lines shown in **bold** are the ones containing strings that need to be extracted. The other lines contain text that does not need to be extracted, such as class names, identifiers, filenames, and version numbers.

Each string is replaced with a descriptive key that starts with a percent (%) sign. These are the same keys that will be used in the associated `plugin.properties` file. The only rule is that the keys need to be unique within the plug-in. You should also endeavor to give the keys descriptive names so that they are easily identifiable within the `plugin.xml` and `plugin.properties` files.

After extraction, the fragment will look like this:

```
<plugin
    ...
    <extension point="org.eclipse.ui.views">
       <category
             name="%favorites.category.name"
             id="com.qualityeclipse.favorites">
       </category>
       <view
             name="%favorites.view.name"
             icon="icons/sample.gif"
             category="com.qualityeclipse.favorites"
             class="com.qualityeclipse.favorites.
                  views.FavoritesView"
             id="com.qualityeclipse.favorites.
                  views.FavoritesView">
       </view>
    </extension>
    ...
</plugin>
```

The `plugin.properties` file (created using the **File > New > File** command) would then look like this:

```
# Contains translated strings for the Favorites plug-in
favorites.category.name=Quality Eclipse
favorites.view.name=Favorites
```

When the strings have been extracted to the `plugin.properties` file, they can be translated. The translated files for each targeted language should be named `plugin_<language>_<country>.properties`, where `<language>` and `<country>` represent the two-letter codes (ISO 639 and ISO 3166) used to signify the language and country (the country component is optional).

> **Tip:** A list of ISO 639 language codes can be found at:
> *www.unicode.org/onlinedat/languages.html*
> A list of ISO 3166 country codes can be found at:
> *www.unicode.org/onlinedat/countries.html*

For example, the standard German translation would be named `plugin_de.properties` and would look something like this:

```
# Enthält übersetzten Text für die steckbaren Lieblingeh
favorites.category.name= Qualitätseklipse
favorites.view.name=Lieblinge
```

Likewise, the standard French translation would be named `plugin_fr.`
`properties` and would look something like this:

```
# Contient le texte traduit pour les favoris plugin
favorites.category.name= Éclipse De Qualité
favorites.view.name=Favoris
```

16.2 Externalizing Plug-in Strings

When the plug-in manifest has been externalized, the other major source of
human-readable strings is the Java source for the plug-in. Within the **Favorites**
example, there are dozens of strings that are presented to the user in the form
of UI elements and messages.

To show the process for externalizing the strings in your Java source files,
the following will take you through the process of extracting the strings from
the `FavoritesView` class. The **Favorites** view contains several hard-coded
strings that are used for UI elements such as menu labels and table column
headers (see Figure 16–1).

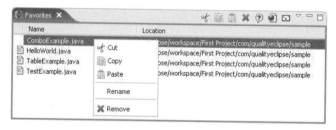

Figure 16–1 The Favorites view showing various strings.

Within the `FavoritesView` class, you should focus on the following hard-
coded string definitions (extracted to constants using the **Refactor > Extract
Constant...** command):

```
private static final String CUT = "Cut";
private static final String COPY = "Copy";
private static final String PASTE = "Paste";
private static final String RENAME = "Rename";
private static final String REMOVE = "Remove";
private static final String NAME = "Name";
private static final String LOCATION = "Location";
```

Eclipse includes a powerful string externalization tool that will do most of the work. Start by selecting the `FavoritesView` class. Next, select the **Source > Externalize Strings…** command to open the **Externalize Strings** wizard (see Figure 16–2).

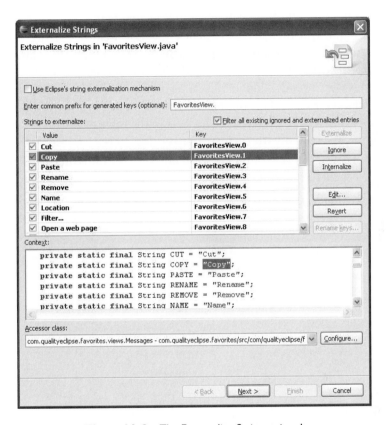

Figure 16–2   The Externalize Strings wizard.

Externalizing Manifest Files   Eclipse 3.2 includes a new wizard for extracting strings from plug-in manifest files (`MANIFEST.MF` and `plugin.xml`). Access it using the **PDE Tools > Externalize Strings…** command in the context menu of your plug-in project or manifest files.

The wizard scans the class for any string literals and presents them in the **Strings to externalize** list. The first column of the table is used to determine whether the string is translated, never translated, or skipped (until the next time the wizard is run on this class). The key column contains the wizard's first attempt at generating a unique key for the string (initially numbered 1 through *n*). The value column contains the strings that were found. Selecting an entry in the table will highlight it in context in the text pane below the table.

Prior to Eclipse 3.1, the default string-extraction mechanism used by Eclipse relied on dynamically looking up each string at runtime using a message lookup class and a call to a `getString()` method. Eclipse 3.1 introduced a much more efficient mechanism that is used here.

At the top of the wizard, click the **Use Eclipse's string externalization mechanism** option to use the new string-extraction mechanism. The **common prefix** field has been prepopulated with the name of the class in which the strings were found. Change this value to "FavoritesView_" (note the use of the underscore rather than the period to make each key a valid Java identifier). This value will be prefixed to the keys in the table to create the final keys that will be associated with each string.

Because the generated keys are not very meaningful, the first thing to do is edit them to represent the strings they will replace. Since the strings you want to replace are simple, have the keys duplicate the values (see Figure 16-3).

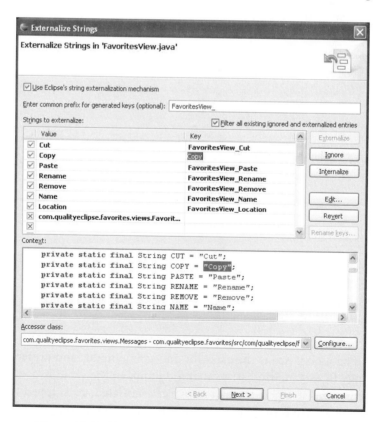

Figure 16–3   Externalize Strings wizard with better key names.

After providing better keys for the strings you want to extract, you need to go through the list and identify which strings to extract and which ones should never be translated (see Figure 16–4).

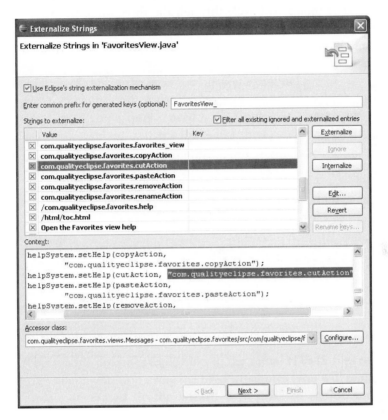

Figure 16–4   Externalize Strings wizard with strings marked as "Ignore."

By default, all the strings will be extracted. This means that each string with its key will be added to the properties file. Within the Java source file, the string will be replaced by references to a field which has been populated with the corresponding string from the properties file. If you know that a string should not be extracted, manually mark it with a special end-of-line comment (e.g., //$NON-NLS-1$) during development to make the string extraction process easier later on.

The number that is at the end of the comment indicates which string should be ignored when there is more than one string on the same line. If more than one string should be ignored on the line, each string will have its own end-of-line comment in that exact same format (including the leading double slashes).

Selecting a string and clicking the **Internalize** button will tell the wizard to mark the string as nontranslatable using the same end-of-line comment used earlier. Clicking the **Ignore** button will cause the wizard to take no action. Alternatively, you can click on the checkbox image in the first column of the table. The image will cycle through the three options: ☑ **Externalize,** ☒ **Internalize,** and ⊞ **Ignore.**

Tip: Think carefully about how you write your code, since it can cause more strings that need externalization than is strictly necessary. Replace single-character strings with single characters, look for opportunities to reuse keys rather than creating new ones, and use message binding to reduce the number of strings that need to be externalized. For example, assuming that "Count" has already been externalized, you might encounter the following three scenarios:

```
// Bad, we don't want to externalize "Count ("
label.setText("Count (" + count + ")");
// Good, we already have "Count" externalized.
label.setText("Count" + " (" + count + ')');//$NON-NLS-2$
// Better, use binding patterns whenever possible.
label.setText(
    MessageFormat.format("Count (%1)",
    new String[] {count})
```

In the second scenario, you can reuse the key assigned to "Count" and reduce the number of keys needed. In the third scenario, you can create a single new key that encodes a dynamic argument in a translation-relative position (in other languages, the %1 argument might appear elsewhere in the string).

Clicking the **Configure...** button will take you to a dialog where you can specify where the strings will be externalized and how they will be accessed (see Figure 16–5). The **Package** field specifies the location where the property file will be created, and the **Property file name** field specifies the name of the property file that will be created. It will default to messages.properties. Unless you have a reason to do otherwise, you should simply accept the defaults.

By default, a resource bundle accessor class will be created with the name Messages. This class will define fields corresponding to each extracted string as well as the code needed to populate those fields.

If you are using the older Eclipse string-extraction mechanism and don't want to have this class created, blank the **Class name** field. If you do that— possibly because you want to use an alternative mechanism—you might also want to specify an alternative **string substitution pattern** (the default pattern is designed to match the accessor class that the wizard would create).

Since the **Externalize Strings** wizard is actually built using the Eclipse refactoring framework, the next two pages are common to all refactoring wizards. The first of these pages (see Figure 16–6) will show any errors or informational messages. The only message you should see at this point is a notification that the properties file does not exist and needs to be created. Click the **Next** button to continue.

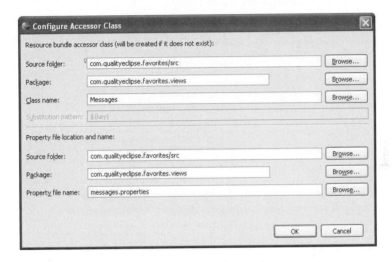

Figure 16–5   Define resource bundle and access settings.

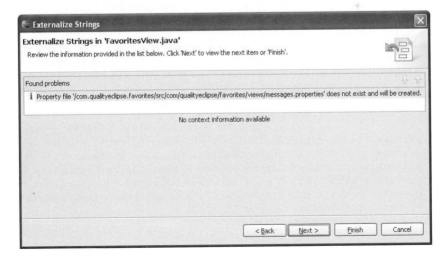

Figure 16–6   The `messages.properties` file needs to be created.

The final page of the wizard will present a list of all the proposed changes that the wizard wants to make (see Figure 16–7). First, you will see all the string substitutions that will be made to the FavoritesView class. After that, you will see the contents of the properties file and the resource bundle accessor class.

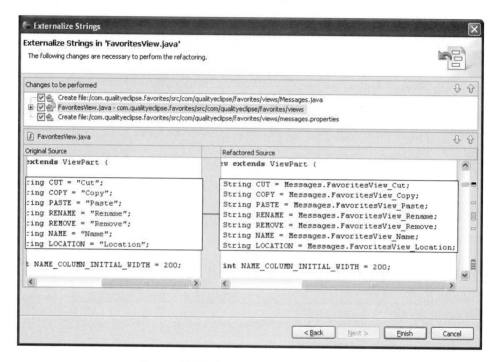

Figure 16–7   Review the proposed changes.

Clicking the **Finish** button will implement all the proposed changes. The original lines from the FavoritesView that you concentrated on earlier will be replaced by the following:

```
private static final String CUT = Messages.FavoritesView_Cut;
private static final String COPY = Messages.FavoritesView_Copy;
private static final String PASTE = Messages.FavoritesView_Paste;
private static final String RENAME = Messages.FavoritesView_Rename;
private static final String REMOVE = Messages.FavoritesView_Remove;
private static final String NAME = Messages.FavoritesView_Name;
private static final String LOCATION =
    Messages.FavoritesView_Locatiion;
```

Every string literal is replaced by a reference to its matching field defined in the Messages class. Every field is populated with the value of its corresponding string. Any string literals that were initially ignored will be marked with the //$NON-NLS-1$ tag, which will prevent them from being extracted in the future.

The code for the resource bundle accessor class will look something like this:

```
package com.qualityeclipse.favorites.views;
import org.eclipse.osgi.util.NLS;
public class Messages extends NLS {
    private static final String BUNDLE_NAME =
        "com.qualityeclipse.favorites.views.messages"; //$NON-NLS-1$
    private Messages() {
    }
    static {
        // initialize resource bundle
        NLS.initializeMessages(BUNDLE_NAME, Messages.class);
    }
    public static String FavoritesView_Cut;
    public static String FavoritesView_Copy;
    public static String FavoritesView_Paste;
    public static String FavoritesView_Rename;
    public static String FavoritesView_Remove;
    public static String FavoritesView_Name;
    public static String FavoritesView_Location;
    public static String FavoritesView_Filter;
}
```

Finally, the messages.properties file will look like this:

```
FavoritesView_Cut=Cut
FavoritesView_Copy=Copy
FavoritesView_Paste=Paste
FavoritesView_Rename=Rename
FavoritesView_Remove=Remove
FavoritesView_Name=Name
FavoritesView_Location=Location
```

As with the `plugin.properties` file, the translated properties files for every targeted language should be named `<basename>_<language>_<country>.properties`, where `<language>` and `<country>` represent the two-letter codes used to signify the language and country and `<basename>` is the name of the original properties file.

> **Tip:** To make sure that you have externalized all your plug-in's strings (or marked them as nontranslatable), consider changing the **Usage of non-externalized strings** option from "Ignore" to "Warning". This option can be found on the **Java > Compiler > Errors/Warnings** preference page. Alternatively, CodePro includes a **String Literals** code audit rule that will flag hard-coded string literals (with options to ignore single-character strings, strings containing only whitespace or digits, static final field initializers, strings matching certain patterns, etc.).

While externalizing strings, the following suggestions have been found to be helpful:

- Remove any punctuation characters such as "&" that appear in the key. If you want to separate words within your keys, standardize on a specific character such as a period, dash, or underscore.

- Edit the `.properties` file and keep the entries sorted. Sort the entries first based on the file they apply to, and then sort them alphabetically within the file.

- Factor out any common values and create a common key. Move all common keys to their own section of the file. Prefix your common keys with `common_` and move them to the top of the file. This reduces the number of translations and removes the possibility of variation in translations.

- When you edit the keys, strive to keep them as close to the original language strings as possible, since this will make the Java code and XML easier to read for the native developer. If you decide to do this, strive to rename the keys when the original language strings are changed, otherwise this might lead to confusion. Of course, numeric keys don't have this problem.

- When the original string contains a colon, such as "`Name:`", the generated key will contain double underscores. Never define keys such as this, but rather go back to the original string and change "`Name:`" to "`Name`"+`':'`. This not only keeps the keys simple, but it also ensures that the colon does not get dropped during translation. The only issue here is whether you truly want to respect local punctuation rules; however, that can be fairly tricky.

- You should always consider including an error number with internationalized error messages so that an error displayed in one language could be addressed by others.

- In the generated static `getString(String key)` method (used by the older Eclipse string-extraction mechanism), edit the catch clause to include the following line that will log any missing resource keys to the console. This is much easier than looking for "`!  <key>  !`" in your application.

```
System.err.println(e.getMessage());
```

16.3 Using Fragments

All the translated properties files could be included in the main plug-in, but this is less than ideal in a situation where the translations will be delivered later than the product itself. If all the translated files need to be included with the main plug-in, you would either need to delay the release of the main plug-in or rerelease it when the translations are available. Fortunately, Eclipse includes a mechanism called a *plug-in fragment* that provides an elegant solution to this problem.

Fragments are used to extend the functionality of another plug-in. Fragments are typically used to supply alternative language packs, maintenance updates, and platform-specific implementation classes. When a fragment is loaded, its features and capabilities are merged with those of the base plug-in such that they appear to have come from the base plug-in itself.

The developer does not need to know whether the plug-in or one of its fragments contributes a specific resource because the plug-in class loader handles this transparently. This makes it easy to deliver translated versions of plug-in files (e.g., HTML, XML, INI, and properties files) independently of the main plug-in.

The properties files follow the resource bundle-naming rules (as noted earlier). Other resources, such as HTML, XML, and INI files are placed into `nl/<language>` or `nl/<language>/<country>` directories, where `<language>` and `<country>` represent the two-letter codes used to signify the language and country (this directory structure was first introduced in Section 15.2.3, Table of contents (toc) files, on page 548).

> **Tip:** Fragments can also be used for smoothing out differences between different versions of Eclipse (see Section 19.2.6.4, Fragments, on page 698) and for accessing internal classes and methods (see Section 20.2.6, Using fragments, on page 714).

16.3.1 New Fragment Project wizard

Creating a new fragment is easy using the **New Fragment Project** wizard. From the **File** menu, select **New > Project** to launch the new project wizard (see Figure 16–8). On this first page of the wizard, select **Plug-in Development > Fragment Project,** followed by the **Next** button.

Figure 16–8   New Project wizard with Fragment Project selected.

On the next page of the wizard (see Figure 16–9), enter the name of the project; in this case, it should be "`com.qualityeclipse.favorites.nl1`", which is the same as the plug-in fragment identifier. The Eclipse convention is to name a plug-in fragment project that contributes national language support to a base plug-in with the same name as the base plug-in plus the suffix "`.nl1`". Click the **Next** button.

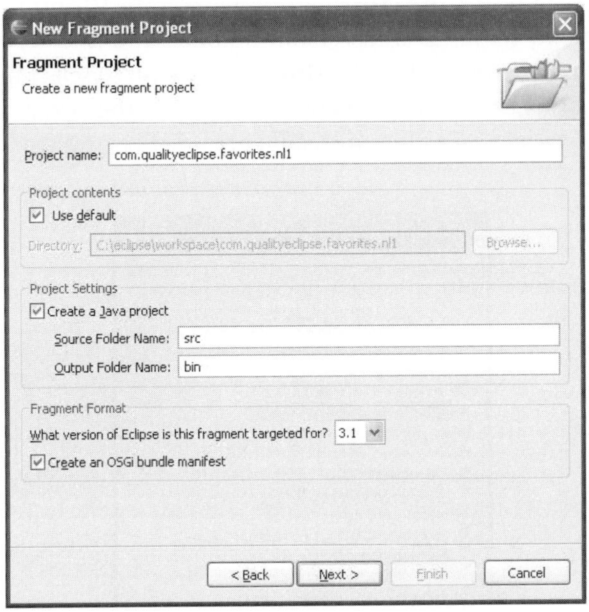

Figure 16–9   New Fragment Project wizard.

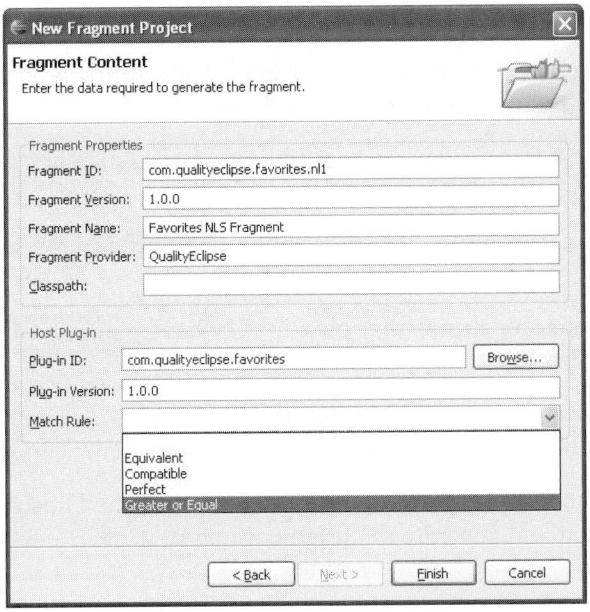

Figure 16–10   Required data for initial fragment files.

The **Fragment Content** page (see Figure 16–10) provides fields to name the fragment, set its ID and version number, and identify the plug-in ID and version that it extends. Use the **Browse...** button to select the plug-in, if necessary. In this case, you want to extend the existing `com.quality-eclipse.favorites` plug-in (see Figure 16–11).

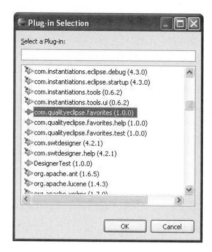

Figure 16–11   The manifest editor for the fragment.

The choices available in the **Match Rule** field control the versions of the associated plug-in that can be extended.

- **Perfect** means that the base plug-in exactly matches the supplied version number.

- **Equivalent** means that the version may differ at the service or qualifier level.

- **Compatible** means that plug-in may have a newer minor version number.

- **Greater or Equal** means that the plug-in may have any newer version number. This is the option you should normally choose.

Choose the **Greater or Equal** option and click the **Finish** button to complete the wizard and generate the fragment manifest file.

16.3.2   Fragment manifest file

Double-clicking in the fragment manifest file, MANIFEST.MF, will open the fragment manifest editor (see Figure 16–12). The editor looks very similar to the plug-in manifest editor with **Overview, Dependencies, Runtime, Extension Points,** etc. pages.

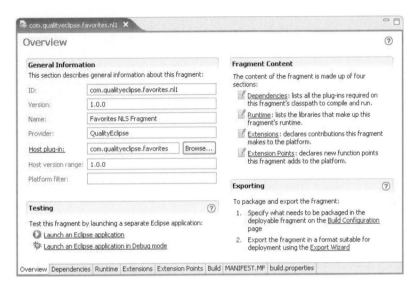

Figure 16–12   Fragment manifest editor.

If you switch to the **Runtime** page (see Figure 16–13), you will see that nothing is included in the runtime classpath for the fragment. Various files, such as translated HTML, XML, and INI files, are located in specially named subdirectories based on the associated locale (language and country combination).

To get those directories to show up in the runtime classpath, click the **New...** button to add a "New Library" entry to the list. Right-click on that entry and **Rename** it to "nl/". This is special syntax that will cause the system to substitute the correct classpath entry at runtime based on the current locale. If the locale is set to Germany, for example, "nl" would be substituted by "de", and the "de/" subdirectory would be added to the runtime path.

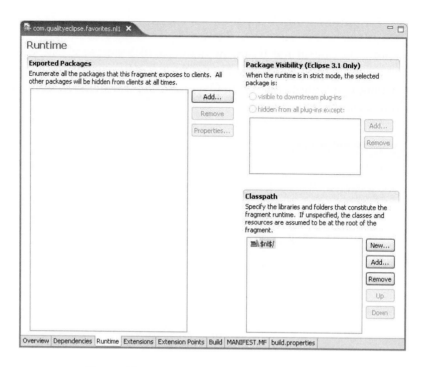

Figure 16–13　Fragment Runtime Information page.

Next, let's switch to the **MANIFEST.MF** page and take a look at the generated text:

```
Manifest-Version: 1.0
Bundle-ManifestVersion: 2
Bundle-Name: Favorites NLS Fragment
Bundle-SymbolicName: com.qualityeclipse.favorites.nl1
Bundle-Version: 1.0.0
Bundle-Vendor: QualityEclipse
Fragment-Host: com.qualityeclipse.favorites;
    bundle-version="1.0.0"
Bundle-Localization: plugin
Bundle-ClassPath: $nl$/
```

This source is very similar to what you would expect to see for a plug-in. The first major difference is that fragments don't have their own plug-in lifecycle (they conform to the lifecycle of their associated plug-in), and thus, they don't need their own `Bundle-Activator` attribute. The second difference is that the fragment does not declare any of its own dependencies (again, they are inherited from the associated plug-in).

The interesting attributes relative to those found in full plug-ins are the `Fragment-Host` and the `bundle-version` attributes. The `Fragment-Host` identifies the plug-in that this fragment will extend. The `bundle-version` specifies the version of the target plug-in that this fragment expects to be able to extend.

16.3.3   *Fragment project contents*

The last thing you need to do is add all the translated files to the appropriate directories within the fragment project folder (see Figure 16–14). Assuming that you want to supply German and French translations of various files, the project would have `nl/de` and `nl/fr` directories to contain any translated HTML, XML, and INI files (like those mentioned in Section 15.2.3, Table of contents (toc) files, on page 548).

The translated versions of the `plugin.properties` files are placed at the root of the fragment, and the translated versions of the `messages.properties` files are placed in the `com.qualityeclipse.favorites.views` directory.

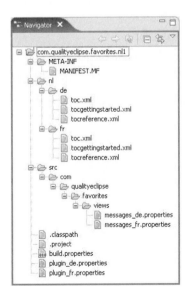

Figure 16–14   Fragment project contents.

16.4   Summary

To make your plug-in accessible to a worldwide audience, it should be internationalized. Extracting the plug-in's human-readable strings into a format that can be easily translated is the most important step. As presented in this chapter, Eclipse provides a number of tools to facilitate this. The **Externalize Strings** wizard makes it easy to extract the strings from your Java code, while fragments provide a convenient packaging mechanism for delivering translated content independent of your main plug-ins.

References

Chapter source (*www.qualityeclipse.com/projects/source-ch-16.zip*).

Java internationalization tutorial (*java.sun.com/docs/books/tutorial/i18n/intro/index.html*).

Kehn, Dan, Scott Fairbrother, and Cam-Thu Le, "How to Internationalize Your Eclipse Plug-in," IBM, August 23, 2002 (*eclipse.org/articles/Article-Internationalization/how2I18n.html*).

Kehn, Dan, "How to Test Your Internationalized Eclipse Plug-in," IBM, August 23, 2002 (*eclipse.org/articles/Article-TVT/how2TestI18n.html*).

Kehn, Dan, Scott Fairbrother and Cam-Thu Le, "Internationalizing Your Eclipse Plug-in," IBM, June 1, 2002 (*www-128.ibm.com/developerworks/opensource/library/os-i18n*).

ISO 639 language codes (*www.unicode.org/onlinedat/languages.html*).

ISO 3166 country codes (*www.unicode.org/onlinedat/countries.html*).

Eclipse Help: **Java Development User Guide > Tasks > Externalizing Strings**

CHAPTER 17

Creating New Extension Points

Eclipse facilitates enhancements by defining *extension points*, but that technique is not reserved only for Eclipse itself. Each plug-in can define its own extension points that can be used either internally as part of a disciplined and flexible programming approach, or externally as a way for third-party plug-ins to enhance an existing plug-in in a controlled yet loosely coupled, flexible manner. This chapter discusses the API involved and provides examples of creating extension points so that a third party can extend the plug-in's functionality.

17.1 The Extension Point Mechanism

Up to this point, we have been discussing extension points as a consumer; now we need to delve into the mechanism behind the curtain so that ultimately you can produce your own extension points for others to consume. Not only will extension points make products more flexible, but also, by carefully exposing specific aspects of your plug-in, you can make your products more flexible and customizable. The goal is to empower your customers to take products and do things that were never envisioned.

Extension points are used throughout Eclipse as a mechanism for loosely coupling chunks of functionality. One plug-in declares an extension point in its plug-in manifest, exposing a minimal set of interfaces and related classes for others to use; other plug-ins declare extensions to that extension point, implementing the appropriate interfaces and referencing or building on the classes provided (see Figure 17–1).

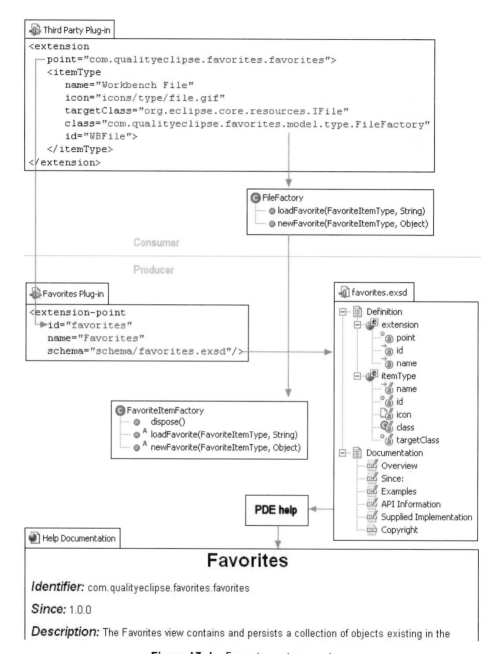

Figure 17–1   Extension point overview.

Each extension point has a unique identifier composed of the plug-in's unique identifier, a period, and a simple identifier containing only alphanumeric characters and underscores. When declaring an extension point (see Section 17.2.1, Creating an extension point, below), only the simple identifier is used. When declaring an extension to an extension point (see Section 17.5, Using the Extension Point, on page 615), the full identifier for the extension point is used.

Every extension point can have a schema defining how they should be used. Although the schema is not necessary for proper extension point usage, the Eclipse PDE can use the schema for basic automated verification of extensions and automatically generated Javadoc-like documentation for the extension point.

The schema is an XML-formatted file, traditionally having the name `<extension-point-id>.exsd` and is located in a schema subdirectory of the plug-in's install directory. For example, the extension point schema discussed later in this chapter will be stored in `<Eclipse_install_dir>/plugins/com.qualityeclipse.favorites_1.0.0/schema/favorites.exsd`.

17.2 Defining an Extension Point

In the **Favorites** product, you would like other plug-ins to extend your product to provide additional types of **Favorites** objects. To accomplish this goal, create a new `favorites` extension point and schema plus related infrastructure types that others can extend. As part of this process, recast the current **Favorites** objects as extensions to this new extension point to prove to yourself that the new extension point does indeed work.

17.2.1 Creating an extension point

Begin by opening the **Favorites** plug-in manifest editor and switching to the **Extension Points** page. Click the **Add...** button to open the **New Extension Point** wizard, and then enter "favorites" for the identifier and "Favorites" for the name (see Figure 17–2).

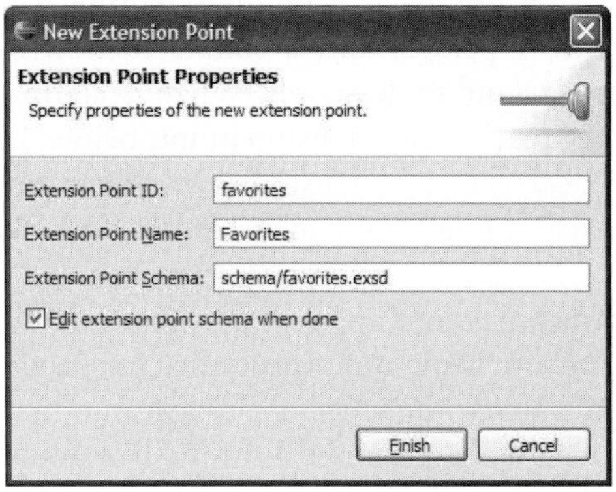

Figure 17–2   The New Extension Point wizard.

Click **Finish** to create the new extension point and open the schema file (more on schemas in Section 17.2.2, Creating an extension point schema, on page 599). After switching back to the plug-in manifest editor, the **Extension Points** page should show the newly defined extension point (see Figure 17–3).

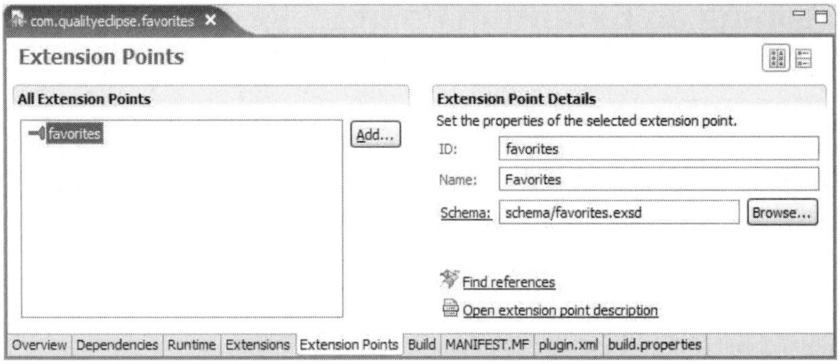

Figure 17–3   The Extension Points page in the plug-in manifest editor.

Switching to the **plugin.xml** page of the plug-in manifest editor reveals a new extension point declaration specifying the identifier, the human-readable name, and the relative location of the schema.

```
<extension-point
   id="favorites"
   name="Favorites"
   schema="schema/favorites.exsd"/>
```

The aforementioned declaration specifies the local identifier of the extension point. The full identifier is the plug-in identifier plus the local identifier and is used when referencing the extension point; in this case, the full identifier is com.qualityeclipse.favorites.favorites.

17.2.2 Creating an extension point schema

The **New Extension Point** wizard automatically opens the schema editor to edit the newly created favorites.exsd file in the schema directory of the **Favorites** project (see Figure 17–4). If you ever need to open the schema editor again, you can either navigate to the schema directory and double-click on the favorites.exsd file, or select the favorites extension point in the **Favorites** plug-in manifest, right-click, and then select **Open Schema**.

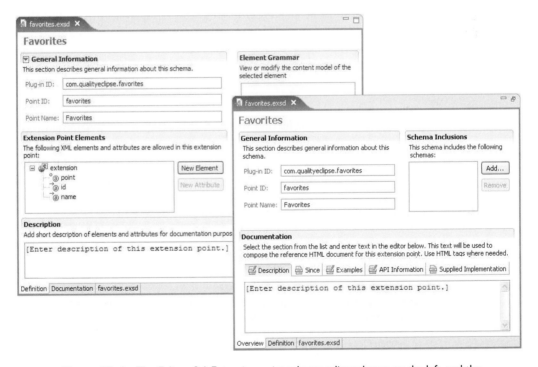

Figure 17–4 The Eclipse 3.1 Extension point schema editor shown on the left, and the Eclipse 3.2 Extension point schema editor shown on the right.

The schema editor has several major parts: **General Information, Extension Point Elements, Element Grammar,** and **Documentation.** Note that between Eclipse 3.1 and 3.2, the pages and sections of this editor have been rearranged; however, the basic principles in using it remain the same.

The **Extension Point Elements** list contains elements and their associated attributes, which appear as extensions to the extension points (see Section 17.2.3, Extension point elements and attributes, on the next page).

In Eclipse 3.1, the **Element Grammar** list contains a description of how the XML elements should appear in the extension (see Section 17.2.4, Extension point element grammar, on page 605). In Eclipse 3.2, this section has been combined with the **Extension Point Elements** list.

To start, document the goal so that you have a clear view of what you are trying to accomplish. An extension point schema is used by the PDE to dynamically assemble a help page for the extension point (see Section 17.4, Extension Point Documentation, on page 614). In the **Description** section of the schema editor (on the **Definition** page of the editor in Eclipse 3.1 and on the **Overview** page in Eclipse 3.2), enter the following description, and then click the **Apply** button.

```
The Favorites view contains and persists a collection of objects
existing in the Eclipse workspace. This Favorites extension point
allows third-party plug-ins to define new types of objects for the
Favorites view.
```

Repeat this process by selecting the **Examples** tab in the **Documentation** section and entering the following text (see below). Note the use of the `<pre>` and `</pre>` XML tags to denote preformatted text in which whitespace should be preserved; all other whitespace greater than a single space outside those tags is discarded in the automatically generated HTML help text (see Section 17.4, Extension Point Documentation, on page 614).

```
The following is an example
of the Favorites extension point usage:
<p>
<pre>
   <extension point="com.qualityeclipse.favorites.favorites">
      <itemType
         id="com.example.xyz.myNewFavoriteItemId"
         name="New Favorites Item Name"
         class="com.example.xyz.MyFavoriteItem"
         targetClass="com.example.xyz.MyObjectClass"/>
   </extension>
</pre>
</p>
```

Then, for **API Information,** enter the following:

Plug-ins that want to extend this extension point must subclass
<samp>com.qualityeclipse.favorites.model.FavoriteItemType</samp> and
generate objects that implement the <samp>com.qualityeclipse.-
favorites.model.IFavoriteItem</samp> interface.

> Note the use the <samp> </samp> XML tags to denote code in a
> sentence similar to the way that many of the Eclipse plug-ins are
> documented; the <code> </code> XML tags should work just as well.

17.2.3   *Extension point elements and attributes*

Extension point elements correspond to XML elements that appear in the
extension declaration. Extension point attributes correspond to XML
attributes that appear in the extension declaration. For example, in the following extension declaration, itemType is an extension point element, while id,
name, class, and targetClass are extension point attributes.

```
<extension point=
   "com.qualityeclipse.favorites.favorites">
   <itemType
      id="com.example.xyz.myNewFavoriteItemId"
      name="New Favorites Item Name"
      class="com.example.xyz.MyFavoriteItem"
      targetClass="com.example.xyz.MyObjectClass"/>
</extension>
```

Extension point attributes have several different properties associated
with them. In Eclipse 3.1, double-clicking on an attribute in the schema editor
opens the **Properties** view and displays the properties (see Figure 17–5). In
Eclipse 3.2, the **Properties** view is no longer used to edit the properties as they
are now shown directly in the **Attribute Details** section of the scheme editor.
The properties for extension attributes are:

Name—The name of the attribute as it appears in the extension's declaration. For example, in the aforementioned extension declaration, id,
name, class, and targetClass are all attribute names.

Type—The type of the attribute: string or Boolean. At this time, these are
the only two types recognized by the schema editor and PDE. If your
attribute should only be true or false, then select boolean; for all
other attributes, select string.

Use—Indicates whether this attribute is required in an extension and
thus must be explicitly declared, or whether it is optional, indicating
that it may be omitted from an extension declaration. Alternately, the

Use may be declared as `default`, indicating that if it is not explicitly declared, then it defaults to the value specified by the **Value** property listed later.

Kind—If the aforementioned **Type** property is `string`, then this property indicates how that string should be interpreted: as a `java` class, as a `resource` path to an image, or simply as a `string` for the extension point code to interpret as it likes.

Based On—If the **Kind** is `java`, then this property indicates the fully qualified name of the class or interface that this attribute must extend or implement. In Eclipse 3.2, this property has been split into separate **Extends** and **Implements** properties (see Figure 17–5).

Restriction—If the **Type** is `string` and the **Kind** is `string`, then this property can restrict the value of the attribute to an enumeration or discrete list of valid strings. For example, using this field, you could specify that an attribute could only have the value "one", "two", or "three".

Translatable—A boolean indicating whether this attribute is human readable and should be translated.

Value—If the **Use** is specified as `default`, then this property indicates the default value that will be used if this attribute is not explicitly specified in the extension's declaration.

Figure 17–5   The Eclipse 3.1 Properties view showing attribute property values on the left and the Eclipse 3.2 Attribute Details area showing those same properties on the right.

For the **Favorites** product, you want extensions to this extension point to specify information about the type of **Favorites** item being added. The following are the extension point attributes to include.

- **name**—The human-readable name.
- **id**—The unique identifier.
- **icon**—The relative path to an image (optional).

- **class**—The `FavoriteItemFactory` for creating items of this type.
- **targetClass**—The type of object being wrapped by this type.

> **Tip:** If your extension point is intended for general consumption, then have a plan for lazy extension initialization so that you do not cause more plug-ins than need to be loaded, resulting in memory bloat and slowing down the system. For example, in this case, the `targetClass` is used to determine which **Favorites** item type should be used *before* the plug-in that defines it is actually loaded. If you do not have this information specified in the extension, then when users drag and drop new objects onto the **Favorites** view, they would need to load and query each **Favorites** type to determine which type should handle the dropped objects. This could potentially pull in many more plug-ins than necessary, bloating and slowing down the workspace.
>
> Instead, you pre-screen the types based on the `targetClass` to determine which type may be able to handle the dropped object. If your extension point is intended for use only within your own plug-in, then you do not need the extra complexity and overhead associated with a proxy.

First, you need to add an `itemType` element representing the **Favorites** item type being defined, to which you will add these attributes. To accomplish this, switch to the **Definition** page, click on the **New Element** button, select the `new_element1` that was created, and change the name to "itemType".

To change the name in Eclipse 3.1, you will need to double-click on the element to open the **Properties** view. In Eclipse 3.2, the name is shown directly in the **Attribute Details** section of the scheme editor.

With `itemType` selected in the schema editor, click the **New Attribute** button to add a new attribute to the `itemType` element. Change its name to "name". With the `name` attribute selected in the schema editor, enter "A human-readable name for this type of Favorites object." for the description of the name attribute and then click **Apply**.

Repeat this process to add four more attributes. When you are done, you should have defined the following attributes for the `itemType` element with the properties specified here.

- **attribute #1**
    name = "name"
    use = "optional"
    kind = "string"
    translatable = "true"
    description =
        "A human-readable name for this type of Favorites object."

- **attribute #2**
  name = "id"
  use = "required"
  kind = "string"
  description =
  "The unique identifier for this type of Favorites object."

- **attribute #3**
  name = "icon"
  use = "optional"
  kind = "resource"
  description =
  "An option image associated with this type of Favorites object."

- **attribute #4**
  name = "class"
  use = "required"
  kind = "java"
  basedOn/extends =
  "com.qualityeclipse.favorites.model.FavoriteItemFactory"
  description =
  "The fully qualified name of the class that extends
  <samp>com.qualityeclipse.favorites.model.
  FavoriteItemFactory</samp>."

- **attribute #5**
  name = "targetClass"
  use = "required"
  kind = "string"
  description =
  "The fully qualified name of the class wrapped by this item
  type. This is not the class name for the IFavoriteItem object
  returned by either
  <samp>FavoriteItemType.loadFavorite(String)</samp> or
  <samp>FavoriteItemType.newFavorite(Object)</samp>, but
  rather the object wrapped by that IFavoriteItem object that
  causes the IFavoriteItem.isFavoriteFor(Object) to return true."

> **Tip:** How should an extension provide behavior for your extension point? Do you need extensions to implement an interface or instead extend an abstract base class? If you need extensions to implement an interface, then you grant more flexibility to the extension writer. On the downside, any change to that interface will break existing extensions. Instead, if you need extensions to extend an abstract base class, then you keep some flexibility while still retaining advantages of loose coupling. Adding a concrete method to an abstract base class will not break existing extensions, giving you the opportunity to change the API in future implementations, all without sacrificing much of the extension writer's flexibility. If you are *sure* that your API will not change, then an interface is a great way to go; otherwise, an abstract base class gives you the flexibility you need to evolve the API.
>
> If you *need* the flexibility of an interface where an abstract base class will not do, then consider requiring the interface but providing an abstract base class that implements that interface for extensions to build on if they choose. Given this approach, you can change the interface API and mitigate disruption by adding concrete methods in your abstract base class that implement any new interface methods. Any extension that uses the abstract base class will be unperturbed by your interface API changes, whereas any extension that implements the interface directly must be modified to fit the new API.

17.2.4 *Extension point element grammar*

After the extension point elements have been defined, construct the element grammar describing how the elements are assembled in a way that can be validated by the PDE. When you select an element in the **Extension Point Elements** list on the left, the grammar associated with the element is displayed in the **Element Grammar** on the right. The grammar on the right describes the child elements of the selected element on the left. If you select an element on the left and no grammar appears on the right, then the selected element on the left cannot have any child elements. Double-clicking on a grammar element on the right opens the **Properties** view and displays the properties associated with the grammar element. Note that in Eclipse 3.2, the grammar elements are shown nested in the **Extension Point Elements** list, and their attributes can be edited directly in the schema editor without using the **Properties** view.

Rather than present all possible grammar elements, several common scenarios and the associated grammar are presented in Table 17–1. The desired XML structure appears on the left. On the right is the grammar used to describe the structure with property values between brackets—[ ].

Table 17.1   XML Grammar

XML	Grammar

```<parentElement ... >```
    ```<childElement ... />```
```</parentElement>```
	+ Sequence
	    childElement

```<parentElement ... >```
    ```<childElement ... />```
    ```<childElement ... />```
    ```...```
```</parentElement>```
	+ Sequence
	    childElement
	        [minOccurs = "0"]
	        [maxOccurs = "unbounded"]

```<parentElement ... >```
    ```<childElement1 ... />```
    ```<childElement1 ... />```
    ```...```
    ```<childElement2 ... />```
    ```<childElement2 ... />```
    ```...```
```</parentElement>```
	+ Sequence
	    childElement1
	        [minOccurs = "0"]
	        [maxOccurs = "unbounded"]
	    childElement2
	        [minOccurs = "0"]
	        [maxOccurs = "unbounded"]

```<parentElement ... >```
    ```<childElement1 ... />```
    ```<childElement2 ... />```
```</parentElement>```
  - OR -
```<parentElement ... >```
    ```<childElement1 ... />```
    ```<childElement3 ... />```
```</parentElement>```
	+ Sequence
	    childElement1
	    + Choice
	        childElement2
	        childElement3

Whenever anyone extends the extension point, you want there to be one or more `itemType` elements as part of that extension declaration. In the schema editor, select the extension point element `extension` in the **Extension Point Elements** list, causing `Sequence` to appear in the **Element Grammar** list on the right. Select `Sequence`, then right-click and select **New > Reference > itemType**. Expand `Sequence` so that `itemType` appears as a child hierarchically under `Sequence`, and then double-click on `itemType` to open the **Properties** view. In the **Properties** view select **maxOccurs** and enter "unbounded". After this is complete, you should see `itemType (1-*)` in the **Element Grammar** list (see Figure 17–6).

In Eclipse 3.2, the `Sequence` and `itemType` items are shown nested under the `extension` element in the **Extension Point Elements** list, and their attributes can be edited in the details area of the schema editor.

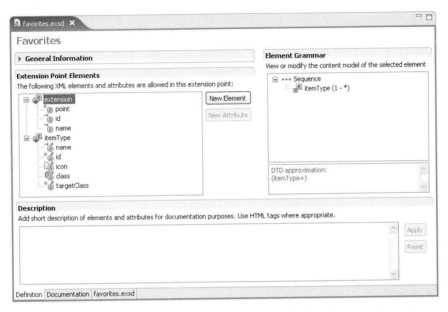

Figure 17–6   The Eclipse 3.1 schema editor showing the Favorites extension point. This editor has a different layout in Eclipse 3.2.

17.3   Code Behind an Extension Point

After the extension point has been defined, you must write the code behind it that builds **Favorites** item types and **Favorites** objects based on the information declared in extensions of the extension point. Following the Eclipse theme of lazy initialization, you want to keep the memory footprint down, so each **Favorites** item type and plug-in containing it must be loaded only if necessary. To achieve this, refactor portions of FavoriteItemType (see Section 17.2.3, Extension point elements and attributes, on page 601) into a new FavoriteItemFactory and then reorganize FavoriteItemType to build types from extension information. This is followed by recasting the **Favorites** item type constants as extensions to the new **Favorites** extension point.

17.3.1   Parsing extension information

The first modification to the FavoriteItemType involves building instances of this class from the extension information rather than hard-coding the information in the class as constants. Rename the TYPES array to cachedTypes to more accurately represent the purpose of this static field. Modify the getTypes() method to build a new instance of FavoriteItemType for each extension found.

```java
private static final String TAG_ITEMTYPE = "itemType";

private static FavoriteItemType[] cachedTypes;

public static FavoriteItemType[] getTypes() {
   if (cachedTypes != null)
      return cachedTypes;
   IExtension[] extensions = Platform.getExtensionRegistry()
      .getExtensionPoint(FavoritesPlugin.ID, "favorites")
      .getExtensions();
   List found = new ArrayList(20);
   found.add(UNKNOWN);
   for (int i = 0; i < extensions.length; i++) {
      IConfigurationElement[] configElements =
         extensions[i].getConfigurationElements();
      for (int j = 0; j < configElements.length; j++) {
         FavoriteItemType proxy =
            parseType(configElements[j], found.size());
         if (proxy != null)
            found.add(proxy);
      }
   }
   cachedTypes =
      (FavoriteItemType[]) found.toArray(
         new FavoriteItemType[found.size()]);
   return cachedTypes;
}

private static FavoriteItemType parseType(
   IConfigurationElement configElement, int ordinal
) {
   if (!configElement.getName().equals(TAG_ITEMTYPE))
      return null;
   try {
      return new FavoriteItemType(configElement, ordinal);
   }
   catch (Exception e) {
      String name = configElement.getAttribute(ATT_NAME);
      if (name == null)
         name = "[missing name attribute]";
      String msg =
         "Failed to load itemType named "
            + name
            + " in "
            + configElement.getDeclaringExtension().getNamespace();
            // Eclipse 3.2 - replace getNamespace()
            // with getContributor().getName()
      FavoritesLog.logError(msg, e);
      return null;
   }
}
```

> **Tip:** As always, proper exception handling is necessary, especially when handling loosely coupled code via extension points. In this case, the instance creation is wrapped in an exception handler so that an improperly declared extension will not cause this method to fail, but instead will generate a log entry containing enough information for the culprit to be tracked down and corrected.

17.3.2   Constructing proxies

Next, you modify the `FavoriteItemType` constructor to extract the basic information from the extension without loading the plug-in that declared the extension. This instance stands in as a proxy for the factory contained in the declaring plug-in. If a required attribute is missing, then an `Illegal-ArgumentException` is thrown, to be caught in the exception handler of the `parseType()` method described earlier.

```
private static final String ATT_ID = "id";
private static final String ATT_NAME = "name";
private static final String ATT_CLASS = "class";
private static final String ATT_TARGETCLASS = "targetClass";
private static final String ATT_ICON = "icon";

private final IConfigurationElement configElement;
private final int ordinal;
private final String id;
private final String name;
private final String targetClassName;
private FavoriteItemFactory factory;
private ImageDescriptor imageDescriptor;

public FavoriteItemType(
   IConfigurationElement configElem, int ordinal
) {
   this.configElement = configElem;
   this.ordinal = ordinal;
   id = getAttribute(configElem, ATT_ID, null);
   name = getAttribute(configElem, ATT_NAME, id);
   targetClassName =
      getAttribute(configElem, ATT_TARGETCLASS, null);

   // Make sure that class is defined,
   // but don't load it.
   getAttribute(configElem, ATT_CLASS, null);
}
```

```
private static String getAttribute(
   IConfigurationElement configElem,
   String name,
   String defaultValue
) {
   String value = configElem.getAttribute(name);
   if (value != null)
      return value;
   if (defaultValue != null)
      return defaultValue;
   throw new IllegalArgumentException(
      "Missing " + name + " attribute");
}
```

> **Tip:** How do you determine what information to load from an extension immediately versus what should be deferred via lazy initialization to an accessor method? Methods that load extension attribute values, such as `IConfigurationElement.getAttribute (String)`, are very quick to execute because they return already cached information. Other methods, such as `IConfigurationElement.createExecutableExtension(String)`, are quite slow because they will load the declaring plug-in into memory if it has not been loaded already. Our philosophy is to cache and validate attribute values up-front, providing immediate validation and "fast fail" for much of the extension information, but to defer via lazy initialization anything that would cause the declaring plug-in to be loaded.

Potentially, every extension could be invalid and you could end up with no valid instances of `FavoriteItemType` returned by `getTypes()`. To alleviate this problem, hard-code a single `FavoriteItemType` named `UNKNOWN` and add this as the first object in the collection returned by `getTypes()`.

```
public static final FavoriteItemType UNKNOWN =
   new FavoriteItemType()
{
   public IFavoriteItem newFavorite(Object obj) {
      return null;
   }
   public IFavoriteItem loadFavorite(String info) {
      return null;
   }
};

private FavoriteItemType() {
   this.id = "Unknown";
   this.ordinal = 0;
   this.name = "Unknown";
   this.configElement = null;
   this.targetClassName = "";
}
```

Now, revise the accessors for obtaining information about the item type based on the cached extension information. The `icon` attribute is assumed to have a path relative to the declaring plug-in, and the image descriptor is constructed accordingly. Images take precious native resources and load comparatively slowly, thus they are lazily initialized on an as-needed basis. Loaded images are cached so that they can be reused and then properly disposed of when the plug-in is shut down (see Section 7.7, Image Caching, on page 315 for `ImageCache` information).

```
private static final ImageCache imageCache = new ImageCache();

public String getId() {
   return id;
}
public String getName() {
   return name;
}
public Image getImage() {
   return imageCache.getImage(getImageDescriptor());
}
public ImageDescriptor getImageDescriptor() {
   if (imageDescriptor != null)
      return imageDescriptor;
   String iconName = configElement.getAttribute(ATT_ICON);
   if (iconName == null)
      return null;
   IExtension extension =
      configElement.getDeclaringExtension();
   String extendingPluginId = extension.getNamespace();
   // Eclipse 3.2 - replace getNamespace()
   // with getContributor().getName()
   imageDescriptor =
      AbstractUIPlugin.imageDescriptorFromPlugin(
         extendingPluginId,
         iconName);
   return imageDescriptor;
}
```

17.3.3 Creating executable extensions

The `loadFavorite(String)` and `newFavorite(Object)` methods are redirected to the `factory` object as specified in the extension. Since instantiating the `factory` object involves loading the plug-in that contains it, this operation is deferred until needed. The `targetClassName` is used by the `newFavorite(Object)` method to determine whether the associated `factory` can handle the specified object and thus whether the associated `factory` needs to be loaded. The code that instantiates the `factory` object is wrapped in an exception handler so that detailed information can be logged concerning the failure that occurred and which plug-in and extension are involved.

```java
public IFavoriteItem newFavorite(Object obj) {
    if (!isTarget(obj)) {
        return null;
    }
    FavoriteItemFactory factory = getFactory();
    if (factory == null) {
        return null;
    }
    return factory.newFavorite(this, obj);
}

private boolean isTarget(Object obj) {
    if (obj == null) {
        return false;
    }
    Class clazz = obj.getClass();
    if (clazz.getName().equals(targetClassName)) {
        return true;
    }
    Class[] interfaces = clazz.getInterfaces();
    for (int i = 0; i < interfaces.length; i++) {
        if (interfaces[i].getName().equals(targetClassName)) {
            return true;
        }
    }
    return false;
}

public IFavoriteItem loadFavorite(String info) {
    FavoriteItemFactory factory = getFactory();
    if (factory == null) {
        return null;
    }
    return factory.loadFavorite(this, info);
}

private FavoriteItemFactory getFactory() {
    if (factory != null) {
        return factory;
    }
    try {
        factory = (FavoriteItemFactory) configElement
            .createExecutableExtension(ATT_CLASS);
    } catch (Exception e) {
        FavoritesLog.logError(
            "Failed to instantiate factory: "
                + configElement.getAttribute(ATT_CLASS)
                + " in type: "
                + id
                + " in plugin: "
               + configElement.getDeclaringExtension().getNamespace(),e);
                // Eclipse 3.2 - replace getNamespace()
                // with getContributor().getName()
    }
    return factory;
}
```

> **Tip:** Whenever instantiating an object specified in an extension, always use
> the `IConfigurationElement.createExecutable(String)` method. This
> method automatically handles references from extensions in one plug-in's
> manifest to code located in another plug-in's runtime library as well as various
> forms of post-instantiation initialization specified in the extension (see Section
> 20.5, Types Specified in an Extension Point, on page 723). If you use
> `Class.forName(String)`, then you will only be able to instantiate objects
> already known to your plug-in because `Class.forName(String)` uses your
> plug-in's class loader and thus will only instantiate objects in your plug-in's
> classpath (see Section 20.9, Plug-in ClassLoaders, on page 742 for more on
> class loaders).

The new `factory` type is an abstract base class that must be extended by
other plug-ins providing new types of **Favorites** objects. See the "**Tip**" in Section 17.2.3, Extension point elements and attributes, on page 601 for a discussion of interface versus abstract base class. The `factory` type includes a
concrete `dispose` method so that subclasses can perform cleanup if necessary,
but are not required to implement this method if cleanup is not needed.

```
package com.qualityeclipse.favorites.model;

public abstract class FavoriteItemFactory
{
   public abstract IFavoriteItem newFavorite(
      FavoriteItemType type, Object obj);

   public abstract IFavoriteItem loadFavorite(
      FavoriteItemType type, String info);

   public void dispose() {
      // Nothing to do... subclasses may override.
   }
}
```

17.3.4   Cleanup

When the plug-in shuts down, you must dispose of all cached images and give
each of the `factory` objects an opportunity to clean up. Add the methods,
`disposeTypes()` and `dispose()`, to the `FavoriteItemType`. Modify the
`FavoritesPlugin` `stop()` method to call this new `disposeTypes()`
method.

```
public static void disposeTypes() {
   if (cachedTypes == null) return;
   for (int i = 0; i < cachedTypes.length; i++)
      cachedTypes[i].dispose();
   imageCache.dispose();
   cachedTypes = null;
}

public void dispose() {
   if (factory == null) return;
   factory.dispose();
   factory = null;
}
```

17.4 Extension Point Documentation

Now that the extension point and related schema (see Section 17.2, Defining an Extension Point, on page 597) have been declared, the PDE will include them in any list of known plug-in extension points. In addition, the documentation snippets added as part of the schema (see Section 17.2.2, Creating an extension point schema, on page 599 and Section 17.2.3, Extension point elements and attributes, on page 601) are dynamically built by the PDE into extension point help pages as requested. Navigate to the plug-in manifest editor's **Extensions** page and click on the **Add...** button. The **New Extensions** wizard now includes the new `favorites` extension point (see Figure 17–7).

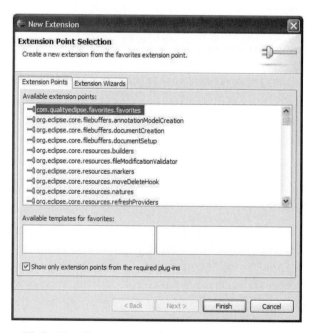

Figure 17–7 New Extension wizard showing Favorites extension point.

To see the dynamically generated help pages, add the `favorites` extension point to the plug-in manifest (see next section), select the `favorites` extension in the plug-in manifest, and then click on **Open extension point description**. This opens a browser to display the HTML help page for the `favorites` extension point (see Figure 17–8).

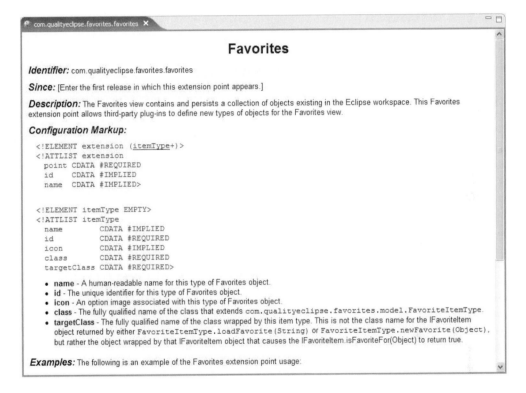

Figure 17–8   Dynamically generated help for the Favorites extension point.

17.5   Using the Extension Point

The `FavoriteItemType` has been refactored to use information from the `favorites` extension point. So now, the constants in that class must be recast as extensions and associated `factory` classes. This modification will help you test your new extension point.

On the plug-in manifest editor's **Extensions** page, click the **Add...** button to open the **New Extensions** wizard. When the wizard appears, select the new `favorites` extension point (see Figure 17–7) and then click **Finish**.

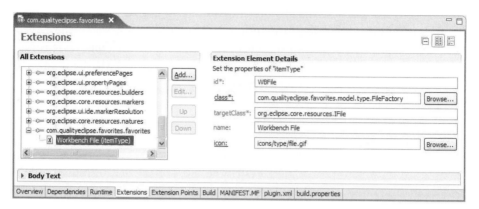

Figure 17–9   The Extension Element Details showing Workbench File item type properties.

Now that you have created an extension, you need to add a new item-Type representing the **Workbench File** item type. Right-click on the new favorites extension and select **New > itemType** to add a new **Favorites** item type. Click on the new itemType and change the properties as follows (see Figure 17–9).

For the icon attribute specified, icons from the Eclipse UI and JDT UI plug-ins have been copied into the **Favorites** plug-in. Clicking the **Browse...** button at the right of the icon attribute field opens an image selection dialog so that you can select the appropriate image for the item type from images defined in the plug-in.

For the class attribute, select the **class:** label at the left of the **class** attribute field to open the **Java Attribute Editor** wizard. Enter "com.quality-eclipse.favorites.model.type" as the package name and "FileFactory" as the type name. Click on the **Finish** button to generate the new class. Move the newFavorite() and loadFavorite() methods from the WORKBENCH_FILE constant in the FavoriteItemType class so that the new FileFactory class looks like this:

```
package com.qualityeclipse.favorites.model.type;

import ...

public class FileFactory extends FavoriteItemFactory
{
   public IFavoriteItem newFavorite(
     FavoriteItemType type, Object obj
   ) {
     if (!(obj instanceof IFile))
        return null;
     return new FavoriteResource(type, (IFile) obj);
   }
}
```

```
    public IFavoriteItem loadFavorite(
        FavoriteItemType type, String info
    ) {
        return FavoriteResource.loadFavorite(type, info);
    }
}
```

Once complete, the first of several **Favorites** item types have been converted from a constant to an extension. Repeat this process multiple times to recast each constant **Favorites** item type in `FavoriteItemType`, except for the UNKNOWN item type discussed earlier (see Section 17.3.2, Constructing proxies, on page 609).

17.6 RFRS Considerations

The "Extension Point" section of the *RFRS Requirements* includes five items—three requirements and two best practices—dealing with defining new extension points.

17.6.1 *Document extension points*   (RFRS 3.10.5)

Requirement #1 states:

> *For each extension point that you define that is considered public, you must supply an extension point schema file. By describing your extension point with an extension point schema, it allows the* `plugin.xml` *editor to validate the extensions, it offers assistance during creation of the extension and it allows the editor to provide assistance for settings values to attributes that require Java syntax by interacting with Java platform features. In addition, you must also include documentation in the extension point schema file that describes how to implement this extension point.*

For this test, attempt to implement the **Favorites** extension point. Add the extension via the **Extensions** page of the `plugin.xml` editor and verify that the editor is providing assistance to the elements that should be added to the extension. Also verify that you are able to open an `html` page for the **Favorites** extension point that provides documentation on how to implement it properly.

17.6.2   Log errors   *(RFRS 5.3.10.1)*

Best Practice #2 states:

> *The registry processing code must log any errors that it detects in the plug-in log.*

Show that the registry processing code handles any errors in the specification of extensions to your plug-in's extension points. For the **Favorites** extension point, create an extension that was missing the `name` attribute. This would create an entry in the Eclipse **Error Log** view (see Figure 17–10).

Figure 17–10   Error Log showing error in extension specification.

17.7   Summary

Extension points are the primary mechanism used to extend Eclipse. Every Eclipse plug-in makes use of dozens of them to contribute new views, actions, editors, and so on. Extension points are not limited, however, to Eclipse itself. Your plug-ins can define extension points either for their internal consumption only or for other third-party plug-ins to use. This chapter demonstrated in detail the process of creating and using a new extension point.

References

Chapter source (*www.qualityeclipse.com/projects/source-ch-17.zip*).

D'Anjou, Jim, Scott Fairbrother, Dan Kehn, John Kellerman, and Pat McCarthy, *The Java Developer's Guide to Eclipse, Second Edition*, Addison-Wesley, Boston, 2004.

Gamma, Eric and Kent Beck, *Contributing to Eclipse*, Addison-Wesley, Boston, 2003.

"Eclipse Platform Technical Overview," Object Technology International, Inc., February 2003 (*www.eclipse.org/whitepapers/eclipse-overview.pdf*).

Bolour, Azad, "Notes on the Eclipse Plug-in Architecture," Bolour Computing, July 3, 2003 (*www.eclipse.org/articles/Article-Plug-in-architecture/plugin_architecture.html*).

CHAPTER 18

Features, Branding, and Updates

One or more Eclipse plug-ins can be grouped together into an Eclipse *feature* so that a user can easily load, manage, and brand those plug-ins as a single unit. This chapter includes an overview of the Eclipse feature framework and shows how to create a simple feature using the built-in feature-creation wizard.

It will also discuss using features to commercialize or brand a plug-in-based product and will conclude with a description of how to package and deliver features via an update-enabled Web site.

So far, several plug-ins have been created, which have contributed different features to the **Favorites** view. Each plug-in has been loosely coupled to other plug-ins, and collectively have not exhibited any unifying structure or identity. A feature provides this structure and a home for branding elements such as the **About** pages and images (see Figure 18–1).

Once packaged as a feature, you will then be able to load and unload your plug-ins as a single unit using the Eclipse **Update Manager**.

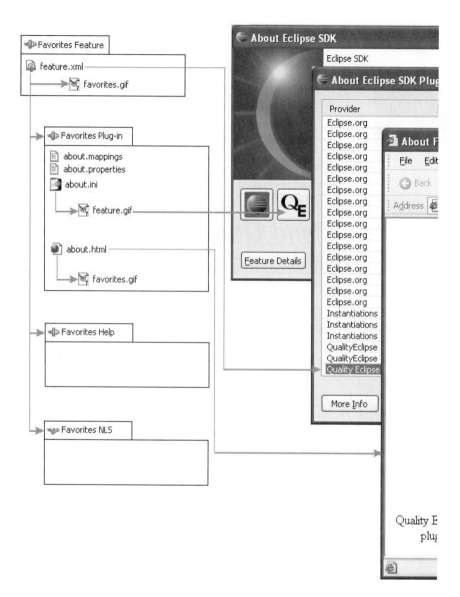

Figure 18–1   Feature file relationships and branding elements.

18.1   Feature Projects

The **Favorites** example includes three projects—"Favorites Plug-in," "Favorites Help," and "Favorites NLS Fragment"—that you would like to combine together into a single feature.

18.1.1 Creating a new feature project

To create the new feature, you will begin by using the **New Project** wizard to create a new **Feature Project** (see Figure 18–2).

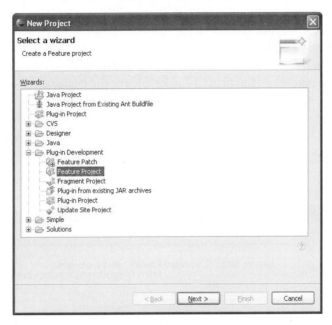

Figure 18–2 The New Project wizard.

On the first page of the **New Feature** wizard (see Figure 18–3), enter "com.qualityeclipse.favorites.feature" as the project name. Click the **Next** button.

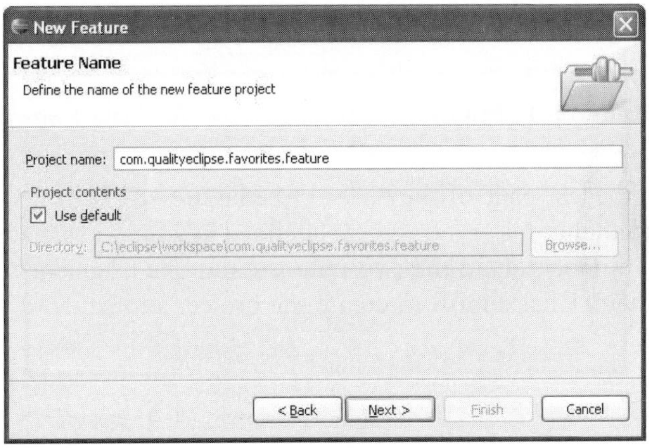

Figure 18–3 The New Feature wizard.

On the second page of the wizard (see Figure 18–4), change the feature ID to "com.qualityeclipse.favorites" so that it matches the ID of the main plug-in. This is important because the generally accepted practice in the Eclipse world is to locate feature branding files (such as about.ini and about. properties) in the plug-in with the same ID as the feature (as you will see a bit later, this is not strictly required—see Section 18.1.3, Feature manifest editor, on page 624).

A couple of other fields should be filled in on this page as well: Change the **Feature Name** to "Favorites Feature"; leave the **Feature Version** set to "1.0.0"; and set the **Feature Provider** to "QualityEclipse". The section at the bottom of this page deals with setting up a custom install handler. This is an advanced feature, which won't be covered in this book. Leave those settings unchanged and click the **Next** button.

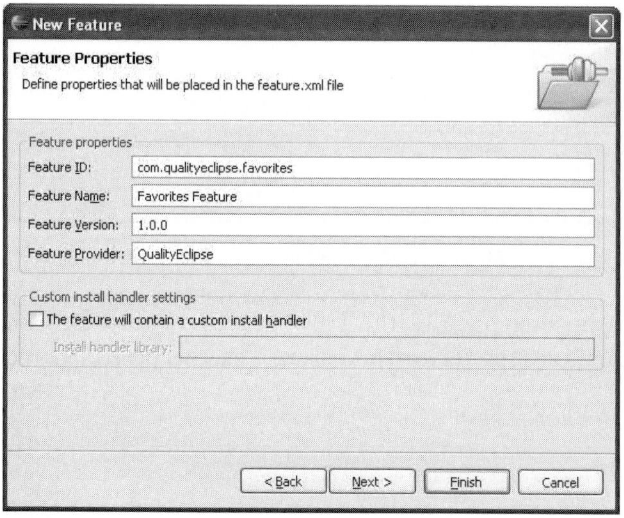

Figure 18–4　Feature Properties page of the New Feature wizard.

On the last page of the wizard (see Figure 18–5), you will see a list of all the loaded plug-ins and fragments defined in your workspace along with their version numbers. Find the two plug-ins and one fragment created earlier and select them. Click **Finish** to create the project and generate the feature manifest file.

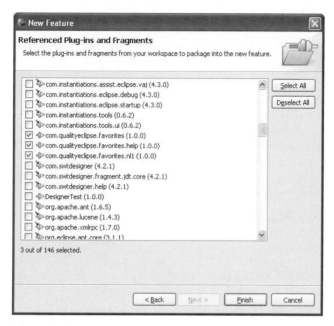

Figure 18–5   Referenced Plug-ins and Fragments page of the New Feature wizard.

18.1.2   Feature manifest files

The wizard created a single file of interest: the feature manifest file. Based on the options selected in the wizard, the feature manifest file (`feature.xml`) will look like this:

```xml
<?xml version="1.0" encoding="UTF-8"?>
<feature
      id="com.qualityeclipse.favorites"
      label="Favorites Feature"
      version="1.0.0"
      provider-name="QualityEclipse">

   <description url="http://www.example.com/description">
      [Enter Feature Description here.]
   </description>

   <copyright url="http://www.example.com/copyright">
      [Enter Copyright Description here.]
   </copyright>

   <license url="http://www.example.com/license">
      [Enter License Description here.]
   </license>
```

```
<plugin
      id="com.qualityeclipse.favorites"
      download-size="0"
      install-size="0"
      version="0.0.0"/>

<plugin
      id="com.qualityeclipse.favorites.help"
      download-size="0"
      install-size="0"
      version="0.0.0"/>

<plugin
      id="com.qualityeclipse.favorites.nl1"
      download-size="0"
      install-size="0"
      version="0.0.0"
      fragment="true"/>
</feature>
```

The structure is fairly simple. At the beginning of the file, you will find the id, label, version, and provider-name attributes. The description, copyright, and license sections contain information meant to be presented to the user of the feature.

The remainder of the file lists the individual plug-ins and fragments that compose this feature. Each plug-in is identified by its plug-in ID, and the version attribute specifies the specific version of the plug-in that is part of this feature. In general, the version numbers of the included plug-ins should match the version number of the feature. Having the fragment attribute set to true identifies any included fragments.

18.1.3   *Feature manifest editor*

The feature manifest generated by the wizard contains the barest essential elements needed to define a feature. Numerous other attributes can be defined to enhance a feature. The feature manifest editor provides a convenient interface for editing the existing attributes of a feature or adding new attributes.

Double-clicking on the feature manifest file, feature.xml, will open the feature manifest editor (see Figure 18–6). The editor looks very similar to the plug-in manifest editor with **Overview, Information, Plug-ins, Included Features, Dependencies, Installation, Build, feature.xml,** and **build.properties** pages.

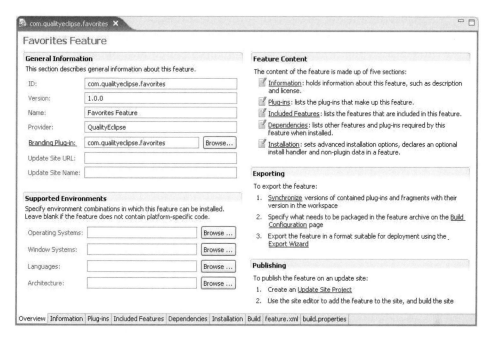

Figure 18–6   Feature manifest editor.

There are a lot of things happening on this page. Initially, the **ID, Version, Name,** and **Provider** fields will be filled in based on inputs to the wizard pages. There are other fields to make note of here. **Branding Plug-in** contains the name of the plug-in that will contain the feature branding files. Use the **Browse...** button to select the main plug-in or manually change the value to "com.qualityeclipse.favorites" so that it matches the ID of the main plug-in.

The **Update Site URL** and **Update Site Name** fields are used to specify the Web address and name of the update site that will be used to load the feature using the Eclipse **Update Manager.** When the **Update Manager** is looking for updates to your plug-in, it will look at the sites defined by your update URLs. This is discussed in more detail in Section 18.3, Update Sites, on page 637.

For most plug-ins written against the public Eclipse API, portability to different Eclipse platforms won't be a problem. Eclipse does not prevent you, however, from making use of platform-specific functionality (such as ActiveX support under Windows). In situations like that, you need to be able to specify which environments are appropriate for your plug-in. In the **Supported Environments** section, you can supply a comma-separated list of valid values for **Operating Systems, Window Systems, Languages,** and **Architecture.**

Clicking on the **Browse...** button to the right of each field will open a selection dialog appropriate to the chosen environment type. For example, the choices available for **Operating Systems** include **aix, hpux, linux, macosx, qnx, solaris,** and **win32** (see Figure 18–7).

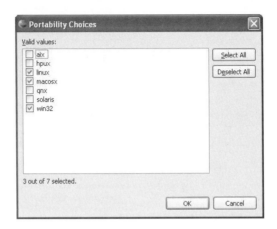

Figure 18–7   Portability Choices for operating systems.

On the right side of the page, the **Exporting** section includes a couple of interesting options. The **Synchronize** button is used to synchronize the version numbers of the included plug-ins and fragments with the version number of the feature. If these version numbers don't match, the **Update Manager** won't be able to install the feature properly. Clicking the button will open the **Version Synchronization** dialog (see Figure 18–8).

That dialog contains three options: The first, and most useful option, is **Synchronize versions on build (recommended)**. This will update the manifest files of all included plug-ins and fragments so that their version numbers match the version number of the feature. The second option, **Copy versions from plug-in and fragment manifests**, will copy the individual version numbers from each plug-in and fragment and update the corresponding plug-in entry in the feature manifest file. The final option, **Force feature version into plug-in and fragment manifests**, does the reverse and takes the individual version numbers defined for each plug-in in the feature manifest file and updates the manifest files of the corresponding plug-ins and fragments. Select the first option and click **Finish** to return to the manifest editor.

The **Export Wizard** button is used to build and deploy the feature. Ignore this option and focus on a much more comprehensive build operation in Chapter 19, Building a Product.

Figure 18–8   Version Synchronization dialog.

The **Information** page of the editor provides tabs for specifying **Feature Description, Copyright Notice, License Agreement,** and **Sites to Visit** information about the feature (see Figure 18–9). The feature description will be displayed by the **Update Manager** when the feature is selected. This information, as well as the license and copyright text, is displayed in the **Properties** dialog that appears when the **Show Properties** link is clicked within the **Update Manager.**

For each of these items, you can either enter text into the **Text** field or you can specify a URL in the **Optional URL** field. Unless the URL is an absolute reference to a site, the URL is assumed to point to an HTML file that is located relative to the root of the feature.

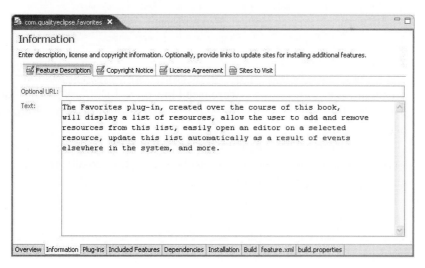

Figure 18–9   Description, license, and copyright information page.

The **Plug-ins** page of the editor lists the plug-ins and fragments contained in your feature (see Figure 18–10). In this case, you will see the same three items that were selected when the feature was originally created. Double-clicking on any of these items will open the appropriate manifest editor.

As your project gets more complex, you may need to add plug-ins or fragments and update the list of required features and plug-ins. Clicking the **Add...** button will open a dialog showing a list of all the plug-in and fragment projects available in your workspace. Select one or more and then click **Finish** to add them to the list.

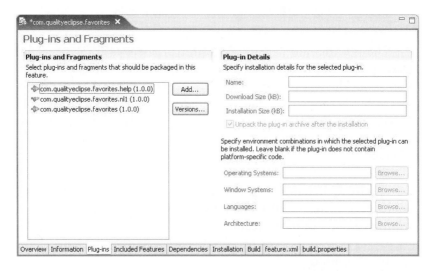

Figure 18–10 Plug-ins and Fragments page.

The **Included Features** page of the editor contains a list of subfeatures that are included as part of this feature (see Figure 18–11). Clicking the **Add...** button will allow you to select the features that should become children of the current feature.

If a feature has its **The feature is optional** field enabled, it is not required to be present for the parent feature to be successfully loaded (it may be loaded and installed later as necessary).

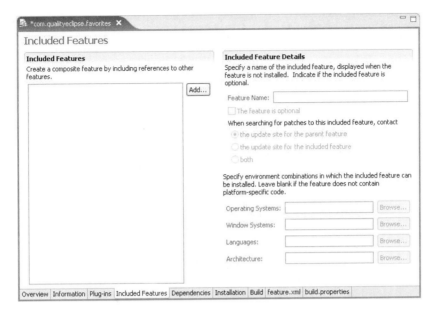

Figure 18–11   Included Features page.

Optional subfeatures can also be enabled or disabled via the **Update Manager** independent of their parent features. The **Feature Name** field is used to supply a name for this feature (for display purposes) in the event that it is missing.

The **Dependencies** page contains a list of all the features and plug-ins that must be available to install your feature (see Figure 18–12). If any of them are missing, your feature won't be able to load. As stated earlier, the list of required plug-ins was initially computed based on merging the required plug-ins specified by the plug-ins in your feature.

You can manually add plug-ins or features to the list by clicking the **Add Plug-in...** or **Add Feature...** buttons. Clicking the **Compute** button will recompute the list based on the requirements specified by the plug-ins included in the feature.

For each required plug-in, you, optionally, can specify a **Version to match** and a **Match Rule**. The following choices that are available in the **Match Rule** field control what versions of the plug-in are acceptable prerequisites.

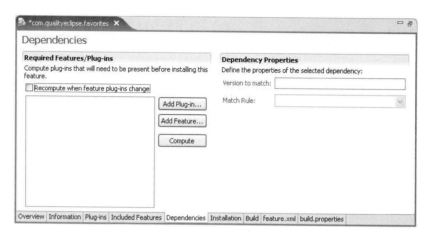

Figure 18–12   Dependencies page.

- **Perfect** means that the plug-in must exactly match the supplied version number.

- **Equivalent** means that the version may differ at the service or qualifier level.

- **Compatible** means that the plug-in may have a newer minor version number.

- **Greater or Equal** means that the plug-in may have any newer version number.

If the version number does not match the chosen criteria, that prerequisite will be missing and your feature will not load. In general, you will probably leave these fields blank unless your feature has very specific requirements that will cause it to fail when faced with the wrong version of some expected plug-in (as might be the case if you were using an Eclipse 3.1-specific API that was not available in earlier releases).

The **Installation Details** page specifies whether the feature cannot be installed simultaneously with other features or must be installed in the same directory as another feature (see Figure 18–13). The **This feature requires exclusive installation** option is used to prevent your feature from being installed simultaneously with a number of other features. Unless there is something unique about your feature that would prevent it from being installed properly in conjunction with other features, you should leave this option unchecked.

The remaining fields on the **Installation Details** page are used for specifying optional non-plug-in items that should be included with this feature as well as advanced installation handlers. These are beyond the scope of this book and won't be discussed further here.

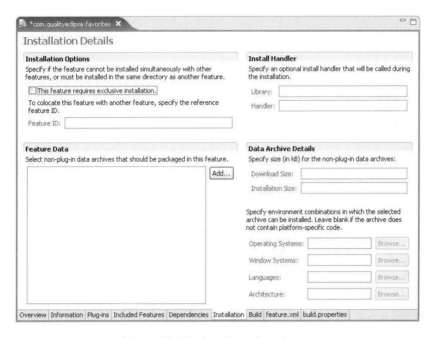

Figure 18–13   Installation Details page.

18.2   **Branding**

In addition to providing structure to your collection of plug-ins and fragments, a feature also provides a single location for all your branding information (e.g., **About** pages, images, etc.). As stated earlier, the branding elements (such as the banner image shown in the **Update Manager**) aren't located in the feature project itself; most of the branding elements are located in the feature's associated branding plug-in.

There are quite a few different branding files that come into play at this point. Several of them only apply to Eclipse *products* (a stand-alone program built with the Eclipse platform) while the rest apply to any feature. The files that apply to any type of feature include:

- `about.html`
- `about.ini`
- `about.properties`
- `about.mappings`
- `<featureImage>` (named in the `about.ini` file)

The remaining files, which apply only to products, include:

- `<aboutImage>`
- `<windowImages>`
- `plugin_customization.ini`
- `plugin_customization.properties`
- `splash.bmp`

18.2.1   The about.html file

Every feature and plug-in should include an `about.html` file. This is a simple HTML file that is displayed when the user opens the Eclipse **About** dialog, opens the **Plug-in Details** dialog, selects a plug-in, and then clicks the **More Info** button (see Figure 18–14).

Figure 18–14   The About page for the Favorites plug-in.

Note that to satisfy the RFRS requirements, the about.html must contain the following phrase: "This offering is powered by Eclipse technology and includes Eclipse plug-ins that can be installed and used with other Eclipse (3.1)-based offerings".

18.2.2 The about.ini file

The about.ini file located in the feature's branding plug-in controls most of the feature branding information. It is a standard Java properties file that contains specific keys (see Table 18-1) such as the feature's about text, the name of the image displayed in the Eclipse **About** dialog (see Figure 18–15), and so on.

Table 18–1 about.ini Keys

Key	Description
aboutText	Short multiline description of the feature
featureImage	32x32 pixel image used in the **About** dialog
tipsAndTricksHref	Link to tips and tricks help page

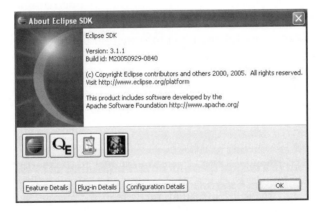

Figure 18–15 The About Eclipse dialog.

The first key, aboutText, is a short multiline description of the feature that should give its name, version number, relevant build information, copyright information, and so on. The text will be visible in the **About Features** dialog (see Figure 18–16), which is accessible by clicking the **Feature Details** button in the **About** dialog.

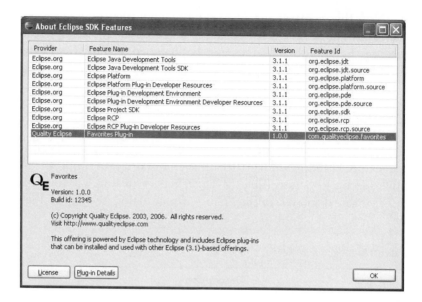

Figure 18–16   The About Eclipse Features dialog.

To localize (translate) this information, the text can be located in an associated `about.properties` file with a localization key placed in the `about.ini` file itself. The about text can also be parameterized with values supplied by the `about.mappings` file.

This can be useful encoding information that changes based on the product build (such as a build number) or the product install (such as the user's name or license key). For example, the about text might include the phrase "this product is licensed to {0}", where "{0}" represents an argument number that matches a corresponding value, such as "0=Joe User", in the mappings file.

The next key in the `about.ini` file, `featureImage`, is used to reference a 32x32 pixel image that will be used to represent the feature in the main **About** dialog (see Figure 18–15) and the **About Features** dialog (see Figure 18–16). If multiple features are installed, those features' images will be lined up along the bottom of the **About** dialog.

If a feature's documentation includes a "tips and tricks" section, you can reference it with the `tipsAndTricksHref` key. You can access the tips and tricks for any feature that includes them by selecting the **Help > Tips and Tricks** command.

The `about.ini` file for the **Favorites** feature should end up looking like this:

```
# about.ini
# contains information about a feature
# java.io.Properties file (ISO 8859-1 with "\" escapes)
# "%key" are externalized strings defined in about.properties
# This file does not need to be translated.

# Property "aboutText" contains blurb for About dialog. (translated)
aboutText=%blurb

# Property "featureImage" contains path to feature image. (32x32)
featureImage=feature.gif
```

The `about.properties` file contains any translatable strings from the `about.ini` file. For the **Favorites** feature, the file should look like:

```
# about.properties
# contains externalized strings for about.ini
# java.io.Properties file (ISO 8859-1 with "\" escapes)
# fill-ins are supplied by about.mappings
# This file should be translated.

blurb=Favorites\n\
\n\
Version: 1.0.0\n\
Build id: {0}\n\
\n\
(c) Copyright Quality Eclipse. 2003, 2006. All rights reserved.\n\
Visit http://www.qualityeclipse.com\n\
\n\
This offering is powered by Eclipse technology and includes\n\
Eclipse plug-ins that can be installed and used with other\n\
Eclipse (3.1)-based offerings.
```

18.2.3   Product branding

The remaining branding files are only applicable to products and are specified by contributing to the `org.eclipse.core.runtime.products` extension point (see Figure 18–17). As an example, here is the extension definition found in the `org.eclipse.platform` plug-in:

```
<extension id="ide" point="org.eclipse.core.runtime.products">
   <product name="%productName"
            application="org.eclipse.ui.ide.workbench"
            description="%productBlurb">
      <property name="windowImages"
                value="eclipse.png,eclipse32.png"/>
      <property name="aboutImage" value="eclipse_lg.png"/>
      <property name="aboutText" value="%productBlurb"/>
      <property name="appName" value="Eclipse"/>
      <property name="preferenceCustomization"
                value="plugin_customization.ini"/>
   </product>
</extension>
```

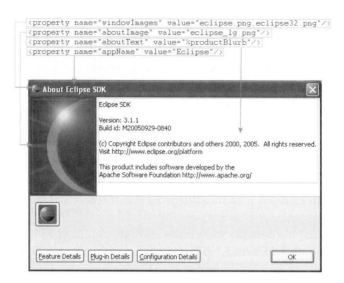

Figure 18–17   Product branding properties.

The `windowImages` property points to a 16x16 pixel image used as the icon in the upper-left corner of windows and dialogs. For the Eclipse workbench itself, this is the ubiquitous Eclipse icon.

The `aboutImage` property points to a larger image that is placed next to the about text in the main **About** dialog. If the image is less than 250x330 pixels in size, the image is shown next to the about text. If the image is larger (up to 500x330 pixels in size), the about text will be suppressed.

As described for the `about.ini` file earlier, the `aboutText` property is a short multiline description of the product that should give its name, version number, relevant build information, copyright information, and so on. This text will be displayed in the product **About** dialog (see Figure 18–15).

The `appName` property is used to provide a non-translatable name for the application. For Eclipse, this is just the string "Eclipse".

If the product needs to change the default preferences of any other installed plug-ins, it can place those new settings in a file specified by the `preference-Customization` property (e.g., the `plugin_customization.ini` file). Every line in the file should follow this form:

```
<plug-in id>/<preference id>=<value>
```

If any of the values need to be localized, the translated values should be placed in the `plugin_customization.properties` file, which follows the pattern established in Chapter 16, Internationalization.

The location of the product splash screen is specified by the `osgi.splashPath` property in the `config.ini` contained in the product's configuration directory. The splash.bmp file, which Eclipse specifically looks for by name, contains the product splash screen. It should be a 24-bit color bitmap, and its size should be approximately 500x330 pixels. If the text in the splash screen needs to be localized, the splash.bmp file can be located in a fragment.

18.3 Update Sites

After you have created a feature and provided a unifying structure and brand identity to your plug-ins, you need to deliver your feature to users. While you can package a feature as a compressed ZIP file or create your own installer (using InstallShield or something similar), Eclipse provides an attractive Web-based alternative that can manage the delivery, installation, and eventual updating of your feature.

An Eclipse update site is a specially constructed Web site designed to host your features and plug-ins (packaged as JAR files) and describe them with a special site manifest file (the site.xml file). The Eclipse **Update Manager** can read this site manifest file and automatically load and install any updates (or new products) that it finds.

18.3.1 Creating an update site project

Just as plug-ins, fragments, and features are represented as projects in your workspace, so too are update sites. To create the update site, begin by using the **New Project** wizard to create a new **Update Site Project** (see Figure 18–18).

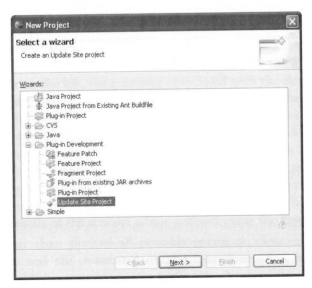

Figure 18–18 The New Project wizard—selecting an Update Site Project.

On the first and only page of the **New Update Site** wizard (see Figure 18-19), enter "com.qualityeclipse.favorites.update" as the project name. The **Web Resources** options control whether the wizard will generate a default home page for the update site. If a user visits the update site manually, this is the page they will see. Turn on the **Generate a sample web page listing all available features within the site** checkbox and leave the **Web resources location** field set to "web". Click the **Finish** button to create the project and its initial files.

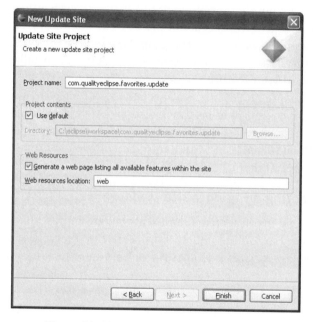

Figure 18–19   The New Update Site wizard.

Several files and directories are created by default:

```
/web
    site.css
    site.xls
index.html
site.xml
```

After you have added a feature to the site, two additional directories, /features and /plugins, will hold the JAR files containing the feature and plug-in files. When these files are uploaded to the update site, they will be accessible by the **Update Manager**. The /web directory contains the style sheet files used to provide the look of the update site. The index.html file is the

main entry Web page for the site. Most of its contents are dynamically constructed based on the contents of the update site.

18.3.2   The site.xml file

The most important file is the site manifest file—site.xml. Initially, it is
empty for all practical purposes, so you will need to flesh out its definition.
The site manifest editor provides a convenient interface for editing the existing
characteristics of the site or adding new attributes.

Double-clicking on the site manifest file will open the site manifest editor
(see Figure 18–20). The editor has three pages—**Site Map, Archives,** and
site.xml.

If more than one feature will be made available via the update site, you
might want to place them in categories. Click the **New Category** button to create a new category. Every category should have a unique **Name,** a **Label,** and
a **Description** that will appear in the update site and within the **Update
Manager.** For the update site, enter "Favorites" for the **Name** and "Favorites
Features" for the **Label.**

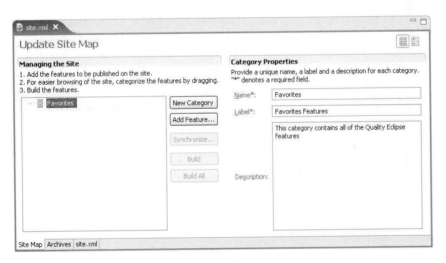

Figure 18–20   The site manifest editor.

Each category that you create is added to the **Managing the Site** list and
acts as a drop target. If you want a specific feature to show up in more than
one category, drag and drop the feature on each category.

To add a feature to the **Managing the Site** list, click the **Add Feature...** button to see a list of features defined in the workspace in the **Feature Selection**
dialog (see Figure 18–21). Select the "com.qualityeclipse.favorites" feature
and click **OK** to add the **Favorites** feature to the list.

Figure 18–21   The Feature Selection dialog.

Clicking on any feature in the **Managing the Site** list displays the **Feature Properties** and **Feature Environments** (see Figure 18–22). You will see one required and a number of optional fields that can be used to provide details about each feature. The required (and uneditable) **URL** field is used to specify the location (relative to the site.xml file) on the update site where the **Update Manager** can expect to find the feature's JAR file. For the **Favorites** feature, this should appear as "features/com.qualityeclipse. favorites_1.0.0.jar". The **This feature is a patch for another feature** option specifies whether this feature will be used to patch an existing feature (as opposed to updating it to a new version).

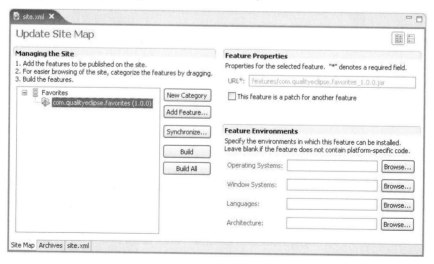

Figure 18–22   The site manifest editor showing Feature Properties.

The remaining fields are optional and used to specify in which environments the selected feature is appropriate. These are very similar to the fields you saw within the feature manifest editor (see Figure 18–6 on page 625). You will generally leave these fields blank unless your feature has specific runtime requirements.

Clicking the **Build All** button at this point will add the /features and /plugins directories to the project and populate them with the JAR files containing the feature and plug-in files.

```
/features
    com.qualityeclipse.favorites_1.0.0.jar
/plugins
    com.qualityeclipse.favorites_1.0.0.jar
    com.qualityeclipse.favorites.help_1.0.0.jar
    com.qualityeclipse.favorites.nl1_1.0.0.jar
```

The **Archives** page (Figure 18–23) describes the update site and specifies its Web address, description, and any additional data archives. The **URL** field contains the root Web address of the update site. For the **Favorites** example, you will enter "http://com.qualityeclipse.com/update." Finally, enter a description for the site in the **Description** field and leave the **Archive Mapping** section blank.

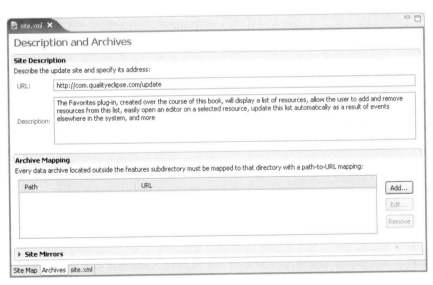

Figure 18–23   The Archives page of the site manifest editor.

At this point, if you switch to the **site.xml** page of the editor, the source of the site.xml file will look something like this:

```xml
<?xml version="1.0" encoding="UTF-8"?>
<site>
   <description url="http://com.qualityeclipse.com/update">
      The Favorites plug-in, created over the course of this book,
      will display a list of resources, allow the user to add and
      remove resources from this list, easily open an editor on a
      selected resource, update this list automatically as a result
      of events elsewhere in the system, and more.
   </description>
   <feature
      url="features/com.qualityeclipse.favorites_1.0.0.jar"
      id="com.qualityeclipse.favorites"
      version="1.0.0">
      <category name="Favorites"/>
   </feature>
   <category-def
      name="Favorites"
      label="Favorites Features">
      <description>
         The Favorites feature includes the Favorites
         plugin, the Favorites help plugin, and the
         Favorites NLS fragment.
      </description>
   </category-def>
</site>
```

18.3.3   *The update Web site*

Now you can see what the update site will look like. Copy the various site map and JAR files within the update project to the update Web site—*www.qualityeclipse.com/update* in the case of the **Favorites** example.

Once the files are uploaded, you can point your Web browser at the update site's URL. The **Favorites** update site will show the description, categories, and features that you defined in the site manifest editor (see Figure 18–24).

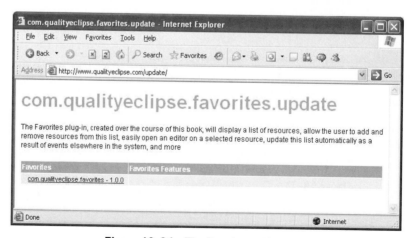

Figure 18–24   The Favorites update site.

18.3.4   Revisiting the feature manifest

When the feature manifest file was first discussed earlier in this chapter, we skipped over discussing the **Update Site URL**. As stated before, when the **Update Manager** is looking for updates to your plug-in, it will look at the site defined by your update URL.

Reopen the feature manifest editor (see Section 18.1.3, Feature manifest editor, on page 624) and access the **Overview** page. In the **General Information** section of the editor, change the **Update Site URL** to "http://www.quality-eclipse.com/update" and the **Update Site Name** to "Quality Eclipse" (see Figure 18–25). Any time the **Favorites** feature needs to check for updates, it will search the specified update site.

Figure 18–25   Feature URLs within the feature manifest file.

18.3.5   Accessing the update site

The update site can be accessed using the Eclipse **Update Manager** in a variety of ways. Selecting the **Help > Software Updates > Manage Configuration** command will open the **Product Configuration** dialog (see Figure 18–26). Expanding the tree on the left will display a list of all the features loaded in the workspace. Clicking on a feature will show the feature's details on the right.

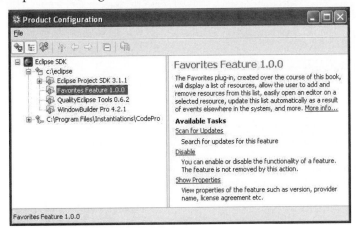

Figure 18–26   The Product Configuration dialog.

For each feature, several different tasks are available. The **Disable** task can be used to disable the feature, causing all its contributions to disappear from the workspace. If a feature has been disabled, the **Disable** task will be replaced with a matching **Enable** task. The **Show Properties** task will open a properties dialog showing the version, provider name, license agreement, and so on for the feature (see Figure 18–27).

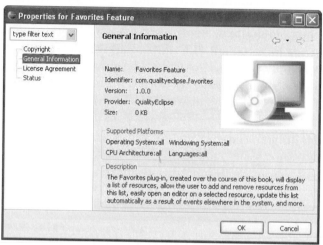

Figure 18–27   Properties for the Favorites feature.

Any feature defining an update site URL will also show a **Scan for Updates** task. Clicking on that task will cause the **Update Manager** to go to the update site and read the site manifest file. It will then determine whether any newer updates for the feature are available. If any updates are available, they will appear in the **Search Results** wizard (see Figure 18–28).

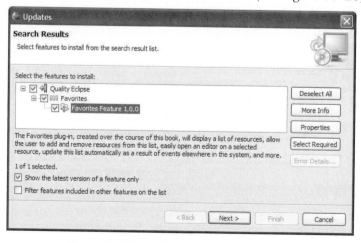

Figure 18–28   Update Manager search results.

Clicking the **Next** button will switch to the **Feature License** page displaying the feature's license, which must be accepted before clicking the **Next** button to get to the **Installation** page (see Figure 18–29). Clicking the **Finish** button will initiate the installation process. Click the **Install** button in the **Feature Verification** dialog to install the update into your workspace.

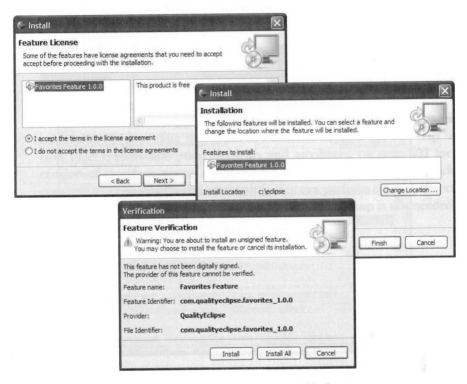

Figure 18–29   Feature Installation and Verification.

In addition to updating via the **Product Configuration** dialog, you can use the **Feature Updates** wizard, which can be accessed via the **Help > Software Updates > Find and Install** command (see Figure 18–30). Selecting the **Search for updates of the currently installed features** radio button and clicking the **Next** button will cause the **Update Manager** to scan the update sites for all the installed features and display any available updates in the **Search Results** wizard you saw earlier.

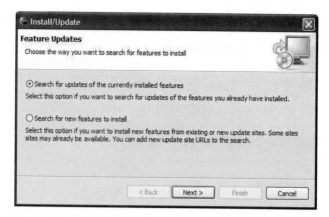

Figure 18–30   The Feature Updates wizard.

If you select the **Search for new features to install** option instead, you will be presented with the option of manually specifying any update sites to search for new features.

If you click the **New Remote Site...** button and specify a site named "Quality Eclipse" with a URL of "http://www.qualityeclipse.com/update", the wizard will scan the update site, read the site manifest, and automatically discover the "Favorites Example" feature (see Figure 18–31). Clicking **Finish** will show any available features in the **Search Results** wizard (see Figure 18–28 on page 644). Clicking **Next**, accepting the license, and then clicking **Finish** will load the feature into your workspace as seen earlier (see Figure 18–29).

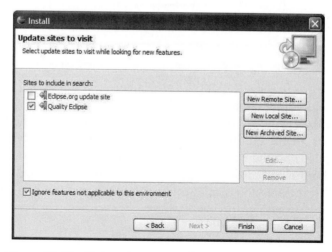

Figure 18–31   Update sites to visit while looking for new features.

18.4 RFRS Considerations

The "Feature Branding" section of the *RFRS Requirements* includes one requirement and four best practices dealing with branding issues.

18.4.1 Do not override product branding (RFRS 3.1.8)

Requirement #1 states:

> *Product branding and launch points are limited to the Product installation that has included the Eclipse platform. Extension installations may not override the existing product branding by overwriting the existing product configuration. Extension installations may not create shortcuts to launch the platform with an alternative configuration. If an Extension wants to launch the Eclipse platform, they must install their own copy.*

To pass this test, show that your feature does not override any of the existing product branding (either by replacing any files or by using the feature startup option).

18.4.2 Branded feature visibility (RFRS 5.3.1.9)

Best Practice #2 states:

> *At least one branded feature must be visible in the **About product_name** and **About product_name Features** dialogs when the Extension has been installed and is enabled. Business Partners should consider providing feature branding for at least one feature and include appropriate documentation for each plug-in referenced by any installed feature. The feature branding content, when provided, must be complete and correct.*

Open the Eclipse **About** dialog and show that your feature icon appears above the pushbuttons. Next, open the **About Eclipse SDK Features** dialog, select your feature in the list, and show that your feature details are displayed (see Figure 18–15 on page 633 for an example).

18.4.3 Include attribution information (RFRS 5.3.1.10)

Best Practice #3 states:

> *A Business Partner's features and plug-ins must include appropriate attribution information (company name, version id, name) in the attribution dialogs started using the **Feature Details...** and **Plug-in Details...** buttons found on the **About product_name** dialog.*

Show that the about text for your feature (see Figure 18–15 on page 633) includes your company name, the feature version ID, and so on.

18.4.4   *about.html file contents*   *(RFRS 5.3.1.11)*

Best Practice #4 states:

> The plug-in must include an `about.html` file in the plug-in install directory. At a minimum it must contain:
>
> a. The Eclipse attribution, using the following text:
> "Company_Name Software_Name offering includes Eclipse plug-ins that can be installed and used with other Eclipse (x.y)-based offerings."
>
> b. Any attribution required by any dependent technology used by the plug-in (as defined by the provider of that technology)
>
> c. Any other legal information that the provider is mandated to provide

Show that each of your plug-ins includes an `about.html` file that properly mentions the use of the Eclipse technology (see Figure 18–13 on page 631) as well as any other relevant legal information.

18.4.5   *Splash screen restrictions*   *(RFRS 5.3.1.12)*

Best Practice #5 states:

> The display of a splash image for a feature is permitted only when the software is installed in an evaluation or demonstration mode. The display of the splash image may not interfere with the user or require a special action to disappear. Once a license is purchased, the software must be automatically modified during the application of the license to remove the display of any feature-specific splash images.

For this test, show that your feature either does not have its own splash screen or that it properly deactivates its own splash screen after the evaluation period has expired.

18.5   Summary

Once you have created your product's plug-ins, features provide a mechanism for adding structure and branding. Branding elements, such as **About** pages are tied to the feature. The Eclipse **Update Manager** can load and unload a group of plug-ins packaged as a feature and can search Web-based update sites for new versions.

References

Chapter source (*www.qualityeclipse.com/projects/source-ch-18.zip*).

Eidsness, Andrew, and Pascal Rapicault, "Branding Your Application," OTI, September 16, 2004 (*www.eclipse.org/articles/Article-Branding/branding-your-application.html*).

Adams, Greg, "Creating Product Branding," OTI, November 27, 2001 (*www.eclipse.org/articles/product-guide/guide.html*).

Glozic, Dejan, and Dorian Birsan, "How to Keep Up to Date," IBM, August 27, 2003 (*www.eclipse.org/articles/Article-Update/keeping-up-to-date.html*).

McCarthy, Pat, "Put Eclipse Features to Work for You," IBM, October 14, 2003 (*www-128.ibm.com/developerworks/opensource/library/os-ecfeat/*).

Eclipse Help: **PDE Guide > Exporting a plug-in**

CHAPTER 19

Building a Product

As introduced in Section 2.4, Building a Product, on page 81, building a commercial product involves packaging up only those elements to be delivered to the customer in a form that the customer can install into his or her environment. Although you can build your product manually, it is better to spend some time constructing an automated build process that is more rigorous and will save time in the long run. This chapter discusses just such an automated build process for the **Favorites** product and enhances the build script introduced in Section 2.4.2, Building with Apache Ant, on page 83.

19.1 A Brief Introduction to Ant

Ant is a build tool on the Apache Web site (*ant.apache.org/*) that ships as part of Eclipse. It differs from *make* and others of its ilk because Ant is written entirely in Java, can be extended without any native platform-dependent code, and has an XML-based syntax. What follows is a very brief introduction to Ant and its syntax. For more information, see the Ant Web site.

19.1.1 Build projects

An Ant build script is XML-based with the following structure:

```
<?xml version="1.0" encoding="UTF-8"?>
<project default="target2" basedir=".">
   <target name="target1">
      <task 1a>
      <task 1b>
      ... more tasks here ...
   </target>
```

```
<target name="target2" depends="target1">
  <task 2a>
  <task 2b>
  ... more tasks here ...
</target>
... more targets here ...
</project>
```

Every Ant build script has exactly one project element that has the following attributes:

basedir (optional)—Specifies the working directory to be used while the script is being executed.

default (required)—Specifies the default target that is to be run when the script is run and no targets are specified.

name (optional)—Specifies a human-readable name for the project.

To execute a build script, select the build script in an Eclipse view, such as the **Resource Navigator**, and select the **Run As > Ant Build...** command (see Section 2.4.2, Building with Apache Ant, on page 83).

19.1.2   Build targets

A project contains one or more internal and external targets. The only thing that differentiates an internal target from an external target is that external targets have a description associated with them while internal targets do not. Every target can have the following attributes:

description (optional)—A description of the task. If this attribute is defined then the target is considered to be external, if not then it is an internal target.

depends (optional)—A comma-delimited list of names of tasks on which this task depends (see discussion later in this section).

name (required)—The name of the task used by other tasks to reference this task.

if (optional)—The name of a property that must be set for this task to be executed. For example, for a task to be executed only if the Ant build script is being launched from Eclipse, then you could use the ${eclipse. running} property (see Section 19.1.4.1, Predefined properties, on page 658):

```
<target name="myTarget" if="${eclipse.running}">
  ... do something Eclipse related ...
</target>
```

unless (optional)—The name of a property that must *not* be set for this task to be executed. For example, for a task to be executed only if the Ant build script is *not* being launched from Eclipse, you could use the `${eclipse.running}` property (see Section 19.1.4.1, Predefined properties, on page 658):

```
<target name="myTarget" unless="${eclipse.running}">
   ... do something non-Eclipse related ...
</target>
```

One build target can explicitly call another build target in the same build script using the `<antcall>` task, or in a different build script using the `<ant>` task. Alternatively, one target can *depend* on another target to achieve a similar effect, *but only within the same build script*. If target A depends on target B, which in turn depends on target C (see Figure 19–1), then if you execute target A, the Ant framework will execute first target C, then target B, and finally target A. This same effect could be achieved by having target A call target B, which in turn calls target C.

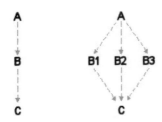

Figure 19–1   Example build target dependencies.

The difference between these two approaches lies in how many times a target is executed. For example, let's assume a more complicated script in which A depends on B1, B2, and B3, and each of these depends on C. In this case, if you execute A then the Ant framework will execute C first, then B1, B2, and B3 in some undetermined order, and finally A. Note that in this case, target C was only executed *once* and not three times as you would expect.

19.1.3   Build tasks

Build targets are composed of a sequence of tasks to be executed. There are many different types of Ant tasks, some of which are listed on the next three pages. In this list, tasks with names that start with "eclipse" are not built into Ant, but are available either as part of Eclipse or as plug-ins for Eclipse (see

Section 19.1.8, Ant extensions, on page 669). Much more complete documentation for Apache Ant tasks can be found on the Apache Ant Web site
(*ant.apache.org/*).

ant—Runs Ant on another build file. For example:

```
<ant
        antfile="subproject/subbuild.xml"
        dir="subproject"
        target="compile"/>
```

By default, all the properties in the current build script will be available in
the build script being called. Alternatively, you can set the inheritAll
attribute to false and only user properties (i.e., those passed on the command line) will be available to the build script being called. In either case,
the set of properties being passed will override any properties with the
same name in the build script being called.

```
<ant
        antfile="subproject/subbuild.xml"
        dir="subproject"
        inheritAll="false"
        target="compile"/>
```

antcall—Calls another target within the same build file (see Section
19.1.5, <antcall> task, on page 664). For example:

```
<antcall target="doSomethingElse">
        <param name="foo.name" value="someValue"/>
</antcall>
```

copy—Copies a file or a set of files specified by a <fileset> to a new
file or directory. By default, files are only copied if the source file is
newer than the destination file, or when the destination file does not
exist. However, you can explicitly overwrite files with the overwrite
attribute. For example:

```
        <copy file="myfile.txt" todir="../some/other/dir"/>
or
        <copy todir="../new/dir">
           <fileset dir="src_dir" includes="**/*.java"/>
        </copy>
```

The <fileset> structure in the code above specifies the files to be
included in the operation. The two asterisks (**) indicate that the operation should include files in the directory specified by the dir attribute,
along with files in any of its subdirectories to an infinite depth.

delete—Deletes a single file, a specified directory and all its files and subdirectories, or a set of files specified by a `<fileset>` (see **copy** for more information about `<filesets>`). When specifying a set of files, empty directories are not removed by default. To remove empty directories, use the `includeEmptyDirs` attribute. For example:

```
<delete dir="lib"/>
```
or
```
<delete>
    <fileset dir="." includes="**/*.bak"/>
</delete>
```

echo—Echoes a message to the current loggers and listeners, which in this case means the **Console** view. For example:

```
<echo message="Hello, world"/>
<echo level="info">Hello, World</echo>
```

eclipse.buildScript—Generates an Ant script to build a specified plug-in, fragment, or feature.

eclipse.convertPath—Converts a filesystem path to a resource path, and vice versa, assigning the result to the specified property (see Section 19.1.7, Headless Ant, on page 668). For example:

```
<eclipse.convertPath
     fileSystemPath="${basedir}"
     property="myPath"/>
```
or
```
<eclipse.convertPath
     resourcePath="MyProject/MyFile"
     property="myPath"/>
```

eclipse.fetch—Generates an Ant script that when executed will retrieve content from a CVS repository.

eclipse.incrementalBuild—Triggers an incremental build of either a project or the entire workspace, depending on whether the project attributed is specified.

eclipse.refreshLocal—Refreshes the specified resources in the workspace (see Section 19.1.7, Headless Ant, on page 668). For example:

```
<eclipse.refreshLocal
     resource="MyProject/MyFolder"
     depth="infinite"/>
```

where `resource` is a resource path relative to the workspace and `depth` can be one of the following: `zero`, `one`, or `infinite`. This is useful when an Ant build script has created, modified, or deleted a file or folder residing within the Eclipse workspace. Eclipse will not reflect the change in the workspace until after this task executes.

`eclipsetools.getclasspath`—Resolves a project's classpath and places the result into an Ant property. Optionally, the classpath can be translated from referencing one Eclipse installation to referencing another (see Section 19.1.7, Headless Ant, on page 668, Section 19.2.3, Compiling during the build process, on page 689 and Section 19.2.7, Classpath tools, on page 701).

`eclipsetools.preprocessor`—Translates source written for one version of Eclipse into source written for another version of Eclipse prior to compilation (see Section 19.1.7, Headless Ant, on page 668 and Section 19.2.6.3, Preprocessor, on page 695).

`javac`—Compiles Java source files into class files (see Section 19.2.3, Compiling during the build process, on page 689). For example:

```
<javac srcdir="${src}"
    destdir="${build}"
    classpath="xyz.jar"
    debug="on"/>
```

`mkdir`—Creates a directory, and nonexistent parent directories are created, when necessary. For example:

```
<mkdir dir="${dist}"/>
```

`property`—Sets a property (by name and value) or a set of properties (from file or resource) in the project (see the next section). For example:

```
<property name="foo.dist" value="dist"/>
```

or

```
<property file="foo.properties"/>
```

`zip`—Creates a ZIP file containing one or more files from a directory, or as specified by a `<zipfileset>` (a `<zipfileset>` is similar to a `<fileset>`; see preceding **copy** for more information about `<fileset>`). For example:

```
<zip
    destfile="${dist}/manual.zip"
    basedir="htdocs/manual"/>
```

or

```
<zip destfile="${dist}/manual.zip">
    <zipfileset
        dir="htdocs/manual"
        prefix="docs/user-guide"/>
</zip>
```

19.1.4 Build properties

A property is a name/value pair, where the name is case-sensitive. Properties can be used in the value of various task attributes by placing the property name between "${" and "}" in the attribute value.

```
<property name="builddir" value="c:\build"/>
<mkdir dir="${builddir}/temp"/>
```

In this build script, the `builddir` property is assigned the value "`c:\build`" in the first task, and then this property is resolved in the `dir` attribute of the second task so that the `c:\build\temp` directory is created.

An alternative form of the `property` task uses the `location` attribute:

```
<property name="builddir" location="dir/subdir"/>
```

When specified this way, the value is resolved relative to the `${basedir}` before being associated with the `builddir` property. For example, if the `${basedir}` is `c:\temp`, then the statement above would have associated `builddir` with the value `c:\temp\dir\subdir`. If the `property` task is modified slightly (notice the slash added before the `dir/subdir`):

```
<property name="builddir" location="/dir/subdir"/>
```

and ${basedir} is `c:\temp`, then the statement above would have associated `builddir` with the value `c:\dir\subdir`.

Tip: Using the `location` attribute without a drive letter is more portable; if you specify a drive letter, then your build scripts will only run on a Windows platform.

Unfortunately, a reference to an undefined property will not be reported during Ant execution, but silently ignored. If a property has not been defined, then no string substitution is made. For example, if you reference the **foo** property before it has been defined:

```
<echo message="the foo property is ${foo}"/>
```

then Ant will leave `${foo}` unchanged and the message displayed will be:

```
the foo property is ${foo}
```

This makes it more difficult to spot problems, and you might end up with some unusual file or directory names, such as:

```
/temp/${plug-in.id}_3.1.0/icons
```

19.1.4.1   Predefined properties

Ant provides several predefined properties including all the Java system properties, such as ${os.name}, as well as the built-in properties shown in Table 19–1.

Table 19–1   Predefined Ant Properties

Property	Description
${basedir}	The absolute path of the project's basedir as set with the basedir attribute of the <project> element.
${ant.file}	The absolute path of the build file.
${ant.version}	The version of Ant.
${ant.project.name}	The name of the project that is currently executing as defined by the name attribute of the <project> element.
${ant.java.version}	The JVM version Ant detected, such as "1.1", "1.2", "1.3", "1.4", or "1.5".

Eclipse provides two additional predefined properties, as shown in Table 19–2.

Table 19–2   Predefined Eclispe Ant Properties

Property	Description
${eclipse.home}	The location of the Eclipse installation directory.
${eclipse.running}	true if the Ant build has been launched from Eclipse, else undefined.

19.1.4.2   Property scoping

Properties are global within a build script from the moment they are declared. If one task assigns a value to a property, another task within the same script can then use that property. In the following script, the foo and bar properties are each declared in separate targets and referenced in others:

```
<?xml version="1.0" encoding="UTF-8"?>
<project name="Test" default="test" basedir=".">
   <target name="init">
      <property name="foo" value="xyz"/>
      <echo message="foo=${foo}"/>
   </target>
   <target name="sub1" depends="init">
      <echo message="foo=${foo}"/>
      <property name="bar" value="abc"/>
      <echo message="bar=${bar}"/>
   </target>
   <target name="sub2" depends="init">
      <echo message="foo=${foo}"/>
      <echo message="bar=${bar}"/>
   </target>
   <target name="test" depends="sub1,sub2">
      <echo message="foo=${foo}"/>
      <echo message="bar=${bar}"/>
   </target>
</project>
```

Looking at the output, you can see that the properties `foo` and `bar` can be referenced anytime after they are declared.

```
Buildfile: scoping_test_1.xml
init:
     [echo] foo=xyz
sub1:
     [echo] foo=xyz
     [echo] bar=abc
sub2:
     [echo] foo=xyz
     [echo] bar=abc
test:
     [echo] foo=xyz
     [echo] bar=abc
BUILD SUCCESSFUL
Total time: 234 milliseconds
```

Closer inspection of both the script and the output reveals something disturbing. The `bar` property is declared in target `sub1` and then referenced in target `sub2` even though *sub2 does not depend on sub1*. This is important because **Ant does not guarantee the order in which nondependent targets will be executed.**

In this first case, target `sub1` just happened to be executed before target `sub2`, and thus `sub2` could reference the `bar` property as expected. If you modify the `test` target's `depends` attribute as follows:

```
<target name="test" depends="sub2,sub1">
```

then the `sub2` target will be executed before the `sub1` target, causing the `bar` property to be declared after it is referenced.

```
Buildfile: scoping_test_2.xml
init:
     [echo] foo=xyz
sub2:
     [echo] foo=xyz
     [echo] bar=${bar}
sub1:
     [echo] foo=xyz
     [echo] bar=abc
test:
     [echo] foo=xyz
     [echo] bar=abc
BUILD SUCCESSFUL
Total time: 265 milliseconds
```

In the simple test build script, the problem and solution are obvious, but as your product, and thus your build scripts, become more complex, this problem could be harder to diagnose.

Tip: The bottom line is that when task A references a property declared in task B, care must be taken to ensure that task A is directly or indirectly dependent on task B so that the build order is deterministic and the property will be declared before it is referenced.

19.1.4.3 *Property mutability*

Properties are immutable once declared. For example, in the following build script:

```
<?xml version="1.0" encoding="UTF-8"?>
<project name="Test" default="test" basedir=".">
   <target name="init">
      <property name="foo" value="xyz"/>
      <echo message="foo=${foo}"/>
      <property name="foo" value="123"/>
      <echo message="foo=${foo}"/>
   </target>
   <target name="test" depends="init">
      <echo message="foo=${foo}"/>
      <property name="foo" value="abc"/>
      <echo message="foo=${foo}"/>
   </target>
</project>
```

the **foo** property is assigned in the `init` target; and once assigned, it *cannot* be modified (the exception to this rule is the `<antcall>` task—see Section 19.1.5, <antcall> task, on page 664). Unfortunately, multiple assignments are quietly ignored and thus are quite a source of confusion.

```
Buildfile: mutability_test_1.xml

init:
     [echo]  foo=xyz
     [echo]  foo=xyz
test:
     [echo]  foo=xyz
     [echo]  foo=xyz

BUILD SUCCESSFUL
Total time: 203 milliseconds
```

19.1.4.4   *Properties outside targets*

Properties are special in that they can be declared outside the scope of a target. A property declared in such a manner is defined before any target is executed and is immutable. For example, in the following build script:

```
<project name="Test" default="test" basedir=".">
   <property name="foo" value="xyz"/>
   <target name="test">
      <echo message="foo=${foo}"/>
      <property name="foo" value="abc"/>
      <echo message="foo=${foo}"/>
   </target>
</project>
```

the **foo** property is assigned its value before the **test** target is executed, and its value is *not* changed by the second `property` task within the test target.

```
Buildfile: mutability_test_2.xml

test:
     [echo]  foo=xyz
     [echo]  foo=xyz

BUILD SUCCESSFUL
Total time: 188 milliseconds
```

19.1.4.5   Properties on the command line

Properties can also be declared outside the build script. A property declared
on the command line is defined before the build is launched and is immutable.

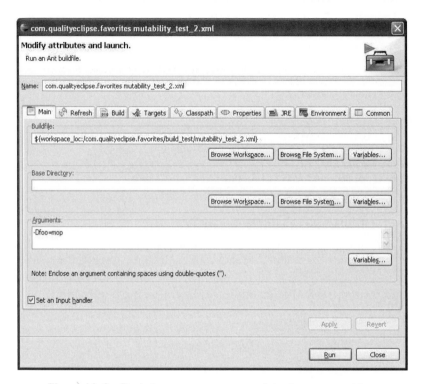

Figure 19–2   Declaring a property as part of the Ant command line.

For example, if you execute the build script described in the previous section using the **Run As > Ant Build...** command, switch to the **Main** tab panel
(see Figure 19–2) and then enter the following in the **Arguments** field.

```
-Dfoo=mop
```

Then, the **foo** property is assigned its value before the build script is executed,
and its value is *not* changed by the property declaration or property task
within the build script.

```
Buildfile: mutability_test_2.xml
test:
     [echo] foo=mop
     [echo] foo=mop
BUILD SUCCESSFUL
Total time: 297 milliseconds
```

Alternatively, properties can be specified by switching to the **Properties** tab panel (see Figure 19–3) and unchecking the **Use global properties as specified in the Ant runtime preferences** checkbox. The top part of the page contains individual property declarations, while the bottom part displays a list of files containing property declarations.

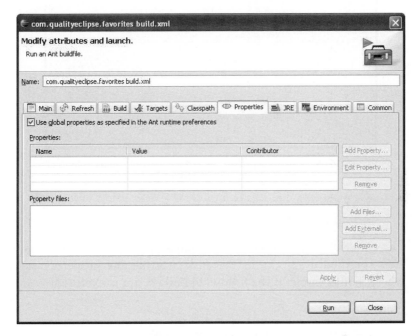

Figure 19–3   Declaring properties and property files applicable to an individual build script.

To specify properties applicable to *all* the build scripts in the workspace, open the Eclipse **Preferences** dialog and navigate to the **Ant > Runtime** preference page (see Figure 19–4). Similar to the **Properties** tab panel shown earlier, the top part of the preference page contains individual property declarations, while the bottom part displays a list of files that contain the property declarations.

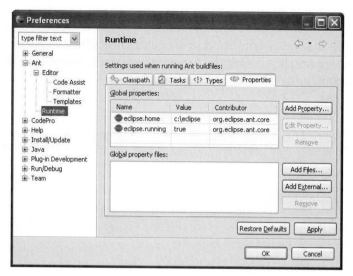

Figure 19–4   Declaring properties and property files applicable to all
build scripts in the workspace.

19.1.5 *<antcall> task*

The <antcall> task has some unusual aspects worthy of discussion. Parameters specified in an <antcall> task override any properties specified elsewhere. For example, if the following build script is executed:

```
<?xml version="1.0" encoding="UTF-8"?>
<project name="Test" default="test" basedir=".">
   <target name="init">
      <property name="foo" value="xyz"/>
      <echo message="in init, foo=${foo}"/>
      <property name="foo" value="123"/>
      <echo message="in init, foo=${foo}"/>
   </target>
   <target name="test" depends="init">
      <echo message="in test, foo=${foo}"/>
      <antcall target="sub">
         <param name="foo" value="gob"/>
      </antcall>
      <echo message="in test, foo=${foo}"/>
   </target>
   <target name="sub">
      <echo message="in sub,  foo=${foo}"/>
      <property name="foo" value="abc"/>
      <echo message="in sub,  foo=${foo}"/>
   </target>
</project>
```

The **foo** property is assigned in the init target and should be immutable (see Section 19.1.4.3, Property mutability, on page 660). However, because **foo** is specified as a parameter in the <antcall> task, the value *is modified* for the duration of the <antcall> task; its original value is restored when the <antcall> task completes.

```
Buildfile: mutability_test_3.xml
init:
     [echo] in init, foo=xyz
     [echo] in init, foo=xyz
test:
     [echo] in test, foo=xyz
sub:
     [echo] in sub,  foo=gob
     [echo] in sub,  foo=gob
     [echo] in test, foo=xyz
BUILD SUCCESSFUL
Total time: 282 milliseconds
```

The <antcall> task resets the depends calculations so that targets can be executed twice. Consider the previous build script with a slight modification.

```
<?xml version="1.0" encoding="UTF-8"?>
<project name="Test" default="test" basedir=".">
   <target name="init">
      <property name="foo" value="xyz"/>
      <echo message="in init, foo=${foo}"/>
      <property name="foo" value="123"/>
      <echo message="in init, foo=${foo}"/>
   </target>
   <target name="test" depends="init">
      <echo message="in test, foo=${foo}"/>
      <antcall target="sub">
         <param name="foo" value="gob"/>
      </antcall>
      <echo message="in test, foo=${foo}"/>
   </target>
   <target name="sub" depends="init">
      <echo message="in sub,  foo=${foo}"/>
      <property name="foo" value="abc"/>
      <echo message="in sub,  foo=${foo}"/>
   </target>
</project>
```

This modification makes the sub target dependent on the init target. Even though the init target is executed prior to the test target, the init target is executed a second time before the sub target because the sub target was executed using the <antcall> task. In addition, the value for the **foo** property is different the second time the init target is executed, but as discussed before, returns to its original value when the <antcall> task completes.

```
Buildfile: mutability_test_4.xml
init:
     [echo] in init, foo=xyz
     [echo] in init, foo=xyz
test:
     [echo] in test, foo=xyz
init:
     [echo] in init, foo=gob
     [echo] in init, foo=gob
sub:
     [echo] in sub,  foo=gob
     [echo] in sub,  foo=gob
     [echo] in test, foo=xyz
BUILD SUCCESSFUL
Total time: 375 milliseconds
```

19.1.6 macrodef

When building complex Ant build scripts, you will find groups of similar
operations. One way to refactor and parameterize these operations is by placing them in their own target and then calling them via <antcall> (see Section
19.1.5, <antcall> task, on page 664). Another way to group and parameterize
operations is to create a new task using a *macrodef*. For example, modify the
script from the previous example to use a macrodef.

```xml
<?xml version="1.0" encoding="UTF-8"?>
<project name="Test" default="test" basedir=".">
   <target name="init">
      <sub fooval="xyz"/>
      <echo message="in init, foo=${foo}"/>
      <sub fooval="123"/>
      <echo message="in init, foo=${foo}"/>
   </target>
   <target name="test" depends="init">
      <echo message="in test, foo=${foo}"/>
      <sub fooval="gob"/>
      <echo message="in test, foo=${foo}"/>
   </target>
   <macrodef name="sub">
      <attribute name="fooval"/>
      <sequential>
         <echo message="in sub,  foo=${foo}"/>
         <property name="foo" value="@{fooval}"/>
         <echo message="in sub,  foo=${foo}"/>
      </sequential>
   </macrodef>
</project>
```

The first thing to notice in the script is that calls to the sub macrodef look
exactly like calls to a built-in Ant task such as echo. The permitted attributes
in that call are specified by the *attribute* tag as in the following.

```
<attribute name="fooval"/>
```

If the attribute is optional and need not be specified by the caller, then supply a default value for the attribute as in the following.

```
<attribute name="fooval" default="a default value"/>
```

Attributes can only be referenced in the macrodef in which they are defined and are preceded by "@" rather than "$" prefix.

- `${foo}`—refers to the build property "`foo`"
- `@{foo}`—refers to the macrodef attribute named "`foo`"

Attributes are resolved in the order that they are defined and before any build properties, leading to some interesting techniques. First, an attribute defined earlier can be used in the default value of an attribute defined later. For example, "`foo`" could be used in the default value of "`bar`" as shown here.

```
<attribute name="foo"/>
<attribute name="bar" default="a @{foo} value"/>
```

Because attributes are resolved before properties, attributes can be used in the name of a property. For example, the "`foo`" attribute could be used to specify which property should be passed to the javac task.

```
<macrodef name="sub">
   <attribute name="foo"/>
   <sequential>
      <javac classpath="${classpath_@{foo}}" ... />
```

Finally, property mutability behaves exactly as if sub is a task.

```
Buildfile: mutability_test_5.xml
init:
     [echo] in sub,  foo=${foo}
     [echo] in sub,  foo=xyz
     [echo] in init, foo=xyz
     [echo] in sub,  foo=xyz
     [echo] in sub,  foo=xyz
     [echo] in init, foo=xyz
test:
     [echo] in test, foo=xyz
     [echo] in sub,  foo=xyz
     [echo] in sub,  foo=xyz
     [echo] in test, foo=xyz
BUILD SUCCESSFUL
Total time: 437 milliseconds
```

19.1.7 Headless Ant

Running Ant headless (from the command line—without a UI) is well-documented (see *ant.apache.org/*), but using Eclipse-specific Ant tasks will cause the build script to fail; Eclipse-specific Ant tasks need Eclipse to execute properly. The following is a Windows batch file (batch files for other platforms will be similar) used to build the **Favorites** product by launching Eclipse headless and executing the **Favorites** build.xml file (the ==> denotes a continuation of the previous line and the characters must not be included).

```
echo off
setlocal

REM ****************************************************
set JAVAEXE="C:\j2sdk1.4.2_02\jre\bin\java.exe"
set STARTUPJAR="C:\eclipse_310\startup.jar"
set WORKSPACE="C:\eclipse_310\workspace"
set BUILDFILE=build.xml

REM ****************************************************
if not exist %JAVAEXE% echo ERROR:
==>         incorrect java.exe=%JAVAEXE%, edit this file
==>         and correct the JAVAEXE envar
if not exist %JAVAEXE% goto done
if not exist %STARTUPJAR% echo ERROR:
==>         incorrect startup.jar=%STARTUPJAR%, edit this file
==>         and correct the STARTUPJAR envar
if not exist %STARTUPJAR% goto done
if not exist %WORKSPACE% echo ERROR:
==>         incorrect workspace=%WORKSPACE%, edit this file
==>         and correct the WORKSPACE envar
if not exist %WORKSPACE% goto done
if not exist %BUILDFILE% echo ERROR:
==>         incorrect buildfile=%BUILDFILE%, edit this file
==>         and correct the BUILDFILE envar
if not exist %BUILDFILE% goto done
REM ****************************************************
:run
@echo on
%JAVAEXE% -cp %STARTUPJAR% org.eclipse.core.launcher.Main
==>         -application org.eclipse.ant.core.antRunner
==>         -data %WORKSPACE% -buildfile %BUILDFILE%

REM ****************************************************
:done
pause
```

Copy this batch file into an external_build.bat file located in the same directory as the build.xml file you want to run, and modify the batch variables shown in Table 19–3 to suit your environment.

Table 19–3   Batch Variables

Script Variable	Description
JAVAEXE	The JRE `java.exe` to be used when running Ant in a headless Eclipse environment. Typically, this would be the same JRE used to run the Eclipse UI.
STARTUPJAR	The `startup.jar` located in the Eclipse install directory.
WORKSPACE	The workspace directory containing the projects to be built.
BUILDFILE	The relative path from the batch file to the build script used to build the product. Typically, the batch file is located in the same directory as the build script, so this would specify only the name of the build script.

The first part of the batch file assigns the script variables while the second part validates the existence of files specified by those script variables. The real work is accomplished in the third part, where Eclipse is launched without a UI and the build script is executed.

19.1.8   Ant extensions

Several of the tasks just listed are not part of Ant; some are part of Eclipse and others must be downloaded from the *QualityEclipse* Web site (*www.quality-eclipse.com/*). The additional tasks listed in Table 19–4 will not work outside of Eclipse.

Table 19–4   Eclipse Ant Task Providers

Ant Task	Provider
eclipse.convertPath	Built into Eclipse as part of the `org.eclipse.core.resources` plug-in
eclipse.refreshLocal	Built into Eclipse as part of the `org.eclipse.core.resources` plug-in
eclipsetools.getclasspath	Downloadable from the *QualityEclipse* Web site as part of the `com.instantiations.preprocessor` plug-in (see Section 19.2.7, Classpath tools, on page 701)
eclipsetools.preprocessor	Downloadable from the *QualityEclipse* Web site as part of the `com.instantiations.preprocessor` plug-in (see Section 19.2.6.3, Preprocessor, on page 695).

By default, Eclipse executes Ant using an alternate JRE. If you are using Eclipse-specific tasks such as those listed before, and you encounter an error similar to the following:

```
Buildfile: com.qualityeclipse.favorites\build.xml
init:
BUILD FAILED: file: com.qualityeclipse.favorites/build.xml:56: Could
not create task or type of type:
eclipsetools_classpath_modifications.

Ant could not find the task or a class this task relies on.
... etc ...
Total time: 406 milliseconds
```

then you may need to execute the build script in the same JRE as the workspace. To accomplish this, select the build script, right-click, and then select **Run As > Ant Build....** In the launch dialog, select the **JRE** tab and select the **Run in the same JRE as the workspace** radio button (see Figure 19–5). This enables the Eclipse-specific Ant tasks to access the underlying Eclipse functionality.

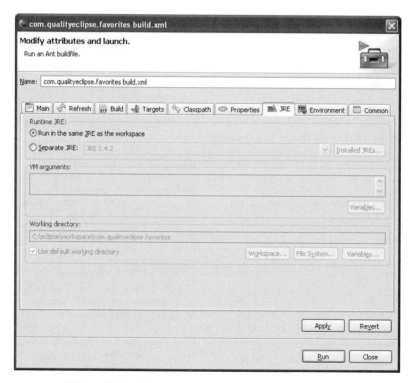

Figure 19–5   JRE tab page in the Ant launch configuration.

19.2   Building the Favorites Product

Now let's revisit the **Favorites** product build script introduced in Section 2.4.2,
Building with Apache Ant, on page 83 and compare that with a build script
automatically generated by the plug-in development tools. Following that,
enhance your build script to take into account all the new bells and whistles
that have been added since the build script was introduced in Chapter 2, A
Simple Plug-in Example.

19.2.1   Auto-generated build script

The Eclipse plug-in development tools can generate a build.xml file containing a skeleton of a build script. In the **Navigator** view, right-click on the
pugin.xml file and select **PDE Tools > Create Ant Build File** (the ==> denotes
a continuation of the previous line and must not be included).

```xml
<project name="com.qualityeclipse.favorites"
        default="build.jars"
        basedir=".">

  <property name="basews" value="${ws}" />
  <property name="baseos" value="${os}" />
  <property name="basearch" value="${arch}" />
  <property name="basenl" value="${nl}" />

  <!-- Compiler settings. -->
  <property name="javacFailOnError" value="false" />
  <property name="javacDebugInfo" value="on" />
  <property name="javacVerbose" value="true" />
  <property name="javacSource" value="1.3" />
  <property name="javacTarget" value="1.2" />
  <property name="compilerArg" value="" />
  <path id="path_bootclasspath">
     <fileset dir="${java.home}/lib">
        <include name="*.jar" />
     </fileset>
  </path>
  <property name="bootclasspath" refid="path_bootclasspath" />

  <target name="init" depends="properties">
     <condition property="pluginTemp"
                value="${buildTempFolder}/plugins">
        <isset property="buildTempFolder" />
     </condition>
     <property name="pluginTemp" value="${basedir}" />
     <condition property="build.result.folder"
                value="${pluginTemp}/com.qualityeclipse.favorites">
        <isset property="buildTempFolder" />
     </condition>
     <property name="build.result.folder" value="${basedir}" />
     <property name="temp.folder" value="${basedir}/temp.folder" />
     <property name="plugin.destination" value="${basedir}" />
  </target>
```

```
        <target name="properties" if="eclipse.running">
          <property name="build.compiler"
                    value="org.eclipse.jdt.core.JDTCompilerAdapter" />
        </target>

        <target name="build.update.jar"
                depends="init"
                description="Build the plug-in:
 ==>          com.qualityeclipse.favorites for an update site.">
          <delete dir="${temp.folder}" />
          <mkdir dir="${temp.folder}" />
          <antcall target="build.jars" />
          <antcall target="gather.bin.parts">
            <param name="destination.temp.folder"
                   value="${temp.folder}/" />
          </antcall>
          <zip destfile="${plugin.destination}/
 ==>            com.qualityeclipse.favorites_1.0.0.jar"
               basedir="${temp.folder}/
 ==>            com.qualityeclipse.favorites_1.0.0"
               filesonly="false"
               whenempty="skip"
               update="false" />
          <delete dir="${temp.folder}" />
        </target>

        <target name="favorites.jar"
                depends="init"
                unless="favorites.jar"
                description="Create jar:
 ==>            com.qualityeclipse.favorites favorites.jar.">
          <delete dir="${temp.folder}/favorites.jar.bin" />
          <mkdir dir="${temp.folder}/favorites.jar.bin" />
          <!-- compile the source code -->
          <javac destdir="${temp.folder}/favorites.jar.bin"
                 failonerror="${javacFailOnError}"
                 verbose="${javacVerbose}"
                 debug="${javacDebugInfo}"
                 includeAntRuntime="no"
                 bootclasspath="${bootclasspath}"
                 source="${javacSource}"
                 target="${javacTarget}">
            <compilerarg line="${compilerArg}" />
            <classpath>
              <pathelement path="..\..\plugins\
 ==>                        org.eclipse.core.runtime_3.1.2.jar" />
              <pathelement path="..\..\plugins\
 ==>                        org.eclipse.osgi_3.1.2.jar" />
              <pathelement path="..\..\plugins\
 ==>                        org.eclipse.core.resources_3.1.2.jar" />

                ... lots more of the same ...

            </classpath>
            <src path="src/" />
          </javac>
```

```
          <!-- Copy necessary resources -->
          <copy todir="${temp.folder}/favorites.jar.bin"
                failonerror="true"
                overwrite="false">
            <fileset dir="src/"
                     excludes="**/*.java, **/package.htm*,null" />
          </copy>
          <mkdir dir="${build.result.folder}" />
          <jar destfile="${build.result.folder}/favorites.jar"
               basedir="${temp.folder}/favorites.jar.bin" />
          <delete dir="${temp.folder}/favorites.jar.bin" />
       </target>

       <target name="favoritessrc.zip"
               depends="init"
               unless="favoritessrc.zip">
          <mkdir dir="${build.result.folder}" />
          <zip destfile="${build.result.folder}/favoritessrc.zip"
               filesonly="false"
               whenempty="skip"
               update="false">
            <fileset dir="src/" includes="**/*.java" />
          </zip>
       </target>

       <target name="build.jars"
               depends="init"
               description="Build all the jars for the plug-in:
==>            com.qualityeclipse.favorites.">
          <available property="favorites.jar"
                     file="${build.result.folder}/favorites.jar" />
          <antcall target="favorites.jar" />
       </target>

       <target name="build.sources" depends="init">
          <available property="favoritessrc.zip"
                     file="${build.result.folder}/favoritessrc.zip" />
          <antcall target="favoritessrc.zip" />
       </target>

       <target name="gather.bin.parts"
               depends="init"
               if="destination.temp.folder">
          <mkdir dir="${destination.temp.folder}/
==>            com.qualityeclipse.favorites_1.0.0" />
          <copy todir="${destination.temp.folder}/
==>            com.qualityeclipse.favorites_1.0.0"
                failonerror="true"
                overwrite="false">
            <fileset dir="${build.result.folder}"
                     includes="favorites.jar" />
          </copy>
          <copy todir="${destination.temp.folder}/
==>            com.qualityeclipse.favorites_1.0.0"
                failonerror="true"
                overwrite="false">
```

```
              <fileset dir="${basedir}"
                      includes="plugin.xml,META-INF/,favorites.jar,
==>                          icons/,plugin.properties,
==>                          about.html,about.ini,about.mappings,
==>                          about.properties, favorites.gif,
==>                          feature.gif,schema/" />
        </copy>
    </target>

    <target name="build.zips" depends="init">
    </target>

    <target name="gather.sources"
            depends="init"
            if="destination.temp.folder">
        <mkdir dir="${destination.temp.folder}/
==>            com.qualityeclipse.favorites_1.0.0" />
        <copy file="${build.result.folder}/favoritessrc.zip"
            todir="${destination.temp.folder}/
==>            com.qualityeclipse.favorites_1.0.0"
            failonerror="false"
            overwrite="false" />
    </target>

    <target name="gather.logs"
            depends="init"
            if="destination.temp.folder">
        <mkdir dir="${destination.temp.folder}/
==>            com.qualityeclipse.favorites_1.0.0" />
        <copy file="${temp.folder}/favorites.jar.bin.log"
            todir="${destination.temp.folder}/
==>            com.qualityeclipse.favorites_1.0.0"
            failonerror="false"
            overwrite="false" />
    </target>

    <target name="clean"
            depends="init"
            description="Clean the plug-in:
==>            com.qualityeclipse.favorites of all the zips,
==>            jars and logs created.">
        <delete file="${build.result.folder}/favorites.jar" />
        <delete file="${build.result.folder}/favoritessrc.zip" />
        <delete file="${plugin.destination}/
==>            com.qualityeclipse.favorites_1.0.0.jar" />
        <delete file="${plugin.destination}/
==>            com.qualityeclipse.favorites_1.0.0.zip" />
        <delete dir="${temp.folder}" />
    </target>

    <target name="refresh"
            depends="init"
            if="eclipse.running"
            description="Refresh this folder.">
```

```
                    <eclipse.convertPath fileSystemPath="
==>                     C:/eclipse/workspace/com.qualityeclipse.favorites"
                                    property="resourcePath" />
                    <eclipse.refreshLocal resource="${resourcePath}"
                                    depth="infinite" />
            </target>


        <target name="zip.plugin"
                depends="init"
                description="Create a zip containing all the elements
==>                 for the plug-in: com.qualityeclipse.favorites.">
            <delete dir="${temp.folder}" />
            <mkdir dir="${temp.folder}" />
            <antcall target="build.jars" />
            <antcall target="build.sources" />
            <antcall target="gather.bin.parts">
                <param name="destination.temp.folder"
                        value="${temp.folder}/" />
            </antcall>
            <antcall target="gather.sources">
                <param name="destination.temp.folder"
                        value="${temp.folder}/" />
            </antcall>
            <delete>
                <fileset dir="${temp.folder}" includes="**/*.bin.log" />
            </delete>
            <zip destfile="${plugin.destination}/
==>                 com.qualityeclipse.favorites_1.0.0.zip"
                basedir="${temp.folder}"
                filesonly="true"
                whenempty="skip"
                update="false" />
            <delete dir="${temp.folder}" />
        </target>

</project>
```

This auto-generated build script is a bit more complicated than the **Favorites** build script, containing five external targets and seven internal targets (see Figure 19–6). The `zip.plugin` and `build.update.jar` targets call other targets, and all the targets depend on the `init` target, which in turn depends on the `properties` target.

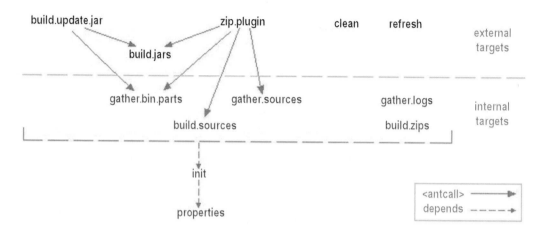

Figure 19–6   The PDE-generated build script.

You would not manually edit this script, but rather use the PDE Build process (not covered here) to auto-generate and execute this and other scripts—one per plug-in, fragment, and feature—then package the result. For a more complete description of the PDE Build process, check out Chapter 24 of the *Eclipse Rich Client Platform* book. The PDE Build process has its advantages, but does not lend itself to building products against multiple versions of Eclipse as we wish to do, so we are going to stick with our script and enhance it over the next several sections to perform the necessary tasks.

19.2.2   Refactoring the Favorites build script

Before proceeding, you need to review the build script introduced in Section 2.4.2, Building with Apache Ant, on page 83, examining each chunk and refactoring it into separate targets, macrodefs, and build files. Each plug-in, fragment and feature should be responsible for building itself using its own `build-bundle.xml` script. A master build script named `build-favorites.xml` initializes the build process, calls the appropriate target in each `build-bundle.xml` script (see Figure 19–7), then packages the result. Common macrodefs are placed in the `build-macros.xml` file and shared by all scripts. This new structure scales well as more plug-ins, fragments and features are added and will be helpful in building the **Favorites** product for more than just the Eclipse 3.1 platform.

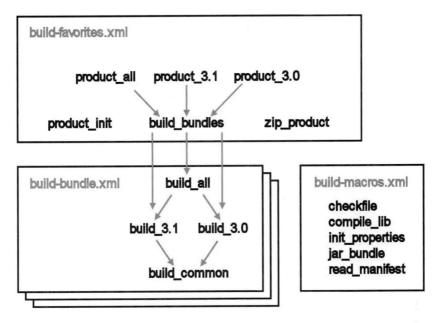

Figure 19–7   Favorites build script structure.

During the build process, scripts need a well-defined place for temporary files generated during the build process and product files that will be shipped to the customer. The ${build.root} property defines a root directory for the build process, from which other properties are derived. Developers can override these build properties to suit their own build situations (see Section 19.2.2.2, Build initialization, on page 679). If the user has defined the ${build.root} property to be /Build/QualityEclipse and not overridden any of the other build properties, then the directory structure would look something like this:

```
/Build/QualityEclipse   <---- ${build.root}

   product                 <---- ${build.out} files ready for Customer
      Favorites_v1.0.0_for_Eclipse3.0.zip
      Favorites_v1.0.0_for_Eclipse3.1.zip

   temp                    <---- ${build.temp}

      3.0                   <---- files specific to Eclipse 3.0
         com.qualityeclipse.favorites
            src             <---- preprocessed source files
            bin             <---- compiled preprocessed source files
            out             <---- jars, etc.
         com.qualityeclipse.favorites.nl1
            out
         . . .
```

```
    out                     <---- Eclipse 3.0 files ready for product
        plugins
            com.qualityeclipse.favorites_1.0.0
            com.qualityeclipse.favorites.nl1_1.0.0
            . . .


  3.1                       <---- files specific to Eclipse 3.1
    com.qualityeclipse.favorites
        out
    com.qualityeclipse.favorites.nl1
        out
    . . .
    out                     <---- Eclipse 3.1 files ready for product
        plugins

  common                    <---- files common to all versions
    com.qualityeclipse.favorites
        out
    com.qualityeclipse.favorites.feature
        out
    . . .
    out                     <---- common files ready for product
        features
            com.qualityeclipse.favorites_1.0.0
        plugins
            com.qualityeclipse.favorites.help_1.0.0
```

19.2.2.1 Build macros and fast fail

Create a new `build-macros.xml` file containing build elements shared by all build files. Over the course of this and the next several sections, macrodefs will be added to this file. Reference this new file at the top of the `build-favorites.xml` file and each `build-bundle.xml` file like this:

```xml
<?xml version="1.0" encoding="UTF-8"?>
<project default="product_all">
   <import file="../com.qualityeclipse.favorites/build-macros.xml"/>
   . . .
```

In build scripts, as with any program, it is better to find a problem earlier rather than later; it is better for a build script to fail immediately, near the problem, so that it is obvious and can be fixed rather than failing later on (or worse not at all) making the process of finding and fixing the problem more difficult. To this end, declare a new `checkfile` macro in the `build-macros.xml` file. This new macro is used in various other macros and targets, providing a sanity check in the build process by checking for the existence of a specified file and causing the build to fail if that file is not present.

```
<macrodef name="checkfile">
  <attribute name="file" />
   <sequential>
     <fail message="Cannot find file: @{file}">
        <condition>
           <not>
              <available file="@{file}" />
           </not>
        </condition>
     </fail>
   </sequential>
</macrodef>
```

In addition, sanity checking code is sprinkled throughout the build scripts but omitted from the following sections for brevity. For example, when a macrodef expects a property such as ${build.temp} to be defined, you add the following line near the beginning of the macrodef:

```
<fail unless="build.temp" />
```

Sometimes a macrodef contains an attribute that should only have one of a limited range of values. For example, the @{target} attribute used in several macros in later sections should be "3.1", "3.0", or "common". In this case, add the following lines near the beginning of the macrodef.

```
<fail message="invalid value for target: @{target}">
   <condition>
      <not>
         <or>
            <equals arg1="@{target}" arg2="3.1" />
            <equals arg1="@{target}" arg2="3.0" />
            <equals arg1="@{target}" arg2="common" />
         </or>
      </not>
   </condition>
</fail>
```

19.2.2.2 *Build initialization*

The next step is to gather all the product build initialization, such as property assignments and directory deletion, into a single product_init target. This new product_init target will be responsible for initializing common properties used in building multiple binaries (see Section 19.2.4, Single versus multiple binaries, on page 691) and clearing out the temporary directories used during the build process to ensure a clean build.

Developers need to have the ability to build this product on their own machines, so different build properties for different developers are necessary. One approach is for each developer to modify their own local copy of this script, changing the build properties to suit the machine, but then there would be multiple versions of that same build script file, and synchronization would be complicated.

Alternatively, developers could specify build properties on the command line or in the Ant launch configuration dialog (see Section 19.1.4.5, Properties on the command line, on page 662), but then when they switched machines or changed workspaces their settings would be lost. A better approach is to have the build script load properties from a developer-specific file in a known location so that each developer can mantain their own set of build properties in the repository.

To accomplish this use the ${user.name} property, which Ant initializes to the user's account name, to read properties from a file located in the /com.qualityeclipse.favorites/build directory. This file (e.g. danrubel.properties) must define at least the ${build.root} property from which many other build-related properties are derived. Because it appears first in the build process, it, optionally, can define properties such as ${build.out} and ${build.temp}.

```
<target name="product_init">
  <checkfile file="build/${user.name}.properties" />
  <property file="build/${user.name}.properties" />

  <!-- At least one property must be defined -->
  <fail unless="build.root" />

  <!-- Properties derived from ${build.root} -->
  <property name="build.out" location="${build.root}/product" />
  <property name="build.temp" location="${build.root}/temp" />

  <!-- Define product info -->
  <property name="product.name" value="Favorites" />
  <property name="product.version" value="1.0.0" />
```

The product_init target also initializes getclasspath properties (see Section 19.2.3, Compiling during the build process, on page 689), preprocessor properties (see Section 19.2.6.3, Preprocessor, on page 695) and deletes the temporary build directory.

```
  <!-- GetClasspath and preprocessor initialization -->
  <property name="build.map"
            value="../com.qualityeclipse.favorites/.buildmap" />
  <property name="eclipsetools.preprocessor.version.valid"
            value="3.1,3.0"/>
  <property name="eclipsetools.preprocessor.version.source"
            value="3.1"/>

  <!-- Delete the temporary directory -->
  <delete dir="${build.temp}" />
</target>
```

19.2.2.3 Building multiple projects

As the **Favorites** product grows, you will be adding plug-ins, fragments, and features, so you need a build script that scales with your needs. To this end, split the build script along project lines with each project containing its own `build-bundle.xml` script. These build scripts are called by a new macrodef in the `build-favorites.xml` script. As new projects are added in the sections following this one, you must continue to update this macrodef with references to the `build-bundle.xml` script for those new projects. The order in which projects are built is important because one project can depend on build artifacts generated by another.

```
<macrodef name="build_bundles">
    <attribute name="target" />
    <sequential>
       <ant antfile="build-bundle.xml"
            target="@{target}"
            dir="../com.qualityeclipse.favorites" />
       <ant antfile="build-bundle.xml"
            target="@{target}"
            dir="../com.qualityeclipse.favorites.nl1" />
       <ant antfile="build-bundle.xml"
            target="@{target}"
            dir="../com.qualityeclipse.favorites.help" />
       <ant antfile="build-bundle.xml"
            target="@{target}"
            dir="../com.qualityeclipse.favorites.feature" />
    </sequential>
</macrodef>
```

This macro plus the `zip_product` macro (see below) are called from three new top-level targets in `build-favorites.xml`. Each target calls the `build_bundles` macro with a different `@{target}` attribute, causing the product to be built for different versions of Eclipse.

```
<target name="product_3.0" depends="product_init">
    <build_bundles target="build_3.0" />
    <zip_product target="3.0" />
</target>

<target name="product_3.1" depends="product_init">
    <build_bundles target="build_3.1" />
    <zip_product target="3.1" />
</target>

<target name="product_all" depends="product_init">
    <build_bundles target="build_all" />
    <zip_product target="3.1" />
    <zip_product target="3.0" />
</target>
```

Every `build-bundle.xml` file has roughly the same structure: three top-level targets called by the `build_bundles` macro previously mentioned plus a common target on which all three targets rely.

```
<?xml version="1.0" encoding="UTF-8"?>
<project default="build_all">
   <import file="../com.qualityeclipse.favorites/build-macros.xml"/>

   <target name="build_common">
      ... build processes common to all versions of Eclipse here ...
   </target>

   <target name="build_3.0" depends="build_common">
      ... build processes specific to Eclipse 3.0 here ...
   </target>

   <target name="build_3.1" depends="build_common">
      ... build processes specific to Eclipse 3.1 here ...
   </target>

   <target name="build_all" depends="build_3.1, build_3.0">
   </target>
</project>
```

Finally, a `zip_product` macro in the `build-favorites.xml` file, called by the top-level targets above, packages the files in Eclipse-specific files for the customer. All the files from the `${build.out}/common/out` and `${build.out}/@{target}/out` directories are combined to form a single deliverable for a specific version of Eclipse (the `==>` in the code below denotes a continuation of the line above and must not be included).

```
<macrodef name="zip_product">
   <attribute name="target" />
   <attribute name="prefix"
         default="QualityEclipse/Favorites/E-@{target}/eclipse"/>

   <sequential>
      <mkdir dir="${build.out}" />
      <zip destfile="${build.out}/${product.name}
==>                   _v${product.version}_for_Eclipse@{target}.zip">
         <zipfileset dir="${build.temp}/common/out"
                     prefix="@{prefix}" />
         <zipfileset dir="${build.temp}/@{target}/out"
                     prefix="@{prefix}" />
      </zip>
   </sequential>
</macrodef>
```

> **Tip:** In the `zip_product` macro above, the `@{prefix}` attribute
> determines the structure of the ZIP file that is created. The `@{prefix}`
> attribute default specified above is for product installation in a directory
> hierarchy separate from the Eclipse install directory as per the RFRS
> requirements (see Section 3.2.1, Link files, on page 105). For a simpler
> installation that does not necessitate a link file, change the `@{prefix}`
> attribute to "" (blank) so that the product can be unzipped directly into the
> Eclipse install directory.

19.2.2.4 *Building each project*

The specific elements for building each plug-in, fragment, and feature project
are moved out of the `build-favorites.xml` file and into the appropriate
`build-bundle.xml` file. Within each project-specific build script, the elements,
such as initialization and building of shared files, common to both Eclipse 3.1
and 3.0 are placed in a `build_common` target while elements specific to Eclipse
3.1 are placed into a `build_3.1` target.

For the **com.qualityeclipse.favorites** project, the common elements
include things such as reading manifest information and generating the
`favoritessrc.zip`.

```
<target name="build_common">
   <init_properties />
   <read_manifest />
   <read_build />
   <jar_lib target="common" lib="favoritessrc.zip">
      <fileset dir=".">
         <include name="${source.favorites.jar}" />
      </fileset>
   </jar_lib>
</target>
```

This target references several new macros that need to be added to the shared
`build-macros.xml` file. The first macro referenced in the code above,
`init_properties`, initializes properties that are common to all projects
being built. In this case, the `${Bundle-Proj}` property is initialized to the
name of the project being built.

```
<macrodef name="init_properties">
   <sequential>
      <basename file="." property="Bundle-Proj" />
   </sequential>
</macrodef>
```

The next macro in `build-macros.xml` referenced by the `build_common` target, `read_manifest`, reads build information such as plug-in or fragment name, identifier, and version from the `META-INF/MANIFEST.MF` file. Because the information in the manifest is not in a form that can be read directly into Ant, you must first make a copy of the file in a temporary location, rework that copy into a more usable format, then read the copy into Ant. In the future, an Ant task could be created specifically to read build information out of a `META-INF/MANIFEST.MF` file.

```xml
<macrodef name="read_manifest">
    <attribute name="file" default="META-INF/MANIFEST.MF" />
    <attribute name="temp"
               default="${build.temp}/common/${Bundle-Proj}" />

    <sequential>

        <!-- Copy and rewrite the MANIFEST.MF
             so that it can be loaded as properties -->

        <mkdir dir="@{temp}" />

        <copy file="@{file}"
              tofile="@{temp}/MANIFEST.MF"
              overwrite="true" />

        <replace file="@{temp}/MANIFEST.MF">
           <replacefilter token=":=" value="=" />
           <replacefilter token=":" value="=" />
           <replacetoken>;</replacetoken>
           <replacevalue>
           </replacevalue>
        </replace>

        <!-- Load properties from the rewritten manifest -->
        <property file="@{temp}/MANIFEST.MF" />

        <!-- Rename properties for clarity -->
        <property name="Bundle-Id" value="${Bundle-SymbolicName}" />

    </sequential>
</macrodef>
```

Every project contains a `build.properties` file describing various files and directories to be included in the build. This file is convenient because Eclipse provides a nice **Build Configuration** editor that also appears as part of the plug-in manifest editor. The `build.properties` file in the **com.quality-eclipse.favorites** project looks something like what is shown in Figure 19–8.

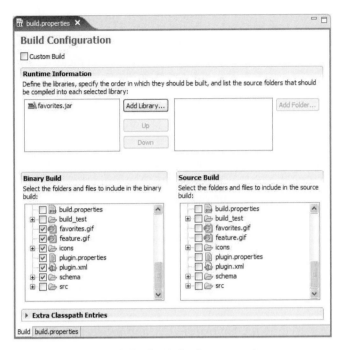

Figure 19–8   Build Configuration editor

Switching to the **build.properties** tab in the editor shows the properties being manipulated by the editor. In this case, the `source.favorites.jar` property is a comma-separated list of source directories for the `favorites.jar`, the `output.favorites.jar` property is a comma-separated list of directories containing binary files for the `favorites.jar`, and the `bin.includes` property is a comma-separated list of files and directories to be included in the plug-in itself.

```
source.favorites.jar = src/
output.favorites.jar = bin/
bin.includes = plugin.xml,\
               favorites.jar,\
               icons/,\
               plugin.properties,\
               about.html,\
               about.ini,\
               about.mappings,\
               about.properties,\
               favorites.gif,\
               feature.gif,\
               schema/
```

The various properties that can appear in this file include the following:

- source.<library>—a comma-separated list of files and directories to be included when compiling <library>. Typically, this is either the project root represented by ".\u200b" or the "src/" directory.

- extra.<library>—a comma separated list of files and directories to be included on the classpath when compiling <library> but not in the library itself.

- output.<library>—the directory into which Eclipse compiles files specified in source.<library>. Typically this is either the project root represented by ".\u200b" or the "bin/" directory.

- bin.includes—a comma-eparated list of files and directories to be included in the plug-in, fragment, or feature.

The bin.includes typically contains elements common for all versions of Eclipse. For example, the bin.includes of the various **Favorites** product projects have such things as:

- Icons used by the **Favorites** view and model (see Chapter 7, Views)

- preferences.ini (see Section 16.2, Externalizing Plug-in Strings, on page 578)

- The schema files (see Section 17.2.2, Creating an extension point schema, on page 599)

- META-INF/MANIFEST.MF, plugin.xml, and feature.xml files

- The entire **Favorites** feature plug-in and related files (see Chapter 18, Features, Branding, and Updates)

- The entire **Favorites** help plug-in (see Chapter 15, Implementing Help)

The read_build macro referenced in the build_common target resides in the build-macros.xml file, asserts that the build.properties file exists, and loads the properties in the build.properties file into Ant.

```
<macrodef name="read_build">
    <attribute name="file" default="build.properties" />
    <sequential>
        <checkfile file="@{file}" />
        <property file="@{file}" />
        <!-- Rename some properties for clarity -->
        <property name="Bundle-CommonFiles" value="${bin.includes}" />
    </sequential>
</macrodef>
```

Finally, the last call in the the `build_common` target, the `jar_lib` macro, gathers the source files for this project into the `favoritessrc.zip` file, placing that file in the `${build.temp}/@{target}/${Bundle-Proj}/out` directory to be picked up later by either the `jar_bundle` or `dir_bundle` macros. As mentioned earlier, assertions for various macro inputs, such as the `${build.temp}` property and the `@{target}` attribute, are omitted here for brevity (the `==>` in the code below denotes a continuation of the previous line and must not be included).

```
<macrodef name="jar_lib">
   <attribute name="target" />
   <attribute name="lib" />
   <element name="content" implicit="true" />
   <sequential>
      <mkdir dir="${build.temp}/@{target}/${Bundle-Proj}/out" />
      <zip destfile="${build.temp}/@{target}
==>                                 /${Bundle-Proj}/out/@{lib}">
         <content />
      </zip>
   </sequential>
</macrodef>
```

The `build_3.1` target in the `build-bundle.xml` file of the **com.quality-eclipse.favorites** project assembles the Eclipse 3.1-specific elements, gathers the artifacts generated by `build_common`, and places them all in a common location ready for inclusion in the product.

```
<target name="build_3.1" depends="build_common">
   <jar_bundle target="3.1" type="plugins">
      <fileset dir="." includes="META-INF/MANIFEST.MF" />
      <fileset dir="${output.favorites.jar}" />
   </jar_bundle>
</target>
```

> **Tip:** When packaging a plug-in as a single JAR file, it is best to include the class files directly in that plug-in's JAR file rather than in a separate classes JAR file which is then contained in the plug-in JAR file. If you do this, then be sure to exclude the `Bundle-ClassPath` attribute from the `META-INF/MANIFEST.MF` either by editing the file directly or by removing all JAR files from the **Classpath** section of the **Runtime** page in the **Plug-in manifest** editor (see Figure 2–11 on page 75).

The `jar_bundle` macro referenced in the preceding `build_3.1` target appears in the `build-macros.xml` file so that it can be reused by multiple build-bundle.xml scripts (the ==> in the code below denotes a continuation of the previous line and must not be included).

```
<macrodef name="jar_bundle">
   <attribute name="target" />
   <attribute name="type" />
   <attribute name="id" default="${Bundle-Id}" />
   <attribute name="version" default="${Bundle-Version}" />
   <element name="content" implicit="true" optional="true" />
   <sequential>
      <mkdir dir="${build.temp}/@{target}/out/@{type}" />
      <mkdir dir="${build.temp}/common/${Bundle-Proj}/out" />
      <mkdir dir="${build.temp}/@{target}/${Bundle-Proj}/out" />
      <zip destfile="${build.temp}
==>                       /@{target}/out/@{type}/@{id}_@{version}.jar">
       <zipfileset dir="." includes="${Bundle-CommonFiles}" />
       <zipfileset dir="${build.temp}/common/${Bundle-Proj}/out" />
       <zipfileset dir="${build.temp}/@{target}/${Bundle-Proj}/out"/>
       <content />
      </zip>
   </sequential>
</macrodef>
```

This code assembles the following elements into a single bundle JAR file (a plug-in can be deployed as a single JAR file as of Eclipse 3.1) and places that JAR in the ${build.temp}/@{target}/out file for inclusion in the product.

- Files and directories in the ${Bundle-CommonFiles} property (same as the ${bin.includes} property)

- Anything in ${build.temp}/common/${Bundle-Proj}/out

- Anything in ${build.temp}/@{target}/${Bundle-Proj}/out

- Anything specified as a fileset subelement

All the other projects—**com.qualityeclipse.favorites.feature, com.quality-eclipse.favorites.help,** and **com.qualityeclipse.favorites.nl1**—are assembled in a similar fashion using their own build-bundle.xml scripts.

All this refactoring has resulted in a new and more flexible build structure that can easily be adapted to generate new binaries for other versions of Eclipse (see Figure 19–7 on page 677). Currently, the product_31 target depends on the build_31 and build_common targets in each build-bundle.xml file.

This structure scales nicely in that by adding new `build-bundle.xml` files you can easily build additional projects as part of the **Favorites** product; and by adding new `product_xx` and `build_xx` targets you can easily build additional binaries to support different versions of Eclipse. For example, in the next section new `product_30` and `build_30` targets are added to support Eclipse 3.0.

> **Tip:** When installing the newly built **Favorites** product, be sure to adjust the link file discussed in Section 3.2.1, Link files, on page 105 from
>
>   path=C:/QualityEclipse/Favorites
>
> to
>
>   path=C:/QualityEclipse/Favorites/E-3.1
>
> so that the newly built **Favorites** product will be used.

19.2.3   Compiling during the build process

The current build script simply copies the Java class files produced by the Eclipse environment into the `favorites.jar` file. You need to compile the source files during the build process to ensure that you have a full and complete compilation, verifying the work of the Eclipse IDE. In addition, this step will be necessary if you want to produce a binary for each different version of Eclipse that is supported. In the `build-bundle.xml` file of the **com.qualityeclipse.favorites** project, modify the `build_3.1` target to compile the source before packaging it rather than packaging what the Eclipse IDE has already compiled.

```
<target name="build_3.1" depends="build_common">
   <compile_dir target="3.1" />
   <jar_bundle target="3.1" type="plugins">
      <fileset dir="." includes="META-INF/MANIFEST.MF" />
   </jar_bundle>
</target>
```

The `build_3.1` target above calls a new `compile_dir` macro that must be added to the `build-macros.xml` file. This new macro runs the source through the `eclipsetools.preprocessor` (see Section 19.2.6.3, Preprocessor, on page 695), obtains the project's classpath using the `eclipsetools.getclasspath` task (see Section 19.2.7, Classpath tools, on page 701), and finally compiles the source into the specified directory.

```
<macrodef name="compile_dir">
   <attribute name="target" />
   <attribute name="source" default="src" />
   <attribute name="destdir"
             default="${build.temp}/@{target}/${Bundle-Proj}/bin" />
   <attribute name="extraClasspath" default="" />
   <attribute name="debug" default="on" />
   <sequential>

      <eclipsetools.preprocessor
         targetVersion="@{target}"
         dir="@{source}"
         todir="${build.temp}/@{target}/${Bundle-Proj}/src" />

      <eclipsetools.getclasspath
         config="eclipse_@{target}"
         binroot="${build.temp}/@{target}"
         buildmap="${build.map}"
         property="classpath_@{target}" />

      <mkdir dir="${build.temp}/@{target}/${Bundle-Proj}/bin" />

      <javac srcdir="${build.temp}/@{target}/${Bundle-Proj}/src"
            destdir="@{destdir}"
            classpath="${classpath_@{target}};@{extraClasspath}"
            debug="@{debug}" />

      <copy todir="@{destdir}">
         <fileset dir="@{source}">
            <exclude name="**/*.class" />
            <exclude name="**/*.java" />
            <exclude name="**/Thumbs.db" />
         </fileset>
      </copy>

   </sequential>
</macrodef>
```

If you get a build error similar to this:

```
BUILD FAILED: file:    .../workspace/com.qualityeclipse.favorites/
build.xml:182:
Unable to find a javac compiler;
com.sun.tools.javac.Main is not on the classpath.
Perhaps JAVA_HOME does not point to the JDK
```

you may not have the JDK `tools.jar` file on your Ant classpath. Open the
Ant > Runtime preference page (see Figure 19–9) and verify that the
`tools.jar` file appears under **Global Entries**. If it does not, then select **Global
Entries**, click **Add External JARS...**, navigate to your `<JDK>\lib\tools.jar`
file, and click **Open** so that `tools.jar` is added to your Ant classpath.

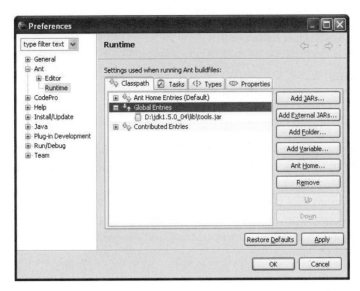

Figure 19–9   The **Ant > Runtime** preference page showing tools.jar.

By default, the `javac` task uses the Java compiler found on the Ant class-path as just specified. To use the Eclipse compiler, set the `build.compiler` property.

```
<property
    name="build.compiler"
    value="org.eclipse.jdt.core.JDTCompilerAdapter"/>
```

19.2.4   *Single versus multiple binaries*

What if the public API used by your plug-in has not changed and the code compiles against each version of Eclipse successfully? Why should you ship a different binary of your product for each version of Eclipse? Given this scenario, a single binary might run correctly on different versions of Eclipse, *but can you be sure*? There are cases where the same source compiled against two different versions of Eclipse will produce two different binaries, each of which will only execute correctly on one version of Eclipse, not the other. For example, if your code had a method called `yourMethod()`:

```
Your code:
    public void yourMethod() {
        foo(0);
    }
```

```
Eclipse 3.1:
   public void foo(int value) {
      ... some operation ...
   }

Eclipse 3.0:
   public void foo(long value) {
      ... some operation ...
   }
```

then `yourMethod()` method would compile under Eclipse 3.1 and Eclipse 3.0 without any code changes, but would the version compiled under Eclipse 3.1 run in Eclipse 3.0?

Things like this make it well worth the up-front time and effort to deliver one binary for each version of Eclipse you intend to support rather than spending that same amount of time and more later on debugging problems in the field.

19.2.5 *Editing with different versions of Eclipse*

Sometimes, different developers using different versions of Eclipse want to work on the same project. If the project in question does not involve any Eclipse plug-ins, then there is no problem. The problem arises when a project uses the `ECLIPSE_HOME` classpath variable, which is automatically managed by the environment to point to the current Eclipse installation. As a result, any project using `ECLIPSE_HOME` references plug-ins in the current Eclipse installation.

For example, a developer using Eclipse 3.1 will have the project compiled against the Eclipse 3.1 plug-ins, whereas someone using Rational Application Developer 6.0, which is based on Eclipse 3.0, will have that same project compiled against Eclipse 3.0 plug-ins.

One solution is to use the PDE **Target Platform** preference page (see Figure 19–10). Using this page, you can retarget the `ECLIPSE_HOME` classpath variable at a different Eclipse installation. The problem with this approach is that it does not address the problem of different projects compiled against different versions of Eclipse. With this solution, you will have all projects compiled against the same Eclipse installation.

Another solution is to never use the `ECLIPSE_HOME` classpath variable at all. Assuming that you want to support Eclipse 2.1, 3.0, and 3.1, install all three Eclipse versions into separate directories with names such as `c:\eclipse2.1`, `c:\eclipse3.0`, and `c:\eclipse3.1`.

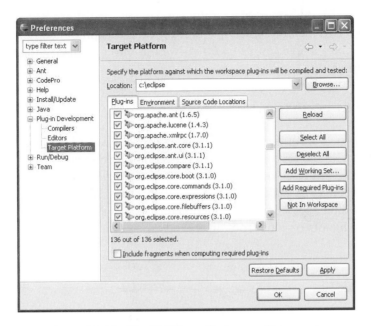

Figure 19–10 The PDE Target Platform preference page.

Then, set up three classpath variables named ECLIPSE21_HOME, ECLIPSE30_HOME, and ECLIPSE31_HOME, which point to their respective Eclipse installations. If a project has been compiled against Eclipse 3.1, you would use ECLIPSE31_HOME rather than ECLIPSE_HOME.

With this approach, it doesn't matter which version of Eclipse is being used as the code is always compiled against one specific Eclipse version. The downside of this approach is that the PDE will not keep the plug-in manifest dependency list in sync with the project's classpath file.

19.2.6 Building against different versions of Eclipse

Many developers, especially tool developers who write code for Eclipse itself, like to use bleeding-edge code; however, large IT departments and other paying customers tend to prefer to lag the edge, using older, more established and supported software. This disparity creates a problem because you want to develop plug-ins using the latest and greatest, but your client base, the ones who pay for your development fun, may not have caught up yet. Therefore, you need to ship a product with one binary for each version of Eclipse supported.

To complicate matters, different versions of Eclipse have different public APIs. This means one set of source for each version of Eclipse, or does it? Can there be a single source base that is built into one binary for each version of Eclipse?

19.2.6.1   Code branches

One tried-and-true approach to this problem is to have one code stream or branch in the repository for each version of Eclipse you intend to support (see Figure 19–11). Another is to have separate projects, one per version of Eclipse. Unfortunately, with each of these approaches, there is no single code base, so providing the same new functionality for each version of Eclipse involves merging lots of code from one branch to another.

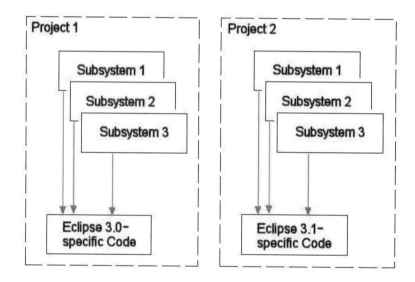

Figure 19–11   Code branches, or multiple projects.

19.2.6.2   Façade pattern

Another approach is a single code base with a façade pattern to handle differences between the versions of Eclipse. One project contains the common code, typically well over 95 percent of the code, accessing the Eclipse API that has not changed across the versions supported. Additional projects, one for each version of Eclipse, provide glue code for accessing just those public APIs that have changed (see Figure 19–12). This approach could produce a single binary that will provide the same functionality across different versions of Eclipse, but you could have the hidden runtime problems outlined in Section 19.2.4, Single versus multiple binaries, on page 691.

Another drawback is that related functionality and methods that should be clustered together tend to become spread out across different packages and projects due to the façade pattern being used.

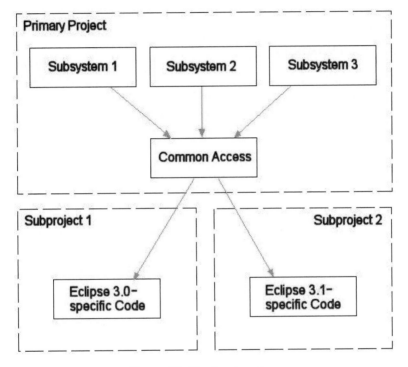

Figure 19–12 Façade pattern.

19.2.6.3 Preprocessor

After trying the first two approaches, we settled on using a Java preprocesssor to handle the differences between versions of Eclipse. This way, there is a single code base that is compiled against each different version of Eclipse, verifying that the calls to Eclipse methods match the public APIs available in that version. A build process takes one code base and produces one binary for each version of Eclipse (see Figure 19–13). In contrast to the façade pattern approach, related functionality and methods tend to stay logically clumped together in the same package rather than being spread out across the product, which leads to a more maintainable product.

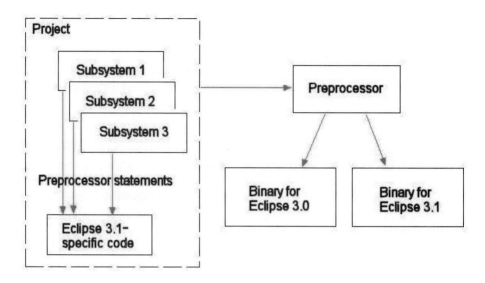

Figure 19–13   Preprocessor approach.

The following lines of code from Section 19.2.2.2, Build initialization, on page 679 define which versions are being targeted and which version of Eclipse contains the source. These properties are used by the `eclipsetools.preprocessor` Ant task to sanity check the situation and globally specify the version of Eclipse in which the source was developed.

```
<property name="eclipsetools.preprocessor.version.valid"
        value="3.1,3.0"/>
<property name="eclipsetools.preprocessor.version.source"
        value="3.1"/>
```

In the `compile_dir` macro discussed in Section 19.2.3, Compiling during the build process, on page 689, the `eclipsetools.preprocessor` is used to translate source developed for one version of Eclipse into source targeted against another version of Eclipse.

```
<eclipsetools.preprocessor
   targetVersion="@{target}"
   dir="@{source}"
   todir="${build.temp}/@{target}/${Bundle-Proj}/src" />
```

Download the Preprocessor

The `<eclipsetools.preprocessor>` task just mentioned is not part of Ant or Eclipse, but is an Ant extension that we wrote. We needed it to build our products, and it is freely available for anyone to use at *www.qualityeclipse.com/ant/preprocessor.*

Code to be translated by the preprocessor involves structured Java comments. The preprocessor statements embedded in comments expose the API call for only one version of Eclipse while hiding the different API calls for the other versions. During the build process, the source is parsed and some sections are commented while others are uncommented, all before the source is sent to the Java compiler (see Figure 19–14).

For example, the code on the next page was developed against the Eclipse 3.1 environment, and thus the Eclipse 3.1-specific code is uncommented, while the Eclipse 2.1- and 3.0-specific code are commented.

In addition, differences in the `plugin.xml` can be handled in a similar manner. For example, the `org.eclipse.ui.ide` plug-in only exists in Eclipse 3.0 and 3.1, not in Eclipse 2.1.

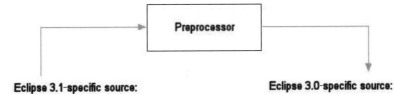

Figure 19–14   Preprocessor translating code.

```
<?xml version="1.0" encoding="UTF-8"?>
<plugin
   id="com.mycompany.myapp"
   name="%pluginName"
   version="1.0.0"
   provider-name="My Company"
   class="com.mycompany.myapp.MyPlugin">

   <requires>
      <import plugin="org.apache.xerces"/>
      <import plugin="org.eclipse.core.runtime"/>
      <import plugin="org.eclipse.core.resources"/>
      <import plugin="org.eclipse.ui"/>
      <!-- $if version >= 3.0 $ -->
      <import plugin="org.eclipse.ui.ide" optional="true"/>
      <!--$endif $ -->
   </requires>

   ... etc ...
</plugin>
```

> **Tip:** If you modify the `<requires>` section of the `plugin.xml` without changing the plug-in's version number and then install it over an earlier version of that plug-in, you may need to delete some information in `<eclipseInstallDir>/configuration` because Eclipse caches plug-in dependency information in that directory.

19.2.6.4 *Fragments*

Fragments can be used to smooth out differences between versions of Eclipse (see Section 16.3, Using Fragments, on page 587 and Section 20.2.6, Using fragments, on page 714 for more about fragments). If a newer version of Eclipse has an API you want to use but an older version does not, use a fragment to insert a helper class into the older version of Eclipse, allowing you access to the necessary internal code. If a class has been added to a newer version of Eclipse that was not present in the older version, then you can backport the entire class to the older version of Eclipse using a fragment. Be aware that your fragment may collide with someone else's fragment doing the same thing; it is safer to add uniquely named helper classes than to backport Eclipse classes.

> **Tip:** When creating a fragment to backport functionality, be sure to adjust the **Host version range** attribute on the **Overview** page of the manifest editor (see Figure 16–12 on page 591) to include the version of Eclipse for which the functionality applies (see Section 3.3.3, Plug-in dependencies, on page 110 for examples of valid version ranges).

19.2.6.5   *Favorites in Eclipse 3.0*

Since you want to support Eclipse 3.0, the next step is to modify the **Favorites** project so that the source correctly compiles against Eclipse 3.0. First, retarget the ECLIPSE_HOME classpath variable so that it points to the Eclipse 3.0 installation (see Section 19.2.5, Editing with different versions of Eclipse, on page 692). Then, modify the code so that it properly compiles against Eclipse 3.0, placing any Eclipse 3.1-specific code in comments. Finally, revert the classpath variable so that it again points to the Eclipse 3.1 installation, and adjust the preprocessor comments accordingly.

> **Tip:** A tool for automatically adjusting the classpath of a project between versions of Eclipse is available on the *QualityEclipse* Web site (*www.qualityeclipse.com/tools/classpath*).

When preparing the **Favorites** view for Eclipse 3.0, one of the issues encountered is the addHelpButtonToToolBar() method. In this case, the Eclipse 3.1 help public API differs from the Eclipse 3.0 help public API. To handle this situation, modify the addHelpButtonToToolBar() method:

```
private void addHelpButtonToToolBar() {
    final IWorkbenchHelpSystem helpSystem = getHelpSystem();
    ... etc ...
```

extracting help system access into a new getHelpSystem() method:

```
private IWorkbenchHelpSystem getHelpSystem() {

    /* $eclipsetools.preprocessor.if version >= 3.1 $ */
    return getSite().getWorkbenchWindow().getWorkbench()
        .getHelpSystem();

    /* $eclipsetools.preprocessor.elseif version < 3.1 $
    return org.eclipse.ui.help.WorkbenchHelpSystem30
        .getHelpSystem();

    $eclipsetools.preprocessor.endif $ */
}
```

In addition, because Eclipse 3.0 lacks a IWorkbenchHelpSystem interface, you should create a new fragment named com.qualityeclipse. e30f.ui.workbench to backport this functionality. Create a WorkbenchHelpSystem30 class in this fragment to access the help system interface because IWorkbench does not have a getHelpSystem() method in Eclipse 3.0.

```
public class WorkbenchHelpSystem30
{
   private WorkbenchHelpSystem30() {}      // No instances

   public static IWorkbenchHelpSystem getHelpSystem() {
      return new IWorkbenchHelpSystem() {
         public boolean hasHelpUI() {
            return true;
         }
         public void displayHelp() {
            WorkbenchHelp.displayHelp();
         }
         public void displaySearch() {
            // no corresponding function in Eclipse 3.0
         }
         ... etc ...
      };
   }
}
```

Another difference you will encounter in the FavoritesView involves trees and columns. Eclipse 3.1 added support for columns in the Tree control, but Eclipse 3.0 does not have this support. Backporting functionality into SWT is tricky at best and involves platform-specific code so that option is out. Another option would be to modify the FavoritesView to use the Table-Tree control—a precursor to tree columns available in Eclipse 3.0 and 3.1 (and 3.2) but deprecated in Eclipse 3.1 (and 3.2). In this case, use preprocessor code to use Tree in Eclipse 3.1 and TableTree in 3.0. To minimize the amount of preprocessor code, method references and variable types are generalized whenever possible. For example, wherever you can, replace

```
viewer.getTree()
```

with

```
viewer.getControl()
```

Since you are using TreeViewer in Eclipse 3.1 and TableTreeViewer in Eclipse 3.0, replace specific local variable declarations in RemoveProperties-Operation such as

```
TreeViewer viewer
```

with more general declarations that work with both TreeViewer and TableTreeViewer:

```
AbstractTreeViewer viewer
```

There is much more of the same to get the **Favorites** product working in Eclipse 3.0 as well as 3.1 including backporting NLS, help system, and undo framework support that are not covered here. In general we use the following approaches to smooth out differences between versions of Eclipse.

- Backporting functionality using plug-ins and fragments.

- Older deprecated API in newer versions of Eclipse.

- More generalized accessors and variable declarations.

- Preprocessor comments when all else fails.

This process of retargeting the `ECLIPSE_HOME` classpath variable only needs to be performed once per project to get the code to compile against a different version of Eclipse. To support multiple versions in an ongoing manner, simply code against one version of Eclipse, and then build the product to make sure that it compiles against the others, adding preprocessor statements only as necessary. In practice, this is not a big deal as only a fraction of your code base will include any preprocessor statements (typically less than one percent of the files).

The final step is to run the code through the preprocessor before it is compiled. Required preprocessor properties have already been added to the `product_init` target described in Section 19.2.2.2, Build initialization, on page 679; and the source before compilation in the `compile_lib` macro was translated in Section 19.2.3, Compiling during the build process, on page 689.

19.2.7   Classpath tools

The `eclipsetools.getclasspath` task introduced in Section 19.2.3, Compiling during the build process, on page 689 can modify the classpath for different versions of Eclipse after it retrieves the classpath. The `${build.map}` property defined in Section 19.2.2.2, Build initialization, on page 679 points to a `.buildmap` file that specifies the differences between the Eclipse 3.0 and 3.1 classpaths.

```
<?xml version="1.0" encoding="UTF-8"?>
<buildmap>
   <config name="eclipse_3.2" marker="ECLIPSE32_HOME">
      <replace variable="ECLIPSE_HOME"
             withVariable="ECLIPSE32_HOME" />
   </config>
   <config name="eclipse_3.1" marker="ECLIPSE_HOME">
      <replace variable="ECLIPSE30_HOME"
             withVariable="ECLIPSE_HOME" />
   </config>
```

```
<config name="eclipse_3.0" marker="ECLIPSE30_HOME">
   <replace variable="ECLIPSE21_HOME"
            withVariable="ECLIPSE30_HOME" />
</config>
<config name="eclipse_2.1" marker="ECLIPSE21_HOME">
   <replace variable="ECLIPSE20_HOME"
            withVariable="ECLIPSE21_HOME" />
</config>
</buildmap>
```

The preceding `.buildmap` file defines the modifications necessary to convert the **Favorites** product Eclipse 3.1 classpath to a classpath compatible with other versions of Eclipse. Each configuration contains instructions for converting a classpath from an *older* version to a *newer* version of Eclipse. For example, the "`eclipse_3.2`" configuration specifies that the `ECLIPSE_HOME` classpath variable should be replaced with the `ECLIPSE32_HOME` classpath variable when converting an older classpath to Eclipse 3.2. When converting a classpath from a newer to an older version of Eclipse, the `eclipsetools.getclasspath` Ant task reverses the process.

The `config` element's `marker` attribute provides a way for the `eclipsetools.getclasspath` Ant task to determine which configuration is the current one. By scanning the specified project's classpath and looking for the use of classpath variables matching the specified markers, the Ant task can automatically determine which is the current configuration for a project.

The `config` element's `name` attribute provides a way to reference that configuration from within the build script. When retrieving the **Favorites** project's classpath in the not yet existing `build_30` target, reference the "`eclipse_3.0`" configuration. The `eclipsetools.getclasspath` Ant task determines the differences between the "`eclipse_3.1`" and "`eclipse_3.0`" configurations, replaces the `ECLIPSE_HOME` classpath variable with the `ECLIPSE30_HOME` classpath variable and finally adjusts the results classpath elements to take plug-in version changes into account.

The configuration's subelements specify the changes necessary to convert a classpath for one version of Eclipse to a classpath for another version. The `replace` element can specify that a `variable` should be replaced `withVariable` or a `project` should be replaced `withProject`.

Download the getclasspath Task

The `<eclipsetools.getclasspath>` task just mentioned is not part of Ant or Eclipse, but is an Ant extension we wrote. We needed it to build our products, and it is freely available for anyone to use at *www.qualityeclipse.com/ant/getclasspath*.

19.2.8   *Building against Eclipse 3.0*

With the preprocessor and classpath tools in place, you are ready to build the **Favorites** project for Eclipse 3.0 by fleshing out the `build_3.0` target in the **Favorites** project's `build-bundle.xml` file. In Eclipse 3.0, plug-ins must be directories, not JAR files, so the classes comprising the **Favorites** plug-in must be compiled and placed in a `favorites.jar` file (rather than in the plug-in JAR file). The classpath must also include all the backported projects and fragments for successful compilation. Add the following to the `build_3.0` target.

```
<compile_lib target="3.0" lib="favorites.jar" extraClasspath="
  ../com.qualityeclipse.e30f.core.runtime/bin;
  ../com.qualityeclipse.e30f.ui.workbench/bin;
  ../com.qualityeclipse.e30p.core.commands/bin;
  ../com.qualityeclipse.e30p.ui.workbench.commands/bin" />
```

This references a new `compile_lib` macro to be added to the `build-macros.xml` file. This convenience macro combines two other earlier defined macros.

```
<macrodef name="compile_lib">
   <attribute name="target" />
   <attribute name="source" default="src" />
   <attribute name="lib" />
   <attribute name="extraClasspath" default="" />
   <attribute name="debug" default="on" />
   <sequential>
      <compile_dir target="@{target}"
                   source="@{source}"
                   extraClasspath="@{extraClasspath}"
                   debug="@{debug}" />

      <jar_lib target="@{target}" lib="@{lib}">
         <fileset dir="${build.temp}/@{target}/${Bundle-Proj}/bin" />
      </jar_lib>
   </sequential>
</macrodef>
```

The `META-INF/MANIFEST.MF` file for Eclipse 3.1 does not contain a class-path declaration because the plug-in is packaged as a single JAR file. In Eclipse 3.0, the `Bundle-ClassPath` specification must be reintroduced so that Eclipse 3.0 can find the **Favorites** plug-in's classes. You must also add the backported plug-ins to the `Require-Bundle` specification. Because you are modifying the `META-INF/MANIFEST.MF` file, it must be removed from the build configuration (see Figure 19–8 on page 685) and explicitly included in both the `build_3.0` and `build_3.1` targets.

The following addition to the `build_3.0` target modifies the `META-INF/MANIFEST.MF` and copies it to `${build.temp}/3.0/${Bundle-Proj}/out` so that the `dir_bundle` macro discussed later will include it in the build (the ==> in the code below denotes a continuation of the previous line and must not be included but lines that do **not** start with ==> must be entered as they appear).

```
<mkdir dir="${build.temp}/3.0/${Bundle-Proj}/out" />
<copy todir="${build.temp}/3.0/${Bundle-Proj}/out">
   <fileset dir="." includes="META-INF/MANIFEST.MF" />
</copy>
<replace file="${build.temp}/3.0/${Bundle-Proj}/out
==>                                /META-INF/MANIFEST.MF">
   <replacetoken>Bundle-Localization: plugin</replacetoken>
   <replacevalue>Bundle-Localization: plugin
Bundle-ClassPath: favorites.jar</replacevalue>
</replace>
<replace file="${build.temp}/3.0/${Bundle-Proj}/out
==>                                /META-INF/MANIFEST.MF">
   <replacetoken> org.eclipse.ui.ide,</replacetoken>
   <replacevalue> org.eclipse.ui.ide,
 com.qualityeclipse.e30p.core.commands,
 com.qualityeclipse.e30p.ui.workbench.commands,</replacevalue>
</replace>
```

Finally, the `build_3.0` target calls the `dir_bundle` macro.

```
<dir_bundle target="3.0" type="plugins" />
```

The `dir_bundle` macro located in the `build-macros.xml` file is very similar to the `jar_bundle` macro discussed earlier except that the bundle's content is placed into a directory rather than a JAR file (the ==> in the code below denotes a continuation of the previous line and must not be included).

```
<macrodef name="dir_bundle">
   <attribute name="target" />
   <attribute name="type" />
   <attribute name="id" default="${Bundle-Id}" />
   <attribute name="version" default="${Bundle-Version}" />
   <element name="content" implicit="true" optional="true" />
   <sequential>
      <mkdir dir="${build.temp}/@{target}/out/@{type}
==>                                /@{id}_@{version}" />
      <mkdir dir="${build.temp}/common/${Bundle-Proj}/out" />
      <mkdir dir="${build.temp}/@{target}/${Bundle-Proj}/out" />
      <copy todir="${build.temp}/@{target}/out/@{type}
==>                                /@{id}_@{version}">
         <fileset dir="." includes="${Bundle-CommonFiles}" />
         <fileset dir="${build.temp}/common/${Bundle-Proj}/out" />
        <fileset dir="${build.temp}/@{target}/${Bundle-Proj}/out" />
         <content />
      </copy>
   </sequential>
</macrodef>
```

The other projects are built in a similar fashion but not covered here. The backported plug-ins and fragments are not needed for Eclipse 3.1 and thus the `build_3.1` target in their `build-bundle.xml` files are empty, but must appear first in the `build_bundles` macro discussed in Section 19.2.2.3, Building multiple projects, on page 681.

19.2.9 *Retargeting source code*

Using the preprocessor approach outlined in the previous sections involves source targeted at one version, but generating binaries for other versions of Eclipse. In other words, the code contains some source that is surrounded by preprocessor statements, but uncommented, for the targeted version of Eclipse, while source for the other versions of Eclipse is commented out. At some point, you'll want to change the targeted version of Eclipse from, say, Eclipse 3.0 to Eclipse 3.1. To accomplish this involves using the preprocessor itself to regenerate your source and the introduction of a new classpath tool.

The first step when retargeting the code from Eclipse 3.0 to Eclipse 3.1 involves running the preprocessor over the code to produce revised source that targets the newer version of Eclipse. This is what happens every time the build process runs, only this time, you are taking the result and checking the revised version back into the repository as the basis for new development. The capability to generate multiple binaries, one for each version of Eclipse, is not lost, only the targeted version of Eclipse has changed.

The second step involves updating the projects' Java build paths by modifying the `.classpath` file (see the end of Section 19.2.5, Editing with different versions of Eclipse, on page 692) to use the appropriate classpath variable.

For example, if you are moving from development in Eclipse 3.0 to Eclipse 3.1, replace all occurrences of `ECLIPSE30_HOME` with `ECLIPSE31_HOME`. In addition, you'll need to update the plug-in's directory suffix in the `.classpath` file to match the target version of Eclipse (e.g., `plugins/org.eclipse. swt_3.0.1` changes to `plugins/org.eclipse. swt_3.1.0`).

> **Tip:** A tool for automatically adjusting the classpath of a project between versions of Eclipse is available on the *QualityEclipse* Web site (*www.qualityeclipse.com/tools/classpath*).

19.2.10 *Version checking*

Having one product binary for each version of Eclipse solves one problem while causing another: What if the user installs the wrong binary for the version of Eclipse he or she is using?

To solve this, you can add version checking to the plug-in startup method to compare the version of Eclipse for which the binary was produced with the version of Eclipse on which the code is currently executing. If the versions don't match, the code immediately informs the user.

```
public static final PluginVersionIdentifier IDE_VERSION_EXPECTED =
   /* $if version == 3.1 $ */
      new PluginVersionIdentifier(3, 1, 0);
   /* $elseif version == 3.0 $
      new PluginVersionIdentifier(3, 0, 0);
   $endif $ */

public static final PluginVersionIdentifier IDE_VERSION_ACTUAL =
   new PluginVersionIdentifier(
      (String) ResourcesPlugin.getPlugin().getBundle().getHeaders()
         .get(org.osgi.framework.Constants.BUNDLE_VERSION));

public static boolean isValidProductVersionForIDE() {
   return
        IDE_VERSION_EXPECTED.getMajorComponent()
        == IDE_VERSION_ACTUAL.getMajorComponent()
   &&
        IDE_VERSION_EXPECTED.getMinorComponent()
        == IDE_VERSION_ACTUAL.getMinorComponent();
}
```

This code can be easily added to the `FavoritesPlugin` class. Once that is in place, you can modify the `createPartControl(Composite)` method in the `FavoritesView` by adding the following code to be the beginning of the method.

```
if (!FavoritesPlugin.isValidProductVersionForIDE()) {
   Label label = new Label(parent, SWT.NONE);
   label.setText(
      "This Favorites binary is compiled for "
         + FavoritesPlugin.IDE_VERSION_EXPECTED
         + " but being executed on "
         + FavoritesPlugin.IDE_VERSION_ACTUAL);
   return;
}
```

Now, if the user installs the **Favorites** product binary compiled for Eclipse 3.1 into Eclipse 3.0, he or she will see the message in the **Favorites** view as shown in Figure 19–15.

Figure 19–15   The Favorites view containing an IDE version message.

19.2.11 *Building for internationalization*

If you are targeting an international market and have generated a language-specific fragment project (see Section 16.3, Using Fragments, on page 587), you need to generate separate deliverables containing language-specific code and resources. For the **Favorites** product, generate two new files:

- `Favorites_v1.0.0_for_Eclipse3.1.zip`
- `Favorites_v1.0.0_for_Eclipse3.0.zip`

These files contain the contents of the `com.qualityeclipse.favorites.nl1` project. Customers desiring language support for French and German would install this language-specific ZIP file in the same location as the main product.

To accomplish all this, modify the `zip_product` macro discussed in Section 19.2.2.3, Building multiple projects, on page 681 to exclude the `com.qualityeclipse.favorites.nl1` project from the main `zip` and place it into a separate `zip` file (the `==>` in the code below denotes a continuation of the previous line and must not be included).

```
<zip destfile="${build.out}/${product.name}_v${product.version}
==>                                    _for_Eclipse@{target}.zip">
   <zipfileset dir="${build.temp}/common/out"
               prefix="@{prefix}" />
   <zipfileset dir="${build.temp}/@{target}/out"
               prefix="@{prefix}" >
      <exclude
         name="plugins/com.qualityeclipse.favorites.nl1_*.jar" />
      <exclude
         name="plugins/com.qualityeclipse.favorites.nl1_*/**/*.*" />
   </zipfileset>
</zip>
<zip destfile="${build.out}/${product.name}_I18N_v${product.version}
==>                                    _for_Eclipse@{target}.zip">
   <zipfileset dir="${build.temp}/@{target}/out"
               prefix="@{prefix}" >
      <include
         name="plugins/com.qualityeclipse.favorites.nl1_*.jar" />
      <include
         name="plugins/com.qualityeclipse.favorites.nl1_*/**/*.*" />
   </zipfileset>
</zip>
```

19.3 Summary

While you can build your plug-ins manually, this can introduce errors and subtle differences between builds. Creating a one-click, repeatable build process is essential for delivering (and redelivering) a commercial Eclipse plug-in.

This chapter introduced Ant and then went into detail about how to create an Ant-based build process. It then went on to discuss some of the issues you will face in building and delivering a plug-in for more than one version of Eclipse.

References

Ant Web site (*ant.apache.org/*).

Eclipse Ant FAQ (*eclipsewiki.editme.com/ANTFaq*).

Loughran, Steve, "Ant in Anger: Using Apache Ant in a Production Development System," November 9, 2002 (*ant.apache.org/ant_in_anger.html*).

QualityEclipse Web site (*www.qualityeclipse.com/ant*).

McAffer, Jeff, and Jean-Michel Lemieux, *Eclipse Rich Client Platform: Designing, Coding, and Packaging Java Applications*, Addison-Wesley, Boston, 2005.

CHAPTER 20

Advanced Topics

When organizing anything, more than likely you will end up with a handful of items that do not fit into any of the existing categories yet are not large or numerous enough to warrant a new category; this book is no exception.

This chapter contains miscellaneous topics that bear discussing, but don't really fit anywhere else in the book, including:

- Advanced search—reference projects

- Accessing internal code

- Adapters

- Opening a browser or creating an email

- Types specified in an extension point

- Modifying Eclipse to find part identifiers

- Label decorators

- Background tasks—jobs API

- Plug-in ClassLoaders

- Early startup

- Rich Client Platform

20.1   Advanced Search—Reference Projects

Eclipse provides an excellent Java search facility for locating source (see Section 1.6.2, Java Search, on page 30), yet the scope of any search is limited to the projects loaded in the workspace; if a Java class is located in a plug-in's jar file, and the plug-in is not on the Java build path of an open project, then the class will not be found. When building Eclipse plug-ins, it is advantageous to include *all* Eclipse plug-ins in the search scope, even those not referenced by any projects under development.

One approach is to load all the plug-in projects from the Eclipse CVS server (see Section 20.6.1, Modifying the Eclipse base, on page 727). Unfortunately, this chews up memory and clutters your workspace with hundreds of additional projects.

Another approach is to create binary projects, one for each Eclipse plug-in. To create one or more binary projects, open the **PDE > Plug-ins** view using the **Show View** dialog (see **Show View** in Section 2.5, Installing and Running the Product, on page 86), select the plug-ins to be imported as projects, then right-click and select **Import > As Binary Project**. Although binary projects take up less memory than source projects, this too will clutter your workspace with hundreds of additional projects.

The approach here—useful for searching and supporting multiple versions of Eclipse at the same time (see Section 19.2.6, Building against different versions of Eclipse, on page 693)—is to create one *reference project* for each version of Eclipse to be searched. This project contains no source of its own, but contains all the Eclipse plug-ins on its classpath so that a search can include the entire source for Eclipse. To include or exclude a particular version of Eclipse from your searches, simply open or close the corresponding reference project.

To create a reference project, first create a Java project (see Section 1.4.1, Using the new Java Project wizard, on page 19), and then add each jar file in each Eclipse plug-in to the project's Java build path (see Section 1.4.2, .classpath and .project files, on page 22). Adding each plug-in can be a tedious process, so a new project wizard to automate this process was created (see Section 11.2, Wizards, on page 430 for specific information about creating wizards).

> **Tip:** A wizard for creating reference projects is available as part of the QualityEclipse Tools plug-in, downloadable from *www.qualityeclipse.com/tools*.

20.2 Accessing Internal Code

Eclipse separates classes into two categories: public API and "for internal use only." Any classes located in a package that has "`internal`" in its name (e.g., `org.eclipse.core.internal.boot`) are internal to the plug-in, should not be referenced by any code outside the plug-in itself, and may change drastically between different versions of Eclipse. All other classes are considered public API, can be called from outside the plug-in, and follow strict Eclipse guidelines for how and when the class and method signatures can change. Needless to say, it is easier to stick to the public API when supporting multiple versions of Eclipse.

During the course of development, you may need to access classes and methods marked internal to a particular Eclipse plug-in. Every time you have such a need, the first thing you should do is double-check that there is not an existing public API that will do the trick instead. If no public API exists, then search the *Eclipse.org* archives or related sites (see Section A.2, Resources, on page 761) for a similar problem with a solution you can use. Failing that, post a message on the Eclipse newsgroup describing your situation and asking for suggestions (see the next section).

If you don't find a solution, then proceed to file a bug report or feature request in the Eclipse Bugzilla tracking system (see Section 20.2.2, Bugzilla— Eclipse bug tracking system, on page 712). If needed, you can create a fragment (see Section 20.2.6, Using fragments, on page 714) to access the code necessary until a public API is made available.

20.2.1 Eclipse newsgroup

The Eclipse newsgroup—*www.eclipse.org/newsgroups/*—provides novices and experts alike with an avenue for sharing knowledge. You'll need a user-name name and password, so if you do not have one, browse *www.eclipse.org/*, then go to **Newsgroups > Request a Password**. The more information you provide regarding what you are trying to accomplish and code showing what you have tried so far, the more likely you are to get a response and the information you need. A vague question will likely be ignored or bounced back to you for more information.

Do your homework, and above all, don't expect an answer—these are smart folks who will answer depending on their area of expertise, their interest in your question, and their available time. Nobody is being paid to help you. The Eclipse newsgroup is open to everyone, so don't be afraid to contribute to the community by offering help to others when you can.

20.2.2   Bugzilla—Eclipse bug tracking system

Once you have double-checked that no public API exists and no one else on the newsgroup has a suggestion as to how your task can be accomplished, submit a bug report or feature request to the Eclipse Bugzilla tracking system:

```
bugs.eclipse.org/bugs/
```

Again, you'll need a username and password, so if you don't have one, browse *www.eclipse.org/*, and then select **Bugs > Create a Bugzilla account**. As with the newsgroup, the more information you provide regarding what you are trying to accomplish and code showing what you have tried so far, the more likely the Eclipse team will provide the public API you need in future versions of Eclipse. To increase your odds of success even further, be sure to include details concerning how you think Eclipse should be modified to suit your needs; or better yet, make and submit the modifications yourself (see Section 20.6.1, Modifying the Eclipse base, on page 727), along with test cases so that the Eclipse development team can simply install your changes, test them, and move on with the rest of their work. Your modifications may involve modifying existing Eclipse code, adding new code, or even adding a new extension point (see Section 17.2, Defining an Extension Point, on page 597).

Be sure to vote for the bugs that you want fixed so that the Eclipse team can get a better feel for which changes are important and which are not. As with the newsgroup, do your homework and don't expect to get everything you want. The Eclipse team is trying to satisfy a diverse community's needs and keep quite busy doing so.

20.2.3   Options for accessing internal code

Submitting a request to the Eclipse development team will help with future versions of Eclipse; but, what is to be done to support the current and prior versions? There are several techniques for accessing internal code, including:

- Calling a method directly if it is publicly accessible
- Creating a utility class in the same package
- Copying the code into your own plug-in
- Subclassing
- Using fragments (see Section 20.2.6, Using fragments, on page 714)

> **Note:** If you reference internal code, either directly or indirectly via a fragment, then the onus is on you to change your code if the internal code changes or goes away.

20.2.4   How Eclipse is different

Eclipse imposes more restrictions on plug-in interaction than in a typical Java application. Each plug-in has its own ClassLoader, restricting its visibility of the system to code in the plug-ins specified via the plug-in manifest (see Section 2.3.1, The Plug-in manifests, on page 71). This means that even though class A in one plug-in resides in a package with the same name as class B in a required plug-in, class A will *not* be able to access the `protected` and default methods in class B. The Eclipse Java development environment will correctly compile the code as if those methods can be accessed, but when the code is executed inside an Eclipse framework, the plug-in ClassLoader will restrict the access, throwing an `IllegalAccessException`.

This situation can also arise if the library is not exported by its plug-in manifest (see Section 3.3.2, Plug-in runtime, on page 110), even if the class and methods are all marked as `public`. Since you do not want to modify an existing Eclipse plug-in, you must be a bit more resourceful to work around these restrictions.

> **Tip:** If a third party will be referencing and building on your plug-ins' code, then consider exporting all classes in your plug-in as shown in Section 3.3.2, Plug-in runtime, on page 110. Your classes may be used to build things not originally envisioned by you, and hiding classes prevents others from supporting different Eclipse versions and your code (see Section 19.2.6, Building against different versions of Eclipse, on page 693). Obviously, wherever you can, provide controlled third-party enhancements through the use of extension points (see Section 17.1, The Extension Point Mechanism, on page 595).

20.2.5   Related plug-ins

Eclipse 3.1 introduces a couple of enhanced package-level visibility directives—`x-internal` and `x-friends`—to more exactly define which plug-ins have access to which packages. When exporting packages using the **Runtime** page of the manifest editor (see Figure 2–11 on page 75), use the **Package Visibility** section to explicitly specify which plug-ins, if any, have access to the selected packages.

For example, in Section 2.8.1, Test preparation, on page 92, you could limit visibility of the exported packages to the test plug-in. This would result in an `Export-Package` declarations something like this.

```
Export-Package: com.qualityeclipse.favorites.actions
   ;x-friends:="com.qualityeclipse.favorites.test",
 com.qualityeclipse.favorites.model
   ;x-friends:="com.qualityeclipse.favorites.test",
 com.qualityeclipse.favorites.views
   ;x-friends:="com.qualityeclipse.favorites.test"
```

In this way, other plug-ins can be granted access to internal packages in a controlled manner.

20.2.6 Using fragments

When neither referencing the code directly nor copying the code into your own plug-in will work, you can try using fragments. Fragments are chunks of code defined in a plug-in-like structure that Eclipse automatically attaches to an existing plug-in (see Section 16.3, Using Fragments, on page 587).

As far as the Eclipse system is concerned, code contributed by a fragment is treated exactly the same as code that exists in the target plug-in. Originally, fragments were created to insert different National Language Support (NLS) code into a plug-in based on the intended audience, but you can exploit this mechanism to solve your own problems. Using this technique, you cannot override classes that already exist in the plug-in, but you can insert new utility classes used to access methods that were previously not accessible because they had default or protected visibility.

20.3 Adapters

Eclipse provides an adapter framework for translating one type of object into a corresponding object of another type. This allows for new types of objects to be systematically translated into existing types of objects already known to Eclipse.

When a user selects elements in one view or editor, other views can request adapted objects from those selected objects that implement the `org.eclipse.core.runtime.IAdaptable` interface. This means that items selected in the **Favorites** view can be translated into resources and Java elements as requested by existing Eclipse views without any code modifications to them (see Section 7.4, Linking the View, on page 305).

20.3.1 IAdaptable

For objects to participate in the adapter framework, they must first implement the `IAdaptable` interface, as was done with `IFavoriteItem` (see Section 7.4.2, Adaptable objects, on page 306). The `IAdaptable` interface contains this single method for translating one type of object into another:

> `getAdapter(Class)`—Returns an object that is an instance of the given class and is associated with this object. Returns `null` if no such object can be provided.

Implementers of the `IAdaptable` interface attempt to provide an object of the specified type. If they cannot translate themselves, then they call the adapter manager to see whether a factory exists for translating them into the specified type.

```
private IResource resource;

public Object getAdapter(Class adapter) {
    if (adapter.isInstance(resource)) {
        return resource;
    }
    return Platform.getAdapterManager()
        .getAdapter(this, adapter);
}
```

20.3.2   Using adapters

Code that needs to translate an object passes the desired type, such as `IResource.class`, into the `getAdapter()` method, and either obtains an instance of `IResource` corresponding to the original object or `null` indicating that such a translation is not possible.

```
if (!(object instanceof IAdaptable)) {
    return;
}

MyInterface myObject
    = ((IAdaptable) object).getAdapter(MyInterface.class);

if (myObject == null) {
    return;
}
... do stuff with myObject ...
```

20.3.3   Adapter factory

Implementing the `IAdaptable` interface allows new types of objects, such as the **Favorites** items to be translated into existing types such as `IResource`, but how are existing types translated into new types? To accomplish this, implement the `org.eclipse.core.runtime.IAdapterFactory` interface to translate existing types into new types.

For example, in the **Favorites** product, you cannot modify the implementers of `IResource`, but can implement an adapter factory to translate `IResource` into `IFavoriteItem`. The `getAdapterList()` method returns an array indicating the types to which this factory can translate, while the `getAdapter()` method performs the translation. In this case, the factory can translate `IResource` and `IJavaElement` objects into `IFavoriteItem` objects so the `getAdapterList()` method returns an array containing the `IFavoriteItem.class`.

```
package com.qualityeclipse.favorites.model;

import org.eclipse.core.runtime.*;

public class FavoriteAdapterFactory
   implements IAdapterFactory
{
   private static Class[] SUPPORTED_TYPES =
      new Class[] { IFavoriteItem.class };

   public Class[] getAdapterList() {
      return SUPPORTED_TYPES;
   }

   public Object getAdapter(Object object, Class key) {
      if (IFavoriteItem.class.equals(key)) {
         FavoritesManager mgr = FavoritesManager.getManager();
         IFavoriteItem item = mgr.existingFavoriteFor(object);
         if (item == null) {
            item = mgr.newFavoriteFor(object);
         }
         return item;
      }
      return null;
   }
}
```

Adapter factories must be registered with the adapter manager before they are used. Typically, a plug-in registers adapters with adapter managers when it starts up and unregisters them when it shuts down. For example, in the **Favorites** product, add the following field to the `FavoritesPlugin` class:

```
private FavoriteAdapterFactory favoriteAdapterFactory;
```

The following code, added to the `FavoritesPlugin`'s `start()` method, registers the adapter. The `FavoriteAdapterFactory` translates `IResource` and `IJavaElement` objects into `IFavoriteItem` objects, so you can register the adapter once with `IResource.class` as the argument and a second time with `IJavaElement.class` indicating that the adapter factory can translate from these types to others.

```
favoriteAdapterFactory = new FavoriteAdapterFactory();
IAdapterManager mgr = Platform.getAdapterManager();
mgr.registerAdapters(favoriteAdapterFactory, IResource.class);
mgr.registerAdapters(favoriteAdapterFactory, IJavaElement.class);
```

In addition, the `FavoritesPlugin`'s `stop()` method must be modified to unregister the adapter:

```
Platform.getAdapterManager().unregisterAdapters(
   favoriteAdapterFactory);
favoriteAdapterFactory = null;
```

The introduction of an adapter factory allows code in the **Favorites** product and any plug-ins that depend on it to be more loosely coupled with the `FavoritesManager`. For example, rather than directly calling the `FavoritesManager` class, the `FavoritesView.pageSelectionChanged()` method (see Section 7.4.3, Selection listener, on page 306) can be revised to use the adaptable interface.

```
protected void pageSelectionChanged(
   IWorkbenchPart part, ISelection selection)
{
   if (part == this) {
      return;
   }
   if (!(selection instanceof IStructuredSelection)) {
      return;
   }

   IStructuredSelection sel = (IStructuredSelection) selection;

   List items = new ArrayList();
   Iterator iter = sel.iterator();
   while (iter.hasNext()) {
      Object object = iter.next();
      if (!(object instanceof IAdaptable)) {
         continue;
      }

      IFavoriteItem item = (IFavoriteItem)
         ((IAdaptable) object).getAdapter(IFavoriteItem.class);

      if (item == null) {
         continue;
      }
      items.add(item);
   }

   if (items.size() > 0) {
      viewer.setSelection(new StructuredSelection(items), true);
   }
}
```

Using an adapter factory has a bit more overhead than referencing the FavoritesManager directly. When considering this for your own product, you will need to determine whether the advantage of looser coupling out-weighs the additional complexity and slightly slower execution time inherent in this approach.

20.3.4 IWorkbenchAdapter

Eclipse uses the IWorkbenchAdapter interface to display information. Many Eclipse views, such as the **Navigator** view, create an instance of Workbench-LabelProvider. This label provider uses the IAdaptable interface to trans-late unknown objects into instances of IWorkbenchAdapter, and then queries this translated object for displayable information such as text and images.

For your object to be displayed in an Eclipse view, such as the **Navigator**, implement the IAdaptable interface and return an object that implements IWorkbenchAdapter or extends the WorkbenchAdapter abstract base class.

20.4 Opening a Browser or Creating an Email

In your product, you may want to provide an easy way for users to reach your Web site or quickly compose an email to your company. Start by creating a button that opens a browser on your product's Web page or creates an email message in the user's default email client when clicked. The simple approach is to use the launch() method in the org.eclipse.swt.program.Program class (see Section 15.4.2, Opening a Web page, on page 562), but unfortu-nately, that approach does not work with platforms other than Windows. First, Eclipse provides the IWorkbenchBrowserSupport interface for opening an embedded browser and an external browser. Second, construct an action for launching the default email client.

20.4.1 IWorkbenchBrowserSupport

To use IWorkbenchBrowserSupport in the FavoritesView, modify the addWebButtonToToolBar() method to construct the URL and then open a browser inside the Eclipse workbench window showing the QualityEclipse Web site. To launch an external browser rather than an embedded browser, change the first argument of the createBrowser() call to IWorkbench-BrowserSupport.AS_EDITOR.

```java
private void addWebButtonToToolBar() {
    Action webAction = new Action() {
        public void run() {
            IWorkbenchBrowserSupport browserSupport = getSite()
                    .getWorkbenchWindow().getWorkbench()
                    .getBrowserSupport();

            URL webUrl;
            try {
                webUrl = new URL("http://www.qualityeclipse.com");
            }
            catch (MalformedURLException e) {
                FavoritesLog.logError(e);
                return;
            }

            IWebBrowser browser;
            try {
                browser = browserSupport.createBrowser(
                        IWorkbenchBrowserSupport.AS_EDITOR, null,
                        "Quality Eclipse", "The Quality Eclipse website");
                browser.openURL(webUrl);
            }
            catch (PartInitException e) {
                FavoritesLog.logError(e);
                return;
            }
        }
    };

    webAction.setToolTipText("Open a web page"); //$NON-NLS-1$
    webAction.setImageDescriptor(ImageDescriptor.createFromFile(
            FavoritesView.class, "web.gif")); //$NON-NLS-1$
    getViewSite().getActionBars().getToolBarManager().add(webAction);
}
```

If you are building an RCP application and not building on top of the Eclipse Workbench, you will need to extract some functionality from the `org.eclipse.ui.browser` plug-in and build on top of the basic browser support provided in the SWT and JFace plug-ins. If you head down this path, be sure to review `DefaultBrowserSupport`, `WebBrowserEditor`, and `BrowserViewer` in the `org.eclipse.ui.browser` plug-in and `Browser` in the `org.eclipse.swt` plug-in.

> **Tip:** See *www.qualityeclipse.com/util/browser* for more on using functionality similar to `IWorkbenchBrowserSupport` in an RCP application.

20.4.2   LaunchURL

The `org.eclipse.help.ui.browser.LaunchURL` class provides another mechanism for opening a browser. This action delegate, part of the `org.eclipse.help.ui` plug-in, can be used to add a workbench menu (see Section 6.2.3, Defining a menu item and toolbar button, on page 212) that opens a browser on a predefined Web page (reading the code, this action appears to have cross-platform support, but we've only tried this on Windows). For example, in the **Favorites** product, you could add a new action to the top-level **Favorites** menu by adding the following declaration to the "Favorites ActionSet" in the plug-in manifest.

```
<action
   id="com.qualityeclipse.favorites.browseWeb"
   menubarPath="com.qualityeclipse.favorites.workbenchMenu/content"
   label="Browse QualityEclipse"
   icon="icons/web.gif"
   style="push"
   tooltip="Use the LaunchURL class to open a browser"
   class="org.eclipse.help.ui.browser.LaunchURL"
   url="http://www.qualityeclipse.com"/>
```

The `url` attribute in the declaration above specifies the Web page displayed by the `LaunchURL` action delegate. Unfortunately, the plug-in manifest editor does not support the `url` attribute, so you must switch to the **plugin.xml** page to hand-code the attribute.

20.4.3   OpenEmailAction

The `launch()` method in the `org.eclipse.swt.program.Program` class is useful for opening the default email client in Windows, but not so in Linux. What you need is a separate action that opens email clients differently based on the current platform. To start, create a new `OpenEmailAction` class with fields and setters for standard email elements.

```
public class OpenEmailAction extends Action
{
   private String recipient;
   private String subject;
   private String body;

   public void setRecipient(String recipient) {
      this.recipient = recipient;
   }
```

```
    public void setSubject(String subject) {
        this.subject = subject;
    }

    public void setBody(String body) {
        this.body = body;
    }
}
```

Next add a `run()` method that determines a platform-specific template, fills in the specified email elements, and then launches the email client. Over time, you can enhance this method to check for additional Linux email clients.

```
public void run() {
    String template;
    if (SWT.getPlatform().equals("win32")) {
        template = "mailto:${recipient}" +
            "?Subject=${subject}&Body=${body}";
    }
    else {
        // Put code here to test for various Linux email clients
        template = "netscape mailto:${recipient}" +
            "?Subject=${subject}&Body=${body}";
    }

    String mailSpec = buildMailSpec(template);

    if (mailSpec.startsWith("mailto:")) {
        Program.launch(mailSpec);
    }
    else {
        try {
            Runtime.getRuntime().exec(mailSpec);
        }
        catch (IOException e) {
            FavoritesLog.logError(
                "Failed to open mail client: " + mailSpec,
                e);
        }
    }
}
```

> **Tip:** The platform-specific code that appears above is inherently more fragile than the less specific Java code, so see *www.qualityeclipse.com/util/email* for the latest notes and code.

The preceding `run()` method calls the `buildMailSpec()` method to generate an email specification based on the platform-specific template provided. It replaces tokens, such as `${subject}`, in the template with their respective values.

```java
private String buildMailSpec(String template) {
   StringBuffer buf = new StringBuffer(1000);
   int start = 0;
   while (true) {
      int end = template.indexOf("${", start);
      if (end == -1) {
         buf.append(template.substring(start));
         break;
      }
      buf.append(template.substring(start, end));
      start = template.indexOf("}", end + 2);
      if (start == -1) {
         buf.append(template.substring(end));
         break;
      }
      String key = template.substring(end + 2, start);
      if (key.equalsIgnoreCase("recipient")) {
         buf.append(recipient);
      }
      else if (key.equalsIgnoreCase("subject")) {
         buf.append(subject);
      }
      else if (key.equalsIgnoreCase("body")) {
         appendBody(buf);
      }
      start++;
   }
   return buf.toString();
}
```

The buildMailSpec() method calls appendBody() to append email content to the email specification. Carriage return and line feed characters are replaced with "%0A" to create separate lines when appending the email's content.

```java
private void appendBody(StringBuffer buf) {
   if (body == null)
      return;
   int start = 0;
   while (true) {
      int end = body.indexOf('\n', start);
      if (end == -1) {
         buf.append(body.substring(start));
         return;
      }
      if (end > 0 && body.charAt(end - 1) == '\r')
         buf.append(body.substring(start, end - 1));
      else
         buf.append(body.substring(start, end));
      buf.append("%0A");
      start = end + 1;
   }
}
```

Now you can modify the `addEMailButtonToToolBar()` method in the `FavoritesView` to use this new action.

```
private void addEMailButtonToToolBar() {
    OpenEmailAction emailAction = new OpenEmailAction();
    emailAction.setRecipient("info@qualityeclipse.com");
    emailAction.setSubject("Question");
    emailAction.setBody("My question is ..." +
        "\nSecond line\nThird line.");
    emailAction.setToolTipText("Send an email"); //$NON-NLS-1$
    emailAction.setImageDescriptor(
        ImageDescriptor.createFromFile(
            FavoritesView.class, "mail.gif")); //$NON-NLS-1$

    getViewSite().getActionBars().getToolBarManager()
        .add(emailAction);
}
```

This does not send the message, but signals the email client to create the message with the specific information so that the user can review and send it. The code above creates an email message that looks something like this:

```
To: info@qualityeclipse.com
Subject: Question

My question is ...
Second line
Third line.
```

> **Tip:** Not all systems or browsers support all `mailto` options. For a complete listing of what can be encoded in a `mailto` request, google "mailto syntax" or see *www.qualityeclipse.com/util/mailtoSyntax.htm*

20.5 Types Specified in an Extension Point

All plug-ins declaring an extension point use the `IConfiguration-Element.createExecutable()` method to instantiate types specified by other plug-ins (see Section 17.3.3, Creating executable extensions, on page 611). For example, given the following declaration, the `org.eclipse.ui` plug-in will instantiate the `myPackage.MyActionDelegate` class when necessary using the `createExecutable()` method.

```
<extension point="org.eclipse.ui.actionSets">
   <action
      label="Open Favorites View"
      icon="icons/sample.gif"
      tooltip="Open the favorites view"
      menubarPath="myMenu/content"
      toolbarPath="Normal/additions"
      id="myProduct.openFavoritesView">
      class="myPackage.MyActionDelegate"
   </action>
</extension>
```

In the declaration above, only the fully qualified class name is specified, but there are a few hidden surprises that are explored in the following sections.

20.5.1 Parameterized types

Types specified in a plug-in manifest are instantiated using their default no argument constructor, so how can they be parameterized? For example, let's suppose that you have two very similar functions in your menu. How should those functions be implemented? One approach is to have two different action delegates, one for each function, with a shared superclass containing all the common behavior. Another approach is to have a single action delegate, but somehow initialize each instance differently to perform a slightly different operation, but how? It is this second option being explored here.

Parameterizing a type—passing additional information to that type during its initialization phase—is accomplished by implementing the `org.eclipse.core.runtime.IExecutableExtension` interface. If additional information is provided in the plug-in manifest, then Eclipse passes the additional information to the type using the `setInitializationData` method. The information arrives via the `setInitializationData` method in different formats depending on how it is structured in the plug-in manifest.

20.5.1.1 Unstructured parameters

One way to parameterize a type is to place a colon at the end of the type's class name followed by a string of information. This string is unstructured and has as much or as little information as desired. Eclipse parses the `class` attribute, using the information before the colon to determine the class to be instantiated, while the information after the colon is passed as a string to the type via the `setInitializationData` method.

For example, in the following declaration (see Figure 20–1), the action delegate `myPackage.MyActionDelegate` would be instantiated using its no argument constructor and then the `setInitializationData` method would be called with the string "`one two three`" as its third argument.

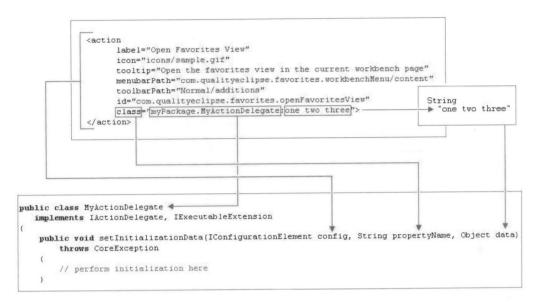

Figure 20–1   IExecutableExtension with unstructured parameters.

20.5.1.2   *Structured parameters*

A second more structured approach is to define parameters formally. Rather than all parameters being declared in a single string, each parameter is declared separately as key/value pairs. Each key/value pair is placed into a `java.util.Hashtable` that is passed to the `setInitializationData` method.

For example, in the following `IExecutableExtension` declaration (see Figure 20–2), the action delegate `myPackage.MyActionDelegate` would be instantiated using its no argument constructor and then the `setInitialization-`
`tionData` method would be called with a `Hashtable` as its third argument. The `Hashtable` would contain the key/value pairs "`p1`"/"`one`", "`p2`"/"`two`", and "`p3`"/"`three`". All other aspects of this second approach are the same as those of the first.

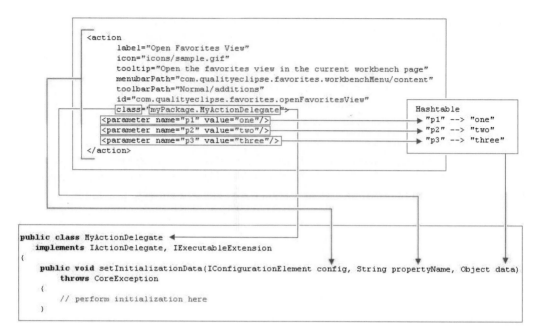

Figure 20–2   IExecutableExtension with structured parameters.

20.5.2   *Referencing a class in a different plug-in*

Most of the time, the class being referenced in a plug-in's manifest resides in the same plug-in. But, what if one plug-in manifest references a class that is contained in a `jar` file of another plug-in? By default, if the fully qualified class name is specified, then Eclipse makes the assumption that the class resides in the plug-in making the declaration, so it will not find a class that resides in a different plug-in. In this case, precede the class name with the other plug-in's identifier followed by a slash.

For example, if `plugin.A` provides an action delegate class that can be parameterized (see Section 20.5.1, Parameterized types, on page 724) and `plugin.B` provides an action that launches a parameterized copy of that class, then the action declaration in `plugin.B` might look something like this:

```
<action
    id="com.qualityeclipse.favorites.showPartInfo"
    label="Show My View Info"
    menubarPath="myMenu/content"
    class="plugin.A/
        plugin.A.actions.ShowPartInfoActionDelegate">
    <parmeter
        name="partClass"
        value="plugin.B.view.myView"/>
</action>
```

20.6   Modifying Eclipse to Find Part Identifiers

Defining new actions using the plug-in manifest editor is a straightforward process, except for finding those pesky identifiers for extending the context menus of specific views and editors (see Section 6.4, View Actions, on page 237 and Section 6.5, Editor Actions, on page 244). This information is not part of any plug-in manifest and thus must be obtained in some other manner.

One approach is to start with the `registerContextMenu` method in the `org.eclipse.ui.internal.PartSite` class and search for references, exploring the code and recording identifiers as you go. This is a viable but time-consuming approach that tends to become out of date as new versions of Eclipse arrive.

An alternate approach is a development utility that interrogates the active workbench part, be it an editor or a view, and dumps information about that part, such as the context menu identifiers, to the console. Unfortunately, the API for obtaining this information does not exist (see Section 20.2, Accessing Internal Code, on page 711), so before creating an action delegate, you need to modify the underlying Eclipse system to provide the appropriate accessor methods.

> **Tip:** You can download and install this part information utility from *www.qualityeclipse.com/util.*

20.6.1   *Modifying the Eclipse base*

To modify the Eclipse base, you first need to check out the appropriate project from the Eclipse repository so that later you can create and submit a CVS patch. Submitting a CVS patch is how such changes are fed back to the Eclipse committers with the hope of getting integrated into the development stream. Connect to the *Eclipse.org* development repository by opening the **CVS Repositories** view (see Section 1.8.1, Getting started with CVS, on page 49) and selecting **New > Repository Location**. In the **Add CVS Repository** dialog, enter the following values.

Host—"dev.eclipse.org"

Repository Path—"/home/eclipse"

User—"anonymous"

Password—Leave this blank.

Connection Type—"pserver"

Once connected, expand the **HEAD** tree element, locate the `org.eclipse.ui.workbench` project, and check it out in the workspace (see Section 1.8.2, Checking out a project from CVS, on page 50). Once it is checked out in the workspace, there may be some compile errors in the **Problems** view because the Eclipse being used may be different from the Eclipse against which the plug-in project was compiled. The plug-in project is compiled against the **HEAD** versions of other plug-in projects, but since it cannot locate those other plug-in projects in your workspace, it compiles them against the plug-ins in the current Eclipse installation. The following are several different ways to remedy this situation.

- Check out each Eclipse plug-in project on which this plug-in project directly or indirectly depends.

- Download and install (but do not launch) the latest Eclipse integration build, then retarget your current Eclipse environment to compile against plug-ins in the integration build using the **Plug-in Development > Target Platform** preference page (see Section 19.2.5, Editing with different versions of Eclipse, on page 692). The disadvantage is that all other plug-in projects in your workspace will also be compiled against this target platform.

- Check out a prior version of the plug-in project that compiles against the plug-ins contained in your Eclipse installation. The disadvantage is that if any of the code you write depends on functionality that has changed between the version you checked out and the **HEAD**, then it may not compile when you submit it back to *Eclipse.org*.

- Do as much as you can using one of the preceding approaches, then wait until the next Eclipse milestone build is released (they are usually very stable, whereas various integration builds are not). Download, install, and code against the new build and submit your changes as soon as possible back to *Eclipse.org*.

When the `org.eclipse.ui.workbench` project is loaded and its compile errors cleaned up, add the following methods.

org.eclipse.ui.internal.PopupMenuExtender

```
public String getMenuId() {
    return menuID;
}
```

org.eclipse.ui.internal.PartSite

```
public String[] getContextMenuIds() {
   if (menuExtenders == null)
      return new String[0];
   String[] menuIds = new String[menuExtenders.size()];
   int index = 0;
   Iterator iter = menuExtenders.iterator();
   PopupMenuExtender extender;
   while (iter.hasNext()) {
      extender = (PopupMenuExtender) iter.next();
      menuIds[index] = extender.getMenuId();
      index++;
   }
   return menuIds;
}
```

20.6.2   *Creating the global action*

Next, you will create an action delegate capable of using this newly introduced API. In the plug-in project of your choice (e.g., the **Favorites** plug-in
project, but not the `org.eclipse.ui.workbench` plug-in project), define a
new workbench menu and menu item in the plug-in manifest (see Section 6.2,
Workbench Window Actions, on page 209), give it a name similar to "Show
Part Info," and associate it with the action delegate that follows. Be sure to
modify that plug-in's classpath to reference the `org.eclipse.ui.workbench`
project in the workspace rather than the `org.eclipse.ui.workbench` external plug-in, and make sure that `org.eclipse.ui.workbench` is in the
required plug-ins list in the plug-in manifest.

```
package com.qualityeclipse.favorites.actions;

import ...

public class ShowPartInfoActionDelegate
   implements IWorkbenchWindowActionDelegate
{
   public void init(IWorkbenchWindow window) {
      // ignored
   }

   public void selectionChanged(IAction action, ISelection selection)
   {
      // Ignored.
   }
```

```java
public void run(IAction action) {

    // Determine the active part.
    IWorkbenchPage activePage =
        PlatformUI
            .getWorkbench()
            .getActiveWorkbenchWindow()
            .getActivePage();

    IWorkbenchPart activePart =
        activePage.getActivePart();

    // Search editor references.
    IEditorReference[] editorRefs =
        activePage.getEditorReferences();

    for (int i = 0; i < editorRefs.length; i++) {
        IEditorReference eachRef = editorRefs[i];
        if (eachRef.getEditor(false) == activePart) {
            printEditorInfo(
                eachRef,
                (IEditorPart) activePart);
        }
    }

    // Search view references.
    IViewReference[] viewRefs =
        activePage.getViewReferences();

    for (int i = 0; i < viewRefs.length; i++) {
        IViewReference eachRef = viewRefs[i];
        if (eachRef.getView(false) == activePart) {
            printViewInfo(eachRef, (IViewPart) activePart);
        }
    }
}

private void printEditorInfo(
    IEditorReference editorRef,
    IEditorPart editor) {

    printPartInfo(editorRef, editor);
}

private void printViewInfo(
    IViewReference viewRef,
    IViewPart view) {

    printPartInfo(viewRef, view);
}
```

```
   private void printPartInfo(
      IWorkbenchPartReference partRef,
      IWorkbenchPart part) {

      println(partRef.getTitle());
      println("  id = " + partRef.getId());
      IWorkbenchPartSite site = part.getSite();
      if (site instanceof PartSite) {
         String[] menuIds =
            ((PartSite) site).getContextMenuIds();
         if (menuIds != null) {
            for (int i = 0; i < menuIds.length; i++)
               println("  menuId = " + menuIds[i]);
         }
      }
   }

   public void println(String line) {
      System.out.println(line);
   }

   public void dispose() {
      // Ignored.
   }
}
```

20.6.3 Testing the new utility

Create a new launch configuration (see Section 2.6, Debugging the Product, on page 88) and launch a **Runtime Workbench** to test the new utility. Be sure to modify the launch configuration so that it references the org.eclipse. ui.workbench project in the workspace rather than the org.eclipse.ui. workbench external plug-in. When you activate an editor or view and then select the new global action from the workbench menu bar, you will see the workbench part's information appear in the **Console** view of the **Development Workbench**.

20.6.4 Submitting the change to Eclipse

After you've created a useful addition to Eclipse and decided that it's of no real commercial value yet it might really help other developers, you can post it to a Web site for others to download and use as they choose; or better still, you can submit it to *Eclipse.org* for inclusion in the Eclipse base via Bugzilla (see Section 20.2.2, Bugzilla—Eclipse bug tracking system, on page 712).

For example, if you were to submit the modifications made to the Eclipse base (see Section 20.6.1, Modifying the Eclipse base, on page 727), you would follow these steps:

1. Open a Web browser to the Eclipse Bugzilla page (*bugs.eclipse.org/bugs*) and search the submissions to see whether someone has already had the same thoughts you have had and already posted a bug or feature request (e.g., we've already posted this code to Bug # 39782).

2. If, after a search you've determined that your contribution has not been made by anyone else, then package up your modifications to the Eclipse base code in a CVS *patch*. To create a patch for submission to *Eclipse.org*, select the Eclipse project containing your modifications, right-click, and then select **Team > Create Patch...** . Note that the patch creation functionality can only be used on a project checked out from a repository, such as *dev.eclipse.org* (see Section 20.6.1, Modifying the Eclipse base, on page 727), not from imported binary or source plug-in projects.

3. Either create a new bug report and append your patch or append your patch to an existing bug report. Be sure to explain what the patch contains and why you think it should be included in the Eclipse base code.

20.7 Label Decorators

Label decorators visually indicate specific attributes of an object. For example, if a project is stored in a repository, then it has a small cylinder below and to the right of its folder icon in the **Navigator** view. The **Navigator's** label provider (see Section 7.2.5, Label provider, on page 277) returns a folder image, which is then decorated by the repository's label decorator with a small cylinder. The final composite image is then rendered in the **Navigator** view. Label decorators are not restricted to decorating images only; an object's text can be enhanced by adding characters to the beginning or end.

The org.eclipse.ui.decorators extension point provides a mechanism for adding new label decorators. Label decorators appear in the **General > Appearance > Label Decorations** preference page (see Figure 20–3) and can be enabled or disabled by the user. Behavior for a label decorator is supplied by implementing ILabelDecorator, and optionally IFontDecorator and/or IColorDecorator. If the information to decorate an object is not immediately available, for example the type of decoration depends on a network query, then implement IDelayedLabelDecorator.

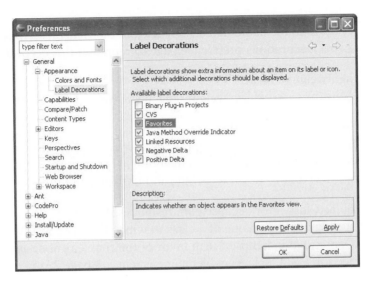

Figure 20–3   The Label Decorations preference page.

20.7.1 *Declaring a label decorator*

In the **Favorites** product, you want to decorate objects in other views that also appear in the **Favorites** view. To accomplish this, create a new `org.eclipse.ui.decorators` extension (see Section 6.2.1, Defining a workbench window menu, on page 209 for an example of creating extensions) with the following values.

adaptable—"true"
A flag that indicates whether types that adapt to `IResource` should use this object contribution. This flag is used only if `objectClass` adapts to `IResource`. The default value is `false`.

class—"com.qualityeclipse.favorites.views.FavoritesLightweightDecorator"
A fully qualified name of a class that implements `org.eclipse.jface.viewers.ILightweightLabelDecorator` (see the next section) or is unspecified if this decorator has only an icon and no behavior (see Section 20.7.3, Decorative label decorators, on page 736).

icon—Leave blank
If the decorator is lightweight and the class is not specified, this is the path to the overlay image to apply (see the next section).

id— "com.qualityeclipse.favorites.favoritesLightweightDecorator"
A unique name that will be used to identify this decorator.

label—"Favorites"
A translatable name that will be used in the **General > Appearance > Label Decorations** preference page to represent this decorator.

lightweight—"true"
Must be `true`. Heavyweight label decorators are deprecated.

location—"TOP_LEFT"
The location at which to apply the decorator image. Defaults to `BOTTOM_RIGHT`. Valid values include `TOP_LEFT`, `TOP_RIGHT`, `BOTTOM_LEFT`, `BOTTOM_RIGHT`, and `UNDERLAY`.

objectClass—"org.eclipse.core.resources.IResource"
A fully qualified name of a class to which this decorator will be applied. Deprecated in Eclipse 2.1 in favor of the enablement nested element (see Section 6.3.2.5, The enablement element, on page 231).

state—"true"
A flag that indicates whether the decorator is on by default. The default value is `false`.

Use this description nested element to provide a brief description of what the label decorator does:

```
<description>
Indicates whether an object appears in the Favorites view.
</description>
```

You can add the `enablement` (see Section 6.3.2.5, The enablement element, on page 231), the `and`, the `or`, and the `not` subelements (see Section 6.3.2.2, The visibility element, on page 228) if you want to more exactly specify when this label decorator is to be used (see Section 20.7.3, Decorative label decorators, on page 736 for an example).

20.7.2 ILightweightLabelDecorator

Instances of `ILightweightLabelDecorator` can modify the image, text, font, and color displayed for an object. Create the class that contains the decorative behavior when you specify the `class` attribute by clicking the `class` label to the left of the `class` attribute's value. In the Java Attribute Editor, select **Generate a new Java class**, enter the package name and class name, and click the **Finish** button.

When the initial class has been generated, make sure that the decorator implements `ILightweightLabelDecorator` and not `ILabelDecorator`. The `decorate()` method appends " `[favorite]` " and overlays a small green `F` to any resource that has been added to the **Favorites** view.

```
package com.qualityeclipse.favorites.views;

import ...

public class FavoritesLightweightDecorator
   implements ILightweightLabelDecorator, FavoritesManagerListener
{
   private static final String SUFFIX = " [favorite]";
   private final ImageDescriptor OVERLAY =
      FavoritesPlugin.imageDescriptorFromPlugin(
         FavoritesPlugin.ID, "icons/favorites_overlay.gif");

   private final FavoritesManager manager =
      FavoritesManager.getManager();

   public void decorate(Object element, IDecoration decoration) {
      if (manager.existingFavoriteFor(element) != null) {
         decoration.addOverlay(OVERLAY);
         decoration.addSuffix(SUFFIX);
      }
   }
}
```

The decorator must also notify label listeners when the decoration for an element has changed. In this case, whenever an element has been added to or removed from the **Favorites** view, notify listeners that the state of associated resources has changed. This entails registering for change events from the `FavoritesManager` and then rebroadcasting those events to all registered `ILabelProviderListener` instances.

```
private final List listenerList = new ArrayList();

public FavoritesLightweightDecorator() {
   // Make sure that the Favorites are loaded.
   manager.getFavorites();
   manager.addFavoritesManagerListener(this);
}

public void dispose() {
   manager.removeFavoritesManagerListener(this);
}

public void addListener(ILabelProviderListener listener) {
   if (!listenerList.contains(listener))
      listenerList.add(listener);
}
```

```
public void removeListener(ILabelProviderListener listener) {
    listenerList.remove(listener);
}

public void favoritesChanged(FavoritesManagerEvent favoritesEvent) {
    Collection elements = new HashSet();
    addResourcesTo(favoritesEvent.getItemsAdded(), elements);
    addResourcesTo(favoritesEvent.getItemsRemoved(), elements);

    LabelProviderChangedEvent labelEvent =
        new LabelProviderChangedEvent(this, elements.toArray());

    Iterator iter = listenerList.iterator();
    while (iter.hasNext()) {
        ((ILabelProviderListener) iter.next())
            .labelProviderChanged(labelEvent);
    }
}

private void addResourcesTo(
    IFavoriteItem[] items, Collection elements)
{
    for (int i = 0; i < items.length; i++) {
        IFavoriteItem item = items[i];
        Object res = item.getAdapter(IResource.class);
        if (res != null) {
            elements.add(res);
        }
    }
}

public boolean isLabelProperty(Object element, String property) {
    return false;
}
```

When this behavior is in place, any elements added to the **Favorites** view will have a small "F" overlay and the suffix [favorite] in the **Navigator** view (see Figure 20–4).

20.7.3   Decorative label decorators

If you simply want to decorate a label by adding a static image in one of the quadrants without any text modifications, then you can specify the icon attribute instead of the class attribute. If the class attribute is not specified, Eclipse places the image specified by the icon attribute in the quadrant specified by the location attribute.

In this case, there is no need to create a class that implements ILightweightLabelDecorator because Eclipse provides this behavior for you. A read-only file decorator is one example of a decorative label decorator.

```
<decorator
   lightweight="true"
   location="BOTTOM_LEFT"
   label="Locked"
   icon="icons/locked_overlay.gif"
   state="true"
   id="com.qualityeclipse.favorites.locked">
   <description>
     Indicates whether a file is locked
   </description>
   <enablement>
      <and>
         <objectClass
             name="org.eclipse.core.resources.IResource"/>
         <objectState name="readOnly" value="true"/>
      </and>
   </enablement>
</decorator>
```

With this declaration in the plug-in manifest, a small lock icon appears in the lower left corner of the icon associated with any locked resource (see Figure 20–4).

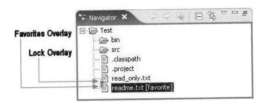

Figure 20–4 Navigator view with Favorites and locked decoration.

20.7.4 IDecoratorManager

Now that you have added decorations to other views, it is time to decorate your own view. Eclipse provides a `DecoratingLabelProvider` and an decorator manager via the `getDecoratorManager()` method in `IWorkbench`. If the view contained a simple list, then you could wrap the `FavoritesViewLabelProvider` with a `DecoratingLabelProvider` by modifying the `FavoritesView createTableViewer()` method something like this:

```
IWorkbench workbench =
   getSite().getWorkbenchWindow().getWorkbench();
viewer.setLabelProvider(new DecoratingLabelProvider(
   new FavoritesViewLabelProvider(),
   workbench.getDecoratorManager())));
```

Unfortunately, the **Favorites** view contains a table, so a bit more work is involved to add the decorator. Start by adding the workbench decorator to the FavoritesViewLabelProvider.

```
final IDecoratorManager decorator;

public FavoritesViewLabelProvider() {
   decorator = PlatformUI.getWorkbench().getDecoratorManager();
}
```

Next, override the listener methods so that your view is notified when the workbench decoration has changed.

```
public void addListener(ILabelProviderListener listener) {
   decorator.addListener(listener);
   super.addListener(listener);
}

public void removeListener(ILabelProviderListener listener) {
   decorator.removeListener(listener);
   super.removeListener(listener);
}
```

Finally, modify the getColumnText() and getColumnImage() methods to query the workbench decorator before returning the requested text or image, respectively.

```
public String getColumnText(Object obj, int index) {
   switch (index) {
   case 0: // Type column
      return "";
   case 1: // Name column
      String name;
      if (obj instanceof IFavoriteItem)
         name = ((IFavoriteItem) obj).getName();
      else if (obj != null)
         name = obj.toString();
      else
         name = "";
      String decorated = decorator.decorateText(name, obj);
      if (decorated != null)
         return decorated;
      return name;
   case 2: // Location column
      if (obj instanceof IFavoriteItem)
         return ((IFavoriteItem) obj).getLocation();
      return "";
   default:
      return "";
   }
}
```

```
public Image getColumnImage(Object obj, int index) {
    if ((index == 0) && (obj instanceof IFavoriteItem)) {
        Image image = ((IFavoriteItem) obj).getType().getImage();
        Image decorated = decorator.decorateImage(image, obj);
        if (decorated != null)
            return decorated;
        return image;
    }
    return null;
}
```

20.8 Background Tasks—Jobs API

Long-running operations should be executed in the background so that the UI stays responsive. One solution is to fork a lower-priority thread to perform the operation rather than performing the operation in the UI thread. But, how do you keep the user informed as to the progress of the background operation? Eclipse provides a *Jobs API* for creating, managing, and displaying background operations.

In the **Favorites** product, you want to periodically check for the availability of a newer version. Rather than interrupt the user, you want to have this check performed in the background and provide the user with nonintrusive progress information as the operation proceeds. To accomplish this, create NewVersionCheckJob. The goal is to exercise the Jobs API, not Internet access, so NewVersionCheckJob only simulates a version check.

```
package com.qualityeclipse.favorites.jobs;
import ...
public class NewVersionCheckJob extends Job
{
    private NewVersionCheckJob(String name) {
        super(name);
    }
    protected IStatus run(IProgressMonitor monitor) {
        // Simulate check for new version.
        monitor.beginTask("check for new version", 20);
        for (int i = 20; i > 0; --i) {
            monitor.subTask("seconds left = " + i);
            try {
                Thread.sleep(1000);
            } catch (InterruptedException e) {
                // Ignored.
            }
            monitor.worked(1);
        }
        monitor.done();
        // Reschedule job to execute in 2 minutes.
        schedule(120000);
        return Status.OK_STATUS;
    }
}
```

The user will control this operation via a new checkbox on the **Favorites** preference page, so first add a new constant to the `PreferenceConstants` (see Section 12.2.4, Favorites preference page, on page 461).

```
public static final String
   FAVORITES_NEW_VERSION_CHECK_PREF =
      "favorites.newVersionCheck";
```

Next, expose this new preference on the **Favorites** preference page by adding a new checkbox. This entails a new field plus additional code at the end of the `createFieldEditors()` method (see Section 12.2.4, Favorites preference page, on page 461).

```
private BooleanFieldEditor newVersionCheckEditor;

public void createFieldEditors() {
   … original code here …
   newVersionCheckEditor = new BooleanFieldEditor(
      PreferenceConstants.FAVORITES_NEW_VERSION_CHECK_PREF,
      "Periodically check for new version"
         + " of Favorites product (simulated)",
      getFieldEditorParent());
      addField(newVersionCheckEditor);
}
```

Now you want to tie the new version check job to this preference by adding a preference listener to `NewVersionCheckJob`. The preference listener either schedules or cancels the job depending on the preference setting as specified by the user.

```
private static final String JOB_NAME =
   "Favorites check for new version";

private static NewVersionCheckJob job = null;

public boolean shouldSchedule() {
   return equals(job);
}

private static final Preferences preferences =
   FavoritesPlugin.getDefault().getPluginPreferences();

private static final Preferences.IPropertyChangeListener
   propertyListener = new Preferences.IPropertyChangeListener() {
      public void propertyChange(PropertyChangeEvent event) {
         update();
      }
   };
```

```
private static void update() {
    if (preferences.getBoolean(
        PreferenceConstants.FAVORITES_NEW_VERSION_CHECK_PREF))
    {
        if (job == null) {
            job = new NewVersionCheckJob(JOB_NAME);
            job.schedule();
        }
    }
    else {
        if (job != null) {
            job.cancel();
            job = null;
        }
    }
}
```

Next, create additional methods that are called by `FavoritesPlugin` when the plug-in starts up and shuts down.

```
public static void startup() {
    preferences.addPropertyChangeListener(propertyListener);
    update();
}

public static void shutdown() {
    preferences.removePropertyChangeListener(propertyListener);
}
```

When all this is in place, selecting the **Periodically check for new version of Favorites product (simulated)** checkbox on the **Favorites** preference page will cause the new version check operation to be performed periodically. Feedback to the user is automatically provided as part of the Jobs API through the **Progress** view (see Figure 20–5). The "**% done**" shown in the **Progress** view is based on the total work specified in the `beginTask()` method and the number of units worked is based on calls to the `worked()` method. The "seconds left = n" is specified by calling the `subTask()` method (see Section 9.4.1, IProgressMonitor, on page 383).

Figure 20–5   Progress view for a background operation.

Typically, jobs are executed in the background, but the IProgressService provides the showInDialog() method for executing them in the foreground (see Section 9.4.4, IProgressService, on page 386). In addition, if setUser(true) is called after the job is instantiated but before it is scheduled, and if the user has the **General > Always run in background** preference unchecked, then it will execute in the foreground.

```
job = new NewVersionCheckJob(JOB_NAME);
job.setUser(true);
job.schedule();
```

20.9 Plug-in ClassLoaders

Most of the time you can easily ignore ClassLoaders, knowing that as long as your classpath is correct—or in this case, the dependency declaration in the plug-in manifest (see Section 2.3.1, The Plug-in manifests, on page 71)—class loading will happen automatically, without intervention. But what if you want to load classes that are not known when a plug-in is compiled? Information about code developed by the user in the workspace is accessible via the JDT interfaces such as ICompilationUnit, IType, and IMethod; however, it is not normally on a plug-in's classpath and thus cannot be executed. Normally, this is a good thing, because code under development can throw exceptions, or under rare circumstances, crash Eclipse without any warning.

The Eclipse debugger (see Section 1.10, Introduction to Debugging, on page 58) executes user-developed code in a separate VM to avoid these problems, but it is a heavyweight, involving the overhead of launching a separate VM and communicating with it to obtain results. If you need a quick way to execute user-developed code in the same VM as Eclipse and are willing to accept the risks involved in doing so, then you need to write a ClassLoader.

To illustrate and test the ClassLoader, you first declare a new action in the "Favorites ActionSet" of the **Favorites** plug-in manifest to appear in the top-level **Favorites** menu (see Section 6.2.3, Defining a menu item and toolbar button, on page 212).

```
<action
   class="com.qualityeclipse.favorites.actions.
         ExecuteMethodActionDelegate"
   label="Execute method"
   menubarPath="com.qualityeclipse.favorites.workbenchMenu/content"
   id="com.qualityeclipse.favorites.executeMethod"/>
</actionSet>
```

The ExecuteMethodActionDelegate obtains the selected Java method, loads the type declaring the method, instantiates a new instance of that type, and prints the result of executing the method to the **Console** view. For simplicity, the selected method must be public with no arguments.

```
package com.qualityeclipse.favorites.actions;

import ...

public class ExecuteMethodActionDelegate
    implements IWorkbenchWindowActionDelegate
{
    IStructuredSelection selection;

    public void init(IWorkbenchWindow window) {
    }

    public void selectionChanged(IAction action, ISelection selection)
    {
        this.selection = selection instanceof IStructuredSelection
            ? (IStructuredSelection) selection : null;
    }

    public void run(IAction action) {
        System.out.println(executeMethod());
    }

    public void dispose() {
    }
}
```

The run() method calls the executeMethod() to perform the actual operation and return a message. This message is then appended to the system console.

```
private String executeMethod() {
    if (selection == null || selection.isEmpty())
        return "Nothing selected";
    Object element = selection.getFirstElement();
    if (!(element instanceof IMethod))
        return "No Java method selected";
    IMethod method = (IMethod) element;
    try {
        if (!Flags.isPublic(method.getFlags()))
            return "Java method must be public";
    }
    catch (JavaModelException e) {
        FavoritesLog.logError(e);
        return "Failed to get method modifiers";
    }
```

```
   if (method.getParameterTypes().length != 0)
      return "Java method must have zero arguments";
   IType type = method.getDeclaringType();
   String typeName = type.getFullyQualifiedName();
   ClassLoader loader =
      new ProjectClassLoader(type.getJavaProject());
   Class c;
   try {
      c = loader.loadClass(typeName);
   }
   catch (ClassNotFoundException e) {
      FavoritesLog.logError(e);
      return "Failed to load: " + typeName;
   }
   Object target;
   try {
      target = c.newInstance();
   }
   catch (Exception e) {
      FavoritesLog.logError(e);
      return "Failed to instantiate: " + typeName;
   }
   Method m;
   try {
      m = c.getMethod(method.getElementName(), new Class[] {});
   }
   catch (Exception e) {
      FavoritesLog.logError(e);
      return "Failed to find method: " + method.getElementName();
   }
   Object result;
   try {
      result = m.invoke(target, new Object[] {});
   }
   catch (Exception e) {
      FavoritesLog.logError(e);
      return "Failed to invoke method: " + method.getElementName();
   }
   return "Return value = " + result;
}
```

The ExecuteMethodActionDelegate uses ProjectClassLoader to load the selected class into the **Favorites** plug-in to be executed. This Class-Loader locates the class file using the project's Java build path, reads the class file using standard java.io, and creates the class in memory using the superclass' defineClass() method. It is not complete as it only loads source-based classes; loading classes from a jar file or reference project is left as an exercise for the reader.

```java
package com.qualityeclipse.favorites.util;

import ...

public class ProjectClassLoader extends ClassLoader
{
   private IJavaProject project;

   public ProjectClassLoader(IJavaProject project) {
      if (project == null || !project.exists() || !project.isOpen())
         throw new IllegalArgumentException("Invalid project");
      this.project = project;
   }

   protected Class findClass(String name)
      throws ClassNotFoundException
   {
      byte[] buf = readBytes(name);
      if (buf == null)
         throw new ClassNotFoundException(name);
      return defineClass(name, buf, 0, buf.length);
   }

   private byte[] readBytes(String name) {
      IPath rootLoc = ResourcesPlugin
         .getWorkspace().getRoot().getLocation();
      Path relativePathToClassFile =
         new Path(name.replace('.', '/') + ".class");
      IClasspathEntry[] entries;
      IPath outputLocation;
      try {
         entries = project.getResolvedClasspath(true);
         outputLocation =
            rootLoc.append(project.getOutputLocation());
      }
      catch (JavaModelException e) {
         FavoritesLog.logError(e);
         return null;
      }
      for (int i = 0; i < entries.length; i++) {
         IClasspathEntry entry = entries[i];
         switch (entry.getEntryKind()) {

            case IClasspathEntry.CPE_SOURCE :
               IPath path = entry.getOutputLocation();
               if (path != null)
                  path = rootLoc.append(path);
               else
                  path = outputLocation;
               path = path.append(relativePathToClassFile);
               byte[] buf = readBytes(path.toFile());
               if (buf != null)
                  return buf;
               break;
```

```
                           case IClasspathEntry.CPE_LIBRARY:
                           case IClasspathEntry.CPE_PROJECT:
                              // Handle other entry types here.
                              break;

                           default :
                              break;
                  }
            }
            return null;
      }

      private static byte[] readBytes(File file) {
            if (file == null || !file.exists())
               return null;
            InputStream stream = null;
            try {
               stream =
                  new BufferedInputStream(
                     new FileInputStream(file));
               int size = 0;
               byte[] buf = new byte[10];
               while (true) {
                  int count =
                     stream.read(buf, size, buf.length - size);
                  if (count < 0)
                     break;
                  size += count;
                  if (size < buf.length)
                     break;
                  byte[] newBuf = new byte[size + 10];
                  System.arraycopy(buf, 0, newBuf, 0, size);
                  buf = newBuf;
               }
               byte[] result = new byte[size];
               System.arraycopy(buf, 0, result, 0, size);
               return result;
            }
            catch (Exception e) {
               FavoritesLog.logError(e);
               return null;
            }
            finally {
               try {
                  if (stream != null)
                     stream.close();
               }
               catch (IOException e) {
                  FavoritesLog.logError(e);
                  return null;
               }
            }
      }
}
```

20.10 Early Startup

As discussed in Section 3.4.2, Early plug-in startup, on page 114, use the `org.eclipse.ui.startup` extension point to ensure that your plug-in will be started when Eclipse starts. Doing so should not be done lightly because it defeats the Eclipse lazy-loading mechanism, causing Eclipse to always load and execute your plug-in thus consuming precious memory and startup time. If you *must* do this, then keep your early startup plug-in small so that it takes up less memory and executes quickly when it starts.

20.10.1 Managing early startup

Eclipse does not provide a mechanism for programmatically specifying whether a plug-in should be started immediately when it is launched. If you have one or more plug-ins that *may* need early startup, then consider creating a small plug-in that manages early startup (see Figure 20–6). For example, if you have a large plug-in that only needs early startup if the user has enabled some functionality, then create a small early startup plug-in that determines whether that functionality has been enabled, and if so, starts the larger plug-in.

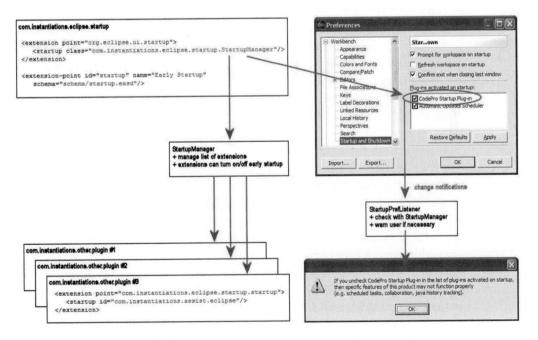

Figure 20–6 Plug-in for managing early startup of other plug-ins.

20.10.2 *Disabling early startup*

The user can disable early plug-in startup using the **General > Startup and Shutdown** preference page. If you have added an early startup extension, then your plug-in will appear in this list, and the user can disable its startup. You can detect this situation and warn the user that some of your plug-in's functionality will be compromised.

```
public static boolean isEarlyStartupDisabled() {
    String plugins = PlatformUI.getPreferenceStore().getString(
        /*
         * Copy constant out of internal Eclipse interface
         * IPreferenceConstants.PLUGINS_NOT_ACTIVATED_ON_STARTUP
         * so that we are not accessing internal type.
         */
        "PLUGINS_NOT_ACTIVATED_ON_STARTUP");
    return plugins.indexOf(FavortesPlugin.ID) != -1;
}
```

20.11 Rich Client Platform

Even though Eclipse started life with the mantra "an open extensible IDE (integrated development environment) for anything but nothing in particular" (from *www-128.ibm.com/developerworks/opensource/library/os-plat*), it did not stop there. The first major refactoring of the Eclipse platform involved separating the generic tool elements from the IDE-specific elements so that it became a framework for more than just Java development. The Rich Client Platform represents the second major refactoring of the Eclipse platform, separating the application infrastructure such as views, editors, and perspectives, from the generic tool elements. After this latest restructuring, the Eclipse IDE rests on a generic tooling framework which in turn rests on a generic application framework called the Rich Client Platform, or simply RCP.

RCP at its core consists of a small handful of plug-ins or bundles providing a basic application framework including action sets, perspectives, views, and editors without any of the tooling or IDE-specific aspects such as source editing, refactoring, compiling, or building. Any of the tooling and IDE-specific plug-ins can be used as part of an RCP application but are not necessary. Everything that has been covered so far from actions and views to cheat sheets and jobs is part of building an RCP application, but there is still more. The book, *Eclipse Rich Client Platform* (McAffer and Lemieux 2005), forms a perfect companion to this book, providing additional detail specific to RCP applications.

20.12 Conclusion

Throughout this book, we have provided in-depth discussion of the complete process involved in building a commercial-quality Eclipse plug-in. To us, "commercial-quality" means going above and beyond the minimal requirements needed to integrate with Eclipse. To that end, we have tried to present numerous suggestions and examples intended to help you take your plug-in to the next level. If you have followed the guidelines presented in this book, you will also be in a good position to submit your plug-in to IBM for RFRS certification.

We hope that you found this book to be both informative and useful. We also hope that you will use it as a reference to improve the plug-ins that you create, whether they are high-quality, open source or commercial offerings.

References

Chapter source (*www.qualityeclipse.com/projects/source-ch-20.zip*).

Krish-Sampath, Balaji, "Understanding Decorators in Eclipse," IBM, January 16, 2003 (*www.eclipse.org/articles/Article-Decorators/decorators.html*).

Valenta, Michael, "On the Job: The Eclipse Jobs API," IBM, September 20, 2004 (*www.eclipse.org/articles/Article-Concurrency/jobs-api.html*).

Erickson, Marc, "Working the Eclipse Platform," IBM, November 1, 2001 (*www-128.ibm.com/developerworks/opensource/library/os-plat*).

McAffer, Jeff, and Jean-Michel Lemieux, *Eclipse Rich Client Platform: Designing, Coding, and Packaging Java Applications*, Addison-Wesley, Boston, 2005.

APPENDIX A

Eclipse Plug-ins and Resources

The widespread availability and adoption of Eclipse has spawned an entire cottage industry devoted to adding new features to the environment. As of this writing, there are more than 1,000 plug-ins available to extend Eclipse in almost any conceivable direction. These range from high-quality, commercial, and open source offerings to not-so-high-quality experiments.

In working with Eclipse over the last several years, we have identified (and in some cases, created for ourselves) a number of very useful Eclipse add-ons.

A.1 Plug-ins

The following list of plug-ins—some commercial, some open source, some expensive, some very inexpensive or free—represents our short list of plug-ins that you should seriously take a look at. All of these are very high-quality and very well-respected in the Eclipse community.

A.1.1 CodePro AnalytiX and CodePro PlusPak

CodePro AnalytiX and CodePro PlusPak (available for $899 and $299, respectively, with a noncommercial combined version available for $99) adds more than 500 enhancements to Eclipse in the areas of best practices, analytics, testing, usability, and collaboration.

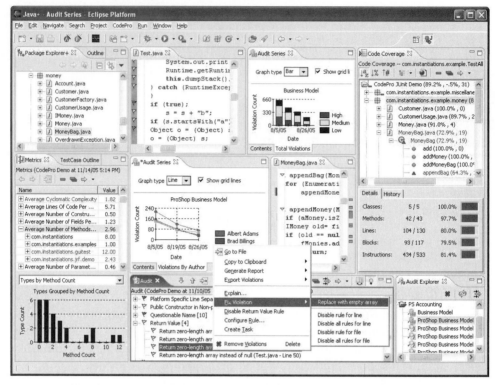

URL: *www.instantiations.com/codepro/*

Key features include code audit, metrics, Javadoc repair, JUnit test generation, code coverage, design patterns, dependency analyzer, Ant integration enhancements, task scheduler, and team collaboration tools.

- Code audit catches more than 750 audit violations with full support for Ant scripts and headless operation. Dynamic code audit mode catches errors as they occur, while built-in "quick fix" integration automatically fixes most violations. Easily add your own audit rules via an Eclipse extension point and exchange audit rule sets with other developers. Generate detailed audit reports in multiple formats.

- Code metrics have drilldown capability and trigger points.

- The project/package dependency analyzer graphically examines cycles and closures. It generates detailed dependency reports and metrics.

- Support for design patterns (including all 23 of the "Gang of Four").

- Javadoc repair tool.

- Spellchecker for comments, identifiers, literals, properties, and XML files.

- Automatic JUnit Test Case generation.

- Code Coverage analysis.

- Color-enhanced Java views.

- Java History view, Modified Types and Members views.

- VisualAge Java-style views and perspective.

- Ant script wizard and enhanced Ant tasks.

- Powerful task scheduler for Eclipse scripting.

- Many editor enhancements.

- Memory Monitor view.

- Preferences import/export/exchange tool.

- Global workspace administration.

- Inter-workspace messaging.

- Eclipse-based (Koi) collaboration server.

A.1.2   EclipseProfiler

This is a free Eclipse plug-in that provides Java profiling tools. It allows a Java developer to tune the performance of his or her Java programs all within the comfort of Eclipse.

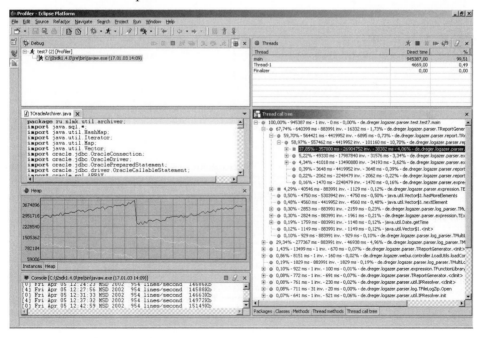

URL: *sourceforge.net/projects/eclipsecolorer/*

Key features include:

- Tomcat CPU profiling
- Tomcat heap profiling
- JBoss profiling
- WebLogic profiling
- Resin profiling
- CPU profiling

A.1.3   EclipseUML

EclipseUML is a visual modeling tool, natively integrated with Eclipse and CVS. It is capable of managing hundreds of simultaneous connections and is therefore suitable for large software development projects.

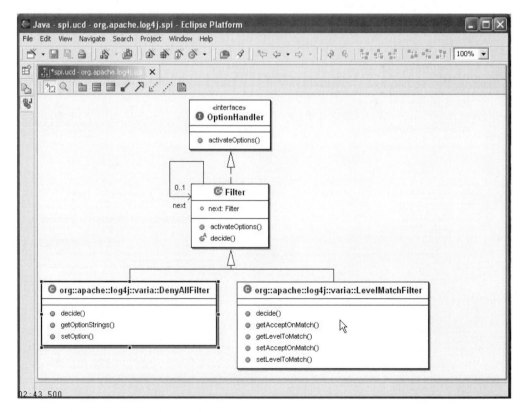

URL: *www.eclipseuml.com/*

Key features of the free edition include:

- Live bidirectional code and model synchronization.
- Native Graphical Editor Framework (GEF) integration.
- Native Eclipse Modeling Framework (EMF) integration.

An Enterprise version (available for $1,990) adds the following features:

- Complete Java Version 2 Enterprise Edition (J2EE) lifecycle.
- Complete database modeling lifecycle.
- Open API and UML profiles are being merged and will offer a unique opportunity to fully customize your applications.

A.1.4   MyEclipse Enterprise Workbench

MyEclipse Enterprise Workbench (available for $29 for the standard edition or $49 for the professional edition via yearly subscription) is a completely integrated product extension for Eclipse and offers a full-featured J2EE IDE based on the Eclipse platform. MyEclipse supports the full development lifecycle (code, deploy, test, and debug) for JavaServer Pages (JSP), Enterprise JavaBeans (EJB), XML, JSF, AJAX, and Struts.

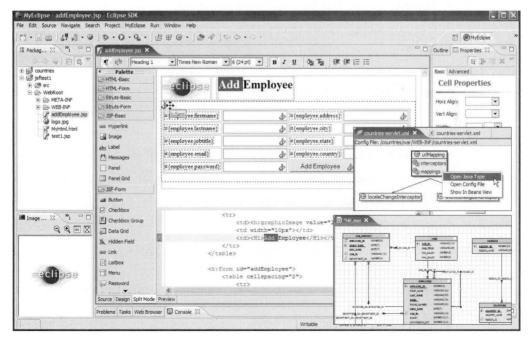

URL: *www.myeclipseide.com/*

Its main features include:

- Smart editors with code completion and syntax coloring for JSP, HTML, Struts, XML, Cascading Style Sheets (CSS), and J2EE deployment descriptors.
- XML editing with smart code completion, DTD caching for offline support, and an outline navigation viewer.
- Visual HTML Designer with round trip code generation.
- Struts support via a configuration editor with code completion and a layout flow viewer.
- Java Server Faces (JSF) Developer with graphical navigation flow designer, advanced XML editor, and multimode outline view.
- Hibernate development tools with productivity tools, code generation, and DB Explorer connector integration.
- Database explorer and SQL editor.
- JSP syntax validation and native JSP debugging, plus full support for JSR045.
- Step-through debugging for included JSP files.
- JSP rendering.
- Support for the JSP 2.0 expression language.
- Customizable creation templates for JSPs HTML, XML, servlets, and applets.
- Integrated browser for real-time rendering.
- Spring IDE integration.
- Tapestry support.
- J2EE 1.4 support.
- XDoclet support.
- Ad-hoc image preview for GIF, JPG, BMP, PNG, and ICO images.
- Creation of Web, EAR, and EJB projects.
- Java project-to-Web project enablements.
- WAR, JAR, and EAR import and export.
- EJB wizards.
- Sync-on-demand, or automated deployment of applications to integrated servers.
- Archive-based deployment (EAR and WAR).
- Integrated controls for starting and stopping servers.

- More than 20 application server connectors, including Bejy Tiger, JBoss, Jetty, Jonas, JRun, Oracle, Orion, Resin, Tomcat, WebLogic, and Web-Sphere.

- Full hot-swap debugging support for deployed applications.

A.1.5   WindowBuilder Pro

WindowBuilder Pro is a powerful and easy-to-use two-way Java GUI designer capable of building Swing, SWT and RCP interfaces.

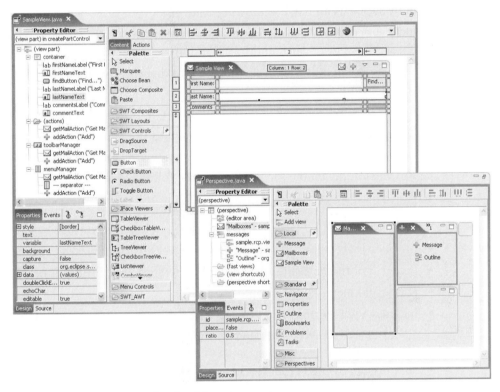

URL: *www.windowbuilderpro.com/*

Key features of the free version include:

- Implements what you see is what you get (WYSIWYG) GUI editing with native SWT and Swing controls by dragging and dropping composites, layouts, and controls.

- When implemented as a two-way tool, WindowBuilder directly generates Java code that can be changed in the graphical editor or directly in source. All changes made directly to the source code will be reflected in the graphical designer.

- Uses only pure SWT and Swing classes, resulting in zero overhead at runtime. There are no special libraries added to projects.

- Contains a handy property editor for easy and intuitive property editing. All changes will be immediately displayed in the code editor and in the graphical designer.

- Displays a component tree, which makes navigation through components much easier.

- Includes SWT applications and JFace dialog creation wizards.

- Fully supports all SWT and Swing controls.

- Fully supports SWT grid, fill, and row layout managers as well as Swing border, flow, grid, card, and box layout managers.

- Seamlessly integrates with the Eclipse workbench. Just unpack it and restart Eclipse.

- Allows on-the-fly testing of UIs without compiling by clicking one button.

- Fully integrated into the Eclipse help system.

- Fully configurable UI with dockable flyout palette and property editor.

The Pro version (available for $299) adds the following features:

- Fully supports all JFace dialogs and viewers.

- Fully supports RCP perspectives, advisors, views, and editors.

- Includes JFace applications and JFace viewer creation wizards.

- Fully supports the Eclipse Forms and Preference Page Field Editor APIs.

- Has visual menu design support.

- Includes SWT FormLayout, Swing GridBagLayout, Swing SpringLayout and JGoodies FormLayout support with intelligent layout assist and dynamic snap points.

- Supports all Swing layout managers in SWT for easy Swing-to-SWT conversion.

- Allows a user to select and edit multiple widgets simultaneously.

- Supports visual inheritance of windows and panels.

- Creates and embeds custom composites and groups.

- Morph widgets from one type into another.

- Defines custom widget templates.

- Includes support for nonvisual beans.

- Supports visual tab order editing.

- Supports the SWT_AWT bridge allowing SWT and Swing to be mixed.

A.1.6   XMLBuddy

XMLBuddy is the ultimate XML editor for Eclipse supporting XML, DTD, XML schema, RELAX NG, RELAX NG compact syntax, and XSLT.

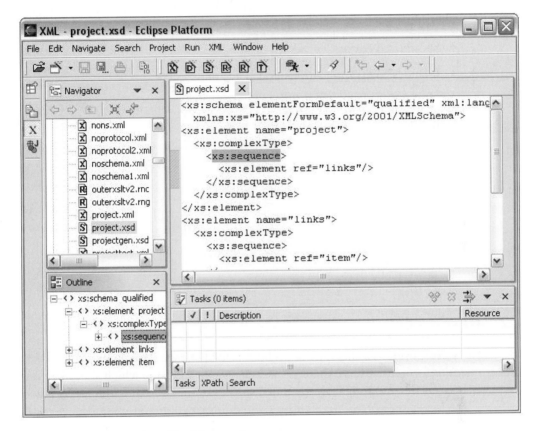

URL: *www.xmlbuddy.com/*

Key features of the free edition include:

- User-configurable syntax coloring for XML and DTD.
- Dynamic code assist for XML driven by DTD or current document contents.
- Dynamically updated outline (tree) view.
- Generates DTD from example XML document.
- Validates XML documents with DTDs or XML schemas.
- Automatically validates XML in background while user edits.
- Formats XML documents, on command or while user edits (auto-flow).

The Pro version (available for $35) adds the following features:

- User-configurable syntax coloring and code assist for XML schema, RELAX NG, RELAX NG compact syntax, and XSLT.

- Dynamic code assist for XML driven by XML schema, RELAX NG, or RELAX NG compact syntax.

- Specialized editors for XML schema, RELAX NG, RELAX NG compact syntax, and XSLT, providing code assist and validation based on built-in schemas.

- Generates XML instance from DTD or XML schema, RELAX NG, or RELAX NG compact syntax schema.

- Converts between DTD, XML schema, RELAX NG, or RELAX NG compact syntax in both directions.

- Applies XSLT transformations.

- Automatically validates DTD, XML schema, RELAX NG, and RELAX NG compact syntax in the background while user edits.

- Opens definition in DTDs, XML schemas, or RELAX NG schemas (XML or compact syntax).

A.2   Resources

The following is a short list of Web links for Eclipse-related plug-ins, projects, and information. First, there is the *Eclipse.org* Web site, which should always be your first stop for Eclipse-related information. Following that are a few of the larger sites providing Eclipse-related information and lists of plug-ins. At the end is a smattering of sites containing plug-ins, projects, notes, and information of varying quality that caught our eye.

A.2.1   Eclipse.org

www.eclipse.org/—The place to start concerning Eclipse and Eclipse-related technology for downloads, documentation, articles, mailing lists, and more. The main projects at *Eclipse.org* are further divided into subprojects:

- **The Eclipse Project**—The primary platform and its tools
- Platform—Frameworks and common services
- JDT—Java development tools
- PDE—Plug-in development environment

- Equinox—an OSGi framework
- **The Eclipse Tools Project**—Secondary tools for Eclipse
- CDT—C/C++ development tools
- GEF—Graphical editor framework
- COBOL—A fully functional COBOL IDE
- EMF—A Java/XML framework for generating models
- VE—Visual editor; Framework for creating GUI builders
- UML2—Framework for UML 2.0 modeling tools
- **The Eclipse Web Tools Platform (WTP)**—J2EE Web Applications
- WST—Web Standard Tools
- JST—J2EE Standard Tools
- JSF—JavaServer Faces Tools
- **Test & Performance Tools (TPTP)**—Testing and Performance
- TPTP Platform
- Monitoring tools
- Testing tools
- Tracing and profiling tools
- **The Business Intelligence and Reporting Tools Project (BIRT)**
- **The Eclipse Data Tools Platform Project**
- **Device Software Development Platform (DSDP)**
- **The Eclipse Technology Project**—Eclipse-based technology incubators
- AJDT—AspectJ Development Tools Project
- ECESIS—Eclipse Community Education Project
- ECF—Eclipse Communications Framework
- Generative Model Transformer—Tools for model-driven software development

The *Eclipse.org* Web site also has a community page (*www.eclipse.org/community/index.html*) that lists upcoming events, courses, and links to related Web sites containing more information on Eclipse.

A.2.2   Eclipse Plug-in Central

www.eclipseplugincentral.com—A site dedicated to supporting the growth of the Eclipse community by helping developers locate, evaluate, and acquire plug-ins that can help them deliver their projects faster, better, and cheaper. Eclipse Plug-in Central (EPiC) adds value by offering marketplace updates, reviews, ratings, news, forums, community listings for products and services, and support for the Eclipse Foundation.

A.2.3   Eclipse plug-in site

www.eclipse-plugins.info/—A site containing lists of plug-ins sliced and diced by category and hit count (a very rough popularity statistic). Each plug-in has a short description, a place for anyone to comment, statistics, and a link to the plug-in's home page.

A.2.4   Eclipse wiki wiki

eclipse-wiki.info—A wiki wiki site containing information about Eclipse gleaned from newsgroups, mailing lists, and the like. The availability of this site has been unpredictable, but when available, it contains a wealth of information.

A.2.5   EclipseCon

www.eclipsecon.org—The Web site for information about the EclipseCon technical conference.

A.2.6   ANTLR plug-in for Eclipse

antlreclipse.sourceforge.net—A plug-in providing support for the parser generator ANTLR, including an editor and builder.

A.2.7   Bugzilla plug-in

kered.org/project-eclipse_bugzilla_plugin—Proof of concept for integrating Bugzilla into Eclipse. Looks promising, but we have not tried it.

A.2.8   Coloring editor

www.gstaff.org/coloreditor/—A free syntax color highlighting editor for Eclipse that uses JEdit's syntax highlighting mode files. There are several other projects and plug-ins on this site, including cSpy and a widget/plug-in inspector.

A.2.9   Eclipse Easter eggs

mmoebius.gmxhome.de/eclipse/eastereggs.htm—A list of links and resources for Eclipse, plus a page of Eclipse Easter eggs for fun.

A.2.10   IBM Alphaworks on Eclipse

www.alphaworks.ibm.com/eclipse—A site filled with Eclipse-related technology and articles from the IBM Alphaworks labs.

A.2.11   IBM Eclipse research

www.research.ibm.com/eclipse/—A source of information regarding IBM grants and programs centered on Eclipse-based technology.

A.2.12   PHP plug-in for Eclipse

sourceforge.net/projects/phpeclipse—An open source plug-in providing support for PHP, structured query language (SQL), HTML, and Jtidy. It includes syntax highlighting, command completion, and a preview of pages.

A.2.13   QNX's Momentics

www.qnx.com/products/ps_momentics/—An IDE build on Eclipse for writing code around a real-time OS.

A.2.14   QuickShare: XP programming for Eclipse

www.scs.carleton.ca/~skaegi/cdt/—A lightweight code sharing plug-in for XP-like pair programming in a distributed environment.

A.2.15   Sangam: XP programming for Eclipse

sangam.sourceforge.net/—Another code sharing plug-in for XP-like pair programming in a distributed environment.

APPENDIX B

Ready for Rational Software

IBM Rational Software Development Platforms (SDP) is IBM's open, comprehensive, multi-language development environment for WebSphere. Three main products are in the Rational Software family: Web Developer, Application Developer, and Software Architect. There are also many toolkits that add tools for particular components of WebSphere and other IBM middleware (e.g., Voice Toolkit for WebSphere Studio). Customers use a mix of the core products and toolkits depending on the components of the WebSphere platform and other middleware used in their applications. The products and toolkits are generally supported on both Microsoft Windows and Linux systems.

Rational SDP is built on the open source Eclipse tools platform, which provides a complete extensibility architecture. Eclipse plug-in tools products from IBM Business Partners can thus integrate tightly to the SDP and extend the SDP with the Business Partner tool's unique capabilities.

However, for customers to obtain value from a Business Partner plug-in, the plug-in must install safely into Rational Software and interoperate well with the Eclipse platform and other plug-ins. The plug-in must also support the common Eclipse/Rational Software UI and common Eclipse/Rational behaviors.

The RFRS software validation program defines integration criteria for plug-ins integrating to the SDP via the Eclipse platform and components. Compliance with these criteria can help assure your customers that your plug-in product meets SDP standards for installation, interoperation, and UI.

The RFRS software validation program is part of IBM's family of "Ready for" technical validation programs (*www.ibm.com/partnerworld/isv/rational/readyfor.html*). Any IBM Business Partner that is a member of PWD (Partner World for Developers) can validate plug-in products to the RFRS criteria and join the RFRS program. Business Partners can then use the "Ready for IBM Rational Software" mark with any validated product as visible confirmation of the product's validation to the integration criteria. Use of the mark enables Business Partners to differentiate their RFRS-validated offerings from their competition and enables a shorter sales cycle through increased customer confidence and reduced customer evaluation time.

RFRS is also the gateway to a variety of incremental co-marketing resources to help program members extend their marketing reach. These benefits include RFRS presence at trade shows and IBM road shows, a listing of validated products on the *RFRS Plug-in Central* Web site (*www.ibm.com/developerworks/websphere/downloads/plugin/*), and Business Partner content in newsletters and IBM sales flashes.

Trademarks

The following terms are registered trademarks of the International Business Machines Corporation in the United States, other countries, or both:

- IBM
- Rational
- PartnerWorld
- WebSphere

Microsoft and Windows are trademarks of the Microsoft Corporation in the United States, other countries, or both.

Other company, product, and service names may be trademarks or service marks of others.

INDEX

Safari®
BOOKS ONLINE
ENABLED

THIS BOOK IS SAFARI ENABLED

INCLUDES FREE 45-DAY ACCESS TO THE ONLINE EDITION

The Safari® Enabled icon on the cover of your favorite technology book means the book is available through Safari Bookshelf. When you buy this book, you get free access to the online edition for 45 days.

Safari Bookshelf is an electronic reference library that lets you easily search thousands of technical books, find code samples, download chapters, and access technical information whenever and wherever you need it.

TO GAIN 45-DAY SAFARI ENABLED ACCESS TO THIS BOOK:

● Go to **http://www.awprofessional.com/safarienabled**

● Complete the brief registration form

● Enter the coupon code found in the front of this book on the "Copyright" page

Addison
Wesley

If you have difficulty registering on Safari Bookshelf or accessing the online edition, please e-mail customer-service@safaribooksonline.com.